Student Solutions Guide

to Accompany

Brief Calculus
with
Applications

Fourth Edition

Larson/Hostetler/Edwards

Dianna L. Zook
Indiana University, Purdue University at Fort Wayne

Bruce H. Edwards
University of Florida

D. C. Heath and Company
Lexington, Massachusetts   Toronto

Address editorial correspondence to:

D. C. Heath and Company
125 Spring Street
Lexington, MA 02173

Published simultaneously in Canada.

Printed in the United States of America.

International Standard Book Number: 0–669–35167–9

10   9   8   7   6   5   4   3   2

Preface

This student solutions guide is a supplement to *Brief Calculus with Applications*, Fourth Edition, by Roland E. Larson, Robert P. Hostetler, and Bruce H. Edwards, as well as to *Brief Calculus with Applications*, Alternate Fourth Edition, and all custom-published versions of these two texts. All references to chapters, theorems, and definitions apply to these texts. The purpose of this supplement is to guide you through calculus by providing the basic solution steps for each of the odd-numbered exercises in the text. This solutions guide is not intended to be used as a substitute for working homework problems yourself. It is one thing to be able to read and understand a solution, but quite another thing to be able to derive the solution on you own. Remember, mathematics is not a spectator sport!

To use this solutions guide correctly, we suggest the following study pattern.

1. Attempt each problem before looking at its solution.

2. Even if you have attempted to solve a problem, don't be too anxious to look up the solution. Check your work or try to come up with an alternative approach. It is through trial and error that you will sharpen your mathematical skills. These skills, like muscles, will develop only with consistent exercise.

3. Once you have completed an exercise, compare your solution with the one given in this guide. Sometimes the given solution will be more efficient than your own and will provide you with a better way of doing that type of problem in the future. Other times your own solution may require fewer steps and you can claim a small victory for your ingenuity. Be careful, however, not to sacrifice accuracy for efficiency.

Good luck in your study of calculus. If you have any corrections or suggestions for improving this guide, we would appreciate hearing from you.

Dianna L. Zook
Indiana University
Purdue University at Fort Wayne
Fort Wayne, Indiana 46805

Bruce H. Edwards
Department of Mathematics
University of Florida
Gainesville, Florida 32611
be@math.ufl.edu

CONTENTS

A Precalculus Review

Functions, Graphs, and Limits

Differentiation

Applications of the Derivative

Exponential and Logarithmic Functions

Integration and Its Applications

Techniques of Integration

Functions of Several Variables

Probability and Calculus

Differential Equations

Series and Taylor Polynomials

Trigonometric Functions

CHAPTER 0
A Precalculus Review

Section 0.1   The Real Line and Order

1. Determine whether 0.7 is rational or irrational.

   Solution:

   Since $0.7 = \frac{7}{10}$, it is rational.

3. Determine whether $\dfrac{3\pi}{2}$ is rational or irrational.

   Solution:

   $\dfrac{3\pi}{2}$ is irrational because π is irrational.

5. Determine whether $4.3451\overline{451}$ is rational or irrational.

   Solution:

   $4.3451\overline{451}$ is rational because it has a repeating decimal expansion.

7. Determine whether $\sqrt[3]{64}$ is rational or irrational.

   Solution:

   Since $\sqrt[3]{64} = 4$, it is rational.

9. Determine whether $\sqrt[3]{60}$ is rational or irrational.

   Solution:

   $\sqrt[3]{60}$ is irrational.

11. Determine whether the given value of x satisfies the inequality $5x - 12 > 0$.

    (a) $x = 3$ (b) $x = -3$

    (c) $x = \frac{5}{2}$ (d) $x = \frac{3}{2}$

    Solution:

    (a) Yes, if $x = 3$, then $5(3) - 12 = 3 > 0$.   (b) No, if $x = -3$, then $5(-3) - 12 = -27 < 0$.

    (c) Yes, if $x = \frac{5}{2}$, then $5\left(\frac{5}{2}\right) - 12 = \frac{1}{2} > 0$.   (d) No, if $x = \frac{3}{2}$, then $5\left(\frac{3}{2}\right) - 12 = -\frac{9}{2} < 0$.

1

13. Determine whether the given value of x satisfies the inequality $0 < \dfrac{x-2}{4} < 2$.

(a) $x = 4$ (b) $x = 10$

(c) $x = 0$ (d) $x = \frac{7}{2}$

Solution:

$$0 < \frac{x-2}{4} < 2$$
$$0 < x - 2 < 8$$
$$2 < x < 1°$$

(a) Yes, if $x = 4$, then $2 < x < 10$.   (b) No, if $x = 10$, then x is not less than 10.

(c) No, if $x = 0$, then x is not greater than 2.   (d) Yes, if $x = \frac{7}{2}$, then $2 < x < 10$.

15. Solve the inequality $x - 5 \geq 7$ and sketch the graph of the solution on the real line.

    Solution:

$$x - 5 \geq 7$$
$$x - 5 + 5 \geq 7 + 5$$
$$x \geq 12$$

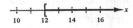

17. Solve the inequality $4x + 1 < 2x$ and sketch the graph of the solution on the real line.

    Solution:

$$4x + 1 < 2x$$
$$2x < -1$$
$$x < -\frac{1}{2}$$

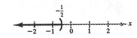

19. Solve the inequality $2x - 1 \geq 0$ and sketch the graph of the solution on the real line.

    Solution:

$$2x - 1 \geq 0$$
$$2x \geq 1$$
$$x \geq \frac{1}{2}$$

21. Solve the inequality $4 - 2x < 3x - 1$ and sketch the graph of the solution on the real line.

    Solution:

$$4 - 2x < 3x - 1$$
$$4 - 5x < -1$$
$$-5x < -5$$
$$x > 1$$

23. Solve the inequality $-4 < 2x - 3 < 4$ and sketch the graph of the solution on the real line.

Solution:

$$-4 < 2x - 3 < 4$$
$$-4 + 3 < 2x - 3 + 3 < 4 + 3$$
$$-1 < 2x < 7$$
$$-\tfrac{1}{2} < x < \tfrac{7}{2}$$

25. Solve the inequality $\tfrac{3}{4} > x + 1 > \tfrac{1}{4}$ and sketch the graph of the solution on the real number line.

Solution:

$$\tfrac{3}{4} > x + 1 > \tfrac{1}{4}$$
$$-\tfrac{1}{4} > x > -\tfrac{3}{4}$$
$$-\tfrac{3}{4} < x < -\tfrac{1}{4}$$

27. Solve the inequality $\dfrac{x}{2} + \dfrac{x}{3} > 5$ and sketch the graph of the solution on the real line.

Solution:

$$\frac{x}{2} + \frac{x}{3} > 5$$
$$3x + 2x > 30$$
$$5x > 30$$
$$x > 6$$

29. Solve the inequality $x^2 \le 3 - 2x$ and sketch the graph of the solution on the real line.

Solution:

$$x^2 \le 3 - 2x$$
$$x^2 + 2x - 3 \le 0$$
$$(x + 3)(x - 1) \le 0$$

Therefore, the solution is $-3 \le x \le 1$.

31. Solve the inequality $x^2 + x - 1 \le 5$ and sketch the graph of the solution on the real line.

Solution:

$$x^2 + x - 1 \le 5$$
$$x^2 + x - 6 \le 0$$
$$(x + 3)(x - 2) \le 0$$

Therefore, the solution is $-3 \le x \le 2$.

33. *Simple Interest* P dollars is invested at a (simple) interest rate of r. After t years, the balance in the account is given by

$A = P + Prt,$

where the interest rate r is expressed in decimal form. In order for an investment of $1000 to grow to *more than* $1250 in 2 years, what must the interest rate be?

Solution:

$P = 1000$ and $t = 2$ and we have $A > 1250$ and

$$P + Prt > 1250$$
$$1000 + 1000r(2) > 1250$$
$$2000r > 250$$
$$r > \tfrac{250}{2000} = 0.125 = 12.5\%$$

35. *Profit* The revenue for selling x units of a product is

$R = 115.95x,$

and the cost of producing x units is

$C = 95x + 750.$

In order to obtain a profit, the revenue must be *greater than* the cost. For what values of x will this product return a profit?

Solution:

$R = 115.95x$ and $C = 95x + 750$ and we have

$$R > C$$
$$115.95x > 95x + 750$$
$$20.95x > 750$$
$$x > \tfrac{750}{20.95} = 35.7995\dots$$

Therefore, $x \geq 36$ units.

37. *Area* A square region is to have an area of *at least* 500 square meters. What must the length of the sides of the region be?

Solution:

Let $x = $ length of the side of the square. Then, the area of the square is x^2, and we have

$$x^2 \geq 500$$
$$x \geq \sqrt{500}$$
$$x \geq 10\sqrt{5}.$$

39. Determine whether each statement is true or false, given $a < b$.

(a) $-2a < -2b$ (b) $a + 2 < b + 2$

(c) $6a < 6b$ (d) $\dfrac{1}{a} < \dfrac{1}{b}$

Solution:

(a) The statement $-2a < -2b$ is false.

(b) The statement $a + 2 < b + 2$ is true.

(c) The statement $6a < 6b$ is true.

(d) The statement $(1/a) < (1/b)$ is true if $ab < 0$ and false if $ab > 0$.

Section 0.2   Absolute Value and Distance on the Real Line

1. Find (a) the directed distance from a to b, (b) the directed distance from b to a, and (c) the distance
between a and b.

$$a = 126, b = 75$$

Solution:

(a) The directed distance from a to b is $75 - 126 = -51$.

(b) The directed distance from b to a is $126 - 75 = 51$.

(c) The distance between a and b is $|75 - 126| = 51$.

3. Find (a) the directed distance from a to b, (b) the directed distance from b to a, and (c) the distance
between a and b.

$$a = 9.34, b = -5.65$$

Solution:

(a) The directed distance from a to b is $-5.65 - 9.34 = -14.99$.

(b) The directed distance from b to a is $9.34 - (-5.65) = 14.99$.

(c) The distance between a and b is $|-5.65 - 9.34| = 14.99$.

5. Find the midpoint of the given interval.

$[7, 21]$

Solution:

$$\text{Midpoint} = \frac{7 + 21}{2} = 14$$

7. Find the midpoint of the given interval.

$[-6.85, 9.35]$

Solution:

$$\text{Midpoint} = \frac{-6.85 + 9.35}{2} = 1.25$$

9. Solve the inequality $|x| < 5$ and sketch the graph of the solution on the real line.

Solution:

$-5 < x < 5$

11. Solve the inequality $|\frac{x}{2}| > 3$ and sketch the graph of the solution on the real line.

Solution:

$\frac{x}{2} < -3$ or $\frac{x}{2} > 3$

$x < -6 \qquad x > 6$

13. Solve the inequality $|x + 2| < 5$ and sketch the graph of the solution on the real line.

Solution:

$-5 < x + 2 < 5$

$-7 < x < 3$

15. Solve the inequality $\left|\frac{x - 3}{2}\right| \geq 5$ and sketch the graph of the solution on the real line.

Solution:

$$\frac{x - 3}{2} \leq -5 \qquad \text{or} \qquad \frac{x - 3}{2} \geq 5$$

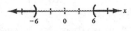

$$\frac{x - 3}{2}(2) \leq -5(2) \qquad \frac{x - 3}{2}(2) \geq 5(2)$$

$$x - 3 \leq -10 \qquad x - 3 \geq 10$$

$$x - 3 + 3 \leq -10 + 3 \qquad x - 3 + 3 \geq 10 + 3$$

$$x \leq -7 \qquad x \geq 13$$

17. Solve the inequality $|10 - x| > 4$ and sketch the graph of the solution on the real line.

Solution:

$$10 - x < -4 \quad \text{or} \quad 10 - x > 4$$

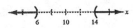

$$-x < -14 \qquad -x > -6$$

$$x > 14 \qquad x < 6$$

19. Solve the inequality $|9 - 2x| < 1$ and sketch the graph of the solution on the real line.

Solution:

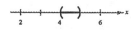

$$-1 < 9 - 2x < 1$$
$$-10 < -2x < -8$$
$$5 > x > 4$$
$$4 < x < 5$$

21. Solve the inequality $|x - a| \le b$ and sketch the graph of the solution on the real line.

Solution:

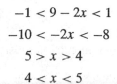

$$-b \le x - a \le b$$
$$a - b \le x \le a + b$$

23. Use absolute values to describe the given interval $[-2, 2]$ on the real line.

Solution:

$$|x| \le 2$$

25. Use absolute values to describe the pair of intervals $(-\infty, -2) \cup (2, \infty)$ on the real line.

Solution:

$$|x| > 2$$

27. Use absolute values to describe the given interval $[2, 6]$ on the real line.

Solution:

$$|x - 4| \le 2$$

29. Use absolute values to describe the pair of intervals $(-\infty, 0) \cup (4, \infty)$ on the real line.

Solution:

$$|x - 2| > 2$$

31. Use absolute values to describe "All numbers *less than* two units from 4".

Solution:

$$|x - 4| < 2$$

33. Use absolute values to describe "y is *at most* two units from a".

Solution:

$$|y - a| \leq 2$$

35. *Statistics* The heights h of two-thirds of the members of a certain population satisfy the inequality

$$\left|\frac{h - 68.5}{2.7}\right| \leq 1,$$

where h is measured in inches. Determine the interval on the real line in which these heights lie.

Solution:

$$\left|\frac{h - 68.5}{2.7}\right| \leq 1$$

$$-1 \leq \frac{h - 68.5}{2.7} \leq 1$$

$$-2.7 \leq h - 68.5 \leq 2.7$$

$$65.8 \leq h \leq 71.2$$

37. *Production* The estimated daily production x at a refinery is given by

$$|x - 200{,}000| \leq 125{,}000,$$

where x is measured in barrels of oil. Determine the high and low production levels.

Solution:

$$|x - 200{,}000| < 125{,}000$$

$$-125{,}000 < x - 200{,}000 < 125{,}000$$

$$175{,}000 < x < 225{,}000$$

39. *Budget Variance* Use absolute value notation to represent (a) the two intervals in which expenses must lie if they are to be within \$500 and within 5% of the specified budget amount, and (b) using the more stringent constraint, determine whether the given expense is at variance with the budget restriction.

Item	Budget	Expense
Utilities	\$4,750.00	\$5,116.37

Solution:

(a) $|E - 4750| \leq 500 \Rightarrow 4250 \leq E \leq 5250$

$0.05(4750) = 237.50$

$|E - 4750| \leq 237.50 \Rightarrow 4512.50 \leq E \leq 4987.50$

(b) \$5116.37 is not within 5% of the specified budgeted amount.

41. Use absolute value notation to represent (a) the two intervals in which expenses must lie if they are to be within $500 and within 5% of the specified budget amount, and (b) using the more stringent constraint, determine whether the given expense is at variance with the budget restriction.

Item	Budget	Expense
Maintenance	$20,000.00	$22,718.35

Solution:

(a) $|E - 20,000| \leq 500 \Rightarrow 19,500 \leq E \leq 20,500$

$0.05(20,000) = 1000$

$|E - 20,000| \leq 1000 \Rightarrow 19,000 \leq E \leq 21,000$

(b) $22,718.35 is at variance with both budget restrictions.

Section 0.3   Exponents and Radicals

1. Evaluate the expression for the indicated value of x.

     Expression   *x-value*

     $-3x^3$ $x = 2$

Solution:

     $-3(2)^3 = -3(8) = -24$

3. Evaluate the expression for the indicated value of x.

     Expression   *x-value*

     $4x^{-3}$ $x = 2$

Solution:

     $4(2)^{-3} = 4\left(\frac{1}{8}\right) = \frac{1}{2}$

5. Evaluate the expression for the indicated value of x.

     Expression   *x-value*

     $\dfrac{1 + x^{-1}}{x^{-1}}$ $x = 2$

Solution:

     $\dfrac{1 + (2)^{-1}}{(2)^{-1}} = \dfrac{1 + (1/2)}{1/2} = 3$

A Precalculus Review

7. Evaluate the expression for the indicated value of x.

> *Expression*   *x-value*
> $3x^2 - 4x^3$ $x = -2$

Solution:

$$3(-2)^2 - 4(-2)^3 = 3(4) - 4(-8) = 12 + 32 = 44$$

9. Evaluate the expression for the indicated value of x.

> *Expression*   *x-value*
> $6x^0 - (6x)^0$ $x = 10$

Solution:

$$6(10)^0 - (6(10))^0 = 6(1) - 1 = 5$$

11. Evaluate the expression for the indicated value of x.

> *Expression*   *x-value*
> $\sqrt[3]{x^2}$ $x = 27$

Solution:

$$\sqrt[3]{27^2} = \left(\sqrt[3]{27}\right)^2 = 3^2 = 9$$

13. Evaluate the expression for the indicated value of x.

> *Expression*   *x-value*
> $x^{-1/2}$ $x = 4$

Solution:

$$4^{-1/2} = \frac{1}{\sqrt{4}} = \frac{1}{2}$$

15. Evaluate the expression for the indicated value of x.

> *Expression*   *x-value*
> $x^{-2/5}$ $x = -32$

Solution:

$$(-32)^{-2/5} = \frac{1}{\left(\sqrt[5]{-32}\right)^2} = \frac{1}{(-2)^3} = \frac{1}{4}$$

17. Evaluate the expression for the indicated value of x.

> *Expression*   *x-value*
> $500x^{60}$ $x = 1.01$

Solution:

$$500(1.01)^{60} \approx 908.3483$$

19. Evaluate the expression for the indicated value of x.

    Expression   *x-value*

    $\sqrt[3]{x}$ $x = -154$

Solution:

$$\sqrt[3]{-154} \approx -5.3601$$

21. Simplify the expression $5x^4(x^2)$.

Solution:

$$5x^4(x^2) = 5x^6$$

23. Simplify the expression $6y^2(2y^4)^2$.

Solution:

$$6y^2(2y^4)^2 = 6y^2(4y^3) = 24y^{10}$$

25. Simplify the expression $10(x^2)^2$.

Solution:

$$10(x^2)^2 = 10x^4$$

27. Simplify the expression $\dfrac{7x^2}{x^{-3}}$.

Solution:

$$\frac{7x^2}{x^{-3}} = 7x^5$$

29. Simplify the expression $\dfrac{12(x+y)^3}{9(x+y)}$.

Solution:

$$\frac{12(x+y)^3}{9(x+y)} = \frac{4}{3}(x+y)^2$$

31. Simplify the expression $\dfrac{3x\sqrt{x}}{x^{1/2}}$.

Solution:

$$\frac{3x\sqrt{x}}{x^{1/2}} = \frac{3x\sqrt{x}}{\sqrt{x}} = 3x$$

33. Simplify the expression $\left(\dfrac{\sqrt{2}\sqrt{x^3}}{\sqrt{x}}\right)^4$.

Solution:

$$\left(\frac{\sqrt{2}\sqrt{x^3}}{\sqrt{x}}\right)^4 = \left(\frac{\sqrt{2}(x\sqrt{x})}{\sqrt{x}}\right)^4$$
$$= \left(\sqrt{2}x\right)^4 = \left(\sqrt{2}\right)^4 x^4 = 4x^4$$

35. Simplify (a) $\sqrt{8}$ and (b) $\sqrt{18}$ by removing all possible factors from the radical.

Solution:

(a) $\sqrt{8} = \sqrt{4 \cdot 2} = \sqrt{4}\sqrt{2} = 2\sqrt{2}$

(b) $\sqrt{18} = \sqrt{9 \cdot 2} = \sqrt{9}\sqrt{2} = 3\sqrt{2}$

37. Simplify (a) $\sqrt[3]{16x^5}$ and (b) $\sqrt[4]{32x^4z^5}$ by removing all possible factors from the radical.

Solution:

(a) $\sqrt[3]{16x^5} = \sqrt[3]{(8x^3)(2x^2)} = \sqrt[3]{8x^3}\sqrt[3]{2x^2} = 2x\sqrt[3]{2x^2}$

(b) $\sqrt[4]{32x^4z^5} = \sqrt[4]{16x^4z^42z} = \sqrt[4]{16x^4z^4}\sqrt[4]{2z} = 2|x|z\sqrt[4]{2z}$

[Note: Since x^4 is under the radical, x could be positive or negative. For z^5 to be under the radical,
z must be positive.]

39. Simplify (a) $\sqrt{75x^2y^{-4}}$ and (b) $\sqrt{5(x-y)^3}$ by removing all possible factors from the radical.

Solution:

(a) $\sqrt{75x^2y^{-4}} = \sqrt{\dfrac{25x^2}{y^4} \cdot 3} = \dfrac{5\sqrt{3}|x|}{y^2}$

(b) $\sqrt{5(x-y)^3} = \sqrt{(x-y)^2 5(x-y)} = (x-y)\sqrt{5(x-y)}$

41. Find the domain of $\sqrt{x-1}$

Solution:

$\sqrt{x-1}$ is defined when $x \geq 1$. Therefore, the domain is $[1, \infty)$.

43. Find the domain of $\sqrt{x^2+3}$

Solution:

$\sqrt{x^2+3}$ is defined for all real numbers. Therefore, the domain is $(-\infty, \infty)$.

45. Find the domain of $\dfrac{1}{\sqrt[3]{x-1}}$

Solution:

$\dfrac{1}{\sqrt[3]{x-1}}$ is defined for all real numbers except $x = 1$. Therefore, the domain is $(-\infty, 1)$ and $(1, \infty)$.

47. Find the domain of $\dfrac{1}{\sqrt[4]{2x-6}}$

Solution:

$\dfrac{1}{\sqrt[4]{2x-6}}$ is defined when $x > 3$. Therefore, the domain is $(3, \infty)$.

49. Find the domain of $\sqrt{x-1} + \sqrt{5-x}$

Solution:

$\sqrt{x-1}$ is defined when $x \geq 1$, and $\sqrt{5-x}$ is defined when $x \leq 5$. Therefore, the domain of $\sqrt{x-1} + \sqrt{5-x}$ is $1 \leq x \leq 5$.

51. *Compound Interest* A certificate of deposit has a principal of P and an annual percentage rate of r (expressed as a decimial) compounded n times per year. Use the compound interest formula

$$A = P\left(1 + \frac{r}{n}\right)^N$$

to find the balance after N compoundings.

$P = \$10,000$

$r = 9.5\%, n = 12$

$N = 120$

Solution:

$$A = 10,000\left(1 + \frac{0.095}{12}\right)^{120} \approx \$25,760.55$$

53. *Installment Loan* A 5-year auto loan for $P = \$7000$ with an annual percentage rate of $r = 0.14$ requires a monthly payment of $M = \$162.88$. Payments have been made on the loan for 2 years ($N = 24$ monthly payments). Determine the balance B due on the loan if that balance is given by the formula

$$B = \left(1 + \frac{r}{12}\right)^N \left(P - \frac{12M}{r}\right) + \frac{12M}{r}.$$

Solution:

$$B = \left(1 + \frac{0.14}{12}\right)^{24}\left(7000 - \frac{12(162.88)}{0.14}\right) + \frac{12(162.88)}{0.14} \approx \$4765.56$$

Section 0.4   Factoring Polynomials

1. Use the Quadratic Formula to find all real zeros of $6x^2 - x - 1$.

Solution:

Since $a = 6$, $b = -1$, and $c = -1$, we have $x = \dfrac{1 \pm \sqrt{1 - (-24)}}{12} = \dfrac{1 \pm 5}{12}$.

Thus, $x = \dfrac{1 + 5}{12} = \dfrac{1}{2}$ or $x = \dfrac{1 - 5}{12} = -\dfrac{1}{3}$.

3. Use the Quadratic Formula to find all real zeros of $4x^2 - 12x + 9$.

Solution:

Since $a = 4$, $b = -12$, and $c = 9$, we have $x = \dfrac{12 \pm \sqrt{144 - 144}}{8} = \dfrac{12}{8} = \dfrac{3}{2}$.

5. Use the Quadratic Formula to find all real zeros of $y^2 + 4y + 1$.

Solution:

Since $a = 1$, $b = 4$, and $c = 1$, we have $y = \dfrac{-4 \pm \sqrt{16 - 4}}{2} = \dfrac{-4 \pm 2\sqrt{3}}{2} = -2 \pm \sqrt{3}$.

7. Write $x^2 - 4x + 4$ as the product of two linear factors.

Solution:

$$x^2 - 4x + 4 = (x - 2)^2$$

9. Write $4x^2 + 4x + 1$ as the product of two linear factors.

Solution:

$$4x^2 + 4x + 1 = (2x + 1)^2$$

11. Write $x^2 + x - 2$ as the product of two linear factors.

Solution:

$$x^2 + x - 2 = (x + 2)(x - 1)$$

13. Write $3x^2 - 5x + 2$ as the product of two linear factors.

Solution:

$$3x^2 - 5x + 2 = (3x - 2)(x - 1)$$

15. Write $x^2 - 4xy + 4y^2$ as the product of two linear factors.

Solution:

$$x^2 - 4xy + 4y^2 = (x - 2y)^2$$

17. Completely factor $81 - y^4$.

  Solution:

$$81 - y^4 = (9 + y^2)(9 - y^2)$$
$$= (9 + y^2)(3 + y)(3 - y)$$

19. Completely factor $x^3 - 8$.

  Solution:

$$x^3 - 8 = x^3 - 2^3 = (x - 2)(x^2 + 2x + 4)$$

21. Completely factor $y^3 + 64$.

  Solution:

$$y^3 + 64 = y^3 + 4^3 = (y + 4)(y^2 - 4y + 16)$$

23. Completely factor $x^3 - 27$.

  Solution:

$$x^3 - 27 = x^3 - 3^3 = (x - 3)(x^2 + 3x + 9)$$

25. Completely factor $x^3 - 4x^2 - x + 4$.

  Solution:

$$x^3 - 4x^2 - x + 4 = x^2(x - 4) - (x - 4)$$
$$= (x - 4)(x^2 - 1)$$
$$= (x - 4)(x + 1)(x - 1)$$

27. Completely factor $2x^3 - 3x^2 + 4x - 6$.

  Solution:

$$2x^3 - 2x^2 + 4x - 6 = x^2(2x - 3) + 2(2x - 3)$$
$$= (2x - 3)(x^2 + 2)$$

29. Completely factor $2x^3 - 4x^2 - x + 2$

  Solution:

$$2x^3 - 4x^2 - x + 2 = 2x^2(x - 2) - (x - 2)$$
$$= (x - 2)(2x^2 - 1)$$

31. Find all real solutions of $x^2 - 5x = 0$.

Solution:

$$x^2 - 5x = 0$$
$$x(x - 5) = 0$$
$$x = 0, 5$$

33. Find all real solutions of $x^2 - 9 = 0$.

Solution:

$$x^2 - 9 = 0$$
$$(x + 3)(x - 3) = 0$$
$$x = -3, 3$$

35. Find all real solutions of $x^2 - 3 = 0$.

Solution:

$$x^2 - 3 = 0$$
$$\left(x + \sqrt{3}\right)\left(x - \sqrt{3}\right) = 0$$
$$x = \pm\sqrt{3}$$

37. Find all real solutions of $(x - 3)^2 - 9 = 0$.

Solution:

$$(x - 3)^2 - 9 = 0$$
$$x^2 - 6x + 9 - 9 = 0$$
$$x(x - 6) = 0$$
$$x = 0, 6$$

39. Find all real solutions of $x^2 + x - 2 = 0$.

Solution:

$$x^2 + x - 2 = 0$$
$$(x + 2)(x - 1) = 0$$
$$x = -2, 1$$

41. Find all real solutions of $x^2 - 5x + 6 = 0$.

Solution:

$$x^2 - 5 + 6 = 0$$
$$(x - 2)(x - 3) = 0$$
$$x = 2, 3$$

43. Find all real solutions of $x^3 + 64 = 0$.

Solution:

$$x^3 + 64 = 0$$
$$x^3 = -64$$
$$x = \sqrt[3]{-64} = -4$$

45. Find all real solutions of $x^4 - 16 = 0$.

Solution:

$$x^4 - 16 = 0$$
$$x^4 = 16$$
$$x = \pm\sqrt[4]{16} = \pm 2$$

47. Find all real solutions of $x^3 - x^2 - 4x + 4 = 0$.

Solution:

$$x^3 - x^2 - 4x + 4 = 0$$
$$x^2(x - 1) - 4(x - 1) = 0$$
$$(x - 1)(x^2 - 4) = 0$$
$$(x - 1)(x - 2)(x + 2) = 0$$
$$x = 1, \pm 2$$

49. Find the interval (or intervals) on which $\sqrt{x^2 - 7x + 12}$ is defined.

Solution:

Since

$$\sqrt{x^2 - 7x + 12} = \sqrt{(x - 3)(x - 4)},$$

the roots are $x = 3$ and $x = 4$. By testing points inside and outside the interval [3, 4], we find that the expression is defined when $x \leq 3$ or $x \geq 4$. Thus, the domain is $(-\infty, 3] \cup [4, \infty)$.

51. Find the interval (or intervals) on which $\sqrt{4 - x^2}$ is defined.

Solution:

Since

$$\sqrt{4 - x^2} = \sqrt{(2 + x)(2 - x)},$$

the roots are $x = \pm 2$. By testing points inside and outside the interval $[-2, 2]$, we find that the expression is defined when $-2 \leq x \leq 2$. Thus, the domain is $[-2, 2]$.

53. Use synthetic division to complete the indicated factorization $x^3 + 8 = (x + 2)(\quad)$.

Solution:

$$
\begin{array}{r|rrrr}
-2 & 1 & 0 & 0 & 8 \\
   &   & -2 & 4 & -8 \\
\hline
   & 1 & -2 & 4 & 0
\end{array}
$$

Therefore, the factorization is $x^3 + 8 = (x + 2)(x^2 - 2x + 4)$.

55. Use synthetic division to complete the indicated factorization $2x^3 - x^2 - 2x + 1 = (x - 1)(\quad)$

Solution:

$$
\begin{array}{r|rrrr}
1 & 2 & -1 & -2 & 1 \\
  &   & 2 & 1 & -1 \\
\hline
  & 2 & 1 & -1 & 0
\end{array}
$$

Therefore, the factorization is $2x^3 - x^2 - 2x + 1 = (x - 1)(2x^2 + x - 1)$.

57. Use the Rational Zero Theorem as an aid in finding all real solutions of $x^3 - x^2 - x + 1 = 0$.

Solution:

Possible rational roots: ± 1

Using synthetic division for $x = 1$, we have the following.

$$
\begin{array}{r|rrrr}
1 & 1 & -1 & -1 & 1 \\
  &   & 1 & 0 & -1 \\
\hline
  & 1 & 0 & -1 & 0
\end{array}
$$

Therefore, we have

$$x^3 - x^2 - x + 1 = 0$$
$$(x - 1)(x^2 - 1) = 0$$
$$(x - 1)(x - 1)(x + 1) = 0$$
$$x = \pm 1.$$

59. Use the Rational Zero Theorem as an aid in finding all real solutions of $x^3 - 6x^2 + 11x - 6 = 0$.

Solution:

Possible rational roots: $\pm 1, \pm 2, \pm 3, \pm 6$

Using synthetic division for $x = 1$, we have the following.

$$
\begin{array}{r|rrrr}
1 & 1 & -6 & 11 & -6 \\
  &   & 1 & -5 & 6 \\
\hline
  & 1 & -5 & 6 & 0
\end{array}
$$

Therefore, we have

$$x^3 - 6x^2 + 11x - 6 = 0$$
$$(x - 1)(x^2 - 5x + 6) = 0$$
$$(x - 1)(x - 2)(x - 3) = 0$$
$$x = 1, 2, 3.$$

61. Use the Rational Zero Theorem as an aid in finding all real solutions of $4x^3 - 4x^2 - x + 1 = 0$.

Solution:

Possible rational roots: $\pm 1, \pm \frac{1}{2}, \pm \frac{1}{4}$

Using synthetic division for $x = 1$, we have the following.

$$
\begin{array}{r|rrrr}
1 & 4 & -4 & -1 & 1 \\
  &   & 4 & 0 & -1 \\
\hline
  & 4 & 0 & -1 & 0
\end{array}
$$

Therefore, we have

$$4x^3 - 4x^2 - x + 1 = 0$$
$$(x - 1)(4x^2 - 1) = 0$$
$$(x - 1)(2x + 1)(2x - 1) = 0$$
$$x = 1, \pm\frac{1}{2}.$$

63. Use the Rational Zero Theorem as an aid in finding all real solutions of $x^3 - 3x^2 - 3x - 4 = 0$.

Solution:

Possible rational roots: $\pm 1, \pm 2, \pm 4$.

Using synthetic division for $x = 4$, we have the following.

$$
\begin{array}{r|rrrr}
4 & 1 & -3 & -3 & -4 \\
  &   & 4 & 4 & 4 \\
\hline
  & 1 & 1 & 1 & 0
\end{array}
$$

Therefore, we have

$$x^3 - 3x^2 - 3x - 4 = 0$$

$$(x - 4)(x^2 + x + 1) = 0.$$

Since $x^2 + x + 1$ has no real solutions, $x = 4$ is the only real solution.

65. *Average Cost* The minimum average cost of producing x units of a certain product occurs when the production level is set at the (positive) solution of

$$0.0003x^2 - 1200 = 0$$

Determine the production level.

Solution:

$$0.0003x^2 - 1200 = 0$$

$$0.0003x^2 = 1200$$

$$x^2 = 4,000,000$$

$$x = 2000 \text{ units}$$

Section 0.5   Fractions and Rationalization

1. Perform the indicated operations and simplify your answer.

$$\frac{5}{x-1} + \frac{x}{x-1}$$

Solution:

$$\frac{5}{x-1} + \frac{x}{x-1} = \frac{5+x}{x-1} = \frac{x+5}{x-1}$$

3. Perform the indicated operations and simplify your answer.

$$\frac{2x}{x^2+2} - \frac{1-3x}{x^2+2}$$

Solution:

$$\frac{2x}{x^2+2} - \frac{1-3x}{x^2+2} = \frac{2x-(1-3x)}{x^2+2}$$
$$= \frac{5x-1}{x^2+2}$$

5. Perform the indicated operations and simplify your answer.

$$\frac{4}{x} - \frac{3}{x^2}$$

Solution:

$$\frac{4}{x} - \frac{3}{x^2} = \frac{4x}{x^2} - \frac{3}{x^2} = \frac{4x-3}{x^2}$$

7. Perform the indicated operations and simplify your answer.

$$\frac{2}{x+2} - \frac{1}{x-2}$$

Solution:

$$\frac{2}{x+2} - \frac{1}{x-2} = \frac{2(x-2)-(x+2)}{(x+2)(x-2)}$$
$$= \frac{x-6}{x^2-4}$$

9. Perform the indicated operations and simplify your answer.

$$\frac{5}{x-3} + \frac{3}{3-x}$$

Solution:

$$\frac{5}{x-3} + \frac{3}{3-x} = \frac{5}{x-3} + \frac{-3}{x-3} = \frac{2}{x-3}$$

11. Perform the indicated operations and simplify your answer.

$$\frac{A}{x-6} + \frac{B}{x+3}$$

Solution:

$$\frac{A}{x-6} + \frac{B}{x+3} = \frac{A(x+3) + B(x-6)}{(x-6)(x+3)} = \frac{Ax + 3A + Bx - 6B}{(x-6)(x+3)}$$

$$= \frac{(A+B)x + 3(A-2B)}{(x-6)(x+3)}$$

13. Perform the indicated operations and simplify your answer.

$$-\frac{1}{x} + \frac{2}{x^2+1}$$

Solution:

$$-\frac{1}{x} + \frac{2}{x^2+1} = \frac{-(x^2+1) + 2x}{x(x^2+1)} = \frac{-x^2 + 2x - 1}{x(x^2+1)} = \frac{-(x^2 - 2x + 1)}{x(x^2+1)} = \frac{-(x-1)^2}{x(x^2+1)}$$

15. Perform the indicated operations and simplify your answer.

$$\frac{-x}{(x+1)^{3/2}} + \frac{2}{(x+1)^{1/2}}$$

Solution:

$$\frac{-x}{(x+1)^{3/2}} + \frac{2}{(x+1)^{1/2}} = \frac{-x + 2(x+1)}{(x+1)^{3/2}} = \frac{x+2}{(x+1)^{3/2}}$$

17. Perform the indicated operations and simplify your answer.

$$\frac{2-t}{2\sqrt{1+t}} - \sqrt{1+t}$$

Solution:

$$\frac{2-t}{2\sqrt{1+t}} - \sqrt{1+t} = \frac{2-t}{2\sqrt{1+t}} - \frac{\sqrt{1+t}}{1} \cdot \frac{2\sqrt{1+t}}{2\sqrt{1+t}} = \frac{(2-t) - 2(1+t)}{2\sqrt{1+t}} = \frac{-3t}{2\sqrt{1+t}}$$

19. Perform the indicated operations and simplify your answer.

$$\frac{1}{x^2 - x - 2} - \frac{x}{x^2 - 5x + 6}$$

Solution:

$$\frac{1}{x^2 - x - 2} - \frac{x}{x^2 - 5x + 6} = \frac{1}{(x+1)(x-2)} - \frac{x}{(x-2)(x-3)}$$

$$= \frac{(x-3) - x(x+1)}{(x+1)(x-2)(x-3)}$$

$$= \frac{-x^2 - 3}{(x+1)(x-2)(x-3)}$$

$$= \frac{x^2 + 3}{(x+1)(x-2)(x-3)}$$

21. Perform the indicated operations and simplify your answer.

$$\frac{A}{x+1} + \frac{B}{(x+1)^2} + \frac{C}{x-2}$$

Solution:

$$\frac{A}{x+1} + \frac{B}{(x+1)^2} + \frac{C}{x-2} = \frac{A(x+1)(x-2) + B(x-2) + C(x+1)^2}{(x+1)^2(x-2)}$$

$$= \frac{A(x^2-x-2) + B(x-2) + C(x^2+2x+1)}{(x+1)^2(x-2)}$$

$$= \frac{Ax^2 - Ax - 2A + Bx - 2B + Cx^2 + 2Cx + C}{(x+1)^2(x-2)}$$

$$= \frac{(A+C)x^2 - (A-B-2C)x - (2A+2B-C)}{(x+1)^2(x-2)}$$

23. Perform the indicated operations and simplify your answer.

$$\left(2x\sqrt{x^2+1} - \frac{x^3}{\sqrt{x^2+1}}\right) \div (x^2+1)$$

Solution:

$$\left(2x\sqrt{x^2+1} - \frac{x^3}{\sqrt{x^2+1}}\right) \div (x^2+1) = \frac{2x(x^2+1) - x^3}{\sqrt{x^2+1}} \cdot \frac{1}{x^2+1}$$

$$= \frac{x^3+2x}{\sqrt{x^2+1}(x^2+1)} = \frac{x(x^2+2)}{(x^2+1)^{3/2}}$$

25. Perform the indicated operations and simplify your answer.

$$\frac{(x^2+2)^{1/2} - x^2(x^2+2)^{-1/2}}{x^2}$$

Solution:

$$\frac{(x^2+2)^{1/2} - x^2(x^2+2)^{-1/2}}{x^2} = \frac{(x^2+2)^{-1/2}[(x^2+2) - x^2]}{x^2} = \frac{2}{x^2\sqrt{x^2+2}}$$

27. Perform the indicated operations and simplify your answer.

$$\frac{\dfrac{\sqrt{x+1}}{\sqrt{x}} - \dfrac{\sqrt{x}}{\sqrt{x+1}}}{2(x+1)}$$

Solution:

$$\frac{\dfrac{\sqrt{x+1}}{\sqrt{x}} - \dfrac{\sqrt{x}}{\sqrt{x+1}}}{2(x+1)} = \frac{(x+1) - x}{\sqrt{x}\sqrt{x+1}} \cdot \frac{1}{2(x+1)} = \frac{1}{2\sqrt{x}(x+1)^{3/2}}$$

29. Rationalize the denominator and simplify.

$$\frac{3}{\sqrt{27}}$$

Solution:

$$\frac{3}{\sqrt{27}} = \frac{3}{3\sqrt{3}} = \frac{1}{\sqrt{3}} \cdot \frac{\sqrt{3}}{\sqrt{3}} = \frac{\sqrt{3}}{3}$$

31. Rationalize the numerator and simplify.

$$\frac{\sqrt{2}}{3}$$

Solution:

$$\frac{\sqrt{2}}{3} = \frac{\sqrt{2}}{3} \cdot \frac{\sqrt{2}}{\sqrt{2}} = \frac{2}{3\sqrt{2}}$$

33. Rationalize the denominator and simplify.

$$\frac{x}{\sqrt{x-4}}$$

Solution:

$$\frac{x}{\sqrt{x-4}} = \frac{x}{\sqrt{x-4}} \cdot \frac{\sqrt{x-4}}{\sqrt{x-4}} = \frac{x\sqrt{x-4}}{x-4}$$

35. Rationalize the numerator and simplify.

$$\frac{\sqrt{y^3}}{6y}$$

Solution:

$$\frac{\sqrt{y^3}}{6y} = \frac{y\sqrt{y}}{6y} = \frac{\sqrt{y}}{6} = \frac{y}{6\sqrt{y}}$$

37. Rationalize the denominator and simplify.

$$\frac{49(x-3)}{\sqrt{x^2-9}}$$

Solution:

$$\frac{49(x-3)}{\sqrt{x^2-9}} = \frac{49(x-3)}{\sqrt{x^2-9}} \cdot \frac{\sqrt{x^2-9}}{\sqrt{x^2-9}} = \frac{49(x-3)\sqrt{x^2-9}}{(x+3)(x-3)} = \frac{49\sqrt{x^2-9}}{x+3}$$

39. Rationalize the denominator and simplify.

$$\frac{5}{\sqrt{14}-2}$$

Solution:

$$\frac{5}{\sqrt{14}-2} = \frac{5}{\sqrt{14}-2} \cdot \frac{\sqrt{14}+2}{\sqrt{14}+2} = \frac{5(\sqrt{14}+2)}{14-4} = \frac{\sqrt{14}+2}{2}$$

41. Rationalize the denominator and simplify.

$$\frac{2x}{5 - \sqrt{3}}$$

Solution:

$$\frac{2x}{5 - \sqrt{3}} = \frac{2x}{5 - \sqrt{3}} \cdot \frac{5 + \sqrt{3}}{5 + \sqrt{3}} = \frac{2x(5 + \sqrt{3})}{25 - 3} = \frac{x(5 + \sqrt{3})}{11}$$

43. Rationalize the denominator and simplify.

$$\frac{1}{\sqrt{6} + \sqrt{5}}$$

Solution:

$$\frac{1}{\sqrt{6} + \sqrt{5}} = \frac{1}{\sqrt{6} + \sqrt{5}} \cdot \frac{\sqrt{6} - \sqrt{5}}{\sqrt{6} - \sqrt{5}} = \frac{\sqrt{6} - \sqrt{5}}{6 - 5} = \sqrt{6} - \sqrt{5}$$

45. Rationalize the numerator and simplify.

$$\frac{\sqrt{3} - \sqrt{2}}{x}$$

Solution:

$$\frac{\sqrt{3} - \sqrt{2}}{x} = \frac{\sqrt{3} - \sqrt{2}}{x} \cdot \frac{\sqrt{3} + \sqrt{2}}{\sqrt{3} + \sqrt{2}} = \frac{3 - 2}{x(\sqrt{3} + \sqrt{2})} = \frac{1}{x\sqrt{3} + \sqrt{2})}$$

47. Rationalize the numerator and simplify.

$$\frac{2x - \sqrt{4x - 1}}{2x - 1}$$

Solution:

$$\frac{2x - \sqrt{4x - 1}}{2x - 1} = \frac{2x - \sqrt{4x - 1}}{2x - 1} \cdot \frac{2x + \sqrt{4x - 1}}{2x + \sqrt{4x - 1}}$$

$$= \frac{4x^2 - (4x - 1)}{(2x - 1)(2x + \sqrt{4x - 1})}$$

$$= \frac{(2x - 1)^2}{(2x - 1)(2x + \sqrt{4x - 1})}$$

$$= \frac{2x - 1}{2x + \sqrt{4x - 1}}$$

49. *Installment Loan* Determine the monthly payment M for an installment loan of $P = \$10,000$ at an annual percentage rate of 14% ($r = 0.14$) for 5 years ($N = 60$ monthly payments) given the formula

$$M = P \left[\frac{r/12}{1 - \left(\dfrac{1}{(r/12) + 1} \right)^N} \right].$$

Solution:

$$P = 10,000, r = 0.14, N = 60$$

$$M = 10,000 \left[\frac{0.14/12}{1 - \left(\dfrac{1}{(0.14/12) + 1} \right)^{60}} \right] \approx \$232.68$$

Practice Test for Chapter 0

1. Determine whether $\sqrt[4]{81}$ is rational or irrational.

2. Determine whether the given value of x satisfies the inequality $3x + 4 \leq x/2$.
   - (a) $x = -2$
   - (b) $x = 0$
   - (c) $x = -8/5$
   - (d) $x = -6$

3. Solve the inequality $3x + 4 \geq 13$.

4. Solve the inequality $x^2 < 6x + 7$.

5. Determine which of the two given real numbers is greater, $\sqrt{19}$ or $\frac{13}{3}$.

6. Given the interval $[-3, \ 7]$, find (a) the distance between -3 and 7 and (b) the midpoint of the interval.

7. Solve the inequality $|3x + 1| \leq 10$.

8. Solve the inequality $|4 - 5x| > 29$.

9. Solve the inequality $\left| 3 - \dfrac{2x}{5} \right| < 8$.

10. Use absolute values to describe the interval $[-3, \ 5]$.

11. Simplify $\dfrac{12x^3}{4x^{-2}}$.

12. Simplify $\left(\dfrac{\sqrt{3}\sqrt{x^3}}{x} \right)^0$, $\quad x \neq 0$.

13. Remove all possible factors from the radical $\sqrt[3]{32x^4 y^3}$.

14. Complete the factorization.
$$\tfrac{3}{2}(x + 1)^{-1/3} + \tfrac{1}{4}(x + 1)^{2/3} = \tfrac{1}{4}(x + 1)^{-1/3}(\quad)$$

15. Find the domain: $\quad \dfrac{1}{\sqrt{5 - x}}$.

16. Factor completely: $3x^2 - 19x - 14$.

17. Factor completely: $25x^2 - 81$.

18. Factor completely: $x^3 + 8$.

19. Use the Quadratic Formula to find all real roots of $x^2 + 6x - 2 = 0$.

20. Use the Rational Zero Theorem to find all real roots of $x^3 - 4x^2 + x + 6 = 0$.

21. Combine terms and simplify: $\dfrac{x}{x^2 + 2x - 3} - \dfrac{1}{x-1}$.

22. Combine terms and simplify: $\dfrac{3-x}{2\sqrt{x+5}} + \sqrt{x+5}$.

23. Combine terms and simplify: $\dfrac{\dfrac{\sqrt{x+2}}{\sqrt{x}} - \dfrac{\sqrt{x}}{\sqrt{x+2}}}{2(x+2)}$.

24. Rationalize the denominator: $\dfrac{3y}{\sqrt{y^2+9}}$.

25. Rationalize the numerator: $\dfrac{\sqrt{x} + \sqrt{x+7}}{14}$.

Graphing Calculator Required

26. Use a graphing calculator to find the real solutions of $x^3 - 5x^2 + 2x + 8 = 0$ by graphing $y = x^3 - 5x^2 + 2x + 8$ and finding the x-intercepts.

CHAPTER 1
Functions, Graphs, and Limits

Section 1.1   The Cartesian Plane and the Distance Formula

1. (a) Find the length of each side of the right triangle shown in the accompanying graph.
   (b) Show that these lengths satisfy the Pythagorean Theorem.

   Solution:

   (a) $a = 4$

   $b = 3$

   $c = \sqrt{(4-0)^2 + (3-0)^2} = 5$

   (b) $a^2 + b^2 = 16 + 9 = 25 = c^2$

   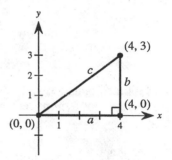

3. (a) Find the length of each side of the right triangle shown in the accompanying graph.
   (b) Show that these lengths satisfy the Pythagorean Theorem.

   Solution:

   (a) $a = 10$

   $b = 3$

   $c = \sqrt{(7+3)^2 + (4-1)^2} = \sqrt{109}$

   (b) $a^2 + b^2 = 100 + 9 = 109 = c^2$

   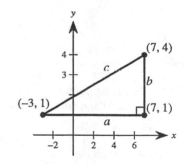

5. (a) Plot the points (3, 1), (5, 5), (b) find the distance between the points, and (c) find the midpoint of the line segment joining the points.

Solution:

(a) see graph

(b) $d = \sqrt{(5-3)^2 + (5-1)^2}$

$\quad = \sqrt{4+16} = \sqrt{20} = 2\sqrt{5}$

(c) Midpoint $= \left(\dfrac{3+5}{2}, \dfrac{1+5}{2}\right) = (4, 3)$

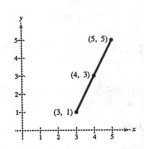

7. (a) Plot the points $\left(\frac{1}{2}, 1\right)$, $\left(-\frac{3}{2}, -5\right)$, (b) find the distance between the points, and (c) find the midpoint of the line segment joining the points.

Solution:

(a) see graph

(b) $d = \sqrt{[-(3/2) - (1/2)]^2 + (-5-1)^2}$

$\quad = \sqrt{4+36} = \sqrt{4(1+9)} = 2\sqrt{10}$

(c) Midpoint $= \left(\dfrac{(1/2) + (-3/2)}{2}, \dfrac{1 + (-5)}{2}\right)$

$\quad = \left(-\dfrac{1}{2}, -2\right)$

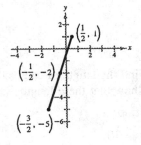

9. (a) Plot the points (2, 2), (4, 14) (b) find the distance between the points, and (c) find the midpoint of the line segment joining the points.

Solution:

(a) see graph

(b) $d = \sqrt{(4-2)^2 + (14-2)^2}$

$\quad = \sqrt{4+144} = \sqrt{4(1+36)} = 2\sqrt{37}$

(c) Midpoint $= \left(\dfrac{2+4}{2}, \dfrac{2+14}{2}\right) = (3, 8)$

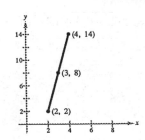

11. (a) Plot the points $(1, \sqrt{3})$, $(-1, 1)$ (b) find the distance between the points, and (c) find the midpoint of the line segment joining the points.

Solution:

(a) see graph

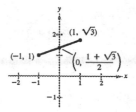

(b) $d = \sqrt{(-1 - 1)^2 + (1 - \sqrt{3})^2} = \sqrt{8 - 2\sqrt{3}}$

(c) Midpoint $= \left(\dfrac{1 + (-1)}{2}, \dfrac{\sqrt{3} + 1}{1} \right)$

$\qquad = \left(0, \dfrac{\sqrt{3} + 1}{2} \right)$

13. Show that the points form the vertices of the indicated figure.

Vertices	Figure
$(0, 1)$, $(3, 7)$, $(4, -1)$	Right triangle

Solution:

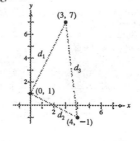

$d_1 = \sqrt{(3 - 0)^2 + (7 - 1)^2} = \sqrt{45} = 3\sqrt{5}$

$d_2 = \sqrt{(4 - 0)^2 + (-1 - 1)^2} = \sqrt{20} = 2\sqrt{5}$

$d_3 = \sqrt{(3 - 4)^2 + (7 - (-1))^2} = \sqrt{65}$

Since $d_1^2 + d_2^2 = d_3^2$, the triangle is a right triangle.

15. Show that the points form the vertices of the indicated figure.

Vertices	Figure
$(0, 0)$, $(1, 2)$, $(2, 1)$, $(3, 3)$	Rhombus

Solution:

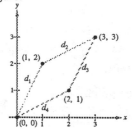

$d_1 = \sqrt{(1 - 0)^2 + (2 - 0)^2} = \sqrt{5}$

$d_2 = \sqrt{(3 - 1)^2 + (3 - 2)^2} = \sqrt{5}$

$d_3 = \sqrt{(2 - 3)^2 + (1 - 3)^2} = \sqrt{5}$

$d_4 = \sqrt{(0 - 2)^2 + (0 - 1)^2} = \sqrt{5}$

17. Use the Distance Formula to determine whether the points $(0, -4)$, $(2, 0)$, $(3, 2)$ are collinear.

Solution:

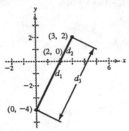

$$d_1 = \sqrt{(2-0)^2 + (0+4)^2} = \sqrt{20} = 2\sqrt{5}$$

$$d_2 = \sqrt{(3-2)^2 + (2-0)^2} = \sqrt{5}$$

$$d_3 = \sqrt{(3-0)^2 + (2+4)^2} = \sqrt{45} = 3\sqrt{5}$$

Since $d_1 + d_2 = d_3$, the points are collinear.

19. Use the Distance Formula to determine whether the points $(-2, -6)$, $(1, -3)$, $(5, 2)$ are collinear.

Solution:

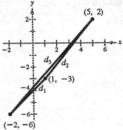

$$d_1 = \sqrt{(1-(-2))^2 + (-3-(-6))^2} = \sqrt{18} = 3\sqrt{2}$$

$$d_2 = \sqrt{(5-1)^2 + (2-(-3))^2} = \sqrt{41}$$

$$d_3 = \sqrt{(5-(-2))^2 + (2-(-6))^2} = \sqrt{113}$$

Since $d_1 + d_2 \neq d_3$, the points are not collinear.

21. Find x so that the distance between $(1, 0)$, $(x, -4)$ is 5.

Solution:

$$d = \sqrt{(x-1)^2 + (-4-0)^2} = 5$$

$$\sqrt{x^2 - 2x + 17} = 5$$

$$x^2 - 2x + 17 = 25$$

$$x^2 - 2x - 8 = 0$$

$$(x-4)(x+2) = 0$$

$$x = 4, -2$$

23. Find y so that the distance between $(0, 0)$, $(3, y)$ is 8.

Solution:

$$d = \sqrt{(3 - 0)^2 + (y - 0)^2} = 8$$

$$\sqrt{9 + y^2} = 8$$

$$9 + y^2 = 64$$

$$y^2 = 55$$

$$y = \pm\sqrt{55}$$

25. Use the Midpoint Formula successively to find the three points that divide the line segment joining (x_1, y_1) and (x_2, y_2) into four equal parts.

Solution:

$$\text{Midpoint} = \left(\frac{x_1 + x_2}{2}, \frac{y_1 + y_2}{2}\right)$$

The point one-fourth of the way between (x_1, y_1) and (x_2, y_2) is the midpoint of the line segment from (x_1, y_1) to

$\left(\dfrac{x_1 + x_2}{2}, \dfrac{y_1 + y_2}{2}\right)$, which is

$$\left(\frac{x_1 + \dfrac{x_1 + x_2}{2}}{2}, \frac{y_1 + \dfrac{y_1 + y_2}{2}}{2}\right) = \left(\frac{3x_1 + x_2}{4}, \frac{3y_1 + y_2}{4}\right).$$

The point three-fourths of the way between (x_1, y_1) and (x_2, y_2) is the midpoint of the line segment from

$\left(\dfrac{x_1 + x_2}{2}, \dfrac{y_1 + y_2}{2}\right)$ to (x_2, y_2), which is

$$\left(\frac{\dfrac{x_1 + x_2}{2} + x_2}{2}, \frac{\dfrac{y_1 + y_2}{2} + y_2}{2}\right) = \left(\frac{x_1 + 3x_2}{4}, \frac{y_1 + 3y_2}{4}\right).$$

Thus, $\left(\dfrac{3x_1 + x_2}{4}, \dfrac{3y_1 + y_2}{4}\right)$, $\left(\dfrac{x_1 + x_2}{2}, \dfrac{y_1 + y_2}{2}\right)$, and $\left(\dfrac{x_1 + 3x_2}{4}, \dfrac{y_1 + 3y_2}{4}\right)$ are the three points that divide the line segment joining (x_1, y_1) and (x_2, y_2) into four equal parts.

27. Use the result of Exercise 25 to find the points that divide the line segment joining the given points into four equal parts.

(a) $(1, -2)$, $(4, -1)$ (b) $(-2, -3)$, $(0, 0)$

Solution:

(a) $\left(\dfrac{3(1)+4}{4}, \dfrac{3(-2)-1}{4}\right) = \left(\dfrac{7}{4}, -\dfrac{7}{4}\right)$ (b) $\left(\dfrac{3(-2)+0}{4}, \dfrac{3(-3)+0}{4}\right) = \left(-\dfrac{3}{2}, -\dfrac{9}{4}\right)$

$\left(\dfrac{1+4}{2}, \dfrac{-2-1}{2}\right) = \left(\dfrac{5}{2}, -\dfrac{3}{2}\right)$ $\left(\dfrac{-2+0}{2}, \dfrac{-3+0}{2}\right) = \left(-1, -\dfrac{3}{2}\right)$

$\left(\dfrac{1+3(4)}{4}, \dfrac{-2+3(-1)}{4}\right) = \left(\dfrac{13}{4}, -\dfrac{5}{4}\right)$ $\left(\dfrac{-2+3(0)}{4}, \dfrac{-3+3(0)}{4}\right) = \left(-\dfrac{1}{2}, -\dfrac{3}{4}\right)$

29. *Building Dimensions* The base and height of the trusses for the roof of a house are 32 feet and 5 feet, respectively. (a) Find the distance from the eaves to the peak of the roof. (b) Use the result of part (a) to find the number of square feet of roofing required for the house if the length of the house is 40 feet.

Solution:

(a) $x^2 = 16^2 + 5^2, \quad x > 0$

       $x^2 = 281$

       $x = \sqrt{281} \approx 16.76$ feet

(b) $A = 2(40)(\sqrt{281}) = 80\sqrt{281} \approx 1341.04$ square feet

31. *Cable TV* For 1983–1992, the number (in millions) of cable television subscribers in the United States is given in the table.

Year	1983	1984	1985	1986	1987
Subscribers	25.0	37.3	39.9	42.2	44.9

Year	1988	1989	1990	1991	1992
Subscribers	48.6	52.6	54.9	55.8	57.2

Use a scatter plot, a bar graph, or a line graph to represent the data. Describe any trends that appear.

Solution:

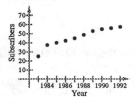

33. Use the figure in the text showing the Dow Jones Industrial Average for common stocks.

Solution:

(a) In August 1990, the Dow Jones Average was approximately 2900.

(b) In November 1990, the Dow Jones Average was approximately 2450.

(c) In December 1991, the Dow Jones Average was approximately 2970.

(d) In March 1992, the Dow Jones Average was approximately 3270.

35. *Housing Starts* Use the figure shown in the text showing the number of housing starts (in millions) in the United States from 1990 through 1992.

Estimate the number of housing starts for the following.

(a) February 1990   (b) October 1990

(c) January 1991   (d) April 1992

Solution:

(a) Approximately 1.42 million housing starts in February 1990.

(b) Approximately 1.04 million housing starts in October 1990.

(c) Approximately 0.85 million housing starts in January 1991.

(d) Approximately 1.13 million housing starts in April 1992.

37. (a) Use the Midpoint Formula to estimate the revenue and profit of the company in 1990. (b) Then use your school's library or some other reference source to find the actual revenue and profit for 1990. (c) Did the revenue and profit increase in a linear pattern from 1988 to 1992? Explain your reasoning. (d) What were the company's expenses during each of the given years? (e) How would you rate the company's growth from 1988 to 1992?

Solution:

$$\text{Revenue midpoint} = \left(\frac{1988 + 1992}{2}, \frac{3581.2 + 5162.8}{2} \right)$$

$$= (1990, 4372.0)$$

$$\text{Profit midpoint} = \left(\frac{1988 + 1992}{2}, \frac{268.5 + 513.4}{2} \right)$$

$$= (1990, 390.95)$$

Thus, in 1990, the revenue was approximately 4372.0 million and the profit 390.95 million.

39. The red figure is translated to a new position in the plane to form the blue figure. (a) Find the vertices of the transformed figure. (b) Then use a graphing utility to draw the figure.

Solution:

(a) $(0, 0)$ is translated to $(0 + 2, 0 + 3) = (2, 3)$ (b)
$(-3, -1)$ is translated to $(-3 + 2, -1 + 3) = (-1, 2)$.
$(-1, -2)$ is translated to $(-1 + 2, -2 + 3) = (1, 1)$.

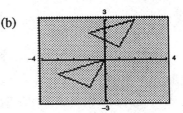

Section 1.2   Graphs of Equations

1. Determine whether the points are solutions points for the equation $2x - y - 3 = 0$.

(a) $(1, 2)$ (b) $(1, -1)$ (c) $(4, 5)$

Solution:

(a) This is not a solution point since $2x - y - 3 = 2(1) - 2 - 3 = -3 \neq 0$.
(b) This is a solution point since $2x - y - 3 = 2(1) - (-1) - 3 = 0$.
(c) This is a solution point since $2x - y - 3 = 2(4) - 5 - 3 = 0$.

3. Determine whether the points are solutions points for the equation $x^2y + x^2 - 5y = 0$.

   (a) $\left(0, \frac{1}{5}\right)$ (b) $(2, 4)$ (c) $(-2, -4)$

   Solution:

   (a) This is not a solution point since $x^2y + x^2 - 5y = 0^2\left(\frac{1}{5}\right) + 0^2 - 5\left(\frac{1}{5}\right) = -1 \neq 0$.

   (b) This is a solution point since $x^2y + x^2 - 5y = 2^2(4) + 2^2 - 5(4) = 0$.

   (c) This is not a solution point since $x^2y + x^2 - 5y = (-2)^2(-4) + (-2)^2 - 5(-4) = 8 \neq 0$.

5. Match $y = x - 2$ with one of the six graphs shown in the text.

   Solution:

   The graph of $y = x - 2$ is a straight line with y-intercept at $(0, -2)$. Thus, it matches (e).

7. Match $y = x^2 + 2x$ with one of the six graphs shown in the text.

   Solution:

   The graph of $y = x^2 + 2x$ is a parabola opening up with vertex at $(-1, -1)$. Thus, it matches (c).

9. Match $y = |x| - 2$ with one of the six graphs shown in the text.

   Solution:

   The graph of $y = |x| - 2$ has a y-intercept at $(0, -2)$ and has x-intercepts at $(-2, 0)$ and $(2, 0)$. Thus, it matches (a).

11. Find the intercepts of the graph of $2x - y - 3 = 0$.

    Solution:

    To find the y-intercept, let $x = 0$ to obtain

    $$2(0) - y - 3 = 0$$
    $$y = -3.$$

    Thus, the y-intercept is $(0, -3)$. To find the x-intercept, let $y = 0$ to obtain

    $$2x - (0) - 3 = 0$$
    $$x = \frac{3}{2}.$$

    Thus, the x-intercept is $\left(\frac{3}{2}, 0\right)$.

13. Find the intercepts of the graph of $y = x^2 + x - 2$.

Solution:

The y-intercept occurs at $(0, -2)$. To find the x-intercepts, let $y = 0$ to obtain

$$x^2 + x - 2 = 0$$
$$(x + 2)(x - 1) = 0$$
$$x = -2, \ 1.$$

Thus, the x-intercepts are $(-2, \ 0)$ and $(1, 0)$.

15. Find the intercepts of the graph of $y = x^2\sqrt{9 - x^2}$.

Solution:

The y-intercept occurs at $(0, 0)$. To find the x-intercepts, let $y = 0$ to obtain

$$x^2\sqrt{9 - x^2} = 0$$
$$x = 0, \ \pm 3.$$

Thus, the x-intercepts are $(0, \ 0)$, $(-3, \ 0)$, and $(3, 0)$.

17. Find the intercepts of the graph of $y = \dfrac{x^2 - 4}{x - 2}$.

Solution:

The y-intercept occurs at $(0, 2)$.

The x-intercept occurs when the numerator equals zero and the denominator does not equal zero.

Thus, $(-2, 0)$ is the only x-intercept.

19. Find the intercepts of the graph of $x^2y - x^2 + 4y = 0$.

Solution:

The x-intercept and y-intercept both occur at $(0, 0)$.

21. Sketch the graph of $y = x$ and plot the intercepts.

Solution:

The graph of $y = x$ is a straight line with intercept at $(0, 0)$.

x	0	1	2	3
y	0	1	2	3

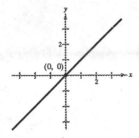

23. Sketch the graph of $y = -3x + 2$ and plot the intercepts.

Solution:

The graph of $y = -3x + 2$ is a straight line with intercepts at $\left(\frac{2}{3}, 0\right)$ and $(0, 2)$.

x	0	$\frac{2}{3}$	1	2
y	2	0	-1	-4

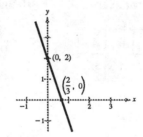

25. Sketch the graph of $y = -3 - x^2$ and plot the intercepts.

Solution:

The graph of $y = -3 - x^2$ is a parabola with vertex at $(0, -3)$, which is also the only intercept.

x	0	± 1	± 2
y	-3	-4	-7

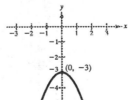

27. Sketch the graph of $y = x^3 + 2$ and plot the intercepts.

Solution:

Intercepts: $(-\sqrt[3]{2},\ 0)$ and $(0, 2)$

x	-2	-1	0	1	2
y	-6	1	2	3	10

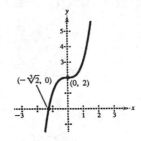

29. Sketch the graph of $y = (x + 2)^2$ and plot the intercepts.

Solution:

The graph is a parabola with vertex at $(-2,\ 0)$ and intercepts at $(-2,\ 0)$ and $(0, 4)$.

x	-3	-2	-1	0	1
y	1	0	1	4	9

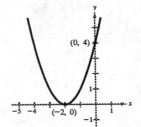

31. Sketch the graph of $y = \sqrt{x + 1}$ and plot the intercepts.

Solution:

$x \geq -1$, intercept: $(0, 0)$

x	-1	0	3	8
y	0	1	2	3

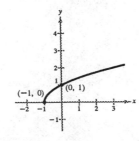

33. Sketch the graph of $y = |x + 1|$ and plot the intercepts.

Intercepts: $(-1, 0)$, $(0, 1)$

Solution:

x	-3	-2	-1	0	1	2
y	2	1	0	1	2	3

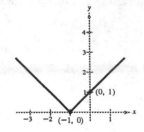

35. Sketch the graph of the equation $y = \dfrac{1}{x - 3}$ and plot the intercepts.

Intercept $\left(0, -\frac{1}{3}\right)$

Solution:

x	-1	0	1	2	2.5	3.5	4	5	6
y	$-\frac{1}{4}$	$-\frac{1}{3}$	$-\frac{1}{2}$	-1	-2	2	1	$\frac{1}{2}$	$\frac{1}{3}$

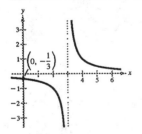

37. Sketch the graph of $x = y^2 - 4$ and plot the intercepts.

Solution:

The graph is a parabola with vertex at $(-4, \ 0)$ and intercepts at $(-4, \ 0)$, $(0, \ 2)$, and $(0, \ -2)$.

x	5	0	-3	-4
y	± 3	± 2	± 1	0

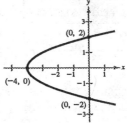

39. Write the general form of the equation of a circle with a center at $(0, 0)$ and a radius of 3.

Solution:

$$(x - 0)^2 + (y - 0)^2 = 3^2$$
$$x^2 + y^2 = 9$$
$$x^2 + y^2 - 9 = 0$$

41. Write the general form of the equation of a circle with a center at $(2, \ -1)$ and a radius of 4.

Solution:

$$(x - 2)^2 + (y + 1)^2 = 4^2$$
$$x^2 - 4x + 4 + y^2 + 2y + 1 = 16$$
$$x^2 + y^2 - 4x + 2y - 11 = 0$$

43. Write the general form of the equation of a circle with a center at $(-1, \ 2)$ and solution point $(0, 0)$.

Solution:

Since the point $(0, 0)$ lies on the circle, the radius must be the distance between $(0, 0)$ and $(-1, \ 2)$.

$$\text{Radius} = \sqrt{(0 + 1)^2 + (0 - 2)^2} = \sqrt{5}$$
$$(x + 1)^2 + (y - 2)^2 = 5$$
$$x^2 + y^2 + 2x - 4y = 0$$

45. Write the general form of the equation of a circle with the endpoints of a diameter $(3, 3)$, $(-3, 3)$.

Solution:

Center = midpoint = $(0, 3)$.

Radius = distance from center to an endpoint = $\sqrt{(0 - 3)^2 + (3 - 3)^2} = 3$

$(x - 0)^2 + (y - 3)^2 = 3^2$

$x^2 + y^2 - 6y = 0$

47. Use the process of completing the square to write $x^2 + y^2 - 2x + 6y + 6 = 0$ in standard form. Sketch the graph of the circle.

Solution:

$(x^2 - 2x + 1) + (y^2 + 6y + 9) = -6 + 1 + 9$

$(x - 1)^2 + (y + 3)^2 = 4$

Center: $(1, -3)$

Radius: 2

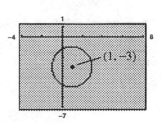

49. Use the process of completing the square to write $x^2 + y^2 + 4x + 6y - 3 = 0$ in standard form. Sketch the graph of the circle.

Solution:

$(x^2 + 4x + 4) + (y^2 + 6y + 9) = 3 + 4 + 9$

$(x + 2)^2 + (y + 3)^2 = 16$

Center: $(-2, -3)$

Radius: 4

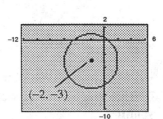

51. Use the process of completing the square to write $2x^2 + 2y^2 - 2x - 2y - 3 = 0$ in standard form. Sketch the graph of the circle.

Solution:

$$x^2 + y^2 - x - y = \frac{3}{2}$$

$$\left(x^2 - x + \frac{1}{4}\right) + \left(y^2 - y + \frac{1}{4}\right) = \frac{3}{2} + \frac{1}{4} + \frac{1}{4}$$

$$\left(x - \frac{1}{2}\right)^2 + \left(y - \frac{1}{2}\right)^2 = 2$$

Center: $\left(\dfrac{1}{2}, \dfrac{1}{2}\right)$

Radius: $\sqrt{2}$

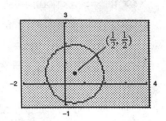

53. Use the process of completing the square to write $16x^2 + 16y^2 + 16x + 40y - 7 = 0$ in standard form. Sketch the graph of the circle.

Solution:

$$x^2 + y^2 + x + \frac{5}{2}y = \frac{7}{16}$$

$$\left(x^2 + x + \frac{1}{4}\right) + \left(y^2 + \frac{5}{2}y + \frac{25}{16}\right) = \frac{7}{16} + \frac{1}{4} + \frac{25}{16}$$

$$\left(x + \frac{1}{2}\right)^2 + \left(y + \frac{5}{4}\right)^2 = \frac{9}{4}$$

Center: $\left(-\dfrac{1}{2}, -\dfrac{5}{4}\right)$

Radius: $\dfrac{3}{2}$

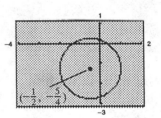

55. Find the point(s) of intersection of the graphs of $x + y = 2$ and $2x - y = 1$ and check your results.

Solution:

Solving for y in the equation $x + y = 2$ yields $y = 2 - x$, and solving for y in the equation $2x - y = 1$ yields $y = 2x - 1$. Then setting these two y-values equal to each other, we have

$$2 - x = 2x - 1$$
$$3 = 3x$$
$$x = 1.$$

The corresponding y-value is $y = 2 - 1 = 1$, so the point of intersection is $(1, 1)$.

57. Find the point(s) of intersection of the graphs of $x + y = 7$ and $3x - 2y = 11$, and check your results.

Solution:

Solving for y in the first equation yields $y = 7 - x$ and substituting this value in the second equation gives us

$$3x - 2(7 - x) = 11$$
$$5x = 25$$
$$x = 5.$$

The corresponding y-value is $y = 7 - 5 = 2$, so the point of intersection is $(5, 2)$.

59. Find the point(s) of intersection of the graphs of $x^2 + y^2 = 5$ and $x - y = 1$, and check your results.

Solution:

Solving for x in the second equation yields $x = y + 1$ and substituting this into the first equation gives us

$$(y + 1)^2 + y^2 = 5$$
$$y^2 + 2y + 1 + y^2 = 5$$
$$2y^2 + 2y - 4 = 0$$
$$2(y - 1)(y + 2) = 0$$
$$y = 1, \ -2.$$

The corresponding x-values are $x = 2$ and $x = -1$, so the points of intersection are $(2, 1)$ and $(-1, \ -2)$.

61. Find the point(s) of intersection of the graphs of $y = x^3$ and $y = 2x$ and check your results.

By equating the y-values for the two equations, we have

$$x^3 = 2x$$
$$x^3 - 2x = 0$$
$$x(x^2 - 2) = 0$$
$$x = 0, \pm\sqrt{2}$$

The corresponding y-values are $y = 0$, $y = -2\sqrt{2}$, and $y = 2\sqrt{2}$, so the points of intersection are $(0, 0)$, $(-\sqrt{2}, -2\sqrt{2})$ and $(\sqrt{2}, 2\sqrt{2})$.

63. Find the point(s) of intersection of the graphs of $y = x^4 - 2x^2 + 1$ and $y = 1 - x^2$ and check your results.

Solution:

By equating the y-values for the two equations, we have

$$x^4 - 2x^2 + 1 = 1 - x^2$$
$$x^4 - x^2 = 0$$
$$x^2(x + 1)(x - 1) = 0$$
$$x = 0, \pm 1.$$

The corresponding y-values are $y = 1$, 0, and 0, so the points of intersection are $(-1, 0)$, $(0, 1)$, and $(1, 0)$.

65. *Break-Even Analysis* You are setting up a part-time business with an initial investment of \$5000. The unit cost of the product is \$11.80, and the selling price is \$19.30.

(a) Find equations for the total cost C and total revenue R for x units.

(b) Find the break-even point by finding the point of intersection of the cost and revenue equations.

(c) How many units would yield a profit of \$100?

Solution:

(a) $C = 11.8x + 5000$

$R = 19.3x$

(b) By equating R and C, we have

$R = C$

$19.3x = 11.8x + 5000$

$7.5x = 5000$

$$x = \frac{5000}{7.5} = 666\tfrac{2}{3} \approx 667 \text{ units}$$

(c) Profit = Revenue − Cost

$$100 = 19.3x - (11.8x + 5000)$$
$$= 7.5x - 5000$$
$$5100 = 7.5x$$
$$x = 5100/7.5 = 680 \text{ units}$$

67. Find the sales necessary to break even for the given cost and revenue equation.

$C = 0.85x + 35,000, R = 1.55x$

Solution:

$R = C$

$1.55x = 0.85x + 35,000$

$.7x = 35,000$

$x = 35,000/.7 = 50,000$ units

69. Find the sales necessary to break even for the given cost and revenue equation.

$C = 8650x + 250,000, R = 9950x$

Solution:

$R = C$

$9950x = 8650x + 250,000$

$1300x = 250,000$

$x = \dfrac{250,000}{1300} \approx 193$ units

71. The amount of money y (in millions of dollars) spent on college textbooks in the United States is given in the table in the text. A mathematical model for the data is $y = 10.40t^2 - 6.52t + 1355.74$, where $t = 0$ corresponds to 1980.

(a) Compare the actual expenses with those given by the model.

(b) Use the model to predict the expenses in 1995.

Solution:

(a)

(b) Using $t = 15$, $y = 10.40(15)^2 - 6.52(15) + 1355.74 \approx 3597.94$ million dollars.

73. *Annual Salary* A mathematical model for the average annual salary y of a person in finance, insurance, or real estate is

$$y = 15{,}848.32 + 1519.23t + 291.82\sqrt{t},$$

where t represents the year, with $t = 0$ corresponding to 1980.

(a) Use the model to complete the table.

(b) This model was created using actual data from 1980 through 1991. How accurate do you think the model is in predicting the 1994 average salary? Explain your reasoning.

(c) What does this model predict the average salary to be in the year 2000? How valid do you think this prediction is?

Solution:

(a)

Year	1980	1985	1990	1991	1994
Salary	15,848.32	24,097.00	3,1963.44	33,527.71	38,209.43

(c) When $t = 20$ (year 2000), $y = 47537.98$

75. Find the point(s) of intersection of the graphs of $y = 2x - 5$, $y = -x + 4$.

Solution:

$2x - 5 = -x + 4$

$3x = 9$

$x = 3 (3, 1)$

77. Find the point(s) of intersection of the graphs of $y = x + 2$, $y = -x^2 + 4$.

Solution:

$$x + 2 = -x^2 + 4$$

$x^2 + x - 2 = 0$

$(x + 2)(x - 1) = 0$

$x = -2, 1 (-2, 0), (1, 3)$

79. Find the point(s) of intersection of the graphs of $y = x^2 + 1$, $y = -x^2 + 9$.

Solution:

$x^2 + 1 = -x^2 + 9$

$2x^2 = 8$

$x^2 = 4$

$x = 2, -2 (2, 5), (-2, 5)$

81. Use a graphing utility to graph the equation $y = 0.24x^2 + 1.32x + 5.36$. Use the graphing utility to approximate the intercepts of the graph.

Solution:

Intercept: $(0, 5.36)$

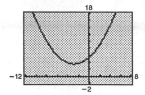

83. Use a graphing utility to graph the equation $y = -0.1x^3 + 1.3x^2 - 4.3$. Use the graphing utility to approximate the intercepts of the graph.

Solution:

Intercepts: $(0, -4.3)$, $(1.9749, 0)$, $(-1.7097, 0)$ $(12.7349, 0)$.

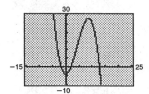

85. Use a graphing utility to graph the equation $y = \sqrt{0.3x^2 - 4.3x + 5.7}$. Use the graphing utility to approximate the intercepts of the graph.

Solution:

Intercepts: $(1.4780, 0)$, $(12.8553, 0)$, $(0, 2.3875)$

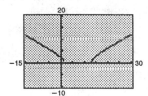

87. Use a graphing utility to graph the equation $y = \dfrac{0.2x^2 + 1}{0.1x + 2.4}$. Use the graphing utility to approximate the intercepts of the graph.

Solution:

Intercepts: $(0, 0.4167)$

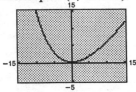

Section 1.3   Lines in the Plane and Slope

1. Estimate the slope of the given line from its graph which is shown in the text.

Solution:

The slope is $m = 1$ since the line rises one unit vertically for each unit of horizontal change from left to right.

3. Estimate the slope of the given line from its graph which is shown in the text.

Solution:

The slope is $m = 0$ since the line is horizontal.

5. Estimate the slope of the given line from its graph which is shown in the text.

Solution:

The slope is $m = -3$ since the line falls three units vertically for each unit of horizontal change from left to right.

7. Plot the points (3, −4) and (5, 2) and find the slope of the line passing through the points.

Solution:

The points are plotted in the accompanying graph and the slope is

$$m = \frac{2 - (-4)}{5 - 3} = 3.$$

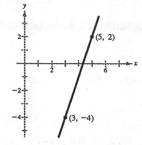

9. Plot the points $\left(\frac{1}{2}, 2\right)$ and (6, 2) and find the slope of the line passing through the points.

Solution:

The points are plotted in the accompanying graph and the slope is

$$m = \frac{2 - 2}{6 - (1/2)} = 0.$$

Thus, the line is horizontal.

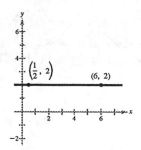

11. Plot the points (−8, −3), (−8, −5) and find the slope of the line passing through the points.

Solution:

The points are plotted in the accompanying graph. The slope is undefined since

$$m = \frac{-5 - (-3)}{-8 - 8}. \text{ (undefined slope)}$$

Thus, the line is vertical.

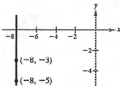

13. Plot the points (1, 2) and (−2, 2) and find the slope of the line passing through the points.

Solution:

The points are plotted in the accompanying graph and the slope is

$$m = \frac{2-2}{-2-1} = 0.$$

Thus, the line is horizontal.

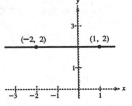

15. A line with a slope of $m = 0$ passes through the point (2, 1). Find three additional points that the line passes through. (The solution is not unique.)

Solution:

The equation of this horizontal line is $y = 1$. Therefore, three additional points are (0, 1), (1, 1), and (3, 1).

17. A line with a slope of $m = -2$ passes through the point (6, −4). Find three additional points that the line passes through. (The solution is not unique.)

Solution:

The equation of this line is

$$y + 4 = -2(x - 6)$$
$$y = -2x + 8$$

Therefore, three additional points are (0, 8), (1, 6) and (2, 4).

19. A line with a slope of $m = -3$ passes through the point (1, 7). Find three additional points that the line passes through. (The solution is not unique.)

Solution:

The equation of the line is

$$y - 7 = -3(x - 1)$$
$$y = -3x + 10.$$

Therefore, three additional points are (0, 10), (2, 4), and (3, 1).

21. A line with an undefined slope passes through the point $(-8,\ 1)$. Find three additional points that the line passes through. (The solution is not unique.)

Solution:

The equation of this vertical line is $x = -8$. Therefore, three additional points are $(-8,\ 0)$, $(-8,\ 2)$, and $(-8,\ 3)$.

23. Find the slope and y-intercept of the line given by $x + 5y = 20$.

Solution:

$$x + 5y = 20$$
$$y = -\tfrac{1}{5}x + 4$$

Therefore, the slope is $m = -\tfrac{1}{5}$ and the y-intercept is $(0, 4)$.

25. Find the slope and y-intercept of the line given by $7x - 5y = 15$.

Solution:

$$7x - 5y = 15$$
$$y = \tfrac{7}{5}x - 3$$

Therefore, the slope is $m = \tfrac{7}{5}$ and the y-intercept is $(0,\ -3)$.

27. Find the slope and y-intercept (if possible) of the line given by $x = 4$.

Solution:

Since the line is vertical, the slope is undefined and there is no y-intercept.

29. Find an equation for the line that passes through the points $(4, 3)$ and $(0,\ -5)$ and sketch the graph of the line.

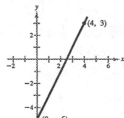

Solution:

The slope of the line is

$$m = \frac{3 - (-5)}{4 - 0} = 2.$$

Using the point-slope form, we have

$$y + 5 = 2(x - 0)$$
$$y = 2x - 5$$

31. Find an equation for the line that passes through the points $(0, 0)$ and $(-1, 3)$ and sketch
the graph of the line.

Solution:

The slope of the line is

$$m = \frac{3 - 0}{-1 - 0} = -3.$$

Using the point-slope form, we have

$$y = -3x$$
$$3x + y = 0.$$

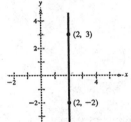

33. Find an equation for the line that passes through the points $(2, 3)$ and $(2, -2)$ and sketch
the graph of the line.

Solution:

The slope of the line is undefined, so
the line is vertical and its equation is

$$x = 2$$
$$x - 2 = 0.$$

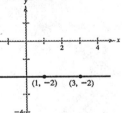

35. Find an equation for the line that passes through the points $(1, -2)$ and $(3, -2)$ and
sketch the graph of the line.

Solution:

The slope of the line is $m = 0$, so the
line is horizontal and its equation is

$$y = -2$$
$$y + 2 = 0.$$

37. Find an equation of the line that passes through the point (0, 3) and has the slope $m = \frac{3}{4}$. Sketch the line.

Solution:

Using the slope-intercept form, we have

$$y = \frac{3}{4}x + 3$$

$$4y = 3x + 12$$

$$3x - 4y + 12 = 0.$$

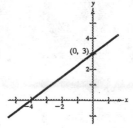

39. Find an equation of the line that passes through the point (0, 0) and has the slope $m = \frac{2}{3}$. Sketch the line.

Solution:

Using the slope-intercept form, we have

$$y = \frac{2}{3}x + 0$$

$$2x - 3y = 0.$$

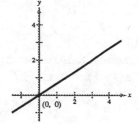

41. Find an equation of the line that passes through the point $(-2, 7)$ and has the slope $m = -3$. Sketch the line.

Solution:

Using the slope-intercept form, we have

$$y - 7 = -3(x + 2)$$

$$y = -3x + 1$$

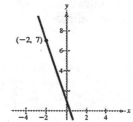

43. Find an equation of the line that passes through the point (0, 2) and has the slope $m = 4$. Sketch the line.

Solution:

Using the slope-intercept form, we have

$$y = 4x + 2$$
$$4x - y + 2 = 0.$$

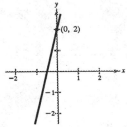

45. Find an equation of the line that passes through the point $\left(0, \frac{2}{3}\right)$ and has the slope $m = \frac{3}{4}$. Sketch the line.

Solution:

Using the slope-intercept form, we have

$$y = \frac{3}{4}x + \frac{2}{3}$$
$$12y = 9x + 8$$
$$9x - 12y + 8 = 0.$$

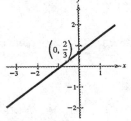

47. Explain how to use the concept of slope to determine whether the three points $(-2, 1)$, $(-1, 0)$, $(2, -2)$ are collinear. Then explain how to use the Distance Formula to determine whether the points are collinear.

Solution:

The slope of the line joining $(-2, 1)$ and $(-1, 0)$ is $\dfrac{1 - 0}{-2 - (-1)} = \dfrac{1}{-1} = -1$.

The slope of the line joining $(-1, 0)$ and $(2, -2)$ is $\dfrac{0 - (-2)}{-1 - 2} = \dfrac{2}{-3} = -\dfrac{2}{3}$.

Since the slopes are different, the points are not collinear.

$$d_1 = \sqrt{(-2 - (-1))^2 + (1 - 0)^2} = \sqrt{1 + 1} = \sqrt{2} \cong 1.41421$$
$$d_2 = \sqrt{(-1 - 2)^2 + (0 - (-0))^2} = \sqrt{9 + 4} = \sqrt{13} \approx 3.60555$$
$$d_3 = \sqrt{(-2 - 2)^2 + (1 - (-2))^2} = \sqrt{6 + 9} = 5$$

Since $d_1 + d_2 \neq d_3$, the points are collinear.

49. Find an equation of the vertical line with x-intercept at 3.

Solution:

Since the line is vertical, it has an undefined slope and its equation is

$$x = 3$$
$$x - 3 = 0.$$

51. Write an equation of the line through the point $(-3, 2)$ (a) parallel to the line $x + y = 7$ and (b) perpendicular to the line.

Solution:

Given line: $y = -x + 7$, $m_1 = -1$

(a) Parallel; $m_1 = -1$

$$y - 2 = -1(x + 3)$$
$$x + y + 1 = 0$$

(b) Perpendicular; $m_2 = 1$

$$y - 2 = -1(x + 3)$$
$$x - y + 5 = 0$$

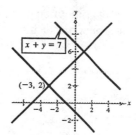

53. Write an equation of the line through the point $(-6, 4)$ (a) parallel to the line $3x + 4y = 7$ and (b) perpendicular to the line.

Solution:

Given line: $y = -\frac{3}{4}x + \frac{7}{4}$, $m_1 = -\frac{3}{4}$

(a) Parallel; $m_1 = -\frac{3}{4}$

$$y - 4 = -\frac{3}{4}(x + 6)$$
$$4y - 16 = -3x - 18$$
$$3x + 4y + 2 = 0$$

(b) Perpendicular; $m_2 = \frac{4}{3}$

$$y - 4 = \frac{4}{3}(x + 6)$$
$$3y - 12 = 4x + 24$$
$$4x - 3y + 36 = 0$$

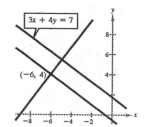

55. Write an equation of the line through the point $(-1,\ 0)$ (a) parallel to the line $y = -3$ and (b) perpendicular to the line.

Solution:

Given line: $y = -3$ is horizontal and
$m_1 = 0$

(a) Parallel: $y = 0$ or the x-axis

(b) Perpendicular: $x = -1$ or $x + 1 = 0$

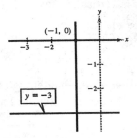

57. Write an equation of the line through the point $(1, 1)$ (a) parallel to the line $-2x + 3y = -3$ and (b) perpendicular to the line.

Solution:

Given line: $y = \frac{2}{3}x - 1$

(a) Parallel: $m_1 = \frac{2}{3}$

$$y - 1 = \frac{2}{3}(x - 1)$$

$$y = \frac{2}{3}x + \frac{1}{3}$$

$3y - 2x - 1 = 0$

(b) Perpendicular; $m_2 = -\frac{3}{2}$

$$y - 1 = -\frac{3}{2}(x - 1)$$

$$y = \frac{-3}{2}x + \frac{5}{2}$$

$2y + 3x - 5 = 0$

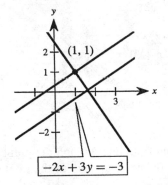

59. Sketch the graph of $y = -2$.

Solution:

$y = -2$ is a horizontal line

x	-2	-1	0	1
y	-2	-2	-2	-2

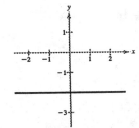

61. Sketch the graph of $2x - y - 3 = 0$.

Solution:

$y = 2x - 3$

x	-1	0	1	2
y	-5	-3	-1	1

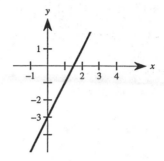

63. Sketch the graph of $y = -2x + 1$.

Solution:

x	-1	0	1	2
y	3	1	-1	-3

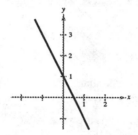

65. Sketch the graph of $y + 2 = -4(x + 1)$.

Solution:

$y = -4x - 6$ has slope -4 and y-intercept $(0, -6)$.

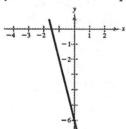

67. *Temperature Conversion* Find an equation of the line giving the relationship between the temperature in degrees Celsius (C) and degrees Fahrenheit (F). Use the fact that water freezes at $0°$ Celsius ($32°$ Fahrenheit) and boils at $100°$ Celsius ($212°$ Fahrenheit).

Solution:

$$m = \frac{212 - 32}{100 - 0} = \frac{9}{5}$$

$$F - 32 = \frac{9}{5}(C - 0)$$

$$F = \frac{9}{5}C + 32$$

69. *Reimbursed Expenses* A company reimburses its sales representative $100 per day for lodging and meals plus $0.25 per mile driven. Write a linear equation giving the daily cost C to the company in terms of x, the number of miles driven.

Solution:

$$C = 0.25x + 100$$

71. *Annual Salary* Your annual salary was $26,300 in 1992 and $29,700 in 1994. Assume your salary can be modeled by a linear equation.

(a) Write a linear equation giving your salary S in terms of the year t where $t = 0$ corresponds to the year 1992.

(b) Use the linear model to predict your salary in 1997.

(c) Does a linear model assume that your salary increases by the same *amount* each year or the same *percent* each year? Explain.

(d) If you assume your salary can be modeled by the equation $S = 26,300(1.0627)^t$, would it be increasing by the same *amount* each year or the same *percent*? Would you prefer this model over the linear one? Explain.

Solution:

(a) $\text{Slope} = \dfrac{29,700 - 26,300}{2 - 0} = 1700.$ (c) Same amount each year (1700)

(d) Same percent.

$$S = 1700t + 26,300$$

(b) In 1997, $t = 5$ and $S = 34,800$

73. *Linear Depreciation* A small business purchases a piece of equipment for $1025. After 5 years the equipment will be outdated, having no value.

(a) Write a linear equation giving the value of the equipment in terms of the time t, $0 \le t \le 5$.

(b) Use a graphing utility to graph the equation.

(c) Move the cursor along the graph and estimate (to two decimal place accuracy) the value of the equipment when $t = 3$.

(d) Move the cursor along the graph and estimate (to two decimal place accuracy) the time when the value of the equipment will be $600.

Solution:

(a) The equipment depreciates
$$\frac{1025}{5} = \$205 \text{ per year,}$$
so the value is
$$y = 1025 - 205t, \text{ where } 0 \le t \le 5.$$

(c) When $t = 3$, the value is $410.00.

(d) The value is $600 when $t = 2.07$ years.

(b)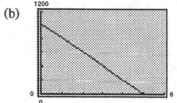

75. *Profit* A contractor purchases a piece of equipment for $26,500. The equipment requires an average expenditure of $5.25 per hour for fuel and maintenance, and the operator is paid $9.50 per hour.

(a) Write a linear equation giving the total cost C of operating this equipment t hours.

(b) Given that customers are charged $25 per hour of machine use, write an equation for the revenue R derived from t hours of use.

(c) Use the formula for profit $(P = R - C)$ to write an equation for the profit derived from t hours of use.

(d) Find the number of hours the equipment must be operated for the contractor to break even.

Solution:

(a) $C = (5.25 + 9.50)t + 26,500 = 14.75t + 26,500$

(b) $R = 25t$

(c) $P = R - C = 25t - (14.75t + 26,500) = 10.25t - 26,500$

(d) $\qquad R = C$

$$25t = 14.75t + 26,500$$

$$10.25t = 26,500$$

$$t \approx 2585.4 \text{ hours}$$

77. *Cost* Use a computer or graphics calculator to sketch the graph of the cost function $C = 23,500 + 3100x$. Determine the maximum production level x given that C cannot exceed $100,000.

Solution:

$$23,500 + 3,100x \leq 100,000$$
$$3,100x \leq 76,500$$
$$x \leq 24.677$$
$$x \leq 24 \text{ units or } 24.67 \text{ units if fractional units are allowed.}$$

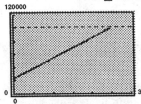

79. Use a graphing utility to graph the cost function $C = 18,275 + 1150x$. Determine the maximum production level x, given that the cost C cannot exceed $100,000.

Solution:

$$C = 18,375 + 1150x \leq 100,000$$
$$1150x \leq 81,625$$
$$x \leq 70.978$$
$$x \leq 70 \text{ unit}$$

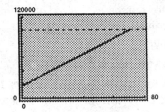

81. Use a graphing utility to graph the cost function $C = 75,000 + 89x$. Determine the maximum production level x, given that the cost C cannot exceed $100,000.

Solution:

$$C = 75,500 + 89x \leq 100,000$$

$$89x \leq 24,500$$

$$x \leq 275.28$$

$$x \leq 275 \text{ units}$$

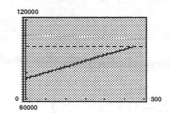

83. *Sales Commission* As a salesperson, you receive a monthly salary of $2000, plus a commission of 7% of sales. You are offered a new job at $2300 per month, plus a commission of 5% of sales.

(a) Write a linear equation for your current monthly wage W in terms of your monthly sales S.

(b) Write a linear equation for the monthly wage W of your job offer in terms of the monthly sales S.

(c) Use a graphing utility to graph both equations on the same viewing rectangle. Find the point of intersection. What does it signify?

(d) You think you can sell $20,000 per month. Should you change jobs? Explain.

Solution:

(a) $W = 2000 + .07S$

(b) $W = 2300 + .05S$

(c)

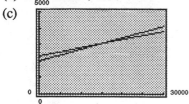

The lines intersect at (15,000, 3050). If you sell $15,000, then both jobs would yield wages of $3050.

(d) No. You will make more money (if sales are $20,000) at your current job ($w = 3400) than in the offered job ($w = 3300).

Section 1.4 Functions

1. Given $f(x) = 2x - 3$, find the following.

   (a) $f(0)$ (b) $f(-3)$
   (c) $f(x - 1)$ (d) $f(1 + \Delta x)$

   Solution:

   (a) $f(0) = 2(0) - 3 = -3$ (b) $f(-3) = 2(-3) - 3 = -9$
   (c) $f(x - 1) = 2(x - 1) - 3 = 2x - 5$ (d) $f(1+\Delta x) = 2(1+\Delta x) - 3 = 2\Delta x - 1$

3. Given $g(x) = \dfrac{1}{2}x^2$, find the following.

   $g(x) = \frac{1}{2}x^2$

   (a) $g(-2)$ (b) $g(6)$
   (c) $g(c)$ (d) $g(x + \Delta x)$

   Solution:

   (a) $g(-2) = \frac{1}{2}(-2)^2 = 2$ (b) $g(6) = \frac{1}{2}(6)^2 = 18$
   (c) $g(c) = \frac{1}{2}(c^2) = c^2/2$ (d) $g(x + \Delta x) = \frac{1}{2}(x + \Delta x)^2$

                                                         $= \frac{1}{2}x^2 + x(\Delta x) + (\Delta x)^2/2$

5. Given $f(x) = \dfrac{|x|}{x}$, find the following.

   (a) $f(2)$ (b) $f(-2)$
   (c) $f(x^2)$ (d) $f(x - 1)$

   Solution:

   (a) $f(2) = \dfrac{|2|}{2} = 1$ (b) $f(-2) = \dfrac{|-2|}{-2} = -1$

   (c) $f(x^2) = \dfrac{|x^2|}{x^2} = 1$ (d) $f(x-1) = \dfrac{|x - 1|}{x - 1} = \begin{cases} -1, & x < 1 \\ 1, & x > 1 \end{cases}$

7. Given $f(x) = 3x - 1$, find and simplify $\dfrac{f(x + \Delta x) - f(x)}{\Delta x}$.

   Solution:

   $$\frac{f(x + \Delta x) - f(x)}{\Delta x} = \frac{[3(x + \Delta x) - 1] - (3x - 1)}{\Delta x}$$

   $$= \frac{3x + 3\Delta x - 1 - 3x + 1}{\Delta x}$$

   $$= \frac{3\Delta x}{\Delta x} = 3$$

9. Given $h(x) = x^2 - x + 1$, find and simplify $\dfrac{h(2 + \Delta x) - h(2)}{\Delta x}$.

Solution:

$$\frac{h(2 + \Delta x) - h(2)}{\Delta x} = \frac{(2 + \Delta x)^2 - (2 + \Delta x) + 1 - [(2)^2 - 2 + 1]}{\Delta x}$$

$$= \frac{4 + 4\Delta x + (\Delta x)^2 - 2 - \Delta x + 1 - 4 + 2 - 1}{\Delta x}$$

$$= \frac{3\Delta x + (\Delta x)^2}{\Delta x}$$

$$= 3 + \Delta x, \ \Delta x \neq 0$$

11. Given $f(x) = x^3 - x$, find and simplify $\dfrac{f(x + \Delta x) - f(x)}{\Delta x}$

Solution:

$$\frac{f(x + \Delta x) - f(x)}{\Delta x} = \frac{(x + \Delta x)^3 - (x + \Delta x) - (x^3 - x)}{\Delta x}$$

$$= \frac{x^3 + 3x^2(\Delta x) + 3x(\Delta x)^2 + (\Delta x)^3 - x - \Delta x - x^3 + x}{\Delta x}$$

$$= \frac{3x^2(\Delta x) + 3x(\Delta x)^2 + (\Delta x)^3 - \Delta x}{\Delta x}$$

$$= 3x^2 + 3x(\Delta x) + (\Delta x)^2 - 1, \ \Delta x \neq 0$$

13. Does the equation $x^2 + y^2 = 4$ determine y as a function of x?

Solution:

$$y = \pm\sqrt{4 - x^2}$$

y is *not* a function of x since there are two values of y for some x.

15. Does the equation $\dfrac{1}{2}x - 6y = -3$ determine y as a function of x.

Solution:

$$\frac{1}{2}x - 6y = -3$$

$$y = \frac{1}{12}x + \frac{1}{2}$$

y *is* a function of x since there is only one value of y for each x.

17. Does the equation $x^2 + y = 4$ determine y as a function of x?

Solution:

$$y = 4 - x^2$$

y *is* a function of x since there is only one value of y for each x.

19. Does the equation $y^2 = x^2 - 1$ determine y as a function of x?

Solution:

$$y = \pm\sqrt{x^2 - 1}$$

y is *not* a function of x since there are two values of y for some x.

21. Find the domain and range of $f(x) = 4 - 2x$. Give your answer using interval notation.

Solution:

Domain: $(-\infty,\ \infty)$

Range: $(-\infty,\ \infty)$

23. Find the domain and range of $f(x) = \sqrt{2x - 3}$. Give your answer using interval notation.

Solution:

Domain: $2x - 3 \geq 0$ or $x \geq \dfrac{3}{2}; \left[\dfrac{3}{2}, \infty\right)$

Range: $[0, \infty)$

25. Find the domain and range of $f(x) = \dfrac{1}{|x|}$. Give your answer using interval notation.

Solution:

Domain: $(-\infty,\ 0) \cup (0, \infty)$

Range: $(0,\ \infty)$

27. Find the domain and range of $g(x) = \sqrt{9 - x^2}$. Give your answer using interval notation.

Solution:

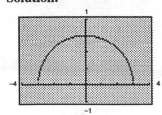

Domain: $[-3,\ 3]$

Range: $[0,\ 3]$

29. Find the domain and range of $f(x) = \dfrac{|x|}{x}$. Give your answer using interval notation.

Solution:

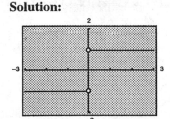

Domain: $(-\infty,\ 0) \cup (0,\ \infty)$

Range: $\{-1,\ 1\}$

31. Find the domain and range of $f(x) = \dfrac{x - 2}{x + 4}$. Give your answer using interval notation.

Solution:

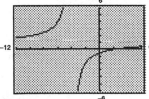

Domain: $(-\infty, -4) \cup (-4, \infty)$

Range: $(-\infty, 1) \cup (1, \infty)$

33. Use the vertical line test to determine whether y is a function of x in $y = x^2$.

Solution:

y *is* a function of x.

35. Use the vertical line test to determine whether y is a function of x in $x^2 + y^2 = 9$.

Solution:

y is *not* function of x.

37. Use the vertical line test to determine whether y is a function of x in $x^2 = xy - 1$.

Solution:

y *is* a function of x.

39. When $f(x) = x + 1$ and $g(x) = x - 1$, find the following.

(a) $f(x) + g(x)$ (b) $f(x) \cdot g(x)$

(c) $\dfrac{f(x)}{g(x)}$ (d) $f(g(x))$

(e) $g(f(x))$

Solution:

(a) $f(x) + g(x) = (x+1) + (x-1) = 2x$ (b) $f(x) \cdot g(x) = (x+1)(x-1) = x^2 - 1$

(c) $\dfrac{f(x)}{g(x)} = \dfrac{x+1}{x-1}, \quad x \neq 1$ (d) $f(g(x)) = f(x-1) = (x-1) + 1 = x$

(e) $g(f(x)) = g(x+1) = (x+1) - 1 = x$

41. When $f(x) = 2x^2$ and $g(x) = x^2 - 1$, find the following.

(a) $f(x) + g(x)$

(b) $f(x) \cdot g(x)$

(c) $f(x)/g(x)$

(d) $f(g(x))$

(e) $g(f(x))$

Solution:

(a) $f(x) + g(x) = 2x^2 + (x^2 - 1) = 3x^2 - 1$

(b) $f(x) \cdot g(x) = 2x^2(x^2 - 1) = 2x^4 - 2x^3$

(c) $f(x)/g(x) = 2x^2/(x^2 - 1), \qquad x \neq \pm 1$

(d) $f(g(x)) = 2(x^2 - 1)^2 = 2(x^4 - 2x^2 + 1) = 2x^4 - 4x^2 + 2$

(e) $g(f(x)) = (2x^2)^2 - 1 = 4x^4 - 1$

43. When $f(x) = x^2 + 5$ and $g(x) = \sqrt{1-x}$, find the following.

(a) $f(x) + g(x)$ (b) $f(x) \cdot g(x)$

(c) $\dfrac{f(x)}{g(x)}$ (d) $f(g(x))$

(e) $g(f(x))$

Solution:

(a) $f(x) + g(x) = x^2 + 5 + \sqrt{1-x}, \quad x \le 1$

(b) $f(x) \cdot g(x) = (x^2 + 5)\sqrt{1-x}, \quad x \le 1$

(c) $\dfrac{f(x)}{g(x)} = \dfrac{x^2 + 5}{\sqrt{1-x}}, \quad x < 1$

(d) $f(g(x)) = f(\sqrt{1-x}) = (\sqrt{1-x})^2 + 5 = 6 - x, \quad x \le 1$

(e) $g(f(x))$ is not defined since the domain of g is $(-\infty, \ 1]$ and the range of f is $[5, \ \infty)$. The range of f is not in the domain of g.

45. When $f(x) = \dfrac{1}{x}$ and $g(x) = \dfrac{1}{x^2}$ find the following.

(a) $f(x) + g(x)$ (b) $f(x) \cdot g(x)$

(c) $\dfrac{f(x)}{g(x)}$ (d) $f(g(x))$

(e) $g(f(x))$

Solution:

(a) $f(x) + g(x) = \dfrac{1}{x} + \dfrac{1}{x^2} = \dfrac{x+1}{x^2}$ (b) $f(x) \cdot g(x) = \left(\dfrac{1}{x}\right)\left(\dfrac{1}{x^2}\right) = \dfrac{1}{x^3}$

(c) $\dfrac{f(x)}{g(x)} = \dfrac{1/x}{1/x^2} = x$ (d) $f(g(x)) = f\left(\dfrac{1}{x^2}\right) = \dfrac{1}{1/x^2} = x^2$

(e) $g(f(x)) = g\left(\dfrac{1}{x}\right) = \dfrac{1}{(1/x)^2} = x^2$

47. When $f(x) = x^3$ and $g(x) = \sqrt[3]{x}$,   (a) show that f and g are inverse functions by showing that $f(g(x)) = x$ and $g(f(x)) = x$, and (b) graph f and g on the same set of coordinate axes.

Solution:

(a) $f(g(x)) = f(\sqrt[3]{x}) = (\sqrt[3]{x})^3 = x$

$\quad g(f(x)) = g(x^3) = \sqrt[3]{x^3} = x$

(b) See accompanying graph.

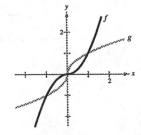

49. When $f(x) = 5x + 1$ and $g(x) = (x-1)/5$,   (a) show that f and g are inverse functions by showing that $f(g(x)) = x$ and $g(f(x)) = x$, and (b) graph f and g on the same set of coordinate axes.

Solution:

(a) $f(g(x)) = f\left(\dfrac{x-1}{5}\right) = 5\left(\dfrac{x-1}{5}\right) + 1 = x$

$\quad g(f(x)) = g(5x+1) = \dfrac{(5x+1) - 1}{5} = x$

(b) See accompanying graph.

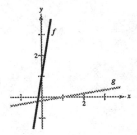

51. When $f(x) = \sqrt{x-4}$, $x \geq 4$ and $g(x) = x^2 + 4$, $x \geq 0$,   (a) show that f and g are inverse functions by showing that $f(g(x)) = x$ and $g(f(x)) = x$, and (b) graph f and g on the same set of coordinate axes.

Solution:

(a) $f(g(x)) = f(x^2 + 4) = \sqrt{(x^2+4) - 4} = x$, $x \geq 0$

$\quad g(f(x)) = g(\sqrt{x-4}) = (\sqrt{x-4})^2 + 4 = x$, $x \geq 4$

(b) See accompanying graph.

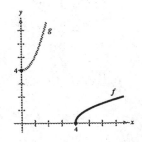

53. Find the inverse of $f(x) = 2x - 3$. Graph both f and f^{-1} on the same set of axes.

Solution:

$$f(x) = 2x - 3 = y$$

$$2y - 3 = x$$

$$y = \frac{x+3}{2}$$

$$f^{-1}(x) = \frac{x+3}{2}$$

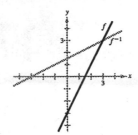

55. Find the inverse of $f(x) = x^5$. Graph both f and f^{-1} on the same set of axes.

Solution:

$$f(x) = x^5 = y$$

$$x = y^5$$

$$y = \sqrt[5]{x}$$

$$f^{-1}(x) = \sqrt[5]{x}$$

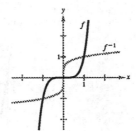

57. Find the inverse of $f(x) = \sqrt{9 - x^2}, 0 \le x \le 3$. Graph both f and f^{-1} on the same set of axes.

Solution:

$$f(x) = \sqrt{9 - x^2} = y, \qquad 0 \le x \le 3$$

$$x = \sqrt{9 - y^2}$$

$$x^2 = 9 - y^2$$

$$y^2 = 9 - x^2$$

$$y = \sqrt{9 - x^2}$$

$$f^{-1}(x) = \sqrt{9 - x^2}, \qquad 0 \le x \le 3$$

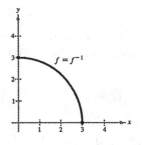

59. Find the inverse of $f(x) = x^{2/3}$, $x \geq 0$. Graph both f and f^{-1} on the same set of axes.

Solution:

$$f(x) = x^{2/3} = y, \quad x \geq 0$$

$$x = y^{2/3}$$

$$y = x^{3/2}$$

$$f^{-1}(x) = x^{3/2}$$

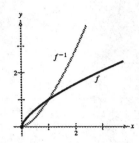

61. Determine whether $f(x) = 3 - 7x$ is one-to-one, and if so, find its inverse.

Solution:

$$f(x) = 3 - 7x \text{ is one-to-one}$$

$$y = 3 - 7x$$

$$x = 3 - 7y$$

$$y = \frac{3 - x}{7}$$

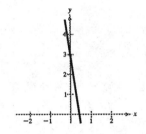

63. Determine whether $f(x) = x^2$ is one-to-one.

Solution:

$$f(x) = x^2 = y$$

f is *not* one-to-one since $f(1) = 1 = f(-1)$.

65. Determine whether $f(x) = |x - 2|$ is one-to-one.

Solution:

$$f(x) = |x - 2| = y$$

f is *not* one-to-one since $f(0) = 2 = f(4)$.

67. Given $f(x) = \sqrt{x}$ and $g(x) = x^2 - 1$, find the composite functions.

(a) $f(g(1))$
(b) $g(f(1))$
(c) $g(f(0))$
(d) $f(g(-4))$
(e) $f(g(x))$
(f) $g(f(x))$

Solution:

$$f(x) = \sqrt{x}, \qquad g(x) = x^2 - 1$$

(a) $f(g(1)) = f(1^2 - 1) = f(0) = 0$
(b) $g(f(1)) = g(\sqrt{1}) = g(1) = 0$
(c) $g(f(0)) = g(0) = -1$
(d) $f(g(-4)) = f(15) = \sqrt{15}$
(e) $f(g(x)) = f(x^2 - 1) = \sqrt{x^2 - 1}$
(f) $g(f(x)) = g(\sqrt{x}) = x - 1, x \geq 0$

69. Select a function from (a) $f(x) = cx$, (b) $g(x) = cx^2$, (c) $h(x) = c\sqrt{|x|}$, or (d) $r(x) = c/x$ and determine the value of the constant c so that the function fits the data in the table.

x	-4	-1	0	1	4
y	-32	-2	0	-2	-32

Solution:

The data fits the function (b) $g(x) = -2x^2$ with $c = -2$.

71. Select a function from (a) $f(x) = cx$, (b) $g(x) = cx^2$, (c) $h(x) = c\sqrt{|x|}$, or (d) $r(x) = c/x$ and determine the value of the constant c so that the function fits the data in the table.

x	-4	-1	0	1	4
y	-8	-32	undef.	32	8

Solution:

The data fits the function (d) $r(x) = \dfrac{32}{x}$, with $c = 32$.

73. Use the graph of $f(x) = \sqrt{x}$ shown in the text to sketch the graph of each of the following.

(a) $y = \sqrt{x} + 2$

(b) $y = -\sqrt{x}$

(c) $y = \sqrt{x} - 2$

(d) $y = \sqrt{x + 3}$

(e) $y = \sqrt{x - 4}$

(f) $y = 2\sqrt{x}$

Solution:

(a)
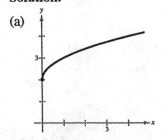

(b)
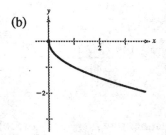

(c)
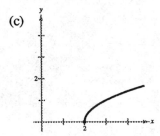

(d)
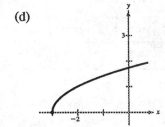

(e)
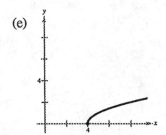

(f)
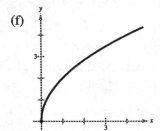

75. *Real Estate* Express the value V of a real estate firm in terms of x, the number of acres of property owned. Each acre is valued at \$2500 and other company assets total \$750,000.

Solution:

Value $= V(x) = 2500x + 750,000$

77. *Demand* The demand function for a particular commodity is given by $p = 14.75/(1 + 0.01x)$, $x \geq 0$, where p is the price per unit and x is the number of units sold.

(a) Find x as a function of p.

(b) Use the result of part (a) to find the number of units sold when the price is $10.

Solution:

(a) $1 + 0.01x = \dfrac{14.75}{p}$

$$x = \frac{(14.75/p) - 1}{0.01} = \frac{14.75 - p}{0.01p} = \frac{100(14.75 - p)}{p} = \frac{1475}{p} - 100$$

(b) $x = \dfrac{100(14.75 - 10)}{10} = 47.5$ units

79. *Market Equilibrium* The supply function for a product relates the number of units x that producers are willing to supply for a given price per unit p. The supply and demand functions for a market are

$p = \frac{2}{5}x + 4$ *Supply*

$p = -\frac{16}{25}x + 30$. *Demand*

(a) Use a graphing utility to graph the supply and demand functions on the same viewing rectangle.

(b) Use the trace feature of the graphing utility to find the *equilibrium point* for the market. That is, find the point of intersection of the two graphs.

(c) For what values of x does the demand exceed the supply?

(d) For what values of x does the supply exceed the demand?

Solution:

(a) Graph utility graph.

(b) (25, 14) is equilibrium point.

(c) Demand exceeds supply for $x < 25$.

(d) Supply exceeds demand for $x > 25$.

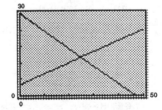

81. *Cost, Revenue, and Profit* A company invests \$98,000 for equipment to produce a new product. Each unit of the product costs \$12.30 and is sold for \$17.98. Let x be the number of units produced and sold.

(a) Write the total cost C as a function of x.

(b) Write the revenue R as a function of x.

(c) Write the profit P as a function of x.

Solution:

(a) Cost $= C = 98{,}000 + 12.30x$

(b) Revenue $= R = 17.98x$

(c) Profit $= R - C = 17.98x - (12.30x + 98{,}000)$

$$= 5.68x - 98{,}000$$

83. Use a graphing utility to graph the function $f(x) = x\sqrt{9 - x^2}$. Then use the zoom and trace features to find the zeros of the function. Is the function one-to-one?

Solution:

$f(x) = x\sqrt{9 - x^2}$ Zeros: $x = 0, \pm 3$

The function is *not* one-to-one.

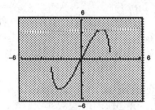

85. Use a graphing utility to graph the function $g(t) = \dfrac{t + 3}{1 - t}$. Then use the zoom and trace features to find the zeros of the function. Is the function one-to-one?

Solution:

$g(t) = \dfrac{t + 3}{1 - t}$ Zero: $t = -3$

The function *is* one-to-one.

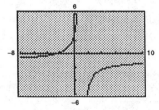

87. Use a graphing utility to graph the function $f(x) = \dfrac{4 - x^2}{x}$. Then use the zoom and trace features to find the zeros of the function. Is the function one-to-one?

Solution:

$f(x) = \dfrac{4 - x^2}{x}$ Zeros: $x = \pm 2$

The function is *not* one-to-one.

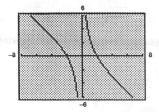

Section 1.5   Limits

1. Complete the table to estimate $\lim\limits_{x \to 2} (5x + 4)$.

Solution:

x	1.9	1.99	1.999	2	2.001	2.01	2.1
$f(x)$	13.5	13.95	13.995	14	14.005	14.05	14.5

$\lim\limits_{x \to 2} (5x + 4) = 14$

3. Complete the table to estimate $\lim\limits_{x \to 2} \dfrac{x - 2}{x^2 - 4}$.

Solution:

x	1.9	1.99	1.999	2	2.001	2.01	2.1
$f(x)$	0.2564	0.2506	0.2501	undefined	0.2499	0.2494	0.2439

$\lim\limits_{x \to 2} \dfrac{x - 2}{x^2 - 4} = \dfrac{1}{4}$

5. Complete the table to estimate $\lim\limits_{x \to 0} \dfrac{\sqrt{x+3} - \sqrt{3}}{x}$.

Solution:

x	-0.1	-0.01	-0.001	0	0.001	0.01	0.1
$f(x)$	0.2911	0.2889	0.2887	undefined	0.2887	0.2884	0.2863

$$\lim_{x \to 0} \frac{\sqrt{x+3} - \sqrt{3}}{x} = \frac{1}{2\sqrt{3}} \approx 0.289$$

7. Complete the table to estimate $\lim\limits_{x \to 2^-} \dfrac{2 - x}{\sqrt{4 - x^2}}$.

Solution:

x	1.5	1.9	1.99	1.999	2
$f(x)$	0.3780	0.1601	0.0501	0.0158	undefined

$$\lim_{x \to 2^-} \frac{2 - x}{\sqrt{4 - x^2}} = 0$$

9. Use the graph shown in the text to visually determine the following.

(a) $\lim\limits_{x \to 0} f(x)$

(b) $\lim\limits_{x \to -1} f(x)$

Solution:

(a) $\lim\limits_{x \to 0} f(x) = 1$

(b) $\lim\limits_{x \to -1} f(x) = 3$

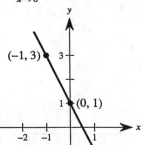

11. Use the graph shown in the text to visually determine the following.

(a) $\lim\limits_{x \to 0} g(x)$

(b) $\lim\limits_{x \to -1} g(x)$

Solution:

(a) $\lim\limits_{x \to 0} g(x) = 1$

(b) $\lim\limits_{x \to -1} g(x) = 3$

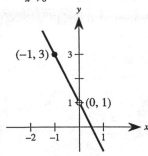

13. Use $\lim\limits_{x \to c} f(x) = 3$ and $\lim\limits_{x \to c} g(x) = 9$ to find (a) $f(x) + g(x)$, (b) $f(x)g(x)$, and (c) $f(x)/g(x)$.

Solution:

(a) $\lim\limits_{x \to c} [f(x) + g(x)] = \lim\limits_{x \to c} f(x) + \lim\limits_{x \to c} g(x) = 3 + 9 = 12$

(b) $\lim\limits_{x \to c} [f(x)g(x)] = \left[\lim\limits_{x \to c} f(x) \right]\left[\lim\limits_{x \to c} g(x) \right] = 3 \cdot 9 = 27$

(c) $\lim\limits_{x \to c} \dfrac{f(x)}{g(x)} = \dfrac{\lim\limits_{x \to c} f(x)}{\lim\limits_{x \to c} g(x)} = \dfrac{3}{0} = \dfrac{1}{3}$

15. Use the graph to visually determine the limit (if it exists).

   (a) $\lim\limits_{x\to3^+} f(x)$ (b) $\lim\limits_{x\to3^-} f(x)$ (c) $\lim\limits_{x\to3} f(x)$

Solution:

   (a) $\lim\limits_{x\to3^+} f(x) = 1$ (b) $\lim\limits_{x\to3^-} f(x) = 1$ (c) $\lim\limits_{x\to3} f(x) = 1$

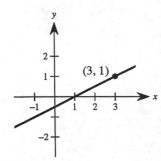

17. Use the graph to visually determine the limit (if it exists).

   (a) $\lim\limits_{x\to3^+} f(x)$ (b) $\lim\limits_{x\to3^-} f(x)$ (c) $\lim\limits_{x\to3} f(x)$

Solution:

   (a) $\lim\limits_{x\to3^+} f(x) = 0$ (b) $\lim\limits_{x\to3^-} f(x) = 0$ (c) $\lim\limits_{x\to3} f(x) = 0$

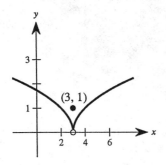

19. Use the graph to visually determine the limit (if it exists).

    (a) $\lim\limits_{x\to3^+} f(x)$ (b) $\lim\limits_{x\to3^-} f(x)$ (c) $\lim\limits_{x\to3} f(x)$

Solution:

    (a) $\lim\limits_{x\to3^+} f(x) = 3$ (b) $\lim\limits_{x\to3^-} f(x) = -3$ (c) $\lim\limits_{x\to3} f(x)$ does not exist.

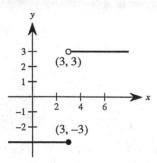

21. Find $\lim\limits_{x\to2} x^2$.

Solution:

$$\lim\limits_{x\to2} x^2 = 2^2 = 4$$

23. Find $\lim\limits_{x\to0} (2x - 3)$.

Solution:

$$\lim\limits_{x\to0} (2x - 3) = 2(0) - 3 = -3$$

25. Find $\lim\limits_{x\to2} (-x^2 + x - 2)$.

Solution:

$$\lim\limits_{x\to2} (-x^2 + x - 2) = -(2)^2 + 2 - 2 = -4$$

27. Find $\lim\limits_{x\to3} \sqrt{x + 1}$.

Solution:

$$\lim\limits_{x\to3} \sqrt{x + 1} - \sqrt{3 + 1} = 2$$

29. Find $\lim\limits_{x \to 2} -\dfrac{2}{x}$.

Solution:

$$\lim_{x \to 2} -\frac{2}{x} = -\frac{2}{2} = -1$$

31. Find $\lim\limits_{x \to 3} \dfrac{3x - 5}{x + 3}$.

Solution:

$$\lim_{x \to 3} \frac{3x - 5}{x + 3} = \frac{3(3) - 5}{3 + 3} = \frac{4}{6} = \frac{2}{3}$$

33. Find $\lim\limits_{x \to -1} \dfrac{x^2 - 1}{x + 1}$.

Solution:

$$\lim_{x \to -1} \frac{x^2 - 1}{x + 1} = \lim_{x \to -1} \frac{(x + 1)(x - 1)}{x + 1} = \lim_{x \to -1} (x - 1) = -2$$

35. Find $\lim\limits_{x \to 2} \dfrac{x - 2}{x^2 - 4x + 4}$.

Solution:

$$\lim_{x \to 2} \frac{x - 2}{x^2 - 4x + 4} = \lim_{x \to 2} \frac{x - 2}{(x - 2)(x - 2)} = \lim_{x \to 2} \frac{1}{x - 2} \text{ does not exist.}$$

37. Find $\lim\limits_{t \to 5} \dfrac{t - 5}{t^2 - 25}$.

Solution:

$$\lim_{t \to 5} \frac{t - 5}{t^2 - 25} = \lim_{t \to 5} \frac{t - 5}{(t + 5)(t - 5)} = \lim_{t \to 5} \frac{1}{t + 5} = \frac{1}{10}$$

39. Find $\lim\limits_{x \to -2} \dfrac{x^3 + 8}{x + 2}$.

Solution:

$$\lim_{x \to -2} \frac{x^3 + 8}{x + 2} = \lim_{x \to -2} \frac{(x + 2)(x^2 - 2x + 4)}{x + 2} = \lim_{x \to -2} (x^2 - 2x + 4) = 12$$

41. Find $\lim\limits_{x \to 0} \dfrac{|x|}{x}$.

Solution:

$$\lim_{x \to 0^-} \frac{|x|}{x} = -1$$

$$\lim_{x \to 0^+} \frac{|x|}{x} = 1$$

Therefore, $\lim\limits_{x \to 0} \dfrac{|x|}{x}$ does not exist.

43. Find $\lim\limits_{x \to 3}$ where $f(x) = \begin{cases} \frac{1}{3}x - 2, & x \le 3 \\ -2x + 5, & x > 3 \end{cases}$

Solution:

$$\lim_{x \to 3^-} f(x) = \lim_{x \to 3^-} \left(\tfrac{1}{3}x - 2\right) = 1 - 2 = -1$$

$$\lim_{x \to 3^+} f(x) = \lim_{x \to 3^+} (-2x + 5) = 6 + 5 = -1.$$

Therefore, $\lim\limits_{x \to 3} = -1.$

45. Find $\lim\limits_{x \to 1} f(x)$ where $f(x) = \begin{cases} x^3 + 1, & x < 1 \\ x + 1, & x \ge 1. \end{cases}$

Solution:

$$\lim_{x \to 1^-} f(x) = \lim_{x \to 1^-} (x^3 + 1) = 2$$

$$\lim_{x \to 1^+} f(x) = \lim_{x \to 1^+} (x + 1) = 2$$

Therefore, $\lim\limits_{x \to 1} f(x) = 2.$

47. Find $\lim\limits_{\Delta x \to 0} \dfrac{2(x + \Delta x) - 2x}{\Delta x}$.

Solution:

$$\lim_{\Delta x \to 0} \frac{2(x + \Delta x) - 2x}{\Delta x} = \lim_{\Delta x \to 0} \frac{2x + 2\Delta x - 2x}{\Delta x} = \lim_{\Delta x \to 0} 2 = 2$$

49. Find $\lim\limits_{\Delta x \to 0} \dfrac{(x + \Delta x)^3 - x^3}{\Delta x}$

Solution:

$$\lim_{\Delta x \to 0} \frac{(x + \Delta x)^3 - x^3}{\Delta x} = \lim_{\Delta x \to 0} \frac{1 + 3x^2 \Delta x + 3x(\Delta x)^2 + (\Delta x)^3 - x^3}{\Delta x}$$

$$= \lim_{\Delta x \to 0} (3x^2 + 3x\Delta x + (\Delta x)^2) = 3x^2$$

51. Find $\displaystyle\lim_{\Delta t \to 0} \frac{(t + \Delta t)^2 - 5(t + \Delta t) - (t^2 - 5t)}{\Delta t}$

Solution:

$$\lim_{\Delta t \to 0} \frac{(t + \Delta t)^2 - 5(t + \Delta t) - (t^2 - 5t)}{\Delta t}$$

$$= \lim_{\Delta t \to 0} \frac{t^2 + 2t(\Delta t) + (\Delta t)^2 - 5t - 5(\Delta t) - t^2 + 5t}{\Delta t}$$

$$= \lim_{\Delta t \to 0} \frac{2t(\Delta t) + (\Delta t)^2 - 5(\Delta t)}{\Delta t}$$

$$= \lim_{\Delta t \to 0} 2t + (\Delta t) - 5 = 2t - 5$$

53. Find $\displaystyle\lim_{x \to 0} \frac{\sqrt{2 + x} - \sqrt{2}}{x}$

Solution:

$$\lim_{x \to 0} \frac{\sqrt{2 + x} - \sqrt{2}}{x} = \lim_{x \to 0} \frac{\sqrt{2 + x} - \sqrt{2}}{x} \cdot \frac{\sqrt{2 + x} + \sqrt{2}}{\sqrt{2 + x} + \sqrt{2}}$$

$$= \lim_{x \to 0} \frac{2 + x - 2}{x(\sqrt{2 + x} + \sqrt{2})} = \lim_{x \to 0} \frac{1}{\sqrt{2 + x} + \sqrt{2}} = \frac{1}{2\sqrt{2}}$$

55. Find $\displaystyle\lim_{x \to 1^-} \frac{2}{x^2 - 1}$

Solution:

$$\lim_{x \to 1^-} \frac{2}{x^2 - 1} = \lim_{x \to 1^-} \frac{2}{(x - 1)(x + 1)} = -\infty$$

57. Find $\displaystyle\lim_{x \to -2^-} \frac{1}{x + 2}.$

Solution:

$$\lim_{x \to -2^-} \frac{1}{x + 2} = -\infty$$

59. Find $\displaystyle\lim_{x \to 5^+} \frac{2}{(x - 5)^2}.$

Solution:

$$\lim_{x \to 5^+} \frac{2}{(x - 5)^2} = \infty$$

61. Given $4 - x^2 \leq f(x) \leq 4 + x^2$ for all x, find $\lim\limits_{x \to 0} f(x)$.

Solution:

$$\lim_{x \to 0} (4 - x^2) \leq \lim_{x \to 0} f(x) \leq \lim_{x \to 0} (4 + x^2)$$

$$4 \leq \lim_{x \to 0} f(x) \leq 4$$

Therefore, $\lim\limits_{x \to 0} f(x) = 4$.

63. Estimate the limit (if it exists).
$$f(x) = \frac{x^2 - 5x + 6}{x^2 - 4x + 4} = \frac{(x-2)(x-3)}{(x-2)(x-2)}$$

Solution:

$$f(x) = \frac{x^2 - 5x + 6}{x^2 - 4x + 4} = \frac{(x-2)(x-3)}{(x-2)(x-2)}$$

$$\lim_{x \to 2} f(x) = \lim_{x \to 2} \frac{x-3}{x-2} \text{ does not exist.}$$

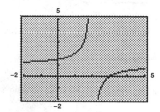

65. Estimate the limit (if it exists).
$$\lim_{x \to -4} \frac{x^3 + 4x^2 + x + 4}{2x^2 + 7x - 4}$$

Solution:

$$\lim_{x \to -4} \frac{x^3 + 4x^2 + x + 4}{2x^2 + 7x - 4} = \lim_{x \to -4} \frac{(x+4)(x^2+1)}{(x+4)(2x-1)}$$

$$= \frac{17}{9} \approx -1.889$$

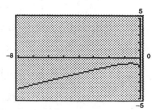

67. Estimate the limit (if it exists).
$$A = 1000 \left(1 + \frac{r}{4}\right)^{40}$$

Solution:

$$\lim_{r \to 0.06} A = \lim_{r \to 0.06} 1000 \left(1 + \frac{r}{4}\right)^{40} = 1814.02.$$

Yes, the limit of A as $r \to 6\%$ exists.

Section 1.6 Continuity

1. Find the discontinuities (if any) for $5x^3 - x^2 + 2$.

Solution:

The polynomial $f(x) = 5x^3 - x^2 + 2$ *is* continuous on the entire real line.

3. Find the discontinuities (if any) for $\dfrac{1}{x^2 - 4}$.

Solution:

The rational function $f(x) = \dfrac{1}{x^2 - 4}$ is *not* continuous on the entire real line. It is not continuous at $x = \pm 2$.

5. Find the discontinuities (if any) for $f(x) = -\dfrac{x^3}{2}$.

Solution:

$f(x) = -\dfrac{x^3}{2}$ *is* continuous on $(-\infty, \infty)$.

7. Find the discontinuities (if any) for $f(x) = \dfrac{x^2 - 1}{x + 1}$.

Solution:

$f(x) = \dfrac{x^2 - 1}{x + 1}$ is continuous on $(-\infty, -1) \cup (-1, \infty)$.

9. Find the discontinuities (if any) for $f(x) = x^2 - 2x + 1$.

Solution:

$f(x) = x^2 - 2x + 1$ *is* continuous on $(-\infty, \infty)$.

11. Find the discontinuities (if any) for $f(x) = \dfrac{1}{x - 1}$.

Solution:

$f(x) = \dfrac{1}{x - 1}$ is continuous on $(-\infty, 1) \cup (1, \infty)$.

13. Find the discontinuities (if any) for $f(x) = \dfrac{x}{x^2 + 1}$.

Solution:

$f(x) = \dfrac{x}{x^2 + 1}$ *is* continuous on $(-\infty, \infty)$.

15. Find the discontinuities (if any) for $f(x) = \dfrac{x-5}{x^2 - 9x + 20}$.

Solution:

$f(x) = \dfrac{x-5}{x^2 - 9 + 20} = \dfrac{x-5}{(x-5)(x-4)}$ *is continuous on* $(-\infty, 4) \cup (4, 5) \cup (5, \infty)$.

17. Find the discontinuities (if any) for the following.

$$f(x) = \begin{cases} -x, & x < 1 \\ 1, & x = 1 \\ x, & x > 1 \end{cases}$$

Solution:

$f(x)$ is continuous on $(-\infty, 1) \cup (1, \infty)$.

19. Find the discontinuities (if any) for the following.

$$f(x) = \begin{cases} x, & x \le 1 \\ x^2, & x > 1 \end{cases}$$

Solution:

$$\lim_{x \to 1^-} f(x) = \lim_{x \to 1^-} x = 1$$

$$\lim_{x \to 1^+} f(x) = \lim_{x \to 1^+} x^2 = 1$$

Since $f(1) = 1$, f is continuous on the entire real line.

21. Find the discontinuities (if any) for the following.

$$f(x) = \begin{cases} \frac{1}{2}x + 1, & x \le 2 \\ 3 - x, & x > 2 \end{cases}$$

Solution:

$$\lim_{x \to 2^-} f(x) = \lim_{x \to 2^-} \left(\frac{x}{2} + 1\right) = 2$$

$$\lim_{x \to 2^+} f(x) = \lim_{x \to 2^+} (3 - x) = 1$$

f is continuous on $(-\infty, 2) \cup (2, \infty)$.

23. Find the discontinuities (if any) for the following.

$$f(x) = \begin{cases} 3 + x, & x \le 2 \\ x^2 + 1, & x > 2 \end{cases}$$

Solution:

$$\lim_{x \to 2^-} f(x) = \lim_{x \to 2^-} (3 + x) = 5$$

$$\lim_{x \to 2^+} f(x) = \lim_{x \to 2^+} (x^2 + 1) = 5$$

Since $f(2) = 5$, f is continuous on the entire real line.

25. Find the discontinuities (if any) for $f(x) = \dfrac{|x + 1|}{x + 1}$.

Solution:

$$\lim_{x \to -1^-} \frac{|x + 1|}{x + 1} = \lim_{x \to -1^-} \frac{-(x + 1)}{x + 1} = -1$$

$$\lim_{x \to -1^+} \frac{|x + 1|}{x + 1} = \lim_{x \to -1^+} \frac{x + 1}{x + 1} = 1.$$

Since $\lim_{x \to -1} f(x)$ does not exist, f is continuous on $(-\infty, -1) \cup (-1, \infty)$.

27. Find the discontinuities (if any) for $f(x) = [\![x - 1]\!]$.

Solution:

$$\lim_{x \to c^-} [\![x - 1]\!] = c - 2, \quad c \text{ is any integer}$$

$$\lim_{x \to c^+} [\![x - 1]\!] = c - 1, \quad c \text{ is any integer}$$

Since $\lim_{x \to c} [\![x - 1]\!]$ does not exist, f is continuous on all intervals $(c, c + 1)$.

29. Find the discontinuities (if any) for $f(x) = [\![x]\!] - 2$.

Solution:

$f(x) = [\![x]\!] - 2$ is continuous on all intervals $(c, c + 1)$, where c is an integer.

31. Find the discontinuities (if any) for the following.

$$h(x) = f(g(x)), \quad f(x) = \frac{1}{\sqrt{x}}, \quad g(x) = x - 1, \quad x > 1$$

Solution:

$$h(x) = f(g(x)) = f(x - 1) = \frac{1}{\sqrt{x - 1}}, \quad x > 1$$

Thus, h is continuous on its entire domain $(1, \infty)$.

33. Discuss the continuity of the function $f(x) = x^2 - 4x - 5$ on the closed interval $[-1, 5]$. If there are any discontinuities, determine whether they are removable.

Solution:

Since $f(x) = x^2 - 4x - 5$ is a polynomial, it is continuous on $[-1, 5]$.

35. Discuss the continuity of the function $f(x) = \dfrac{1}{x - 2}$ on the closed interval $[1, 4]$. If there are any discontinuities, determine whether they are removable.

Solution:

Since $\displaystyle\lim_{x \to 2^+} \dfrac{1}{x - 2} = \infty$, f has a nonremovable discontinuity at $x = 2$ on the closed interval $[1, 4]$.

37. To determine any points of discontinuity, sketch the graph of $f(x) = \dfrac{x^2 - 16}{x - 4}$.

Solution:

$$f(x) = \frac{x^2 - 16}{x - 4} = \frac{(x + 4)(x - 4)}{x - 4} = x + 4, \quad x \neq 4$$

Removable discontinuity at $x = 4$

Continuous on $(-\infty, 4) \cup (4, \infty)$.

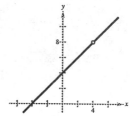

39. To determine any points of discontinuity, sketch the graph of $f(x) = \dfrac{x^3 + x}{x}$.

Solution:

$$f(x) = \frac{x^3 + x}{x} = \frac{x(x^2 + 1)}{x} = x^2 + 1, \quad x \neq 0$$

Removable discontinuity at $x = 0$

Continuous on $(-\infty, 0) \cup (0, \infty)$

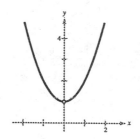

41. To determine any points of discontinuity, sketch the graph of

$$f(x) = \begin{cases} x^2 + 1 & x < 0 \\ x - 1 & x \geq 0 \end{cases}$$

Solution:

$$f(x) = \begin{cases} x^2 + 1 & x < 0 \\ x - 1 & x \geq 0 \end{cases}$$

Nonremovable, discontinue at $x = 0$.

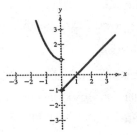

43. Determine the constant a so that the following function is continuous.

$$f(x) = \begin{cases} x^3, & x \leq 2 \\ ax^2, & x > 2 \end{cases}$$

Solution:

$$\lim_{x \to 2^-} f(x) = \lim_{x \to 2^-} x^3 = 8$$

$$\lim_{x \to 2^+} f(x) = \lim_{x \to 2^+} ax^2 = 4a$$

Therefore, $8 = 4a$ and $a = 2$.

45. Graph the function $h(x) = \dfrac{1}{x^2 - x - 2}$, and determine any x-values at which the function is not continuous.

Solution:

$$h(x) = \frac{1}{x^2 - x - 2} = \frac{1}{(x - 2)(x + 1)i} h \text{ is not continuous at } x = 2 \text{ and } x = -1.$$

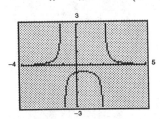

47. Find the interval(s) on which the function $f(x) = \dfrac{x}{x^2 + 1}$ is continuous.

Solution:

$$f(x) = \frac{x}{x^2 + 1} \text{ is continuous on } (-\infty, \infty).$$

49. Find the interval(s) on which the function $f(x) = \frac{1}{2}[\![2x]\!]$ is continuous.

Solution:

$f(x) = \frac{1}{2}[\![2x]\!]$ is continuous on all intervals of the form $\left(\dfrac{c}{2}, \dfrac{c+1}{2}\right)$, where c is an integer.

51. Graph the function $f(x) = \dfrac{x^2 + x}{x}$ on the interval $[-4, 4]$. Does the graph of the function appear continuous on this interval? Is the function continuous on $[-4, 4]$?

Solution:

$f(x) = \dfrac{x^2 + x}{x} = \dfrac{x(x+1)}{x}$ appears to be continuous on $[-4, 4]$. But, it is not continuous at $x = 0$ (removable discontinuity).

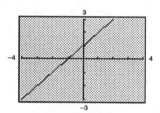

53. *Compound Interest* A deposit of $7500 is made into an account that pays 6% compounded quarterly. The amount A in the account after t years is

$$A = 7500(1.015)^{[\![4t]\!]}, \ t \geq 0.$$

(a) Sketch the graph of A. Is the graph continuous? Explain.

(b) What is the balance after 7 years?

Solution:

$A = 7500(1.015)^{[\![4t]\!]}, \ t \geq 0$

(a)

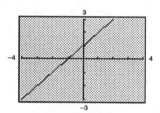

The graph has nonremovable discontinuities at $t = \frac{1}{4}, \frac{1}{2}, \frac{3}{4}, 1, \frac{5}{4}, \ldots$ (every 3 months).

(b) For $t = 7$, $A = 7500(1.015)^{[\![4 \cdot 7]\!]} = \$11{,}379.17$

55. *Telephone Rates* A dial-direct long distance call between two cities costs $1.04 for the first 2 minutes and $0.36 for each additional minute or fraction thereof.

(a) Use the greatest integer function to write the cost C of a call in terms of the time t (in minutes). Graph the cost function and discuss its continuity.

(b) Find the cost of a 9-minute call.

Solution:

(a) $C(t) = \begin{cases} 1.04 & , 0 < t \leq 2 \\ 1.04 & +0.36[\![t-1]\!], t > 2t, \text{ not an integer} \\ 1.04 + 0.36(t-2), t > 2, & t \text{ is an integer.} \end{cases}$

C is not continuous at $t = 2, 3, 4, \ldots$

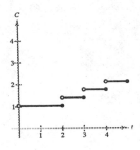

(b) $C(9) = 1.04 + 0.36[\![9-2]\!] = \$3.56.$

57. *Inventory Management* The number of units in inventory in a small company is

$$N = 25\left(2\left[\!\left[\frac{t+2}{2}\right]\!\right] - t\right), \qquad 0 \leq t \leq 12,$$

where the real number t is the time in months.

(a) Graph this function and discuss its continuity.

(b) How often must the company replenish its inventory?

Solution:

Nonremovable discontinuities at $t = 2, 4, 6, 8, \ldots$

$N \to 0$ when $t \to 2^-, 4^-, 6^-, 8^-, \ldots,$

so the inventory is replenished every two months.

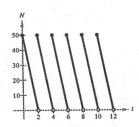

Section 1.R   Review

1. Match the data with the real-life situation that it represents (graphs are shown in the text).

    1. Population of Texas   2. Population of California
    3. Number of U.S. Business Failures 4. IBM Revenues

    Solution:

    1. Population of Texas (a)

3. Match the data with the real-life situation that it represents (graphs are shown in the text).

    1. Population of Texas   2. Population of California
    3. Number of U.S. Business Failures 4. IBM Revenues

    Solution:

    1. Number of U.S. Business Failures (b)

5. Find the distance between the points (0, 0), (5, 2).

    Solution:

    $$\text{Distance} = \sqrt{(0-5)^2 + (0-2)^2} = \sqrt{25+4} = \sqrt{29}$$

7. Find the distance between the points $(-1, 3)$, $(-4, 6)$.

    Solution:

    $$\text{Distance} = \sqrt{(-1-(-4))^2 + (3-6)^2} = \sqrt{9+9} = \sqrt{18} = 3\sqrt{2}$$

9. Find the midpoint of the line segment between the two points (5, 6), (9, 2).

    Solution:

    $$\text{Midpoint} = \left(\frac{5+9}{2}, \frac{6+2}{2}\right) = (7, 4).$$

11. Find the midpoint of the line segment between the two points $(-10, 4)$, $(-6, 8)$.

    Solution:

    $$\text{Midpoint} = \left(\frac{-10-6}{2}, \frac{4+8}{2}\right) = (-8, 6).$$

13. Use the graph shown in the text. Which bars on the graph represent the revenues? Which represent the costs? Which represent the profits? Explain your reasoning. Write an equation that relates the revenue R, cost C, and profit P.

Solution:

The taller bars in the back represent revenues. The middle bars represent costs. The smaller bars in front represent profits, since $P = R - C$.

15. Translate the triangle whose vertices are $(1, 3)$, $(2, 4)$ and $(5, 6)$ three units to the right and four units up. Find the coordinates of the translated vertices.

Solution:

The translated vertices are $(1+3, 3+4) = (4, 7)$, $(2+3, 4+4) = (5, 8)$ and $(5+3, 6+4) = (8, 10)$.

17. Sketch the graph of the equation $y = 4x - 12$.

Solution:

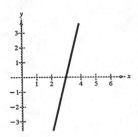

19. Sketch the graph of the equation $y = x^2 + 5$.

Solution:

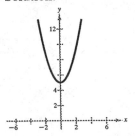

21. Sketch the graph of the equation $y = x^2 + 5x + 6$.

Solution:

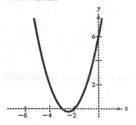

23. Sketch the graph of the equation $y = x^3 + 4$.

Solution:

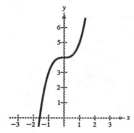

25. Find the intercepts of the graph of the equation $4x + y + 3 = 0$

Solution:

$x = 0 \Rightarrow y = -3 \Rightarrow (0, -3)$ y-intercept
$y = 0 \Rightarrow x = -\frac{3}{4} \Rightarrow (-\frac{3}{4}, 0)$ x-intercept.

27. Write the standard form of the circle for

Center: $(0, 0)$;

Solution point: $\left(2, \sqrt{5}\right)$

Solution:

$$(x - 0)^2 + (y - 0)^2 = r^2$$
$$x^2 + y^2 = r^2$$
$$2^2 + \left(\sqrt{5}\right)^2 = r^2$$
$$9 = r^2$$
$$3 = r$$

elevation: $x^2 + y^2 = 3^2$

29. Complete the square to write the equation of the circle $x^2 + y^2 - 6x + 8y = 0$ in standard form. Determine the radius and center of the circle. Then sketch the circle.

Solution:

$$x^2 + y^2 - 6x + 8y = 0$$
$$(x^2 - 6x + 9) + (y^2 + 8y + 16) = 9 + 16$$
$$(x-3)^2 + (y+4)^2 = 25$$

Center: $(3, -4)$

Radius: 5

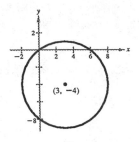

31. Find the points of intersection of the graphs algebraically.

$x + y = 2, \ 2x - y = 1$

Solution:

$$x + y = 2 \Rightarrow y = 2 - x \qquad 2 - x = 2x - 1$$
$$2x - y = 1 \Rightarrow y = 2x - 1 \qquad 3 = 3x$$
$$1 = x$$

Point of intersection: $(1, 1)$

33. Find the points of intersection of the graphs algebraically.

$y = x^3, \ y = x$

Solution:

$$y = x^3 \qquad\qquad x^3 = x$$
$$y = x \qquad\qquad x^3 - x = 0$$
$$x(x-1)(x+1) = 0$$

Points of intersection: $(0, 0), (1, 1), (-1, -1)$.

35. *Break-Even Analysis* The student government association wants to raise money by having a T-shirt sale. Each shirt costs $8. The silk screening costs $200 for the design, plus $2 per shirt. Each shirt will sell for $14.

(a) Find equations for the total cost C and the total revenue R for selling x shirts.

(b) Find the break-even point.

Solution:

(a) $C = 200 + 2x + 8x = 200 + 10x$ (b) $C = R$

  $R = 14x$ $200 + 10x = 14x$

                                                          $200 = 4x$

                                                       $x = 50$ shirts

37. Find the slope and y-intercept (if possible) of the linear equation $3x + y = -2$.

Solution:

  $3x + y = -2$

    $y = -3x - 2$

Slope: -3

y-intercept: $(0, -2)$

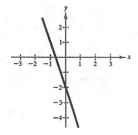

39. Find the slope and y-intercept (if possible) of the linear equation $y = -\frac{5}{3}$.

Solution:

$y = -\frac{5}{3}$

Slope: 0 (horizontal line)

y-intercept: $\left(0, -\frac{5}{3}\right)$

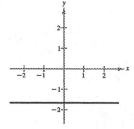

41. Find the slope and y-intercept (if possible) of the linear equation $-2x - 5y - 5 = 0$.

Solution:

$$-2x - 5y - 5 = 0$$
$$5y = -2x - 5$$
$$y = -\tfrac{2}{5}x - 1$$

Slope: $-\tfrac{2}{5}$

y-intercept: $(0, -1)$

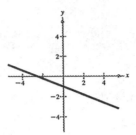

43. Find the slope of the line passing through the two points $(0, 0)$, $(7, 6)$.

Solution:

$$\text{Slope} = \frac{6 - 0}{7 - 0} = \frac{6}{7}$$

45. Find the slope of the line passing through the two points $(10, 17)$, $(-11, -3)$.

Solution:

$$\text{Slope} = \frac{17 - (-3)}{10 - (-11)} = \frac{20}{21}$$

47. Find an equation of the line that passes through the point and has the indicated slope.

Point: $(3, -1)$; Slope: $m = -2$.

Solution:

$$y - (-1) = -2(x - 3)$$
$$y = -2x + 5$$

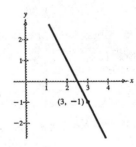

49. Find the general form of the equation of the line passing through the point and satisfying the given condition.

Point: $(-3, 6)$

(a) Slope is $\frac{7}{8}$.

(b) Parallel to the line $4x + 2y = 7$.

(c) Passes through the origin.

(d) Perpendicular to the line $3x - 2y = 2$.

Solution:

(a) $y - 6 = \frac{7}{8}(x - (-3))$

$\qquad y = \frac{7}{8}x + \frac{69}{8}$

(b) $4x + 2y = 7 \Rightarrow y = -2x + \frac{7}{2}$; slope $= -2$

$\qquad y - 6 = -2(x - (-3))$

$\qquad\quad y = -2x$

(c) The line through $(0, 0)$ and $(-3, 6)$ has slope $\frac{6}{-3} = -2 \Rightarrow y = -2x$.

(d) $3x - 2y = 2 \Rightarrow y = \frac{3}{2}x - 1$. Slope of perpendicular is $-\frac{2}{3}$:

$$y - 6 = -\frac{2}{3}(x - (-3))$$

$$y = -\frac{2}{3}x + 4$$

51. *Demand* When a wholesaler sold a product at $32 per unit, sales were 750 units per week. After a price increase of $5 per unit, however, the sales dropped to 700 units per week.

(a) Write the quantity demanded x as a linear function of the price p.

(b) *Linear Interpolation* Predict the number of units sold at a price of $34.50 per unit.

(c) *Linear Extrapolation* Predict the number of units sold at a price of $42.00 per unit.

Solution:

$(32,750), (37,700) \qquad m = \dfrac{750 - 700}{32 - 37} = \dfrac{50}{-5} = -10$

(a) $x - 750 = -10(p - 32)$

$\qquad x = -10p + 1070$

(b) If $p = 34.50$, $x = -10(34.50) + 1070 = 725$

(c) If $p = 42.00$, $x = -10(42.00) + 1070 = 650$.

53. Determine whether y is a function of x if $y = -x^2 + 2$

Solution:

Yes.

55. Determine whether y is a function of x if $y^2 - \frac{1}{4}x^2 = 4$

Solution:

No.

57. Given $f(x) = 3x + 4$, find the following.

(a) $f(1)$ (b) $f(x+1)$ (c) $f(2+\Delta x)$

Solution:

$f(x) = 3x + 4$

(a) $f(1) = 3(1) + 4 = 7$

(b) $f(x+1) = 3(x+1) + 4 = 3x + 7$

(c) $f(2+\Delta x) = 3(2+\Delta x) + 4 = 10 + 3\Delta x$

59. Graph the function $f(x) = x^2 + 3x + 2$, and find the domain and range of the function.

Solution:

$f(x) = x^2 + 3x + 2$

$\quad = (x + \frac{3}{2})^2 - \frac{1}{4}$

Domain: $(-\infty, \infty)$

Range: $[-\frac{1}{4}, \infty)$

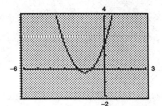

61. Graph the function $f(x) = \sqrt{x+1}$, and find the domain and range of the function.

Solution:

$f(x) = \sqrt{x+1}$

Domain: $[-1, \infty]$

Range: $[0, \infty]$

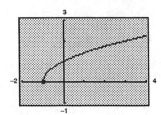

63. Graph the function $f(x) = -|x| + 3$, and find the domain and range of the function.

Solution:

$f(x) = -|x| + 3$

Domain: $(-\infty, \infty)$

Range: $(-\infty, 3]$

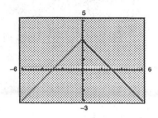

65. Use the functions $f(x) = 1 + x^2$ and $g(x) = 2x - 1$ to find the following.

(a) $f(x) + g(x)$ (b) $f(x) - g(x)$ (c) $f(x)g(x)$

(d) $\dfrac{f(x)}{g(x)}$ (e) $f(g(x))$ (f) $g(f(x))$

Solution:

(a) $f(x) + g(x) = (1 + x^2) + (2x - 1) = x^2 + 2x$

(b) $f(x) - g(x) = (1 + x^2) - (2x - 1) = x^2 - 2x + 2$

(c) $f(x)g(x) = (1 + x^2)(2x - 1) = 2x^3 - x^2 + 2x - 1$

(d) $\dfrac{f(x)}{g(x)} = \dfrac{1 + x^2}{2x - 1}$

(e) $f(g(x)) = f(2x - 1) = 1 + (2x - 1)^2 = 4x^2 - 4x + 2$

(f) $g(f(x)) = g(1 + x^2) = 2(1 + x^2) - 1 = 2x^2 + 1$

67. Find the inverse of $f(x) = \frac{3}{2}x$ (if it exists).

Solution:

$f(x) = \frac{3}{2}x$ has an inverse by the horizontal line test

$y = \frac{3}{2}x$

$x = \frac{3}{2}y$

$y = \frac{2}{3}x$ $f^{-1}(x) = \frac{2}{3}x$

69. Find the inverse of $f(x) = -x^2 + \frac{1}{2}$

Solution:

$f(x) = -x^2 + \frac{1}{2}$ does not have an inverse by the horizontal line test.

71. Find $\lim\limits_{x \to 2} (5x - 3)$.

Solution:

$$\lim\limits_{x \to 2} (5x - 3) = 5(2) - 3 = 7$$

73. Find $\lim\limits_{x \to 2} (5x - 3)(2x + 3)$.

Solution:

$$\lim\limits_{x \to 2} (5x - 3)(2x + 3) = [5(2) - 3][2(2) + 3] = 49$$

75. Find $\lim\limits_{t \to 3} \dfrac{t^2 + 1}{t}$.

Solution:

$$\lim\limits_{t \to 3} \frac{t^2 + 1}{t} = \frac{(3)^2 + 1}{3} = \frac{10}{3}$$

77. Find $\lim\limits_{t \to 0} \dfrac{t^2 + 1}{t}$, if it exists.

Solution:

$$\lim\limits_{t \to 0^-} \frac{t^2 + 1}{t} = -\infty$$

$$\lim\limits_{t \to 0^+} \frac{t^2 + 1}{t} = \infty$$

$$\lim\limits_{t \to 0} \frac{t^2 + 1}{t} \text{ does not exist.}$$

79. Find $\lim\limits_{x \to -2} \dfrac{x + 2}{x^2 - 4}$.

Solution:

$$\lim\limits_{x \to -2} \frac{x + 2}{x^2 - 4} = \lim\limits_{x \to -2} \frac{x + 2}{(x + 2)(x - 2)} = \lim\limits_{x \to -2} \frac{1}{x - 2} = -\frac{1}{4}$$

81. Find $\lim\limits_{x \to 0^+} \left(x - \dfrac{1}{x} \right)$.

Solution:

$$\lim\limits_{x \to 0^+} \left(x - \frac{1}{x} \right) = \lim\limits_{x \to 0^+} \frac{x^2 - 1}{x} = -\infty$$

83. Find $\lim\limits_{x \to 0} \dfrac{[1/(x - 2)] - 1}{x}$.

Solution:

$$\lim\limits_{x \to 0} \frac{[1/(x - 2)] - 1}{x} = \lim\limits_{x \to 0} \frac{1 - (x - 2)}{x(x - 2)} = \lim\limits_{x \to 0} \frac{3 - x}{x(x - 2)} \text{ does not exist.}$$

85. Find $\displaystyle\lim_{\Delta x \to 0} \frac{(x + \Delta x)^3 - (x + \Delta x) - (x^3 - x)}{\Delta x}$.

Solution:

$\displaystyle\lim_{\Delta x \to 0}$

$$\frac{(x + \Delta x)^3 - (x + \Delta x) - (x^3 - x)}{\Delta x}$$

$$= \lim_{\Delta x \to 0} \frac{x^3 + 3x^2 \Delta x + 3x(\Delta x)^2 + (\Delta x)^3 - x - \Delta x - x^3 + x}{\Delta x}$$

$$= \lim_{\Delta x \to 0} \frac{3x^2 \Delta x + 3x(\Delta x)^2 + (\Delta x)^3 - \Delta x}{\Delta x}$$

$$= \lim_{\Delta x \to 0} [3x^2 + 3x \Delta x + (\Delta x)^2 - 1]$$

$$= 3x^2 - 1$$

87. Complete a table to estimate $\displaystyle\lim_{x \to 1^+} \frac{\sqrt{2x + 1} - \sqrt{3}}{x - 1}$.

Solution:

x	1.1	1.01	1.001	1.0001
$f(x)$	0.5680	0.5764	0.5773	0.5773

$$\lim_{x \to 1^+} \frac{\sqrt{2x + 1} - \sqrt{3}}{x - 1} = \frac{1}{\sqrt{3}} \approx 0.5774$$

89. Determine if the statement $\displaystyle\lim_{x \to 0} \frac{|x|}{x} = 1$ is true or false.

Solution:

The statement is false since $\displaystyle\lim_{x \to 0^-} \frac{|x|}{x} = -1$.

91. Determine if the statement $\displaystyle\lim_{x \to 0} \sqrt{x} = 0$ is true or false.

Solution:

The statement is false since $\displaystyle\lim_{x \to 0^-} \sqrt{x}$ is undefined.

93. Determine if the statement $\displaystyle\lim_{x \to 2} f(x) = 3$ is true or false, given

$$f(x) = \begin{cases} 3, & x \leq 2 \\ 0, & x > 2 \end{cases}$$

Solution:

The statement is false since $\displaystyle\lim_{x \to 2^+} f(x) = \lim_{x \to 2^+} 0 = 0$.

95. Find the intervals on which the function $f(x) = \dfrac{1}{(x+4)^2}$ is continuous.

Solution:

$f(x) = \dfrac{1}{(x+4)^2}$ is continuous on the intervals $(-\infty, -4) \cup (-4, \infty)$.

97. Find the intervals on which the function $f(x) = \dfrac{3}{x+1}$ is continuous.

Solution:

$f(x) = \dfrac{3}{x+1}$ is continuous on the invervals $(-\infty, -1) \cup (-1, \infty)$.

99. Find the intervals on which the function $f(x) = [\![x+3]\!]$ is continuous.

Solution:

$f(x) = [\![x+3]\!]$ is continuous on all intervals of the form $(c, c+1)$, where c is an integer.

101. Find the intervals on which the function

$$f(x) = \begin{cases} x, & x \le 0 \\ x+1, & x > 0 \end{cases}$$

is continuous.

Solution:

$f(x)$ is continuous on the intervals $(-\infty, 0) \cup (0, \infty)$.

103. Find a so that f is continuous on $(-\infty, \infty)$, if $f(x) = \begin{cases} -x+1, & x \le 3 \\ ax-8, & x > 3 \end{cases}$

Solution:

$\displaystyle \lim_{x \to 3^-} f(x) = \lim_{x \to 3^-} (-x+1) = -2$

$\displaystyle \lim_{x \to 3^+} f(x) = \lim_{x \to 3^+} (ax-8) = 3a - 8$

Thus, $-2 = 3a - 8$ and $a = 2$.

105. *National Debt* The table lists the national debt D (in billions of dollars) for selected years. A mathematical model for the national debt is

$$D = 0.2t^3 + 2.74t^2 + 8.47t + 358.78,$$

where $t = 0$ represents 1970.

t	0	5	10	15	20	21
D	381	542	909	1817	3206	3599

(a) Use a graphing utility to graph the model.

(b) Create a table that compares the values given by the model with the actual data.

(c) Use the model to estimate the national debt in 1995.

Solution:

(a)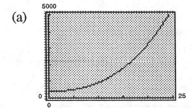

(b)

t	0	5	10	15	20	21
debt	381	542	909	1817	3206	3599
model	358.77	494.63	917.48	1777.33	3224.18	3597.19

(c) In 1995, $t = 25$ and $D \approx 5408.03$

Practice Test for Chapter 1

1. Find the distance between $(3, 7)$ and $(4, -2)$.

2. Find the midpoint of the line segment joining $(0, 5)$ and $(2, 1)$.

3. Determine whether the points $(0, -3)$, $(2, 5)$, and $(-3, -15)$ are collinear.

4. Find x so that the distance between $(0, 3)$ and $(x, 5)$ is 7.

5. Sketch the graph of $y = 4 - x^2$.

6. Sketch the graph of $y = \sqrt{x - 2}$.

7. Sketch the graph of $y = |x - 3|$.

8. Write the equation of the circle in standard form and sketch its graph:
$$x^2 + y^2 - 8x + 2y + 8 = 0.$$

9. Find the points of intersection of the graphs of $x^2 + y^2 = 25$ and $x - 2y = 10$.

10. Find the general equation of the line passing through the points $(7, 4)$ and $(6, -2)$.

11. Find the general equation of the line passing through the point $(-2, -1)$ with a slope of $m = \frac{2}{3}$.

12. Find the general equation of the line passing through the point $(6, -8)$ with undefined slope.

13. Find the general equation of the line passing through the point $(0, 3)$ and perpendicular to the line given by $2x - 5y = 7$.

14. Given $f(x) = x^2 - 5$, find the following.
    (a) $f(3)$ (b) $f(-6)$
    (c) $f(x - 5)$ (d) $f(x + \Delta x)$

15. Find the domain and range of $f(x) = \sqrt{3 - x}$.

16. Given $f(x) = 2x + 3$ and $g(x) = x^2 - 1$, find the following.

(a) $f(g(x))$ (b) $g(f(x))$

17. Given $f(x) = x^3 + 6$, find $f^{-1}(x)$.

18. Find $\lim\limits_{x \to -4} (2 - 5x)$.

19. Find $\lim\limits_{x \to 6} \dfrac{x^2 - 36}{x - 6}$.

20. Find $\lim\limits_{x \to -1} \dfrac{|x + 1|}{x + 1}$.

21. Find $\lim\limits_{x \to 0} \dfrac{\sqrt{x + 5} - \sqrt{5}}{x}$.

22. Find $\lim\limits_{x \to 1} f(x)$, where $f(x) = \begin{cases} 2x + 3, & x \le 1 \\ x^2 + 4, & x > 1. \end{cases}$

23. Find the discontinuities of $f(x) = \dfrac{x - 8}{x^2 - 64}$. Which are removable?

24. Find the discontinuities of $f(x) = \dfrac{|x - 3|}{x - 3}$. Which are removable?

25. Sketch the graph of $f(x) = \dfrac{x^2 - 5x + 6}{x - 3}$.

Graphing Calculator Required

26. Solve the equation for y and graph the resulting two equations on the same set of coordinate axes.

$$x^2 + y^2 + 6x + 5 = 0$$

27. Use a graphing calculator to graph $f(x) = \dfrac{x^2 - 9}{x - 3}$ and find $\lim\limits_{x \to 3} f(x)$. Is the graph displayed correctly at $x = 3$?

CHAPTER 2
Differentiation

Section 2.1   The Derivative and the Slope of a Graph

1. Trace the given curve and sketch the tangent line at each of the points $(x_1, \ y_1)$ and $(x_2, \ y_2)$. Determine whether the slope of each tangent line is positive, negative, or zero.

   Solution:

   The tangent line at $(x_1, \ y_1)$ has a positive slope.

   The tangent line at $(x_2, \ y_2)$ has a negative slope.

   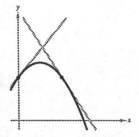

3. Trace the given curve and sketch the tangent line at each of the points $(x_1, \ y_1)$ and $(x_2, \ y_2)$. Determine whether the slope of each tangent line is positive, negative, or zero.

   Solution:

   The tangent line at $(x_1, \ y_1)$ has a positive slope.

   The tangent line at $(x_2, \ y_2)$ has zero slope.

   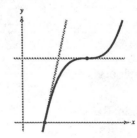

5. Estimate the slope of the curve at the point $(x, \ y)$.

   Solution:

   The slope is $m = 1$.

7. Estimate the slope of the curve at the point $(x, \ y)$.

   Solution:

   The slope is $m = 0$.

9. Estimate the slope of the curve at the point $(x,\ y)$.

Solution:

The slope is $m = -\frac{1}{3}$.

11. *Revenue* The graph shown in the text represents the revenue R (in millions of dollars) for Dairy Queen from 1989 through 1993. Estimate the slope of the graph in 1990 and in 1992.

Solution:

In 1990 $(t = 1)$, the slope is about $\dfrac{300 - 280}{2 - 1} = 20$ million/yr.

In 1992 $(t = 3)$, the slope is about $\dfrac{295 - 291}{3 - 2} = 4$ million/yr.

13. Use the limit definition to find the derivative of $f(x) = 3$.

Solution:

$$f(x + \Delta x) = 3$$
$$f(x + \Delta x) - f(x) = 0$$
$$\frac{f(x + \Delta x) - f(x)}{\Delta x} = 0$$
$$\lim_{\Delta x \to 0} \frac{f(x + \Delta x) - f(x)}{\Delta x} = 0$$

15. Use the limit definition to find the derivative of $f(x) = -5x + 3$.

Solution:

$$f(x + \Delta x) = -5(x + \Delta x) + 3 = -5x - 5\Delta x + 3$$
$$f(x + \Delta x) - f(x) = -5\Delta x$$
$$\frac{f(x + \Delta x) - f(x)}{\Delta x} = -5$$
$$\lim_{\Delta x \to 0} \frac{f(x + \Delta x) - f(x)}{\Delta x} = -5$$

17. Use the limit definition to find the derivative of $f(x) = x^2$.

Solution:

$$f(x + \Delta x) = (x + \Delta x)^2 = x^2 + 2x\Delta x + (\Delta x)^2$$
$$f(x + \Delta x) - f(x) = 2x\Delta x + (\Delta x)^2$$
$$\frac{f(x + \Delta x) - f(x)}{\Delta x} = 2x + \Delta x$$
$$\lim_{\Delta x \to 0} \frac{f(x + \Delta x) - f(x)}{\Delta x} = 2x$$

19. Use the limit definition to find the derivative of the function $f(x) = 3x^2 - 5x - 2$

Solution:

$$f(x + \Delta x) = 3(x + \Delta x)^2 - 5(x + \Delta x) - 2$$
$$= 3x^2 + 6x\Delta x + 3(\Delta x)^2 - 5x - 5(\Delta x) - 2$$
$$f(x + \Delta x) - f(x) = 6x\Delta x + 3(\Delta x)^2 - 5(\Delta x)$$
$$\frac{f(x + \Delta x) - f(x)}{\Delta x} = 6x + 3(\Delta x) - 5$$
$$\lim_{\Delta x \to 0} \frac{f(x + \Delta x)}{\Delta x} = 6x - 5$$

21. Use the limit definition to find the derivative of $h(t) = \sqrt{t - 1}$.

Solution:

$$h(t + \Delta t) = \sqrt{t + \Delta t - 1}$$
$$h(t + \Delta t) - h(t) = \sqrt{t + \Delta t - 1} - \sqrt{t - 1}$$
$$= \frac{\sqrt{t + \Delta t - 1} - \sqrt{t - 1}}{1} \cdot \frac{\sqrt{t + \Delta t - 1} + \sqrt{t - 1}}{\sqrt{t + \Delta t - 1} + \sqrt{t - 1}}$$
$$= \frac{\Delta t}{\sqrt{t + \Delta t - 1} + \sqrt{t - 1}}$$
$$\frac{h(t + \Delta t) - h(t)}{\Delta t} = \frac{1}{\sqrt{t + \Delta t - 1} + \sqrt{t - 1}}$$
$$\lim_{\Delta t \to 0} \frac{h(t + \Delta t) - h(t)}{\Delta t} = \frac{1}{2\sqrt{t - 1}}$$

23. Use the limit definition to find the derivative of $f(t) = t^3 - 12t$.

Solution:

$$f(t + \Delta t) = (t + \Delta t)^3 - 12(t + \Delta t)$$
$$= t^3 + 3t^2\Delta t + 3t(\Delta t)^2 + (\Delta t)^3 - 12t - 12\Delta t$$
$$f(t + \Delta t) - f(t) = 3t^2\Delta t + 3t(\Delta t)^2 + (\Delta t)^3 - 12\Delta t$$
$$\frac{f(t + \Delta t) - f(t)}{\Delta t} = 3t^2 + 3t\Delta t + (\Delta t)^2 - 12$$
$$\lim_{\Delta t \to 0} \frac{f(t + \Delta t) - f(t)}{\Delta t} = 3t^2 - 12$$

25. Use the limit definition to find the derivative of $f(x) = \dfrac{1}{x^2}$

Solution:

$$f(x + \Delta x) = \frac{1}{(x + \Delta x)^2}$$

$$f(x + \Delta x) - f(x) = \frac{1}{(x + \Delta x)^2} - \frac{1}{x^2} = \frac{x^2 - (x^2 + 2x\Delta x + (\Delta x)^2}{(x + \Delta x)^2 x^2}$$

$$= \frac{-2x\Delta x - (\Delta x)^2}{(x + \Delta x)^2 x^2}$$

$$\frac{f(x + \Delta x) - f(x)}{\Delta x} = \frac{-2x - \Delta x}{(x + \Delta x)^2 x^2}$$

$$\lim_{\Delta x \to 0} \frac{f(x + \Delta x) - f(x)}{\Delta x} = \frac{-2x}{x^4} = -\frac{2}{x^3}$$

27. Find the slope of the tangent line to the graph of $f(x) = 6 - 2x$ at the point (2, 2).

Solution:

$$f(x + \Delta x) = 6 - 2(x + \Delta x) = 6 - 2x - 2\Delta x$$

$$f(x + \Delta x) - f(x) = -2\Delta x$$

$$\frac{f(x + \Delta x) - f(x)}{\Delta x} = -2$$

$$\lim_{\Delta x \to 0} \frac{f(x + \Delta x) - f(x)}{\Delta x} = -2$$

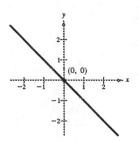

At (2, 2), the slope of the tangent line is $m = -2$. The accompanying figure shows the graph of f and the tangent line.

29. Find the slope of the tangent line to the graph of $f(x) = -x$ at the point (0, 0).

Solution:

$$f(x + \Delta x) = -(x + \Delta x)$$

$$f(x + \Delta x) - f(x) = -(x + \Delta x) - (-x) = -\Delta x$$

$$\frac{f(x + \Delta x) - f(x)}{\Delta x} = -1$$

$$\lim_{\Delta x \to 0} \frac{f(x + \Delta x) - f(x)}{\Delta x} = -1$$

At (0, 0) the slope of the tangent line is -1. The accompany figure shows the graph of f and the tangent line.

31. Find the slope of the tangent line to the graph of $f(x) = x^2 - 2$ at the point $(2, 2)$.

Solution:

$$f(x + \Delta x) = (x + \Delta x)^2 - 2$$
$$= x^2 + 2x\Delta x + (\Delta x)^2 - 2$$
$$f(x + \Delta x) - f(x) = 2x\Delta x + (\Delta x)^2$$
$$\frac{f(x + \Delta x) - f(x)}{\Delta x} = 2x + \Delta x$$
$$\lim_{\Delta x \to 0} \frac{f(x + \Delta x) - f(x)}{\Delta x} = 2x$$

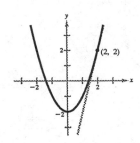

At $(2, 2)$, the slope of the tangent line is $m = 2(2) = 4$. The accompanying figure shows the graph of f and the tangent line.

33. Find the slope of the tangent line to the graph of $f(x) = x^3$ at the point $(2, 8)$.

Solution:

$$f(x + \Delta x) = x^3 + 3x^2\Delta x + 3x(\Delta x)^2 + (\Delta x)^3$$
$$f(x + \Delta x) - f(x) = 3x^2\Delta x + 3x(\Delta x)^2 + (\Delta x)^3$$
$$\frac{f(x + \Delta x) - f(x)}{\Delta x} = 3x^2 + 3x\Delta x + (\Delta x)^2$$
$$\lim_{\Delta x \to 0} \frac{f(x + \Delta x) - f(x)}{\Delta x} = 3x^2$$

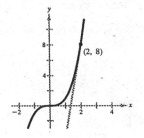

At $(2, 8)$, the slope of the tangent line is $m = 3(2)^2 = 12$.

The accompanying figure shows the graph of f and the tangent line.

35. Find the slope of the tangent line to the graph of $f(x) = \sqrt{x+1}$ at the point (3, 2).

Solution:

$$f(x + \Delta x) = \sqrt{x + \Delta x + 1}$$

$$f(x + \Delta x) - f(x) = \sqrt{x + \Delta x + 1} - \sqrt{x + 1}$$

$$= \frac{\sqrt{x + \Delta x + 1} - \sqrt{x + 1}}{1} \cdot \frac{\sqrt{x + \Delta x + 1} + \sqrt{x + 1}}{\sqrt{x + \Delta x + 1} + \sqrt{x + 1}}$$

$$= \frac{\Delta x}{\sqrt{x + \Delta x + 1} + \sqrt{x + 1}}$$

$$\frac{f(x + \Delta x) - f(x)}{\Delta x} = \frac{1}{\sqrt{x + \Delta x + 1} + \sqrt{x + 1}}$$

$$\lim_{\Delta x \to 0} \frac{f(x + \Delta x) - f(x)}{\Delta x} = \frac{1}{2\sqrt{x + 1}}$$

At (3, 2), the slope of the tangent line is $m = \frac{1}{4}$. The accompanying figure shows the graph of f and the tangent line.

37. Find the slope of the tangent line to the graph of $f(x) = x^3 + 2x$ at the point (1, 3).

Solution:

$$f(x + \Delta x) = (x + \Delta x)^3 + 2(x + \Delta x)$$

$$= x^3 + 3x^2 \Delta x + 3x(\Delta x)^2 + (\Delta x)^3 + 2x + 2\Delta x$$

$$f(x + \Delta x) - f(x) = 3x^2 \Delta x + 3x(\Delta x)^2 + (\Delta x)^3 + 2\Delta x$$

$$\frac{f(x + \Delta x) - f(x)}{\Delta x} = 3x^2 + 3\Delta x + (\Delta x)^2 + 2$$

$$\lim_{\Delta x \to 0} \frac{f(x + \Delta x) - f(x)}{\Delta x} = 3x^2 + 2$$

At (1, 3), the slope of the tangent line is $m = 3(1)^2 + 2 = 5$. The accompanying figure shows the graph of f and the tangent line.

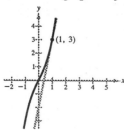

39. Find an equation of the tangent line to the graph of $f(x) = \frac{1}{2}x^2$ at the point $(2, 2)$.

Solution:

$$f(x + \Delta x) = \frac{1}{2}(x + \Delta x)^2$$
$$= \frac{1}{2}x^2 + x\Delta x + \frac{1}{2}\Delta x^2$$
$$f(x + \Delta x) - f(x) = x\Delta x + \frac{1}{2}(\Delta x)^3$$
$$\frac{f(x + \Delta x) - f(x)}{\Delta x} = x + \frac{1}{2}(\Delta x)$$
$$\lim_{\Delta x \to 0} \frac{f(x + \Delta x) - f(x)}{\Delta x} = x$$

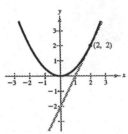

At the point $(2, 2)$, the slope of the tangent line is $m = 2$. The equation of the tangent line is

$$y - 2 = 2(x - 2)$$
$$y = 2x - 2$$

41. Find an equation of the tangent line to the graph of $f(x) = (x - 1)^2$ at the point $(-2, 9)$.

Solution:

$$f(x + \Delta x) = ((x + \Delta x) - 1)^2$$
$$= x^2 + 2x\Delta x + \Delta x^2 - 2x - 2\Delta x + 1$$
$$f(x + \Delta x) - f(x) = 2x\Delta x + (\Delta x)^2 - 2\Delta x$$
$$\frac{f(x + \Delta x) - f(x)}{\Delta x} = 2x + \Delta x - 2$$
$$\lim_{\Delta x \to 0} \frac{f(x + \Delta x) - f(x)}{\Delta x} = 2x - 2$$

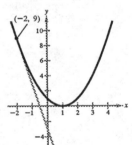

At the point $(-2, 9)$, the slope of the tangent line is $m = 2(-2) - 2 = -6$. The equation of the tangent line is

$$y - 9 = -6(x - (-2))$$
$$y = -6x - 3$$

43. Find an equation of the tangent line to the graph of $f(x) = \sqrt{x} + 1$ at the point $(4, 3)$.

Solution:

$f(x + \Delta x) = \sqrt{x + \Delta x} + 1$

$f(x + \Delta x) - f(x) = \sqrt{x + \Delta x} - \sqrt{x}$

$$= \frac{\sqrt{x + \Delta x} - \sqrt{x}}{1} \cdot \frac{\sqrt{x + \Delta x} + \sqrt{x}}{\sqrt{x + \Delta x} + \sqrt{x}}$$

$$= \frac{\Delta x}{\sqrt{x + \Delta x} + \sqrt{x}}$$

$$\frac{f(x + \Delta x) - f(x)}{\Delta x} = \frac{1}{\sqrt{x + \Delta x} + \sqrt{x}}$$

$$\lim_{\Delta x \to 0} \frac{f(x + \Delta x) - f(x)}{\Delta x} = \frac{1}{\sqrt{x} + \sqrt{x}} = \frac{1}{2\sqrt{x}}$$

At the point $(4, 3)$, $f'(4) = \dfrac{1}{2\sqrt{4}} = \dfrac{1}{4}$.

The equation of the tangent line is

$$y - 3 = \frac{1}{4}(x - 4)$$

$$y = \frac{1}{4}x + 2.$$

45. Find an equation of the line that is tangent to the graph of $f(x) = -\frac{1}{4}x^2$ and parallel to the given line $x + y = 0$.

Solution:

$$f(x + \Delta x) = -\frac{1}{4}(x + \Delta x)^2 = -\frac{1}{4}(x^2 + 2x\Delta x + (\Delta x)^2)$$

$$f(x + \Delta x) - f(x) = -\frac{1}{4}(2x\Delta x + (\Delta x^2))$$

$$f\frac{(x + \Delta x) - f(x)}{\Delta x} = -\frac{x}{2} - \frac{1}{4}\Delta x$$

$$\lim_{\Delta x \to 0} \frac{f(x + \Delta x) - f(x)}{\Delta x} = -\frac{x}{2} \quad \text{(Slope of tangent line)}$$

Since the slope of the given line is -1, we have

$$-\frac{x}{2} = -1$$

$$x = 2$$

Therefore, at the point $(2, -1)$, the tangent line parallel to $x + y = 0$ is

$$y - (-1) = -1(x - 2)$$

$$y = -x + 1$$

47. Find an equation of the line that is tangent to the graph of $f(x) = -\frac{1}{2}x^3$ and parallel to the given line $6x + y + 4 = 0$.

Solution:

$$f(x + \Delta x) = -\frac{1}{2}(x + \Delta x)^3 = -\frac{1}{2}(x^3 + 3x^2\Delta x + 3x(\Delta x)^2 + (\Delta x)^3$$

$$f(x + \Delta x) - f(x) = -\frac{1}{2}(3x^2\Delta x + 3x(\Delta x)^2 + (\Delta x)^3)$$

$$\frac{f(x + \Delta x) - f(x)}{\Delta x} = -\frac{1}{2}(3x^2 + 3x\Delta x + (\Delta x)^2)$$

$$\lim_{\Delta x \to 0} \frac{f(x + \Delta x) - f(x)}{\Delta x} = -\frac{1}{2}(3x^2) = \frac{-3}{2}x^2 \text{ (Slope of tangent line)}.$$

Since the slope of the given line is -6, we have

$$\frac{-3}{2}x^2 = -6$$

$$x^2 = 4$$

$$x = \pm 2$$

At the point $(2, -4)$, the tangent line is

$$y + 4 = -6(x - 2)$$

$$y = -6x + 8$$

At the point $(-2, 4)$, the tangent line is

$$y - 4 = -6(x + 2)$$

$$y = -6x - 8$$

49. Determine where the function $y = |x + 3|$ is not differentiable.

Solution:

y is not differentiable when $x = -3$. At $(-3, \ 0)$, the graph has a node.

51. Determine where the function $y = \dfrac{1}{x + 1}$ is differentiable.

Solution:

This function is differentiable for all values of x except $x = -1$ since $x = -1$ is a nonremovable discontinuity.

53. Determine where the function $y = (x - 3)^{2/3}$ is differentiable.

Solution:

y is differentiable everywhere except at $x = 3$. At $(3, 0)$, the graph has a node.

55. Determine where the following function is differentiable.

$y = \sqrt{x-1}$

Solution:

f is differentiable on the open interval $(1, \infty)$.

57. Determine where the following function is differentiable.

$y = \begin{cases} x^3 + 3, & x < 0 \\ x^3 - 3, & x \geq 0 \end{cases}$

Solution:

f is differentiable everywhere except at $x = 0$, which is a nonremovable discontinuity.

59. Use a graphing utility to graph f over the interval $[-2, 2]$. Then complete the table (shown in the text) by *graphically* estimating the slope of the graph at the indicated points.

Solution:

x	-2	$\dfrac{-3}{2}$	-1	$-\dfrac{1}{2}$	0	$\dfrac{1}{2}$	1	$\dfrac{3}{2}$	2
$f(x)$	-2	-0.8438	-0.25	-0.0313	0	0.0313	0.25	0.8438	2
$f'(x)$	3	1.6875	0.75	0.1875	0	0.1875	0.75	1.6875	3

Analytically, the slope of $f(x) = \dfrac{1}{4}x^3$ is

$$m = \lim_{\Delta x \to 0} \frac{f(x + \Delta x) - f(x)}{\Delta x}$$

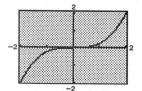

$$= \lim_{\Delta x \to 0} \frac{\frac{1}{4}(x + \Delta x)^3 - \frac{1}{4}x^3}{\Delta x}$$

$$= \lim_{\Delta x \to 0} \frac{\frac{1}{4}(3x^2 \Delta x + 3x(\Delta x) + (\Delta x)^3)}{\Delta x}$$

$$= \lim_{\Delta x \to 0} \frac{1}{4}(3x^2 + 3x\Delta x + (\Delta x)^2)$$

$$= \frac{3}{4}x^2$$

61. Determine whether the following statement is true or false.

The slope of the graph of $y = x^2$ is different at every point on the graph of f.

Solution:

True.

63. Determine whether the following statement is true or false.

If a function is differentiable at a point, then it is continuous at that point.

Solution:

True.

65. Find the derivative of the function $f(x) = x^2 - 4x$. Then graph f and its derivative on the same set of coordinate axes. What does the x-intercept of the derivative indicate about the graph of f?

Solution:

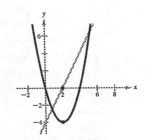

$$f'(x) = \lim_{\Delta x \to 0} \frac{f(x + \Delta x) - f(x)}{\Delta x}$$

$$= \lim_{\Delta x \to 0} \frac{(x + \Delta x)^2 - 4(x + \Delta x) - (x^2 - 4x)}{\Delta x}$$

$$= \lim_{\Delta x \to 0} \frac{2x\,\Delta x + (\Delta x)^2 - 4\Delta x}{\Delta x}$$

$$= \lim_{\Delta x \to 0} (2x + \Delta x - 4) = 2x - 4$$

Graphs of $f(x) = x^2 - 4x$ and $f'(x) = 2x - 4$

The x-intercept of the derivative indicates a point of horizontal tangency for f.

Section 2.2   Some Rules for Differentiation

1. Find the slope of the tangent line at the point $(1, 1)$ to the graphs of the following.

(a) $y = x^2$ 　　　　　　　　　　　　　　　(b) $y = x^{1/2}$

Solution:

(a)
$$y = x^2$$
$$y' = 2x$$
At $(1, 1)$, $y' = 2$.

(b)
$$y = x^{1/2}$$
$$y' = \frac{1}{2}x^{-1/2} = \frac{1}{2\sqrt{x}}$$
At $(1, 1)$, $y' = \frac{1}{2}$.

3. Find the slope of the tangent line at the point (1, 1) to the graphs of the following.

(a) $y = x^{-1}$

(b) $y = x^{-1/3}$

Solution:

(a)
$$y = x^{-1}$$
$$y' = -x^{-2} = -\frac{1}{x^2}$$
At (1, 1), $y' = -1$.

(b)
$$y = x^{-1/3}$$
$$y' = \frac{-1}{3}x^{-4/3} = \frac{-1}{3x^{4/3}}$$
At (1, 1), $y' = -\frac{1}{3}$.

5. Use the differentiation rules to find the derivative of $y = 3$.

Solution:

$$y' = 0$$

7. Use the differentiation rules to find the derivative of $f(x) = x + 1$.

Solution:

$$f'(x) = 1$$

9. Use the differentiation rules to find the derivative of $g(x) = x^2 + 4$.

Solution:

$$g'(x) = 2x$$

11. Use the differentiation rules to find the derivative of $-3t^2 + 2t - 4$.

Solution:

$$f'(t) = -6t + 2$$

13. Use the differentiation rules to find the derivative of $s(t) = t^3 - 2t + 4$.

Solution:

$$s'(t) = 3t^2 - 2$$

15. Use the differentiation rules to find the derivative of $y = 4t^{4/3}$.

Solution:

$$y' = 4\left(\frac{4}{3}\right)t^{1/3} = \frac{16}{3}t^{1/3}$$

17. Use the differentiation rules to find the derivative of $f(x) = 4\sqrt{x}$.

Solution:

$$f(x) = 4\sqrt{x} = 4x^{1/2}$$

$$f'(x) = 4\left(\frac{1}{2}\right)x^{(1/2)-1} = 2x^{-1/2} = \frac{2}{\sqrt{x}}$$

19. Use differentiation rules to find the derivative of $y = 4x^{-2} + 2x^2$.

Solution:

$$y' = 4(-2)x^{-2-1} + 2(2)x^{2-1} = -8x^{-3} + 4x^1 = -\frac{8}{x^3} + 4x$$

In Exercises 21–25, complete the table using Example 7 as a model.

	Function	Rewrite	Derivative	Simplify
21.	$y = \dfrac{1}{4x^3}$	$y = \dfrac{1}{4}x^{-3}$	$y' = -\dfrac{3}{4}x^{-4}$	$y' = \dfrac{-3}{4x^4}$
23.	$y = \dfrac{1}{(4x)^3}$	$y = \dfrac{1}{64}x^{-3}$	$y' = \dfrac{-3}{64}x^{-4}$	$y' = \dfrac{-3}{64x^4}$
25.	$y = \dfrac{\sqrt{x}}{x}$	$y = x^{-(1/2)}$	$y' = -\dfrac{1}{2}x^{-(3/2)}$	$y' = -\dfrac{1}{2x^{3/2}}$

27. Find the value of the derivative of $f(x) = 1/x$ at $(1, 1)$.

Solution:

$$f(x) = \frac{1}{x} = x^{-1}$$

$$f'(x) = -x^{-2} = -\frac{1}{x^2} \Rightarrow f'(1) = -1$$

29. Find the value of the derivative of $f(t) = 4 - \dfrac{4}{3t}$ at $\left(\dfrac{1}{2}, \dfrac{4}{3}\right)$.

Solution:

$$f(t) = 4 - \frac{4}{3t} = 4 - \frac{4}{3}t^{-1}$$

$$f'(t) = \frac{4}{3}t^{-2} = \frac{4}{3t^2}$$

$$f'\left(\frac{1}{2}\right) = \frac{16}{3}$$

31. Find the value of the derivative of $y = (2x + 1)^2$ at the point $(0, 1)$.

Solution:

$$y = (2x + 1)^2 = 4x^2 + 4x + 1$$
$$y' = 8x + 4$$
At $(0, \ 1), \ y' = 4$

33. Find $f'(x)$ for $f(x) = x^2 - (4/x)$.

Solution:

$$f(x) = x^2 - \frac{4}{x} = x^2 - 4x^{-1}$$

$$f'(x) = 2x + 4x^{-2} = 2x + \frac{4}{x^2} = \frac{2(x^3 + 2)}{x^2}$$

35. Find $f'(x)$ for $f(x) = x^2 - 2x - \dfrac{2}{x^4}$.

Solution:

$$f(x) = x^2 - 2x - \frac{2}{x^4} = x^2 - 2 - 2x^{-4}$$

$$f' = 2x - 2 + 8x^{-5} = 2x - 2 + \frac{8}{x^5}$$

37. Find $f'(x)$ for $f(x) = \dfrac{2x^3 - 4x^2 + 3}{x^2}$.

Solution:

$$f(x) = \frac{2x^3 - 4x^2 + 3}{x^2} = 2x - 4 + 3x^{-2}$$

$$f'(x) = 2 - 6x^{-3} = 2 - \frac{6}{x^3} = \frac{2x^3 - 6}{x^3}$$

39. Find $f'(x)$ for $f(x) = x(x^2 + 1)$.

Solution:

$$f(x) = x(x^2 + 1) = x^3 + x$$
$$f'(x) = 3x^2 + 1$$

41. Find $f'(x)$ for $f(x) = x^{4/5}$.

Solution:

$$f'(x) = \frac{4}{5}x^{-1/5} = \frac{4}{5x^{1/5}}$$

43. Find $f'(x)$ for $f(x) = \sqrt[3]{x} + \sqrt[5]{x}$.

Solution:

$$f(x) = \sqrt[3]{x} + \sqrt[5]{x} = x^{1/3} + x^{1/5}$$

$$f'(x) = \frac{1}{3}x^{-2/3} + \frac{1}{5}x^{-4/5} = \frac{1}{3x^{2/3}} + \frac{1}{5x^{4/5}}$$

45. Find an equation of the tangent line to the graph of $y = -2x^4 + 5x^2 - 3$ at the point (1, 0).

Solution:

$$y' = -4x^3 + 6x$$

At (1, 0), the slope is $m = y' = -4 + 6 = 2$. The equation of the tangent line is

$$y - 0 = 2(x - 1)$$

$$y = 2x - 2$$

47. Determine the point(s), if any, at which $y = -x^4 + 3x^2 - 1$ has a horizontal tangent line.

Solution:

$$y' = -4x^3 + 6x = 2x(3 - 2x^2) = 0$$

$$x = 0, \, x = \pm\sqrt{\frac{3}{2}} = \pm\sqrt{\frac{6}{2}}.$$

If $x = \pm\sqrt{\frac{6}{2}}$, then $y = -\left(\frac{\sqrt{6}}{2}\right)^4 + 3\left(\frac{\sqrt{6}}{2}\right)^2 - 1$

$$= -\frac{9}{4} + 3\left(\frac{3}{2}\right) - 1$$

$$= \frac{5}{4}$$

The function has horizontal tangent lines at the points (0, 1), $\left(-\frac{\sqrt{6}}{2}, \frac{5}{4}\right)$ and $\left(\frac{\sqrt{6}}{2}, \frac{5}{4}\right)$.

49. Determine the point(s) (if any) at which $f(x) = x^3 + x$ has a horizontal tangent line.

Solution:

$$f'(x) = 3x^2 + 1$$

$f'(x) \neq 0$ for any value of x. The graph of $f(x)$ has no horizontal tangent lines.

51. Perform the following.

(a) Sketch the graphs of f, g, and h on the same set of coordinate axes.

(b) Find $f'(1)$, $g'(1)$, and $h'(1)$.

(c) Sketch the graph of the tangent lines to each graph when $x = 1$.

Solution:

(a)

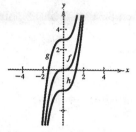

(c)

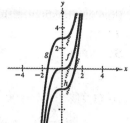

(b) $f'(x) = g'(x) = h'(x) = 3x^2$

$f'(1) = g'(1) = h'(1) = 3$

53. Use the Constant Rule, the Constant Multiple Rule, and the Sum Rule to find $h'(1)$ given that $f'(1) = 3$, where $h(x)$ is defined as follows.

(a) $h(x) = f(x) - 2$ (b) $h(x) = 2f(x)$

(c) $h(x) = -f(x)$ (d) $h(x) = -1 + 2f(x)$

Solution:

(a) $h(x) = f(x) - 2$

$h'(x) = f'(x) - 0 = f'(x)$

$h'(1) = f'(1) = 3$

(b) $h(x) = 2f(x)$

$h'(x) = 2f'(x)$

$h'(1) = 2f'(1) = 2(3) = 6$

(c) $h(x) = -f(x)$

$h'(x) = -f'(x)$

$h'(1) = -f'(1) = -3$

(d) $h(x) = -1 + 2f(x)$

$h'(x) = 0 + 2f'(x) = 2f'(x)$

$h'(1) = 2f'(1) = 2(3) = 6$

55. *Revenue* The revenue R (in billions of dollars) for Chrysler Corporation from 1989 through 1993 can be modeled by

$$R = -6.1t^3 + 23.6t^{5/2} - 22.6t^2 + 35.2,$$

where $t = 0$ represents 1989. (See graph in text.)

(a) Find the slope of the graph in 1990 ($t = 0$) and in 1992 ($t = 3$).

(b) Compare your results with those obtained in Exercise 12 in Section 2.1.

(c) What are the units for the slope of the graph? Interpret the slope of the graph in the context of the problem.

Solution:

$$R = -6.1t^3 + 23.6t^{5/2} - 22.6t^2 + 35.2$$

$$R' = -18.3t^2 + \frac{5}{2}(23.6)t^{3/2} - 45.2t$$

(a) $R'(1) = -4.5$

   $R'(3) = 6.27$

   (c) billions of dollars per year.

57. *Cost* A college club raises funds by selling candy bars for $1.00 each. The club pays $0.60 for each candy bar and has annual fixed costs of $250. Write the profit P as a function of x, the number of candy bars sold. Show that the derivative of the profit function is a constant and that it is equal to the profit on each candy bar sold.

Solution:

$$C = 0.60x + 250$$

$$R = 1.00x$$

$$P = R - C = 1.00x - (0.60x + 250)$$

$$= 0.40x - 250$$

$$\frac{dP}{dx} = 0.40$$

Therefore, the derivative is constant and is equal to the profit on each candy bar sold.

59. Graph f and f' over the interval $[0, 3]$ and determine all horizontal tangents.

Solution:

$$f(x) = x^3 - 1.4x^2 - 0.96x + 1.44$$

$$f'(x) = 3x^2 - 2.8x - 0.96$$

If the tangent line is horizontal,

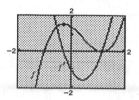

$$f'(x) = 0$$

$$0 = 3x^2 - 2.8x - 0.96.$$

By the Quadratic Formula,

$$x = \frac{2.8 \pm \sqrt{7.84 + 11.52}}{6}$$

$$x = 1.2, \ -0.267$$

The graph has horizontal tangents at the points

$(-0.267, \ 1.577)$ and $(1.2, \ 0)$.

Section 2.3   Rates of Change: Velocity and Marginals

1. *Research and Development*   The graph shown in the text shows the amount A (in billions of constant 1982 dollars) spent on research and development in the United States from 1960 through 1990. Approximate the average rate of change of A during the following periods.

(a) 1960-1968

(b) 1968-1975

(c) 1980-1985

(d) 1960-1990

Solution:

(a) $\dfrac{65 - 45}{1968 - 1960} = \dfrac{20}{8} = 2.5$ billion/year

(b) $\dfrac{60 - 65}{1975 - 1968} = \dfrac{-5}{7} \approx -0.714$ billion/year

(c) $\dfrac{102 - 73}{1985 - 1980} = \dfrac{29}{5} = 5.8$ billion/year

(d) $\dfrac{111 - 45}{1990 - 1960} = \dfrac{66}{30} = 2.2$ billion/year

3. Sketch the graph of $f(t) = 2t + 7$ and find its average rate of change over the interval $[1, 2]$. Compare this to the instantaneous rates of change at the endpoints of the interval.

Solution:

$f'(t) = 2$

Average rate of change: $\dfrac{\Delta y}{\Delta t} = \dfrac{f(2) - f(1)}{2 - 1} = \dfrac{11 - 9}{1} = 2$

Instantaneous rates of change: $f'(1) = 2, \quad f'(2) = 2$

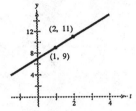

5. Sketch the graph of $h(x) = 1 - x^2$ and find its average rate of change over the interval $[0, 1]$. Compare this to the instantaneous rates of change at the endpoints of the interval.

Solution:

$h'(x) = -2x$

Average rate of change: $\dfrac{\Delta y}{\Delta x} = \dfrac{h(1) - h(0)}{1 - 0} = \dfrac{0 - 1}{1 - 0} = -1$

Instantaneous rates of change: $h'(0) = 0, \quad h'(1) = -2$

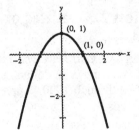

7. Sketch the graph of $f(t) = t^2 + 2$ and find its average rate of change over the interval $[1, 1.1]$. Compare this to the instantaneous rates of change at the endpoints of the interval.

Solution:

$f'(t) = 2t$

Average rate of change: $\dfrac{\Delta y}{\Delta t} = \dfrac{f(1.1) - f(1)}{1.1 - 1} = \dfrac{3.21 - 3}{0.1} = 2.1$

Instantaneous rate of change: $f'(1) = 2, \ f'(1.1) = 2.2$

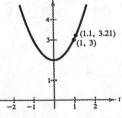

9. Sketch the graph of $f(x) = 1/x$ and find its average rate of change over the interval [1, 4]. Compare this to the instantaneous rates of change at the endpoints of the interval.

Solution:

$$f'(x) = -\frac{1}{x^2}$$

Average rate of change: $\dfrac{\Delta y}{\Delta x} = \dfrac{f(4) - f(1)}{4 - 1} = \dfrac{(1/4) - 1}{3} = -\dfrac{1}{4}$

Instantaneous rates of change: $f'(1) = -1, \quad f'(4) = -\dfrac{1}{16}$

11. Sketch the graph of $g(x) = 4\sqrt{x}$ and find its average rate of change over the interval [1, 9]. Compare this to the instantaneous rates of change at the endpoints of the interval.

Solution:

$$g'(x) = \frac{2}{\sqrt{x}}$$

Average rate of change: $\dfrac{\Delta y}{\Delta x} = \dfrac{g(9) - g(1)}{9 - 1} = \dfrac{12 - 4}{8} = 1$

Instantaneous rates of change: $g'(1) = 2, \quad g'(9) = \dfrac{2}{3}$

13. *Drug Effectiveness* Suppose the effectiveness E (on a scale from 0 to 1) of a painkilling drug t hours after entering the bloodstream is given by

$$E(t) = \frac{1}{27}(9t + 3t^2 - t^3), \quad 0 \le t \le 4.5.$$

Find the average rate of change of E over the indicated interval and compare this to the instantaneous rates of change at the endpoints of the interval.

(a) [0, 1]　　　　　　　　　　　　　(b) [1, 2]

(c) [2, 3]　　　　　　　　　　　　　(d) [3, 4]

Solution:

$$E'(t) = \frac{1}{27}(9 + 6t - 3t^2) = \frac{1}{9}(3 + 2t - t^2)$$

(a) $\dfrac{E(1) - E(0)}{1-0} = \dfrac{(11/27) - 0}{1-0} = \dfrac{11}{27}$　　(b) $\dfrac{E(2) - E(1)}{2-1} = \dfrac{(22/27) - (11/27)}{2-1}$

$$E'(0) = \frac{1}{3}$$

$$E'(1) = \frac{4}{9}$$

$$= \frac{11}{27}$$

$$E'(1) = \frac{4}{9}$$

$$E'(2) = \frac{1}{3}$$

(c) $\dfrac{E(3) - E(2)}{3-2} = \dfrac{1 - (22/27)}{3-2} = \dfrac{5}{27}$　　(d) $\dfrac{E(4) - E(3)}{4-3} = \dfrac{(20/27) - 1}{4-3} = -\dfrac{7}{27}$

$$E'(2) = \frac{1}{3}$$

$$E'(3) = 0$$

$$E'(3) = 0$$

$$E'(4) = -\frac{5}{9}$$

15. *Velocity* The height s (in feet) at time t (in seconds) of a silver dollar dropped from the top of the Washington Monument is

$$s = -16t^2 + 555$$

(a) Find the average velocity on the interval [2, 3].

(b) Find the instantaneous velocity when $t = 2$ and when $t = 3$.

(c) How long will it take the dollar to hit the ground?

(d) Find the velocity of the dollar when it hits the ground.

Solution:

$s = -16t^2 + 555$

(a) average velocity $= \dfrac{5(3) - 5(2)}{3 - 2} = \dfrac{411 - 491}{1} = -80$ ft/sec

(b) $v = s'(t) = -32t$, $v(2) = -64$ ft/sec, $v(3) = -96$ ft/sec

(c) $s = -16t^2 + 555 = 0$

$$16t^2 = 555$$

$$t^2 = \frac{555}{16}$$

$$t \approx 5.89 \text{ seconds}$$

(d) $v(5.89) \approx -188.5$ ft/sec.

17. *Velocity* Suppose the position of an accelerating car is given by $s(t) = 10t^{3/2}$, $0 \le t \le 10$ where s is measured in feet and t is measured in seconds. Find the velocity of the car when

(a) $t = 0$,   (b) $t = 1$,   (c) $t = 4$, and
(d) $t = 9$.

Solution:

$$s'(t) = 15\sqrt{t} = v(t)$$

(a) $v(0) = 0$ ft/sec   (b) $v(1) = 15$ ft/sec

(c) $v(4) = 30$ ft/sec   (d) $v(9) = 45$ ft/sec

19. *Marginal Cost* Use the cost function to find the marginal cost for producing x units if $C = 4500 + 1.47x$.

Solution:

$$\frac{dC}{dx} = 1.47$$

21. *Marginal Cost* Use the cost function to find the marginal cost for producing x units if

$$C = 55,000 + 470x - (0.25)x^2, \quad 0 \le x \le 940.$$

Solution:

$$\frac{dC}{dx} = 470 - 0.5x$$

23. *Marginal Revenue* Use the revenue function to find the marginal revenue for selling x units if $R = 50x - 0.5x^2$.

Solution:

$$\frac{dR}{dx} = 50 - x$$

25. *Marginal Revenue* Use the revenue function to find the marginal revenue for selling x units if

$$R = -6x^3 + 8x^2 + 200x.$$

Solution:

$$\frac{dR}{dx} = -18x^2 + 16x + 200$$

27. *Marginal Profit* Use the profit function to find the marginal profit for selling x units if $P = -2x^2 + 72x - 145.$

Solution:

$$\frac{dP}{dx} = -4x + 72$$

29. *Marginal Profit* Use the profit function to find the marginal profit for selling x units if

$$P = -0.00025x^2 + 12.2x - 25,000.$$

Solution:

$$\frac{dP}{dx} = -0.0005x + 12.2$$

31. *Marginal Revenue*   The revenue (in dollars) from producing x units of a product is

$$R = 125x - 0.002x^2$$

(a) Find the additional revenue when production is increased from 15,000 units to 15,001 units.

(b) Find the marginal revenue when $x = 15,000$.

(c) Compare the results of parts (a) and (b).

Solution:

$R = 125x - 0.002x^2$

(a) $R(15,001) - R(15,000) = 64.998$

(b) $R' = 125 - 0.004x$

   $R'(15,000) = 65$

(c) The answers to (a) and (b) are very close.

33. *Marginal Cost*   The cost (in dollars) of producing x units of a product is given by

$$C = 3.6\sqrt{x} + 500$$

(a) Find the additional cost when the production increases from nine to ten units.

(b) Find the marginal cost when $x = 9$.

(c) Compare the results of parts (a) and (b).

Solution:

$C = 3.6\sqrt{x} + 500$

(a) $C(10) - C(9) \approx 0.584$

(b) $C' = 1.8/\sqrt{x}$

   $C'(9) = 0.6$.

(c) The answers to (a) and (b) are very close.

35. *Marginal Profit*   The profit for producing x units of a product is given by

$$P = 2400 - 403.4x + 32x^2 - 0.664x^3, \quad 10 \le x \le 25.$$

Find the marginal profit when (a) $x = 10$, (b) $x = 20$, (c) $x = 23$, and (d) $x = 25$.

Solution:

$$\frac{dP}{dx} = -403.4 + 64x - 1.992x^2$$

(a) $P'(10) = 37.40$ (b) $P'(20) = 79.80$

(c) $P'(23) = 14.83$ (d) $P'(25) = -48.40$

37. *Profit*   The monthly demand function and cost function for x newspapers at a newsstand are

$$p = 5 - 0.001x \text{ and } C = 35 + 1.5x$$

(a) Find the monthly revenue as a function of x.

(b) Find the monthly profit as a function of x.

(c) Complete the table shown in the text.

Solution:

$p = 5 - 0.001x, \ C = 35 + 1.5x$

(a) $R = xp = x(5 - 0.001x) = 5x - 0.001x^2$

(b) $P = R - C = (5x - 0.001x^2) - (35 + 1.5x)$

$$= 3.5x - 0.001x^2 - 35$$

(c) $R'(x) = 5 - 0.002x \ P'(x) = 3.5 - 0.002x$

x	600	1200	1800	2400	3000
dR/dx	3.8	2.6	1.4	0.2	−1.0
dP/dx	2.3	1.1	−0.1	−1.3	−2.5
P	1705	2725	3025	2605	1465

39. *Marginal Profit*   When the admission price to a baseball game was $6 per ticket, 36,000 tickets were sold. When the price was raised to $7, only 33,000 tickets were sold. Assume that the demand function is linear and that the variable and fixed costs for the ballpark owners are $0.20 and $85,000, respectively.

(a) Find the profit P as a function of x, the number of tickets sold.

(b) Find the marginal profit when 18,000 tickets are sold.

Solution:

$(36,000, 6), (33,000, 7)$

$$\text{Slope} = \frac{7 - 6}{33,000 - 36,000} = \frac{1}{-3000}$$

$$p - 6 = \frac{-1}{3000}(x - 36,000)$$

$$p = \frac{-1}{3000}x + 18 \text{ (demand function)}$$

(a) $P = R - C = xp - (0.20x + 85,000)$

$$= x\left(\frac{-1}{3000}x + 18\right) - 0.2x - 85,000$$

$$= \frac{x^2}{3000} + 17.8x - 85,000$$

(b) $P'(x) = \frac{-x}{1500} + 17.8$ $P'(18,000) = 5.8$ dollars

41. *Marginal Cost* The cost C of producing x units is modeled by

$$C = v(x) + k$$

where v represents the variable cost and k represents the fixed cost. Show that the marginal cost is independent of the fixed cost.

Solution:

$$C = v(x) + k$$

Marginal cost: $C' = v'(x) + 0 = v'(x)$

Thus, the marginal cost is independent of the fixed cost.

43. *Inventory Management* The annual inventory cost for a manufacturer is

$$C = \frac{1,008,000}{Q} + 6.3Q.$$

where Q is the order size when the inventory is replenished. Find the change in annual cost when Q is increased from 350 to 351, and compare this with the instantaneous rate of change when $Q = 350$.

Solution:

$$\frac{dC}{dQ} = -\frac{1,008,000}{Q^2} + \frac{63}{10}$$

$$C(351) - C(350) \approx -1.91$$

$$\frac{dC}{dQ} = -1.93 \text{ when } Q = 350.$$

45. *Fuel Cost* A car is driven 15,000 miles a year and gets x miles per gallon. The average fuel cost is \$1.10 per gallon. Find the annual cost C of fuel as a function of x and use this function to complete the table shown in the text.

Who would benefit more from a 1 mile per gallon increase in fuel efficiency–the driver of a car that gets 15 or 35 miler per gallon? Explain.

Solution:

$$C(x) = \frac{15,000}{x}(1.10) \text{ dollars/mile}$$

$$C'(x) = \frac{-16,500}{x^2}$$

x	10	15	20	25	30	35	40
C	1650	1100	825	660	550	471.43	412.50
dc/dx	−165	−73.33	−41.25	−26.40	−18.33	−13.47	−10.31

The car that gets 15 miles/gallon would benefit more.

47. Use a graphing utility to sketch the graph of $f(x) = \frac{1}{4}x^3$ and its derivative on $[-2, 2]$ and determine the points (if any) at which f has a horizontal tangent.

Solution:

$$f(x) = \frac{1}{4}x^3, \quad f'(x) = \frac{3}{4}x^2$$

f has a horizontal tangent at $x = 0$.

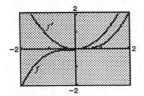

Section 2.4   The Product and Quotient Rules

1. Find the value of the derivative of $f(x) = x^2(3x^3 - 1)$ at the point $(1, 2)$.

Solution:

$$f'(x) = x^2(9x^2) + 2x(3x^3 - 1) = 15x^4 - 2x$$
$$f'(1) = 13$$

3. Find the value of the derivative of $f(x) = \frac{1}{3}(2x^3 - 4)$ at the point $\left(0, -\frac{4}{3}\right)$.

Solution:

$$f'(x) = \frac{1}{3}(6x^2) = 2x^2$$
$$f'(0) = 0$$

5. Find the value of the derivative of $g(x) = (x^2 - 4x + 3)(x - 2)$ at the point $(4, 6)$.

Solution:

$$g'(x) = (x^2 - 4x + 3)(1) + (2x - 4)(x - 2) = 3x^2 - 12x + 11$$
$$g'(4) = (16 - 16 + 3) + (8 - 4)(4 - 2) = 3 + 8 = 11$$

7. Find the value of the derivative of $h(x) = x/(x - 5)$ at the point $(6, 6)$.

Solution:

$$h'(x) = \frac{(x - 5)(1) - (x)(1)}{(x - 5)^2} = \frac{-5}{(x - 5)^2}$$
$$h'(6) = -5$$

9. Find the value of the derivative of $f(t) = \dfrac{2t^2 - 3}{3t}$ at the point $\left(2, \dfrac{5}{6}\right)$

Solution:

$$f'(t) = \frac{3t(4t) - (2t^2 - 3)(3)}{(3t)^2} = \frac{6t^2 + 9}{9t^2} = \frac{2t^2 + 3}{3t^2} .$$

$$f'(2) = \frac{2(2)^2 + 3}{3(2)^2} = \frac{11}{12}$$

Find the derivative of the function.

Function	Rewrite	Derivative	Simplify
11. $y = \dfrac{x^2 + 2x}{x}$	$y = x + 2$	$y' = 1$	$y' = 1$
13. $y = \dfrac{7}{3x^3}$	$y = \dfrac{7}{3}x^{-3}$	$y' = -7x^{-4}$	$y' = -\dfrac{7}{x^4}$
15. $y = \dfrac{4x^2 - 3x}{8\sqrt{x}}$	$y = \dfrac{1}{2}x^{3/2} - \dfrac{3}{8}x^{1/2}$	$y' = \dfrac{3}{4}x^{1/2} - \dfrac{3}{16}x^{-1/2}$	$y' = \dfrac{3}{4}\sqrt{x} - \dfrac{3}{16\sqrt{x}}$
17. $y = \dfrac{x^2 - 4x + 3}{x - 1}$	$y = x - 3, x \neq 1$	$y' = 1, x \neq 1$	$y' = 1, x \neq 1$

19. Differentiate $f(x) = (x^3 - 3x)(2x^2 + 3x + 5)$.

Solution:

$$\begin{aligned}
f'(x) &= (x^3 - 3x)(4x + 3) + (3x^2 - 3)(2x^2 + 3x + 5) \\
&= 4x^4 + 3x^3 - 12x^2 - 9x + 6x^4 + 9x^3 + 9x^2 - 9x - 15 \\
&= 10x^4 + 12x^3 - 3x^2 - 18x - 15
\end{aligned}$$

21. Differentiate $h(t) = (t^5 - 1)(4t^2 - 7t - 3)$.

Solution:

$$\begin{aligned}
h'(t) &= (t^5 - 1)(8t - 7) + (5t^4)(4t^2 - 7t - 3) \\
&= 8t^6 - 7t^5 - 8t + 7 + 20t^6 - 35t^5 - 15t^4 \\
&= 28t^6 - 42t^5 - 15t^4 - 8t + 7
\end{aligned}$$

23. Differentiate $h(p) = (p^3 - 2)^2$.

Solution:

$$h(p) = p^6 - 4p^3 + 4$$

$$h'(p) = 6p^5 - 12p^2 = 6p^2(p^3 - 2)$$

25. Differentiate $f(x) = \sqrt[3]{x}(\sqrt{x} + 3)$.

Solution:

$$f(x) = \sqrt[3]{x}(\sqrt{x} + 3) = x^{1/3}(x^{1/2} + 3) = x^{5/6} + 3x^{1/3}$$

$$f'(x) = \frac{5}{6}x^{-1/6} + x^{-2/3} = \frac{5}{6x^{1/6}} + \frac{1}{x^{2/3}}$$

27. Differentiate $f(x) = \dfrac{3x - 2}{2x - 3}$.

Solution:

$$f(x) = \frac{3x - 2}{2x - 3}$$

$$f'(x) = \frac{(2x - 3)(3) - (3x - 2)(2)}{(2x - 3)^2} = \frac{-5}{(2x - 3)^2}$$

29. Differentiate $f(x) = \dfrac{3 - 2x - x^2}{x^2 - 1}$.

Solution:

$$f(x) = \frac{3 - 2x - x^2}{x^2 - 1} = \frac{(3 + x)(1 - x)}{(x + 1)(x - 1)} = \frac{-(3 + x)}{x + 1}, x \neq 1$$

$$f'(x) = \frac{(x + 1)(-1) + (3 + x)(1)}{(x + 1)^2} = \frac{2}{(x + 1)^2}, x \neq -1$$

31. Differentiate $f(x) = (x^5 - 3x)(1/x^2)$.

Solution:

$$f(x) = (x^5 - 3x)\left(\frac{1}{x^2}\right) = x^3 - \frac{3}{x}$$

$$f'(x) = 3x^2 + \frac{3}{x^2} = \frac{3x^4 + 3}{x^2} = \frac{3(x^4 + 1)}{x^2}$$

33. Differentiate $h(t) = \dfrac{t + 2}{t^2 + 5t + 6}$.

Solution:

$$h(t) = \frac{t + 2}{t^2 + 5t + 6}$$

$$h'(t) = \frac{(t^2 + 5t + 6)(1) - (t + 2)(2t + 5)}{(t^2 + 5t + 6)^2} = \frac{-t^2 - 4t - 4}{(t + 2)^2(t + 3)^2}$$

$$= -\frac{(t + 2)^2}{(t + 2)^2(t + 3)^2} = \frac{-1}{(t + 3)^2}, t \neq -2$$

Equivalently, note that $h(t) = \dfrac{t + 2}{(t + 2)(t + 3)} = \dfrac{1}{t + 3}, t \neq -2.$

35. Differentiate $f(x) = \dfrac{x+1}{\sqrt{x}}$.

Solution:

$$f(x) = \frac{x+1}{\sqrt{x}} = x^{1/2} + x^{-1/2}$$

$$f'(x) = \frac{1}{2}x^{-1/2} - \frac{1}{2}x^{-3/2} = \frac{1}{2}\left(\frac{1}{x^{1/2}} - \frac{1}{x^{3/2}}\right) = \frac{1}{2}\left(\frac{x-1}{x^{3/2}}\right) = \frac{x-1}{2x^{3/2}}$$

37. Differentiate $g(x) = \left(\dfrac{x-3}{x+4}\right)(x^2 + 2x + 1)$.

Solution:

$$g(x) = \frac{x-3}{x+4}(x^2 + 2x + 1) = \frac{x^3 - x^2 - 5x - 3}{x+4}$$

$$g'(x) = \frac{(x+4)(3x^2 - 2x - 5) - (x^3 - x^2 - 5x - 3)(1)}{(x+4)^2}$$

$$= \frac{3x^3 + 10x^2 - 13x - 20 - x^3 + x^2 + 5x + 3}{(x+4)^2}$$

$$= \frac{2x^3 + 11x^2 - 8x - 17}{(x+4)^2}$$

39. Differentiate $f(x) = (3x^3 + 4x)(x - 5)(x + 1)$.

Solution:

$$f(x) = (3x^3 + 4x)(x - 5)(x + 1) = (3x^3 + 4x)(x^2 - 4x - 5)$$

$$f'(x) = (3x^3 + 4x)(2x - 4) + (x^2 - 4x - 5)(9x^2 + 4)$$

$$= (6x^4 - 12x^3 + 8x^2 - 16x) + (9x^4 - 36x^3 - 41x^2 - 16x - 20)$$

$$= 15x^4 - 48x^3 - 33x^2 - 32x - 20$$

41. Find an equation of the tangent line to the graph of $f(x) = \dfrac{2x}{x+2}$ at the point (2, 1).

Solution:

$$f'(x) = \frac{(x+2)(2) - 2x(1)}{(x+2)^2} = \frac{4}{(x+2)^2}$$

At (2, 1), $f'(2) = \dfrac{4}{(2+2)^2} = \dfrac{1}{4}$. The equation of the tangent line is

$$y - 1 = \frac{1}{4}(x - 2)$$

$$y = \frac{1}{4}x + \frac{1}{2}$$

43. Find an equation of the tangent line to the graph of $f(x) = (x^3 - 3x + 1)(x + 2)$ at the point $(1, -3)$.

Solution:

$$f'(x) = (x^3 - 3x + 1)(1) + (x + 2)(3x^2 - 3)$$
$$= 4x^3 + 6x^2 - 6x - 5$$

At $(1, -3)$, the slope is $m = f'(1) = -1$. The equation of the tangent line is

$$y + 3 = -1(x - 1)$$
$$y = -x - 2.$$

45. Determine the points where the graph of $f(x) = x^2/(x - 1)$ has a horizontal tangent.

Solution:

$$f'(x) = \frac{(x - 1)(2x) - x^2(1)}{(x - 1)^2} = \frac{x^2 - 2x}{(x - 1)^2}$$

$f'(x) = 0$ when $x^2 - 2x = x(x - 2) = 0$, which implies that $x = 0$ or $x = 2$. Thus, the horizontal tangent lines occur at $(0, 0)$ and $(2, 4)$.

47. Determine the points where the graph of $f(x) = \dfrac{x^4}{x^3 + 1}$ has a horizontal tangent.

Solution:

$$f'(x) = \frac{(x^3 + 1)(4x^3) - x^4(3x^2)}{(x^3 + 1)^2} = \frac{x^6 + 4x^3}{(x^3 + 1)^2}$$

$f'(x) = 0$ when $x^6 + 4x^3 = x^3(x^3 + 4) = 0$. Thus, the horizontal tangent lines occur at $x = 0$ and $x = \sqrt[3]{-4}$.

49. Use a computer or graphics calculator to sketch the graph of f and f' over the interval $[-2, 2]$, where $f(x) = x(x + 1)$.

Solution:

$$f(x) = x(x + 1) = x^2 + x$$
$$f'(x) = 2x + 1$$

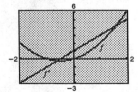

51. Use a computer or graphics calculator to sketch the graph of f and f' over the interval $[-2, 2]$ where $f(x) = x(x+1)(x-1)$.

Solution:

$$f(x) = x(x+1)(x-1) = x^3 - x$$
$$f'(x) = 3x^2 - 1$$

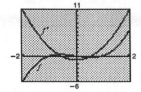

53. Use the demand function to find the rate of change in $x = 275\left(1 - \dfrac{3p}{5p+1}\right)$, for the given price $p = \$4$.

Solution:

$$x = 275\left(1 - \frac{3p}{5p+1}\right)$$
$$\frac{dx}{dp} = -275\left(\frac{(5p+1)3 - (3p)(5)}{(5p+1)^2}\right) = -275\left(\frac{3}{(5p+1)^2}\right)$$

When $p = 4$, $\dfrac{dx}{dp} = -275\left(\dfrac{3}{(21)^2}\right) \approx -1.87$

55. *Oxygen Level* The function

$$f(t) = \frac{t^2 - t + 1}{t^2 + 1}$$

measures the percentage of the normal level of oxygen in a pond, where t is the time in weeks after organic waste is dumped into the pond. Find the rate of change of f with respect to t when (a) $t = 0.5$, (b) $t = 2$, and (c) $t = 8$.

Solution:

$$f'(t) = \frac{(t^2+1)(2t-1) - (t^2 - t + 1)(2t)}{(t^2+1)^2} = \frac{t^2 - 1}{(t^2+1)^2}$$

(a) $f'(0.5) = -0.48$

(b) $f'(2) = 0.12$

(c) $f'(8) \approx 0.015$

57. *Population Growth*   A population of 500 bacteria is introduced into a culture. The number of bacteria in the population at any given time is given by

$$P = 500\left(1 + \frac{4t}{50 + t^2}\right)$$

where t is measured in hours. Find the rate of change of the population when $t = 2$.

Solution:

$$P' = 500\left[\frac{(50 + t^2)(4) - (4t)(2t)}{(50 + t^2)^2}\right] = 500\left[\frac{200 - 4t^2}{(50 + t^2)^2}\right].$$

When $t = 2$,

$$P' = 500\left[\frac{184}{(54)^2}\right] \approx 31.55 \text{ bacteria/hour.}$$

59. *Profit*   The demand x for a given product is inversely proportional to the square of the price p for $x \geq 5$.

(a) Find the demand function if there is a demand for 16 units when the price is $1000.

(b) Write the cost as a function of x if the variable cost is $250 per unit and the fixed cost is $10,000.

(c) See book p. 132.

Solution:

(a) $\qquad x = \dfrac{k}{p^2}, \quad x \geq 5$

$\qquad\qquad 16 = \dfrac{k}{1000^2}$

$\qquad 16,000,000 = k$

$\qquad\qquad x = \dfrac{16,000,000}{p^2}$

$\qquad\qquad p^2 = \dfrac{16,000,000}{x}$

$\qquad\qquad p = \dfrac{4000}{\sqrt{x}}$

(b) C = 250x + 10,000

(c) $P = R - C = xp - C$

$\qquad = x\left(\dfrac{4000}{\sqrt{x}}\right) - (250x + 10,000)$

$\qquad = 4000\sqrt{x} - 250x - 10,000$

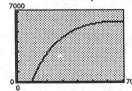

Let $x = 64$, and $p = \$500$.

61. Given the function $f(x) = x^2 + 1$, find the derivatives of each of the following.

(a) $p = f(x)$

(b) $p = xf(x)$

(c) $p = \dfrac{f(x)}{x}$

(d) $p = \dfrac{1}{f(x)}$

Solution:

(a) $f(x) = x^2 + 1$

$f'(x) = 2x$

(b) $\qquad xf(x) = x^3 + x$

$\dfrac{d}{dx}[xf(x)] = 3x^2 + 1$

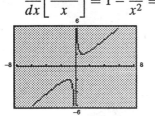

(c) $\qquad \dfrac{f(x)}{x} = \dfrac{x^2 + 1}{x} = x + \dfrac{1}{x}$

$\dfrac{d}{dx}\left[\dfrac{f(x)}{x}\right] = 1 - \dfrac{1}{x^2} = \dfrac{x^2 - 1}{x^2}$

(d) $\qquad \dfrac{1}{f(x)} = \dfrac{1}{x^2 + 1}$

$\dfrac{d}{dx}\left[\dfrac{1}{f(x)}\right] = \dfrac{(x^2 + 1)(0) - (1)(2x)}{(x^2 + 1)^2}$

$= -\dfrac{2x}{(x^2 + 1)^2}$

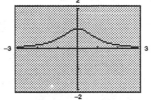

Since (a), (b), and (c) are increasing functions, only (d) could represent a demand function.

63. *Inventory Replenishment* The ordering and transportation cost C (in thousands of dollars) of the components used in manufacturing a product is

$$C = 100 \left(\frac{200}{x^2} + \frac{x}{x + 30} \right), 1 \le x,$$

where x is the order size (in hundreds). Find the rate of change of C with respect to x for the following order sizes. (a) $x = 10$ (b) $x = 15$ (c) $x = 20$

What do these rates of change imply about increasing the size of an order?

Solution:

$$C = 100 \left(\frac{200}{x^2} + \frac{x}{x + 30} \right), x \ge 1$$

$$C' = 100 \left(-2(200x^{-3}) + \frac{(x + 30) - x}{(x + 30)^2} \right) = 100 \left(\frac{-400}{x^3} + \frac{30}{(x + 30)^2} \right)$$

$$C'(10) = 100 \left(\frac{-400}{10^3} + \frac{30}{40^2} \right) = -38.125$$

$$C'(15) \approx -10.37$$

$$C'(20) \approx -3.8$$

Increasing the order size reduces the cost per item.

Section 2.5   The Chain Rule

For Exercises 1–7, complete the table using Example 1 as a model.

	$y = f(g(x))$	$u = g(x)$	$y = f(u)$
1.	$y = (6x - 5)^4$	$u = 6x - 5$	$y = u^4$
3.	$y = (4 - x^2)^{-1}$	$u = 4 - x^2$	$y = u^{-1}$
5.	$y = \sqrt{5x - 2}$	$u = 5x - 2$	$y = \sqrt{u}$
7.	$y = \dfrac{1}{3x + 1}$	$u = 3x + 1$	$y = u^{-1}$

9. Match the function with the rule that you would use to *most efficiently* find the derivative of $f(x) = \dfrac{2}{1 - x^3}$. (a) Simple Power Rule   (b) Constant Rule

(c) General Power Rule   (d) Quotient Rule

Solution:

$$f(x) = \frac{2}{1 - x^3} = 2(1 - x^3)^{-1}$$ is most efficiently done by the General Power Rule (c).

11. Match the function with the rule that you would use to *most efficiently* find the derivative of $f(x) = \sqrt[3]{89^2}$. (a) Simple Power Rule   (b) Constant Rule (c) General Power Rule   (d) Quotient Rule

Solution:

$f(x) = \sqrt[3]{8^2}$ is most efficiently done by the Constant Rule (b).

13. Find the derivative of $y = (2x - 7)^3$.

Solution:

$$y' = 3(2x - 7)^2(2) = 6(2x - 7)^2$$

15. Find the derivative of $f(x) = 2(x^2 - 1)^3$.

Solution:

$$f'(x) = 6(x^2 - 1)^2(2x) = 12x(x^2 - 1)^2$$

17. Find the derivative of $g(x) = (4 - 2x)^3$.

Solution:

$$g'(x) = 3(4 - 2x)^2(-2) = -6(4 - 2x)^2$$

19. Find the derivative of $h(x) = (6x - x^3)^2$.

Solution:

$$h'(x) = 2(6x - x^3)(6 - 3x^2) = 6x(6 - x^2)(2 - x^2)$$

21. Find the derivative of $f(x) = (x^2 - 9)^{2/3}$.

Solution:

$$f'(x) = \frac{2}{3}(x^2 - 9)^{-1/3}(2x) = \frac{4x}{3(x^2 - 9)^{1/3}}$$

23. Find the derivative of $f(t) = \sqrt{t + 1}$.

Solution:

$$f(t) = \sqrt{t + 1} = (t + 1)^{1/2}$$
$$f'(t) = \frac{1}{2}(t + 1)^{-1/2}(1) = \frac{1}{2\sqrt{t + 1}}$$

25. Find the derivative of $s(t) = \sqrt{2t^2 + 5t + 2}$

Solution:

$$s(t) = \sqrt{2t^2 + 5t + 2} = (2t^2 + 5t + 2)^{1/2}$$
$$s'(t) = \frac{1}{2}(2t^2 + 5t + 2)^{-1/2}(4t + 5) = \frac{4t + 5}{2\sqrt{2t^2 + 5t + 2}}$$

27. Find the derivative of $y = \sqrt[3]{9x^2 + 4}$.

Solution:

$$y = \sqrt[3]{9x^2 + 4} = (9x^2 + 4)^{1/3}$$

$$y' = \frac{1}{3}(9x^2 + 4)^{-2/3}(18x) = \frac{6x}{(9x^2 + 4)^{2/3}}$$

29. Find the derivative of $y = 2\sqrt{4 - x^2}$.

Solution:

$$y = 2\sqrt{4 - x^2} = 2(4 - x^2)^{1/2}$$

$$y' = 2\left(\frac{1}{2}\right)(4 - x^2)^{-1/2}(-2x) = -\frac{2x}{\sqrt{4 - x^2}}$$

31. Find the derivative of $f(x) = (25 + x^2)^{-1/2}$.

Solution:

$$f'(x) = -\frac{1}{2}(25 + x^2)^{-3/2}(2x) = -\frac{x}{(25 + x^2)^{3/2}}$$

33. Find the derivative of $h(x) = (4 - x^3)^{-4/3}$.

Solution:

$$h'(x) = -\frac{4}{3}(4 - x^3)^{-7/3}(-3x^2) = \frac{4x^2}{(4 - x^3)^{7/3}}$$

35. Find an equation of the tangent line to the graph of $f(x) = \sqrt{4x^2 - 7}$.

Solution:

$$f(x) = \sqrt{4x^2 - 7} = (4x^2 - 7)^{1/2}. \text{ Point: } (2, f(2)) = (2, 3).$$

$$f'(x) = \frac{1}{2}(4x^2 - 7)^{-1/2}(8x) = \frac{4x}{\sqrt{4x^2 - 7}}$$

When $x = 2$, the slope is $f'(2) = \frac{8}{3}$, and the equation of the tangent line is

$$y - 3 = \frac{8}{3}(x - 2)$$

$$y = \frac{8}{3}x - \frac{7}{3}$$

$$3y - 8x + 7 = 0$$

37. Find the derivative of $f(x) = \dfrac{\sqrt{x}+1}{x^2+1}$.

Solution:

$$f(x) = \frac{\sqrt{x}+1}{x^2+1}$$

$$f'(x) = \frac{1 - 3x^2 - 4x^{3/2}}{2\sqrt{x}(x^2+1)^2}$$

f has a horizontal tangent when $f' = 0$.

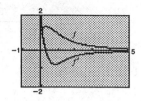

39. Find the derivative of $f(x) = \sqrt{\dfrac{x+1}{x}}$.

Solution:

$$f(x) = \sqrt{\frac{x+1}{x}}$$

$$f'(x) = \frac{-1}{2\sqrt{x+1}\,x^{3/2}}$$

f' is never 0.

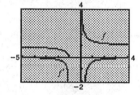

41. Find the derivative of $y = \dfrac{1}{x-2}$.

Solution:

$$y = (x-2)^{-1}$$

$$y' = (-1)(x-2)^{-2}(1) = -\frac{1}{(x-2)^2}$$

43. Find the derivative of $f(t) = \left(\dfrac{6}{3-t}\right)^2$.

Solution:

$$f(t) = \left(\frac{6}{3-t}\right)^2 = 36(3-t)^{-2}$$

$$f'(t) = 36(-2)(3-t)^{-3}(-1) = \frac{72}{(3-t)^3}$$

45. Find the derivative of $f(x) = \dfrac{3}{x^3 - 4}$.

Solution:

$$f(x) = 3(x^3 - 4)^{-1}$$

$$f'(x) = -3(x^3 - 4)^{-2}(3x^2) = -\frac{9x^2}{(x^3 - 4)^2}$$

47. Find the derivative of $y = \dfrac{1}{\sqrt{x + 2}}$.

Solution:

$$y = (x + 2)^{-1/2}$$

$$y' = -\frac{1}{2}(x + 2)^{-3/2}(1) = -\frac{1}{2(x + 2)^{3/2}}$$

49. Find the derivative of $g(x) = \dfrac{3}{\sqrt[3]{x^3 - 1}}$.

Solution:

$$g(x) = 3(x^3 - 1)^{-1/3}$$

$$g'(x) = 3\left(-\frac{1}{3}\right)(x^3 - 1)^{-4/3}(3x^2) = -\frac{3x^2}{(x^3 - 1)^{4/3}}$$

51. Find the derivative of $y = x\sqrt{2x + 3}$.

Solution:

$$y = x(2x + 3)^{1/2}$$

$$y' = x\left[\frac{1}{2}(2x + 3)^{-1/2}(2)\right] + (2x + 3)^{1/2} = (2t + 3)^{-1/2}[x + (2x + 3)] = \frac{3(x + 1)}{\sqrt{2x + 3}}$$

53. Find the derivative of $y = t^2\sqrt{t - 2}$.

Solution:

$$y = t^2(t - 2)^{1/2}$$

$$y' = t^2\left[\frac{1}{2}(t - 2)^{-1/2}(1)\right] + 2t(t - 2)^{1/2}$$

$$= \frac{1}{2}(t - 2)^{-1/2}[t^2 + 4t(t - 2)]$$

$$= \frac{t^2 + 4t(t - 2)}{2\sqrt{t - 2}}$$

$$= \frac{t(5t - 8)}{2\sqrt{t - 2}}$$

55. Find the derivative of $f(x) = x^3(x - 4)^2$.

Solution:

$$f(x) = x^3(x - 4)^2$$
$$f'(x) = x^3 2(x - 4)(1) + (x - 4)^2 3x^2$$
$$= 2x^3(x - 4) + 3x^2(x - 4)^2$$
$$= x^2(x - 4)(2x + 3(x - 4))$$
$$= x^2(x - 4)(5x - 12)$$

57. Find the derivative of $f(t) = (t^2 - 9)\sqrt{t + 2}$.

Solution:

$$f(t) = (t^2 - 9)(t + 2)^{1/2}$$
$$f'(t) = (t^2 - 9)\left[\left(\frac{1}{2}\right)(t + 2)^{-1/2}(1)\right] + (2t)(t + 2)^{1/2}$$
$$= \frac{1}{2}(t + 2)^{-1/2}[(t^2 - 9) + 4t(t + 2)]$$
$$= \frac{5t^2 + 8t - 9}{2\sqrt{t + 2}}$$

59. Find the derivative of $f(x) = \sqrt{\dfrac{3 - 2x}{4x}}$.

Solution:

$$f(x) = \sqrt{\frac{3 - 2x}{4x}} = \sqrt{\frac{3}{4}x^{-1} - \frac{1}{2}} = \left(\frac{3}{4}x^{-1} - \frac{1}{2}\right)^{1/2}$$
$$f'(x) = \frac{1}{2}\left(\frac{3}{4}x^{-1} - \frac{1}{2}\right)^{-1/2}\left(-\frac{3}{4}x^{-2}\right) = \frac{-3}{8x^2\sqrt{\frac{3}{4x} - \frac{1}{2}}} = \frac{-3}{4\sqrt{3 - 2x}x^{3/2}}$$

61. Find the derivative of $g(t) = \dfrac{3t^2}{\sqrt{t^2 + 2t - 1}}$.

Solution:

$$g(t) = \frac{3t^2}{\sqrt{t^2 + 2t - 1}} = 3t^2(t^2 + 2t - 1)^{-1/2}$$
$$g'(t) = 3t^2\left[-\left(\frac{1}{2}\right)(t^2 + 2t - 1)^{-3/2}(2t + 2)\right] + (t^2 + 2t - 1)^{-1/2}(6t)$$
$$= 3t(t^2 + 2t - 1)^{-3/2}[-t(t + 1) + 2(t^2 + 2t - 1)]$$
$$= \frac{3t(t^2 + 3t - 2)}{(t^2 + 2t - 1)^{3/2}}$$

63. Find the derivative of $f(x) = \dfrac{\sqrt[3]{x^3 + 1}}{x}$.

Solution:

$$f(x) = \frac{\sqrt[3]{x^3 + 1}}{x} = \frac{(x^3 + 1)^{1/3}}{x}$$

$$f'(x) = \frac{x\frac{1}{3}(x^3 + 1)^{-2/3}(3x^2) - (x^3 + 1)^{1/3}(1)}{x^2}$$

$$= \frac{(x^3 + 1)^{-2/3}[x^3 - (x^3 + 1)]}{x^2} = \frac{-1}{x^2(x^3 + 1)^{2/3}}$$

65. Find the derivative of $y = \left(\dfrac{6 - 5x}{x^2 - 1}\right)^2$.

Solution:

$$y = \left(\frac{6 - 5x}{x^2 - 1}\right)^2$$

$$y' = 2\left(\frac{6 - 5x}{x^2 - 1}\right)\left(\frac{(x^2 - 1)(-5) - (6 - 5x)(2x)}{(x^2 - 1)^2}\right)$$

$$= \frac{2(6 - 5x)(5x^2 - 12x + 5)}{(x^2 - 1)^3}$$

67. *Compound Interest*   You deposit $1000 in an account with an annual rate of r (in decimal form) compounded monthly. At the end of 5 years, the balance is

$$A = 1000\left(1 + \frac{r}{12}\right)^{60}.$$

Find the rate of change of A with respect to r when (a) $r = 0.08$, (b) $r = 0.10$, and (c) $r = 0.12$.

Solution:

$$A = 1000\left(1 + \frac{r}{12}\right)^{60}$$

$$A' = 1000(60)\left(1 + \frac{r}{12}\right)^{59}\left(\frac{1}{12}\right) = 5000\left(1 + \frac{r}{12}\right)^{59}$$

$$(a)\, A'(0.08) = 50\left(1 + \frac{.08}{12}\right)^{59} \approx \$74.00 \text{ per percentage point}$$

$$(b)\, A'(0.10) = 50\left(1 + \frac{.10}{12}\right)^{59} \approx \$81.59 \text{ per percentage point}$$

$$(c)\, A'(0.12) = 50\left(1 + \frac{.12}{12}\right) \approx \$89.94 \text{ per percentage point}$$

69. *Population Growth* The number N of bacteria in a culture after t days is modeled by

$$N = 400 \left[1 - \frac{3}{(t^2 + 2)^2} \right].$$

Complete the table in the textbook. What can you conclude?

Solution:

$$N = 400[1 - 3(t^2 + 2)^{-2}] = 400 - 1200(t^2 + 2)^{-2}$$

$$\frac{dN}{dt} = 2400(t^2 + 2)^{-3}(2t) = \frac{4800t}{(t^2 + 2)^3}$$

t	0	1	2	3	4
$\dfrac{dN}{dt}$	0	177.78	44.44	10.82	3.29

The rate of growth of N is decreasing.

71. *Depreciation* Repeat Exercise 70 given that the value of the machine t years after it is purchased is inversely proportional to the cube root of $t + 1$.

Solution:

(a) $V = \dfrac{k}{\sqrt[3]{t + 1}}$

When $t = 0$, $V = 10,000 \Rightarrow k = 10,000$.

Therefore, $V = \dfrac{10,000}{\sqrt[3]{t + 1}}$.

(b) $V = 10,000(t + 1)^{-1/3}$

$$\frac{dV}{dt} = -\frac{10,000}{3}(t + 1)^{-4/3}(1) = -\frac{10,000}{3(t + 1)^{4/3}}$$

(c) When $t = 3$,

$$\frac{dV}{dt} = -\frac{10,000}{3(4)^{4/3}}$$

$$\approx -\$524.97 \text{ per year.}$$

Solution:

When $t = 1$,

$$\frac{dV}{dt} = -\frac{10,000}{3(2)^{4/3}}$$

$$\approx -\$1322.83 \text{ per year.}$$

Section 2.6   Higher–Order Derivatives

1. Find the second derivative of $f(x) = 5 - 4x$.

Solution:

$$f'(x) = -4$$
$$f''(x) = 0$$

3. Find the second derivative of $f(x) = x^2 + 7x - 4$.

Solution:

$$f'(x) = 2x + 7$$
$$f''(x) = 2$$

5. Find the second derivative of $g(t) = \frac{1}{3}t^3 - 4t^2 + 2t$.

Solution:

$$g'(t) = t^2 - 8t + 2$$
$$g''(t) = 2t - 8$$

7. Find the second derivative of $g(t) = t^{-1/3}$.

Solution:

$$g'(t) = -\frac{1}{3}t^{-4/3}$$
$$g''(t) = \frac{4}{9}t^{-7/3} = \frac{4}{9t^{7/3}}$$

9. Find the second derivative of $f(x) = 4(x^2 - 1)^2$.

Solution:

$$f'(x) = 8(x^2 - 1)(2x) = 16x(x^2 - 1) = 16x^3 - 16x$$
$$f''(x) = 48x^2 - 16 = 16(3x^2 - 1)$$

11. Find the second derivative of $f(x) = x\sqrt[3]{x}$.

Solution:

$$f(x) = x\sqrt[3]{x} = x^{4/3}$$
$$f'(x) = \frac{4}{3}x^{1/3}$$
$$f''(x) = \frac{4}{9}x^{-2/3} = \frac{4}{9x^{2/3}}$$

13. Find the second derivative of $f(x) = \dfrac{x+1}{x-1}$.

Solution:

$$f'(x) = \frac{(x-1)(1) - (x+1)(1)}{(x-1)^2} = -\frac{2}{(x-1)^2} = -2(x-1)^{-2}$$

$$f''(x) = 4(x-1)^{-3}(1) = \frac{4}{(x-1)^3}$$

15. Find the second derivative of $y = x^2(x^2 + 4x + 8)$.

Solution:

$$y = x^2(x^2 + 4x + 8) = x^4 + 4x^3 + 8x^2$$

$$y' = 4x^3 + 12x^2 + 16x$$

$$y'' = 12x^2 + 24x + 16$$

17. Find the third derivative of $f(x) = x^5 - 3x^4$.

Solution:

$$f'(x) = 5x^4 - 12x^3$$

$$f''(x) = 20x^3 - 36x^2$$

$$f'''(x) = 60x^2 - 72x$$

19. Find the third derivative of $f(x) = 5x(x+4)^3$.

Solution:

$$f(x) = 5x(x+4)^3 = 5x(x^3 + 12x^2 + 48x + 64)$$

$$= 5x^4 + 60x^3 + 240x^2 + 320x$$

$$f'(x) = 20x^3 + 180x^2 + 480x + 320$$

$$f''(x) = 60x^2 + 360x + 480$$

$$f'''(x) = 120x + 360$$

21. Find the third derivative of $f(x) = \dfrac{3}{(4x)^2}$.

Solution:

$$f(x) = \frac{3}{(4x)^2} = \frac{3}{16}x^{-2}$$

$$f'(x) = -\frac{3}{8}x^{-3}$$

$$f''(x) = \frac{9}{8}x^{-4}$$

$$f'''(x) = -\frac{9}{2}x^{-5} = -\frac{9}{2x^5}$$

23. Find the third derivative of $f(x) = \sqrt{4-x}$.

Solution:

$$f(x) = (4-x)^{1/2}$$

$$f'(x) = \frac{1}{2}(4-x)^{-1/2}(-1) = -\frac{1}{2}(4-x)^{-1/2}$$

$$f''(x) = \frac{1}{4}(4-x)^{-3/2}(-1) = -\frac{1}{4}(4-x)^{-3/2}$$

$$f'''(x) = \frac{3}{8}(4-x)^{-5/2}(-1) = -\frac{3}{8(4-x)^{5/2}}$$

25. Given $f'(x) = 2x^2$, find $f''(x)$.

Solution:

$$f''(x) = 4x$$

27. Given $f''(x) = (2x-2)/x$, find $f'''(x)$.

Solution:

$$f''(x) = \frac{2x-2}{x} = 2 - \frac{2}{x}$$

$$f'''(x) = 0 - \left(-\frac{2}{x^2}\right) = \frac{2}{x^2}$$

29. Given $f^{(4)}(x) = (x+1)^2$, find $f^{(6)}(x)$.

Solution:

$$f^{(5)}(x) = 2(x+1)$$

$$f^{(6)}(x) = 2$$

31. Find the second derivative and solve the equation $f''(x) = 0$
if $f(x) = x^3 - 9x^2 + 27x - 27$.

Solution:

$$f'(x) = 3x^2 - 18x + 27$$

$$f''(x) = 6x - 18 = 0$$

$$f''(x) = 0 \text{ when } x = 3.$$

33. Find the second derivative and solve the equation $f(x) = (x+3)(x-4)(x+5)$.

Solution:

$$f(x) = (x+3)(x-4)(x+5)$$
$$= x^3 + 4x^2 - 17x - 60$$
$$f'(x) = 3x^2 + 8x - 17$$
$$f''(x) = 6x + 8$$
$$f''(x) = 0 \qquad \text{when} \qquad 6x + 8 = 0$$

$$x = \frac{-4}{3}$$

35. Find the second derivative and solve the equation $f(x) = 3x^4 - 18x^2$.

Solution:

$$f(x) = 3x^4 - 18x^2$$
$$f'(x) = 12x^3 - 36x$$
$$f''(x) = 36x^2 - 36 = 36(x^2 - 1) = 0$$
$$f''(x) = 0 \text{ when } x = \pm 1.$$

37. Find the second derivative and solve the equation $f''(x) = 0$ if $f(x) = \dfrac{x}{x^2 + 3}$.

Solution:

$$f'(x) = \frac{(x^2+3)(1) - (x)(2x)}{(x^2+3)^2} = \frac{3 - x^2}{(x^2+3)^2} = (3 - x^2)(x^2 + 3)^{-2}$$
$$f''(x) = (3 - x^2)[-2(x^2 + 3)^{-3}(2x)] + (x^2 + 3)^{-2}(-2x)$$
$$= -2x(x^2 + 3)^{-3}[2(3 - x^2) + (x^2 + 3)] = \frac{-2x(9 - x^2)}{(x^2+3)^3} = \frac{2x(x^2 - 9)}{(x^2+3)^3}$$

$$f''(x) = 0 \text{ when } 2x(x^2 - 9) = 0$$

$$x = 0, \ \pm 3.$$

39. *Velocity and Acceleration*   A ball is propelled straight up from ground level with an initial velocity of 144 feet per second.

(a) Write the position function of the ball.

(b) Write the velocity and acceleration functions.

(c) When is the ball at its highest point? How high is this point?

(d) How fast is the ball traveling when it hits the ground? How is this speed related to its initial velocity?

Solution:

(a) $s(t) = -16t + 144t$

(b) $v(t) = s'(t) = -32t + 144$

   $a(t) = v'(t) = -32$

(c) $v(t) = 0 = -32t + 144$ when $t = \dfrac{144}{32} = 4.5$ sec

   $s(4.5) = 324$ feet

(d) $s(t) =$ when $16t^2 = 144t$, or $t = 0, 9$ seconds

   $v(9) = -144$ft/sec, which is the same speed as the initial velocity.

41. *Velocity and Acceleration*   The velocity of an automobile starting from rest is given by

$$\frac{ds}{dt} = \frac{90t}{t+10} \text{ ft/sec.}$$

Complete the table showing the velocity and acceleration at 10-second intervals during the first minute of travel.

Solution:

$$\frac{d^2s}{dt^2} = \frac{(t+10)(90) - (90t)(1)}{(t+10)^2} = \frac{900}{(t+10)^2}$$

t	0	10	20	30	40	50	60
$\dfrac{ds}{dt}$	0	45	60	67.5	72	75	77.14
$\dfrac{d^2s}{dt^2}$	9	2.25	1	0.56	0.36	0.25	0.18

43. Use a computer or graphics calculator to sketch the graphs of f, f', and f'' on the same set of coordinate axes. Observe the reduction of the degree of the polynomial and the resulting graph with each derivative.

$$f(x) = x^2 - 6x + 6$$

Solution:

$$f(x) = x^2 - 6x + 6$$

$$f'(x) = 2x - 6$$

$$f''(x) = 2$$

The degrees of the successive derivatives decrease by 1.

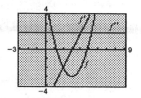

45. The graphs of f, f', and f'' are shown in the textbook. Which is which? Explain your reasoning.

Solution:

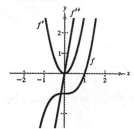

The degree of f is 3, and the degrees of the successive derivatives decrease by 1.

47. Determine if $y = f(x)g(x)$, then $y' = f'(x)g'(x)$ is true or false.

Solution:

False. The product rule is $[f(x)g(x)]' = f'(x)g(x) + f(x)g'(x)$.

49. Determine if $f'(c)$ and $g'(c)$ are zero and $h(x) = f(x)g(x)$, then $h'(c) = 0$ is true or false.

Solution:

True. $h'(c) = f'(c)g(c) + f(c)g'(c) = 0$.

51. Determine whether the statement "The second derivative represents the rate of change of the first derivative" is true or false.

Solution:

True.

53. Determine if $f'(x) = g'(x)$, then $f(x) = g(x)$ is true or false.

Solution:

False. Let $f(x) = x^2$ and $g(x) = x^2 + 1$.

Section 2.7   Implicit Differentiation

1. Find y' for $5xy = 1$.

Solution:

$$5xy = 1$$
$$5xy' + 5y = 0$$
$$5xy' = -5y$$
$$y' = \frac{-y}{x}$$

3. Find y' for $y^2 = 1 - x^2, 0 \le x \le 1$.

Solution:

$$y^2 = 1 - x^2$$
$$2yy' = -2x$$
$$y' = \frac{-x}{y}$$

5. Find y' for $\dfrac{2 - x}{y - 3} = 5$.

Solution:

$$\frac{2 - x}{y - 3} = 5$$
$$2 - x = 5y - 15$$
$$-1 = 5y'$$
$$y' = -\frac{1}{5}$$

7. When $x^2 + y^2 = 49$, find dy/dx by implicit differentiation and evaluate the derivative at the point $(0, 7)$.

Solution:

$$x^2 + y^2 = 49$$

$$2x + 2yy' = 0$$

$$y' = -\frac{x}{y}$$

At $(0, 7)$, $y' = \dfrac{-0}{7} = 0$.

9. When $y + xy = 4$, find dy/dx by implicit differentiation and evaluate the derivative at the point $(-5, -1)$.

Solution:

$$y + xy = 4$$

$$\frac{dy}{dx} + x\frac{dy}{dx} + y = 0$$

$$\frac{dy}{dx}(1 + x) = -y$$

$$\frac{dy}{dx} = -\frac{y}{x + 1}$$

At $(-5, -1)$, $\dfrac{dy}{dx} = -\dfrac{1}{4}$.

11. When $x^2 - y^3 = 3$, find dy/dx by implicit differentiation and evaluate the derivative at the point $(2, 1)$.

Solution:

$$x^2 - y^3 = 3$$

$$2x - 3y^2\frac{dy}{dx} = 0$$

$$\frac{dy}{dx} = \frac{2x}{3y^2}$$

At $(2, 1)$, $\dfrac{dy}{dx} = \dfrac{4}{3}$.

13. When $x^3 - xy + y^2 = 4$, find dy/dx by implicit differentiation and evaluate the derivative at the point $(0, -2)$.

Solution:

$$x^3 - xy + y^2 = 4$$

$$3x^2 - x\frac{dy}{dx} - y + 2y\frac{dy}{dx} = 0 \quad \text{(Product Rule)}$$

$$\frac{dy}{dx}(2y - x) = y - 3x^2$$

$$\frac{dy}{dx} = \frac{y - 3x^2}{2y - x}$$

At $(0, -2)$, $\dfrac{dy}{dx} = \dfrac{1}{2}$.

15. When $x^3 y^3 - y = x$, find dy/dx by implicit differentiation and evaluate the derivative at the point $(0, 0)$.

Solution:

$$x^3 y^3 - y = x$$

$$3x^3 y^2 \frac{dy}{dx} + 3x^2 y^3 - \frac{dy}{dx} = 1$$

$$\frac{dy}{dx}(3x^3 y^2 - 1) = 1 - 3x^2 y^3$$

$$\frac{dy}{dx} = \frac{1 - 3x^2 y^3}{3x^3 y^2 - 1}$$

At $(0, 0)$, $\dfrac{dy}{dx} = -1$.

17. When $x^{1/2} + y^{1/2} = 9$, find dy/dx by implicit differentiation and evaluate the derivative at the point $(16, 25)$.

Solution:

$$x^{1/2} + y^{1/2} = 9$$

$$\frac{1}{2}x^{-1/2} + \frac{1}{2}y^{-1/2}\frac{dy}{dx} = 0$$

$$x^{-1/2} + y^{-1/2}\frac{dy}{dx} = 0$$

$$\frac{dy}{dx} = \frac{-x^{-1/2}}{y^{-1/2}} = -\sqrt{\frac{y}{x}}$$

At $(16, 25)$, $\dfrac{dy}{dx} = -\dfrac{5}{4}$.

19. When $x^{2/3} + y^{2/3} = 5$, find dy/dx by implicit differentiation and evaluate the derivative at the point $(8, 1)$.

Solution:

$$x^{2/3} + y^{2/3} = 5$$

$$\frac{2}{3}x^{-1/3} + \frac{2}{3}y^{-1/3}\frac{dy}{dx} = 0$$

$$\frac{dy}{dx} = \frac{-x^{-1/3}}{y^{-1/3}} = -\frac{y^{1/3}}{x^{1/3}} = -\sqrt[3]{\frac{y}{x}}$$

At $(8, 1)$, $\dfrac{dy}{dx} = -\dfrac{1}{2}$.

21. When $x^3 - 3x^2y + 3xy^2 = 26$, find dy/dx by implicit differentiation and evaluate the derivative at the point $(2, 3)$.

Solution:

$$x^3 - 3x^2y + 3xy^2 = 26$$

$$3x^2 - 3x^2y' - 6xy + 3y^2 + 6xyy' = 0$$

$$(6xy - 3x^2)y' = 6xy - 3y^2 - 3x^2$$

$$y' = \frac{6xy - 3y^2 - 3x^2}{6xy - 3x^2} = \frac{2xy - y^2 - x^2}{2xy - x^2}$$

At $(2, 3)$, $y' = \dfrac{36 - 27 - 12}{36 - 12} = \dfrac{-3}{24} = -\dfrac{1}{8}$.

23. Find dy/dx by implicit differentiation and find the slope of the tangent line at the point $(1, 4)$ on the graph for
$3x^2 - 2y + 5 = 0$.

Solution:

$$3x^2 - 2y + 5 = 0$$

$$6x - 2\frac{dy}{dx} = 0$$

$$\frac{dy}{dx} = 3x$$

At $(1, 4)$, $\dfrac{dy}{dx} = 3$.

25. Find the slope of the graph of $4x^2 + 9y^2 = 36$ at the indicated point $\left(\sqrt{5}, \dfrac{4}{3} \right)$.

Solution:

$$4x^2 + 9y^2 = 36$$

$$8x + 18yy' = 0$$

$$y' = \frac{-4x}{9y}$$

At $\left(\sqrt{5}, \dfrac{4}{3} \right)$, $y' = \dfrac{-4\sqrt{5}}{9\left(\frac{4}{3}\right)} = \dfrac{-\sqrt{5}}{3}$.

27. Find dy/dx implicitly and explicitly (the explicit functions are shown on the graph) and show that the two results are equivalent. Find the slope of the tangent line at the point $(-4, 3)$ given on the graph for $x^2 + y^2 = 25$.

Solution:

Implicitly: $2x + 2y\dfrac{dy}{dx} = 0$

$$\frac{dy}{dx} = -\frac{x}{y}$$

Explicitly: $y = \pm\sqrt{25 - x^2}$

$$\frac{dy}{dx} = \pm\left(\frac{1}{2}\right)(25 - x^2)^{-1/2}(-2x)$$

$$= \pm\frac{-x}{\sqrt{25 - x^2}}$$

$$= -\frac{x}{\pm\sqrt{25 - x^2}} = -\frac{x}{y}$$

At $(-4,\ 3)$, $\dfrac{dy}{dx} = \dfrac{4}{3}$.

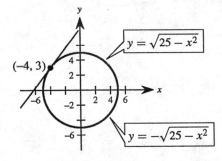

29. Find dy/dx implicitly and explicitly (the explicit functions are shown on the graph) and show that the two results are equivalent. Find the slope of the tangent line at the point $\left(2, \dfrac{3\sqrt{3}}{2}\right)$ given on the graph for $9x^2 + 16y^2 = 144$.

Solution:

Implicitly: $18x + 32y\dfrac{dy}{dx} = 0$

$$\dfrac{dy}{dx} = -\dfrac{9x}{16y}$$

Explicitly: $y = \pm\left(\dfrac{1}{4}\right)\sqrt{144 - 9x^2}$

$$\dfrac{dy}{dx} = \pm\left(\dfrac{1}{8}\right)(144 - 9x^2)^{-1/2}(-18x)$$

$$= \pm\dfrac{-9x}{4\sqrt{144 - 9x^2}}$$

$$= -\dfrac{9x}{16[\pm(1/4)\sqrt{144 - 9x^2}]} = -\dfrac{9x}{16y}$$

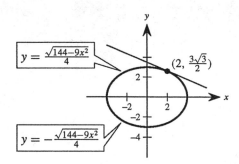

$$y = \dfrac{\sqrt{144-9x^2}}{4}$$

$$\left(2, \dfrac{3\sqrt{3}}{2}\right)$$

$$y = -\dfrac{\sqrt{144-9x^2}}{4}$$

At $\left(2, \dfrac{3\sqrt{3}}{2}\right),\ \dfrac{dy}{dx} = -\dfrac{\sqrt{3}}{4}.$

31. Find equations for the tangent lines to the circle $x^2 + y^2 = 169$ at points (5, 12) and (−12, 5). Sketch the graph of the equation and the tangent lines on the same set of coordinate axes.

Solution:

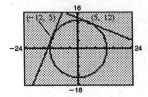

$$x^2 + y^2 = 169$$

$$2x + 2y\frac{dy}{dx} = 0$$

$$\frac{dy}{dx} = -\frac{x}{y}$$

At (5, 12):

$$m = -\frac{5}{12}$$

$$y - 12 = -\frac{5}{12}(x - 5)$$

$$5x + 12y - 169 = 0$$

At (−12, 5):

$$m = \frac{12}{5}$$

$$y - 5 = \frac{12}{5}(x + 12)$$

$$12x - 5y + 169 = 0$$

33. Find equations for the tangent lines to the graphs of $y^2 = 5x^3$ at the points $(1, \sqrt{5})$ and $(1, -\sqrt{5})$. Graph the equation and the tangent lines on the same viewing rectangle.

Solution:

$$y^2 = 5x^3$$

$$2yy' = 15x^2$$

$$y' = \frac{15x^2}{2y}$$

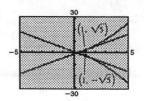

At $(1, \sqrt{5})$:

$$y' = \frac{15}{2\sqrt{5}}$$

$$y - \sqrt{5} = \frac{15}{2\sqrt{5}}(x-1)$$

$$2\sqrt{5}y - 10 = 15x - 15$$

$$2\sqrt{5}y - 15x + 5 = 0$$

At $(1, -\sqrt{5})$:

$$y' = \frac{-15}{2\sqrt{5}}$$

$$y + \sqrt{5} = \frac{-15}{2\sqrt{5}}(x-1)$$

$$2\sqrt{5}y + 10 = -15x + 15$$

$$2\sqrt{5}y + 15x - 5 = 0$$

35. Find the rate of change of x with respect to p.

$p = 0.006x^4 + 0.02x^2 + 10,\ x \geq 0$

Solution:

$$p = 0.006x^4 + 0.02x^2 + 10,\ x \geq 0$$

$$\frac{dp}{dp} = 1 = 0.024x^3\frac{dx}{dp} + 0.04x\frac{dx}{dp}$$

$$1 = (0.024x^3 + 0.04x)\frac{dx}{dp}$$

$$\frac{dx}{dp} = \frac{1}{0.024x^3 + 0.04x}$$

37. Find the rate of change of x with respect to p.

$$p = \frac{200 - x}{2x}, \quad 0 < x \le 200.$$

Solution:

$$p = \frac{200 - x}{2x} = \frac{100}{x} - \frac{1}{2} = 100x^{-1} - \frac{1}{2}$$

$$1 = -100x^{-2}\frac{dx}{dp}$$

$$\frac{dx}{dp} = \frac{-x^2}{100}$$

39. *Production* Let x represent the units of labot and y the capital invested in a manufacturing process. When 135,540 units are produced, the relationship between labor and capital can be modeled by

$$100x^{0.75}y^{0.25} = 135{,}540.$$

(a) Find the rate of change of y with respect to x when $x = 1500$ and $y = 1000$.

(b) The model used in the problem is called the *Cobb-Douglas production function.* Graph the model and describe the relationship between labor and capital.

Solution:

(a)
$$100x^{0.75}y^{0.25} = 135{,}540$$

$$100x^{0.75}\left(0.25y^{-0.75}\frac{dy}{dx}\right) + y^{0.25}(75x^{-0.25}) = 0$$

$$\frac{25x^{0.75}}{y^{0.75}}\frac{dy}{dx} = -\frac{75y^{0.25}}{x^{0.25}}$$

$$\frac{dy}{dx} = -\frac{3y}{x}$$

When $x = 1500$ and $y = 1000$, $\dfrac{dy}{dx} = -2$.

(b)

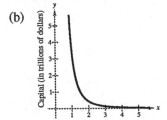

If more labor is used, then less capital is available. If more capital is used, then less labor is available.

Section 2.8   Related Rates

1. For $y = x^2 - \sqrt{x}$, assume that x and y are differentiable functions of t. Find (a) dy/dt given $x = 4$ and $dx/dt = 8$, and (b) dx/dt given $x = 16$ and $dy/dt = 12$.

   Solution:

   $$y = x^2 - \sqrt{x}, \quad \frac{dy}{dt} = 2x\frac{dx}{dt} - \frac{1}{2\sqrt{x}}\frac{dx}{dt} = \left(2x - \frac{1}{2\sqrt{x}}\right)\frac{dx}{dt}$$

   (a) When $x = 4$ and $\frac{dx}{dt} = 8$, $\frac{dy}{dt} = \left(2(4) - \frac{1}{2\sqrt{4}}\right)8 = 62$

   (b) When $x = 16$ and $\frac{dy}{dt} = 12$, we have

   $$12 = \left(2(16) - \frac{1}{2\sqrt{16}}\right)\frac{dx}{dt} = \left(32 - \frac{1}{8}\right)\frac{dx}{dt} = \frac{255}{8}\frac{dx}{dt}\frac{dx}{dt} = \frac{8 \cdot 12}{255} = \frac{32}{85}$$

3. For $xy = 4$, assume that x and y are both differentiable functions of t. Find (a) dy/dt given $x = 8$ and $dx/dt = 10$, and (b) dx/dt given $x = 1$ and $dy/dt = -6$.

   Solution:

   $$xy = 4, \qquad x\frac{dy}{dt} + y\frac{dx}{dt} = 0, \qquad \frac{dy}{dt} = \left(-\frac{y}{x}\right)\frac{dx}{dt}, \qquad \frac{dx}{dt} = \left(-\frac{x}{y}\right)\frac{dy}{dt}$$

   (a) When $x = 8$, $y = \frac{1}{2}$, and $\frac{dx}{dt} = 10$, $\frac{dy}{dt} = -\frac{1/2}{8}(10) = -\frac{5}{8}$.

   (b) When $x = 1$, $y = 4$, and $\frac{dy}{dt} = -6$, $\frac{dx}{dt} = -\frac{1}{4}(-6) = \frac{3}{2}$.

5. *Area* The radius r of a circle is increasing at a rate of 2 in/min. Find the rate of change of the area when
   (a) $r = 6$ inches and (b) $r = 24$ inches.

   Solution:

   $$A = \pi r^2, \qquad \frac{dr}{dt} = 2, \qquad \frac{dA}{dt} = 2\pi r\frac{dr}{dt}$$

   (a) When $r = 6$, $\frac{dA}{dt} = 2\pi(6)(2) = 24\pi$ in²/min.

   (b) When $r = 24$, $\frac{dA}{dt} = 2\pi(24)(2) = 96\pi$ in²/min.

7. *Area* Let A be the area of a circle of radius r that is changing with respect to time. If dr/dt is constant, is dA/dt constant? Explain why or why not.

   Solution:

   $$A = \pi r^2, \qquad \frac{dA}{dt} = 2\pi r\frac{dr}{dt}$$

   If dr/dt is constant, then $\frac{dA}{dt}$ is not constant; dA/dt is proportional to r.

9. *Inflating Balloon* A spherical balloon is inflated with gas at the rate of 20 ft³/min. How fast is the radius of the balloon changing at the instant the radius is (a) 1 foot, and (b) 2 feet?

Solution:

$$V = \frac{4}{3}\pi r^3, \qquad \frac{dV}{dt} = 20, \qquad \frac{dV}{dt} = 4\pi r^2 \frac{dr}{dt}, \qquad \frac{dr}{dt} = \left(\frac{1}{4\pi r^2}\right)\frac{dV}{dt}$$

(a) When $r = 1$, $\dfrac{dr}{dt} = \dfrac{1}{4\pi(1)^2}(20) = \dfrac{5}{\pi}$ ft/min.

(b) When $r = 2$, $\dfrac{dr}{dt} = \dfrac{1}{4\pi(2)^2}(20) = \dfrac{5}{4\pi}$ ft/min.

11. *Falling Sand* At a sand and gravel plant, Sand is falling off a conveyer and is forming a conical pile at the rate of 20 ft³/min. The diameter of the base of the cone is approximately three times the altitude. At what rate is the height of the pile changing when it is 10 feet high?

Solution:

$$V = \frac{1}{3}\pi r^2 h = \frac{1}{3}\pi\left(\frac{9}{4}h^2\right)h \qquad \text{[since } 2r = 3h\text{]}$$

$$= \frac{3\pi}{4}h^3$$

$$\frac{dV}{dt} = 20$$

$$\frac{dV}{dt} = \frac{9\pi}{4}h^2\frac{dh}{dt} \Rightarrow \frac{dh}{dt} = \frac{4(dV/dt)}{9\pi h^2}$$

When $h = 10$, $\dfrac{dh}{dt} = \dfrac{4(20)}{9\pi(10)^2} = \dfrac{8}{90\pi} = \dfrac{4}{45\pi}$ ft/min

13. *Expanding Cube* All edges of a cube are expanding at the rate of 3 cm/sec. How fast is the volume changing when each edge is (a) 1 centimeter, and (b) 10 centimeters?

Solution:

$$V = x^3, \qquad \frac{dx}{dt} = 3, \qquad \frac{dV}{dt} = 3x^2\frac{dx}{dt}$$

(a) When $x = 1$, $\dfrac{dV}{dt} = 3(1)^2(3) = 9$ cm³/sec.

(b) When $x = 10$, $\dfrac{dV}{dt} = 3(10)^2(3) = 900$ cm³/sec.

15. *Moving Point* A point is moving along the graph of $y = x^2$ so that dx/dt is 2 cm/min. Find dy/dt when (a) $x = -3$, (b) $x = 0$, (c) $x = 1$, and (d) $x = 3$.

Solution:

$$y = x^2, \qquad \frac{dx}{dt} = 2, \qquad \frac{dy}{dt} = 2x\frac{dx}{dt}$$

(a) When $x = -3$, $dy/dt = 2(-3)(2) = -12$ cm/min.
(b) When $x = 0$, $dy/dt = 2(0)(2) = 0$ cm/min.
(c) When $x = 1$, $dy/dt = 2(1)(2) = 4$ cm/min.
(d) When $x = 3$, $dy/dt = 2(3)(2) = 12$ cm/min.

17. *Sliding Ladder* A ladder 25 feet long is leaning against a house, as shown in the figure. The base of the ladder is pulled away from the house wall at a rate of 2 ft/sec. How fast is the top of the ladder moving down the wall when the base of the ladder is (a) 7 feet, (b) 15 feet, and (c) 24 feet from the wall?

Solution:

$$x^2 + y^2 = 25^2, \qquad 2x\frac{dx}{dt} + 2y\frac{dy}{dt} = 0, \qquad \frac{dy}{dt} = \frac{-x}{y}\frac{dx}{dt} = \frac{-2x}{y} \text{ since } \frac{dx}{dt} = 2.$$

(a) When $x = 7$, $y = \sqrt{576} = 24$,
$$\frac{dy}{dt} = \frac{-2(7)}{24} = \frac{-7}{12} \text{ ft/sec.}$$

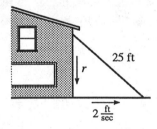

(b) When $x = 15$, $y = \sqrt{400} = 20$,
$$\frac{dy}{dt} = \frac{-2(15)}{20} = \frac{-3}{2} \text{ ft/sec.}$$

(c) When $x = 24$, $y = 7$,
$$\frac{dy}{dt} = \frac{-2(24)}{7} = \frac{-48}{7} \text{ ft/sec.}$$

19. *Air Traffic Control* An air traffic controller spots two planes at the same altitude converging on a point as they fly at right angles to one another, as shown in the figure. One plane is 150 miles from the point and is moving at 450 mi/hr. The other plane is 200 miles from the point and has a speed of 600 mi/hr.

(a) At what rate is the distance between the planes changing?

(b) How much time does the traffic controller have to get one of the planes on a different flight path?

Solution:

(a) $L^2 = x^2 + y^2$, $\dfrac{dx}{dt} = -450$, $\dfrac{dy}{dt} = -600$, and

$\dfrac{dL}{dt} = \dfrac{x(dx/dt) + y(dy/dt)}{L}$

When $x = 150$ and $y = 200$,

$\dfrac{dL}{dt} = \dfrac{150(-450) + 200(-600)}{250} = -750$ mph.

(b) $t = \dfrac{250}{750} = \dfrac{1}{3}$ hr $= 20$ min.

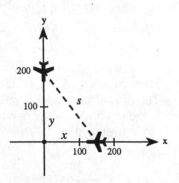

21. *Baseball* A baseball diamond has the shape of a square with sides 90 feet long, as shown in the figure. A player 26 feet from third base is running at a speed of 30 ft/sec. At what rate is the player's distance from home plate changing?

Solution:

$s^2 = 90^2 + x^2$, $x = 26$, $\dfrac{dx}{dt} = -30$

$2s\dfrac{ds}{dt} = 2x\dfrac{dx}{dt} \Rightarrow \dfrac{ds}{dt} = \dfrac{x}{s}\dfrac{dx}{dt}$

When $x = 26$, $s = \sqrt{90^2 + 26^2} \approx 93.68$

$\dfrac{ds}{dt} = -8.85$ ft/sec $\dfrac{26}{93.68}(-30) \approx -8.33$ ft/sec.

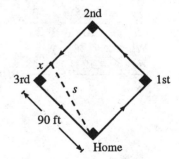

23. *Profit* A company is increasing its production of a certain product at the rate of 25 units per week. The demand and cost functions for this product are given by $p = 50 - (0.01x)$ and $C = 4000 + 40x - 0.02x^2$. Find the rate of change of the profit with respect to time when weekly sales are $x = 800$ units.

Solution:

$$P = R - C = xp - C$$

$$= x\left[50 - 0.01x\right] - (4000 + 40x - 0.02x^2)$$

$$= 50x - 0.01x^2 - 4000 - 40x + 0.2x^2 = 0.01x^2 + 10x - 4000$$

$$\frac{dP}{dt} = 0.02x\frac{dx}{dt} + 10\frac{dx}{dt}$$

When $x = 800$ and $\dfrac{dx}{dt} = 25$, $\dfrac{dP}{dt} = 0.02(800)(25) + (10)(25) = \$650/\text{week}$.

25. *Drug Costs* The annual cost (in millions of dollars) for a government agency to seize 4% of an illegal drug is

$$C = \frac{528p}{100 - p} \quad 0 \le p < 100.$$

Find the rate of change of the cost when

(a) $p = 30\%$ and (b) $p = 60\%$.

Solution:

(a) $\dfrac{dC}{dp} = \dfrac{(100 - p)528 - 528p(-1)}{(100 - p)^2} = \dfrac{52{,}800}{(100 - p)^2}$

When $p = 30$, $\dfrac{dC}{dp} = \dfrac{52{,}800}{(100 - 30)^2} = \dfrac{528}{49} \approx 10.78\dfrac{\text{dollars}}{\text{percent}}$.

(b) From part (a), when $p = 60$, $\dfrac{dC}{dp} = \dfrac{52{,}800}{(100 - 60)^2} = 33\dfrac{\text{dollars}}{\text{percent}}$.

Chapter 2   Review Exercises

1. Approximate the slope of the tangent line to the graph at (x, y). (Shown in the graph in the textbook.)

Solution:

$$\text{Slope} \approx \frac{-4}{2} = -2.$$

3. Approximate the slope of the tangent line to the graph at (x, y). (Shown in the graph in the textbook.)

Solution:

$$\text{Slope} \approx 0$$

5. *Revenue* The graph shown in the textbook approximates the annaul revenue (in millions of dollars) of Bethlehem Steel Corporation for the years 1985–1992, with $t = 0$ corresponding to 1980. Estimate the slope of the graph when $t = 7$ and $t = 10$. Interpret each slope in the context of the problem.

Solution:

When $t = 7$, slope $\approx$ \$600 million per year (revenues are increasing)

When $t = 10$, slope $\approx$ −\$700 million per year (revenues are decreasing)

7. Use the limit definition to find the slope of $f(x) = -3x - 5$; to the graph of f at $(-2, 1)$.

Solution:

$$f(x) = -3x - 5, (-2, 1)$$

$$m = \lim_{\Delta x \to 0} \frac{f(-2 + \Delta x) - f(-2)}{\Delta x}$$

$$= \lim_{\Delta x \to 0} \frac{(-3(-2 + \Delta x) - 5) - 1}{\Delta x}$$

$$= \lim_{\Delta x \to 0} \frac{-3\Delta x}{\Delta x} = -3$$

9. Use the limit definition to find the slope of $f(x) = \sqrt{x + 9}$; to the graph of f at $(-5, 2)$.

Solution:

$$f(x) = \sqrt{x + 9}, (-5, 2)$$

$$m = \lim_{\Delta x \to 0} \frac{\sqrt{-5 + \Delta x + 9} - 2}{\Delta x}$$

$$= \lim_{\Delta x \to 0} \frac{\sqrt{4 + \Delta x} - 2}{\Delta x} \cdot \frac{\sqrt{4 + \Delta x} + 2}{\sqrt{4 + \Delta x} + 2}$$

$$= \lim_{\Delta x \to 0} \frac{\Delta x}{\Delta x \left(\sqrt{4 + \Delta x} + 2 \right)}$$

$$= \lim_{\Delta x \to 0} \frac{1}{\sqrt{4 + \Delta x} + 2} = \frac{1}{4}$$

11. Use the limit definition to find the derivative of the function $f(x) = 7x + 3$.

Solution:

$$f'(x) = \lim_{\Delta x \to 0} \frac{f(x + \Delta x) - f(x)}{\Delta x}$$

$$= \lim_{\Delta x \to 0} \frac{7(x + \Delta x) + 3 - (7x + 3)}{\Delta x}$$

$$= \lim_{\Delta x \to 0} \frac{7\Delta x}{\Delta x} = 7$$

13. Use the limit definition to find the derivative of the function $f(x) = \dfrac{1}{x-5}$.

Solution:

$$f'(x) = \lim_{\Delta x \to 0} \frac{f(x + \Delta x) - f(x)}{\Delta x}$$

$$= \lim_{\Delta x \to 0} \frac{\frac{1}{x + \Delta x - 5} - \frac{1}{x - 5}}{\Delta x}$$

$$= \lim_{\Delta x \to 0} \frac{(x - 5) - (x + \Delta x - 5)}{(x + \Delta x - 5)(x - 5)\Delta x}$$

$$= \lim_{\Delta x \to 0} \frac{-1}{(x + \Delta x - 5)(x - 5)} = \frac{-1}{(x - 5)^2}$$

15. Find the slope of the graph of $f(x) = 8 - 5x$ at the point $(3, -7)$.

Solution:

$$f(x) = 8 - 5x$$
$$f'(x) = -5 \qquad f'(3) = -5$$

17. Find the slope of the graph of $f(x) = \sqrt{x} + 2$ at the point $(9, 5)$.

Solution:

$$f(x) = \sqrt{x} + 2 = x^{1/2} + 2$$
$$f'(x) = \frac{1}{2}x^{-1/2} = \frac{1}{2\sqrt{x}} \qquad f'(9) = \frac{1}{2\sqrt{9}} = \frac{1}{6}$$

19. Find an equation of the tangent line to the graph of $f(x) = \dfrac{x^2 + 3}{x}$ at the point $(1, 4)$.

Solution:

$$f(x) = \frac{x^2 + 3}{x} = x + 3x^{-1}$$
$$f'(x) = 1 - 3x^{-2} \qquad f'(1) = 1 - 3 = -2$$

tangent line: $y - 4 = -2(x - 1)$
$$y = -2x + 6$$

21. Determine the x-value (shown in graph in textbook) at which the function

$$y = \frac{x + 1}{x - 1}$$

is not differentiable.

Solution:

$$y = \frac{x + 1}{x - 1} \text{ is not differentiable at } x = 1.$$

23. Determine the x-value (shown in graph in textbook) at which the function is

$$y = \begin{cases} -x - 2, & x \le 0 \\ x^3 + 2, & x > 0 \end{cases}$$

Solution:

$$y = \begin{cases} -x - 2, & x \le 0 \\ x^3 + 2, & x > 0 \end{cases} \text{ is not differentiable at } x = 0.$$

25. Find the derivative of $f(x) = \sqrt{5}$.

Solution:

$$f'(x) = 0$$

27. Find the derivative of $y = x^5$.

Solution:

$$y' = 5x^4$$

29. Find the derivative of $y = \sqrt{x}$.

Solution:

$$y' = \frac{1}{2\sqrt{x}}$$

31. Find the derivative of $f(x) = 3x^4$.

Solution:

$$f'(x) = 12x^3$$

33. Find the derivative of $g(t) = \dfrac{2}{3t^2}$.

Solution:

$$g(t) = \frac{2}{3t^2} = \frac{2}{3}t^{-2}$$

$$g'(t) = -\frac{4}{3}t^{-3} = -\frac{4}{3t^3}$$

35. Find the derivative of $y = 11x^4 - 5x^2 + 1$.

Solution:

$$f'(x) = 44x^3 - 10x$$

37. Find the derivative of $f(x) = \sqrt{x} - \dfrac{1}{\sqrt{x}}$.

Solution:

$$f(x) = \sqrt{x} - \frac{1}{\sqrt{x}} = x^{1/2} - x^{-1/2}$$

$$f'(x) = \frac{1}{2}x^{-1/2} + \frac{1}{2}x^{-3/2} = \frac{1}{2x^{1/2}} + \frac{1}{2x^{3/2}} = \frac{x+1}{2x^{3/2}}$$

39. Find the average rate of change of the function $f(x) = x^2 + 3x - 4$ over the indicated interval. Then compare the average rate of change with the instantaneous rates of change at the endpoints [0, 1] of the interval.

Solution:

$$f(x) = x^2 + 3x - 4 \qquad [0, 1]$$

$$\text{average rate of change} = \frac{f(1) - f(0)}{1 - 0} = \frac{0 - (-4)}{1} = 4$$

$$f'(x) = 2x + 3 \qquad f'(0) = 3 \qquad f'(1) = 5$$

41. *Revenue* The annual revenue R (in millions of dollars) of Bethelehem Steel Corporation for the years 1984–1992 can be modeled by

$$R = 18.45t^4 - 650.94t^3 + 8292.83t^2 - 45{,}165.42t + 93{,}432.28,$$

where $t = 0$ corresponds to 1980.

(a) Find the average rate of change for the interval from 1986 to 1990.

(b) Find the instantaneous rate of change of the model in 1986 and 1990.

(c) Interpret the results of parts (a) and (b) in the context of the problem.

Solution:

(a) $\dfrac{R(10) - R(6)}{10 - 6} = -\dfrac{4621.08 - 4289.80}{4} = 82.82$ million per year

(b) $\quad R' = 73.8t^3 - 1952.82t^2 + 16{,}585.66t - 45{,}165.42$

$\quad R'(6) = -12.18$

$\quad R'(10) = -790.82$

(c) Revenues were decreasing in 1986 and 1990, but grew during the period 1987–89.

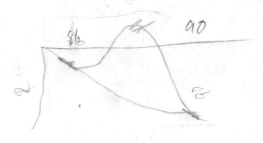

43. *Velocity* A rock is dropped from a tower on the Brooklyn Bridge, 276 feet above the East River. Let t represent the time in seconds.

(a) Write a model for the position function (assume that air resistance is negligible.)

(b) Find the average velocity during the first 2 seconds.

(c) Find the instantaneous velocity when $t = 2$ and $t = 3$.

(d) How long will it take for the rock to hit the water?

(e) When it hits the water, what is the rock's speed?

Solution:

(a) $s(t) = -16t^2 + 276$

(b) average velocity $= \dfrac{s(2) - s(0)}{2 - 0} = \dfrac{-64}{2} = -32$ ft/sec

(c) $v(t) = -32t$ \qquad $v(2) = -64$ ft/sec

$v(3) = -96$ ft/sec

(d) $s(t) = -16t^2 + 276 = 0 \Rightarrow t^2 = \dfrac{276}{16} = 17.25$

$t \approx 14.15$ sec

(e) $v(4.15) \approx -32(4.15) = -132.8$ velocity; speed $= 132.8$ ft/sec at impact

45. *Revenue, Cost, and Profit* The fixed cost of operating a small flower shop is $2500 per month. The average cost of a floral arrangement is $15 and the average price is $27.50. Write the monthly revenue, cost, and profit functions for the floral shop in termns of x, the number of arrangements sold.

Solution:

$R = 27.50x$

$C = 15x + 2500$

$P = R - C = 27.50x - (15x + 2500) = 12.50x - 2500$

47. Find the marginal cost for $C = 25000 + 320x$.

Solution:

$\dfrac{dC}{dx} = 320$

49. Find the marginal revenue for $R = 35x/\sqrt{x-2}$ when $x \geq 6$.

Solution:

$$R = \frac{35x}{\sqrt{x-2}} = 35x(x-2)^{-1/2}$$

$$\frac{dR}{dx} = 35x\left[-\frac{1}{2}(x-2)^{-3/2}\right] + 35(x-2)^{-1/2}$$

$$= \frac{35}{2}(x-2)^{-3/2}[-x + 2(x-2)]$$

$$= \frac{35(x-4)}{2(x-2)^{3/2}}$$

51. Find the marginal profit when $P = -0.0002x^3 + 6x^2 - x - 2000$.

Solution:

$$\frac{dP}{dx} = -0.0006x^2 + 12x - 1$$

53. Find the derivative of $f(x) = x^3(5 - 3x^2)$

Solution:

$$f(x) = x^3(5 - 3x^2) = 5x^3 - 3x^5$$

$$f'(x) = 15x^2 - 15x^4 = 15x^2(1 - x^2)$$

55. Find the derivative of $y = (4x - 3)(x^3 - 2x^2)$

Solution:

$$y = (4x - 3)(x^3 - 2x^2)$$

$$= 4x^4 - 11x^3 + 6x^2$$

$$y' = 16x^3 - 33x^2 + 12x$$

57. Find the derivative of $f(x) = \dfrac{6x - 5}{x^2 + 1}$

Solution:

$$f(x) = \frac{6x - 5}{x^2 + 1}$$

$$f'(x) = \frac{(x^2 + 1)(6) - (6x - 5)(2x)}{(x^2 + 1)^2}$$

$$= \frac{6 + 10x - 6x^2}{(x^2 + 1)^2} = \frac{2(3 + 5x - 3x^2)}{(x^2 + 1)^2}$$

59. Find the derivative of $g(t) = \dfrac{(1/t) - 2t}{t^3 - 1}$

Solution:

$$g(t) = \frac{(1/t) - 2t}{t^3 - 1} = \frac{1 - 2t^2}{t^4 - t}$$

$$g'(t) = \frac{(t^4 - t)(-4t) - (1 - 2t^2)(4t^3 - 1)}{(t^4 - t)^2}$$

$$= \frac{-4t^5 + 4t^2 - 4t^3 + 1 + 8t^5 - 2t^2}{(t^4 - t)^2}$$

$$= \frac{4t^5 - 4t^3 + 2t^2 + 1}{t^2(t^3 - 1)^2}$$

61. Find the derivative of $f(x) = (5x^2 + 2)^3$

Solution:

$$f(x) = (5x^2 + 2)^3$$

$$f'(x) = 3(5x^2 + 2)^2(10x) = 30x(5x^2 + 2)^2$$

63. Find the derivative of $h(x) = \dfrac{2}{\sqrt{x + 1}}$.

Solution:

$$h(x) = \frac{2}{\sqrt{x + 1}} = 2(x + 1)^{-1/2}$$

$$h'(x) = 2\left(-\frac{1}{2}\right)(x + 1)^{-3/2}(1) = -\frac{1}{(x + 1)^{3/2}}$$

65. Find the derivative of $g(x) = x\sqrt{x^2 + 1}$.

Solution:

$$g(x) = x\sqrt{x^2 + 1} = x(x^2 + 1)^{1/2}$$

$$g'(x) = x\left[\frac{1}{2}(x^2 + 1)^{-1/2}(2x)\right] + (1)(x^2 + 1)^{1/2}$$

$$= (x^2 + 1)^{-1/2}[x^2 + (x^2 + 1)]$$

$$= \frac{2x^2 + 1}{\sqrt{x^2 + 1}}$$

67. Find the derivative of $f(t) = (t+1)\sqrt{t^2+1}$

Solution:

$$f(t) = (t+1)\sqrt{t^2+1}$$

$$f' = (t+1)\frac{1}{2}(t^2+1)^{-1/2}(2t) + \sqrt{t^2+1}$$

$$= \frac{t^2+t}{\sqrt{t^2+1}} + \sqrt{t^2+1} = \frac{2t^2+t+1}{\sqrt{t^2+1}}$$

69. Find the derivative of $f(x) = -2(1-4x^2)^2$.

Solution:

$$f'(x) = -2(2)(1-4x^2)(-8x) = 32x(1-4x^2)$$

71. Find the derivative of $h(x) = [x^2(2x+3)]^3$.

Solution:

$$h(x) = [x^2(2x+3)]^3 = x^6(2x+3)^3$$

$$h'(x) = x^6[3(2x+3)^2(2)] + 6x^5(2x+3)^3$$

$$= 6x^5(2x+3)^2[x+(2x+3)]$$

$$= 18x^5(2x+3)^2(x+1)$$

73. Find the derivative of $f(x) = x^2(x-1)^5$

Solution:

$$f(x) = x^2(x-1)^5$$

$$f'(x) = x^2 5(x-1)^4 + 2x(x-1)^5$$

$$= x(x-1)^4(5x + 2(x-1))$$

$$= x(x-1)^4(7x-2)$$

75. Find the derivative of $h(t) = \dfrac{\sqrt{3t+1}}{(1-3t)^2}$

Solution:

$$h(t) = \frac{\sqrt{3t+1}}{(1-3t)^2}$$

$$h'(t) = \frac{(1-3t)^2\frac{1}{2}(3t+1)^{-1/2}3 - (3t+1)^{1/2}2(1-3t)(-3)}{(1-3t)^4}$$

$$= \frac{(3t+1)^{-1/2}[(1-3t)\frac{3}{2} + (3t+1)6]}{(1-3t)^3}$$

$$= \frac{3(9t+5)}{2\sqrt{3t+1}(1-3t)^3}$$

77. *Refrigeration* The temperature T (in degrees Fahrenheit) of food placed in a freezer can be modeled by

$$T = \frac{1300}{t^2 + 2t + 25},$$

where t is the time (in hours).

(a) Find the rate of change of T when $t = 1$, $t = 3$, $t = 5$, and $t = 10$.

(b) Graph the model and describe the rate at which the temperature is changing.

Solution:

$$T = \frac{1300}{t^2 + 2t + 25} = 1300(t^2 + 2t + 25)^{-1}$$

$$T'(t) = -1300(t^2 + 2t + 25)^{-2}(2t + 2) = \frac{-2600(t + 1)}{(t^2 + 2t + 25)^2}$$

(a) $T'(1) = \dfrac{-325}{49} \approx -6.63$

$T'(3) = \dfrac{-13}{2} \approx -6.5$

$T'(5) = \dfrac{-13}{3} \approx -4.33$

$T'(10) = \dfrac{-1144}{841} \approx -1.36$

(b)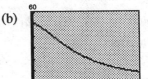

The rate of decrease is approaching zero.

79. Given $f(x) = 3x^2 + 7x + 1x + 1$, find $f''(x)$.

Solution:

$$f(x) = 3x^2 + 7x + 1$$
$$f'(x) = 6x + 7$$
$$f''(x) = 6$$

81. Given $f'''(x) = \dfrac{-6}{x^4}$, find $f^{(5)}(x)$.

Solution:

$$f'''(x) = -6x^{-4}$$
$$f^{(4)}(x) = 24x^{-5}$$
$$f^{(5)}(x) = -120x^{-6} = \frac{-120}{x^6}$$

83. Given $f'(x) = 7x^{5/2}$, find $f'''(x)$.

Solution:

$$f'(x) = 7x^{5/2}$$
$$f'''(x) = \frac{35}{2}x^{3/2}$$

85. Given $f''(x) = 6\sqrt[3]{x}$, find $f'''(x)$.

Solution:

$$f''(x) = 6x^{1/3}$$

$$f'''(x) = 2x^{-2/3} = \frac{2}{x^{2/3}}$$

87. *Diver* A person dives from a 30-foot platform with an initial velocity of 5 feet per second (upward).

(a) Find the position function of the diver.

(b) How long will it take for the diver to hit the water?

(c) What is the diver's velocity at impact?

(d) What is the diver's acceleration at impact?

Solution:

(a) $s(t) = -16t^2 + 5t + 30$

(b) $s(t) = 0 = -16t^2 + 5t + 30$

Using the quadratic formula or a graphing utility, $t \approx 1.534$ seconds.

(c) $v(t) = s'(t) = -32t + 5$

$v(1.534) \approx -44.09$ ft/sec.

(d) $a(t) = v'(t) = -32$ ft/sec²

89. Use implicit differentiation to find dy/dx for $x^2 + 3xy + y^3 = 10$.

Solution:

$$x^2 + 3xy + y^3 = 10$$

$$2x + 3x\frac{dy}{dx} + 3y + 3y^2\frac{dy}{dx} = 0$$

$$\frac{dy}{dx}(3x + 3y^2) = -2x - 3y$$

$$\frac{dy}{dx} = \frac{-2x - 3y}{3x + 3y^2} = -\frac{2x + 3y}{3(x + y^2)}$$

91. Use implicit differentiation to find dy/dx for $y^2 - x^2 = 25$.

Solution:

$$y^2 - x^2 = 49$$

$$2y\frac{dy}{dx} - 2x = 0$$

$$\frac{dy}{dx} = \frac{2x}{2y} = \frac{x}{y}$$

93. Use implicit differentiation to find $\dfrac{dy}{dx}$ for $y^2 = (x - y)(x^2 + y)$.

Solution:

$$y^2 = (x - y)(x^2 + y) = x^3 + xy - yx^2 - y^2$$

$$2yy' = 3x^2 + xy' + y - 2yx - x^2y' - 2yy'$$

$$(4y - x + x^2)y' = 3x^2 + y - 2yx$$

$$y' = \frac{3x^2 + y - 2yx}{4y - x + x^2}$$

95. Use implicit differentiation to find $\dfrac{dy}{dx}$ for $2\sqrt[3]{x} + 3\sqrt{y} = 10$.

Solution:

$$2x^{1/3} + 3y^{1/2} = 10$$

$$\frac{2}{3}x^{-2/3} + \frac{3}{2}y^{-1/2}y' = 0$$

$$\frac{3}{2}y^{-1/2}y' = -\frac{2}{3}x^{-2/3}$$

$$y' = \frac{-4y^{1/2}}{9x^{2/3}}$$

97. *Water Level* A swimming pool is 40 feet long, 20 feet wide, 4 feet deep at the shallow end, and 9 feet deep at the deep end (see figure in textbook). Water is being pumped into the pool at the rate of 10 cubic feet per minute. How fast is the water level rising when there is 4 feet of water in the deep end?

Solution:

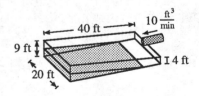

$$b = 8h, \quad 0 \le h \le 5$$

$$V = \frac{1}{2}bh(20) = 10bh = 10(8h)h = 80h^2$$

$$\frac{dV}{dt} = 160h\,\frac{dh}{dt}$$

$$\frac{dh}{dt} = \frac{1}{160h}\frac{dV}{dt} = \frac{1}{16h} \quad \text{[since } dV/dt = 10\text{]}$$

When $h = 4$, $\dfrac{dh}{dt} = \dfrac{1}{16(4)} = \dfrac{1}{64}$ ft/min.

Practice Test for Chapter 2

1. Use the definition of the derivative to find the derivative of $f(x) = 2x^2 + 3x - 5$.

2. Use the definition of the derivative to find the derivative of $f(x) = \dfrac{1}{x-4}$.

3. Use the definition of the derivative to find the equation of the tangent line to the graph of $f(x) = \sqrt{x-2}$ at the point $(6, 2)$.

4. Find $f'(x)$ for $f(x) = 5x^3 - 6x^2 + 15x - 9$.

5. Find $f'(x)$ for $f(x) = \dfrac{6x^2 - 4x + 1}{x^2}$.

6. Find $f'(x)$ for $f(x) = \sqrt[3]{x^2} + \sqrt[5]{x^3}$.

7. Find the average rate of change of $f(x) = x^3 - 11$ over the interval $[0, 2]$. Compare this to the instantaneous rate of change at the endpoints of the interval.

8. Given the cost function $C = 6200 + 4.31x - 0.0001x^2$, find the marginal cost of producing x units.

9. Find $f'(x)$ for $f(x) = (x^3 - 4x)(x^2 + 7x - 9)$.

10. Find $f'(x)$ for $f(x) = \dfrac{x+7}{x^2-8}$.

11. Find $f'(x)$ for $f(x) = x^3\left(\dfrac{x-3}{x+5}\right)$.

12. Find $f'(x)$ for $f(x) = \dfrac{\sqrt{x}}{x^2+4x-1}$.

13. Find $f'(x)$ for $f(x) = (6x - 5)^{12}$.

14. Find $f'(x)$ for $f(x) = 8\sqrt{4-3x}$.

15. Find $f'(x)$ for $f(x) = -\dfrac{3}{(x^2+1)^3}$.

16. Find $f'(x)$ for $f(x) = \sqrt{\dfrac{10x}{x+2}}$.

17. Find $f'''(x)$ for $f(x) = x^4 - 9x^3 + 17x^2 - 4x + 121$.

18. Find $f^{(4)}$ for $f(x) = \sqrt{3-x}$.

19. Use implicit differentiation to find dy/dx for $x^5 + y^5 = 100$.

20. Use implicit differentiation to find dy/dx for $x^2 y^3 + 2x - 3y + 11 = 0$.

21. Use implicit differentiation to find dy/dx for $\sqrt{xy+4} = 5y - 4x$.

22. Use implicit differentiation to find $\dfrac{dy}{dx}$ for $y^3 = \dfrac{x^3 + 4}{x^3 - 4}$.

23. Let $y = 3x^2$. Find dx/dt when $x = 2$ and $dy/dt = 5$.

24. The area A of a circle is increasing at a rate of 10 in^2/min. Find the rate of change of the radius r when $r = 4$ inches.

25. The volume of a cone is $V = \left(\frac{1}{3}\right)\pi r^2 h$. Find the rate of change of the height when dV/dt is 200, $h = r/2$, and $h = 20$ inches.

Graphing Calculator Required

26. Graph $f(x) = \dfrac{x^2}{x-2}$ and its derivative on the same set of coordinate axes. From the graph of $f(x)$ determine any points at which the graph has horizontal tangent lines. What is the value of $f'(x)$ at these points?

27. Use a graphing utility to graph $\sqrt[3]{x} + \sqrt[3]{y} = 3$ then find and sketch the tangent line at the point $(8, 1)$.

CHAPTER 3
Applications of the Derivative

Section 3.1 Increasing and Decreasing Functions

1. Evaluate the derivative of $f(x) = x^2/(x^2 + 4)$ at the indicated points on its graph. Observe the relationship between the sign of the derivative and the increasing or decreasing behavior of the graph.

   Solution:

   $$f'(x) = \frac{(x^2 + 4)(2x) - (x^2)(2x)}{(x^2 + 4)^2} = \frac{8x}{(x^2 + 4)^2}$$

   At $\left(-1, \frac{1}{5}\right)$, f is decreasing since $f'(-1) = -\frac{8}{25}$.

   At $(0, 0)$, f has a critical number since $f'(0) = 0$.

   At $\left(1, \frac{1}{5}\right)$, f is increasing since $f'(1) = \frac{8}{25}$.

   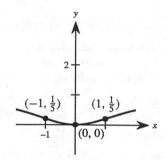

3. Evaluate the derivative of $f(x) = (x+2)^{2/3}$ at the indicated points on its graph. Observe the relationship between the sign of the derivative and the increasing or decreasing behavior of the graph.

   Solution:

   $$f'(x) = \frac{2}{3}(x + 2)^{-1/3}$$

   $$= \frac{2}{3\sqrt[3]{x + 2}}$$

   At $(-3, 1)$, f is decreasing since $f'(-3) = -\frac{2}{3}$.

   At $(-2, 0)$, f has a critical number since $f'(-2)$ is undefined.

   At $(-1, 1)$, f is increasing since $f'(-1) = \frac{2}{3}$.

   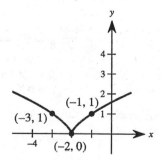

5. Identify the open intervals on which the function $f(x) = -(x + 1)^2$ is increasing or decreasing.

Solution:

$f'(x) = -2(x + 1)$

f has a critical number at $x = -1$. Moreover, f is increasing on $(-\infty, -1)$ and decreasing on $(-1, \infty)$.

7. Identify the open intervals on which the function $f(x) = x^4 - 2x^2$ is increasing or decreasing.

Solution:

$f'(x) = 4x^3 - 4x = 4x(x^2 - 1)$

f has critical numbers at $x = 0, \pm 1$. Moreover, f is increasing on $(-1, 0)$, $(1, \infty)$ and decreasing on $(-\infty, -1)$, $(0, 1)$.

9. Find the critical numbers (if any) and the open intervals on which $f(x) = 2x - 3$ is increasing or decreasing. Sketch the graph of the function.

Solution:

$f'(x) = 2$

Since the derivative is positive for all x, the function is increasing for all x. Thus, there are no critical numbers. Increasing on $(-\infty, \infty)$.

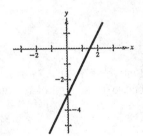

11. Find the critical numbers and the open intervals on which $g(x) = -(x - 1)^2$ is increasing or decreasing. Sketch the graph of the function.

Solution:

$g'(x) = -2(x - 1) = 0$

Critical number: $x = 1$

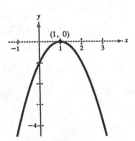

Interval	$-\infty < x < 1$	$1 < x < \infty$
Sign of f'	$f' > 0$	$f' < 0$
Conclusion	Increasing	Decreasing

13. Find the critical numbers and the open intervals on which $y = x^2 - 5x$ is increasing or decreasing. Sketch the graph of the function.

Solution:

$$y' = 2x - 5 = 0$$

Critical number: $x = \frac{5}{2}$

Interval	$-\infty < x < \frac{5}{2}$	$\frac{5}{2} < x < \infty$
Sign of f'	$f' < 0$	$f' > 0$
Conclusion	Decreasing	Increasing

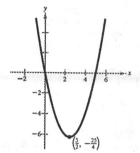

15. Find the critical numbers and the open intervals on which $y = x^3 - 6x^2$ is increasing or decreasing. Sketch the graph of the function.

Solution:

$$y' = 3x^2 - 12x = 3x(x - 4) = 0$$

Critical numbers: $x = 0$ and $x = 4$

Interval	$-\infty < x < 0$	$0 < x < 4$	$4 < x < \infty$
Sign of f'	$f' > 0$	$f' < 0$	$f' > 0$
Conclusion	Increasing	Decreasing	Increasing

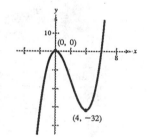

17. Find the critical numbers and the open intervals on which $f(x) = -(x+1)^3$ is increasing or decreasing. Sketch the graph of the function.

Solution:

$$f'(x) = -3(x + 1)^2 = 0$$

Critical number: $x = -1$

Interval	$-\infty < x < -1$	$-1 < x < \infty$
Sign of f'	$f' < 0$	$f' < 0$
Conclusion	Decreasing	Decreasing

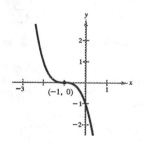

f is decreasing on $(-\infty, \infty)$.

19. Find the critical numbers and open intervals on which $f(x) = -2x^2 + 4x + 3$ is increasing or decreasing.

Solution:

$$f'(x) = -4x + 4 = 0$$

Critical number: $x = 1$

Interval	$-\infty < x < 1$	$1 < x < \infty$
Sign of f'	$f' > 0$	$f' < 0$
Conclusion	Increasing	Decreasing

21. Find the critical numbers and open intervals on which $y = 3x^3 + 12x^2 + 15x$ in increasing or decreasing.

Solution:

$$y' = 9x^2 + 24x + 15 = 3(x + 1)(3x + 5) = 0$$

Critical numbers: $x = -1$, $x = -\frac{5}{3}$

Interval	$-\infty < x < -5/3$	$-5/3 < x < -1$	$-1 < x < \infty$
Sign of f'	$f' > 0$	$f' < 0$	$f' > 0$
Conclusion	Increasing	Decreasing	Increasing

23. Find the critical numbers and the open intervals on which $h(x) = x^{2/3}$ is increasing or decreasing.

Solution:

$$h'(x) = \frac{2}{3}x^{-1/3} = \frac{2}{3\sqrt[3]{x}}$$

Critical number: $x = 0$ (h' is undefined here.)

Interval	$-\infty < x < 0$	$0 < x < \infty$
Sign of h'	$h' < 0$	$h' > 0$
Conclusion	Decreasing	Increasing

25. Find the critical numbers and the open intervals on which $f(x) = x^4 - 2x^3$ is increasing or decreasing.

Solution:

$$f'(x) = 4x^3 - 6x^2 = 2x^2(2x - 3) = 0$$

Critical numbers: $x = 0$ and $x = \frac{3}{2}$

Interval	$-\infty < x < 0$	$0 < x < \frac{3}{2}$	$\frac{3}{2} < x < \infty$
Sign of f'	$f' < 0$	$f' < 0$	$f' > 0$
Conclusion	Decreasing	Decreasing	Increasing

27. Find the critical numbers and the open intervals on which $f(x) = 2x\sqrt{3 - x}$ is increasing or decreasing.

Solution:

$$f'(x) = 2x\left[\frac{1}{2}(3-x)^{-1/2}(-1)\right] + 2\sqrt{3-x} = (3-x)^{-1/2}[-x + 2(3-x)] = \frac{3(2-x)}{\sqrt{3-x}}$$

Domain: $(-\infty, \ 3]$

Critical numbers: $x = 2, \ x = 3$

Interval	$-\infty < x < 2$	$2 < x < 3$
Sign of f'	$f' > 0$	$f' < 0$
Conclusion	Increasing	Decreasing

29. Find the critical numbers and the open intervals on which $f(x) = x/(x^2 + 4)$ is increasing or decreasing.

Solution:

$$f'(x) = \frac{(x^2 + 4)(1) - (x)(2x)}{(x^2 + 4)^2} = \frac{4 - x^2}{(x^2 + 4)^2}$$

Critical numbers: $x = \pm 2$

Interval	$-\infty < x < -2$	$-2 < x < 2$	$2 < x < \infty$
Sign of f'	$f' < 0$	$f' > 0$	$f' < 0$
Conclusion	Decreasing	Increasing	Decreasing

31. Find the critical numbers and the open intervals on which the *discontinuous* function $f(x) = x + (1/x)$ is increasing or decreasing.

Solution:

$$f'(x) = 1 - \frac{1}{x^2} = \frac{x^2 - 1}{x^2}$$

Critical numbers: $x = \pm 1$
Discontinuity: $x = 0$

Interval	$-\infty < x < -1$	$-1 < x < 0$	$0 < x < 1$	$1 < x < \infty$
Sign of f'	$f' > 0$	$f' < 0$	$f' < 0$	$f' > 0$
Conclusion	Increasing	Decreasing	Decreasing	Increasing

33. Find the critical numbers and the open intervals on which the *discontinuous* function $f(x) = \dfrac{2x}{16 - x^2}$ is increasing or decreasing.

Solution:

$$f'(x) = \frac{(16 - x^2)2 - 2x(-2x)}{(16 - x^2)^2} = \frac{2x^2 + 32}{(16 - x^2)^2}$$

No critical numbers.

Discontinuities: $x = \pm 4$

Interval	$-\infty < x < -4$	$-4 < x < 4$	$4 < x < \infty$
Sign of f'	$f' > 0$	$f' > 0$	$f' > 0$
Conclusion	Increasing	Increasing	Increasing

35. Find the critical numbers and the open intervals on which the following *discontinuous* function is increasing or decreasing.

$$f(x) = \begin{cases} 4 - x^2, & x \le 0 \\ -2x, & x > 0 \end{cases}$$

Solution:

$$f'(x) = \begin{cases} -2x, & x < 0 \\ -2, & x > 0 \end{cases}$$

$f'(0)$ is undefined.

Critical number: $x = 0$

Interval	$-\infty < x < 0$	$0 < x < \infty$
Sign of f'	$f' > 0$	$f' < 0$
Conclusion	Increasing	Decreasing

37. *Ordering and Transportation Cost* The ordering and transportation cost C (in hundreds of dollars) for an automobile dealership is

$$C = 10\left(\frac{1}{x} + \frac{x}{x+3}\right), \qquad 1 \le x,$$

where x is the number of automobiles ordered.

(a) Find the intervals on which C is increasing or decreasing.

(b) Use a graphing utility to graph the cost function.

(c) Use the trace feature to determine the order sizes for which the cost is $900. Assuming that the revenue function is increasing for $x \ge 0$, which order size would you use? Explain your reasoning.

Solution:

$$C = 10\left(\frac{1}{x} + \frac{x}{x+3}\right), \ 1 \le x$$

(a) $\dfrac{dC}{dx} = 10\left[-x^{-2} + \dfrac{(x+3)(1) - (x)(1)}{(x+3)^2}\right]$

$= 10\left[-\dfrac{1}{x^2} + \dfrac{3}{(x+3)^2}\right] = 10\left[\dfrac{-(x+3)^2 + 3x^2}{x^2(x+3)^2}\right]$

$= 10\left[\dfrac{2x^2 - 6x - 9}{x^2(x+3)^2}\right]$

By the Quadratic Formula, $2x^2 - 6x - 9 = 0$ when

$$x = \frac{6 \pm \sqrt{108}}{4} = \frac{3 \pm 3\sqrt{3}}{2}.$$

The only critical number in the domain is $x \approx 4.10$. Thus, C is decreasing on the interval $[1, \ 4.10)$ and increasing on $(4.10, \ \infty)$.

(b)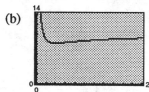

(c) $C = 9$ when $x = 2$ and $x = 15$. Use $x = 4$ to minimize C.

39. *Position Function* The position function, $s(t) = 96t - 16t^2$, $0 \le t \le 6$, gives the height (in feet) of a ball, where the time t is measured in seconds. Find the time interval in which the ball is moving up and the interval in which it is moving down.

Solution:

Since $s'(t) = 96 - 32t = 0$, the critical number is $t = 3$. Therefore, the ball is moving up on the interval $(0, 3)$ and moving down on $(3, 6)$.

41. *Bankers* The number y (in thousands) of people employed in banking and financing can be modeled by

$$y = -1.27t^3 + 6.63t^{5/2} + 1706.88, \qquad 0 \le t \le 21,$$

where $t = 0$ corresponds to 1970.

(a) Use a graphing utility to graph the model. Then graphically estimate the years during which the model is increasing and the years during which it is decreasing.

(b) Use the test for increasing and decreasing functions to verify the result of part (a).

Solution:

$$y = -1.27t^3 + 6.63t^{5/2} + 1706.88, \qquad 0 \le t \le 21$$

(a)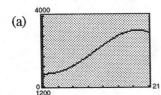

(b) $y' = -3.81t^2 + 16.575t^{3/2}$.

$= 0$ for $t \approx 18.9$

$y' > 0$ on $(0, 18.9)$,

$y' < 0$ on $(18.9, 21)$.

The model is increasing on $(0, 19)$ and decreasing on $(19, 21)$.

43. Use a computer or graphics calculator to (a) sketch the graph of f and f' on the same coordinate axes over the interval $[-3, 3]$ if $f(x) = 2x\sqrt{9 - x^2}$, (b) find the critical numbers of f, and (c) find the interval(s) on which f' is positive and the interval(s) on which it is negative. Note the behavior of f in relation to the sign of f'.

Solution:

$$f(x) = 2x\sqrt{9 - x^2}, \quad -3 \le x \le 3$$

$$f'(x) = 2x\left(-\frac{x}{\sqrt{9 - x^2}}\right) + 2\sqrt{9 - x^2} = \frac{2(9 - 2x^2)}{\sqrt{9 - x^2}}$$

(a)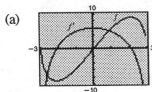

(b) $f'(x) = \dfrac{2(9 - 2x^2)}{\sqrt{9 - x^2}}$

$f'(x) = 0$ when $9 - 2x^2 = 0 \Rightarrow x = \pm\dfrac{3}{\sqrt{2}} = \pm\dfrac{3\sqrt{2}}{2}$

$f'(x)$ is undefined when $x = \pm 3$.

Critical numbers: $x = \pm\dfrac{3\sqrt{2}}{2}$

(c)

Interval	$\left(3, -\dfrac{3\sqrt{2}}{2}\right)$	$\left(-\dfrac{3\sqrt{2}}{2}, \dfrac{3\sqrt{2}}{2}\right)$	$\left(\dfrac{3\sqrt{2}}{2}, 3\right)$
Sign of $f'(x)$	$f' < 0$	$f' > 0$	$f' < 0$
Conclusion	Decreasing	Increasing	Decreasing

Section 3.2   Extrema and the First-Derivative Test

1. Find all relative extrema of $f(x) = -2x^2 + 4x + 3$.

Solution:

$$f'(x) = 4 - 4x = 4(1 - x)$$

Critical number: $x = 1$

Interval	$(-\infty,\ 1)$	$(1,\ \infty)$
Sign of f'	$+$	$-$
f	Increasing	Decreasing

Relative maximum: $(1, 5)$

3. Find all relative extrema of $f(x) = x^2 - 6x$.

Solution:

$$f'(x) = 2x - 6 = 2(x - 3)$$

Critical number: $x = 3$

Interval	$(-\infty,\ 3)$	$(3,\ \infty)$
Sign of f'	$-$	$+$
f	Decreasing	Increasing

Relative minimum: $(3,\ -9)$

5. Find all relative extrema of $g(x) = 6x^3 - 15x^2 + 12x$

Solution:

$$g'(x) = 18x^2 - 30x + 12 = 6(3x^2 - 5x - 12) = 6(x - 1)(3x - 2)$$

Critical numbers: $x = 1, \frac{2}{3}$

Interval	$(-\infty, 2/3)$	$(2/3, 1)$	$(1, \infty)$
Sign of g'	$+$	$-$	$+$
g	Increasing	Decreasing	Increasing

Relative maximum: $\left(\frac{2}{3}, \frac{28}{9}\right)$

Relative minimum: $(1, 3)$

7. Find all relative extrema of $h(x) = -(x + 4)^3$.

Solution:

$$h'(x) = -3(x + 4)^2$$

Critical number: $x = -4$

Interval	$(-\infty, -4)$	$(-4, \infty)$
Sign of h'	$-$	$-$
h	Decreasing	Decreasing

No relative extrema

9. Find all relative extrema of $f(x) = x^3 - 6x^2 + 15$.

Solution:

$$f'(x) = 3x^2 - 12x = 3x(x - 4)$$

Critical numbers: $x = 0$, $x = 4$

Interval	$(-\infty, 0)$	$(0, 4)$	$(4, \infty)$
Sign of f'	$+$	$-$	$+$
f	Increasing	Decreasing	Increasing

Relative maximum: $(0, 15)$

Relative minimum: $(4, -17)$

11. Find all relative extrema of $f(x) = x^4 - 2x^3$.

Solution:

$$f'(x) = 2x^2(2x - 3)$$

Critical numbers: $x = 0$, $x = \frac{3}{2}$

Interval	$(-\infty, 0)$	$\left(0, \frac{3}{2}\right)$	$\left(\frac{3}{2}, \infty\right)$
Sign of f'	$-$	$-$	$+$
f	Decreasing	Decreasing	Increasing

Relative minimum: $\left(\frac{3}{2}, -\frac{27}{16}\right)$

13. Find all relative extrema of $f(x) = x^{1/5} + 2$

Solution:

$$f'(x) = \frac{1}{5}x^{-4/5} = \frac{1}{5x^{4/5}}$$

Critical numbers: $x = 0$

Interval	$(-\infty, 0)$	$(0, \infty)$
Sign of f'	$+$	$+$
f	Increasing	Increasing

No relative extrema.

15. Find all relative extrema of $g(t) = t^{2/3}$.

Solution:

$$g'(t) = \frac{2}{3}t^{-1/3} = \frac{2}{3\sqrt[3]{t}}$$

Critical number: $t = 0$

Interval	$(-\infty, 0)$	$(0, \infty)$
Sign of g'	$-$	$+$
g	Decreasing	Increasing

Relative minimum: $(0, 0)$

17. Find all relative extrema of $f(x) = x + \dfrac{1}{x}$.

Solution:

$$f'(x) = 1 - \frac{1}{x^2} = \frac{x^2 - 1}{x^2}$$

Critical numbers: $x = \pm 1$

Discontinuity: $x = 0$

Interval	$(-\infty, -1)$	$(-1, 0)$	$(0, 1)$	$(1, \infty)$
Sign of f'	$+$	$-$	$-$	$+$
f	Increasing	Decreasing	Decreasing	Increasing

Relative maximum: $(-1, -2)$

Relative minimum: $(1, 2)$

19. Find all relative extrema of $h(x) = \dfrac{4}{x^2 + 1}$.

Solution:

$$h(x) = \frac{4}{x^2 + 1} = 4(x^2 + 1)^{-1}$$

$$h'(x) = -\frac{8x}{(x^2 + 1)^2}$$

Critical number: $x = 0$

Interval	$(-\infty,\ 0)$	$(0,\ \infty)$
Sign of h'	$+$	$-$
h	Increasing	Decreasing

Relative maximum: $(0, 4)$

21. Locate the absolute extrema of $f(x) = 2(3 - x)$ on the interval $[-1,\ 2]$.

Solution:

$$f'(x) = -2$$

No critical numbers

x-value	Endpoint $x = -1$	Endpoint $x = 2$
$f(x)$	8	2
Conclusion	Maximum	Minimum

23. Find the absolute extrema of the function $f(x) = 5 - 2x^3$ on the closed interval $[0, 3]$.

Solution:

$$f(x) = 5 - 2x^2 \qquad [0, 3]$$

$$f'(x) = -4x$$

Critical number: $x = 0$ (also endpoint)

x-value	Endpoint $x = 0$ $x = 0$	Endpoint $x = 3$ $x = 3$
$f(x)$	5	-13
Conclusion	Maximum	Minimum

25. Locate the absolute extrema of $f(x) = x^3 - 3x^2$ on $[-1, \ 3]$.

Solution:

$$f'(x) = 3x^2 - 6x = 3x(x - 2)$$

Critical numbers: $x = 0$ and $x = 2$

x-value	Endpoint $x = -1$	Critical $x = 0$	Critical $x = 2$	Endpoint $x = 3$
$f(x)$	-4	0	-4	0
Conclusion	Minimum	Maximum	Minimum	Maximum

27. Locate the absolute extrema of $f(x) = 3x^{2/3} - 2x$ on the interval $[-1, \ 2]$.

Solution:

$$f'(x) = 2x^{-1/3} - 2 = \frac{2 - 2\sqrt[3]{x}}{\sqrt[3]{x}}$$

Critical numbers: $x = 1$ and $x = 0$

x-value	Endpoint $x = -1$	Critical $x = 0$	Critical $x = 1$	Endpoint $x = 2$
$f(x)$	5	0	1	0.7622
Conclusion	Maximum	Minimum		

29. Find the absolute extrema of the function $h(s) = \dfrac{1}{3 - s}$ on the closed interval $[0, 2]$.

Solution:

$$h(s) = \frac{1}{3 - s} = (3 - s)^{-1} \qquad [0, 2]$$

$$h'(s) = -(3 - s)^{-2}(-1) = \frac{1}{(3 - s)^2}$$

No critical numbers.

s-value	Endpoint $x = 0$	Endpoint $x = 2$
$h(s)$	$1/3$	1
Conclusion	Minimum	Maximum

31. Graphically find the absolute extrema of the function $f(x) = 0.4x^3 - 1.8x^2 + x - 3$ on the closed interval $[0, 5]$.

Solution:

Maximum: $(5, 7)$

Minimum: $(2.69, -5.55)$

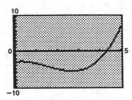

33. Graphically find the absolute extrema of the function $f(x) = 3.2x^5 + 5x^3 - 3.5x$ on the closed interval $[0, 1]$.

Solution:

Maximum: $(1, 4.7)$

Minimum: $(0.4398, -1.0613)$

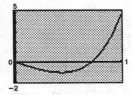

35. Locate the absolute extrema of $f(x) = \dfrac{4x}{x^2 + 1}$ on the interval $[0, \infty)$.

Solution:

$$f'(x) = \frac{(x^2 + 1)(4) - 4x(2x)}{(x^2 + 1)^2} = \frac{4(1 - x^2)}{(x^2 + 1)^2}$$

Critical number: $x = 1$

x-value	Endpoint $x = 0$	Critical $x = 1$	Interval (1∞)
$f(x)$	0	2	$0 < f(x) < 2$
Conclusion	Minimum	Maximum	f is decreasing

37. Locate the absolute extrema of $f(x) = 3 - \dfrac{2}{x^2 - 4x + 5}$ on the interval $[0, \infty)$.

Solution:

$$f(x) = 3 - 2(x^2 - 4x + 5)^{-1} \quad [0, \infty)$$

$$f'(x) = 2(x^2 - 4x + 5)^{-2}(2x - 4) = \frac{4(x - 2)}{(x^2 - 4x + 5)^2}$$

Critical number: $x = 2$

x-value	Endpoint $x = 0$	Critical $x = 2$	Interval $(2, \infty$
$f(x)$	2.6	1	$1 < f(x) < 3$
Conclusion	Neither	Minimum	f is increasing

39. For $f(x) = x^3(3x^2 - 10)$, find the maximum value of $|f''(x)|$ on the closed interval $[0, 1]$.

Solution:

$$f'(x) = 15x^4 - 30x^2$$

$$f''(x) = 60x^3 - 60x$$

$$f'''(x) = 180x^2 - 60 = 60(3x^2 - 1)$$

Critical numbers for f'' in $[0, 1]$: $x = \dfrac{1}{\sqrt{3}}$

x-value	Endpoint $x = 0$	Critical $x = \frac{1}{\sqrt{3}}$	Endpoint $x = 1$
$|f''(x)|$	0	$\frac{40}{\sqrt{3}}$	0
Conclusion		Maximum	

41. Find the maximum value of $|f^{(4)}(x)|$ on the closed interval [0, 1] for the following function.

$$f(x) = 15x^4 - \left(\frac{2x-1}{2}\right)^6$$

Solution:

$$f'(x) = 60x^3 - 6\left(\frac{2x-1}{2}\right)^5$$

$$f''(x) = 180x^2 - 30\left(\frac{2x-1}{2}\right)^4$$

$$f'''(x) = 360x - 120\left(\frac{2x-1}{2}\right)^3$$

$$f^{(4)}(x) = 360 - 360\left(\frac{2x-1}{2}\right)^2$$

$$f^{(5)}(x) = -720\left(\frac{2x-1}{2}\right)$$

Critical number of $f^{(4)}$: $x = \dfrac{1}{2}$

x-value	Endpoint $x = 0$	Critical $x = \frac{1}{2}$	Endpoint $x = 1$
$|f^{(4)}(x)|$	270	360	270
Conclusion		Maximum	

43. *Cost* A retailer has determined the cost C for ordering and storing x units of a product to be

$$C = 3x + \frac{20,000}{x}, \qquad 0 < x \le 200.$$

The delivery truck can bring at most 200 units per order. Find the order size that will minimize the cost.

Solution:

$$C = 3x + 20,000x^{-1}, 0 < x \le 200$$

$$C' = 3 - 20,000x^{-2}$$

$$= \frac{3x^2 - 20,000}{x^2}$$

Critical numbers: $x = \sqrt{\dfrac{20,000}{3}} \approx 81.65 \approx 82$ units.

$C(82) \approx 489.90$, which is the minimum by The First Derivative Test.

45. *Profit* When soft drinks sold for $0.80 per can at football games, approximately 6000 cans were sold. When the price was raised to $1.00 per can, the quantity demanded dropped to 5600. The initial cost is $5000 and the cost per unit is $0.40. Assuming that the demand function is linear, what price will yield a maximum profit?

Solution:

Demand: (6000, 0.80), (5600, 1.00)

$$m = \frac{1 - 0.8}{5600 - 6000} = \frac{0.2}{-400} = -0.0005$$

$$p - 1 = -0.0005(x - 5600)$$

$$p = -0.0005x + 3.80$$

$$\text{Cost} = C = 5000 + 0.40x$$

$$\text{Profit} = P = R - C = xp - C = x(-0.0005x + 3.80) - (5000 + 0.40x)$$

$$= -0.0005x^2 + 3.40x - 5000$$

$$P' = -0.001x + 3.40 = 0 \Rightarrow x = 3400$$

$$p(3400) = \$2.10 \text{ per can}$$

47. *Demographics* From 1940 to 1991, the number r of males to 100 females in the United States can be modeled by

$$r = 0.000045t^3 - 0.2295t + 100.84,$$

where $t = 0$ corresponds to 1940. Determine the year in which the number r was a minimum. In that year, were there more females or more males in the population? Explain.

Solution:

$$r = 0.000045t^3 - 0.2295t + 100.84$$

$$r' = 0.000135t^2 - 0.2295 = 0 \Rightarrow t \approx \pm 41.231$$

$$t = 41 \text{ corresponds to } 1981$$

There were approximately 95 males for every 100 females in 1981.

Section 3.3 Gravity and the Second-Derivative Test

1. Find the intervals on which $y = x^2 - x - 2$ is concave upward and those on which it is concave downward.

   Solution:

   $y' = 2x - 1$

   $y'' = 2$

   Concave upward on $(-\infty, \infty)$

   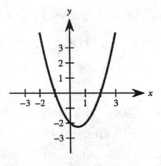

3. Find the intervals on which $f(x) = \dfrac{x^2 - 1}{2x + 1}$ is concave upward and those on which it is concave downward.

   Solution:

   $$f(x) = \frac{x^2 - 1}{2x + 1}$$

   $$f'(x) = \frac{(2x + 1)(2x) - (x^2 - 1)(2)}{(2x + 1)^2} = \frac{2x^2 + 2x + 2}{(2x + 1)^2}$$

   $$= (2x^2 + 2x + 2)(2x + 1)^{-2}$$

   $$f''(x) = (2x^2 + 2x + 2)[-2(2x + 1)^{-3}(2)] + (2x + 1)^{-2}(4x + 2)$$

   $$= -8(x^2 + x + 1)(2x + 1)^{-3} + 2(2x + 1)^{-2}(2x + 1)$$

   $$= 2(2x + 1)^{-3}[-4(x^2 + x + 1) + (2x + 1)(2x + 1)]$$

   $$= 2(2x + 1)^{-3}[-4x^2 - 4x - 4 + 4x^2 + 4x + 1] = \frac{-6}{(2x + 1)^3}$$

   $f''(x) \neq 0$ for any value of x.

   $x = -\frac{1}{2}$ is a discontinuity.

   Concave upward on $\left(-\infty, -\frac{1}{2}\right)$

   Concave downward on $\left(-\frac{1}{2}, \infty\right)$

   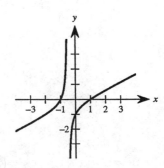

5. Find the intervals on which $f(x) = 24/(x^2 + 12)$ is concave upward and those on which it is concave downward.

Solution:

$$f(x) = 24(x^2 + 12)^{-1}$$

$$f'(x) = -24(2x)(x^2 + 12)^{-2}$$

$$f''(x) = -48[x(-2)(2x)(x^2 + 12)^{-3} + (x^2 + 12)^{-2}]$$

$$= \frac{-48(-4x^2 + x^2 + 12)}{(x^2 + 12)^3}$$

$$= \frac{144(x^2 - 4)}{(x^2 + 12)^3}$$

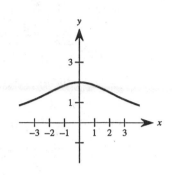

$f''(x) = 0$ when $x = \pm 2$.

Concave upward on $(-\infty, -2)$ and $(2, \infty)$

Concave downward on $(-2, 2)$

7. For $f(x) = 6x - x^2$, identify all relative extrema. Use the Second-Derivative Test if applicable.

Solution:

$$f'(x) = 6 - 2x = 0$$

Critical number: $x = 3$

$$f''(x) = -2$$

$$f''(3) = -2 < 0$$

Thus, $(3, 9)$ is a relative maximum.

9. For $f(x) = (x - 5)^2$, identify all relative extrema. Use the Second-Derivative Test if applicable.

Solution:

$$f'(x) = 2(x - 5) = 0$$

Critical number: $x = 5$

$$f''(x) = 2$$

$$f''(5) = 2 > 0$$

Thus, $(5, 0)$ is a relative minimum.

11. Find all relative extrema of the function $f(x) = x^3 - 5x^2 + 7x$. Use the Second-Derivative Test if applicable.

Solution:

$$f(x) = x^3 - 5x^2 + 7x$$

$$f'(x) = 3x^2 - 10x + 7 = (3x - 7)(x - 1)$$

Critical numbers: $x = 1$, $x = \frac{7}{3}$

$$f''(x) = 6x - 10$$

$$f''(1) = -4 < 0 \Rightarrow (1, 3) \text{ is a relative maximum.}$$

$$f''\left(\frac{7}{3}\right) = 4 > 0 \Rightarrow \left(\frac{7}{3}, 1.\overline{814}\right) \text{ is a relative minimum.}$$

13. For $f(x) = x^4 - 4x^3 + 2$, identify all relative extrema. Use the Second-Derivative Test if applicable.

Solution:

$$f'(x) = 4x^3 - 12x^2 = 4x^2(x - 3)$$

Critical numbers: $x = 0$, $x = 3$

$$f''(x) = 12x^2 - 24x$$

$$f''(0) = 0 \quad \text{(Test fails)}$$

$$f''(3) = 36 > 0$$

Thus, $(3, -25)$ is a relative minimum. [Note: By the First-Derivative Test, $(0, 2)$ is not a relative extrema. In fact, it is an inflection point.]

15. For $f(x) = x^{2/3} - 3$, identify all relative extrema. Use the Second-Derivative Test if applicable.

Solution:

$$f'(x) = \frac{2}{3}x^{-1/3} = \frac{2}{3\sqrt[3]{x}}$$

Critical number: $x = 0$

The Second-Derivative Test does not apply, so we use the First-Derivative Test to conclude that $(0, -3)$ is a relative minimum.

17. For $f(x) = x + (4/x)$, identify all relative extrema. Use the Second-Derivative Test if applicable.

Solution:

$$f'(x) = 1 - \frac{4}{x^2} = \frac{x^2 - 4}{x^2}$$

Critical numbers: $x = \pm 2$

$$f''(x) = \frac{8}{x^3}$$

$$f''(2) = 1 > 0$$

$$f''(-2) = -1 < 0$$

Thus, $(2, 4)$ is a relative minimum and $(-2, -4)$ is a relative maximum.

19. State the sign of $f'(x)$ and $f''(x)$ in the interval $(0, 2)$. (See the graph in the textbook.)

Solution:

$f' > 0$ (increasing)

$f'' > 0$ (concave upward).

21. State the sign of $f'(x)$ and $f''(x)$ in the interval $(0, 2)$. (See the graph in the textbook.)

Solution:

$f' < 0$ (decreasing)

$f'' < 0$ (concave downward).

23. Find any points of inflection for the function $f(x) = x^3 - 9x^2 + 24x - 18$.

Solution:

$$f(x) = x^3 - 9x^2 + 24x - 18$$

$$f'(x) = 3x^2 - 18x + 24$$

$$f''(x) = 6x - 18 = 0 \Rightarrow x = 3$$

Intervals	$(-\infty, 3)$	$(3, \infty)$
Sign of f''	$-$	$+$
Conclusion	Concave downward	Concave upward

Inflection point: $(3, 0)$

25. Find any inflection points for the function $f(x) = (x-1)^3(x-5)$.

Solution:

$$f(x) = (x-1)^3(x-5)$$
$$f'(x) = (x-1)^3(1) + (x-5)(3)(x-1)^2(1)$$
$$= (x-1)^2[(x-1)+3(x-5)] = (x-1)^2(4x-16) = 4(x-1)^2(x-4)$$
$$f''(x) = 4(x-1)^2(1) + (x-4)8(x-1)(1)$$
$$= 4(x-1)[(x-1)+2(x-4)]$$
$$= 4(x-1)(3x-9)$$
$$= 12(x-1)(x-3) = 0 \Rightarrow$$
$$x = 1 \text{ or } x = 3$$

Intervals	$(-\infty,\ 1)$	$(1,\ 3)$	$(3,\ \infty)$
Sign of f''	+	−	+
Conclusion	Concave upward	Concave downward	Concave upward

Inflection points: $(1,\ 0)$, $(3,\ -16)$

27. Find the points of inflection of the graph of $g(x) = 2x^4 - 8x^3 + 12x^2 + 12x$

Solution:

$$g(x) = 2x^4 - 8x^3 + 12x^2 + 12x$$
$$g'(x) = 8x^3 - 24x^2 + 24x + 12$$
$$g'' = 24x^2 - 48x + 24 = 24(x-1)^2$$
$$g'' < 0 \text{ on } (-\infty, 1) \text{ and } (1, \infty) \Rightarrow \text{ no inflection points}$$

29. Find the points of inflection of the graph of $h(x) = (x-2)^3(x-1)$

Solution:

$$h(x) = (x-2)^3(x-1)$$
$$h'(x) = (4x-5)(x-2)^2$$
$$h''(x) = 6(2x-3)(x-2)$$

Inflection points: $\left(\dfrac{3}{2}, \dfrac{-1}{16}\right)$, $(2, 0)$

31. Sketch the graph of $f(x) = x^3 - 12x$ and identify all relative extrema and points of inflection.

Solution:

$$f'(x) = 3x^2 - 12 = 3(x^2 - 4)$$

Critical numbers: $x = \pm 2$

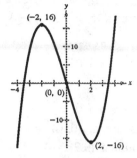

$$f''(x) = 6x$$

$$f''(2) = 12 > 0$$

$$f''(-2) = -12 < 0$$

Relative maximum: $(-2, \; 16)$

Relative minimum: $(2, \; -16)$

$$f''(x) = 0 \text{ when } x = 0$$

$$f''(x) < 0 \text{ on } (-\infty, \; 0)$$

$$f''(x) > 0 \text{ on } (0, \; \infty)$$

Inflection point: $(0, 0)$

33. Sketch the graph of $f(x) = x^3 - 6x^2 + 12x$ and identify all relative extrema and points of inflection.

Solution:

$$f'(x) = 3x^2 - 12x + 12 = 3(x - 2)^2$$

Critical number: $x = 2$

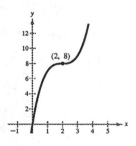

$$f''(x) = 6(x - 2)$$

$$f''(x) = 0 \text{ when } x = 2$$

Since $f'(x) > 0$ when $x \neq 2$ and the concavity changes at $x = 2$, $(2, \; 8)$ is an inflection point. No relative extrema.

35. Sketch the graph of $f(x) = \frac{1}{4}x^4 - 2x^2$ and identify all relative extrema and points of inflection.

Solution:

$$f'(x) = x^3 - 4x = x(x+2)(x-2)$$

Critical numbers: $x = \pm 2, \; x = 0$

$$f''(x) = 3x^2 - 4$$
$$f''(-2) = 8 > 0$$
$$f''(0) = -4 < 0$$
$$f''(2) = 8 > 0$$

Relative maximum: $(0, 0)$

Relative minima: $(\pm 2, \; -4)$

$$f''(x) = 3x^2 - 4 = 0 \text{ when } x = \pm\frac{2\sqrt{3}}{3}$$

$$f''(x) > 0 \text{ on } \left(-\infty, \; -\frac{2\sqrt{3}}{3}\right)$$

$$f''(x) < 0 \text{ on } \left(-\frac{2\sqrt{3}}{3}, \; \frac{2\sqrt{3}}{3}\right)$$

$$f''(x) > 0 \text{ on } \left(\frac{2\sqrt{3}}{3}, \; \infty\right)$$

Inflection points:

$$\left(-\frac{2\sqrt{3}}{3}, \; -\frac{20}{9}\right), \; \left(\frac{2\sqrt{3}}{3}, \; -\frac{20}{9}\right)$$

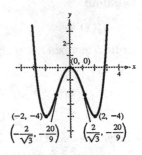

37. Sketch the graph of the function $g(x) = (x - 2)(x + 1)^2$ and identify all relative extrema and points of inflection.

Solution:

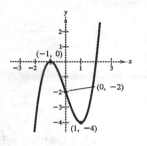

$$g(x) = (x - 2)(x + 1)^2 = x^3 - 3x - 2$$

$$g'(x) = 3x^2 - 3 = 3(x - 1)(x + 1)$$

Critical; numbers: $x = \pm 1$

$$f''(x) = 6x$$

$$f''(-1) = -6 < 0$$

$$f''(1) = 6 > 0$$

Relative Maximum: $(-1, 0)$

Relative Minimum: $(1, -4)$

$$f''(x) = 6x = 0 \text{ when } x = 0$$

$$f''(x) < 0 \text{ on } (-\infty, 0)$$

$$f''(x) > 0 \text{ on } (0, \infty)$$

Inflection point: $(0, 2)$

39. Sketch the graph of $g(x) = x\sqrt{x + 3}$ and identify all relative extrema and points of inflection.

Solution:

The domain of g is $[-3, \infty)$.

$$g'(x) = x\left[\frac{1}{2}(x + 3)^{-1/2}\right] + \sqrt{x + 3} = \frac{3x + 6}{2\sqrt{x + 3}}$$

Critical numbers: $x = -3, \quad x = -2$

By the First-Derivative Test, $(-2, -2)$ is a relative minimum.

$$g''(x) = \frac{(2\sqrt{x + 3})(3) - (3x + 6)(1/\sqrt{x + 3})}{4(x + 3)}$$

$$= \frac{3(x + 4)}{4(x + 3)^{3/2}}$$

$x = -4$ is not in the domain of g.

On $[-3, \infty)$, $g''(x) > 0$ and is concave upward.

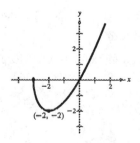

41. Sketch the graph of $f(x) = 4/(1 + x^2)$ and identify all relative extrema and points of inflection.

Solution:

$$f'(x) = \frac{-8x}{(1 + x^2)^2}$$

Critical number: $x = 0$

$$f''(x) = \frac{-8(1 - 3x^2)}{(1 + x^2)^3}$$

$$f''(0) = -8 < 0$$

Thus, $(0, 4)$ is a relative maximum.

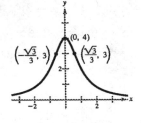

$$f''(x) = 0 \text{ when } 1 - 3x^2 = 0, \quad x = \pm\frac{\sqrt{3}}{3}$$

$$f''(x) > 0 \text{ on } \left(-\infty, \ -\frac{\sqrt{3}}{3}\right)$$

$$f''(x) < 0 \text{ on } \left(-\frac{\sqrt{3}}{3}, \ \frac{\sqrt{3}}{3}\right)$$

$$f''(x) > 0 \text{ on } \left(\frac{\sqrt{3}}{3}, \ \infty\right)$$

Inflection points: $\left(\frac{\sqrt{3}}{3}, \ 3\right), \ \left(-\frac{\sqrt{3}}{3}, \ 3\right)$

43. Sketch a graph of function f having the given characteristics.

Function	First Derivative	Second Derivative
$f(2) = 0$	$f'(x) < 0, \quad x < 3$	$f''(x) > 0$
$f(4) = 0$	$f'(3) = 0$	
	$f'(x) > 0, \quad x > 3$	

Solution:

The function has x-intercepts at $(2, 0)$ and $(4, 0)$. On $(-\infty, 3)$, f is decreasing and on $(3, \infty)$, f is increasing. A relative minimum occurs when $x = 3$. The graph of f is concave upward.

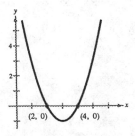

45. Use the graph to sketch the graph of f'. Find the intervals (if any) on which (a) $f'(x)$ is positive, (b) $f'(x)$ is negative, (c) f' is increasing, and (d) f' is decreasing. For each of these intervals describe the corresponding behavior of f.

Solution:

(a) $f'(x) > 0$ on $(-\infty, \ 0)$ where f is increasing.

(b) $f'(x) < 0$ on $(0, \ \infty)$ where f is decreasing.

(c) f' is not increasing. f is not concave upward.

(d) f' is decreasing on $(-\infty, \ \infty)$ where f is concave downward.

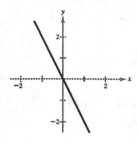

47. *Point of Diminishing Returns* Identify the point of diminishing returns for

$$R = \frac{1}{50,000}(600x^2 - x^3), \quad 0 \le x \le 400$$

where R is revenue and x is the amount spent on advertising. Assume that R and x are measured in thousands of dollars.

Solution:

$$R' = \frac{1}{50,000}(1200x - 3x^2)$$

$$R'' = \frac{1}{50,000}(1200 - 6x) = 0 \text{ when } x = 200$$

$$R'' > 0 \text{ on } (0, \ 200)$$

$$R'' < 0 \text{ on } (200, \ 400)$$

Since (200, 320) is a point of inflection, it is the point of diminishing returns.

49. *Point of Diminishing Returns*   Identify the point of diminishing returns for

$$R = -\tfrac{4}{9}(x^3 - 9x^2 - 27), \quad 0 \le x < 5$$

where R is revenue and x is the amount spent on advertising. Assume that R and x are measured in thousands of dollars.

Solution:

$$R' = -\tfrac{4}{9}(3x^2 - 18x)$$

$$R'' = -\tfrac{4}{9}(6x - 18) = 0 \text{ when } x = 3$$

$$R'' > 0 \text{ on } (0, \ 3)$$

$$R'' < 0 \text{ on } (3, \ 5)$$

Since $(3, 36)$ is a point of inflection, it is the point of diminishing returns.

51. *Average Cost*   When $C = 0.5x^2 + 15x + 5000$ is the total cost function for producing x units, determine the production level that minimizes the average cost per unit. (The average cost per unit is given by $\overline{C} = C/x$.)

Solution:

$$C = 0.5x^2 + 15x + 5000$$

$$\overline{C} = 0.5x + 15 + \frac{5000}{x}$$

$$\overline{C}' = 0.5 - \frac{5000}{x^2}$$

Critical numbers: $x = \pm 100$

$$x = 100 \text{ units}$$

53. *Average Cost*   When $C = 0.002x^3 + 20x + 500$ is the total cost function for producing x units, determine the production level that minimizes the average cost per unit. (The average cost per unit is given by $\overline{C} = C/x$.)

Solution:

$$C = 0.002x^3 + 20x + 500$$

$$\overline{C} = 0.002x^2 + 20 + \frac{500}{x}$$

$$\overline{C}' = 0.004x - \frac{500}{x^2} = 0$$

$$x^3 = \frac{500}{0.004}$$

$$x = 50 \text{ units}$$

55. *Productivity* Consider a college student who works from 7 P.M. to 11 P.M. assembling mechanical components. The cumulative number N of components assembled after working t hours is determined by the given function. At what time is the student assembling components at the greatest rate? (Find the point of diminishing returns.)

$$N(t) = -0.12t^3 + 0.54t^2 + 8.22t, \, 0 \le t \le 4$$

We need to determine when $N'(t)$ is greatest.

Solution:

$$N(t) = -0.12t^3 + 0.54t^2 + 8.22t, \quad 0 \le t \le 4$$

$$N'(t) = -0.36t^2 + 1.08t + 8.22$$

$$N''(t) = -0.72t + 1.08 = 0$$

$$t = \frac{1.08}{0.72} = 1.5 \text{ hours}$$

Thus, the time is 8:30 P.M.

57. *Sales Growth* Find the time t in years when the sales x of a new product is increasing at the greatest rate.

$$x = \frac{10,000t^2}{9 + t^2}$$

Solution:

$$x = 10,000 \left[\frac{t^2}{9 + t^2} \right]$$

$$x = 10,000 \left[\frac{(9 + t^2)(2t) - (t^2)(2t)}{(9 + t^2)^2} \right] = 10,000 \left[\frac{18t}{(9 + t^2)^2} \right] = 180,000 \left[\frac{t}{(9 + t^2)^2} \right]$$

$$x = 180,000 \left[\frac{(9 + t^2)^2(1) - t(2)(9 + t^2)(2t)}{(9 + t^2)^4} \right] = 180,000 \left[\frac{9 - 3t^2}{(9 + t^2)^3} \right] = 0$$

$$9 = 3t^2 \Rightarrow t = \sqrt{3} \approx 1.732 \text{ years}$$

59. *Sales* A company introduces a new product line and the sales increase over time as shown in the figure in the textbook. Visually locate the point of inflection on the graph and state its significance to the rate of growth of sales.

Solution:

Point of inflection: $(4, 5000)$

The sales of the new product are increasing at the greatest rate when $t = 4$.

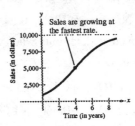

61. Use a graphing utility to graph f, f', and f'' on the same viewing rectangle. Graphically locate the relative extrema and points of inflection of the graph.

$$f(x) = \frac{2x}{x^2 - x + 1}, [-2, 2]$$

Solution:

$$f(x) = \frac{2x}{x^2 - x + 1}$$

$$f'(x) = \frac{(x^2 - x + 1)(2) - 2x(2x - 1)}{(x^2 - x + 1)^2} = \frac{2(1 - x^2)}{(x^2 - x + 1)^2}$$

$$f''(x) = \frac{(x^2 - x + 1)^2(-4x) - 2(1 - x^2)2(x^2 - x + 1)(2x - 1)}{(x^2 - x + 1)^4} = \frac{4(x^3 - 3x + 1)}{(x^2 - x + 1)^3}$$

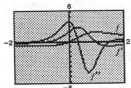

Relative extrema:

$f'(x) = 0$ when $x = \pm 1$

$f''(1) < 0 \Rightarrow (1, 2)$ is a relative maximum.

$f''(-1) > 0 \Rightarrow \left(-1, -\frac{2}{3}\right)$ is a relative minimum.

Points of inflection:

$f''(x) = 0$ when $x^3 - 3x + 1 = 0$

$x \approx -1.88, 0.35, 1.53$

Points of inflection:

$(-1.88, -0.59), (0.35, 0.90), (1.53, 1.69)$

63. Use a graphing utility to graph f, f', and f'' on the same viewing rectangle. Graphically locate the relative extrema and points of inflection of the graph.

$f(x) = \frac{1}{2}x^3 - x^2 + 3x - 5$, $[0, 3]$

Solution:

$$f(x) = \frac{1}{2}x^3 - x^2 + 3x - 5, \ [0, 3]$$

$$f'(x) = \frac{3}{2}x^2 - 2x + 3$$

$$f''(x) = 3x - 2$$

Minimum: $(0, -5)$

Maximum: $(3, 8.5)$

Point of inflection: $\left(\frac{2}{3}, -3.2963\right)$

65. *Millionaires* The number N (in thousands) of millionaires having a net worth of x dollars (in millions) in 1986 can be modeled by

$$N = -\frac{4211.02}{x^2} + \frac{5897.24}{x^{3/2}} - 135.91.$$

Use a graphing utility to graph the function.

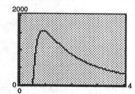

Solution:

$$N = -\frac{4211.02}{x^2} + \frac{5897.24}{x^{3/2}} - 135.91$$

Section 3.4   Optimization Problems

1. Find two positive numbers whose sum is 110 and the product is a maximum.

Solution:

Let x be the first number and y be the second number. Then $x + y = 110$ and $y = 110 - x$. Thus, the product of x and y is given by the following.

$$P = xy = x(110 - x)$$

$$P' = 110 - 2x$$

$P' = 0$ when $x = 55$. Since $P''(55) = -2 < 0$, the product is a maximum when $x = 55$ and $y = 110 - 55 = 55$.

3. Find two positive numbers for which the sum of the first and twice the second is 36 and the product is a maximum.

Solution:

Let x be the first number and y be the second number. Then $x + 2y = 36$ and $x = 36 - 2y$. The product of x and y is given by the following.

$$P = xy = (36 - 2y)y$$
$$P' = 36 - 4y$$

$P' = 0$ when $y = 9$. Since $P''(9) = -4 < 0$, the product is a maximum when $y = 9$ and $x = 36 - 2(9) = 18$.

5. Find two positive numbers whose product is 192 and the sum is a minimum.

Solution:

Let x be the first number and y be the second number. Then $xy = 192$ and $y = 192/x$. The sum of x and y is given by the following.

$$S = x + y = x + \frac{192}{x}$$
$$S' = 1 - \frac{192}{x^2}$$

$S' = 0$ when $x = \sqrt{192}$. Since $S''(x) > 0$ when $x > 0$, S is minimum when $x = \sqrt{192} = 8\sqrt{3}$ and $y = 192/\sqrt{192} = \sqrt{192} = 8\sqrt{3}$.

7. What positive number x minimizes the sum of x and its reciprocal?

Solution:

$$S = x + \frac{1}{x}, \quad x > 0$$
$$S' = 1 - \frac{1}{x^2} = \frac{x^2 - 1}{x^2}$$

Critical number: $x = 1$

$$S'' = \frac{2}{x^3}$$

Since $S''(1) = 2 > 0$, $(1, 2)$ is a relative minimum and the sum is a minimum when $x = 1$.

9. Verify that each of the rectangular solids shown in the figure in the textbook has a surface area of 150 square inches. Find the volume of each.

Solution:

(a) $A = 4(11)(3) + 2(3)(3) = 150$ square inches

   $V = 11(3)(3) = 99$ cubic inches

(b) $A = 6(5)(5) = 150$ square inches

   $V = (5)(5)(5) = 125$ cubic inches

(c) $A = 4(6)(3.25) + 2(6)(6) = 150$ square inches

   $V = 6(6)(3.25) = 117$ cubic inches

11. Find the length and width of a rectangle of maximum area with a perimeter of 100 feet.

Solution:

Let x be the length and y be the width of the rectangle. Then $2x + 2y = 100$ and $y = 50 - x$. The area is given by the following.

$$A = xy = x(50 - x)$$
$$A' = 50 - 2x$$

$A' = 0$ when $x = 25$. Since $A''(25) = -2 < 0$, A is maximum when $x = 25$ feet and $y = 50 - 25 = 25$ feet.

13. *Area* A rancher has 200 feet of fencing to enclose two adjacent rectangular corrals, as shown in the figure. What dimensions should be used so that the enclosed area will be a maximum?

Solution:

Let x and y be the lengths shown in the figure. Then $4x + 3y = 200$ and $y = (200 - 4x)/3$. The area of the corrals is given by

$$A = 2xy = 2x\left(\frac{200 - 4x}{3}\right) = \frac{8}{3}(50x - x^2)$$

$$A' = \frac{8}{3}(50 - 2x)$$

$A' = 0$ when $x = 25$. Since $A'' = -\frac{16}{3} < 0$, A is maximum when $x = 25$ feet and $y = \frac{100}{3}$ feet.

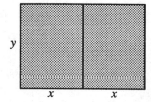

15. *Volume*   An open box is to be made from a square piece of material, 6 inches on a side, by cutting equal squares from each corner and turning up the sides, as shown in the figure. Find the volume of the largest box that can be made in this manner.

Solution:

Let x be the length shown in the figure. Then the volume of the box is given by the following.

$$V = x(6 - 2x)^2, \quad 0 < x < 3$$
$$V' = 12(x - 1)(x - 3)$$

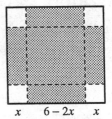

$V' = 0$ when $x = 3$ and $x = 1$. Since $V = 0$ when $x = 3$ and $V = 16$ when $x = 1$, we conclude that the volume is maximum when $x = 1$. The corresponding volume is $V = 16$ cubic inches.

$$x \qquad 6 - 2x \qquad x$$

17. *Surface Area*   A net enclosure for golf practice is open at one end (see figure). The volume of the enclosure is $83\frac{1}{3}$ cubic meters. Find the dimensions that require the least amount of netting.

Solution:

Let x and y be the lengths shown in the figure. Then $x^2 y = \dfrac{250}{3}$ and $y = \dfrac{250}{3x^2}$. The surface area of the enclosure is given by the following.

$$A = 3xy + x^2 = 3x\left(\frac{250}{3x^2}\right) + x^2 = \frac{250}{x} + x^2$$
$$A' = -\frac{250}{x^2} + 2x = \frac{2x^3 - 250}{x^2}$$
$$A' = 0 \text{ when } x = 5$$

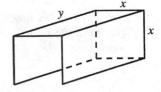

The surface area is minimum when $x = 5$ meters and

$$y = \frac{250}{3(5)^2} = \frac{10}{3} \text{ meters.}$$

19. *Area* An indoor physical fitness room consists of a rectangular region with a semicircle on each end. The perimeter of the room is to be a 200-meter running track. Find the dimensions that will make the area of the rectangular region as large as possible.

Solution:

Let x and y be the length and width of the rectangle. The radius of the semicircle is $r = y/2$, and the perimeter is

$$200 = 2x + 2\pi r = 2x + 2\pi \left(\frac{y}{2}\right) = 2x + \pi y$$

which implies that $y = (200-2x)/\pi$. The area of the rectangle is given by the following.

$$A = xy = x \left[\frac{200 - 2x}{\pi}\right] = \frac{2}{\pi}(100x - x^2)$$

$$A' = \frac{2}{\pi}(100 - 2x)$$

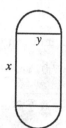

$A' = 0$ when $x = 50$. Thus, A is maximum when

$x = 50$ meters and $y = \dfrac{200 - 2(50)}{\pi} = \dfrac{100}{\pi}$ meters.

21. *Area* A rectangle is bounded by the x- and y-axes and the graph of $y = (6 - x)/2$, as shown in the figure. What length and width should the rectangle have so that its area is a maximum?

Solution:

The area of the rectangle is

$$A = xy = x\left(\frac{6 - x}{2}\right) = \frac{1}{2}(6x - x^2)$$

$$A' = \frac{1}{2}(6 - 2x).$$

$A' = 0$ when $x = 3$. Thus, A is maximum when $x = 3$ and

$$y = \frac{6 - 3}{2} = \frac{3}{2}.$$

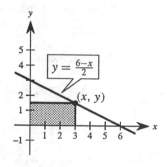

23. *Area* A rectangle is bounded by the x-axis and the semicircle $y = \sqrt{25 - x^2}$, as shown in the figure. What length and width should the rectangle have so that its area is a maximum?

Solution:

The area is given by the following.

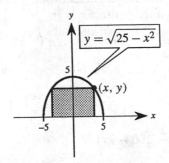

$$A = 2xy = 2x\sqrt{25 - x^2}$$

$$A' = 2\left(\frac{25 - 2x^2}{\sqrt{25 - x^2}}\right)$$

$A' = 0$ when $x = \dfrac{5}{\sqrt{2}}$.

Thus, A is maximum when the length is

$$2x = \frac{10}{\sqrt{2}} \approx 7.07 \text{ and the width is}$$

$$y = \sqrt{25 - (5/\sqrt{2})^2} = \frac{5}{\sqrt{2}} \approx 3.54.$$

25. *Volume* A right circular cylinder is to be designed to hold 12 fluid ounces of a soft drink and to use a minimal amount of material in its construction. Find the dimensions for the container (1 fluid ounce ≈ 1.80469 in^3).

Solution:

The volume of the cylinder is

$$V = \pi r^2 h = 12(1.80469) \approx 21.66$$

which implies that $h = 21.66/\pi r^2$. The surface area of the cylinder is

$$S = 2\pi r^2 + 2\pi rh = 2\pi r^2 + 2\pi r\left(\frac{21.66}{\pi r^2}\right) = 2\left(\pi r^2 + \frac{21.66}{r}\right)$$

$$S' = 2\left(2\pi r - \frac{21.66}{r^2}\right).$$

$S' = 0$ when $2\pi r^3 - 21.66 = 0$, which implies that

$$r = \sqrt[3]{21.66/2\pi} \approx 1.51 \text{ inches}$$

$$h = \frac{21.66}{\pi(1.51)^2} \approx 3.02 \text{ inches.}$$

(Note that in the solution, $h = 2r$.)

27. *Closest Point* Find the point on the graph of $y = x^2 + 1$ that is closest to the point $(0, 4)$.

Solution:

The distance between a point (x, y) on the graph and the point $(0, 4)$ is
$$d = \sqrt{(x - 0)^2 + (y - 4)^2} = \sqrt{x^2 + (x^2 + 1 - 4)^2} = \sqrt{x^2 + (x^2 - 3)^2}$$
We can minimize d by minimizing its square $L = d^2$.
$$L = x^2 + (x^2 - 3)^2 = x^4 - 5x^2 + 9$$
$$L' = 4x^3 - 10x = 2x(2x^2 - 5) \Rightarrow x = 0, \pm\sqrt{\tfrac{5}{2}}$$
Hence, the points are $\left(\pm\sqrt{\tfrac{5}{2}}, \tfrac{7}{2}\right)$

29. *Volume* A rectangular package to be sent by a postal service can have a maximum combined length and girth (perimeter of a cross section) of 108 inches, as shown in the figure. Find the dimensions of the package of maximum volume that can be sent. (Assume that the cross section is square.)

Solution:

The length and girth is $4x + y = 108$. Thus, $y = 108 - 4x$. The volume is
$$V = x^2 y = x^2(108 - 4x) = 108x^2 - 4x^3$$
$$V' = 216x - 12x^2 = 12x(18 - x).$$

$V' = 0$ when $x = 0$ and $x = 18$.

Thus, the maximum volume occurs when $x = 18$ inches and $y = 36$ inches. The dimensions are 18 inches by 18 inches by 36 inches.

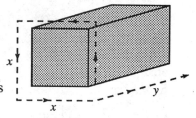

31. *Area* The combined perimeter of a circle and a square is 16. Find the dimensions of the circle and square that produce a minimum total area.

Solution:

Let x be the length of a side of the square and r the radius of the circle. Then the combined perimeter is $4x + 2\pi r = 16$, which implies that

$$x = \frac{16 - 2\pi r}{4} = 4 - \frac{\pi r}{2}.$$

The combined area of the circle and square is

$$A = x^2 + \pi r^2 = \left(4 - \frac{\pi r}{2}\right)^2 + \pi r^2$$

$$A' = 2\left(4 - \frac{\pi r}{2}\right)\left(-\frac{\pi}{2}\right) + 2\pi r = \frac{1}{2}(\pi^2 r + 4\pi r - 8\pi).$$

$A' = 0$ when $r = \dfrac{8\pi}{\pi^2 + 4\pi} = \dfrac{8}{\pi + 4}$ and the corresponding x-value is

$$x = 4 - \frac{\pi[8/(\pi + 4)]}{2} = \frac{16}{\pi + 4}.$$

This is a minimum by the second derivative test $(A'' = \frac{1}{2}(\pi^2 + 4\pi) > 0)$.

33. *Time* You are in a boat 2 miles from the nearest point on the coast. You are is to go to a point Q, 3 miles down the coast and 1 mile inland, as shown in the figure. If you can row at 2 mi/hr and walk at 4 mi/hr, toward what point on the coast should you row in order to reach point Q in the least time?

Solution:

Using the formula Distance = (Rate)(Time), we have $T = D/R$.

$$T = T_{\text{rowed}} + T_{\text{walked}} = \frac{D_{\text{rowed}}}{R_{\text{rowed}}} + \frac{D_{\text{walked}}}{R_{\text{walked}}} = \frac{\sqrt{x^2 + 4}}{2} + \frac{\sqrt{1 + (3 - x)^2}}{4}$$

$$T' = \frac{x}{2\sqrt{x^2 + 4}} - \frac{3 - x}{4\sqrt{1 + (3 - x)^2}}$$

By setting $T' = 0$, we have the following.

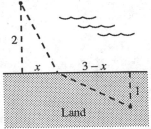

$$\frac{x^2}{4(x^2 + 4)} = \frac{(3 - x)^2}{16[1 + (3 - x)^2]}$$

$$\frac{x^2}{x^2 + 4} = \frac{9 - 6x + x^2}{4(10 - 6x + x^2)}$$

$$4(x^4 - 6x^3 + 10x^2) = (x^2 + 4)(9 - 6x + x^2)$$

$$x^4 - 6x^3 + 9x^2 + 8x - 12 = 0$$

Using a graphing utility, the solution on $[0, 3]$ is $x = 1$ mile on equivalent: possible rational roots: $\pm 1, \pm 2, \pm 3, \pm 4, \pm 6, \pm 12$. By testing, we find that $x = 1$ mile.

35. *Strength of a Beam* A wooden beam has a rectangular cross section of height h and width w, as shown in the figure. The strength S of the beam is directly proportional to the width and the square of the height. What are the dimensions of the strongest beam that can be cut from a round log of diameter 24 inches? (Hint: $S = kh^2w$, where k is the proportionality constant.)

Solution:

Since $h^2 + w^2 = 24^2$, we have $h^2 = 24^2 - w^2$.

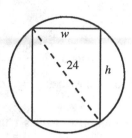

$$S = kh^2w = k(24^2 - w^2)w = k(576w - w^3) \quad S' =$$

$$S' = k(576 - 3w^2)$$

0 when $w = \sqrt{192} = 8\sqrt{3}$.

Thus, S is maximum when $h^2 = 24^2 - 192 = 384 \Rightarrow h = \sqrt{384} = 8\sqrt{6}$.

The dimensions are:

$$w = 8\sqrt{3} \approx 13.856 \text{ inches}$$
$$h = 8\sqrt{6} \approx 19.596 \text{ inches}.$$

37. *Area* Use a graphing utility to graph the primary equation and its first derivative to find the dimensions of the rectangle of maximum area that can be inscribed in a semicircle of radius 10.

Solution:

The area is given by $A = l \cdot w = 2x\sqrt{100 - x^2}$.

From Exercise 24, we have $A' = \dfrac{2(100 - 2x^2)}{\sqrt{100 - x^2}}$.

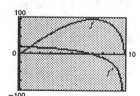

Length: $l = 10\sqrt{2}$

Width: $w = 5\sqrt{2}$

Section 3.5   Business and Economics Applications

1. Find the number of units x that produces a maximum revenue R if $R = 800x - 0.2x^2$.

   Solution:

$$R = 800x - 0.2x^2$$

$$R' = 800 - 0.4x$$

$$R' = 0 \text{ when } x = \frac{800}{0.4} = 2000$$

R is maximum when $x = 2000$.

3. Find the number of units x that produce a maximum revenue R if $R = 400x - x^2$.

   Solution:

$$R = 400x - x^2$$

$$R' = 400 - 2x = 0 \text{ when } x = 200.$$

Thus, R is maximum when $x = 200$ units.

5. For $C = 1.25x^2 + 25x + 8000$, find the number of units x that produces the minimum average cost per unit $\overline{C}$.

   Solution:

$$\overline{C} = 1.25x + 255 + \frac{8000}{x}$$

$$\overline{C}' = 1.25 - \frac{8000}{x^2}$$

$$\overline{C}' = 0 \text{ when } \quad 1.25x^2 = 8000$$

$$x^2 = 6400$$

$$x = 80 \text{ units}$$

7. For $C = 3000x - x^2\sqrt{300 - x}$, find the number of units x that produces the minimum average cost per unit $\overline{C}$.

   Solution:

$$\overline{C} = 3000 - x\sqrt{300 - x}$$

$$\overline{C}' = -x\left[\frac{1}{2}(300 - x)^{-1/2}(-1)\right] - \sqrt{300 - x} = \frac{x}{2\sqrt{300 - x}} - \sqrt{300 - x}$$

$\overline{C}' = 0$ when $2(300 - x) = x$, which implies that $600 = 3x$ and $x = 200$ units.

9. When the cost function is $C = 100 + 30x$ and the demand function is $p = 90 - x$, find the price per unit p that produces the maximum profit P.

Solution:

$$P = xp - C = (90x - x^2) - (100 + 30x) = -x^2 + 60x - 100$$
$$P' = -2x + 60$$

$P' = 0$ when $x = 30$. Thus, the maximum profit occurs at $x = 30$ units and $p = 90 - 30 = \$60$.

11. When the cost function is $C = 8000 + 50x + 0.03x^2$ and the demand function is $p = 70 - 0.001x$, find the price per unit p that produces the maximum profit P.

Solution:

$$P = xp - C = x(70 - 0.001x) - (8000 + 50x + 0.03x^2)$$
$$= -0.031x^2 + 20x - 8000$$
$$P' = -0.062x + 20$$
$$P' = 0 \text{ when } x \approx 322.58 \text{ and } p \approx \$69.68.$$

13. *Average Cost* For the cost function $C = 2x^2 + 5x + 18$, find the value of x for which the average cost is minimum. For this value of x, show that the marginal cost and average cost are equal.

Solution:

$$\overline{C} = 2x + 5 + \frac{18}{x}$$
$$\overline{C}' = 2 - \frac{18}{x^2}$$

$\overline{C}' = 0$ when $x = 3$. Thus, the average cost is minimum when $x = 3$ units and $\overline{C}(3) = \$17$ per unit.

$$C' = \text{Marginal cost} = 4x + 5$$
$$C'(3) = 17 = \overline{C}(3)$$

Applications of the Derivative

15. *Profit* A given commodity has a demand function given by $p = 100 - \frac{1}{2}x^2$ and a total cost function given by $C = 40x + 37.5$.

(a) What price gives the maximum profit?

(b) What is the average cost per unit if production is set to give maximum profit?

Solution:

(a) $P = xp - C = x\left(100 - \frac{1}{2}x^2\right) - (40x + 37.5) = -\frac{1}{2}x^3 + 60x - 37.5$

$P' = -\frac{3}{2}x^2 + 60$

$P' = 0$ when $x = \sqrt{40} = 2\sqrt{10} \approx 6.32$ units. The price is $p = 100 - \frac{1}{2}(40) = \$80$.

(b) $\overline{C} = 40 + (37.5/x)$. When $x = 2\sqrt{10}$, the average price is

$\overline{C}(2\sqrt{10}) = 40 + \dfrac{37.5}{2\sqrt{10}} \approx \$45.93$.

17. *Profit* For $P = -2s^3 + 35s^2 - 100s + 200$, find the amount of advertising s (in 1000s of dollars) that yields the maximum profit P (in 1000s of dollars) and find the point of diminishing returns.

Solution:

$$P' = -6s^2 + 70s - 100 = -2(3s^2 - 35s + 50) = -2(3s - 5)(s - 10)$$

Critical numbers: $s = \frac{5}{3}$ and $s = 10$

$$P'' = -12s + 70$$

$$P''\left(\tfrac{5}{3}\right) = 50 > 0 \Rightarrow \text{Minimum}$$

$$P''(10) = -50 < 0 \Rightarrow \text{Maximum}$$

$P'' = -12s + 70 = 0$ when $s = \frac{35}{6}$. The maximum profit occurs when $s = 10$ (or $\$10,000$) and the point of diminishing returns occurs at $s = \frac{35}{6}$ (or $\$5,833.33$).

19. *Profit* A manufacturer of radios charges $90 per unit when the average production cost per unit is $60. However, to encourage large orders from distributors, the manufacturer will reduce the charge by $0.10 per unit for each unit ordered in excess of 100 (for example, there would be a charge of $89.90 per radio for an order size of 101). Find the largest order the manufacturer should allow so as to realize maximum profit.

Solution:

Let x = number of units purchased, p = price per unit, and P = profit.

$$p = 90 - (0.10)(x - 100) = 100 - 0.10x, \; x \geq 100$$
$$P = xp - C$$
$$= x(100 - 0.10x) - 60x$$
$$= 40x - 0.10x^2$$
$$P' = 40 - 0.20x$$

$P' = 0$ when $x = 200$ radios.

21. *Revenue* When a wholesaler sold a certain product at $40 per unit, sales were 300 units each week. After a price increase of $5, however, the average number of units sold dropped to 275 each week. Assuming that the demand function is linear, what price per unit will yield a maximum total revenue?

Solution:

$(40,300), (45,275)$
$$\text{slope} = \frac{275 - 300}{45 - 40} = -5$$
$$x - 300 = -5(p - 40)$$
$$x = -5p + 500$$
$$R = xp = (-5p + 500)p = -5p^2 + 500p$$
$$R' = -10p + 500 = 0 \Rightarrow p = \$50$$

23. *Cost* A power station is on one side of a river that is $\frac{1}{2}$ mile wide, and a factory is 6 miles downstream on the other side. It costs $6 per foot to run power lines overland and $8 per foot to run them underwater. Find the most economical path for the transmission line from the power station to the factory.

Solution:

Let T be the total cost.

$$T = 8(5280)\sqrt{x^2 + (1/4)} + 6(5280)(6 - x)$$

$$= 2(5280)[4\sqrt{x^2 + (1/4)} + 18 - 3x]$$

$$= 2(5280)[2\sqrt{4x^2 + 1} + 18 - 3x]$$

$$\frac{dT}{dx} = 2(5280)\left[\frac{2(8x)}{2\sqrt{4x^2 + 1}} - 3\right] = 2(5280)\left(\frac{8x - 3\sqrt{4x^2 + 1}}{\sqrt{4x^2 + 1}}\right)$$

$\dfrac{dT}{dx} = 0$ when $8x = 3\sqrt{4x^2 + 1}$ which implies that $64x^2 = 9(4x^2 + 1)$

$$28x^2 = 9$$

$$x^2 = \frac{9}{28}$$

$$x = \frac{3}{2\sqrt{7}} \approx 0.57 \text{ mile.}$$

25. *Cost* A small business uses a minivan to make deliveries. The cost per hour for fuel for the van is $C = v^2/600$, where v is the speed of the minivan (in miles per hour). The driver of the minivan is paid $10 per hour. Find the speed that minimizes the cost of a 110-mile trip. (Assume there are no costs other than fuel and wages.)

Solution:

$$C = \left(\frac{v^2}{600} + 10\right)\left(\frac{110}{v}\right) = \frac{11}{60}v + \frac{1100}{v}$$

$$C' = \frac{11}{60} - \frac{1100}{v^2} = \frac{11v^2 - 66,000}{60v^2}$$

$$C' = 0 \text{ when } v = \sqrt{\frac{66,000}{11}} \approx 77.46 \text{ mph.}$$

27. *Elasticity* Find η (the price elasticity of demand) for $p = 400 - 3x$ when $x = 20$. Is the demand elastic or inelastic (or neither) at the indicated x-value?

Solution:

Since $dp/dx = -3$, the price elasticity of demand is

$$\eta = \frac{p/x}{dp/dx} = \frac{(400 - 3x)/x}{-3} = 1 - \frac{400}{3x}.$$

When $x = 20$, we have

$$\eta = 1 - \frac{400}{3(20)} = -\frac{17}{3}.$$

Since $|\eta(20)| = \frac{17}{3} > 1$, the demand is elastic.

29. *Elasticity* Find η (the price elasticity of demand) for $p = 300 - 0.2x^2$ when $x = 30$. Is the demand elastic, inelastic, or of unit elasticity at the indicated x-value?

Solution:

$$p = 300 - 0.2x^2 \cdot \frac{dp}{dx} = -0.4x$$

$$\eta = \frac{p/x}{dp/dx} = \frac{(300 - 0.2x^2)/x}{-0.4x} = 0.5 - \frac{750}{x^2}$$

When $x = 30$, $\eta = 0.5 - \frac{750}{30^2} = -0.3\overline{3}$.

Since $|\eta(30)| = \frac{1}{3} < 1$, the demand is inelastic.

31. *Elasticity* Find η (the price elasticity of demand) for $p = (100/x^2) + 2$ when $x = 10$. Is the demand elastic or inelastic (or neither) at the indicated x-value?

Solution:

Since $dp/dx = -200/x^3$, the price elasticity of demand is

$$\eta = \frac{p/x}{dp/dx} = \frac{[(100/x^2) + 2]/x}{-(200/x^3)} = -\frac{1}{2} - \frac{x^2}{100}.$$

When $x = 10$, we have

$$\eta = -\frac{1}{2} - \frac{(10)^2}{100} = -\frac{3}{2}.$$

Since $|\eta(10)| = \frac{3}{2} > 1$, the demand is elastic.

33. *Elasticity* The demand function for a product is $x = 20 - 2p^2$.

   (a) Consider a price of $2. If the price increases by 5%, determine the corresponding percentage change in quantity demanded.

   (b) Average elasticity of demand is defined to be the percentage change in quantity divided by the percentage change in price. Use the percentage of part (a) to find the average elasticity over the interval [2, 2.1].

   (c) Find the elasticity for a price of $2 and compare the result with that of part (b).

   (d) Find an expression for total revenue and find the values of x and p that maximize R.

Solution:

(a) If $p = 2$, $x = 12$, and p increases by 5%,

$$p = 2 + 2(0.05) = 2.1$$

$$x = 20 - 2(2.1)^2 = 11.18.$$

The percentage increase in x is

$$\frac{11.18 - 12}{12} = -\frac{41}{600} \approx -6.83\%.$$

(b) At (2, 12), the average elasticity of demand is

$$\frac{\% \text{ change in } x}{\% \text{ change in } p} = \frac{-41/600}{0.05} = \frac{-41}{30} \approx -1.37.$$

(c) The exact elasticity of demand at (2, 12) is

$$\eta = \left(\frac{p}{x}\right)\left(\frac{dx}{dp}\right)$$

$$= \left(\frac{p}{x}\right)(-4p) = \left(\frac{2}{12}\right)[-4(2)] = -\frac{4}{3}.$$

(d) The total revenue is

$$R = xp = (20 - 2p^2)p = 20p - 2p^3$$

$$\frac{dR}{dp} = 20 - 6p^2.$$

$dR/dp = 0$ when $6p^2 = 20$ which implies that

$$p = \sqrt{10/3} \approx \$1.83$$

$$x = 20 - 2(\sqrt{10/3})^2 = \frac{40}{3} \text{ units.}$$

35. *Elasticity* The demand function for a particular commodity is given by
$p = (16 - x)^{1/2}, \quad 0 < x < 16.$

(a) Find η when $x = 9$.

(b) Find the values of x and p that maximize the total revenue.

(c) Show that $|\eta| = 1$ for the value of x found in part (b).

Solution:

(a) $\dfrac{dp}{dx} = -\dfrac{1}{2\sqrt{16 - x}}$

$\eta = \dfrac{p/x}{dp/dx} = \dfrac{(16 - x)^{1/2}/x}{-[1/(2\sqrt{16 - x})]}$

$= -\dfrac{2(16 - x)}{x}$

When $x = 9$, $\eta = -\dfrac{14}{9}$.

(b) $R = px = x(16 - x)^{1/2}$

$R' = x\left(-\dfrac{1}{2\sqrt{16 - x}}\right) + (16 - x)^{1/2}$

$= \dfrac{32 - 3x}{2\sqrt{16 - x}}$

$R' = 0$ when $x = \dfrac{32}{3}$ and $p = \dfrac{4\sqrt{3}}{3}$.

(c) $\left|\eta\left(\dfrac{32}{3}\right)\right| = \left|-\dfrac{2[16 - (32/3)]}{32/3}\right| = \left|-\dfrac{2(16/3)}{32/3}\right| = |-1| = 1$

37. *Revenue* The demand for a car wash in a small town is given by $x = 800 - 40p$ where the current price is \$5. If the business is in financial difficulty, could revenues by increased by lowering the price and thus attracting more customers? [Hint: Determine if the demand is elastic.]

Solution:

$$x = 800 - 40p$$

$$p = 20 - \dfrac{x}{40}$$

$$\dfrac{dp}{dx} = \dfrac{-1}{40}$$

When $p = 5, x = 600$; $\eta = \dfrac{p/x}{dp/dx}$

Since $|\eta| < 1$, the demand is inelastic.

39. *Railroad Revenues* The annual revenue (in millions of dollars) for Union Pacific for the years 1985–1994 can be modeled by

$$R = 4.74t^4 - 193.5t^3 + 2941.7t^2 - 19{,}294.7t + 52{,}012$$

where $t = 0$ corresponds to 1980.

(a) During which year, between 1985 and 1994, was Union Pacific's revenue the least?

(b) During which year was the revenue the greatest?

(c) Find the revenue for each year in parts (a) and (b).

(d) Use a graphing utility to graph the revenue function. Then use the zoom and trace features to confirm the results in parts (a), (b), and (c).

Solution:

$$R = 4.7t^4 - 193.5t^3 + 2941.7t^2 - 19{,}294.7t + 52{,}012$$

(a) Revenue was least for $t = 7.2$ (1987).

(b) Revenue was greatest for $t = 14$ (1994).

(c) Least revenue 6006.6 million

Greatest revenue 8050.6 million

(d)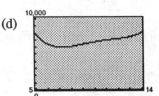

41. Match each graph with the function it best represents-a demand function, a revenue function, a cost function, or a profit function. Explain your reasoning. [The graphs are labeled (a) $\frac{1}{n}$ (d).] (See textbook.)

Solution:

(a) Demand function

(b) Cost function

(c) Revenue function

(d) Profit function

Section 3.6   Asymptotes

1. Find the vertical and horizontal asymptotes for $f(x) = \dfrac{x^2 + 1}{x^2}$.

    Solution:

    A horizontal asymptote occurs at $y = 1$ since

    $$\lim_{x \to \infty} \frac{x^2 + 1}{x^2} = 1, \quad \lim_{x \to -\infty} \frac{x^2 + 1}{x^2} = 0.$$

    A vertical asymptote occurs at $x = 0$ since

    $$\lim_{x \to 0^-} \frac{x^2 + 1}{x^2} = \infty, \quad \lim_{x \to 0^+} \frac{x^2 + 1}{x^2} = \infty.$$

3. Find the vertical and horizontal asymptotes for

    $$f(x) = \frac{x^2 - 2}{x^2 - x - 2}.$$

    Solution:

    A horizontal asymptote occurs at $y = 1$ since

    $$\lim_{x \to \infty} \frac{x^2 - 2}{x^2 - x - 2} = 1, \quad \lim_{x \to -\infty} \frac{x^2 - 2}{x^2 - x - 2} = 1.$$

    Vertical asymptotes occur at $x = -1$ and $x = 2$ since

    $$\lim_{x \to -1^-} \frac{x^2 - 2}{x^2 - x - 2} = -\infty, \quad \lim_{x \to -1^+} \frac{x^2 - 2}{x^2 - x - 2} = \infty$$

    $$\lim_{x \to 2^-} \frac{x^2 - 2}{x^2 - x - 2} = -\infty, \quad \lim_{x \to 2^+} \frac{x^2 - 2}{x^2 - x - 2} = \infty.$$

5. Find the vertical and horizontal asymptotes for

    $$f(x) = \frac{x^3}{x^2 - 1}.$$

    Solution:

    There are no horizontal asymptotes. Vertical asymptotes occur at $x = -1$ and $x = 1$ since

    $$\lim_{x \to -1^-} \frac{x^3}{x^2 - 1} = -\infty, \quad \lim_{x \to -1^+} \frac{x^3}{x^2 - 1} = \infty$$

    $$\lim_{x \to 1^-} \frac{x^3}{x^2 - 1} = -\infty, \quad \lim_{x \to 1^+} \frac{x^3}{x^2 - 1} = \infty.$$

7. Find the vertical and horizontal asymptotes for

$$f(x) = \frac{x^2 - 1}{2x^2 - 8}.$$

Solution:

A horizontal asymptote occurs at $y = \dfrac{1}{2}$ since

$$\lim_{x \to \infty} \frac{x^2 - 1}{2x^2 - 8} = \lim_{x \to -\infty} \frac{x^2 - 1}{2x^2 - 8} = \frac{1}{2}$$

Vertical asymptotes occur at $x = \pm 2$ since

$$\lim_{x \to 2^-} \frac{x^2 - 1}{2x^2 - 8} = -20 \qquad \lim_{x \to 2^+} \frac{x^2 - 1}{2x^2 - 8} = \infty$$

$$\lim_{x \to -2^-} \frac{x^2 - 1}{2x^2 - 8} = \infty \qquad \lim_{x \to -2^+} \frac{x^2 - 1}{2x^2 - 8} = -\infty.$$

9. Using horizontal asymptotes as an aid, match the following function with the correct graph.

$$f(x) = \frac{3x^2}{x^2 + 2}$$

Solution:

The graph of f has a horizontal asymptote at $y = 3$. It matches graph (f).

11. Using horizontal asymptotes as an aid, match the following function with the correct graph.

$$f(x) = \frac{x}{x^2 + 2}$$

Solution:

The graph of f has a horizontal asymptote at $y = 0$. It matches graph (c).

13. Using horizontal asymptotes as an aid, match the following function with the correct graph.

$$f(x) = 5 - \frac{1}{x^2 + 1}$$

The graph of f has a horizontal asymptote at $y = 5$. It matches graph (e).

15. Find $\displaystyle\lim_{x \to -2^-} \frac{1}{(x + 2)^2}.$

Solution:

$$\lim_{x \to -2^-} \frac{1}{(x + 2)^2} = \infty$$

17. Find $\lim\limits_{x\to 3^+} \dfrac{x-4}{x-3}$.

Solution:

$$\lim_{x\to 3^+} \frac{x-4}{x-3} = -\infty$$

19. Find $\lim\limits_{x\to 4^-} \dfrac{x^2}{x^2-16}$.

Solution:

$$\lim_{x\to 4^-} \frac{x^2}{x^2-16} = -\infty$$

21. Find $\lim\limits_{x\to 0^-} \left(1 + \dfrac{1}{x}\right)$.

Solution:

$$\lim_{x\to 0^-} \left(1 + \frac{1}{x}\right) = -\infty$$

23. Find $\lim\limits_{x\to\infty} \dfrac{2x-1}{3x+2}$.

Solution:

$$\lim_{x\to\infty} \frac{2x-1}{3x+2} = \frac{2}{3}$$

25. Find $\lim\limits_{x\to\infty} \dfrac{3x}{4x^2-1}$.

Solution:

$$\lim_{x\to\infty} \frac{3x}{4x^2-1} = 0$$

27. Find $\lim\limits_{x\to-\infty} \dfrac{5x^2}{x+3}$.

Solution:

$$\lim_{x\to-\infty} \frac{5x^2}{x+3} = -\infty$$

29. Find $\lim\limits_{x\to\infty} \left(2x - \dfrac{1}{x^2}\right)$.

Solution:

$$\lim_{x\to\infty} \left(2x - \frac{1}{x^2}\right) = \lim_{x\to\infty} \frac{2x^3-1}{x^2} = \infty$$

31. Find $\lim\limits_{x\to-\infty} \left(\dfrac{2x}{x-1} + \dfrac{3x}{x+1}\right)$.

Solution:

$$\lim_{x\to-\infty} \left(\frac{2x}{x-1} + \frac{3x}{x+1}\right) = \lim_{x\to-\infty} \frac{5x^2-x}{x^2-1} = 5$$

33. Complete the table and estimate the limit of $f(x)$ as x approaches infinity for

$$f(x) = \frac{x+1}{x\sqrt{x}}.$$

Solution:

x	10^0	10^1	10^2	10^3	10^4	10^5	10^6
$f(x)$	2.000	0.348	0.101	0.032	0.010	0.003	0.001

$$\lim_{x\to\infty} \frac{x+1}{x\sqrt{x}} = 0$$

35. Complete the table and estimate the limit of $f(x)$ as x approaches infinity and as x approaches negative infinity for

$$f(x) = \frac{2x}{\sqrt{x^2 + 4}}.$$

Solution:

x	-10^6	-10^4	-10^2	10^0	10^2	10^4	10^6
$f(x)$	-2	-2	-1.9996	0.8944	1.9996	2	2

$$\lim_{x \to \infty} \frac{2x}{\sqrt{x^2 + 4}} = 2, \quad \lim_{x \to -\infty} \frac{2x}{\sqrt{x^2 + 4}} = -2$$

37. Using intercepts, relative extrema, and asymptotes as sketching aids, sketch the graph of

$$y = \frac{2 + x}{1 - x}.$$

Solution:

x-intercept: $(-2, \ 0)$
y-intercept: $(0, \ 2)$
Horizontal asymptote: $y = -1$
Vertical asymptote: $x = 1$

$$y' = \frac{3}{(1 - x)^2}$$

No relative extrema

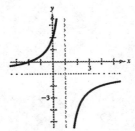

39. Using intercepts, relative extrema, and asymptotes as sketching aids, sketch the graph of

$$f(x) = \frac{x^2}{x^2 + 9}.$$

Solution:

Intercept: $(0, \ 0)$
Horizontal asymptote: $y = 1$

$$f'(x) = \frac{18x}{(x^2 + 9)^2}$$

Relative minimum: $(0, \ 0)$

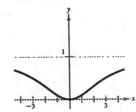

41. Using intercepts, relative extrema, and asymptotes as sketching aids, sketch the graph of

$$g(x) = \frac{x^2}{x^2 - 16}.$$

Solution:

Intercept: $(0, 0)$
Horizontal asymptote: $y = 1$
Vertical asymptotes: $x = \pm 4$

$$g'(x) = \frac{-32x}{(x^2 - 16)^2}$$

Relative maximum: $(0, 0)$

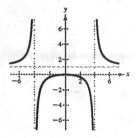

43. Using intercepts, relative extrema, and asymptotes as sketching aids, sketch the graph of $xy^2 = 4$.

Solution:

$$x = \frac{4}{y^2}$$

No intercepts
Horizontal asymptote: $y = 0$
Vertical asymptote: $x = 0$
No relative extrema

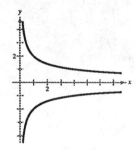

45. Using intercepts, relative extrema, and asymptotes as sketching aids, sketch the graph of

$$y = \frac{2x}{1 - x}.$$

Solution:

Intercept: $(0, 0)$
Horizontal asymptote: $y = -2$

$$y = \frac{2x}{1 - x}$$

Vertical asymptote: $x = 1$

$$y' = \frac{2}{(1 - x)^2}$$

No relative extrema

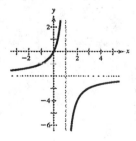

47. Using intercepts, relative extrema, and asymptotes as sketching aids, sketch the graph of

$$y = 3\left(1 - \frac{1}{x^2}\right).$$

Solution:

x-intercepts: $(\pm 1, \ 0)$
Horizontal asymptote: $y = 3$

$$y = \frac{3(x^2 - 1)}{x^2}$$

Vertical asymptote: $x = 0$

$$y' = \frac{6}{x^3}$$

No relative extrema

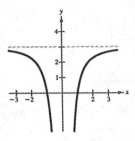

49. Using intercepts, relative extrema, and asymptotes as sketching aids, sketch the graph of

$$f(x) = \frac{1}{x^2 - x - 2}.$$

Solution:

y-intercept: $(0, \ -1/2)$
Horizontal asymptote: $y = 0$

$$f(x) = \frac{1}{(x + 1)(x - 2)}$$

Vertical asymptotes: $x = -1, \ x = 2$

$$f'(x) = -\frac{2x - 1}{(x^2 - x - 2)^2}$$

Relative maximum: $(1/2, \ -4/9)$

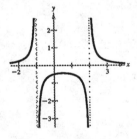

51. Using intercepts, relative extrema, and asymptotes as sketching aids, sketch the graph of

$$g(x) = \frac{x^2 - x - 2}{x - 2}.$$

Solution:

$$g(x) = \frac{x^2 - x - 2}{x - 2} = x + 1 \text{ for } x \neq 2$$

x-intercept: $(-1, \ 0)$
y-intercept: $(0, 1)$
No asymptotes
No relative extrema

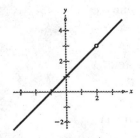

53. Using intercepts, relative extrema, and asymptotes as sketching aids, sketch the graph of
$$y = \frac{2x^2 - 6}{(x-1)^2}.$$

Solution:

$$y = \frac{2(x^2 - 3)}{x^2 - 2x + 1}$$

x-intercepts: $(\pm\sqrt{3},\ 0)$

y-intercept: $(0,\ -6)$

Vertical asymptote: $x = 1$

Horizontal asymptote: $y = 2$

$$y' = \frac{4(3-x)}{(x-1)^3}$$

Relative maximum: $(3, 3)$

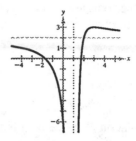

55. *Cost* The cost function for a certain product is given by $C = 1.35x + 4570$ where C is measured in dollars and x is the number of units produced.

(a) Find the average cost per unit when $x = 100$ and when $x = 1000$.

(b) What is the limit of the average cost function as x approaches infinity?

Solution:

(a) $\overline{C} = 1.35 + \dfrac{4570}{x}$. When $x = 100$, $\overline{C} = \$47.05$. When $x = 1000$, $\overline{C} = \$5.92$.

(b) $\displaystyle\lim_{x \to \infty} \left(1.35 + \frac{4570}{x} \right) = 1.35 + 0 = \$1.35$

57. *Cost* The cost in millions of dollars for the federal government to seize $p\%$ of a certain illegal drug as it enters the country is given by
$$C = \frac{528p}{100 - p}, \quad 0 \le p < 100.$$

(a) Find the cost of seizing 25%.   (b) Find the cost of seizing 50%.

(c) Find the cost of seizing 75%.   (d) Find the limit of C as $p \to 100^-$.

Solution:

(a) $C(25) = \dfrac{528(25)}{100 - 25} = \$176$ million

(b) $C(50) = \dfrac{528(50)}{100 - 50} = \$528$ million

(c) $C(75) = \dfrac{528(75)}{100 - 75} = \$1584$ million

(d) $\displaystyle\lim_{p \to 100^-} \frac{528p}{100 - p} = \infty$

59. *Learning Curve* Psychologists have developed mathematical models to predict performance as a function of the number of trials n for a certain task. One such model is

$$P = \frac{b + \theta a(n-1)}{1 + \theta(n-1)}$$

where P is the percentage of correct responses after n trials and a, b, and θ are constants depending on the actual learning situation. Find the limit of P as n approaches infinity.

Solution:

$$\lim_{n \to \infty} \frac{\theta an - \theta a + b}{\theta n - \theta + 1} = \frac{\theta a}{\theta} = a$$

61. *Wildlife Management* The state game commission introduces 30 elk into a new state park. The population N of the herd is modeled by

$$N = \frac{10(3 + 4t)}{1 + 0.1t}.$$

where t is the time in years.

(a) Find the size of the herd after 5, 10, and 25 years.

(b) According to this model, what is the limiting size of the herd as time progresses?

Solution:

$$N = \frac{10(3 + 4t)}{1 + 0.1t} = \frac{40t + 30}{0.1t + 1} = \frac{400t + 300}{t + 10}$$

(a) $N(5) = 153.3\overline{3} \approx 153$ elk

$N(10) = 215$ elk

$N(25) \approx 294.29 \approx 294$ elk

(b) $\lim_{t \to \infty} N(t) = 400$ elk

63. Use a graphing utility to graph

$$f(x) = \frac{3x}{\sqrt{4x^2 + 1}}$$

and locate any horizontal asymptotes.

Solution:

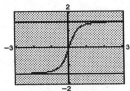

Horizontal asymptotes: $y = \pm\dfrac{3}{2}$.

Section 3.7   Curve Sketching: A Summary

1. Sketch the graph of $y = -x^2 - 2x + 3$. Choose a scale that allows all relative extrema and points of inflection to be identified on the sketch.

Solution:

$$y = -x^2 - 2x + 3 = -(x + 3)(x - 1)$$

$$y' = -2x - 2 = -2(x + 1)$$

$$y'' = -2$$

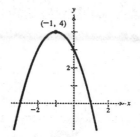

Intercepts: $(0, 3)$, $(1, 0)$, $(-3, \ 0)$
Relative maximum: $(-1, \ 4)$
Concave downward

3. Sketch the graph of $y = x^3 - 4x^2 + 6$. Choose a scale that allows all relative extrema and points of inflection to be identified on the sketch.

Solution:

$$y = x^3 - 4x^2 + 6$$

$$y' = 3x^2 - 8x = x(3x - 8)$$

$$y'' = 6x - 8 = 2(3x - 4)$$

Relative maximum: $(0, 6)$
Relative minimum: $(\frac{8}{3}, -3.\overline{481})$
Point of inflection: $(\frac{4}{3}, 1.\overline{259})$

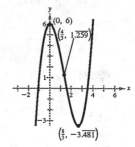

5. Sketch the graph of $y = 2 - x - x^3$. Choose a scale that allows all relative extrema and points of inflection to be identified on the sketch.

Solution:

$$y = 2 - x - x^3$$

$$y' = -1 - 3x^2$$

$$y'' = -6x$$

No relative extrema
Point of inflection: $(0, 2)$

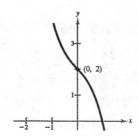

Applications of the Derivative

7. Sketch the graph of $y = 3x^3 - 9x + 1$. Choose a scale that allows all relative extrema and points of inflection to be identified on the sketch.

Solution:

$$y = 3x^3 - 9x + 1$$

$$y' = 9x^2 - 9 = 9(x - 1)(x + 1)$$

$$y'' = 18x$$

Relative maximum: $(-1,\ 7)$
Relative minimum: $(1,\ -5)$
Point of inflection: $(0,\ 1)$

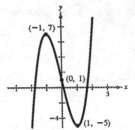

9. Sketch the graph of $y = 3x^4 + 4x^3$. Choose a scale that allows all relative extrema and points of inflection to be identified on the sketch.

Solution:

$$y = 3x^4 + 4x^3 = x^3(3x + 4)$$

$$y' = 12x^3 + 12x^2 = 12x^2(x + 1)$$

$$y'' = 36x^2 + 24x = 12x(3x + 2)$$

Intercepts: $(0,\ 0),\ \left(-\frac{4}{3},\ 0\right)$
Relative minimum: $(-1,\ -1)$
Points of inflection: $(0,\ 0),\ \left(-\frac{2}{3},\ -\frac{16}{27}\right)$

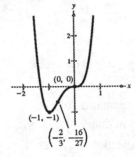

11. Sketch the graph of $y = (x + 1)(x - 2)(x - 5)$. Choose a scale that allows all relative extrema and points of inflection to be identified on the sketch.

Solution:

$$y = (x + 1)(x - 2)(x - 5)$$

$$= x^3 - 6x^2 + 3x + 10$$

$$y' = 3x^2 - 12x + 3 = 3(x^2 - 4x + 1)$$

$$y'' = 6x - 12 = 6(x - 2)$$

Intercepts: $(0, 10), (-1,\ 0), (2, 0), (5, 0)$
Relative maximum: $(2 - \sqrt{3},\ 10.392)$
Relative minimum: $(2 + \sqrt{3},\ -10.392)$
Point of inflection: $(2, 0)$

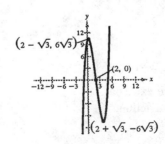

13. Sketch the graph of $y = x^4 - 8x^3 + 18x^2 - 16x + 5$. Choose a scale that allows all relative extrema and points of inflection to be identified on the sketch.

Solution:

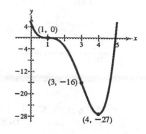

$$y = x^4 - 8x^3 + 18x^2 - 16x + 5$$
$$y' = 4x^3 - 24x^2 + 36x - 16 = 4(x^3 - 6x^2 + 9x - 4)$$
$$= 4(x - 4)(x - 1)^2$$
$$y'' = 12x^2 - 48x + 36 = 12(x^2 - 4x + 3)$$
$$= 12(x - 1)(x - 3)$$

Intercepts: $(0, 5)$, $(1, 0)$, $(5, 0)$

Relative minimum: $(4, -27)$

Points of inflection: $(1, 0)$, $(3, -16)$

15. Sketch the graph of $y = x^4 - 4x^3 + 16x$. Choose a scale that allows all relative extrema and points of inflection to be identified on the sketch.

Solution:

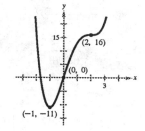

$$y = x^4 - 4x^3 + 16x$$
$$y' = 4x^3 - 12x^2 + 16 = 4(x + 1)(x - 2)^2$$
$$y'' = 12x^2 - 24x = 12x(x - 2)$$

Relative minimum: $(-1, -11)$

Points of inflection: $(0, 0)$, $(2, 16)$

17. Sketch the graph of $y = x^5 - 5x$. Choose a scale that allows all relative extrema and points of inflection to be identified on the sketch.

Solution:

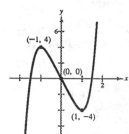

$$y = x^5 - 5x$$
$$y' = 5x^4 - 5 = 5(x + 1)(x - 1)(x^2 + 1)$$
$$y'' = 20x^3$$

Intercepts: $(0, 0)$, $(\pm\sqrt[4]{5}, 0)$

Relative maximum: $(-1, 4)$

Relative minimum: $(1, -4)$

Point of inflection: $(0, 0)$

19. Sketch the graph of $y = |2x - 3|$. Choose a scale that allows all relative extrema and points of inflection to be identified on the sketch.

Solution:

$$y = |2x - 3|$$

$$y' = (2)\frac{2x - 3}{|2x - 3|}$$

$$y'' = 0$$

Relative minimum: $\left(\frac{3}{2}, 0\right)$
No points of inflection

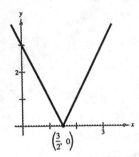

21. Sketch the graph of $y = \dfrac{x^2 + 2}{x^2 + 1}$. Choose a scale that allows all relative extrema and points of inflection to be identified on the sketch.

Solution:

$$y = \frac{x^2 + 2}{x^2 + 1}$$

$$y' = \frac{-2x}{(x^2 + 1)^2}$$

$$y'' = \frac{2(3x^2 - 1)}{(x^2 + 1)}$$

Relative maximum $(0, 2)$

Points of inflection: $x = \left(\dfrac{\sqrt{3}}{3}, \dfrac{7}{4}\right), \left(-\dfrac{\sqrt{3}}{3}, \dfrac{7}{4}\right)$

Horizontal asymptote: $y = 1$

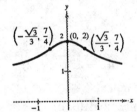

23. Sketch the graph of $y = 3x^{2/3} - 2x$. Choose a scale that allows all relative extrema and points of inflection to be identified on the sketch.

Solution:

$$y = 3x^{2/3} - 2x$$

$$y' = 2x^{-1/3} - 2 = 2(x^{-1/3} - 1)$$

$$y'' = -\frac{2}{3x^{4/3}}$$

Intercepts: $(0, 0), \left(\frac{27}{8}, 0\right)$
Relative maximum: $(1, 1)$
Relative minimum: $(0, 0)$

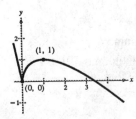

25. Sketch the graph of $y = 1 - x^{2/3}$. Choose a scale that allows all relative extrema and points of inflection to be identified on the sketch.

Solution:

$$y = 1 - x^{2/3}$$

$$y' = -\frac{2}{3}x^{-1/3} = -\frac{2}{3\sqrt[3]{x}}$$

$$y'' = \frac{2}{9}x^{-4/3} = \frac{2}{9\sqrt[3]{x^4}}$$

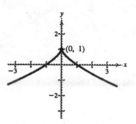

Intercepts: $(0,\ 1)$, $(\pm 1,\ 0)$
Relative maximum: $(0,\ 1)$

27. Sketch the graph of $y = x^{1/3} + 1$. Choose a scale that allows all relative extrema and points of inflection to be identified on the sketch.

Solution:

$$y = x^{1/3} + 1$$

$$y' = \frac{1}{3}x^{-2/3} = \frac{1}{3\sqrt[3]{x^2}}$$

$$y'' = -\frac{2}{9}x^{-5/3} = -\frac{2}{9\sqrt[3]{x^5}}$$

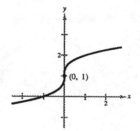

Intercepts: $(0,\ 1)$, $(-1,\ 0)$
Point of inflection: $(0,\ 1)$

29. Sketch the graph of $y = x^{5/3} - 5x^{2/3}$. Choose a scale that allows all relative extrema and points of inflection to be identified on the sketch.

Solution:

$$y = x^{5/3} - 5x^{2/3} = x^{2/3}(x - 5)$$

$$y' = \frac{5}{3}x^{2/3} - \frac{10}{3}x^{-1/3} = \frac{5}{3}x^{-1/3}(x - 2)$$

$$y'' = \frac{10}{9}x^{-1/3} + \frac{10}{9}x^{-4/3} = \frac{10}{3}x^{-4/3}(x + 1)$$

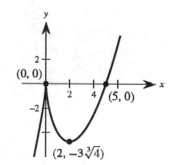

Intercepts: $(0, 0)$, $(5, 0)$
Relative maximum: $(0, 0)$
Relative minimum: $(2,\ -3\sqrt[3]{4})$
Point of inflection: $(-1,\ -4)$

31. Sketch the graph of $y = [1/(x-2)] - 3$. Label the intercepts, relative extrema, points of inflection, and asymptotes, and give the domain of the function.

Solution:

$$y = \frac{1}{x-2} - 3$$

$$y' = -\frac{1}{(x-2)^2}$$

$$y'' = \frac{2}{(x-2)^3}$$

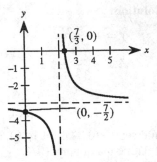

Intercepts: $\left(\frac{7}{3}, 0\right)$, $\left(0, -\frac{7}{2}\right)$
No relative extrema
Horizontal asymptote: $y = -3$
Vertical asymptote: $x = 2$
Domain: $(-\infty, 2)$, $(2, \infty)$

33. Sketch the graph of $y = 2x/(x^2 - 1)$. Label the intercepts, relative extrema, points of inflection, and asymptotes, and give the domain of the function.

Solution:

$$y = \frac{2x}{x^2 - 1}$$

$$y' = \frac{-2(x^2 + 1)}{(x^2 - 1)^2}$$

$$y'' = \frac{4x(x^2 + 3)}{(x^2 - 1)^3}$$

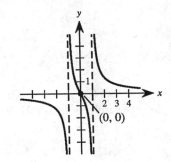

Point of inflection: $(0, 0)$
Intercept: $(0, 0)$
Horizontal asymptote: $y = 0$
Vertical asymptotes: $x = \pm 1$ Domain: $(-\infty, -1)$, $(-1, 1)$, $(1, \infty)$
Symmetry with respect to the origin   No relative extrema

35. Sketch the graph of $y = x\sqrt{4-x}$. Label the intercepts, relative extrema, points of inflection, and asymptotes, and give the domain of the function.

Solution:

$$y = x\sqrt{4-x}$$

$$y' = \frac{8-3x}{2\sqrt{4-x}}$$

$$y'' = \frac{3x-16}{4(4-x)^{3/2}}$$

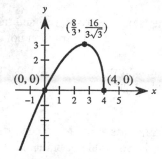

Intercepts: $(0, 0)$, $(4, 0)$
Relative maximum: $(8/3, \; 16/(3\sqrt{3}))$
Domain: $(-\infty, \; 4]$

37. Sketch the graph of $y = \dfrac{x-3}{x}$. Label the intercepts, relative extrema, points of inflection, and asymptotes, and give the domain of the function.

Solution:

$$y = \frac{x-3}{x} = 1 - \frac{3}{x}$$

$$y' = \frac{3}{x^2}$$

$$y'' = \frac{-6}{x^3}$$

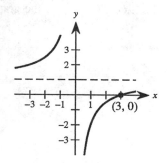

Intercept: $(3, 0)$
Horizontal asymptote: $y = 1$
Vertical asymptote: $x = 0$
Domain: $(-\infty, 0), \; (0, \infty)$

39. Sketch the graph of $y = \dfrac{x^3}{x^3-1}$. Label the intercepts, relative extrema, points of inflection, and asymptotes, and give the domain of the function.

Solution:

$$y = \frac{x^3}{x^3-1}$$

$$y' = \frac{-3x^2}{(x^3-1)^2}$$

$$y'' = \frac{6x(2x^3+1)}{(x^3-1)^3}$$

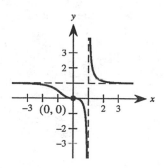

Points of inflection: $(0, 0)$, $\left(-\dfrac{1}{\sqrt[3]{2}}, \dfrac{1}{3}\right)$
Intercept: $(0, 0)$
Horizontal asymptote: $y = 1$
Vertical asmyptote: $x = 1$
Domain: $(-\infty, 1), \; (1, \infty)$

41. Determine the sign of a for which the graph of $f(x) = ax^3 + bx^2 + cx + d$ will resemble the graph shown in the text.

Solution:

Since the graph rises as $x \to -\infty$ and falls as $x \to \infty$, a must be negative.
$f(x) = -x^3 + x^2 + x + 1$ (Solution not unique).

43. Determine the sign of a for which the graph of $f(x) = ax^3 + bx^2 + cx + d$ will resemble the graph shown in the text.

Solution:

Since the graph falls as $x \to -\infty$ and rises as $x \to \infty$, a must be positive.
$f(x) = x^3 + 1$ (Solution not unique).

45. Use the graph of f' (shown in the text) to sketch a graph of the function f. (The solution is not unique.)

Solution:

Since $f'(x) = 2$, the graph of f is a line with a slope of 2.

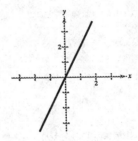

47. Use the graph of f'' (shown in the text) to sketch a graph of the function f. (The solution is not unique.)

Solution:

Since $f''(x) = 2$, the graph of f' is a line with a slope of 2, and the graph of f is a parabola opening upward.

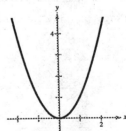

49. Sketch a graph of a function f having the given characteristics. (The solution is not unique.)

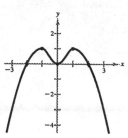

Function	First derivative
$f(-2) = 0$	$f'(x) > 0, \quad -\infty < x < -1$
$f(0) = 0$	$f'(-1) = 0$
$f(2) = 0$	$f'(x) < 0, \quad -1 < x < 0$
	$f'(0) = 0$
	$f'(x) > 0, \quad 0 < x < 1$
	$f'(1) = 0$
	$f'(x) < 0, \quad 1 < x < \infty$

Solution:

x	$-\infty < x < -1$	$-1 < x < 0$	$0 < x < 1$	$1 < x < \infty$
$f'(x)$	$+$	$-$	$+$	$-$
$f(x)$	Increasing	Decreasing	Increasing	Decreasing

Relative maxima: $(-1, \ f(-1)), \ (1, \ f(1))$
Relative minimum: $(0, \ f(0)) = (0, \ 0)$
Intercepts: $(-2, \ 0), \ (2, \ 0), \ (0, \ 0)$

51. *Cost* An employee of a delivery company earns $9 per hour driving a delivery van in an area where gasoline costs $1.20 per gallon. When the van is driven at a constant speed s (in miles per hour with $40 \le s \le 65$), the van gets $500/s$ miles per gallon.

(a) Find the cost C as a function of s for a 100-mile trip on an interstate highway.

(b) Sketch the graph of the function found in part (a) and determine the most economical speed.

Solution:

(a) $C = 1.20 \left(\dfrac{100}{500/s} \right) + 9 \left(\dfrac{100}{s} \right)$

$= 0.245 + \dfrac{900}{s}, \quad 40 \le s \le 65$

(b) $C' = 0.24 - \dfrac{900}{s^2}$

$= 0$ when $s \approx 61.2$ mph.

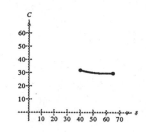

53. *Consumer Preference* Use a graphing utility to sketch the graph of the consumer indifference curve

$$5 = \frac{xy}{x+y}, \quad x > 5, \ y > 5$$

where x and y are measures of preference of two products.

Solution:

$$5 = \frac{xy}{x+y}$$

$$5x + 5y = xy$$

$$(5 - x)y = -5x$$

$$y = \frac{5x}{x-5}, \quad x > 5$$

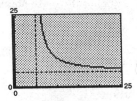

Horizontal asymptote: $y = 5$
Vertical asymptote: $x = 5$

Section 3.8   Differentials and Marginal Analysis

1. Find the differential dy of $y = 3x^2 - 4$.

Solution:

$$dy = 6x\,dx$$

3. Find the differential dy of $y = (4x - 1)^3$.

Solution:

$$dy = 3(4x - 1)^2(4)dx$$

$$= 12(4x - 1)^2 dx$$

5. Find the differential dy of $y = \sqrt{x^2 + 1}$.

Solution:

$$dy = \frac{1}{2}(x^2 + 1)^{-1/2}(2x)\,dx = \frac{x}{\sqrt{x^2 + 1}}\,dx$$

7. Find the differential dy of $y = x\sqrt{1 - x^2}$.

Solution:

$$dy = \left[x\left(\frac{1}{2}\right)(1 - x^2)^{-1/2}(-2x) + \sqrt{1 - x^2} \right] dx = \frac{1 - 2x^2}{\sqrt{1 - x^2}}\,dx$$

9. Find the differential dy of $y = \frac{x - 3}{1 - 3x}$.

Solution:

$$dy = \frac{(1 - 3x)(1) - (x - 3)(-3)}{(1 - 3x)^2}\,dx = \frac{-8}{(1 - 3x)^2}\,dx$$

11. Let $x = 1$ and $\Delta x = 0.01$. Find Δy.

$f(x) = 5x^2 - 1$

Solution:

$$f(x) = 5x^2 - 1, \qquad x = 1, \qquad \Delta x = 0.01$$

$$\Delta y = f(x + \Delta x) - f(x) = (5(1.01)^2 - 1) - (5(1)^2 - 1) = 0.1005$$

13. Let $x = 1$ and $\Delta x = 0.01$. Find Δy.

$$f(x) = \frac{4}{\sqrt[3]{x}}$$

Solution:

$$f(x) = \frac{4}{x^{1/3}}, \qquad x = 1, \qquad \Delta x = 0.01$$

$$\Delta y = f(x + \Delta x) - f(x) = \frac{4}{(1.01)^{1/3}} - \frac{4}{1} \approx -0.013245$$

15. Compare the values of dy and y.

$$y = x^3 \qquad x = 1 \qquad \Delta x = dx = 0.1$$

Solution:

$$dy = 3x^2 dx = 0.3$$

$$\Delta y = (1.1)^3 - 1^3 = 0.331$$

17. Compare the values of dy and y.

$$y = x^4 + 1 \qquad x = -1 \qquad \Delta x = dx = 0.01$$

Solution:

$$dy = 4x^3 dx = -0.04$$

$$\Delta y = ((-0.99)^4 + 1) - ((-1)^4 + 1) \approx -0.0394$$

19. Use $y = x^2$ and the value of $\Delta x = dx$ to complete the table. (Let $x = 2$.)

Solution:

$$dy = 2x\,dx$$

$dx = \Delta x$	dy	Δy	$\Delta y - dy$	$\dfrac{dy}{\Delta y}$
1.0000	4.0000	5.0000	1.0000	0.8000
0.5000	2.0000	2.2500	0.2500	0.8889
0.1000	0.4000	0.4100	0.0100	0.9756
0.0100	0.0400	0.0401	0.0001	0.9975
0.0010	0.0040	0.0040	0.0000	0.9998

21. Use $y = x^5$ and the value of $\Delta x = dx$ to complete the table. (Let $x = 2$.)

Solution:

$$dy = 5x^4\,dx$$

$dx = \Delta x$	dy	Δy	$\Delta y - dy$	$\dfrac{dy}{\Delta y}$
1.0000	80.0000	211.0000	131.0000	0.3791
0.5000	40.0000	65.6562	25.6562	0.6092
0.1000	8.0000	8.8410	0.8410	0.9049
0.0100	0.8000	0.8080	0.0080	0.9901
0.0010	0.0800	0.0801	0.0001	0.9990

23. *Demand* The demand function for a product is modeled by $p = 75 - 0.25x$.

(a) If x changes from 7 to 8, what is the corresponding change in p? Compare the values of Δp and dp.

(b) Repeat part (a) when x changes from 70 to 71 units.

Solution:

$$p = 75 - 0.25x \qquad dp = -0.25$$

(a) $x = 7$, $\Delta x = 1$

$\Delta p = (75 - 0.25(8)) - (75 - 0.25(7)) = -0.25 = dp$

(b) $x = 70$, $\Delta x = 1$

$\Delta p = (75 - 0.25(71)) - (75 - 0.25(70)) = -0.25 = dp$

25. *Marginal Analysis* Use differentials to approximate the change in cost corresponding to an increase in sales of one unit for $C = 0.05x^2 + 4x + 10$, $x = 12$.

Solution:

$x = 12$, $dx = \Delta x = 1$

$\Delta C \approx dC = (0.10x + 4)\,dx = [0.10(12) + 4](1) = \$5.20$

27. *Marginal Analysis* Use differentials to approximate the change in profit corresponding to an increase in sales of one unit for $P = -0.5x^3 + 2500x - 6000$, $x = 50$.

Solution:

$x = 50$, $dx = \Delta x = 1$

$\Delta P \approx dP = (-1.5x^2 + 2500)dx = [-1.5(50)^2 + 2500](1) = -1250$

29. *Marginal Analysis* A retailer has determined that the monthly sales x of a watch is 150 units when the price is \$50, but decreases to 120 units when the price is \$60. If the demand is a linear function of the price, find the revenue R as a function of x and use differentials to approximate the change in revenue for a one unit increase in sales when $x = 141$.

Solution:

$(150, 50)$, $(120, 60)$

$$m = \frac{60 - 50}{120 - 150} = -\frac{1}{3}$$

$$p - 50 = -\frac{1}{3}(x - 150)$$

$$p = -\frac{1}{3}x + 100$$

$$R = xp = -\frac{1}{3}x^2 + 100x$$

When $x = 141$ and $dx = \Delta x = 1$, we have $\Delta R \approx dR =$

$\left(-\dfrac{2}{3}x + 100\right)dx = \left[-\dfrac{2}{3}(141) + 100\right](1) = \$6.00.$

31. *Marginal Analysis* The demand x for a radio is 30,000 units per week when the price is $25 and 40,000 units when the price is $20. The initial investment is $275,000 and the cost per unit is $17. Assume that the demand is a linear function of the price. Find the profit P as a function of x and approximate the change in profit for a one-unit increase in sales when $x = 28,000$. Make a sketch showing dP and ΔP.

Solution:

$(30{,}000, 25) \ (40{,}000, 20)$

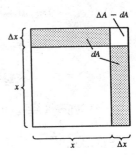

$y = -5x + 117{,}000$

$(28{,}000, -23{,}000)$
$(28{,}001, -23{,}005)$

$\Delta R \{\quad dR\{$

$P = -\frac{1}{2{,}000}x^2 + 23x - 275{,}000$

$$m = \frac{20 - 25}{40{,}000 - -30{,}000} = \frac{-5}{10{,}000} = \frac{-1}{2000}$$

$$p - 25 = \frac{-1}{2000}(x - 30{,}000)$$

$$p = \frac{-1}{2000}x + 40$$

$$C = 275{,}000 + 17x$$

$$P = R - C = xp - C = \left(\frac{-1}{2000}x^2 + 40x\right) - (275{,}000 + 17x)$$

$$= \frac{-1}{2000}x^2 + 23x - 275{,}000$$

When $x = 28{,}000$ and $ds = \Delta x = 1$, we have $\Delta P \approx dp \approx \frac{-1}{1000}x + 23 =$

$\frac{-1}{1000}(28{,}000) + 23 = -\$5.00$

33. The area of a square of side x is given by $A = x^2$.

(a) Compute dA and ΔA in terms of x and Δx.

(b) Identify the region whose area is dA in the figure.

(c) Identify the region whose area is $\Delta A - dA$ in the figure.

Solution:

(a) $dA = 2x \, dx = 2x \Delta x$

$\Delta A = (x + \Delta x)^2 - x^2 = 2x \Delta x + (\Delta x)^2$

(b) See accompanying graph.

(c) $\Delta A - dA = (\Delta x)^2$

    (See accompanying graph.)

35. *Area* The radius of a circle is measured to be 10 inches, with a possible error of $\frac{1}{8}$ inch. Use differentials to approximate the possible error and the relative error in computing the area of the circle.

Solution:

$$A = \pi r^2 \qquad dr = \Delta r = \frac{1}{8} \qquad r = 10$$

$$dA = 2\pi r \cdot dr$$

$$= 2\pi(10)\left(\pm\frac{1}{8}\right) = \pm\frac{5}{2}\pi \text{ in}^2$$

Relative error $= \dfrac{dA}{A} = \dfrac{\pm\frac{5}{2}\pi}{100\pi} = \pm\dfrac{1}{40}$

37. *Volume* The radius of a sphere is measured to be 6 inches, with a possible error of 0.02 inch. Use differentials to approximate the possible error and the relative error in calculating the volume of the sphere.

Solution:

Let $\Delta r = dr = 0.02$ inch.

$$V = \frac{4}{3}\pi r^3$$

$$dV = 4\pi r^2\, dr = 4\pi(6)^2(\pm 0.02) = \pm 2.88\pi \text{ in}^3$$

When $r = 6$, the relative error is

$$\frac{dV}{V} = \frac{4\pi r^2\, dr}{(4/3)\pi r^3} = \frac{3\, dr}{r} = \frac{3(\pm 0.02)}{6} = \pm 0.01.$$

39. *Profit* The profit P for a company selling x units is given by the following.

$$P = R - C = (500x - x^2) - \left(0.5x^2 - 77x + 3000\right)$$

Approximate the change in the profit as production changes from $x = 115$ to $x = 120$ units.

Solution:

Since x changes from 115 to 120, we have $dx = 120 - 115 = 5$.

$$P = R - C = (500x - x^2) - \left(0.5x^2 - 77x + 3000\right)$$

$$dP = (500 - 2x - x + 77)\, dx = (577 - 3x)\, dx = [577 - 3(115)](5) = \$1160$$

Chapter 3 Review Exercises

1. Find the critical numbers of the function
$f(x) = -x^2 + 2x + 4.$
$f(x) = -x^2 + 2x + 4$
$f'(x) = -2x + 2 = 0$ when $x = 1$
Critical number: $x = 1$.

3. Find the critical numbers of the function
$f(x) = \sqrt{x}(x - 3).$
$f(x) = x^{3/2} - 3x^{1/2}$ where $x \geq 0$
$f'(x) = \frac{3}{2}x^{1/2} - \frac{3}{2}x^{-1/2} = \frac{3}{2}x^{-1/2}(x - 1) = \frac{3(x - 1)}{2\sqrt{x}}$
Critical numbers: $x = 0$ and $x = 1$.

5. Determine the open intervals on which the function $f(x) = x^2 + x - 2$ is increasing or decreasing. Solve the problem analytically and graphically.

Solution:

$$f(x) = x^2 + x - 2$$
$$f'(x) = 2x + 1$$

Critical number: $x = -\dfrac{1}{2}$

Increasing on $\left(-\frac{1}{2}, \infty\right)$

Decreasing on $\left(-\infty, -\frac{1}{2}\right)$

7. Determine the open intervals on which the function $h(x) = \dfrac{x^2 - 3x - 4}{x - 3}$ is increasing or decreasing. Solve the problem analytically and graphically.

Solution:

$$h(x) = \frac{x^2 - 3x - 4}{(x - 3)}$$

$$h'(x) = \frac{x^2 - 6x + 13}{(x - 3)^2} > 0 \text{ for all } x \neq 3$$

Increasing on $(-\infty, 3)$, $(3, \infty)$.

9. *Temperature* The daily maximum temperature T (in degrees Fahrenheit) for New York City can be modeled by

$$T = 0.036t^4 - 0.909t^3 + 5.874t^2 - 2.599t + 37.789,$$

where $0 \le t \le 12$ and $t = 0$ corresponds to January 1.

(a) Find the intervals in which the model is increasing.

(b) Find the intervals in which the model is decreasing.

(c) Interpret the results of parts (a) and (b).

(d) Sketch a graph of the model.

Solution:

$$T = 0.036t^4 - 0.909t^3 + 5.874t^2 - 2.599t + 37.789$$

$$T' = 0.144t^3 - 2.727t^2 + 11.748t - 2.599$$

$T' = 0$ for $t \approx 0.23$, $t \approx 6.15$

(a) T increasing on $(0.23, 6.15)$

(b) T decreasing on $(0, 0.23)$, $(6.15, 12)$

(c) The maximum daily temperature is rising from early January to June.

(d)

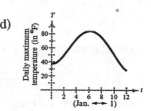

11. Use the First-Derivative Test to find the relative extrema of the function $f(x) = 4x^3 - 6x^2 - 2$. Then use a graphing utility to confirm your result.

Solution:

$$f(x) = 4x^3 - 6x^2 - 2$$

$$f'(x) = 12x^2 - 12x = 12x(x - 1)$$

Critical numbers: $x = 0$, $x = 1$

Intervals	$(-\infty, 0)$	$(0, 1)$	$(1, \infty)$
Sign of $f'(x)$	$+$	$-$	$+$
Conclusion	Increasing	Decreasing	Increasing

Relative maximum: $(0, -2)$

Relative minimum: $(1, -4)$

13. Use the First-Derivative Test to find the relative extrema of the function $g(x) = x^2 - 16x + 12$. Then use a graphing utility to confirm your result.

    Solution:

    $$g(x) = x^2 - 16x + 12$$
    $$g'(x) = 2x - 16 = 2(x - 8)$$

    Critical number: $x = 8$
    Increasing on $(8, \infty)$; Decreasing on $(-\infty, 8)$
    Relative minimum: $(8, -32)$.

15. Use the First-Derivative Test to find the relative extrema of the function $h(x) = 2x^2 - x^4$. Then use a graphing utility to confirm your result.

    Solution:

    $$h(x) = 2x^2 - x^4$$
    $$h'(x) = 4x - 4x^3 = 4x(1 - x^2) = 4x(1 - x)(1 + x)$$

    Critical numbers: $x = 0, 1, -1$

Interval	$(-\infty, -1)$	$(-1, 0)$	$(0, 1)$	$(1, \infty)$
Sign of f	$+$	$-$	$+$	$-$
Conclusion	Increasing	Decreasing	Increasing	Decreasing

    Relative maxima: $(-1, 1)$, $(1, 1)$
    Relative minimum: $(0, 0)$

17. Use the First-Derivative Test to find the relative extrema of the function $f(x) = \dfrac{6}{x^2 + 1}$. Then use a graphing utility to confirm your result.

    Solution:

    $$f(x) = \frac{6}{x^2 + 1}$$
    $$f'(x) = \frac{-12x}{(x^2 + 1)^2}$$

    Critical number: $x = 0$

Interval	$(-\infty, 0)$	$(0, \infty)$
Sign of f'	$+$	$-$
Conclusion	Increasing	Decreasing

    Relative maximum: $(0, 6)$

19. Use the First-Derivative Test to find the relative extrema of the function $h(x) = \dfrac{x^2}{x-2}$. Then use a graphing utility to confirm your result.

Solution:

$$h(x) = \frac{x^2}{x-2}$$

$$h'(x) = \frac{x(x-4)}{(x-2)^2}$$

Critical numbers: $x = 0, 4$; discontinuity $x = 2$

Interval	$(-\infty, 0)$	$(0, 2)$	$(2, 4)$	$(4, 8)$
Sign of f'	$+$	$-$	$-$	$+$
Conclusion	Increasing	Decreasing	Decreasing	Increasing

Relative maximum: $(0, 0)$
Relative minimum: $(4, 8)$

21. Find the absolute extrema of the function $f(x) = x^2 + 5x + 6$ on the interval $[-3, 0]$. Then use a graphing utility to confirm your result.

Solution:

$$f(x) = x^2 + 5x + 6 \qquad [-3, 0]$$

$$f'(x) = 2x + 5$$

Critical number: $x = -\dfrac{5}{2}$

x	$f(x)$	
-3	0	
0	6	Maximum
$-\dfrac{5}{2}$	$-\dfrac{1}{4}$	Minimum

23. Find the absolute extrema of the function $f(x) = x^3 - 12x + 1$ on the interval $[-4, 4]$. Then use a graphing utility to confirm your result.

Solution:

$$f(x) = x^3 - 12x + 1$$

$$f'(x) = 3x^2 - 12 = 3(x - 2)(x + 2)$$

Critical numbers: $x = \pm 2$

x	$f(x)$	
-4	-15	Minimum
4	17	Maximum
-2	17	Maximum
2	-15	Minimum

25. Find the absolute extrema of the function $f(x) = 3x^4 - 6x^2 + 2$ on the interval $[0, 2]$. Then use a graphing utility to confirm your result.

Solution:

$$f(x) = 3x^4 - 6x^2 + 2 \qquad [0, 2]$$

$$f'(x) = 12x^3 - 12x = 12x(x - 1)(x + 1)$$

Critical numbers: $x = 0, 1$

x	$f(x)$	
0	2	
2	26	Maximum
1	-1	Minimum

27. Find the absolute extrema of the function $f(x) = \dfrac{2x}{x^2 + 1}$ on the interval $[-1, 2]$. Then use a graphing utility to confirm your result.

Solution:

$$f(x) = \frac{2x}{x^2 + 1} \qquad [-1, 2]$$

$$f'(x) = \frac{-2(x^2 - 1)}{(x^2 + 1)^2}$$

Critical numbers: $x = 1, -1$

x	$f(x)$	
-1	-1	Minimum
2	$\frac{4}{5}$	
1	1	Maximum

29. *Diamond Prices* During the 1980s, the average price p (in dollars) on the Antwerp Index of a 1-carat diamond can be modeled by

$$p = -0.7t^3 + 16.25t^2 - 106t + 388,$$

where $2 \le t \le 10$ and $t = 2$ corresponds to 1982.

(a) Estimate the maximum average price between 1982 and 1990. When did this price occur?

(b) Estimate the minimum average price between 1982 and 1990. When did this price occur?

Solution:

$$p = 0.7t^3 + 16.25t^2 - 106t + 388$$

The graph of p is:

(a) The maximum of \$253.00 occurs at $t = 10$ (1990).

(b) The minimum of \$176.08 occurs at $t = 4.67$ (around August 1984).

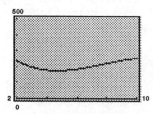

31. Determine the open intervals on which the graph of the function $f(x) = (x - 2)^3$ is concave upward or concave downward. Then use a graphing utility to confirm your result.

Solution:

$$f(x) = (x - 2)^3$$
$$f'(x) = 3(x - 2)^2$$
$$f''(x) = 6(x - 2)$$

$f''(x) > 0$ for $x > 2$: concave upward on $(2, \infty)$

$f''(x) < 0$ for $x < 2$: concave downward on $(-\infty, 2)$

33. Determine the open intervals on which the graph of the function $g(x) = \frac{1}{4}(-x^4 + 8x^2 - 12)$ is concave upward or concave downward. Then use a graphing utility to confirm your result.

Solution:

$$h(x) = x^5 - 10x^2$$

$$h'(x) = 5x^4 - 20x$$

$$h''(x) = 20x^3 - 20 = 20(x-1)(x^2 + x + 1)$$

$f''(x) > 0$ for $x > 1$: concave upward on $(1, \infty)$

$f''(x) < 0$ for $x < 1$: concave downward on $(-\infty, 1)$

35. Find the points of inflection of the graph of the function $f(x) = \frac{1}{2}x^4 - 4x^3$.

Solution:

$$f(x) = \frac{1}{2}x^4 - 4x^3$$

$$f'(x) = 2x^3 - 12x^2$$

$$f''(x) = 6x^2 - 24x = 6x(x-4)$$

$$f''(x) = 0 \text{ when } x = 0, 4$$

Since f changes concavity at $x = 0$ and $x = 4$, the points of inflection are $(0, 0)$ and $(4, -128)$.

37. Find the points of inflection of the graph of the function $f(x) = x^3(x-3)^2$.

Solution:

$$f(x) = x^3(x-3)^2$$

$$f'(x) = x^2(5x-9)(x-3)$$

$$f''(x) = 2x(10x^2 - 36x + 27)$$

Since f changes concavity at $x = 0$, $x = 1.0652$, and $x = 2.5348$, the points of inflection are $(0, 0)$, $(1.0652, 4.5244)$, and $(2.5348, 3.5246)$.

39. Use the Second-Derivative Test to find the relative extrema of the function $f(x) = x^5 - 5x^3$.

Solution:

$$f(x) = x^5 - 5x^3$$
$$f'(x) = 5x^4 - 15x^2 = 5x^2(x^2 - 3)$$
$$f''(x) = 20x^3 - 30x$$

Critical numbers: $x = 0, \pm\sqrt{3}$

$f''(\sqrt{3}) > 0 \Rightarrow (\sqrt{3}, -6\sqrt{3})$ is a relative minimum.

$f''(-\sqrt{3}) < 0 \Rightarrow (-\sqrt{3}, 6\sqrt{3})$ is a relative maximum.

$f''(0) = 0 \Rightarrow$ text fails.

(By First Derivative Test, $(0, 0)$ is not a relative extrema.)

41. Use the Second-Derivative Test to find the relative extrema of the function $f(x) = (x-1)^3(x+4)^2$.

Solution:

$$f(x) = (x-1)^3(x+4)^2$$
$$f''(x) = 5(x+4)(x+2)(x-1)^2$$
$$f''(x) = 10(x-1)(2x^2 + 8x + 5)$$

Critical numbers: $x = -4, -2, 1$

$f''(-4) < 0 \Rightarrow (-4, 0)$ is a relative maximum.

$f''(-2) > 0 \Rightarrow (-2, -108)$ is a relative minimum.

$f''(1) = 0 \Rightarrow$ test fails.

By First Derivative Test, $(1, 0)$ is not a relative extrema.

43. Identify the point of diminishing returns for the input-output function $R = \frac{1}{1500}(150x^2 - x^3), 0 \le x \le 100$. For each function, R is the refenue (in thousands of dollars) and x is the amount spent on advertising (in thousands of dollars).

Solution:

$$R = \frac{1}{1500}(150x^2 - x^3) \qquad 0 \le x \le 100$$
$$R' = \frac{1}{1500}(300x - 3x^2)$$
$$R'' = \frac{1}{1500}(300 - 6x)$$

$R'' = 0$ when $x = 50$. The point of diminishing returns is $(50, 166\frac{2}{3})$.

45. *Minimum Sum* Find two positive numbers whose product is 169 and whose sum is a minimum. Solve the problem analytically *and* graphically.

Solution:

$$xy = 169 \text{ (product is 169)}$$

$$\text{Sum} = S = x + y = x + \frac{169}{x}$$

$$S' = 1 - \frac{169}{x^2} = 0 \Rightarrow x = 13, \, y = 13$$

47. *Charitable Contributions* The percent P of income that Americans give to charities can be modeled by

$$P = 0.0014x^2 - 0.1529x + 5.855, \qquad 5 \le x \le 100,$$

where x is the annual income in thousands of dollars.

(a) What income level corresponds to the least percent of charitable contributions?

(b) What income level corresponds to the greatest percent of charitable contributions?

Solution:

$$P = 0.0014x^2 - 0.1529x + 5.855 \qquad 5 \le x \le 100$$

$$P' - 0.0028x - 0.1529$$

$$P' = 0 \text{ when } x = 54.607$$

(a) $x = 54.607$ ($\$54,607$) corresponds to the least percent.

(b) $x = 5$ ($\$5000$) corresponds to the greatest percent.

49. *Profit* The demand and cost functions for a product are $p = 36 - 4x$ and $C = 2x^2 + 6$.

(a) What level of production will produce a maximum profit?

(b) What level of production will produce a minimum average cost per unit?

Solution:

$$p = 36 - 4x, \, C = 2x^2 + 6$$

(a) $P - R - C = xp - C = x(36 - 4x) - (2x^2 + 6) = -6x^2 + 36x - 6$

$$P' = -12x + 36 = 0 \Rightarrow x = 3 \text{ for maximum profit}$$

(b) $\overline{C} = \dfrac{C}{x} = 2x + \dfrac{6}{x}$

$$\overline{C}' = 2 - \frac{6}{x^2} = 0 \Rightarrow 2x^2 = 6 \Rightarrow x = \sqrt{3} \approx 1.73 \text{ units.}$$

51. *Revenue* For groups of 20 or more, a theater determines the ticket price p according to the formula

$$p = 15 - 0.1(n - 20), \qquad 20 \leq n \leq N,$$

where n is the number in the group. What should the value of N be? Explain your reasoning.

Solution:

$$p = 15 - 0.1(n - 20) = 17 - 0.1n, \qquad 20 \leq n \leq N$$

Let x be the number of people over 20 in the group.

$$\text{Revenue } = R = (x + 20)(15 - 0.1(n - 20))$$
$$= (x + 20)(15 - 0.1x) \qquad (x + 20 = n)$$
$$R' = 13 - 0.2x = 0 \Rightarrow x = 65$$

Thus, $N = 65 + 20 = 85$ people would maximize revenue.

53. *Inventory Cost* The cost C of inventory depends on ordering cost and storage cost. In the following inventory model, assume that sales occur at a constant rate, Q is the number of units sold per year, r is the cost of storing 1 unit for 1 year, s is the cost of placing an order, and x is the number of units per order.

$$C = \left(\frac{Q}{x}\right)s + \left(\frac{x}{2}\right)r$$

Determine the order size that will minimize the cost when $Q = 10,000$, $N = 4.5$ and $r = 5.76$.

Solution:

$$\frac{dC}{dx} = -\frac{Qs}{x^2} + \frac{r}{2}$$

$$\frac{dC}{dx} = 0 \text{ when } x^2 = \frac{2Qs}{r} \text{ or } x = \sqrt{2Qs/r}$$

Since $Q = 10,000$, $s = 4.5$ and $r = 5.76$, $x = 125$.

55. Find the intervals on which the demand is elastic, inelastic, and of unit elasticity.

$$p = \frac{36}{\sqrt[3]{x}}, \qquad x > 0$$

Solution:

$$p = \frac{36}{x^{1/3}} = 36x^{-1/3}, \qquad x > 0$$

$$\frac{dp}{dx} = -12x^{-4/3}$$

$$\eta = \frac{\frac{p}{x}}{\frac{dp}{dx}} = \frac{\frac{36}{x^{4/3}}}{\frac{-12}{x^{4/3}}} = -3$$

Since $|\eta| = 3 > 1$, the demand is elastic.

57. Find any vertical and horizontal asymptotes to the graph of the following function, then sketch the graph.

$$h(x) = \frac{2x+3}{x-4}$$

Solution:

Since $x = 4$ is an infinite discontinuity, it is a vertical asymptote. Since

$$\lim_{x \to \infty} \frac{2x+3}{x-4} = \frac{2}{1} = 2$$

$y = 2$ is a horizontal asymptote.

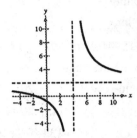

59. Find any vertical and horizontal asymptotes to the graph of the following function, then sketch the graph.

$$f(x) = \frac{1-3x}{x}$$

Solution:

Since $x = 0$ is an infinite discontinuity, it is a vertical asymptote. Since

$$\lim_{x \to \infty} \left(\frac{1-3x}{x} \right) = -3$$

$y = -3$ is a horizontal asymptote.

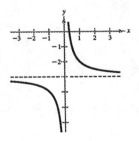

61. Find the vertical and horizontal asymptotes of the graph $f(x) = \dfrac{3}{x^2 - 5x + 4}$, then sketch the graph.

Solution:

$$f(x) = \frac{3}{x^2 - 5x + 4} = \frac{3}{(x-4)(x-1)}$$

$x = 1$ and $x = 4$ are vertical asymptotes. $y = 0$ is the horizontal asymptote.

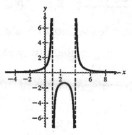

63. Find $\displaystyle \lim_{x \to 0^+} \left(x - \frac{1}{x^3} \right)$.

Solution:

$$\lim_{x \to 0^+} \left(x - \frac{1}{x^3} \right) = -\infty$$

65. Find $\displaystyle \lim_{x \to \infty} \frac{5x^2 + 3}{2x^2 - x + 1}$.

Solution:

$$\lim_{x \to \infty} \frac{5x^2 + 3}{2x^2 - x + 1} = \lim_{x \to \infty} \frac{5 + (3/x^2)}{2 - (1/x) + (1/x^2)} = \frac{5}{2}$$

67. Find the limit $\displaystyle \lim_{x \to -\infty} \frac{3x^2}{x + 2}$, if it exists.

Solution:

$$\lim_{x \to -\infty} \frac{3x^2}{x + 2} = -\infty.$$

Applications of the Derivative

69. *Ultraviolet Radiation* For a person with sensitive skin, the amount T (in hours) of exposure to the sun can be modeled by

$$T = \frac{0.37s + 23.8}{s}, \qquad 0 < s \le 120,$$

where s is the Sunsor Scale reading.

(a) Use a graphing utility to graph the model. Compare your result with the graph at the right.

(b) Describe the value of T as s increases.

Solution:

$$T = \frac{0.37s + 23.8}{s} \qquad 0 < s \le 120$$

(a)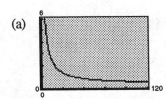

(b) $\displaystyle \lim_{s \to \infty} T = \lim_{s \to \infty} \frac{0.37s + 23.8}{s} = 0.37$

71. Make use of domain, range, asymptotes, intercepts, and relative extrema to sketch the graph of $f(x) = 4x - x^2$.

Solution:

$$f(x) = 4x - x^2 = x(4 - x)$$
$$f'(x) = 4 - 2x = -2(x - 2)$$
$$f''(x) = -2$$

Intercepts: $(0, 0)$, $(4, 0)$
Domain: $(-\infty, \infty)$
Range: $(-\infty, 4]$
Relative maximum: $(2, 4)$
Concave downward on $(-\infty, \infty)$

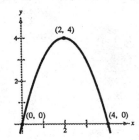

73. Make use of domain, range, asymptotes, intercepts, relative extrema, and points of inflection to sketch the graph of $f(x) = x\sqrt{16 - x^2}$.

Solution:

$$f(x) = x\sqrt{16 - x^2}$$

$$f'(x) = \frac{16 - 2x^2}{\sqrt{16 - x^2}}$$

$$f''(x) = \frac{2x(x^2 - 24)}{(16 - x^2)^{3/2}}$$

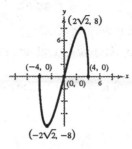

Domain: $[-4,\ 4]$
Range: $[-8,\ 8]$
Intercepts: $(0,\ 0),\ (4,\ 0),\ (-4,\ 0)$
Relative maximum: $(2\sqrt{2},\ 8)$
Relative minimum: $(-2\sqrt{2},\ -8)$
Point of inflection: $(0,\ 0)$
Concave upward on $(-4,\ 0)$
Concave downward on $(0,\ 4)$

75. Make use of domain, range, asymptotes, intercepts, relative extrema, and points of inflection to sketch the graph of the following function.

$$f(x) = \frac{x + 1}{x - 1}$$

Solution:

$$f(x) = \frac{x + 1}{x - 1}$$

$$f'(x) = \frac{-2}{(x - 1)^2}$$

$$f''(x) = \frac{4}{(x - 1)^3}$$

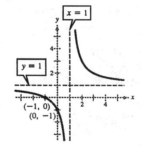

Domain: all real numbers except 1
Range: all real numbers except 1
Intercepts: $(-1,\ 0),\ (0,\ -1)$
Horizontal asymptote: $y = 1$
Vertical asymptote: $x = 1$
Concave upward on $(1,\ \infty)$
Concave downward on $(-\infty,\ 1)$

77. Make use of domain, range, asymptotes, intercepts, relative extrema, and points of inflection to sketch the graph of $f(x) = x^3(x+1)$.

Solution:

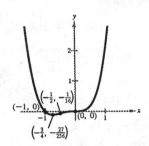

$$f(x) = x^3(x+1)$$

$$f'(x) = x^2(4x+3)$$

$$f''(x) = 6x(2x+1)$$

Domain: all real numbers

Range: $\left[-\frac{27}{256}, \infty\right)$

Intercepts: $(0, 0)$, $(-1, 0)$

Relative minimum: $\left(-\frac{3}{4}, -\frac{27}{256}\right)$

Points of inflection: $(0, 0)$, $\left(-\frac{1}{2}, -\frac{1}{16}\right)$

79. Make use of domain, range, asymptotes, intercepts, relative extrema, and points of inflection to sketch the graph of $f(x) = x^{4/5}$.

Solution:

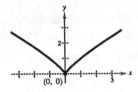

$$f(x) = x^{4/5}$$

$$f'(x) = \frac{4}{5}x^{-1/5} = \frac{4}{5\sqrt[5]{x}}$$

$$f''(x) = -\frac{4}{25}x^{-6/5} = -\frac{4}{25x^{6/5}}$$

Domain: $(-\infty, \infty)$

Range: $[0, \infty)$

Intercept: $(0, 0)$

Relative minimum: $(0, 0)$

Concave downward on $(-\infty, 0)$ and $(0, \infty)$

81. Find the differential dy of $y = 6x^2 - 5$.

Solution:

$$y = 6x^2 - 5$$

$$dy = 12x\,dx$$

83. Find the differential dy of $y = -\dfrac{5}{\sqrt[3]{x}}$.

Solution:

$$y = \frac{-5}{x^{1/3}} = -5x^{-1/3}$$

$$dy = \frac{5}{3}x^{-4/3}dx = \frac{5}{3x^{4/3}}dx$$

85. Use differentials , to approximate the change in cost $C = 40x^2 + 1225$, at $x = 10$ corresponding to an increase in sales of one unit.

Solution:

$$C = 40x^2 + 1225, \qquad x = 10$$
$$dC = 80x \cdot dx = 80(10)(1) = 800$$

87. Use differentials , to approximate the change in revenue, $R = 6.25x + 0.4x^{3/2}$ at $x = 225$ corresponding to an increase in sales of one unit.

Solution:

$$P = 0.003x^2 + 0.019x - 1200, \quad x = 750$$
$$dP = (0.006x + 0.019)dx = 4.519$$

89. *Surface Area and Volume* The diameter of a sphere is measured to be 18 inches with a possible error of 0.05 inch. Use differentials to approximate the possible error in the surface area and the volume of the sphere.

Solution:

The radius is 9 inches with a possible error of 0.025 inch.

$$S = 4\pi r^2$$
$$dS = 8\pi r \, dr$$
$$V = \tfrac{4}{3}\pi r^3$$
$$dV = 4\pi r^2 \, dr$$

When $r = 9$ and $dr = \pm0.025$ we have the following.

$$dS = 8\pi(9)(\pm0.025)$$
$$= \pm1.8\pi \text{ in.}^2$$
$$dV = 4\pi(9)^2(\pm0.025)$$
$$= \pm8.1\pi \text{ in.}^3$$

Practice Test for Chapter 3

1. Find the critical numbers and the intervals on which f is increasing or decreasing for $f(x) = x^3 - 6x^2 + 5$.

2. Find the critical numbers and the intervals on which f is increasing or decreasing for $f(x) = 2x\sqrt{1-x}$.

3. Find the relative extrema of $f(x) = x^4 - 32x + 3$.

4. Find the relative extrema of $f(x) = (x+3)^{4/3}$.

5. Find the extrema of $f(x) = x^2 - 4x - 5$ on $[0, 5]$.

6. Find the points of inflection of $f(x) = 3x^4 - 24x + 2$.

7. Find the points of inflection of $f(x) = \dfrac{x^2}{1+x^2}$.

8. Find two positive numbers whose product is 200 such that the sum of the first plus three times the second is a minimum.

9. Three rectangular fields are to be enclosed by 3000 feet of fencing, as shown in the accompanying figure. What dimensions should be used so that the enclosed area will be a maximum?

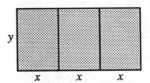

10. Find the number of units that produces a maximum revenue for $R = 400x^2 - 0.02x^3$.

11. Find the price per unit p that produces a maximum profit P given the cost function $C = 300x + 45{,}000$ and the demand function $p = 21{,}000 - 0.03x^2$.

12. Given the demand function $p = 600 - 0.02x^2$, find η (the price elasticity of demand) when $x = 100$.

13. Find $\displaystyle\lim_{x \to 3^-} \dfrac{x+4}{x-3}$.

14. Find $\displaystyle\lim_{x \to \infty} \frac{4x^3 - 9x^2 + 1}{1 - 2x^3}$.

15. Sketch the graph of $f(x) = \dfrac{x^2}{x^2 - 9}$.

16. Sketch the graph of $f(x) = \dfrac{x + 2}{x^2 + 5}$.

17. Sketch the graph of $f(x) = x^3 + 3x^2 + 3x - 1$.

18. Sketch the graph of $f(x) = |4 - 2x|$.

19. Sketch the graph of $f(x) = (2 - x)^{2/3}$.

20. Use differentials to approximate $\sqrt[3]{65}$.

Graphing Calculator Required

21. Graph $y = \dfrac{5x}{\sqrt{x^2 + 4}}$ on a graphing calculator and find any asymptotes that exist. Are there any relative extrema?

22. Graph $y = \dfrac{2x^4 - 5x + 1}{x^4 + 1}$ on a graphing calculator. Is it possible for a graph to cross its horizontal asymptote?

CHAPTER 4
Exponential and Logarithmic Functions

Section 4.1   Exponential Functions

1. Evaluate the following.

   (a) $5(5^3)$ (b) $27^{2/3}$ (c) $64^{3/4}$

   (d) $81^{1/2}$ (e) $25^{3/2}$ (f) $32^{2/5}$

   Solution:

   (a) $5(5^3) = 5^4 = 625$ (b) $27^{2/3} = (\sqrt[3]{27})^2 = 3^2 = 9$

   (c) $64^{3/4} = (2^6)^{3/4}$ (d) $81^{1/2} = \sqrt{81} = 9$

   $\qquad = 2^{9/2} = \sqrt{2^9} = 2^4 \sqrt{2} = 16\sqrt{2}$

   (e) $25^{3/2} = (\sqrt{25})^3 = 5^3 = 125$ (f) $32^{2/5} = (\sqrt[5]{32})^2 = 2^2 = 4$

3. Use the properties of exponents to simplify the following.

   (a) $(5^2)(5^3)$ (b) $(5^2)(5^{-3})$

   (c) $(5^2)^2$ (d) 5^{-3}

   Solution:

   (a) $(5^2)(5^3) = 5^5 = 3125$ (b) $(5^2)(5^{-3}) = 5^{-1} = \dfrac{1}{5}$

   (c) $(5^2)^2 = 5^4 = 625$ (d) $5^{-3} = \dfrac{1}{5^3} = \dfrac{1}{125}$

5. Use the properties of exponents to simplify the following.

   (a) $\dfrac{5^3}{25^2}$ (b) $(9^{2/3})(3)(3^{2/3})$

   (c) $[(25^{1/2})(5^2)]^{1/3}$ (d) $(8^2)(4^3)$

   Solution:

   (a) $\dfrac{5^3}{25^2} = \dfrac{5^3}{(5^2)^2} = \dfrac{5^3}{5^4} = \dfrac{1}{5}$

   (b) $(9^{2/3})(3)(3^{2/3}) = (3^2)^{2/3}(3)(3^{2/3})$

   $\qquad\qquad\qquad\qquad = (3^{4/3})(3^{5/3})$

   $\qquad\qquad\qquad\qquad = 3^{9/3} = 3^3 = 27$

   (c) $[(25^{1/2})t^2] = [5 \cdot 5^2]^{1/3}$ (d) $(8^2)(4^3) = (64)(64) = 4096$

   $\qquad\qquad = [5^3]^{1/3} = 5$

7. Use the properties of exponents to simplify the following.

(a) $e^3(e^4)$

(b) $(e^3)^4$

(c) $(e^3)^{-2}$

(d) e^0

Solution:

(a) $e^3(e^4) = e^7$

(b) $(e^3)^4 = e^{12}$

(c) $(e^3)^{-2} = e^{-6} = \dfrac{1}{e^6}$

(d) $e^0 = 1$

9. If $3^x = 81$, solve for x.

Solution:

$$3^x = 81 = 3^4$$
$$x = 4$$

11. If $\left(\frac{1}{3}\right)^{x-1} = 27$, solve for x.

Solution:

$$\left(\tfrac{1}{3}\right)^{x-1} = 27$$
$$3^{-(x-1)} = 3^3$$
$$-(x-1) = 3$$
$$-x + 1 = 3$$
$$x = -2$$

13. If $4^3 = (x+2)^3$, solve for x.

Solution:

$$4^3 = (x+2)^3$$
$$4 = x + 2$$
$$x = 2$$

15. If $x^{3/4} = 8$, solve for x.

Solution:

$$x = 8^{4/3} = (\sqrt[3]{8})^4 = 2^4 = 16$$

17. If $e^{3x} = e$, solve for x.

Solution:

$$e^{-3x} = e$$
$$-3x = 1$$
$$x = -\frac{1}{3}$$

19. If $e^{\sqrt{x}} = e^3$, solve for x.

Solution:

$$e^{\sqrt{x}} = e^3$$
$$\sqrt{x} = 3$$
$$x = 9$$

21. If $x^{2/3} = \sqrt[3]{e^2}$, solve for x.

Solution:

$$x^{2/3} = \sqrt[3]{e^2} = e^{2/3}$$
$$x = e$$

23. Match $f(x) = 3^x$ with the correct graph from the text.

Solution:

The graph is an exponential curve with the following characteristics.

Passes through $(0, 1)$, $(1, 3)$, $\left(-1, \frac{1}{3}\right)$

Horizontal asymptote: x-axis

Therefore, it matches graph (e).

25. Match $f(x) = -3^x$ with the correct graph from the text.

Solution:

The graph of $f(x) = -3^x = (-1)(3^x)$ is an exponential curve with the following characteristics.

Passes through $(0, -1)$, $(1, -3)$, $\left(-1, -\frac{1}{3}\right)$

Horizontal asymptote: x-axis

Therefore, it matches graph (a).

27. Match $f(x) = 3^{-x} - 1$ with the correct graph.

Solution:

The graph of $f(x) = 3^{-x} - 1 = \left(\frac{1}{3}\right)^x - 1$ is an exponential curve with the following characteristics.

Passes through $(0, 0)$, $\left(1, -\frac{2}{3}\right)$, $(-1, 2)$

Horizontal asymptote: $y = -1$

Therefore, it matches graph (d).

29. Sketch the graph of $f(x) = 6^x$

Solution:

x	-2	-1	0	1	2
$f(x)$	$\frac{1}{36}$	$\frac{1}{6}$	1	6	36

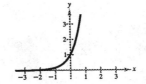

31. Sketch the graph of $f(x) = \left(\frac{1}{5}\right)^x$.

Solution:

x	-2	-1	0	1	2
$f(x)$	25	5	1	$\frac{1}{5}$	$\frac{1}{25}$

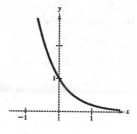

33. Sketch the graph of $y = 3^{-x^2}$.

Solution:

x	-2	-1	0	1	2
y	$\frac{1}{81}$	$\frac{1}{3}$	1	$\frac{1}{3}$	$\frac{1}{81}$

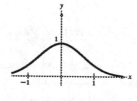

35. Sketch the graph of $y = 3^{-|x|}$.

Solution:

x	-2	-1	0	1	2
y	$\frac{1}{9}$	$\frac{1}{3}$	1	$\frac{1}{3}$	$\frac{1}{9}$

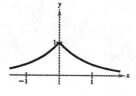

37. Sketch the graph of $s(t) = \dfrac{3^{-t}}{4}$.

Solution:

$$s(t) = \frac{3^{-t}}{4} = \frac{1}{4(3^t)}$$

t	-2	-1	0	1	2
$s(t)$	$\frac{9}{4}$	$\frac{3}{4}$	$\frac{1}{4}$	$\frac{1}{12}$	$\frac{1}{36}$

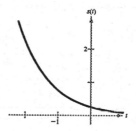

39. Sketch the graph of $h(x) = e^{x-2}$.

Solution:

x	-1	0	1	2	3
$h(x)$	0.050	0.135	0.368	1	2.718

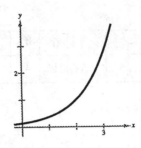

41. Sketch the graph of $N(t) = 500e^{-0.2t}$.

Solution:

t	-5	0	5	10	20
$N(t)$	1359.1	500	183.9	67.7	9.16

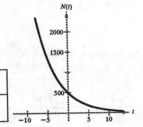

43. Sketch the graph of $g(x) = \dfrac{2}{1 + e^{x^2}}$.

Solution:

x	-2	-1	0	1	2
$g(x)$	0.036	0.538	1	0.538	0.036

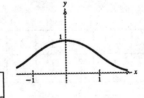

45. Complete the table in the textbook to determine the balance A for $P = \$1000$ dollars invested at rate $r3\%$ for $t = 10$ years, compounded n times per year.

Solution:

$$A = P\left(1 + \frac{r}{n}\right)^{nt}, r = 0.03, t = 10, P = 1000$$

$$= 1000\left(1 + \frac{0.03}{n}\right)^{10n}$$

Continuous compounding: $A = Pe^{rt} = 1000e^{(0.03)(10)}$

n	1	2	4	12	365	Continuous
A	1343.92	1346.86	1348.35	1349.35	1349.84	1349.86

47. Complete the table in the textbook to determine the balance A for $P = \$1000$ dollars invested at rate $r = 3\%$ for $t = 40$ years, compounded n times per year.

Solution:

$$A = P\left(1 + \frac{r}{n}\right)^{nt}, P = 1000, r = 0.03, t = 40$$

$$= 1000\left(1 + \frac{0.03}{n}\right)^{40n}$$

Continuous compounding: $A = Pe^{rt} = 1000e^{(0.03)(40)}$

n	1	2	4	12	365	Continuous
A	3264.04	3290.66	3305.28	3315.15	3319.95	3320.12

49. Complete the table in the textbook to determine the balance $A = \$100,000$ for P dollars invested at rate $r = 4\%$ for t years, compounded continuously.

Solution:

$$A = Pe^{rt}, A = 100,000, r = 0.04 \Rightarrow P = 100,000e^{-0.04t}$$

t	1	10	20	30	40	50
P	96,078.94	67,032.00	44,932.90	30,119.42	20,189.65	13,533.53

51. Complete the table in the textbook to determine the balance $A = \$100,000$ for P dollars invested at rate $r = 4\%$ for t years, compounded continuously.

Solution:

$$A = P\left(1 + \frac{r}{n}\right)^{nt}, A = 100,000, r = 0.05, n = 12 \Rightarrow P = \frac{100,000}{\left(1 + \frac{0.05}{12}\right)^{12}}$$

t	1	10	20	30	40	50
P	95,152.82	60,716.10	36,864.45	22,382.66	13,589.88	8251.24

53. *Demand* The demand function for a certain product is given by

$$p = 5000\left(1 - \frac{4}{4 + e^{-0.002x}}\right).$$

Find the price of the product if the quantity demanded is (a) $x = 100$ units, and (b) $x = 500$ units. What is the limit of the price as x increases without bound?

Solution:

(a) $p(100) = 5000\left(1 - \frac{4}{4 + e^{-0.002(100)}}\right) \approx \$849.53$

(b) $p(500) = 5000\left(1 - 1 - \frac{4}{4 - e^{-0.002(500)}}\right) \approx \$421.12 \lim\limits_{x \to \infty} p = 0$

55. *Probability* The average time between incoming calls at a switchboard is 3 minutes. If a call has just come in, the probability that the next call will come within the next t minutes is given by $P(t) = 1 - e^{-t/3}$. Find
(a) $P\left(\frac{1}{2}\right)$, (b) $P(2)$, and (c) $P(5)$.

Solution:

(a) $P\left(\frac{1}{2}\right) = 1 - e^{-1/6} \approx 0.1535 = 15.35\%$

(b) $P(2) = 1 - e^{-2/3} \approx 0.4866 = 48.66\%$

(c) $P(5) = 1 - e^{-5/3} \approx 0.8111 = 81.11\%$

57. *Population Growth* The population of a bacterial culture is given by the logistics growth function

$y = 925/(1 + e^{-0.3t})$ where y is the number of bacteria and t is the time in days.

(a) Sketch the graph of the model.

(b) Does the population have a limit as t increases without bound?

Solution:

(a)

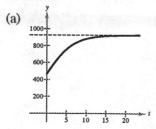

(b) $\displaystyle \lim_{t \to \infty} \frac{925}{1 + e^{-0.3t}} = \frac{925}{1 + 0} = 925$

59. *Learning Theory* In a learning theory project, the proportion P of correct responses after n trials can be modeled by

$$P = \frac{0.83}{1 + e^{-0.2n}}.$$

(a) Use a graphing utility to estimate the proportion of correct responses after ten trials. Check your result analytically.

(b) Use a graphing utility to estimate the number of trials required to have a proportion of correct responses of 0.75.

(c) Does the proportion of correct responses have a limit as n increases without bound? Explain your answer.

Solution:

$$p = \frac{0.83}{1 + e^{-0.2n}}$$

(a) $n = 10 \Rightarrow P = 0.731$

(b) $P = 0.75 \Rightarrow n \approx 11.19$ or 11 trials

(c) $\displaystyle \lim_{n \to \infty} \frac{0.83}{1 + e^{-0.2n}} = \frac{0.83}{1 + 0} = 0.83$

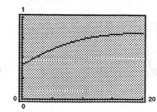

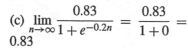

61. Use a computer or graphics calculator to sketch the graph of $f(x) = (e^x + e^{-x})/2$, find any horizontal asymptotes, and determine if the function is continuous on the entire real line.

Solution:

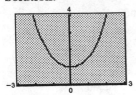

(b) $\lim\limits_{x \to \pm\infty} \dfrac{e^x + e^{-x}}{2} = \infty$

No horizontal asymptotes

Continuous on the entire real line

63. Use a computer or graphics calculator to sketch the graph of $f(x) = 2/(1 + e^{1/x})$, find any horizontal asymptotes, and determine if the function is continuous on the entire real line.

Solution:

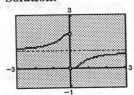

(b) $\lim\limits_{x \to \pm\infty} \dfrac{2}{1 + e^{1/x}} = \dfrac{2}{1+1} = 1$

Horizontal asymptote: $y = 1$

Discontinuous at $x = 0$

Section 4.2   Derivatives of Exponential Functions

1. Find the slope of the tangent line to $y = e^{3x}$ at the point $(0, 1)$.

Solution:

$$y' = 3e^{3x}$$
$$y'(0) = 3$$

3. Find the slope of the tangent line to $y = e^{-x}$ at the point $(0, 1)$.

Solution:

$$y' = -e^{-x}$$
$$y'(0) = -1$$

5. Find the derivative of $y = e^{4x}$.

Solution:

$$y' = 4e^{4x}$$

7. Find the derivative of $y = e^{-2x+x^2}$.

Solution:

$$y' = (-2 + 2x)e^{-2x+x^2} = 2(x-1)e^{-2x+x^2}$$

9. Find the derivative of $f(x) = e^{1/x}$.

Solution:

$$f'(x) = \left(-\frac{1}{x^2}\right)e^{1/x} = -\frac{e^{1/x}}{x^2}$$

11. Find the derivative of $g(x) = e^{\sqrt{x}}$.

Solution:

$$g'(x) = \left(\frac{1}{2}x^{-1/2}\right)e^{\sqrt{x}} = \frac{e^{\sqrt{x}}}{2\sqrt{x}}$$

13. Find the derivative of $f(x) = (x^2 + 1)e^{4x}$.

Solution:

$$f'(x) = (x^2 + 1)4e^{4x} + (2x)e^{4x} = e^{4x}[4x^2 + 2x + 4]$$

15. Find the derivative of $y = (e^{-x} + e^x)^3$.

Solution:

$$y' = 3(e^{-x} + e^x)^2(-e^{-x} + e^x) = 3(e^x - e^{-x})(e^{-x} + e^x)^2$$

17. Find the derivative of $f(x) = \dfrac{2}{e^x + e^{-x}}$.

Solution:

$$f(x) = \frac{2}{e^x + e^{-x}} = 2(e^x + e^{-x})^{-1}$$

$$f'(x) = -2(e^x + e^{-x})^{-2}(e^x - e^{-x}) = -\frac{2(e^x - e^{-x})}{(e^x + e^{-x})^2}$$

19. Find the derivative of $y = xe^x - 4e^{-x}$.

Solution:

$$y' = xe^x + e^x + 4e^{-x}$$

21. Given $xe^x + 2ye^x = 0$, find dy/dx implicitly.

Solution:

$$xe^x + 2ye^x = 0$$

$$xe^x + e^x + 2ye^x + 2\frac{dy}{dx}e^x = 0$$

$$x + 1 + 2y + 2\frac{dy}{dx} = 0$$

$$\frac{dy}{dx} = \frac{1}{2}(-x - 1 - 2y)$$

Alternatively,

$$x + 2y = 0$$

$$y = -\frac{x}{2}$$

$$\frac{dy}{dx} = -\frac{1}{2}$$

These answers are the same since $2ye^x = -xe^x$ implies $2y = -x$.

23. Find the second derivative of $f(x) = 2e^{3x} + 3e^{-2x}$.

Solution:

$$f'(x) = 6e^{3x} - 6e^{-2x}$$

$$f''(x) = 18e^{3x} + 12e^{-2x} = 6(3e^{3x} + 2e^{-2x})$$

25. Find the second derivative of $f(x) = 5e^{-x} - 2e^{-5x}$

Solution:

$$f'(x) = -5e^{-x} + 10e^{-5x}$$

$$f''(x) = 5e^{-x} - 50e^{-5x}$$

27. Graph and analyze the function $f(x) = \dfrac{1}{2 - e^{-x}}$.

Solution:

$$f(x) = \frac{1}{2 - e^{-x}}$$

$$f'(x) = \frac{-e^{-x}}{(2 - e^{-x})^2}$$

$$f''(x) = \frac{e^{-x}(2 + e^{-x})}{(2 - e^{-x})^3}$$

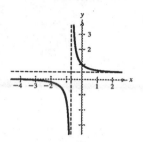

Horizontal asymptote to the right: $y = \dfrac{1}{2}$

Horizontal asymptote to the left: $y = 0$

Vertical asymptote when $2 = e^{-x} \Rightarrow x \approx -0.693$

No relative extrema nor inflection points.

29. Find the extrema and the points of inflection and sketch the graph of $f(x) = x^2 e^{-x}$.

Solution:

$$f(x) = x^2 e^{-x}$$

$$f'(x) = -x^2 e^{-x} + 2xe^{-x} = xe^{-x}(2 - x)$$

$$f'(x) = 0 \text{ when } x = 0 \text{ and } x = 2$$

Since $f''(0) > 0$ and $f''(2) < 0$, we have the following.

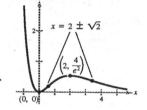

Relative minimum: $(0, 0)$

Relative maximum: $(2, 4/e^2)$

Since $f''(x) = 0$ when $x = 2 \pm \sqrt{2}$, the inflection points occur at $(2 - \sqrt{2},\ 0.191)$ and $(2 + \sqrt{2},\ 0.384)$.

x	-2	-1	0	1	2	3
$f(x)$	29.556	2.718	0	0.368	0.541	0.448

31. Use a graphing utility to graph the function $f(x) = \dfrac{8}{1 + e^{-0.5x}}$

Solution:

$$f(x) = \frac{8}{1 + e^{-0.5x}}$$

Horizontal asymptotes: $y = 8$(as $x \to \infty$)

$$y = 0(\text{ as } x \to -\infty)$$

No vertical asymptotes.

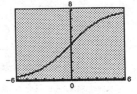

33. *Depreciation* The value V of an item that is being depreciated is given as a function of the time t, where t is measured in years.

$$V = 15{,}000e^{-0.6286t}$$

(a) Sketch the graph of the function over the interval $[0, 10]$.

(b) Find the rate at which V is changing when $t = 1$.

(c) Find the rate at which V is changing when $t = 5$.

(d) Sketch this depreciation model with a linear model. What are the advantages of each?

Solution:

(a)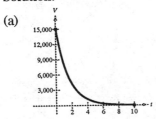

(b) $V'(1) = -9429e^{-0.6286} \approx -\$5028.84$ per year

(c) $V'(5) = -9429e^{-0.6286(5)} \approx -\$406.89$ per year

(d) In this model, the initial rate of depreciation is greater than in a linear model.

35. *Forest Defoliation* To estimate the defoliation p (in percent of foliage) caused by gypsy moths during a year, a forester counts the number x (in thousands) of egg masses on $\frac{1}{40}$ of an acre the preceding fall. The defolilation is modeled by

$$p = \frac{300}{3 + 17e^{-1.57x}}$$

(a) Use a graphing utility to graph the model.

(b) Estimate the percent of defoliation if 2000 egg masses are counted.

(c) Estimate the number of egg masses for which the amount of defoliation is increasing most rapidly.

Solution:

$$p = \frac{300}{3 + 17e^{-1.57x}}$$

(a)

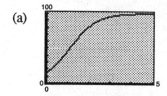

(b) When $x = 2$, $p = 80.3\%$

(c) p' is increasing most rapidly when $x \approx 1.1$ (point of inflection).

37. *Compound Interest* The balance A (in dollars) in a savings accout is given by $A = 5000e^{0.08t}$, where t is measured in years. Find the rate at which the balance is changing when (a) $t = 1$ year, (b) $t = 10$ years, and (c) $t = 50$ years.

Solution:

$$A' = 400^{0.08t}$$

(a) $A'(1) \approx \$433.31$ per year.

(b) $A'(10) \approx \$890.22$ per year.

(c) $A'(50) \approx \$21,839.26$ per year.

39. *Orchard Yield* The yield V (in pounds per acre) for an orchard at age t (in years) is modeled by

$$V = 7955.6e^{-0.0458/t}$$

At what rate is the yield changing when $t = 5$ years? When $t = 10$ years? When $t = 25$ years?

Solution:

$$V' = \frac{364.36648e^{-0.0458/t}}{t^2}$$

When $t = 5$, $V' = 14.44$.
When $t = 10$, $V' = 3.63$.
When $t = 25$, $V' = 0.58$.

41. Use a graphing utility to graph the normal probability density function with $\mu = 0$ and $\sigma = 2$, 3, and 4 on the same viewing rectangle. What effect does the standard deviation σ have on the function? Explain.

Solution:

$$f(x) = \frac{1}{\sigma\sqrt{\pi}}e^{-(x-\mu)^2/2\sigma^2} = \frac{1}{\sigma\sqrt{2\pi}}e^{-x^2/2\sigma^2}$$

For larger σ, the graph becomes flatter.

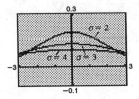

Section 4.3   Logarithmic Functions

1. Write the logarithmic equation $\ln 2 = 0.6931\ldots$ as an exponential equation.

Solution:

$$e^{0.6931\ldots} = 2$$

3. Write the logarithmic equation $\ln 0.2 = -1.6094\ldots$ as an exponential equation.

Solution:

$$e^{-1.6094\ldots} = 0.2$$

5. Write the exponential equation $e^0 = 1$ as a logarithmic equation.

Solution:

$$\ln 1 = 0$$

7. Write the exponential equation $e^{-3} = 0.0498\ldots$ as a logarithmic equation.

Solution:

$$\ln 0.0498 = -3$$

9. Use the graph of $y = \ln x$ to match $f(x) = 2 + \ln x$ with the correct graph from the text.

Solution:

The graph is a logarithmic curve that passes through the point (1, 2) with a vertical asymptote at $x = 0$. Therefore, it matches graph (c).

11. Use the graph of $y = \ln x$ to match $f(x) = \ln(x + 2)$ with the correct graph from the text.

Solution:

The graph is a logarithmic curve that passes through the point $(-1, \ 0)$ with a vertical asymptote at $x = -2$. Therefore, it matches graph (b).

13. Sketch the graph of $y = \ln(x - 1)$.

Solution:

x	1.5	2	3	4	5
y	−0.69	0	0.69	1.10	1.39

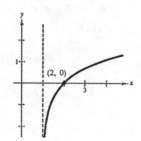

15. Sketch the graph of $y = \ln 2x$.

Solution:

x	.0.25	0.5	1	3	5
y	−0.69	0	0.69	1.79	2.30

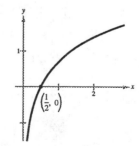

17. Sketch the graph of $y = 3 \ln x$.

Solution:

x	0.5	1	2	3	4
y	-2.08	0	2.08	3.30	4.16

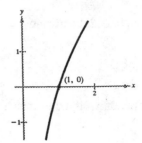

19. Show that $f(x) = e^{2x}$ and $g(x) = \ln \sqrt{x}$ are inverses of each other and sketch their graphs on the same coordinate axes.

Solution:

$$g(x) = \ln \sqrt{x} = \tfrac{1}{2} \ln x$$
$$f(g(x)) = f\left(\tfrac{1}{2} \ln x\right)$$
$$= e^{2(1/2 \ln x)} = e^{\ln x} = x$$
$$g(f(x)) = g(e^{2x})$$
$$= \tfrac{1}{2} \ln e^{2x} = \tfrac{1}{2}(2x) \ln e = x$$

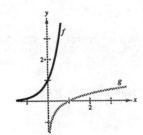

21. Show that $f(x) = e^{2x-1}$ and $g(x) = \tfrac{1}{2} + \ln \sqrt{x}$ are inverses of each other and sketch their graphs on the same coordinate axes.

Solution:

$$f(g(x)) = f(\tfrac{1}{2} + \ln \sqrt{x}) = e^{2(\frac{1}{2} + \ln \sqrt{x}) - 1} = e^{2 \ln x^{1/2}} = e^{\ln x} = x$$
$$g(f(x)) = g(e^{2x-1}) = \frac{1}{2} + \ln \sqrt{e^{2x-1}} = \frac{1}{2} + \frac{1}{2} \ln e^{2x-1}$$
$$= \frac{1}{2} + \frac{1}{2}(2x - 1) = x$$

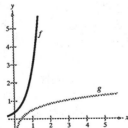

23. Apply the inverse properties of $\ln x$ and e^x to simplify $\ln e^{x^2}$.

Solution:

$$\ln e^{x^2} = x^2$$

25. Apply the inverse properties of $\ln x$ and e^x to simplify $e^{\ln(5x+2)}$.

Solution:

$$e^{\ln(5x+2)} = 5x + 2$$

27. Apply the inverse properties of $\ln x$ and e^x to simplify $e^{\ln \sqrt{x}}$.

Solution:

$$e^{\ln \sqrt{x}} = \sqrt{x}$$

29. Use the properties of logarithms and the fact that $\ln 2 \approx 0.6931$ and $\ln 3 \approx 1.0986$ to approximate the following.

(a) $\ln 6$ (b) $\ln \frac{3}{2}$

(c) $\ln 81$ (d) $\ln \sqrt{3}$

Solution:

(a) $\ln 6 = \ln(2 \cdot 3) = \ln 2 + \ln 3 = 0.6931 + 1.0986 = 1.7917$

(b) $\ln \frac{3}{2} = \ln 3 - \ln 2 = 1.0986 - 0.6931 = 0.4055$

(c) $\ln 81 = \ln 3^4 = 4 \ln 3 = 4(1.0986) = 4.3944$

(d) $\ln \sqrt{3} = \left(\frac{1}{2}\right) \ln 3 = \left(\frac{1}{2}\right)(1.0986) = 0.5493$

31. Use the properties of logarithms to write $\ln\left(\frac{2}{3}\right)$ as a sum, difference, or multiple of logarithms.

Solution:

$$\ln \frac{2}{3} = \ln 2 - \ln 3$$

33. Use the properties of logarithms to write $\ln xyz$ as a sum, difference, or multiple of logarithms.

Solution:

$$\ln xyz = \ln x + \ln y + \ln z$$

35. Use the properties of logarithms to write $\ln \sqrt{x^2 + 1}$ as a sum, difference, or multiple of logarithms.

Solution:

$$\ln \sqrt{x^2 + 1} = \ln(x^2 + 1)^{1/2} = \frac{1}{2} \ln(x^2 + 1)$$

37. Use the properties of logarithms to write the following as a sum, difference, or multiple of logarithms.

$$\ln \frac{2x}{\sqrt{x^2 - 1}}$$

Solution:

$$\ln \frac{2x}{\sqrt{x^2 - 1}} = \ln 2x - \ln \sqrt{x^2 - 1}$$

$$= \ln 2 + \ln x - \frac{1}{2} \ln[(x+1)(x-1)]$$

$$= \ln 2 + \ln x - \frac{1}{2}[\ln(x+1) + \ln(x-1)]$$

$$= \ln 2 + \ln x - \frac{1}{2} \ln(x+1) - \frac{1}{2} \ln(x-1)$$

39. Use the properties of logarithms to write $\ln \dfrac{3x(x+1)}{(2x+1)^2}$ as a sum, difference, or multiple of logarithms.

Solution:

$$\ln \frac{3x(x+1)}{(2x+1)^2} = \ln[3x(x+1)] - \ln(2x+1)^2$$

$$= \ln 3 + \ln x + \ln(x+1) - 2\ln(2x+1)$$

41. Write $\ln(x-2) - \ln(x+2)$ as a single logarithm.

Solution:

$$\ln(x-2) - \ln(x+2) = \ln \frac{x-2}{x+2}$$

43. Write $3\ln x + 2\ln y - 4\ln z$ as a single logarithm.

Solution:

$$3\ln x + 2\ln y - 4\ln z = \ln x^3 + \ln y^2 - \ln z^4 = \ln\left(\frac{x^3 y^2}{z^4}\right)$$

45. Write $3[\ln x + \ln(x+3) - \ln(x+4)]$ as a single logarithm.

Solution:

$$3[\ln x + \ln(x+3) - \ln(x+4)] = 3\ln \frac{x(x+3)}{x+4}$$

$$= \ln\left(\frac{x(x+3)}{x+4}\right)^3$$

47. Write $\frac{3}{2}[\ln x(x^2+1) - \ln(x+1)]$ as a single logarithm.

Solution:

$$\frac{3}{2}[\ln x(x^2+1) - \ln(x+1)] = \frac{3}{2}\ln\frac{x(x^2+1)}{x+1} = \ln\left[\frac{x(x^2+1)}{x+1}\right]^{3/2}$$

49. Write $2[\ln x - \ln(x+1)] - 3[\ln x - \ln(x-1)]$ as a single logarithm.

Solution:

$$2[\ln x - \ln(x+1)] - 3[\ln x - \ln(x-1)] = 2\ln x - 2\ln(x+1) - 3\ln x + 3\ln(x-1)$$

$$= \ln(x-1)^3 - \ln(x+1)^2 - \ln x$$

$$= \ln\frac{(x-1)^3}{(x+1)^2 x}$$

51. If $e^{\ln x} = 4$, solve for x.

Solution:

$$x = 4$$

53. If $\ln x = 0$, solve for x.

Solution:

$$x = e^0 = 1$$

55. If $e^{x+1} = 4$, solve for x.

Solution:

$$x + 1 = \ln 4$$
$$x = (\ln 4) - 1 \approx 0.3863$$

57. If $300e^{-0.2t} = 700$, solve for t.

Solution:

$$300e^{-0.2t} = 700$$
$$e^{-0.2t} = \frac{7}{3}$$
$$-0.2t = \ln 7 - \ln 3$$
$$t = \frac{\ln 7 - \ln 3}{-0.2} \approx -4.2365$$

59. If $5^{2x} = 15$, solve for x.

Solution:

$$2x \ln 5 = \ln 15$$
$$x = \frac{\ln 15}{2\ln 5} \approx 0.8413$$

61. If $500(1.07)^t = 1000$, solve for t.

Solution:

$$500(1.07)^t = 1000$$
$$t \ln 1.07 = \ln 2$$
$$t = \frac{\ln 2}{\ln 1.07} \approx 10.2448$$

63. If $1000\left(1 + \dfrac{0.07}{12}\right)^{12t} = 3000$, solve for t.

Solution:

$$1000\left(1 + \frac{0.07}{12}\right)^{12t} = 3000$$

$$\left(1 + \frac{0.07}{12}\right)^{12t} = 3$$

$$12t \ln\left(1 + \frac{0.07}{12}\right) = \ln 3$$

$$t = \frac{\ln 3}{12 \ln[1 + (0.07/12)]} \approx 15.7402$$

65. If $\dfrac{36}{1 + e^{-t}} = 20$, solve for t.

Solution:

$$\frac{36}{1 + e^{-t}} = 20$$

$$\frac{1 + e^{-t}}{36} = \frac{1}{20}$$

$$1 + e^{-t} = \frac{36}{20}$$

$$e^{-t} = \frac{16}{20} = \frac{4}{5}$$

$$-t = \ln \frac{4}{5}$$

$$t = -\ln \frac{4}{5} \approx 0.2231$$

67. *Compound Interest* A deposit of \$1000 is made into a fund with an annual interest rate of 5%. Find the time for the investment to double if the interest is compounded (a) annually, (b) monthly, (c) daily, and (d) continuously.

Solution:

$$P = 1000, \quad r = 0.05, \quad A = 2000$$

(a) $2000 = 1000(1 + 0.05)^t$

$$t = \frac{\ln 2}{\ln 1.05} \approx 14.2 \text{ years}$$

(b) $2000 = 1000\left(1 + \dfrac{0.05}{12}\right)^{12t}$

$$t \approx \frac{\ln 2}{12 \ln 1.00417} \approx 13.88 \text{ years}$$

(c) $2000 = 1000\left(1 + \dfrac{0.05}{365}\right)^{365t}$

$$t \approx \frac{\ln 2}{365 \ln 1.000137} \approx 13.87 \text{ years}$$

(d) $2000 = 1000e^{0.05t}$

$$t = \frac{\ln 2}{0.05} \approx 13.86 \text{ years}$$

69. *Compound Interest* Complete the table for the time t necessary for P dollars to triple if interest is compounded continuously at the rate r.

Solution:

$$3P = Pe^{rt}$$

$$3 = e^{rt}$$

$$\ln 3 = rt$$

$$t = \frac{\ln 3}{r}$$

r	2%	4%	6%	8%	10%	12%	14%
t	54.93	27.47	18.31	13.73	10.99	9.16	7.85

71. *Population Growth* The population P of Pensacola, Florida from 1970 through 1990 can be modeled by

$$P = 243{,}000e^{0.0173t},$$

where $t = 0$ corresponds to 1970. According to this model, in what year will Pensacola have a population of 400,000?

Solution:

$$P = 243{,}000e^{0.01737t}$$

$$400{,}000 = 243{,}000e^{0.01737t}$$

$$\frac{400}{243} = e^{0.01737t}$$

$$\ln\left(\frac{400}{243}\right) = 0.01737t$$

$$t = \frac{\ln\left(\frac{400}{243}\right)}{0.01737} \approx 28.69 \text{ years}$$

The city will have a population of 400,000 in the year 1999 (1970 + 29).

Alternatively, you could use a graphing utility to find the point of intersection of $y_1 = 243{,}000e^{0.01737t}$ and $y_2 = 400{,}000$, which is $t \approx 28.69$.

73. *Carbon Dating* When organic material dies, its radioactive carbon isotopes begin to decay, with a half-life of about 5700 years. Thus, the ratio R of carbon isotopes to carbon-14 atoms is

$$R = 10^{-12} \left(\frac{1}{2}\right)^{t/5700},$$

where t is the time (in years) and $t = 0$ represents the time when the organic material died. Use $R = 0.32 \times 10^{-12}$ to estimate the age of the fossil.

Solution:

$$0.32 \times x10^{-12} = 10^{-12} \left(\frac{1}{2}\right)^{t/5700}$$

$$0.32 = \left(\frac{1}{2}\right)^{t/5700}$$

$$\ln 0.32 = \frac{t}{5700} \ln \frac{1}{2}$$

$$t = \frac{5700 \ln 0.32}{\ln \frac{1}{2}} \approx 9370 \text{ years}$$

75. *Carbon Dating* When organic material dies, its radioactive carbon isotopes begin to decay, with a half-life of about 5700 years. Thus, the ratio R of carbon isotopes to carbon–14 atoms is

$$R = 10^{-12} \left(\frac{1}{2}\right)^{t/5700},$$

where t is the time (in years) and $t = 0$ represents the time when the organic material died. Use $R = 0.22 \times 10^{-12}$ to estimate the age of the fossil.

Solution:

$$0.22 \times 10^{-12} = 10^{-12} \left(\frac{1}{2}\right)^{t/5700}$$

$$0.22 = \left(\frac{1}{2}\right)^{t/5700}$$

$$\ln 0.22 = \frac{t}{5700} \ln \frac{1}{2}$$

$$t = \frac{5700 \ln 0.22}{\ln \frac{1}{2}} \approx 12,451 \text{ years}$$

77. *Human Memory Model* Students in a mathematics class were given an exam and then retested monthly with equivalent exams. The average score for the class was given by the model

$$f(t) = 80 - 14\ln(t + 1), \quad 0 \le t \le 12$$

where t is the time in months.

(a) What was the average score on the original exam ($t = 0$)?

(b) What was the average score after four months?

(c) After how many months was the average score 46?

Solution:

(a) $S(0) = 80 - 14\ln 1 = 80$

(b) $S(4) = 80 - 14\ln 5 \approx 57.5$

(c) $46 = 80 - \ln(t + 1) \ln(t + 1) = \frac{34}{14} \Rightarrow \approx 10$ months.

79. Use a calculator to demonstrate that $\dfrac{\ln x}{\ln y} \ne \ln \dfrac{x}{y} = \ln x - \ln y$ by completing the table.

Solution:

x	y	$\dfrac{\ln x}{\ln y}$	$\ln \dfrac{x}{y}$	$\ln x - \ln y$
1	2	0.0000	−0.6931	−0.6931
3	4	0.7925	−0.2877	−0.2877
10	5	1.4307	0.6931	0.6931
4	0.5	−2.0000	2.0794	2.0794

81. Use a graphing utility to show that $f = g$ by sketching f and g on the same coordinate axes. (Assume $x > 0$.)

$$f(x) = \ln \frac{x^2}{4}$$

$$g(x) = 2\ln x - \ln 4$$

Solution:

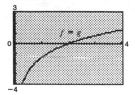

The graphs appear to be identical.

Section 4.4   Derivatives of Logarithmic Functions

1. Find the slope of the tangent line to the graph of $y = \ln x^3$ at the point $(1, 0)$.

   Solution:

$$y = \ln x^3 = 3\ln x$$

$$y' = \frac{3}{x}$$

$$y'(1) = 3$$

3. Find the slope of the tangent line to the graph of $y = \ln x^2$ at the point $(1, 0)$.

   Solution:

$$y = \ln x^2 = 2\ln x$$

$$y' = \frac{2}{x}$$

$$y'(1) = 2$$

5. Find the slope of the tangent line to the graph of $y = \ln x^{3/2}$ at the point $(1, 0)$.

   Solution:

$$y = \ln x^{3/2} = \frac{3}{2}\ln x$$

$$y' = \frac{3}{2x}$$

$$y'(1) = \frac{3}{2}$$

7. Find the derivative of $y = \ln x^2$.

   Solution:

$$y = \ln x^2 = 2\ln x$$

$$y' = \frac{2}{x}$$

9. Find the derivative of $f(x) = \ln 2x$.

   Solution:

$$f(x) = \ln 2x$$

$$f'(x) = \frac{2}{2x} = \frac{1}{x}$$

11. Find the derivative of $y = \ln\sqrt{x^4 - 4x}$.

Solution:

$$y = \ln\sqrt{x^4 - 4x} = \frac{1}{2}\ln(x^4 - 4x)$$

$$y' = \frac{1}{2}\left(\frac{4x^3 - 4}{x^4 - 4x}\right) = \frac{2(x^3 - 1)}{x(x^3 - 4)}$$

13. Find the derivative of $y = \frac{1}{2}(\ln x)^6$.

Solution:

$$y = \frac{1}{2}(\ln x)^6$$

$$y' = \frac{1}{2} \cdot 6(\ln x)^5 \cdot \frac{1}{x} = \frac{3}{x}(\ln x)^5$$

15. Find the derivative of $y = x\ln x$.

Solution:

$$y = x\ln x$$

$$y' = x\left(\frac{1}{x}\right) + \ln x = 1 + \ln x$$

17. Find the derivative of $y = \ln x\sqrt{x^2 - 1}$.

Solution:

$$y = \ln x\sqrt{x^2 - 1} = \ln x + \frac{1}{2}\ln(x^2 - 1)$$

$$y' = \frac{1}{x} + \frac{1}{2}\left(\frac{2x}{x^2 - 1}\right) = \frac{2x^2 - 1}{x(x^2 - 1)}$$

19. Find the derivative of $y = \ln\left(\dfrac{x}{x^2 + 1}\right)$.

Solution:

$$y = \ln\left(\frac{x}{x^2 + 1}\right) = \ln x - \ln(x^2 + 1)$$

$$y' = \frac{1}{x} - \frac{2x}{x^2 + 1} = \frac{1 - x^2}{x(x^2 + 1)}$$

21. Find the derivative of $y = \ln\dfrac{x + 1}{x - 1}$.

Solution:

$$y = \ln\frac{x + 1}{x - 1} = \ln(x + 1) - \ln(x - 1)$$

$$y' = \frac{1}{x + 1} - \frac{1}{x - 1} = -\frac{2}{x^2 - 1} = \frac{2}{1 - x^2}$$

23. Find the derivative of $y = \ln\sqrt{\dfrac{x+1}{x-1}}$.

Solution:

$$y = \ln\sqrt{\frac{x+1}{x-1}} = \frac{1}{2}[\ln(x+1) - \ln(x-1)]$$

$$y' = \frac{1}{2}\left(\frac{1}{x+1} - \frac{1}{x-1}\right) = \frac{-1}{x^2-1} = \frac{1}{1-x^2}$$

25. Find the derivative of $y = \dfrac{\ln x}{x^2}$.

Solution:

$$y = \frac{\ln x}{x^2}$$

$$y' = \frac{x^2(1/x) - (\ln x)(2x)}{x^4} = \frac{1 - 2\ln x}{x^3}$$

27. Find the derivative of $y = \ln\dfrac{\sqrt{4+x^2}}{x}$.

Solution:

$$y = \ln\frac{\sqrt{4+x^2}}{x} = \frac{1}{2}\ln(4+x^2) - \ln x$$

$$y' = \frac{1}{2}\left(\frac{2x}{4+x^2}\right) - \frac{1}{x} = -\frac{4}{x(4+x^2)}$$

29. Find the derivative of $y = \ln\sqrt{2x^2 - 3}$.

Solution:

$$y = \ln\sqrt{2x^2 - 3} = \frac{1}{2}\ln(2x^2 - 3)$$

$$y' = \frac{1}{2} \cdot \frac{4x}{2x^2 - 3} = \frac{2x}{2x^2 - 3}$$

31. Find the derivative of $g(x) = e^{-x}\ln x$.

Solution:

$$g(x) = e^{-x}\ln x$$

$$g'(x) = e^{-x}\left(\frac{1}{x}\right) + (-e^{-x})\ln x$$

$$= e^{-x}\left(\frac{1}{x} - \ln x\right)$$

33. Find the derivative of $f(x) = \ln e^{x^2}$.

Solution:

$$f(x) = \ln e^{x^2} = x^2$$
$$f'(x) = 2x$$

35. Write the expression 2^x with base e.

Solution:

$$2^x = e^{x(\ln 2)}$$

37. Write the expression $\log_4 x$ with base e.

Solution:

$$\log_4 x = \frac{1}{\ln 4} \ln x$$

39. Evaluate the logarithm $\log_2 4$.

Solution:

$$\log_2 4 = 2 \text{ because } 2^2 = 4$$

41. Evaluate the logarithm $\log_3 \frac{1}{2}$.

Solution:

$$\log_3 \frac{1}{2} = \frac{1}{\ln 3} \ln \frac{1}{2} \approx -0.63093 \text{ (calculator)}$$

43. Evaluate the logarithm $\log_{10} 31$.

Solution:

$$\log_{10} 31 = \frac{1}{\ln 10} \cdot \ln 31 \approx 1.49136 \text{ (calculator)}$$

45. Find the derivative of the function $y = 3^x$.

Solution:

$$y = 3^x$$
$$y' = (\ln 3)3^x$$

47. Find the derivative of the function $f(x) = \log_2 x$.

Solution:

$$f(x) = \log_2 x$$

$$f'(x) = \frac{1}{\ln 2} \cdot \frac{1}{x} = \frac{1}{x \ln 2}$$

49. Find the derivative of the function $h(x) = 4^{2x-3}$.

Solution:

$$h(x) = 4^{2x-3}$$

$$h'(x) = (\ln 4)4^{2x-3}(2) = 2\ln 4 \cdot 4^{2x-3}$$

51. Find the derivative of the function $y = \log_3(3x + 7)$.

Solution:

$$y = \log_3(3x + 7)$$

$$y' = \frac{1}{\ln 3} \cdot \frac{3}{3x + 7} = \frac{3}{(3x + 7)\ln 3}$$

53. Find the derivative of the function $f(x) = 10^{x^2}$.

Solution:

$$f(x) = 10^{x^2}$$

$$f'(x) = (\ln 10)10^{x^2}(2x) = 2x(\ln 10)10^{x^2}$$

55. Find the derivative of the function $y = x2^x$.

Solution:

$$y = x2^x$$

$$y' = x(\ln 2)2^x + 2^x = 2^x(1 + x\ln 2)$$

57. Find the derivative of $x^2 - 3\ln y + y^2 = 10$ by using implicit differentiation.

Solution:

$$x^2 - 3\ln y + y^2 = 10$$

$$2x - 3\left(\frac{1}{y}\right)\frac{dy}{dx} + 2y\frac{dy}{dx} = 0$$

$$2x = \frac{dy}{dx}\left(\frac{3}{y} - 2y\right)$$

$$2x = \frac{dy}{dx}\left(\frac{3 - 2y^2}{y}\right)$$

$$\frac{2xy}{3 - 2y^2} = \frac{dy}{dx}$$

59. Given $4x^3 + \ln y^2 + 2y = 2x$, find dy/dx implicitly.

Solution:

$$4x^3 + \ln y^2 + 2y = 2x$$

$$12x^2 + 2\frac{y'}{y} + 2y' = 2$$

$$\left(\frac{2}{y} + 2\right)y' = 2 - 12x^2$$

$$y' = \frac{2 - 12x^2}{\frac{2}{y} + 2} = \frac{1 - 6x^2}{\frac{1}{y} + 1} = \frac{(1 - 6x^2)}{1 + y}y$$

61. Find the second derivative of the function $f(x) = x \ln \sqrt{x} + 2x$.

Solution:

$$f(x) = x \ln \sqrt{x} + 2x = \frac{1}{2}x \ln x + 2x$$

$$f' = \frac{1}{2}x\left(\frac{1}{x}\right) + \frac{1}{2}\ln x + 2 = \frac{1}{2}\ln x + \frac{5}{2}$$

$$f''(x) = \frac{1}{2x}$$

63. Find the second derivative of the function $f(x) = 5^x$.

Solution:

$$f(x) = 5^x$$
$$f'(x) = (\ln 5)5^x$$
$$f''(x) = (\ln 5)(\ln 5)5^x (\ln 5)^2 5^x$$

65. Find the slope of the graph $f(x) = 1 + 2x \ln x$ at the point (1, 1).

Solution:

$$f(x) = 1 + 2x \ln x$$

$$f'(x) = 2x\left(\frac{1}{x}\right) + 2\ln x = 2 + 2\ln x$$

At (1, 1), the slope of the tangent line is $f'(1) = 2$.

Tangent line: $y - 1 = 2(x - 1)$

$$y = 2x - 1$$

67. Find the slope of the graph $f(x) = \ln \dfrac{5(x+2)}{x}$ at the point $(-2.5, 0)$.

Solution:

$$f(x) = \ln \frac{5(x+2)}{x} = \ln 5 + \ln(x+2) - \ln x$$

$$f'(x) = \frac{1}{x+2} - \frac{1}{x}$$

At $(-2.5, 0)$, the slope of the tangent line is

$$f'(-2.5) = \frac{1}{-2.5+2} - \frac{1}{-2.5} = -2 + \frac{2}{5} = -\frac{8}{5}$$

Tangent line: $y - 0 = -\dfrac{8}{5}\left(x + \dfrac{5}{2}\right)$

$$y = -\frac{8}{5}x - 4$$

69. Find the slope of the graph $f(x) = \log_2 x$ at the point $(1, 0)$.

Solution:

$$f(x) = \log_2 x$$

$$f'(x) = \frac{1}{\ln 2} \cdot \frac{1}{x}$$

At the point $(1, 0)$, the slope of the tangent line is $f'(1) = \dfrac{1}{\ln 2}$.

Tangent line: $y - 0 = \dfrac{1}{\ln 2}(x - 1)$

$$y = \frac{1}{\ln 2}x - \frac{1}{\ln 2}$$

71. Find any relative extrema and inflection points and sketch the graph of $y = x - \ln x$.

Solution:

$$y = x - \ln x$$

$$y' = 1 - \frac{1}{x} = \frac{x-1}{x}$$

$$y' = 0 \text{ when } x = 1$$

$$y'' = \frac{1}{x^2}$$

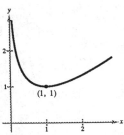

Since $y''(1) = 1 > 0$, there is a relative minimum at $(1, 1)$. Moreover, since $y'' > 0$ on $(0, \infty)$, it follows that the graph is concave upward on its domain and there are no inflection points.

73. Find any relative extrema and inflection points and sketch the graph of $y = (\ln x)/x$.

Solution:

The domain of the function $y = \dfrac{\ln x}{x}$ is $(0, \infty)$.

$$y' = \frac{1 - \ln x}{x^2}$$

$y' = 0$ when $x = e$.

$$y'' = \frac{2 \ln x - 3}{x^3}$$

Since $y''(e) < 0$, it follows that $(e, \ 1/e)$ is a relative maximum. Since $y'' = 0$ when $2 \ln x - 3 = 0$ and $x = e^{3/2}$, there is an inflection point at $(e^{3/2}, \ 3/(2e^{3/2}))$.

75. Find any relative extrema and inflection points and sketch the graph of $y = x^2 \ln x$.

Solution:

$$y = x^2 \ln x$$
$$y' = x(1 + 2 \ln x)$$
$$y' = 0 \text{ when } x = e^{-1/2}$$
$$y'' = 3 + 2 \ln x$$

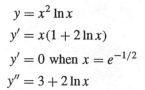

($x = 0$ is not in the domain.)

Since $y''(e^{-1/2}) > 0$, it follows that there is a relative minimum at $(1/\sqrt{e}, \ -1/(2e))$. Since $y'' = 0$ when $x = e^{-3/2}$, it follows that there is an inflection point at $(1/e^{3/2}, \ -3/(2e^3))$

77. Find $\dfrac{dx}{dp}$ for $x = \ln \dfrac{1000}{p}$. Interpret this rate of change when the price is \$10.

Solution:

$$x = \ln \frac{1000}{p} = \ln 1000 - \ln p$$
$$\frac{dx}{dp} = 0 - \frac{1}{p} = -\frac{1}{p}$$
$$\text{when } p = 10, \frac{dy}{dp} = -\frac{1}{10}$$

79. Find $\dfrac{dx}{dp}$ for $x = \dfrac{500}{\ln(p^2 + 1)}$.

Solution:

$$x = \frac{500}{\ln(p^2 + 1)} = 500[\ln(p^2 + 1)]^{-1}$$

$$\frac{dx}{dp} = -500[\ln(p^2 + 1)]^{-2}\frac{1}{p^2 + 1}(2p) = \frac{-1000p}{(p^2 + 1)[\ln(p^2 + 1)]^2}$$

If $p = 10$, $\dfrac{dx}{dp} = \dfrac{-10,000}{101[\ln(101)]^2} \approx -4.65$.

81. Find the demand function in Exercise 77 for p. Use the result to find dp/dx. Then find the value of dp/dx when $p = \$10$. What is the relationship between this derivative and dx/dp?

Solution:

$$x = \ln\frac{1000}{p}$$

$$e^x = \frac{1000}{p}$$

$$p = 1000e^{-x}$$

$$\frac{dp}{dx} = -1000e^{-x}$$

When $p = 10$, $x = \ln\dfrac{1000}{10} = \ln 100$ and $\dfrac{dp}{dx} = -1000e^{-\ln 100} = \dfrac{-1000}{100} = -10$.

Note that $\dfrac{dp}{dx}$ and $\dfrac{dx}{dp}$ are reciprocals of each other.

83. *Minimum Average Cost* The cost of producing x units of a product is

$$C = 500 + 300x - 300 \ln x, \qquad x \geq 1.$$

Use a graphing utility to find the minimum average cost. Then confirm your result analytically.

Solution:

$$C = 500 + 300x - 300 \ln x, \qquad x \geq 1$$

$$\overline{C} = \text{average cost} = \frac{C}{x} = \frac{500}{x} + 300 - 300\frac{\ln x}{x}$$

Using a graphing utility, we determine that the minimum average cost is $\overline{C} \approx 279.15$ when $x \approx 14.39$.

$$\overline{C}' = \frac{-500}{x^2} - 300\left[\frac{x\frac{1}{x} - \ln x}{x^2}\right] = \frac{-500}{x^2} - \frac{300}{x^2}(1 - \ln x)$$

Setting $\overline{C}' = 0$, $\qquad 500 = -300(1 - \ln x)$,

$$\frac{5}{3} = \ln x - 1$$

$$\frac{8}{3} = \ln x$$

$$x = e^{8/3} \approx 14.39$$

which confirms the graphical solution obtained above.

85. *Nonprofit Organizations* The number T (in thousands) of income tax returns filed by nonprofit organizations from 1984 to 1992 can be modeled by

$$T = -\frac{682.83 \ln t}{t} + 0.025t^3 - 15.19t + 317.92,$$

where $t = 4$ corresponds to 1984.

(a) Use a graphing utility to graph T over the interval [4, 12].

(b) Estimate the number of returns filed by nonprofit organizations in 1991.

(c) At what rate was the number of filed returns changing in 1991?

Solution:

$$T = -\frac{682.83 \ln t}{t} + 0.025t^3 - 15.19t + 317.92$$

(a)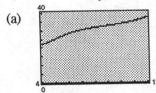

(b) If $t = 11$ (1991), then $T \approx 35.255$, which means that approximately 35,255 returns were filed.

(c) Using a graphing utility, $T'(11) \approx 1.8$.

Section 4.5   Exponential Growth and Decay

1. Find the exponential function $y = Ce^{kt}$ that passes through the points (0, 2) and (4, 3).

Solution:

Since $y = 2$ when $t = 0$, it follows that $C = 2$. Moreover, since $y = 3$ when $t = 4$, we have $3 = 2e^{4k}$ and

$$k = \frac{\ln(3/2)}{4} \approx 0.1014.$$

Thus, $y = 2e^{0.1014t}$.

3. Find the exponential function $y = Ce^{kt}$ that passes through the points (0, 4) and $\left(5, \frac{1}{2}\right)$.

Solution:

Since $y = 4$ when $t = 0$, it follows that $C = 4$. Moreover, since $y = \frac{1}{2}$ when $t = 5$, we have $\frac{1}{2} = 4e^{5k}$ and

$$k = \frac{\ln(1/8)}{5} \approx -0.4159.$$

Thus, $y = 4e^{-0.4159t}$.

5. Find the exponential function $y = Ce^{kt}$ that passes through the points (1, 1) and (5, 5).

Solution:

Using the fact that $y = 1$ when $t = 1$ and $y = 5$ when $t = 5$, we have $1 = Ce^k$ and $5 = Ce^{5k}$. From these two equations, we have $Ce^k = (\frac{1}{5})Ce^{5k}$. Thus,

$$k = \frac{\ln 5}{4} \approx 0.4024$$

and we have $y = Ce^{0.4024t}$. Since $1 = Ce^{0.4024}$, it follows that $C \approx 0.6687$ and $y = 0.6687e^{0.4024t}$.

7. Use the given information $\dfrac{dy}{dt} = 2y$ and $y = 10$ when $t = 0$ to write an equation for y. Confirm your result analytically by showing that the function satisfies the equation $dy/dt = Cy$. Does the function represent exponential growth or decay?

Solution:

$$\frac{dy}{dt} = 2y, \ y = 10 \text{ when } t = 10: \ y = 10e^{2t}$$

$$\frac{dy}{dt} = 10(2e^{2t} = 2(10e^{2t}) = 2y$$

Exponential growth.

9. Use the given information $\dfrac{dy}{dt} = -4y$ and $y = 30$ when $t = 0$ to write an equation for y. Confirm your result analytically by showing that the function satisfies the equation $dy/dt = Cy$. Does the function represent exponential growth or decay?

Solution:

$$\frac{dy}{dt} = -4y, \ y = 30 \text{ when } t = 10: \ y = 30e^{-4t}$$

$$\frac{dy}{dt} = 30(-4)e^{-4t} = -4(30e^{-4t}) = -4y$$

Exponential decay.

11. *Radioactive Decay* The half-life of the isotope Ra^{226} is 1620 years. If the initial amount is 10 grams, how much will remain after (a) 1,000 years and (b) 10,000 years?

Solution:

From Example 1, we have $y = 10e^{[\ln(1/2)/1620]t}$.

(a) When $t = 1,000$, $\ y = 10e^{[\ln(1/2)/1620](1000)} \approx 6.519$ grams.

(b) When $t = 10,000$, $\ y - 10e^{[\ln(1/2)/1620](10,000)} \approx 0.139$ gram.

13. *Radioactive Decay* The half-life of the isotope C^{14} is 5,730 years. If 2 grams remain after 10,000 years
(a) what is the initial amount and (b) how much is present after 1,000 years?

Solution:

Since $y = Ce^{[\ln(1/2)/5730]t}$, we have $2 = Ce^{[\ln(1/2)/5730](10,000)} \Rightarrow C \approx 6.705$ which implies that the initial quantity is 6.705 grams. When $t = 1,000$, we have
$y = 6.705e^{[\ln(1/2)/5730](1000)} \approx 5.941$ grams.

15. *Radioactive Decay* The half-life of the isotope Pu^{230} is 24,360 years. If 2.1 grams remain after 1,000 years,
(a) what is the initial amount and (b) how much will remain after 10,000 years?

Solution:

Since $y = Ce^{[\ln(1/2)/24,360]t}$, we have $2.1 = Ce^{[\ln(1/2)/24,360](1000)} \Rightarrow C \approx 2.161$. Thus, the initial quantity is 2.161 grams. When $t = 10,000$,
$y = 2.161e^{[\ln(1/2)/24,360](10,000)} \approx 1.626$ grams.

17. *Radioactive Decay* What percent of a present amount of radioactive radium (Ra^{226}) will remain after 900 years?

Solution:

$$y = Ce^{[\ln(1/2)/1620t]} \text{ (see Example 1)}$$

when $t = 900$, $y = Ce^{[\ln(1/2)/1620 \cdot 900]} \approx 0.68C$.

After 900 years, approximately 68% of the radioactive radium will remain.

19. *Carbon Dating* C^{14} dating assumes that the carbon dioxide on earth today has the same radioactive content as it did centuries ago. If this is true, then the amount of C^{14} absorbed by a tree that grew several centuries ago should be the same as the amount of C^{14} absorbed by a tree growing today. A piece of ancient charcoal contains only 15% as much of the radioactive carbon as a piece of modern charcoal. How long ago was the tree burned to make the ancient charcoal? [The half-life of C^{14} is 5730 years.]

Solution:

$$0.15C = Ce^{[\ln(1/2)/5730]t}$$

$$\ln 0.15 = \left[\frac{\ln(1/2)}{5730}\right]t$$

$$\frac{5730 \ln 0.15}{\ln 0.5} = t$$

$$t \approx 15,683 \text{ years}$$

21. *Population Growth* The number of a certain type of bacteria increases continuously at a rate proportional to the number present. There are 150 present at a given time and 450 present 5 hours later.

(a) How many will there be 10 hours after the initial time?

(b) How long will it take for the population to double?

(c) Does the answer to part (b) depend on the starting time? Explain.

Solution:

The model is $y = Ce^{kt}$. Since $y = 150$ when $t = 0$, we have $C = 150$. Furthermore,

$$450 = 150e^{k5}$$

$$3 = e^{5k}$$

$$k = \frac{\ln 3}{5}$$

Therefore,

$$y = 150e^{(\frac{\ln 3}{5})t} \approx 150e^{0.2197t}$$

(a) When $t = 10$, $y = 150^{\frac{\ln 3}{5}10} = 1350$ bacteria.

(b) To find the time required for the population to double, solve for t:

$$300 = 150e^{\frac{\ln 3}{5}t}$$

$$2 = e^{\frac{\ln 3}{5}t}$$

$$\ln 2 = \frac{\ln 3}{5}t$$

$$t = \frac{5\ln 2}{\ln 3} \approx 3.15 \text{ hours}$$

(c) No, the doubling time is always 3.15 hours.

23. *Compound Interest* $1000 is deposited in a savings account at a rate of 12% compounded continuously.

(a) Find the time for the amount to double. What is the amount after (b) 10 years, and (c) after 25 years?

Solution:

Since $A = 1000e^{0.12t}$, the time to double is given by $2000 = 1000e^{0.12t}$ and we have

$$t = \frac{\ln 2}{0.12} \approx 5.776 \text{ years}.$$

Amount after 10 years: $A = 1000e^{1.2} \approx \$3320.12$

Amount after 25 years: $A = 1000e^{0.12(25)} \approx \$20,085.54$

25. *Compound Interest* $750 is deposited in an account with continuously compounded interest. If the amount doubles in 7.75 years, what is the rate? How much will be in the account after 10 years and after 25 years?

Solution:

Since $A = 750e^{rt}$ and $A = 1500$ when $t = 7.75$, we have

$$1500 = 750e^{7.75r}$$

$$r = \frac{\ln 2}{7.75} \approx 0.0894 = 8.94\%.$$

Amount after 10 years: $A = 750e^{0.0894(10)} \approx \$1833.67$

Amount after 25 years: $A = 750e^{0.0894(25)} \approx \$7009.86$

27. *Compound Interest* $500 is deposited in an account with continuously compounded interest. If the balance is $1,292.85 after 10 years, what is the rate? How long will it take the amount to double? What is the amount after 25 years?

Solution:

Since $A = 500e^{rt}$ and $A = 1292.85$ when $t = 10$, we have

$$1292.85 = 500e^{10r}$$

$$r = \frac{\ln(1292.85/500)}{10} \approx 0.095 = 9.5\%.$$

The time to double is given by

$$1000 = 500e^{0.095t}$$

$$t = \frac{\ln 2}{0.095} \approx 7.296 \text{ years.}$$

Amount after 25 years: $A = 500e^{0.095(25)} \approx \$5375.51$

29. *Effective Yield* The effective yield is the rate i converted annually that will produce the same interest per year as the nominal rate r compounded n times per year.

(a) Show that the effective yield is given by
$$i = \left(1 + \frac{r}{n}\right)^n - 1.$$

(b) Find the effective yield for a nominal rate of 6%, compounded monthly.

Solution:

(a) $P(1 + i)^t = P\left(1 + \dfrac{r}{n}\right)^{nt}$

$\sqrt[t]{(1 + i)^t} = \sqrt[t]{\left(1 + \dfrac{r}{n}\right)^{nt}}$

$1 + i = \left(1 + \dfrac{r}{n}\right)^n$

$i = \left(1 + \dfrac{r}{n}\right)^n - 1$

(b) If $r = 0.06$ and $n = 12$, then $i = \left(1 + \dfrac{0.06}{12}\right)^{12} - 1 \approx 0.0617$ or 6.17%.

31. *Effective Yield* Use the results of Exercises 29 and 30 to complete the table shown in the textbook showing the effective yield for a nominal rate of 5%.

Solution:

Number of Compoundings Per Year	4	12	365	Continuous
Effective Yield	5.095%	5,116%	5.127%	5.127%

$n = 4 : i = \left(1 + \dfrac{0.05}{4}\right)^4 - 1 \approx 0.05095 \approx 5.095\%$

$n = 12 : i = \left(1 + \dfrac{0.05}{12}\right)^{12} - 1 \approx 0.05116 \approx 5.116\%$

$n = 365 : i = \left(1 + \dfrac{0.05}{365}\right)^{365} - 1 \approx 0.05127 \approx 5.127\%$

Continuous $i = e^{0.05} - 1 \approx 0.05127 \approx 5.127\%$

33. *Rule of 70* Verify that the time necessary for an investment to double its value is approximately $70/r$ if the interest is compounded continuously at rate r. [The formula requires the rate to be entered as a percentage and not a decimal.]

Solution:

$$2P = Pe^{rt}$$

$$2 = e^{rt}$$

$$\ln 2 = rt$$

$$t = \frac{\ln 2}{4} \approx \frac{0.6931}{r} \approx \frac{0.70}{r}$$

If r is entered as a percentage and not as a decimal, then

$$t \approx 100\left(\frac{0.70}{r}\right) = \frac{70}{r}.$$

35. *Revenue* The revenue for La-Z-Boy Chair Company was \$254.9 million in 1983 and \$684.1 million in 1992.

(a) Use an exponential growth model to predict the 1996 revenue.

(b) Use a linear model to predict the 1996 revenue.

Solution:

Let $t = 0$ correspond to 1983: $(0, 254.9)$, $(9, 684.1)$

(a)　　$y = 254.9e^{kt}$

$$684.1 = 254.9e^{9k}$$

$$k = \frac{1}{9}\ln\left(\frac{684.1}{254.9}\right) \approx 0.1097$$

$$y = 254.9e^{0.1097t}$$

When $t = 13$ (1996), $y \approx \$1061.0$ million

(b)　　Slope $= \dfrac{684.1 - 254.9}{9 - 0} = \dfrac{429.2}{9}$

$$y - 254.9 = \frac{429.2}{9}(t - 0)$$

$$y = \frac{429.2}{9}t + 254.9$$

When $t = 13$ (1996), $y \approx \$874.9$ million.

37. Sales The sales S (in thousands of units) of a new product after it has been on the market t years are given by $S(t) = Ce^{k/t}$.

(a) During the first year, 5000 units were sold. The saturation point for the market is 30,000 units. Solve for C and R in the model.

(b) How many units will be sold after five years?

(c) Sketch a graph of this sales function.

Solution:

$S = Ce^{k/t}$

(a) Since $S = 5$ when $t = 1$, we have $5 = Ce^k$ and

$$\lim_{t \to \infty} Ce^{k/t} = C = 30.$$

Therefore, $5 = 30e^k$, $k = \ln(1/6) \approx -1.7918$, and $S = 30e^{-1.7918/t}$.

(b) $S(5) = 30e^{-1.7918/5} \approx 20.9646 \approx 20,965$ units

(c) See graph.

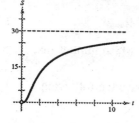

39. Learning Curve The management at a certain factory has found that the maximum number of units a worker can produce in a day is 30. The learning curve for the number of units N produced per day after a new employee has worked t days is given by $N = 30(1 - e^{kt})$. After 20 days on the job, a particular worker produced 19 units.

How many days should pass before this worker is producing 25 units per day?

Solution:

$$N = 30(1 - e^{kt})$$

Since $19 = 30(1 - e^{20k})$, it follows that

$$30e^{20k} = 11$$

$$k = \frac{\ln(11/30)}{20} \approx -0.0502$$

$$N = 30(1 - e^{-0.0502t})$$

$$25 = 30(1 - e^{-0.0502t})$$

$$e^{-0.0502t} = \frac{1}{6}$$

$$t = \frac{\ln 6}{0.0502} \approx 36 \text{ days}$$

41. *Revenue* A small business assumes that the demand function for one of its products is the exponential function $p = Ce^{kx}$. When $p = \$45$, $x = 1000$ units, and when $p = \$40$, $x = 1200$ units.

(a) Solve for C and k.

(b) Find the values of x and p that will maximize revenue for this product.

Solution:

(a) Since $p = Ce^{kx}$ where $p = 45$ when $x = 1000$ and $p = 40$ when $x = 1200$, we have the following.

$$45 = Ce^{1000k} \text{ and } 40 = Ce^{1200k}$$

$$\ln 45 = \ln C + 1000k$$

$$\ln 40 = \ln C + 1200k$$

$$\ln 45 - \ln 40 = -200k$$

$$k = \frac{\ln(45/40)}{-200} \approx -0.0005889$$

Therefore, we have $45 = Ce^{1000(-0.0005889)}$ which implies that $C \approx 81.0915$ and $p = 81.0915e^{-0.0005889x}$.

(b) Since $R = xp = 81.0915xe^{-0.0005889x}$, we have the following.

$$R' = 81.0915[-0.0005889xe^{-0.0005889x} + e^{-0.0005889x}]$$

$$= 81.0915e^{-0.0005889x}[1 - 0.0005889x] = 0$$

Since $R' = 0$ when $x = 1/0.0005889 \approx 1698$ units, we have
$p = 81.0915e^{-0.0005889(1698)} \approx \$29.83$.

43. *Forestry* The value V (in dollars) of a tract of timber can be modeled by
$$V = 100,000e^{0.75\sqrt{t}},$$
where $t = 0$ corresponds to 1990. If money earns interest at a rate of 4%, compounded continuously, then the present value A of the timer at any time t is
$$A = Ve^{-0.04t}$$
Find the year in which the timber should be harvested to maximize the present value.

Solution:

$$A = Ve^{-0.04t}$$
$$= 100,000e^{0.75\sqrt{t}}e^{-0.04t}$$
$$= 100,000e^{(0.75\sqrt{t}-0.04t)}$$
$$A'(t) = 100,000\left(\frac{0.75}{2\sqrt{t}} - 0.04\right)e^{(0.75\sqrt{t}-0.04t)} = 0$$

$$\frac{0.75}{2\sqrt{t}} = 0.04$$

$$\sqrt{t} = \frac{0.75}{(0.04)(2)} = 9.375$$

$$t = 87.89 \approx 88$$

The timber should be harvested in 2078 to maximize the present value.

45. *Earthquake Intensity* On the Richter Scale, the magnitude R of an earthquake of intensity I is given by
$$R = \frac{\ln I - \ln I_0}{\ln 10},$$
where I_0 is the minimum intensity used for comparison. Assume $I_0 = 1$.

(a) Find the intensity of 1906 San Francisco earthquake in which $R = 8.3$.

(b) Find the factor by which the intensity is increased when the value of R is doubled.

(c) Find dR/dI.

Solution:

(a) If $I_0 = 1$, then we have $R = \frac{\ln I}{\ln 10}$ and $8.3 = \frac{\ln I}{\ln 10}$. Therefore
$I = e^{8.3 \ln 10} \approx 199,526,231.5$.

(b) $2R = \frac{\ln I}{\ln 10}$ implies that $I = e^{2R \ln 10} = (e^{R \ln 10})^2$. The intensity is squared if R is doubled.

(c) $\frac{dR}{dI} = \frac{1}{\ln 10}\left(\frac{1}{I}\right) = \frac{1}{I \ln 10}$

Chapter 4   Review Exercises

1. Evaluate the expression $4(4^4)$.

Solution:

$$4(4^4) = 4(256) = 1024$$

3. Evaluate the expression $\left(\dfrac{1}{5}\right)^4$.

Solution:

$$\left(\frac{1}{5}\right)^4 = \frac{1}{625}$$

5. Use the properties of exponents to simplify the expression $\left(\dfrac{25}{4}\right)^0$.

Solution:

$$\left(\frac{25}{4}\right)^0 = 1$$

7. Use the properties of exponents to simplify the expression $\dfrac{6^3}{36^2}$.

Solution:

$$\frac{6^3}{36^2} = \frac{6 \cdot 6^2}{36 \cdot 6^2} = \frac{6}{36} = \frac{1}{6}$$

9. Solve the equation $5^x = 625$ for x.

Solution:

$$5^x = 625$$
$$x = 4$$

11. Solve the equation $e^{-1/2} = e^{x-1}$.

Solution:

$$e^{-1/2} = e^{x-1}$$
$$-\frac{1}{2} = x - 1$$
$$x = \frac{1}{2}$$

13. *New York Stock Exchange* The total number y (in millions) of shares of stocks listed on the New York Stock Exchange between 1940 and 1990 can be modeled by

$$y = 29.619(1.0927)^t, \qquad 40 \le t \le 90,$$

where $t = 40$ corresponds to 1940. Use this model to estimate the total number of shares listed in 1950, 1970, and 1990.

Solution:

$$y = 29.619(1.0927)^t \qquad 40 \le t \le 90$$

For 1950, $t = 50$ and $y = 2492.4$ million shares

For 1970, $t = 70$ and $y = 14{,}677.0$ million shares

For 1990, $t = 90$ and $y = 86{,}428.2$ million shares

15. Sketch the graph of the function $f(x) = 9^{x/2}$.

Solution:

$$f(x) = 9^{x/2}$$

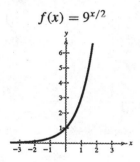

17. Sketch the graph of the function $f(x) = \left(\dfrac{1}{2}\right)^{2x} + 4$.

Solution:

$$f(x) = \left(\frac{1}{2}\right)^{2x} + 4$$

19. *Demand* The demand function for a product is

$$p = 12{,}500 - \frac{10{,}000}{2 + e^{-0.001x}},$$

where p is the price per unit and x is the number of units produced (see figure in textbook). What is the limit of the price as x increases without bound? Explain what this means in the context of the problem.

Solution:

$$p = 12{,}500 - \frac{10{,}000}{2 + e^{-0.001x}}$$

$$\lim_{x \to \infty} p = 12{,}500 - \frac{10{,}000}{2 + 0} = 7500$$

21. Evaluate the function $f(x) = 2e^{x-1}$ at $x = 2$. Then sketch its graph.

Solution:

$$f(x) = 2e^{x-1}$$

$$f(2) = 2e^{2-1} = 2e \approx 5.4366$$

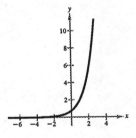

23. Evaluate the function $g(t) = 12e^{-0.2t}$ at $t = 17$. Then sketch its graph.

Solution:

$$g(t) = 12e^{-0.2t}$$

$$g(17) = 12e^{-0.2(17)} \approx 0.4005$$

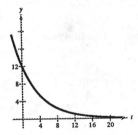

25. *Stocking a Lake with Fish* A lake is stocked with 500 fish and the fish population P begins to increase according to the logistics model

$$P = \frac{10{,}000}{1 + 19e^{-t/5}}, \qquad 0 \le t,$$

where t is measured in months.

(a) Use a graphing utility to graph the function.

(b) Estimate the number of fish in the lake after 4 months.

(c) Does the population have a limit as t increases without bound? Explain your reasoning.

(d) After how many months is the population increasing most rapidly? Explain your reasoning.

Solution:

(a)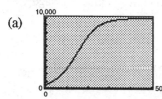

$$P = \frac{10{,}000}{1 + 19e^{-t/5}}, \qquad t \ge 0$$

(b) When $t = 4$, $P \approx 1049$ fish

(c) Yes, P approaches 10,000 fish as $t \to \infty$.

(d) The population is increasing most rapidly at the inflection point, around $t = 15$ months ($P = 5000$).

27. Complete the table in the textbook to determine the balance A when $P = \$1000$ dollars is invested at an annual rate of $r = 4\%$ to $t = 5$ years, compounded n times per year.

Solution:

n	1	2	4	12	365	Continuous
A	1216.65	1218.99	1220.19	1221.00	1221.39	1221.40

$$A = P\left(1 + \frac{r}{n}\right)^{nt} = 1000\left(1 + \frac{0.04}{n}\right)^{5n}$$

$$A = Pe^{rt} = 1000e^{(0.04)5} \approx 1221.50 \text{ (Continuous)}$$

29. $2000 is deposited in an account. Decide which account, (a) or (b), will have the greater balance after 10 years.

(a) 5%, compounded continuously

(b) 6%, compounded quarterly

Solution:

(a) $A = Pe^{rt} = 2000e^{0.05(10)} \approx \$3297.44$

(b) $A = P\left(1 + \dfrac{r}{n}\right)^{nt} = 2000\left(1 + \dfrac{0.06}{4}\right)^{4(10)} \approx \$3628.04$

Accout (b) will be greater.

31. *Age at First Marriage* The average age A of an Anerican man at his first marriage from 1970 to 1990 can be modeled by

$$A = 22.38 + \frac{1}{0.1513 + 9.6155e^{-0.3708t}}, \qquad 0 \le t \le 20,$$

where $t = 0$ corresponds to 1970. Use this model to estimate the average age of an American man at his first marriage in 1970, 1980, and 1990.

Solution:

$$A = 22.38 + \frac{1}{0.1513 + 9.6155e^{-0.3708t}}, \qquad 0 \le t \le 20,$$

1970 $(t = 0)$: $A \approx 22.48$ years

1980 $(t = 10)$: $A \approx 24.96$ years

1990 $(t = 20)$: $A \approx 28.75$ years

33. Find the derivative of the function $y = 4e^{x^2}$.

Solution:

$$y = 4e^{x^2}$$

$$y' = 4e^{x^2}(2x) = 8xe^{x^2}$$

35. Find the derivative of the function $y = \dfrac{x}{e^{2x}}$.

Solution:

$$y = \frac{x}{e^{2x}}$$

$$y' = \frac{e^{2x}(1) - x2e^{2x}}{(e^{2x})^2} = \frac{1 - 2x}{e^{2x}}$$

37. Find the derivative of the function $y = \sqrt{4e^{4x}}$.

Solution:

$$y = \sqrt{4e^{4x}} = (4e^{4x})^{1/2} = 2e^{2x}$$

$$y' = 4e^{2x}$$

39. Find the derivative of the function $y = \dfrac{5}{1 + e^{2x}}$.

Solution:

$$y = \frac{5}{1 + e^{2x}} = 5(1 + e^{2x})^{-1}$$

$$y' = -5(1 + e^{2x})^{-2}(2e^{2x}) = \frac{-10e^{2x}}{(1 + e^{2x})^2}$$

41. Graph and analyze the function $f(x) = 4e^{-x}$.

Solution:

$$f(x) = 4e^{-x}$$

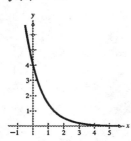

No relative extrema

No inflection point

$y = 0$ is horizontal asymptote.

43. Graph and analyze the function $f(x) = \dfrac{e^x}{x^2}$.

Solution:

$$f(x) = \frac{e^x}{x^2}$$

$$f'(x) = (x - 2)\frac{e^x}{x^3}$$

$$f''(x) = (x - 2)\frac{e^x}{x^3}$$

$$f''(x) = (x^2 - 4x + 6)\frac{e^x}{x^4}$$

(2, 1.847) is a relative minimum.

$y = 0$ is a horizontal asymptote.

$x = 0$ is a vertical asymptote.

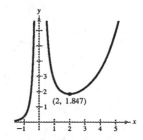

45. Write the logarithmic equation $\ln 12 \approx 2.4849$ as an exponential equation.

Solution:

$$\ln 12 \approx 2.4849$$

$$e^{2.4849} \approx 12$$

47. Write the exponential equation $e^{1.5} \approx 4.4817$ as a logarithmic equation.

Solution:

$$e^{1.5} \approx 4.4817$$

$$\ln 4.4817 \approx 1.5$$

49. Sketch the graph of the function $y = \ln(4 - x)$.

Solution:

$$y = \ln(4 - x)$$

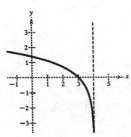

51. Sketch the graph of the function $y = \ln \dfrac{x}{3}$.

Solution:

$$y = \ln \frac{x}{3} = \ln x - \ln 3$$

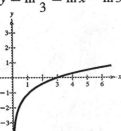

53. Write the expression $\ln \sqrt{x^2(x - 1)}$ as a sum, difference, or multiple of logarithms.

Solution:

$$\ln \sqrt{x^2(x - 1)} = \frac{1}{2} \ln(x^2(x - 1))$$

$$= \frac{1}{2}[\ln x^2 + \ln(x - 1)]$$

$$= \ln x + \frac{1}{2} \ln(x - 1)$$

55. Write the expression $\ln\left(\dfrac{1-x}{3x}\right)^3$ as a sum, difference, or multiple of logarithms.

Solution:

$$\ln\left(\frac{1-x}{3x}\right)^3 = 3\ln\left(\frac{1-x}{3x}\right)$$
$$= 3[\ln(1-x) - \ln 3x]$$
$$= 3[\ln(1-x) - \ln 3 - \ln x]$$

57. Solve the equation $e^{\ln x} = 3$ for x.

Solution:

$$e^{\ln x} = 3$$
$$x = 3$$

59. Solve the equation $\ln 2x - \ln(3x - 1) = 0$ for x.

Solution:

$$\ln 2x - \ln(3x - 1) = 0$$
$$\ln 2x = \ln(3x - 1)$$
$$2x = 3x - 1$$
$$x = 1$$

61. Solve the equation $\ln x + \ln(x - 3) = 0$ for x.

Solution:

$$\ln x + \ln(x - 3) = 0$$
$$\ln(x(x - 3)) = 0$$
$$x(x - 3) = 1$$
$$x^2 - 3x - 1 = 0$$
$$x = \frac{(3 \pm \sqrt{13})}{2}$$
$$x = \frac{(3 + \sqrt{13})}{2} \approx 3.3028 \text{ is only solution in domain.}$$

63. Solve the equation $9^{6x} - 27 = 0$ for x.

Solution:

$$9^{6x} - 27 = 0$$
$$3^{12x} = 3^3$$
$$12x = 3$$
$$x = \frac{1}{4}$$

65. *Home Mortgage* The monthly payment M for a home mortgage of P dollars for t years at an annual interest rate of $r\%$ is given by

$$M = P\left(\frac{\frac{r}{12}}{1 - \left(\frac{1}{(r/12+1)^{12t}}\right)}\right).$$

(a) Use a graphing utility to graph the model when $P = \$100,000$ and $r = 8\%$.

(b) You are given a choice of a 30-year term or a 30-year term. Which would you choose? Explain.

Solution:

(a) $M = 100,000\left(\dfrac{\dfrac{0.08}{12}}{1 - \left(\dfrac{1}{(0.08/12)+1}\right)^{12t}}\right)$

(b) A 30-year term has a smaller monthly payment, but takes more time to pay off than a 20-year term.

67. Find the derivative of the function $f(x) = \ln 3x^2$.

Solution:

$$f(x) = \ln 3x^2 = \ln 3 + 2\ln x$$

$$f'(x) = \frac{2}{x}$$

69. Find the derivative of the function $y = x\sqrt{\ln x}$.

Solution:

$$y = x\sqrt{\ln x}$$

$$y' = \sqrt{\ln x} + \frac{1}{2}x(\ln x)^{-1/2}\frac{1}{x} = \sqrt{\ln x} + \frac{1}{2\sqrt{\ln x}}$$

71. Find the derivative of the function $y = \dfrac{\ln x}{x^3}$.

Solution:

$$y = \frac{\ln x}{x^3}$$

$$y' = \frac{x^3\left(\frac{1}{x}\right) - 3x^2 \cdot \ln x}{x^6} = \frac{1 - 3\ln x}{x^4}$$

73. Find the derivative of the function $f(x) = \ln e^{-x^2}$.

Solution:

$$f(x) = \ln e^{-x} = -x^2$$
$$f'(x) = -2x$$

75. Graph and analyze $y = \ln(x + 3)$.

Solution:

$$y = \ln(x + 3)$$

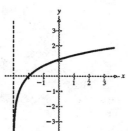

77. Graph and analyze $y = \ln \dfrac{10}{x + 2}$.

Solution:

$$y = \frac{\ln 10}{x + 2} = \ln 10 - \ln(x + 2)$$

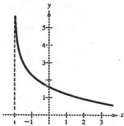

No relative extrema nor inflection points.

79. Evaluate $\log_7 49$.

Solution:

$$\log_7 49 = \log_7 y^2 = 2\log_7 7 = 2$$

81. Evaluate $\log_{10} 1$.

Solution:

$$\log_{10} 1 = 0$$

83. Use the change of base formula to evaluate the logarithm $\log_5 10$ and round the result to four decimal places.

Solution:

$$\log_5 10 = \frac{\ln 10}{\ln 5} \approx 1.4307$$

85. Use the change of base formula to evaluate the logarithm $\log_{16} 64$ and round the result to four decimal places.

Solution:

$$\log_{16} 64 = \frac{\ln 64}{\ln 16} = 1.5$$

87. Find the derivative of the function $y = \log_3 (2x - 1)$.

Solution:

$$y = \log_3 (2x - 1)$$
$$y' = \frac{1}{\ln 3} \cdot \frac{2}{2x - 1} = \frac{2}{(2x - 1) \ln 3}$$

89. Find the derivative of the function $y = \log_2 \frac{1}{x^2}$.

Solution:

$$y = \log_2 \frac{1}{x^2} = \log_2 1 - \log_2 x^2 = -2 \log_2 x$$
$$y' = -2 \frac{1}{\ln 2} \cdot \frac{1}{x} = \frac{-2}{x \ln 2}$$

91. *Depreciation* After t years, the value V of a car purchased for \$20,000 is

$V = 20{,}000(0.75)^t$.

(a) Sketch a graph of the function and determine the value of the car 2 years after it was purchased.

(b) Find the rate of change of V with respect to t when $t = 1$ and when $t = 4$.

(c) After how many years will the car be worth \$5000?

Solution:

$V = 20{,}000(0.75)^t$

(a)

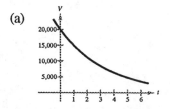

$V(2) = 11{,}250$

(b) $\quad V'(t) = 20{,}000 \cdot \ln\left(\dfrac{3}{4}\right)(0.75)^t$

$\qquad V'(1) = -4315.23$ dollars/year

$\qquad V'(40) = -1820.49$ dollars/year

(c) $V = 5000 = 20{,}000(0.75)^t$

$\qquad \dfrac{1}{4} = (0.75)^t$

$\qquad\quad t = \ln\left(\dfrac{1}{4}\right) / \ln\left(\dfrac{3}{4}\right) \approx 4.8$ years

93. *Drug Decomposition* A medical solution contains 500 milligrams of a drug per milliliter when the solution is prepared. After 40 days, it contains only 300 milligrams per milliliter. Assuming that the rate of decomposition is proportional to the concentration present, find an equation giving the concentration A after t days.

Solution:

$A = Ce^{kt} = 500e^{kt}$

$\quad (A = 500$ when $t = 0)$

$\quad (A = 300$ after 40 days$)$

$300 = 500e^{40k}$

$\dfrac{3}{5} = e^{40k}$

$40k = \ln\left(\dfrac{3}{5}\right)$

$k = \dfrac{\ln(\frac{3}{5})}{40} \approx -0.01277$

$y = 500e^{0.01277t}$

95. *Half-Life* A sample of radioactive waste is taken from a nuclear plant. The sample contains 50 grams of strontium-90 at time $t = 0$ years and 42.031 grams after 7 years. What is the half-life of strontium-90?

Solution:

$y = 50e^{kt}$

$42.031 = 50e^{7k}$

$k = \dfrac{1}{7}\ln\left(\dfrac{42.031}{50}\right) \approx -0.0248$

$25 = 50e^{-0.0248t}$

$\dfrac{1}{2} = e^{-0.0248t}$

$t = \dfrac{\ln(\frac{1}{2})}{-0.0248} \approx 27.9$ years

97. *Profit* The profit for Wendy's was $3.5 million in 1987 and $64.7 million in 1992. Use an exponential growth model to predict the 1996 profit.

Solution:

$$y = 3.5e^{kt}$$

$$64.7 = 3.5e^{5k}$$

$$k = \frac{1}{5} \ln \left(\frac{64.7}{3.5} \right) \approx 0.5834$$

$$y = 3.5e^{0.5834t}$$

In 1996 ($t = 9$), $y \approx 667.4$ million.

Practice Test for Chapter 4

1. Evaluate each of the following expressions.

   (a) $27^{4/3}$ (b) $4^{-5/2}$ (c) $(8^{2/3})(64^{-1/3})$

2. Solve for x.

   (a) $4^{x+1} = 64$ (b) $x^{6/5} = 64$ (c) $(2x+3)^{10} = 13^{10}$

3. Sketch the graph of (a) $f(x) = 3^x$, and (b) $g(x) = \left(\frac{4}{9}\right)^x$.

4. Find the amount in an account in which \$2000 is invested for 7 years at 8.5% if the interest is compounded (a) annually, (b) monthly, and (c) continuously.

5. Differentiate $y = e^{3x^2}$.

6. Differentiate $y = e^{\sqrt[3]{x}}$.

7. Differentiate $y = \sqrt{e^x + e^{-x}}$.

8. Differentiate $y = x^3 e^{2x}$.

9. Differentiate $y = \dfrac{e^x + 3}{4x}$.

10. Write $\ln 5 = 1.6094\ldots$ as an exponential equation.

11. Sketch the graph of (a) $y = \ln(x+2)$, and (b) $y = \ln x + 2$.

12. Write the given expression as a single logarithm.

   (a) $\ln(3x+1) - \ln(2x-5)$ (b) $4\ln x - 3\ln y - \frac{1}{2}\ln z$

13. Solve for x.

   (a) $\ln x = 17$ (b) $5^{3x} = 2$

14. Differentiate $y = \ln(6x - 7)$.

15. Differentiate $y = \ln\left(\dfrac{x^3}{4x+10}\right)$

16. Differentiate $y = \ln \sqrt[3]{\dfrac{x}{x+3}}$.

17. Differentiate $y = x^4 \ln x$.

18. Differentiate $y = \sqrt{\ln x + 1}$.

19. Find the exponential function $y = Ce^{kt}$ that passes through the points
(a) $(0, 7)$, $\left(4, \frac{1}{3}\right)$, and (b) $\left(3, \frac{2}{3}\right)$, $(8, 8)$.

20. If \$5000 is invested in an account in which the interest rate of 12%
is compounded continuously, find the time required for the investment to double.

Graphing Calculator Required

21. Use a graphing calculator to graph both $y = \ln[x^3\sqrt{x+3}]$ and $y = 3\ln x + \dfrac{1}{2}\ln(x+3)$
on the same set of axes. What do you notice about the graphs?

22. Graph the function $f(t) = \dfrac{4200}{7 + e^{-0.9t}}$ and use the graph to find $\lim\limits_{t \to \infty} f(t)$ and $\lim\limits_{t \to -\infty} f(t)$.

CHAPTER 5

Integration and Its Applications

Section 5.1 Antiderivatives and Indefinite Integrals

1. Verify the statement $\displaystyle\int\left(-\frac{9}{x^4}\right)dx = \frac{3}{x^3} + C$ by showing that the derivative of the right side is equal to the integrand on the left side.

Solution:

$$\frac{d}{dx}\left(\frac{3}{x^3} + C\right) = \frac{d}{dx}(3x^{-3} + C) = -9x^{-4} = \frac{-9}{x^4}$$

3. Verify the statement $\displaystyle\int\left(4x^3 - \frac{1}{x^2}\right)dx = x^4 + \frac{1}{x} + C$ by showing that the derivative of the right side is equal to the integrand on the left side.

Solution:

$$\frac{d}{dx}\left(x^4 + \frac{1}{x} + C\right) = 4x^3 - \frac{1}{x^2}$$

5. Verify the statement $\displaystyle\int 2x^3\sqrt{x}\,dx = \frac{4}{9}x^{9/2} + C$ by showing that the derivative of the right side is equal to the integrand on the left side.

Solution:

$$\frac{d}{dx}\left(\frac{4}{9}x^{9/2} + C\right) = \frac{4}{9}\cdot\frac{9}{2}x^{7/2} = 2x^3\sqrt{x}$$

7. Verify the statement $\displaystyle\int \frac{x^2 - 1}{x^{3/2}}dx = \frac{2(x^2 + 3)}{3\sqrt{x}} + C$ by showing that the derivative of the right side is equal to the integrand on the left side.

Solution:

$$\frac{d}{dx}\left(\frac{2(x^2 + 3)}{3\sqrt{x}} + C\right) = \frac{d}{dx}\left(\frac{2}{3}x^{2/3} + 2x^{-1/2} + C\right) = x^{1/2} - x^{-3/2} = \frac{x^2 - 1}{x^{3/2}}$$

9. Evaluate $\int 6\,dx$ and check your result by differentiation.

Solution:

$$\int 6\,dx = 6x + C$$

$$\frac{d}{dx}[6x + C] = 6$$

11. Evaluate $\int 3t^2\,dt$ and check your result by differentiation.

Solution:

$$\int 3t^2\,dt = t^3 + C$$

$$\frac{d}{dt}[t^3 + C] = 3t^2$$

13. Find the indefinite integral of $\int 5x^{-3}\,dx$ and check your result by differentiation.

Solution:

$$\int 5x^{-3}\,dx = \frac{5x^{-2}}{-2} + C = \frac{-5}{2x^2} + C$$

$$\frac{d}{dx}\left[-\frac{5}{2}x^{-2} + C\right] = 5x^{-3}$$

15. Evaluate $\int du$ and check your result by differentiation.

Solution:

$$\int du = u + C$$

$$\frac{d}{du}[u + C] = 1$$

17. Evaluate $\int x^{3/2}\,dx$ and check your result by differentiation.

Solution:

$$\int x^{3/2}\,dx = \frac{2}{5}x^{5/2} + C$$

$$\frac{d}{dx}\left[\frac{2}{5}x^{5/2} + C\right] = x^{3/2}$$

In Exercises 19, 21, and 23, complete the table using Example 3 as a model.

Given	Rewrite	Integrate	Simplify
19. $\displaystyle\int \sqrt[3]{x}\, dx$	$\displaystyle\int x^{1/3}\, dx$	$\dfrac{x^{4/3}}{4/3} + C$	$\dfrac{3}{4}x^{4/3} + C$
21. $\displaystyle\int \dfrac{1}{x\sqrt{x}}\, dx$	$\displaystyle\int x^{-3/2}\, dx$	$\dfrac{x^{-1/2}}{-1/2} + C$	$-\dfrac{2}{\sqrt{x}} + C$
23. $\displaystyle\int \dfrac{1}{2x^3}\, dx$	$\dfrac{1}{2}\displaystyle\int x^{-3}\, dx$	$\dfrac{1}{2}\left(\dfrac{x^{-2}}{-2}\right) + C$	$-\dfrac{1}{4x^2} + C$

25. Find two functions that have the given derivative, and sketch the graph of each. (See textbook.) (There is more than one correct answer.)

    Solution:

    If $f'(x) = 2$, then $f(x) = 2x + C$. For example, $f(x) = 2x$ or $f(x)2x + 1$.

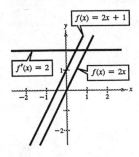

27. Evaluate the indefinite integral and check your result by differentiation.

    $$\int (x^3 + 2)\, dx$$

    Solution:

    $$\int (x^3 + 2)\, dx = \frac{x^4}{4} + 2x + C$$

    $$\frac{d}{dx}\left[\frac{x^4}{4} + 2x + C\right] = x^3 + 2$$

29. Evaluate the indefinite integral and check your result by differentiation.

$$\int (2x^{4/3} + 3x - 1)dx$$

Solution:

$$\int (2x^{4/3} + 3x - 1)dx = \frac{6}{7}x^{7/3} + \frac{3}{2}x^2 - x + C$$

$$\frac{d}{dx}\left[\frac{6}{7}x^{7/3} + \frac{3}{2}x^2 - x + C\right] = 2x^{4/3} - 3x - 1$$

31. Evaluate the indefinite integral and check your result by differentiation.

$$\int \sqrt[3]{x^2}\, dx$$

Solution:

$$\int \sqrt[3]{x^2}\, dx = \int x^{2/3}\, dx = \frac{3}{5}x^{5/3} + C$$

$$\frac{d}{dx}\left[\frac{3}{5}x^{5/3} + C\right] = \sqrt[3]{x^2}$$

33. Evaluate the indefinite integral and check your result by differentiation.

$$\int \frac{1}{x^3}\, dx$$

Solution:

$$\int \frac{1}{x^3}\, dx = \int x^{-3}\, dx = \frac{x^{-2}}{-2} + C = -\frac{1}{2x^2} + C$$

$$\frac{d}{dx}\left[-\frac{1}{2x^2} + C\right] = \frac{1}{x^3}$$

35. Evaluate the indefinite integral and check your result by differentiation.

$$\int \frac{1}{4x^2}\, dx$$

Solution:

$$\int \frac{1}{4x^2}\, dx = \frac{1}{4}\int x^{-2}\, dx = \frac{1}{4}\left(\frac{x^{-1}}{-1}\right) + C = -\frac{1}{4x} + C$$

$$\frac{d}{dx}\left[-\frac{1}{4x} + C\right] = \frac{1}{4x^2}$$

37. Evaluate the indefinite integral and check your result by differentiation.

$$\int \frac{t^2+2}{t^2}\,dt$$

Solution:

$$\int \frac{t^2+2}{t^2}\,dt = \int (1+2t^{-2})\,dt = t+2\left(\frac{t^{-1}}{-1}\right)+C = t-\frac{2}{t}+C$$

$$\frac{d}{dt}\left[t-\frac{2}{t}+C\right] = 1+\frac{2}{t^2} = \frac{t^2+2}{t^2}$$

39. Evaluate the indefinite integral and check your result by differentiation.

$$\int u(3u^2+1)\,du$$

Solution:

$$\int u(3u^2+1)\,du = \int (3u^3+u)\,du = \frac{3}{4}u^4 + \frac{1}{2}u^2 + C$$

$$\frac{d}{du}\left[\frac{3}{4}u^4+\frac{1}{2}u^2+C\right] = 3u^3+u = u(3u^2+1)$$

41. Evaluate the indefinite integral and check your result by differentiation.

$$\int (x-1)(6x-5)\,dx$$

Solution:

$$\int (x-1)(6x-5)\,dx = \int (6x^2-11x+5)\,dx = 2x^3 - \frac{11}{2}x^2 + 5x + C$$

$$\frac{d}{dx}\left[2x^3-\frac{11}{2}x^2+5x+C\right] = 6x^2-11x+5$$

43. Evaluate the indefinite integral and check your result by differentiation.

$$\int y^2\sqrt{y}\,dy$$

Solution:

$$\int y^2\sqrt{y}\,dy = \int y^{5/2}\,dy = \frac{2}{7}y^{7/2} + C$$

$$\frac{d}{dy}\left[\frac{2}{7}y^{7/2}+C\right] = y^{5/2} = y^2\sqrt{y}$$

45. Find the particular solution $y = f(x)$ that satisfies the differential equation $f'(x) = 3\sqrt{x} + 3$ and initial condition $f(1) = 4$.

Solution:

$$f(x) = \int (3x^{1/2} + 3)dx = 2x^{3/2} + 3x + C$$

$$f(1) = 4 = 2(1) + 3(1) + C = 5 + C \Rightarrow C = -1$$

$$f(x) = 2x^{3/2} + 3x - 1$$

47. Find the particular solution $y = f(x)$ that satisfies the differential equation $f'(x) = 6x(x - 1)$ and initial condition $f(1) = -1$.

Solution:

$$f(x) = \int 6x(x - 1)dx = \int (6x^2 - 6x)dx = 2x^3 - 3x^2 + C$$

$$f(1) = -1 = 2 - 3 + C = -1 + C \Rightarrow C = 0$$

$$f(x) = 2x^3 - 3x^2$$

49. Find the particular solution $y = f(x)$ that satisfies the differential equation $f'(x) = \dfrac{2 - x}{x^3}$, $x > 0$ and intitial condition $f(2) = \dfrac{3}{4}$

Solution:

$$f(x) = \int \frac{2 - x}{x^3}dx = \int (2x^{-3} - x^{-2})dx = -x^{-2} + x^{-1} + C = \frac{-1}{x^2} + \frac{1}{x} + C$$

$$f(2) = \frac{3}{4} = -\frac{1}{4} + \frac{1}{2} + C = \frac{1}{4} + C \Rightarrow C = \frac{1}{2}$$

$$f(x) = -\frac{1}{x^2} + \frac{1}{x} + \frac{1}{2}$$

51. Find the equation of the particular solution $\dfrac{dy}{dx} = -5x - 2$ that passes through the indicated point $(0, 2)$. (See graph in textbook.)

Solution:

$$y = \int (-5x - 2)dx = -\frac{5}{2}x^2 - 2x + C$$

At $+(0, 2)$, $2 = C$. Thus, $y = -\dfrac{5}{2}x^2 - 2x + 2$.

53. Find the equation for the function f whose graph passes through the point $(4, 2)$ with slope given by $f'(x) = 6\sqrt{x} - 10$.

Solution:

$$f(x) = \int (6\sqrt{x} - 10)\, dx = \int (6x^{1/2} - 10)\, dx = 4x^{3/2} - 10x + C = 4x\sqrt{x} - 10x + C$$

At $(4, 2)$, $2 = 4(4)\sqrt{4} - 10(4) + C$ which implies that $C = 10$. Thus,

$$f(x) = 4x\sqrt{x} - 10x + 10.$$

55. Find $y = f(x)$ satisfying the conditions $f''(x) = 2$, $f'(2) = 5$, $f(2) = 10$.

Solution:

$$f'(x) = \int 2\, dx = 2x + C_1$$

Since $f'(2) = 4 + C_1 = 5$, we know that $C_1 = 1$. Thus, $f'(x) = 2x + 1$.

$$f(x) = \int (2x + 1)\, dx = x^2 + x + C_2$$

Since $f(2) = 4 + 2 + C_2 = 10$, we know that $C_2 = 4$. Thus, $f(x) = x^2 + x + 4$.

57. Find a function f that satisfies the given conditions $f''(x) = x^{-2/3}$, $f'(8) = 6$, $f(0) = 0$.

Solution:

$$f'(x) = \int x^{-2/3}\, dx = 3x^{1/3} + C_1$$

Since $f'(8) = 3(2) + C_1 = 6$, we have $C_1 = 0$.

Thus $f'(x) = 3x^{1/3}$.

$$f(x) = \int 3x^{1/3}\, dx = \frac{9}{4}x^{4/3} + C_2.$$

Since $f(0) = 0 = C_2$, $f(x) = \frac{9}{4}x^{4/3}$.

59. *Cost* Find the cost function for the marginal cost $\dfrac{dC}{dx} = 85$ and the fixed cost $\$5500\ x = 0$.

Solution:

$$C = \int 85\, dx = 85x + k$$

When $x = 0$, $C = 5500 = k$. Thus, $C = 85x + 5500$.

61. *Cost* Find the cost function for the marginal cost $dC/dx = [1/(20\sqrt{x})] + 4$ and fixed cost of \$750 (cost when $x = 0$).

Solution:

$$C = \int \left(\frac{1}{20} x^{-1/2} + 4 \right) dx = \frac{1}{10} x^{1/2} + 4x + k$$

When $x = 0$,

$$C = \frac{1}{10}(\sqrt{0}) + 4(0) + k = 750 \Rightarrow k = 750.$$

Thus,

$$C = \frac{\sqrt{x}}{10} + 4x + 750.$$

63. *Demand Function* Find the revenue and demand functions for the given marginal revenue $\dfrac{dR}{dx} = 225 - 3x$.

Solution:

$$R = \int (225 - 3x)dx = 225x - \frac{3}{2}x^2 + C.$$

Since $R = 0$ when $x = 0$, it follows that $C = 0$. Thus $R = 225x - \dfrac{3}{2}x^2$ and the demand function is $p = \dfrac{R}{x} = 225 - \dfrac{3}{2}x$.

65. *Profit* Find the profit function for the given marginal profit $\dfrac{dP}{dx} = -18x + 1650$ and initial condition $P(15) = \$22,725$.

Solution:

$$P = \int (-18x + 1650)dx = -9x^2 + 1650x + C$$

$$P(15) = 22,725 = -9(15)^2 + 1650(15) + C \Rightarrow C = 0$$

$$P = -9 \ (\text{as in} -9x^2) + 1650x$$

67. *Vertical Motion* Use $a(t) = -32$ ft/s^2 as the acceleration due to gravity. A ball is thrown upward with an initial velocity of 60 ft/sec. How high will the ball go?

Solution:

$$v(t) = \int -32 \, dt = -32t + C_1$$

Since $v(0) = 60$, it follows that $C_1 = 60$. Thus, we have $v(t) = -32t + 60$.

$$s(t) = \int (-32t + 60) \, dt = -16t^2 + 60t + C_2$$

Since $s(0) = 0$, it follows that $C_2 = 0$. Therefore, the position function is $s(t) = -16t^2 + 60t$. Now, since $v(t) = 0$ when $t = 60/32 = 1.875$ seconds, the maximum height of the ball is $s(1.875) = 56.25$ feet.

69. Use $a(t) = -32$ ft/s^2 as the acceleration due to gravity. With what initial velocity must an object by thrown upward from the ground to reach the height of the Washington Monument (550 feet)?

Solution:

$$v(t) = \int -32 \, dt = -32t + C_1$$

Letting v_0 be the initial velocity, we have $C_1 = v_0$.

$$s(t) = \int (-32t + v_0) \, dt = -16t^2 + v_0 t + C_2$$

Since $s(0) = 0$, we have $C_2 = 0$. Therefore, the position function is $s(t) = -16t^2 + v_0 t$. At the highest point, the velocity is zero. Therefore, we have $v(t) = -32t + v_0 = 0$, and $t = v_0/32$ seconds. Finally, substituting this value into the position function, we have

$$s\left(\frac{v_0}{32}\right) = -16\left(\frac{v_0}{32}\right)^2 + v_0\left(\frac{v_0}{32}\right) = 550$$

which implies that $v_0^2 = 35,200$ and the initial velocity should be $v_0 = 40\sqrt{22} \approx 187.617$ ft/sec.

71. *Cost* A company produces a product for which the marginal cost of producing x units is $dC/dx = 2x - 12$ and fixed costs are $125.

(a) Find the total cost function and the average cost function.

(b) Find the total cost of producing 50 units.

(c) In part (b), how much of the total cost is fixed? How much is variable? Give examples of fixed costs associated with the manufacturing of a product. Give examples of variable costs.

Solution:

(a) $C(x) = \displaystyle\int (2x - 12)\, dx = x^2 - 12x + C_1$

Since $C(0) = 125$, it follows that $C_1 = 125$. Thus, $C(x) = x^2 - 12x + 125$ and the average cost is $C/x = x - 12 + (125/x)$.

(b) $C(50) = 50^2 - 12(50) + 125 = \$2025$

(c) \$125 is fixed, \$1900 is variable.

73. *Natural Gas Consumption* The consumption S (in quadrillion Btu's) of natural gas in the United States increased steadily between 1986 and 1992. The rate of increase can be modeled by

$$\frac{dS}{dt} = -0.175t^2 + 0.4t + 0.81, \qquad 0 \le t \le 6,$$

where $t = 0$ represents 1986. In 1986, the consumption was 16.7 quadrillion Btu's. Find a model for the consumption from 1986 through 1992 and determine the consumption in 1992.

Solution:

$$S = \int (-0.175t^2 + 0.4t^2 + 0.81)dt$$

$$= \frac{-0.175t^3}{3} + 0.2t^2 + 0.81t + C$$

In 1986 $(t = 0)$, $S = 16.7 \Rightarrow C = 16.7$

$$S = \frac{-0.175}{3}t^3 + 0.2t^2 + 0.81t + 16.7$$

In 1992 $(t = 6)$, $S = \dfrac{-0.175}{3}(6)^3 + 0.2(6)^2 + 0.81(6) + 16.7$

$$= 16.16 \text{ quadrillion Btu's}$$

Section 5.2 The General Power Rule

In exercise 1, 3, and 5 complete the table by identifying u and du/dx for the given integral.

$\int u^n \dfrac{du}{dx}\, dx$	u	$\dfrac{du}{dx}$
1. $\displaystyle\int (5x^2 + 1)^2 (10x)\, dx$	$5x^2 + 1$	$10x$
3. $\displaystyle\int \sqrt{1 - x^2}(-2x)\, dx$	$1 - x^2$	$-2x$
5. $\displaystyle\int \left(4 + \dfrac{1}{x^2}\right)\left(\dfrac{-2}{x^3}\right) dx$	$4 + \dfrac{1}{x^2}$	$-\dfrac{2}{x^3}$

7. Evaluate $\displaystyle\int (1 + 2x)^4 (2)\, dx$.

Solution:

$$\int (1 + 2x)^4 (2)\, dx = \frac{(1 + 2x)^5}{5} + C$$

9. Evaluate $\displaystyle\int \sqrt{5x^2 - 4}(10x)dx$.

Solution:

$$\int \sqrt{5x^2 - 4}(10x)dx = \int (5x^2 - 4)^{1/2}(10x)dx$$

$$= \frac{2}{3}(5x^2 - 4)^{3/2} + C$$

11. Evaluate $\displaystyle\int (x - 1)^4\, dx$.

Solution:

$$\int (x - 1)^4\, dx = \int (x - 1)^4 (1)\, dx = \frac{(x - 1)^5}{5} + C$$

13. Evaluate $\displaystyle\int x(x^2 - 1)^7\, dx$.

Solution:

$$\int x(x^2 - 1)^7\, dx = \frac{1}{2}\int (x^2 - 1)^7 (2x)\, dx = \frac{1}{2}\frac{(x^2 - 1)^8}{8} + C = \frac{(x^2 - 1)^8}{16} + C$$

15. Evaluate $\int \dfrac{x^2}{(1+x^3)^2}\,dx$.

Solution:

$$\int \frac{x^2}{(1+x^3)^2}\,dx = \frac{1}{3}\int (1+x^3)^{-2}(3x^2)\,dx = \frac{1}{3}\,\frac{(1+x^3)^{-1}}{-1} + C = -\frac{1}{3(1+x^3)} + C$$

17. Evaluate $\int \dfrac{x+1}{(x^2+2x-3)^2}\,dx$.

Solution:

$$\int \frac{x+1}{(x^2+2x-3)^2}\,dx = \frac{1}{2}\int (x^2+2x-3)^{-2}2(x+1)\,dx$$

$$= \frac{1}{2}\,\frac{(x^2+2x-3)^{-1}}{-1} + C = -\frac{1}{2(x^2+2x-3)} + C$$

19. Evaluate $\int \dfrac{x-2}{\sqrt{x^2-4x+3}}\,dx$.

Solution:

$$\int \frac{x-2}{\sqrt{x^2-4x+3}}\,dx = \frac{1}{2}\int (x^2-4x+3)^{-1/2}(2x-4)\,dx$$

$$= \frac{1}{2}(2)(x^2-4x+3)^{1/2} + C$$

$$= \sqrt{x^2-4x+3} + C$$

21. Evaluate $\int 5x\sqrt[3]{1-x^2}\,dx$.

Solution:

$$\int 5x\sqrt[3]{1-x^2}\,dx = 5\left(-\frac{1}{2}\right)\int (1-x^2)^{1/3}(-2x)\,dx = -\frac{5}{2}\left(\frac{3}{4}\right)(1-x^2)^{4/3} + C =$$
$$\frac{-15(1-x^2)^{4/3}}{8} + C$$

23. Evaluate $\int \dfrac{4x}{\sqrt{1+x^2}}\,dx$.

Solution:

$$\int \frac{4x}{\sqrt{1+x^2}}\,dx = 4\left(\frac{1}{2}\right)\int (1+x^2)^{-1/2}(2x)\,dx = 2(2)(1+x^2)^{1/2}+C = 4\sqrt{1+x^2}+C$$

25. Evaluate $\displaystyle\int \frac{-3}{\sqrt{2x+3}}\,dx.$

Solution:

$$\int \frac{-3}{\sqrt{2x+3}}\,dx = -\frac{3}{2}\int (2x+3)^{-1/2}(2)\,dx$$

$$= -\frac{3}{2}(2)(2x+3)^{1/2} + C = -3\sqrt{2x+3} + C$$

27. Evaluate $\displaystyle\int \frac{x^3}{\sqrt{1-x^4}}\,dx.$

Solution:

$$\int \frac{x^3}{\sqrt{1-x^4}}\,dx = -\frac{1}{4}\int (1-x^4)^{-1/2}(-4x^3)\,dx$$

$$= -\frac{1}{4}(2)(1-x^4)^{1/2} + C = -\frac{\sqrt{1-x^4}}{2} + C$$

29. Evaluate $\displaystyle\int \frac{1}{\sqrt{2x}}\,dx.$

Solution:

$$\int \frac{1}{\sqrt{2x}}\,dx = \frac{1}{\sqrt{2}}\int x^{-1/2}\,dx = \frac{1}{\sqrt{2}}(2x^{1/2}) + C = \sqrt{2x} + C$$

31. Evaluate $\displaystyle\int (x^3+3x)(x^2+1)\,dx.$

Solution:

$$\int (x^3+3x)(x^2+1)\,dx = \frac{1}{3}\int (x^3+3x)^1(3x^2+3)\,dx$$

$$= \frac{1}{3}\frac{(x^3+3x)^2}{2} + C = \frac{1}{6}(x^3+3x)^2 + C$$

33. Use formal substitution to find the following indefinite ingegral.

$$\int x(6x^2-1)^3\,dx.$$

Solution:

$Let\, u = 6x^2 - 1.$ Then $du = 12x\,dx$ and $x\,dx = \dfrac{1}{12}du.$

$$\int x(6x^2-1)^3\,dx = \int (6x^2-1)^3(x\,dx) = \int u^3\frac{1}{12}\,du = \frac{1}{12}\frac{u^4}{4} + C$$

$$= \frac{1}{48}(6x^2-1)^4 + C$$

35. Use formal substitution to find the following indefinite integral.

$$\int x^2 (2 - 3x^3)^{3/2} \, dx$$

Solution:

Let $u = 2 - 3x^3$, then $du = -9x^2 \, dx$ which implies that $x^2 \, dx = -\frac{1}{9} \, du$.

$$\int x^2 (2 - 3x^3)^{3/2} \, dx = \int (2 - 3x^3)^{3/2} (x^2) \, dx$$

$$= \int u^{3/2} \left(-\frac{1}{9}\right) du$$

$$= -\frac{1}{9}\left(\frac{2}{5}\right) u^{5/2} + C$$

$$= -\frac{2}{45}(2 - 3x^3)^{5/2} + C$$

37. Use formal substitution to find the following indefinite integral.

$$\int \frac{x}{\sqrt{x^2 + 25}} \, dx$$

Solution:

Let $u = x^2 + 25$, then $du = 2x \, dx$ which implies that $x \, dx = \frac{1}{2} \, du$.

$$\int \frac{x}{\sqrt{x^2 + 25}} \, dx = \int (x^2 + 25)^{-1/2}(x) \, dx$$

$$= \int u^{-1/2}\left(\frac{1}{2}\right) du$$

$$= \frac{1}{2}(2u^{1/2}) + C$$

$$= \sqrt{u} + C = \sqrt{x^2 + 25} + C$$

39. Use formal substitution to find the following indefinite integral.

$$\int \frac{x^2+1}{\sqrt{x^3+3x+4}}\,dx$$

Solution:

Let $u = x^3 + 3x + 4$, then $du = (3x^2 + 3)\,dx = 3(x^2 + 1)\,dx$ and $(x^2 + 1)\,dx = \frac{1}{3}\,du$.

$$\int \frac{x^2+1}{\sqrt{x^3+3x+4}}\,dx = \int (x^3 + 3x + 4)^{-1/2}(x^2 + 1)\,dx$$

$$= \int u^{-1/2}\left(\frac{1}{3}\right)du$$

$$= \left(\frac{1}{3}\right)2u^{1/2} + C$$

$$= \frac{2}{3}\sqrt{u} + C$$

$$= \frac{2}{3}\sqrt{x^3 + 3x + 4} + C$$

41. Perform the integration in two ways (Simple Power Rule and General Power Rule) and explain the difference in the answers.

$$\int (2x - 1)^2\,dx$$

Solution:

$$\int (2x - 1)^2\,dx = \frac{1}{2}\int (2x - 1)^2(2)\,dx$$

$$= \frac{1}{2}\frac{(2x - 1)^3}{3} + C_1$$

$$= \frac{1}{6}(2x - 1)^3 + C_1$$

$$= \frac{1}{6}(8x^3 - 12x^2 + 6x - 1) + C_1$$

$$= \frac{4}{3}x^3 - 2x^2 + x - \frac{1}{6} + C_1$$

$$\int (2x - 1)^2\,dx = \int (4x^2 - 4x + 1)\,dx = \frac{4}{3}x^3 - 2x^2 + x + C_2$$

The two answers differ by a constant.

43. Perform the integration in two ways (Simple Power Rule and General Power Rule) and explain the difference in the answers.

$$\int x(x^2 - 1)^2 dx$$

Solution:

$$\int x(x^2 - 1)^2 dx = \frac{1}{2}\int (x^2 - 1)^2 (2x)\, dx$$

$$= \frac{1}{2}\frac{(x^2 - 1)^3}{3} + C_1$$

$$= \frac{1}{6}(x^6 - 3x^4 + 3x^2 - 1) + C_1$$

$$= \frac{1}{6}x^6 - \frac{1}{2}x^4 + \frac{1}{2}x^2 - \frac{1}{6} + C_1$$

$$\int x(x^2 - 1)^2 dx = \int (x^5 - 2x^3 + x)\, dx = \frac{1}{6}x^6 - \frac{1}{2}x^4 + \frac{1}{2}x^2 + C_2$$

The two answers differ by a constant.

45. Find the equation of the function f whose graph passes through the point $\left(0, \frac{4}{3}\right)$ and whose derivative is $f'(x) = x\sqrt{1 - x^2}$.

Solution:

$$f(x) = \int x\sqrt{1 - x^2}\, dx$$

$$= -\frac{1}{2}\int (1 - x^2)^{1/2}(-2x)\, dx$$

$$= -\frac{1}{2}\left(\frac{2}{3}\right)(1 - x^2)^{3/2} + C$$

$$= -\frac{1}{3}(1 - x^2)^{3/2} + C$$

Since $f(0) = \frac{4}{3}$, it follows that $C = \frac{5}{3}$ and we have

$$f(x) = -\frac{1}{3}(1 - x^2)^{3/2} + \frac{5}{3} = \frac{1}{3}[5 - (1 - x^2)^{3/2}].$$

47. *Cost* A company has determined the marginal cost for a particular product to be

$$\frac{dC}{dx} = \frac{4}{\sqrt{x+1}}.$$

(a) Find the cost function if $C = 50$ when $x = 15$.

(b) Graph the marginal cost function and the cost function on the same set of axes.

Solution:

(a) $\displaystyle C = \int \frac{4}{\sqrt{x+1}}\, dx$

$\displaystyle \quad = 4\int (x+1)^{-1/2}\, dx$

$\displaystyle \quad = 4(2)(x+1)^{1/2} + K$

$\displaystyle \quad = 8\sqrt{x+1} + K$

Since $C(15) = 50$, it follows that $K = 18$, and we have $C = 8\sqrt{x+1} + 18$.

(b)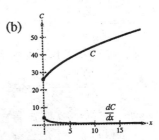

49. Find the supply function $x = f(p)$ that satisfies the given condition $\dfrac{dx}{dp} = p\sqrt{p^2 - 25}$

and $x = 600$ when $p = \$13$.

Solution:

$$x = \int p\sqrt{p^2 - 25}\, dp = \frac{1}{2}\int (p^2 - 25)^{1/2}(2p)\, dp = \frac{1}{2}\cdot\frac{2}{3}(p^2 - 25)^{3/2} + C$$

$$= \frac{1}{3}(p^2 - 25)^{3/2} + C$$

Since $x = 600$ when $p = 13$, it follows that $x = 600 = \frac{1}{3}(13^2 - 25)^{3/2} + C = 576 + C$

and $C = 24$. Therefore, $x = \frac{1}{3}(p^2 - 25)^{3/2} + 24$.

51. *Demand Function* Find the demand function $x = f(p)$ that satisfies the given conditions.

$$\frac{dx}{dp} = -\frac{6000p}{(p^2 - 16)^{3/2}}, \quad x = 5000 \text{ when } p = \$5$$

Solution:

$$x = \int -\frac{6000p}{(p^2 - 16)^{3/2}}\, dp$$

$$= -\frac{6000}{2}\int (p^2 - 16)^{-3/2}(2p)\, dp$$

$$= -3000(-2)(p^2 - 16)^{-1/2} + C$$

$$= \frac{6000}{\sqrt{p^2 - 16}} + C$$

Since $x = 5000$ when $p = 5$, it follows that $C = 3000$, and we have

$$x = \frac{6000}{\sqrt{p^2 - 16}} + 3000.$$

53. *Depreciation* The rate of depreciation dV/dt of a machine is inversely proportional to the square of $t+1$ where V is the value of the machine t years after it was purchased. If the initial value of the machine was \$500,000, and the value after 1 year was \$400,000, estimate its value after 4 years.

Solution:

$$\frac{dV}{dt} = \frac{K}{(t + 1)^2}$$

$$V = \int K(t + 1)^{-2}\, dt = -\frac{K}{t + 1} + C$$

When $t = 0$, $V = 500,000$. Thus, $-K + C = 500,000$.

When $t = 1$, $V = 400,000$. Thus, $-\frac{K}{2} + C = 400,000$.

Solving this system yields $K = -200,000$ and $C = 300,000$.

$$V = \frac{200,000}{t + 1} + 300,000$$

When $t = 4$, $V = \frac{200,000}{5} + 300,000 = \$340,000.$

55. (a) Use the marginal propensity to consume, $d\,Q/dx$, to write Q as a function of x, where x is the income and Q is the income consumed. Assume that 100% of the income is consumed for families that have an annual income of $20,000 or less, (b) Use the result of part (a) to complete the table showing the income consumed and the income saved, $x - Q$, for various incomes. (c) Graphically represent the income consumed and saved.

$$\frac{dQ}{dx} = \frac{0.95}{(x - 19{,}999)^{0.05}}, \; 20{,}000 \le x$$

Solution:

(a) $Q = \displaystyle\int \frac{0.95}{(x - 19{,}999)^{0.05}} dx = (x - 19{,}999)^{0.95} + C$

Since $Q = 20{,}000$ when $x = 20{,}000$

$$20{,}000 = (20{,}000 - 19{,}999)^{0.95} + C = 1 + C$$

$$C = 19{,}999$$

Thus

$$Q = (x - 19{,}999)^{0.95} + 19{,}999$$

(b)

x	20,000	50,000	100,000	150,000
Q	20,000	37,916.56	65,491.59	92,151.16
$X - Q$	0	12,083.44	34,508.41	57,848.84

(c)

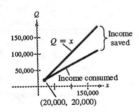

57. Use a symbolic integration utility to find the indefinite integral $\displaystyle\int \frac{1}{\sqrt{x} + \sqrt{x+1}}\,dx$.

Verify the result by differentiating.

Solution:

$$\int \frac{1}{\sqrt{x} + \sqrt{x+1}}\,dx = -\frac{2}{3}x^{3/2} + \frac{2}{3}(x+1)^{3/2} + C.$$

Section 5.3   Exponential and Logarithmic Integrals

1. Use the Exponential Rule to find the indefinite integral $\int 2e^{2x}dx$.

Solution:

$$\int e^{2x}(2)dx = e^{2x} + C$$

3. Use the Exponential Rule to find the indefinite integral $\int e^{4x}dx$.

Solution:

$$\int e^{4x}dx = \frac{1}{4}\int e^{4x}(4)dx = \frac{1}{4}e^{4x} + C$$

5. Use the Exponential Rule to find the indefinite integral $\int 9xe^{-x^2}dx$.

Solution:

$$\int 9xe^{-x^2}dx = -\frac{9}{2}\int e^{-x^2}(-2x)dx = -\frac{9}{2}e^{-x^2} + C$$

7. Use the Exponential Rule to find the indefinite integral $\int 5x^2e^{x^3}dx$.

Solution:

$$\int 5x^2e^{x^3}dx = \frac{5}{3}\int e^{x^3}(3x^2)dx = \frac{5}{3}e^{x^3} + C$$

9. Use the Exponential Rule to find the indefinite integral $\int (x^2 + 2x)e^{x^3+3x^2-1}dx$.

Solution:

$$\frac{1}{3}\int e^{x^3+3x^2-1}(3x^2 + 6x)dx = \frac{1}{3}e^{x^3+3x^2-1} + C$$

11. Use the Exponential Rule to find the indefinite integral $\int 5e^{2-x}dx$.

Solution:

$$\int 5e^{2-x}dx = -5\int e^{2-x}(-1)dx = -5e^{2-x} + C$$

13. Use the Exponential Rule to find the indefinite integral $\int \frac{1}{x^2}e^{2/x}dx$.

Solution:

$$-\frac{1}{2}\int e^{2/x}(-2x^{-2})dx = -\frac{1}{2}e^{2/x} + C$$

15. Use the Exponential Rule to find the indefinite integral $\int \frac{1}{\sqrt{x}} e^{\sqrt{x}} dx$.

Solution:

$$2\int e^{\sqrt{x}} \frac{1}{2\sqrt{x}} dx = 2e^{\sqrt{x}} + C$$

17. Use the Log Rule to find the indefinite integral $\int \frac{1}{x+1} dx$.

Solution:

$$\int \frac{1}{x+1} dx = \ln|x+1| + C$$

19. Use the Log Rule to find the indefinite integral $\int \frac{1}{3-2x} dx$.

Solution:

$$-\frac{1}{2}\int \frac{1(-2)}{3-2x} dx = -\frac{1}{2}\ln|3-2x| + C$$

21. Use the Log Rule to find the indefinite integral $\int \frac{x}{x^2+1} dx$.

Solution:

$$\frac{1}{2}\int \frac{x(2)}{x^2+1} dx = \frac{1}{2}\ln(x^2+1) + C = \ln\sqrt{x^2+1} + C$$

23. Use the Log Rule to find the indefinite integral $\int \frac{x^2}{x^3+1} dx$.

Solution:

$$\int \frac{x^2}{x^3+1} dx = \frac{1}{3}\int \frac{3x^2}{x^3+1} dx$$

$$= \frac{1}{3}\ln|x^3+1| + C$$

25. Use the Log Rule to find the indefinite integral $\int \frac{x+3}{x^2+6x+7} dx$.

Solution:

$$\int \frac{x+3}{x^2+6x+7} dx = \frac{1}{2}\int \frac{2(x+3)}{x^2+6x+7} dx = \frac{1}{2}\ln|x^2+6x+7| + C$$

27. Use the Log Rule to find the indefinite integral $\int \frac{1}{x \ln x} dx$.

Solution:

$$\int \frac{1}{x \ln x} dx = \int \frac{1}{\ln x}\left(\frac{1}{x}\right) dx = \ln|\ln x| + C$$

29. Use the Log Rule to find the indefinite integral $\displaystyle\int \frac{e^{-x}}{1+e^{-x}}$.

Solution:

$$-\int \frac{1}{1+e^{-x}}(-e^{-x})dx = -\ln(1+e^{-x}) + C$$

31. Use the Log Rule to find the indefinite integral $\displaystyle\int \frac{4e^{2x}}{5-e^{2x}}dx$.

Solution:

$$2\int \frac{1}{5-e^{2x}}2e^{2x}dx = 2\ln|5-e^{2x}| + C$$

33. Use any basic integration formula or formulas to find the indefinite integral

$$\int \frac{e^{2x}+2e^{x}+1}{e^{x}}dx.$$

Solution:

$$\int \frac{e^{2x}+2e^{x}+1}{e^{x}}dx = \int (e^{x}+2+e^{-x})dx = e^{x}+2x-e^{-x}+C$$

35. Use any basic integration formula or formulas to find the indefinite integral

$$\int e^{x}\sqrt{1-e^{x}}\,dx.$$

Solution:

$$\int e^{x}\sqrt{1-e^{x}}\,dx = -\int (1-e^{x})^{1/2}(-e^{x})\,dx = -\frac{2}{3}(1-e^{x})^{3/2} + C$$

37. Use any basic integration formula or formulas to find the indefinite integral $\displaystyle\int \frac{1}{(x-1)^{2}}dx$.

Solution:

$$\int (x-1)^{-2}dx = \frac{(x-1)^{-1}}{-1} = \frac{-1}{x-1} + C$$

39. Use any basic integration formula or formulas to find the indefinite integral $\displaystyle\int \frac{x^{2}-4}{x}\,dx$.

Solution:

$$\int \frac{x^{2}-4}{x}\,dx = \int \left[x - 4\left(\frac{1}{x}\right)\right]dx = \frac{x^{2}}{2} - 4\ln|x| + C$$

41. Use any basic integration formula or formulas to find the indefinite integral $\displaystyle\int \frac{x^{3}-8x}{2x^{2}}dx$.

Solution:

$$\int \frac{x^{3}-8x}{2x^{2}}dx = \int \left(\frac{x}{2} - \frac{4}{x}\right)dx = \frac{x^{2}}{4} - 4\ln|x| + C$$

43. Use any basic integration formula or formulas to find the indefinite integral $\int \dfrac{2}{1+e^{-x}}dx.$

Solution:

$$\int \frac{2}{1+e^{-x}}dx = 2\int \frac{1}{e^{x}+1}e^{x}dx = 2\ln(e^{x}+1)+C$$

45. Use any basic integration formula or formulas to find the indefinite integral

$$\int \frac{x^{2}+2x+5}{x-1}dx.$$

Solution:

$$\int \frac{x^{2}+2x+5}{x-1}dx = \int \left(x+3+\frac{8}{x-1}\right)dx = \frac{1}{2}x^{2}+3x+8\ln|x-1|+C$$

47. Use any basic integration formula or formulas to find the indefinite integral

$$\int \frac{x^{3}+4x^{2}+3x}{x^{2}-x}dx.$$

Solution:

$$\int \frac{x^{3}+4x^{2}+3x}{x^{2}-x}dx = \int \frac{x^{2}+4x+3}{x-1}dx = \int x+5+\frac{8}{x-1}dx$$

$$= \frac{1}{2}x^{2}+5x+8\ln|x-1|+C$$

49. Use any basic integration formula or formulas to find the indefinite integral $\int \dfrac{1+e^{-x}}{1+xe^{-x}}dx.$

Solution:

$$\int \frac{1+e^{-x}}{1+xe^{-x}}dx = \int \frac{e^{x}+1}{e^{x}+x}dx = \ln|e^{x}+x|+C$$

51. *Bacteria Growth* A population of bacteria is growing at the rate of $dP/dt = 3000/(1 + 0.25t)$ where t is the time in days. Assuming that the initial population (when $t = 0$) is 1000, (a) write an equation that gives the population P at any time t, (b) find the population when $t = 3$ days, and (c) after how many days will the population be 12,000?

Solution:

(a) $P = \displaystyle\int \frac{3000}{1 + 0.25t} \, dt$

$= \dfrac{3000}{0.25} \displaystyle\int \frac{0.25}{1 + 0.25t} \, dt$

$= 12,000 \ln|1 + 0.25t| + C$

Since $P(0) = 12,000 \ln 1 + C = 1000$, it follows that $C = 1000$. Therefore,

$P(t) = 12,000 \ln|1 + 0.25t| + 1000$.

$= 1000[12 \ln|1 + 0.25t| + 1]$

$= 1000[1 + \ln(1 + 0.25t)^{12}]$

(b) The population when $t = 3$ is $P(3) = 1000[1 + \ln(1 + 0.75)^{12}] \approx 7715$ bacteria.

(c) Using a graphing utility, $12,000 = 1000[1 + \ln)1 + \ln(1 + 0.25t)^{12}] \Rightarrow t \approx 6$ days.

53. *Demand* The marginal price for the demand of a product can be modeled by

$$\frac{dp}{dx} = 0.1e^{-x/500},$$

where x is the quantity demanded. When the demand is 600 units, the price is $30.

(a) Find the demand function, $p = f(x)$.

(b) Use a graphing utility to graph the demand function. Does the price increase or decrease as the demand increases?

(c) Use the zoom and trace features of the graphing utility to find the quantity demanded when the price is $22.

Solution:

(a) $p = \displaystyle\int 0.1e^{-x/500}dx = -50e^{-x/500} + C$

Since $x = 600$ when $p = 30$ we have $30 = -50e^{600/500} + C \Rightarrow C \approx 45.06$.

$p = -50e^{-x/500} + 45.06$

(b)

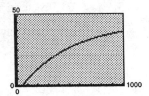

Price increases as demand increases.

(c) When $p = 22$, $x \approx 387$.

55. *ATM Transactions* From 1986 through 1992, the number of automatic teller machine (ATM) transactions T (in millions) in the United States changed at the rate of

$$\frac{dT}{dt} = 23.23t^{3/2} - 7.89t^2 + 44.71e^{-t},$$

where $t = 0$ corresponds to 1986. In 1992, there were 600 million transactions.

(a) Write a model that gives the total number of ATM transactions per year.

(b) Use the model to find the number of ATM transactions in 1987.

Solution:

(a) $T = \displaystyle\int (23.23t^{3/2} - 7.89t^2 + 44.71e^{-t})dt$

$= 9.292t^{5/2} - 2.63t^3 - 44.71e^{-t} + C$

Since $T = 600$ when $t = 6$, $C \approx 348.81$.

Thus, $T = 9.292t^{5/2} - 2.63t^3 - 44.71e^{-t} + 348.81$

(b) When $t = 1$, $T \approx 339$ million transactions.

Section 5.4   Area and the Fundamental Theorem of Calculus

1. Sketch the region whose area is represented by the definite integral $\int_{0}^{2} 3dx$. Then use a geometric formula to evaluate the integral.

   Solution:

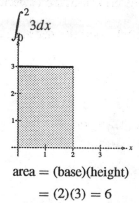

$$\int_{0}^{2} 3dx$$

   area = (base)(height)

   $= (2)(3) = 6$

3. Sketch the region whose area is represented by the definite integral $\int_{0}^{5}(x+1)dx$. Then use a geometric formula to evaluate the integral.

   Solution:

   $$\int_{0}^{5}(x+1)dx$$

   area $= \dfrac{1}{2}$(base)(height)

   $= \dfrac{1}{2}(5)(1+6) = \dfrac{35}{2}$

5. Determine the area of the region bounded by the graphs of $y = x - x^2$ and $y = 0$.

   Solution:

   $$A = \int_{0}^{1}(x - x^2)\,dx = \left[\frac{x^2}{2} - \frac{x^3}{3}\right]_{0}^{1} = \frac{1}{6}$$

7. Determine the area of the region bounded by the graph of $y = 1 - x^4$ and $y = 0$.

Solution:

$$A = \int_{-1}^{1} (1 - x^4)\, dx = 2\int_{0}^{1} (1 - x^4)\, dx = 2\left(x - \frac{x^5}{5}\right)\Bigg]_{0}^{1} = \frac{8}{5} \text{ square units.}$$

9. Determine the area of the region bounded by the graphs of $y = \sqrt[3]{2x}$, $x = 0$, $x = 4$, and $y = 0$.

Solution:

$$A = \int_{0}^{4} \sqrt[3]{2x}\, dx$$

$$= \frac{1}{2}\int_{0}^{4} (2x)^{1/3}(2)\, dx$$

$$= \frac{1}{2}\left(\frac{3}{4}\right)(2x)^{4/3}\Bigg]_{0}^{4}$$

$$= \frac{3}{8}(\sqrt[3]{2x})^4\Bigg]_{0}^{4}$$

$$= \frac{3}{8}(16) - \frac{3}{8}(0) = 6 \text{ square units}$$

11. Evaluate $\displaystyle\int_{0}^{1} 2x\, dx$.

Solution:

$$\int_{0}^{1} 2x\, dx = x^2\Bigg]_{0}^{1} = 1 - 0 = 1$$

13. Evaluate $\displaystyle\int_{-1}^{0} (2x + 1)\,dx$.

Solution:

$$\int_{-1}^{0} (2x + 1),\ dx = \left[x^2 + x\right]_{-1}^{0} = 0 - 0 = 0$$

15. Evaluate $\displaystyle\int_{-1}^{1} (2t - 1)^2\, dt$.

Solution:

$$\int_{-1}^{1} (2t - 1)^2\, dt = \frac{1}{6}(2t - 1)^3\Bigg]_{-1}^{1} = \frac{1}{6} - \left(\frac{-27}{6}\right) = \frac{14}{3}$$

17. Evaluate $\displaystyle\int_0^1 (2t - 1)^2 \, dt$.

Solution:

$$\int_0^1 (2t - 1)^2 \, dt = \frac{1}{2}\int_0^1 (2t - 1)^2(2) \, dt = \frac{1}{6}(2t - 1)^3 \Big]_0^1 = \frac{1}{6} - \left(-\frac{1}{6}\right) = \frac{1}{3}$$

19. Evaluate $\displaystyle\int_{-1}^1 (\sqrt[3]{t} - 2) \, dt$.

Solution:

$$\int_{-1}^1 (\sqrt[3]{t} - 2) \, dt = \left[\frac{3}{4}t^{4/3} - 2t\right]_{-1}^1 = -\frac{5}{4} - \frac{11}{4} = -4$$

21. Evaluate $\displaystyle\int_1^4 \frac{2u - 1}{\sqrt{u}} \, du$.

Solution:

$$\int_1^4 \frac{2u - 1}{\sqrt{u}} \, du = \int_1^4 (2u^{1/2} - u^{-1/2} \, du$$

$$= \left[\frac{4}{3}u^{3/2} - 2u^{1/2}\right]_1^4$$

$$= \left(\frac{32}{3} - 4\right) - \left(\frac{4}{3} - 2\right)$$

$$= \frac{22}{3}$$

23. Evaluate $\displaystyle\int_{-1}^0 (t^{1/3} - t^{2/3}) \, dt$.

Solution:

$$\int_{-1}^0 (t^{1/3} - t^{2/3}) \, dt = \left[\frac{3}{4}t^{4/3} - \frac{3}{5}t^{5/3}\right]_{-1}^0 = 0 - \left(\frac{3}{4} + \frac{3}{5}\right) = -\frac{27}{20}$$

25. Evaluate $\displaystyle\int_0^4 \frac{1}{\sqrt{2x + 1}} \, dx$.

Solution:

$$\int_0^4 \frac{1}{\sqrt{2x + 1}} \, dx = \frac{1}{2}\int_0^4 (2x + 1)^{-1/2}(2) \, dx$$

$$= \left[\frac{1}{2}(2)(2x + 1)^{1/2}\right]_0^4$$

$$= \sqrt{2x + 1}\,\Big]_0^4$$

$$= 3 - 1 = 2$$

27. Evaluate $\displaystyle\int_0^1 e^{-2x}\,dx$.

Solution:

$$\int_0^1 e^{-2x}\,dx = -\frac{1}{2}e^{-2x}\Big]_0^1 = -\frac{e^{-2}}{2} + \frac{1}{2} = \frac{1}{2}(1 - e^{-2}) \approx 0.432$$

29. Evaluate $\displaystyle\int_1^3 \frac{e^{3/x}}{x^2}\,dx$.

Solution:

$$\int_1^3 \frac{e^{3/x}}{x^2}\,dx = -\frac{1}{3}\int_1^3 e^{3/x}\left(-\frac{3}{x^2}\right)dx = -\frac{1}{3}e^{3/x}\Big]_1^3 = -\frac{1}{3}(e - e^3) = \frac{e^3 - e}{3} \approx 5.789$$

31. Evaluate $\displaystyle\int_{-1}^1 |4x|\,dx$

Solution:

$$\int_{-1}^1 |4x|\,dx = \int_{-1}^0 -4x\,dx + \int_0^1 4x\,dx = \left[-2x^2\right]_{-1}^0 = (0 + 2) + (2 - 0) = 4$$

33. Evaluate $\displaystyle\int_0^4 (2 - |x - 2|)\,dx$.

Solution:

$$\int_0^4 (2 - |x - 2|)\,dx = \int_0^2 [2 - [-(x - 2)]]\,dx + \int_2^4 [2 - (x - 2)]\,dx$$

$$= \int_0^2 x\,dx + \int_2^4 (4 - x)\,dx$$

$$= \frac{x^2}{2}\Big]_0^2 + \left[4x - \frac{x^2}{2}\right]_2^4$$

$$= (2 - 0) + (8 - 6) = 4$$

35. Evaluate $\displaystyle\int_{-1}^2 \frac{x}{x^2 - 9}\,dx$.

Solution:

$$\int_{-1}^2 \frac{x}{x^2 - 9} = \left[\frac{1}{2}\ln|x^2 - 9|\right]_{-1}^2 = \frac{1}{2}\ln 5 - \frac{1}{2}\ln 8 \approx -0.235$$

37. Evaluate $\displaystyle\int_0^3 \frac{2e^x}{2 + e^x}\,dx$.

Solution:

$$\int_0^3 \frac{2e^x}{2 + e^x}\,dx = \left[2\ln(2 + e^x)\right]_0^3 = 2\ln(2 + e^3) - 2\ln 3 \approx 3.993$$

39. Evaluate the definite integral and make a sketch of the region whose area is given by the integral.

$$\int_1^3 (4x-3)dx.$$

Solution:

$$\int_1^3 (4x - 3)dx = \left[2x^2 - 3\right]_1^3 = 9 - (-1) = 10$$

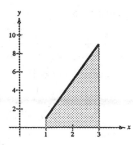

41. Evaluate the definite integral and make a sketch of the region whose area is given by the integral.

$$\int_0^1 (x-x^3)\, dx$$

Solution:

$$\int_0^1 (x - x^3)\, dx = \left[\frac{x^2}{2} - \frac{x^4}{4}\right]_0^1$$

$$= \left(\frac{1}{2} - \frac{1}{4}\right) - 0 = \frac{1}{4}$$

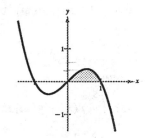

43. Evaluate the definite integral and make a sketch of the region whose area is given by the integral.

$$\int_2^4 \frac{3x^2}{x^3 - 1}\, dx$$

Solution:

$$\int_2^4 \frac{3x^2}{x^3 - 1}\, dx = \left[\ln(x^3 - 1)\right]_2^4$$

$$= \ln 63 - \ln 7 = \ln 9$$

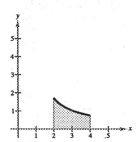

45. Determine the area of the region bounded by the graphs of $y = 3x^2 + 1$, $x = 0$, $x = 2$, and $y = 0$.

Solution:

$$A = \int_0^2 (3x^2 + 1)\, dx = \left[x^3 + x\right]_0^2 = 10 \text{ square units}$$

47. Determine the area of the region bounded by the graphs of $y = (x + 5)/x$, $y = 0$, $x = 1$, and $x = 5$.

Solution:

$$A = \int_1^5 \frac{x+5}{x}\, dx$$

$$= \int_1^5 \left[1 + 5\left(\frac{1}{x}\right)\right] dx = \left[x + 5\ln|x|\right]_1^5$$

$$= (5 + 5\ln 5) - (1 + 0) = 4 + 5\ln 5 \approx 12.047 \text{ square units}$$

49. Use the values of $\int_0^5 f(x)dx = 8$ and $\int_0^5 g(x)dx = 3$ to evaluate the definite integral.

(a) $\displaystyle\int_0^5 [f(x) + g(x)]dx$

(b) $\displaystyle\int_0^5 [f(x) - g(x)]dx$

(c) $\displaystyle\int_0^5 -4f(x)dx$

(d) $\displaystyle\int_0^5 [f(x) - 3g(x)]dx$

Solution:

(a) $\displaystyle\int_0^5 [f(x) + g(x)]dx = \int_0^5 f(x)dx + \int_0^5 g(x)dx = 8 + 3 = 11$

(b) $\displaystyle\int_0^5 [f(x) - g(x)]dx = \int_0^5 f(x)dx - \int_0^5 g(x)dx = 8 - 3 = 5$

(c) $\displaystyle\int_0^5 -4f(x)dx = -4\int_0^5 f(x)dx = -4(8) = -32$

(d) $\displaystyle\int_0^5 [f(x) - 3g(x)]dx = \int_0^5 f(x)dx - 3\int_0^5 g(x)dx = 8 - 3(3) = -1$

51. Find the average value of $f(x) = 6 - x^2$ over the interval $[02, 2]$ and find all the values of x where the function equals its average. Sketch your result.

Solution:

$$\text{Average value} = \frac{1}{2 - (-2)} \int_{-2}^{2} (6 - x^2)dx$$

$$= \frac{1}{4}\left[6x - \frac{x^3}{3}\right]_{-2}^{2} = \frac{1}{4}\left(\frac{28}{3} + \frac{28}{3}\right) = \frac{14}{3}$$

To find the x-values for which $f(x) = \frac{14}{3}$, we let $6 - x^2 = \frac{14}{3}$ and solve for x:

$$x^2 = \frac{4}{3}$$

$$x = \pm 2\sqrt{3} \approx \pm 1.155$$

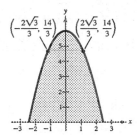

53. Find the average value of $f(x) = x\sqrt{4 - x^2}$ on the interval $[0, 2]$ and find all values of x where the function equals its average. Sketch your result.

Solution:

$$\text{Average value} = \frac{1}{2-0}\int_0^2 x\sqrt{4 - x^2}\,dx = \frac{1}{2}\left(-\frac{1}{2}\right)\int_0^2 (4 - x^2)^{1/2}(-2x)\,dx$$

$$= \frac{1}{2}\left(-\frac{1}{2}\right)\left(\frac{2}{3}\right)(4 - x^2)^{3/2}\Big]_0^2$$

$$= -\frac{1}{6}(4 - x^2)^{3/2}\Big]_0^2 = 0 + \frac{4}{3} = \frac{4}{3}$$

To find the x-values for which $f(x) = \frac{4}{3}$, we let $x\sqrt{4 - x^2} = \frac{4}{3}$ and solve for x to obtain the following.

$$x^2(4 - x^2) = \frac{16}{9}$$

$$36x^2 - 9x^4 = 16$$

$$9x^4 - 36x^2 + 16 = 0$$

$$x^2 = \frac{36 \pm \sqrt{720}}{18} = 2 \pm \frac{2\sqrt{5}}{3}$$

$$x = \sqrt{2 \pm \frac{2\sqrt{5}}{3}} \text{ in the interval } (0, 2).$$

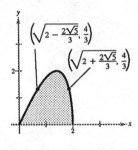

55. Find the average value of $f(x) = x - 2\sqrt{x}$ on the interval $[0, 4]$ and find all values of x where the function equals its average. Sketch your result.

Solution:

$$\text{Average value} = \frac{1}{4-0}\int_0^4 (x - 2\sqrt{x})\,dx = \frac{1}{4}\left(\frac{x^2}{2} - \frac{4}{3}x^{3/2}\right)\Big]_0^4 = \frac{1}{4}\left(8 - \frac{32}{3}\right) = -\frac{2}{3}$$

To find the x-values for which $f(x) = -\frac{2}{3}$, we let $x - 2\sqrt{x} = -\frac{2}{3}$ and solve for x to obtain

$$x + \frac{2}{3} = 2\sqrt{x}$$

$$x^2 + \frac{4}{3}x + \frac{4}{9} = 4x$$

$$x^2 - \frac{8}{3}x + \frac{4}{9} = 0$$

$$9x^2 - 24x + 4 = 0$$

$$x = \frac{24 \pm \sqrt{432}}{18} = \frac{4 \pm 2\sqrt{3}}{3}$$

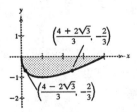

57. State whether $f(x) = 3x^4$ is even, odd, or neither.

Solution:

Since $f(-x) = 3(-x)^4 = 3x^4 = f(x)$, the function is even.

59. State whether $g(t) = 2t^5 - 3tr$ is even, odd, or neither.

Solution:

Since $g(-t) \neq g(t)$ nor $g(-t) = -g(t)$, the function is neither even nor odd.

61. Use the fact that

$$\int_0^2 x^2 \, dx = \frac{8}{3}$$

to evaluate the following definite integrals.

(a) $\displaystyle\int_{-2}^0 x^2 \, dx$

(b) $\displaystyle\int_{-2}^2 x^2 \, dx$

(c) $\displaystyle\int_0^2 -x^2 \, dx$

Solution:

Since $f(x) = x^2$ is an **even** function, we have the following.

(a) $\displaystyle\int_{-2}^0 x^2 \, dx = \int_0^2 x^2 \, dx = \frac{8}{3}$

(b) $\displaystyle\int_{-2}^2 x^2 \, dx = 2\int_0^2 x^2 \, dx = \frac{16}{3}$

(c) $\displaystyle\int_0^2 -x^2 \, dx = -\int_0^2 x^2 \, dx = -\frac{8}{3}$

63. *Marginal Analysis* Find the change in cost C, given the marginal cost $dC/dx = 2.25$, if x increases from 100 to 10?

Solution:

$$\int_{100}^{103} 2.25 \, dx = 2.25x \Big]_{100}^{103} = \$6.75$$

65. Find the change in revenue R, given the marginal revenue $\dfrac{dR}{dx} = 48 - 3x$, if x increases from 12 to 15 units.

Solution:

$$\Delta R = \int_{12}^{15} (48 - 3x)dx = \left[48x - \frac{3}{2}x^2\right]_{12}^{15} = \$22.50.$$

67. Find the change in profit P, given the marginal profit $\dfrac{dP}{dx} = \dfrac{400 - x}{150}$; if x increases from 200 to 203 units.

Solution:

$$\Delta P = \int_{200}^{203} \frac{400 - x}{150}\,dx = \frac{1}{150}\left[400x - \frac{x^2}{2}\right]_{200}^{203} = \$3.97.$$

69. *Capital Accumulation* Find the capital accumulation over a 5-year period if the rate of investment (continuous cash flow in dollars) is given by dI/dt and

$$\text{Capital accumulation} = \int_0^5 \frac{dI}{dt}\,dt$$

where t is the time in years and $dI/dt = 500$.

Solution:

$$\int_0^5 500\,dt = 500t \Big]_0^5 = \$2500$$

71. *Capital Accumulation* Find the capital accumulation over a 5-year period if the rate of investment (continuous cash flow in dollars) is given by dI/dt and

$$\text{Capital accumulation} = \int_0^5 \frac{dI}{dt}\,dt$$

where t is the time in years and $dI/dt = 100t$.

Solution:

$$\int_0^5 100t\,dt = 50t^2 \Big]_0^5 = \$1250$$

73. *Cost* The total cost of purchasing and maintaining a piece of equipment for x years is given by

$$C = 5000\left(25 + 3\int_0^x t^{1/4}\,dt\right).$$

Find (a) $C(1)$, (b) $C(5)$, and (c) $C(10)$.

Solution:

$$C(x) = 5000\left(25 + 3\int_0^x t^{1/4}\,dt\right) = 5000\left(25 + \left[\frac{12}{5}t^{5/4}\right]_0^x\right) = 5000\left(25 + \frac{12}{5}x^{5/4}\right)$$

(a) $C(1) = 5000\left[25 + \left(\dfrac{12}{5}\right)\right] = \$137,000.00$

(b) $C(5) = 5000\left[25 + \left(\dfrac{12}{5}\right)(5)^{5/4}\right] \approx \$214,720.93$

(c) $C(10) = 5000\left[25 + \left(\dfrac{12}{5}\right)(10)^{5/4}\right] \approx \$338,393.53$

75. *Compound Interest* A deposit of \$2250 is made in a savings account at an annual rate of 12%, compounded continuously. Find the average balance in the account during the first 5 years.

Solution:

$$\text{Average balance} = \frac{1}{5-0}\int_0^5 2250e^{0.12t}\,dt$$

$$= 450\int_0^5 e^{0.12t}\,dt$$

$$= 450\left(\frac{1}{0.12}\right)e^{0.12t}\Big]_0^5$$

$$= 3750(e^{0.6} - 1) \approx \$3082.95$$

77. *Computer Industry* The rate of change in revenue for the computer and data processing industry in the United States from 1985 through 1990 can be modeled by

$$\frac{dR}{dt} = 6.972\sqrt{t} - 0.40t^2, \qquad 0 \le t \le 5,$$

where R is revenue (in billions of dollars) and $t = 0$ represents 1985. In 1985, the revenue was \$45.2 billion.

(a) Write a model for the revenue as a function of t.

(b) What was the average revenue for 1985 through 1990?

Solution:

(a) $R(t) = \displaystyle\int (6.972\sqrt{t} - 0.40t^2)\,dt = 4.648t^{3/2} - 0.1333t^3 + C$

Since $R(0) = 45.2 = C$, $R(t) = 4.648t^{3/2} - 0.1333t^3 + 45.2$.

(b) Average revenue $= \dfrac{1}{5-0}\displaystyle\int_0^5 (4.648t^{3/2} - 0.1333t^3 + 45.2)\,dt$

$$\approx \$61.82 \text{ billion}$$

Section 5.5 The Area of a Region Bounded by Two Graphs

1. Find the area of the region bounded by the graphs of $f(x) = x^2 - 6x$ and $g(x) = 0$.

Solution:

$$\int_0^6 [0 - (x^2 - 6x)]dx = -\left(\frac{x^3}{3} - 3x^2\right)\Big]_0^6 = 36.$$

3. Find the area of the region bounded by the graphs of $f(x) = x^2 - 4x + 3$ and $g(x) = -x^2 + 2x + 3$.

Solution:

$$\int_0^3 [(-x^2 + 2x + 3) - (x^2 - 4x + 3)]dx = \int_0^3 (-2x^2 + 6x)dx$$

$$= \left[\frac{-2x^3}{3} + 3x^2 \right]_0^3 = 9$$

5. Find the area of the region bounded by the graphs of $f(x) = 3(x^3 - x)$ and $g(x) = 0$.

Solution:

$$A = 2\int_0^1 [0 - 3(x^3 - x)]\, dx = -6\left(\frac{x^4}{4} - \frac{x^2}{2} \right)\Big]_0^1 = \frac{3}{2} \qquad \text{(By symmetry)}$$

7. Find the area of the region bounded by the graphs of $f(x) = e^x - 1$ and $g(x) = 0$.

Solution:

$$A = \int_0^1 [(e^x - 1) - 0]dx$$

$$= e^x - x \Big]_0^1 = (e - 1) - 1$$

$$= e - 2$$

9. Sketch the region whose area is given by

$$\int_0^4 \left[(x + 1) - \frac{x}{2} \right] dx.$$

Solution:

The region is bounded by the graphs of $y = x + 1$, $y = x/2$, $x = 0$, and $x = 4$, as shown in the accompanying figure.

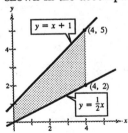

11. Sketch the region bounded by the graphs of $f(x) = x^2 - 4x$ and $g(x) = 0$ and find the area of the region.

Solution:

The points of intersection of f and g are found be setting $f(x) = g(x)$ and solving for x.

$$x^2 - 4x = 0 \qquad A = \int_0^4 [0 - (x^2 - 4x)]\,dx$$

$$x(x - 4) = 0$$

$$x = 0,\ 4 \qquad = -\left(\frac{x^3}{3} - 2x^2\right)\Big]_0^4$$

$$= \frac{32}{3}$$

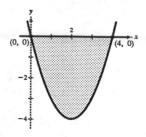

13. Sketch the region bounded by the graphs of the functions $f(x) = x^2 + 2x + 1$, $g(x) = x + 1$ and find the area of the region.

Solution:

The points of intersection are found by setting $f(x) = g(x)$.

$$x^2 + 2x + 1 = x + 1$$

$$x^2 + x = 0$$

$$x(x + 1) = 0$$

$$x = 0,\ -1$$

$$A = \int_{-1}^0 [(x + 1) - (x^2 - 2x + 1)]dx$$

$$= \int_{-1}^0 (-x^2 - x)dx = \frac{-x^3}{3} - \frac{x^2}{2}\Big]_{-1}^0$$

$$= 0 - \left(\frac{1}{3} - \frac{1}{2}\right) = \frac{1}{6}$$

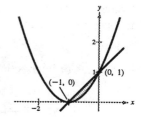

15. Sketch the region bounded by the graphs of the functions $y = 2x$, $y = 4 - 2x$, $y = 0$ and find the area of the region.

Solution:

To find the points of intersection, we solve

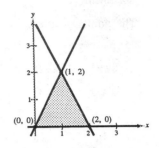

$$2x = 4 - 2x$$
$$4x = 4$$
$$x = 1$$

$$A = \int_0^1 2x\,dx + \int_1^2 (4 - 2x)\,dx$$

$$= x^2 \Big]_0^1 + 4x - x^2 \Big]_1^2$$

$$= 1 + (4 - 3) = 2$$

17. Sketch the region bounded by the graphs of $f(x) = x^2 - x$ and $g(x) = 2(x + 2)$ and find the area of the region.

Solution:

The points of intersection of f and g are found by setting $f(x) = g(x)$ and solving for x.

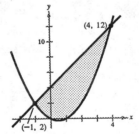

$$x^2 - x = 2(x + 2)$$
$$x^2 - 3x - 4 = 0$$
$$(x + 1)(x - 4) = 0$$
$$x = -1, \ 4$$

$$A = \int_{-1}^4 [2(x + 2) - (x^2 - x)]\,dx$$

$$= \int_{-1}^4 [-x^2 + 3x + 4]\,dx$$

$$= \left[-\frac{x^3}{3} + \frac{3x^2}{2} + 4x \right]_{-1}^4$$

$$= \left(-\frac{64}{3} + 24 + 16 \right)$$

$$\quad - \left(\frac{1}{3} + \frac{3}{2} - 4 \right)$$

$$= \frac{125}{6}$$

19. Sketch the region bounded by the graphs of $y = x^3 - 2x + 1$, $y = -2x$, and $x = 1$ and find the area of the region.

Solution:

The point of intersection of the two graphs is found by equating y-values and solving for x.

$$x^3 - 2x + 1 = -2x$$

$$x^3 + 1 = 0$$

$$x = -1$$

$$A = \int_{-1}^{1} [(x^3 - 2x + 1) - (-2x)] \, dx$$

$$= \int_{-1}^{1} (x^3 + 1) \, dx = \left[\frac{x^4}{4} + x \right]_{-1}^{1} = 2$$

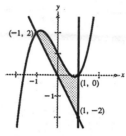

21. Sketch the region bounded by the graphs of $f(x) = \sqrt{3x} + 1$ and $g(x) = x + 1$ and find the area of the region.

Solution:

The points of intersection of f and g are found by setting $f(x) = g(x)$ and solving for x.

$$\sqrt{3x} + 1 = x + 1$$

$$\sqrt{3x} = x$$

$$3x = x^2$$

$$x^2 - 3x = 0$$

$$x(x - 3) = 0$$

$$x = 0, \ 3$$

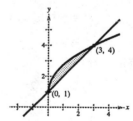

$$A = \int_{0}^{3} [(\sqrt{3x} + 1) - (x + 1)] \, dx = \int_{0}^{3} (\sqrt{3x} - x) \, dx = \left[\frac{2}{9}(3x)^{3/2} - \frac{x^2}{2} \right]_{0}^{3} = \frac{3}{2}$$

23. Sketch the region bounded by the graphs of $y = x^2 - 4x + 3$ and $y = 3 + 4x - x^2$ and find the area of the region.

Solution:

The points of intersection of the two graphs are found be equating y-values and solving for x.

$$x^2 - 4x + 3 = 3 + 4x - x^2$$

$$2x^2 - 8x = 0$$

$$2x(x - 4) = 0$$

$$x = 0, \ 4$$

$$A = \int_0^4 [(3 + 4x - x^2) - (x^2 - 4x + 3)] \, dx$$

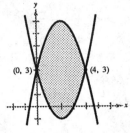

$$= \int_0^4 (-2x^2 + 8x) \, dx = \left[-\frac{2x^3}{3} + 4x^2 \right]_0^4 = \frac{64}{3}$$

25. Sketch the region bounded by the graphs of $f(y) = y^2$ and $g(y) = y + 2$ and find the area of the region.

Solution:

The points of intersection are found by setting $f(y)$ equal to $g(y)$ and solving for y.

$$y^2 = y + 2 \qquad A = \int_{-1}^2 [(y + 2) - y^2] \, dy$$

$$y^2 - y - 2 = 0$$

$$(y + 1)(y - 2) = 0 \qquad = \left[\frac{y^2}{2} + 2y - \frac{y^3}{3} \right]_{-1}^2$$

$$y = -1, \ 2$$

$$= \left(2 + 4 - \frac{8}{3} \right) - \left(\frac{1}{2} - 2 + \frac{1}{3} \right) = \frac{9}{2}$$

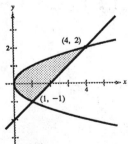

27. Sketch the region bounded by the graphs of $x = y^2 + 2$, $x = 0$, $y = -1$, $y = 2$ and find the area of the region.

Solution:

$$A = \int_{-1}^{2} (y^2 + 2)dy$$

$$= \frac{y^3}{3} + 2y \Big]_{-1}^{2}$$

$$= \left(\frac{8}{3} + 4\right) - \left(-\frac{1}{3} - 2\right) = 9$$

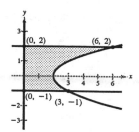

29. Sketch the region bounded by the graphs of $f(x) = e^{0.5x}$, $g(x) = -\frac{1}{x}$, $x = 1$, $x = 2$ and find the area of the region.

Solution:

$$A = \int_{1}^{2} \left[e^{1/2x} - \left(-\frac{1}{x}\right)\right] dx$$

$$= 2e^{1/2x} + \ln x \Big]_{1}^{2}$$

$$= (2e + \ln 2) - 2e^{1/2} \approx 3.832$$

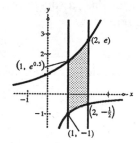

31. Sketch the region bounded by the graphs of $y = \frac{4}{x}$, $y = x$, $x = 1$, $x = 4$ and find the area of the region.

Solution:

$$A = \int_{1}^{2} \left(\frac{4}{x} - x\right) dx + \int_{2}^{4} \left(x - \frac{4}{x}\right) dx$$

$$= \left[4\ln x - \frac{x^2}{2}\right]_{1}^{2} + \left[\frac{x^2}{2} - 4\ln x\right]_{2}^{4}$$

$$= \left(4\ln 2 - \frac{3}{2}\right) + (6 - 4\ln 2)$$

$$= \frac{9}{2}$$

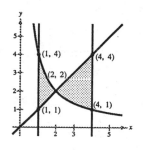

33. Sketch the region bounded by the graphs of $y = xe^{-x^2}$, $y = 0$, $x = 0$, $x = 1$ and find the area of the region.

Solution:

$$A = \int_0^1 xe^{-x^2}\,dx = -\frac{1}{2}e^{-x^2}\bigg]_0^1$$

$$= -\frac{1}{2}e^{-1} + \frac{1}{2}$$

$$\approx 0.316$$

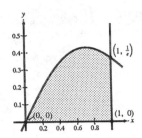

35. Use integration to find the area of the triangle having the vertices (0, 0), (4, 0), and (4, 4).

Solution:

The equation of the line passing through (0, 0) and (4, 4) is $y = x$. Therefore, the area is given by the following.

$$A = \int_0^4 x\,dx = \frac{x^2}{2}\bigg]_0^4 = 8$$

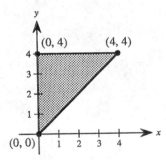

37. *Consumer and Producer Surplus* Find the consumer surplus and producer surplus for the demand function $p_1(x) = 50 - 0.5x$ and the supply function $p_2(x) = 0.125x$.

Solution:

The point of equilibrium is found by equating $50 - 0.5x = 0.125x$ to obtain $x = 80$ and $p = 10$.

$$CS = \int_0^{80} [(50 - 0.5x) - 10]\,dx = \left[-\frac{0.5x^2}{2} + 40x\right]_0^{80} = 1600$$

$$PS = \int_0^{80} (10 - 0.125x)\,dx = \left[10x - \frac{0.125x^2}{2}\right]_0^{80} = 400$$

39. *Consumer and Producer Surplus* Find the consumer surplus and producer surplus for the demand function $p_1(x) = 300 - x$ and the supply function $p_2(x) = 100 + x$.

Solution:

The point of equilibrium is found by equating $300 - x = 100 + x$ to obtain $x = 100$ and $p = 200$.

$$CS = \int_0^{100} [(300 - x) - 200]\,dx = \left[100x - \frac{x^2}{2} \right]_0^{100} = 5000$$

$$PS = \int_0^{100} [200 - (100 + x)]\,dx = \left[100x - \frac{x^2}{2} \right]_0^{100} = 5000$$

41. Find the consumer surplus and producer surplus for the demand function $p_1(x) = 200 - 0.02x^2$ and the supply function $p_2 = 100 + x$.

Solution:

The point of equilibrium is found by equations the demand and supply functions

$$200 - 0.02x^2 = 100 + x$$

$$0.02x^2 + x - 100 = 0$$

$$x^2 + 50x - 5000 = 0$$

$$(x + 100)(x - 50) = 0$$

$$x = 50 \text{ and } p = 150$$

$$CS = \int_0^{50} [(200 - 0.02x^2) - 150]dx = \left[50x - \frac{0.02x^3}{3} \right]_0^{50} \approx 1666.67$$

$$PS = \int_0^{50} [150 - (100 + x)]dx = \left[50x - \frac{x^2}{2} \right]_0^{50} = \$1250.00$$

43. Find the consumer surplus and producer surplus for the demand function $p_1(x) = -0.125x + 50$ and the supply function $p_2(x) = 10 + 0.025x$.

Solution:

The point of equilibrium is found by equating the demand and supply functions

$$-0.125x + 50 = 10 + 0.025x$$

$$40 = 0.15x$$

$$x = 266\tfrac{2}{3} \text{ and } p = 16\tfrac{2}{3}$$

$$CS = \int_0^{266\frac{2}{3}} [(-0.125x + 50) - 16\tfrac{2}{3}]dx \approx \$4444.44$$

$$PS = \int_0^{266\frac{2}{3}} [16\tfrac{2}{3} - (10 + 0.025x)]dx \approx \$888.89.$$

45. *Consumer and Producer Surplus* Find the consumer surplus and producer surplus for the given supply and demand curves.

Demand Function	Supply Function
$p_1(x) = \dfrac{10,000}{\sqrt{x+100}}$	$p_2(x) = 100\sqrt{0.05x+10}$

Solution:

The point of equilibrium is found by equating the demand and supply functions.

$$\frac{10,000}{\sqrt{x+100}} = 100\sqrt{0.05x+10}$$

$$100 = \sqrt{(x+100)(0.05x+10)}$$

$$10,000 = 0.05x^2 + 15x + 1000$$

$$5x^2 + 1500x - 900,000 = 0$$

$$5(x^2 + 300x - 180,000) = 0$$

$$5(x+600)(x-300) = 0$$

$$x = 300 \text{ and } p = 500$$

$$CS = \int_0^{300} \left(\frac{10,000}{\sqrt{x+100}} - 500 \right) dx$$

$$= \left[20,000\sqrt{x+100} - 500x \right]_0^{300}$$

$$= 250,000 - 200,000 = 50,000$$

$$PS = \int_0^{300} (500 - 100\sqrt{0.05x+10})\, dx$$

$$= \left[500x - \frac{4000}{3}(0.05x+10)^{3/2} \right]_0^{300}$$

$$= \frac{-50,000}{3} + \frac{40,000\sqrt{10}}{3}$$

$$= \frac{10,000}{3}(4\sqrt{10} - 5) \approx 25,497$$

47. *Essay* Describe the characteristics of typical demand and supply functions.

Solution:

A typical demand function is decreasing, while a typical supply function is increasing.

49. *Revenue* Two models, R_1 and R_2 are given for revenue (in billions of dollars) for a large corporation. Both models are estimates of revenues for 1996–2000, with $t = 6$ representing 1996. Which model is projecting the greater revenue? How much more total revenue does that model project over the 4-year period?

Solution:

The model R_1 projects greater revenue that R_2. The difference in total revenue is

$$\int_6^{10} (R_1 - R_2)dt = \int_6^{10} [(7.21 - 0.58t) - (7.21 - 0.45t)]dt$$

$$= \int_6^{10} 0.13t\, dt = \frac{0.13t^2}{2}\Bigg]_6^{10} = \$4.16 \text{ billion}$$

51. *Fuel Cost* The projected fuel cost C (in millions of dollars) for an airline company from 1995 through 2005 is

$$C_1 = 568.5 + 7.15t,$$

where $t = 5$ represents 1995. If the company purchases more efficient airplane engines, fuel costs are expected to decrease and follow the model

$$C_2 = 525.6 + 6.43t.$$

How much can the company save on the more efficient engines? Explain your reasoning?

Solution:

The total savings is given by

$$\int_5^{15} (C_1 - C_2)\, dt = \int_5^{15} [(568.50 + 7.15t) - (525.60 + 6.43t)]\, dt$$

$$= \int_5^{15} (42.90 + 0.72t)\, dt = [42.90t + 0.36t^2]\Bigg|_5^{15} = \$501 \text{ million.}$$

53. *Consumer and Producer Surplus* Factory orders for a certain model air conditioner are approximately 6000 units per week when the price is $331. However, orders increase linearly to approximately 8000 units per week when the price is decreased to $303. If the supply function is given by $p = 0.0275x = 11x/400$, find the consumer and producer surplus.

Solution:

Demand: $(6000, 331)$, $(8000, 303)$

$$m = \frac{303 - 331}{8000 - 6000} = \frac{-7}{500}$$

$$p - 331 = -\frac{7}{500}(x - 6000)$$

$$p = -\frac{7x}{500} + 415$$

Point of equilibrium: $-\dfrac{7x}{500} + 415 = \dfrac{11x}{400}$

$$x = 10,000$$

$$p = 275$$

$$CS = \int_0^{10,000} \left[\left(-\frac{7x}{500} + 415\right) - 275\right] dx$$

$$= \int_0^{10,000} \left(-\frac{7x}{500} + 140\right) dx = \left[-\frac{7x^2}{1000} + 140x\right]_0^{10,000} = \$700,000$$

$$PS = \int_0^{10,000} \left[275 - \frac{11x}{400}\right] dx = \left[275x - \frac{11x^2}{800}\right]_0^{10,000} = \$1,375,000$$

55. *Profit* The continuous flow of revenue in millions of dollars per year from a manufacturing process is projected to be $R(t) = 100$ over the next 10 years. Over the same period of time, production costs (in millions of dollars) are projected to be $C(t) = 60 + 0.2t^2$ where t is the time in years. Approximate the profit generated by this production line over the next 10 years.

Solution:

$$\int_0^{10} [R(t) - C(t)] \, dt = \int_0^{10} [100 - (60 + 0.2t^2)] \, dt$$

$$= \int_0^{10} (40 - 0.2t^2) \, dt$$

$$= \left[40t - \frac{2}{30}t^3\right]_0^{10}$$

$$= 333.33 \text{ million dollars}$$

57. *Lorenz Curve* Economists use *Lorenz curves* to illustrate the distribution of income in a country. Letting x represent the percent of families in a country and y represent the percent of total income, the model $x = y$ would represent a country in which each family has the same income. The Lorenz curve, $y = f(x)$, represents the actual income distribution. The area between these two models, for $0 \le x \le 100$, indicates the "income inequality" of a country. In 1990, the Lorenz curve for the United States could be modeled by

$$y = 0.344x + 0.0658x^{2/3}, \qquad 0 \le x \le 100,$$

where x is measured from the poorest to the wealthiest families. Find the income inequality for the United States in 1990.

Solution:

$$\text{Income inequality} = \int_0^{100} (x - f(x)) dx$$

$$= \int_0^{10} (x - 0.344x - 0.0658x^{3/2}) dx$$

$$= 0.328x^2 - 0.02632x^{5/2} \Big]_0^{10} = 648$$

Section 5.6   The Definite Integral as the Limit of a Sum

1. Use the Midpoint Rule with $n = 4$ to approximate the area of the region bounded by the graph of $f(x) = -2x + 3$ and the x-axis on the interval $[0, 1]$. Compare this result with the exact area obtained by using the definite integral.

Solution:

The midpoints of the four intervals are $\frac{1}{8}$, $\frac{3}{8}$, $\frac{5}{8}$, and $\frac{7}{8}$. The approximate area is

$$A \approx \frac{1-0}{4}\left[f\left(\frac{1}{8}\right) + f\left(\frac{3}{8}\right) + f\left(\frac{5}{8}\right) + f\left(\frac{7}{8}\right) \right] = \frac{1}{4}\left[\frac{11}{4} + \frac{9}{4} + \frac{7}{4} + \frac{5}{4} \right] = 2.$$

The exact area is $A = \int_0^1 (-2x + 3) \, dx = \left[-x^2 + 3x \right]_0^1 = 2.$

3. Use the Midpoint Rule with $n = 4$ to approximate the area of the region bounded by the graph of $y = \sqrt{x}$ and the x-axis on the interval $[0, 1]$. Compare this result with the exact area obtained by using the definite integral.

Solution:

The midpoints of the four intervals are $\frac{1}{8}$, $\frac{3}{8}$, $\frac{5}{8}$, and $\frac{7}{8}$. The approximate area is

$$A \approx \frac{1-0}{4}\left[\sqrt{\frac{1}{8}} + \sqrt{\frac{3}{8}} + \sqrt{\frac{5}{8}} + \sqrt{\frac{7}{8}} \right] = \frac{1}{4}\left[\frac{\sqrt{2}}{4} + \frac{\sqrt{6}}{4} + \frac{\sqrt{10}}{4} + \frac{\sqrt{14}}{4} \right] \approx 0.6730.$$

The exact area is $A = \int_0^1 \sqrt{x} \, dx = \frac{2}{3}x^{3/2}\Big]_0^1 = \frac{2}{3} \approx 0.6667.$

5. Use the Midpoint Rule with $n = 4$ to approximate the area of the region bounded by the graph of $f(x) = x^2 + 2$ and the x-axis on the interval $[-1, 1]$. Compare this result with the exact area obtained by using the definite integral. Sketch the region.

Solution:

The midpoints of the four intervals are $-\frac{3}{4}$, $-\frac{1}{4}$, $\frac{1}{4}$, and $\frac{3}{4}$. The approximate area is

$$A \approx \frac{1 - (-1)}{4}\left[\frac{41}{16} + \frac{33}{16} + \frac{33}{16} + \frac{41}{16}\right] = \frac{1}{2}\left[\frac{148}{16}\right] = \frac{37}{8} = 4.625. \quad \text{The exact area}$$

is

$$A = \int_{-1}^{1} (x^2 + 2)\,dx = \left[\frac{x^3}{3} + 2x\right]_{-1}^{1} = \frac{14}{3} \approx 4.6667.$$

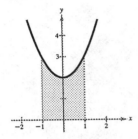

7. Use the Midpoint Rule with $n = 4$ to approximate the area of the region bounded by the graph of $g(x) = 2x^2$ and the x-axis on the interval $[1, 3]$. Compare this result with the exact area obtained by using the definite integral. Sketch the region.

Solution:

The midpoints of the four intervals are $\frac{5}{4}$, $\frac{7}{4}$, $\frac{9}{4}$, and $\frac{11}{4}$. The approximate area is

$$A \approx \frac{3 - 1}{4}\left[f\left(\frac{5}{4}\right) + f\left(\frac{7}{4}\right) + f\left(\frac{9}{4}\right) + f\left(\frac{11}{4}\right)\right]$$

$$= \frac{1}{2}\left[\frac{25}{8} + \frac{49}{8} + \frac{81}{8} + \frac{121}{8}\right] = \frac{69}{4} = 17.25.$$

The exact area is

$$A = \int_{1}^{3} 2x^2\,dx = \frac{2x^3}{3}\Big]_{1}^{3} = \frac{52}{3} \approx 17.3333.$$

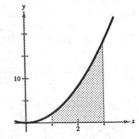

9. Use the Midpoint Rule with $n = 4$ to approximate the area of the region bounded by the graph of $f(x) = x^3 - 1$ and the x-axis on the interval $[1, 2]$. Compare this result with the exact area obtained by using the definite integral. Sketch the region.

Solution:

The midpoints of the four intervals are $\dfrac{9}{8}, \dfrac{11}{8}, \dfrac{13}{8}$ and $\dfrac{15}{8}$. The approximate area is

$$A \approx \frac{2-1}{4}\left[f\left(\frac{9}{8}\right) + f\left(\frac{11}{8}\right) + f\left(\frac{13}{8}\right) + f\left(\frac{15}{8}\right)\right].$$

$$= \frac{1}{4}\left[\frac{217}{512} + \frac{819}{512} + \frac{1685}{512} + \frac{2863}{512}\right] = \frac{5584}{4(512)} \approx 2.7266$$

The exact area is

$$A = \int_1^2 (x^3 - 1)\,dx = \frac{x^4}{4} - x\bigg]_1^2 = 2 + \frac{3}{4} = 2.75$$

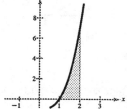

11. Use the Midpoint Rule with $n = 4$ to approximate the area of the region bounded by the graph of $f(x) = x^2 - x^3$ and the x-axis on the interval $[-1, 0]$. Compare this result with the exact area obtained by using the definite integral. Sketch the region.

Solution:

The midpoints of the four intervals are $-\frac{7}{8}, -\frac{5}{8}, -\frac{3}{8}$, and $-\frac{1}{8}$. The approximate area is

$$A \approx \frac{0 - (-1)}{4}\left[\frac{735}{512} + \frac{325}{512} + \frac{99}{512} + \frac{9}{512}\right] = \frac{73}{128} \approx 0.5703.$$

The exact area is

$$A = \int_{-1}^{0} (x^2 - x^3)\,dx$$

$$= \left[\frac{x^3}{3} - \frac{x^4}{4}\right]_{-1}^{0}$$

$$= \frac{7}{12} \approx 0.5833.$$

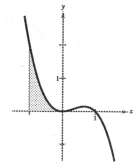

13. Use the Midpoint Rule with $n = 4$ to approximate the area of the region bounded by the graph of $f(x) = x(1-x)^2$ and the x-axis on the interval $[0, 1]$. Compare this result with the exact area obtained by using the definite integral. Sketch the region.

Solution:

The midpoints of the four intervals are $\frac{1}{8}$, $\frac{3}{8}$, $\frac{5}{8}$, and $\frac{7}{8}$. The approximate area is

$$A \approx \frac{1-0}{4}\left[\frac{49}{512} + \frac{75}{512} + \frac{45}{512} + \frac{7}{512}\right]$$

$$= \frac{11}{128} \approx 0.0859.$$

The exact area is

$$A = \int_0^1 x(1-x)^2\,dx$$

$$= \int_0^1 (x^3 - 2x^2 + x)\,dx$$

$$= \left[\frac{x^4}{4} - \frac{2x^3}{3} + \frac{x^2}{2}\right]_0^1 = \frac{1}{12} \approx 0.0833.$$

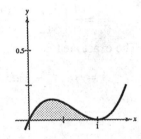

15. Use a program similar to that on page 364 (in the textbook) to approximate the area of the region $\int_0^4 (2x^2 + 3)\,dx$. How large must n be to obtain an approximation that is correct to within 0.01?

Solution:

$$\int_0^4 (2x^2 + 3)\,dx = \frac{164}{3} \approx 54.6667$$

Using the midpoint rule with $n = 40$, we get 54.66.

17. Use the Midpoint Rule with $n = 4$ to approximate the area of the region $f(y) = \frac{1}{4}y$, $[2, 4]$. Compare your result with the exact area obtained with a definite integral.

Solution:

The midpoints of the four intervals are $\frac{9}{4}$, $\frac{11}{9}$, $\frac{13}{4}$, and $\frac{15}{4}$.

The approximate area is

$$A \approx \frac{4-2}{4}\left[f\left(\frac{9}{4}\right) + f\left(\frac{11}{4}\right) + f\left(\frac{13}{4}\right) + f\left(\frac{15}{4}\right)\right] = \frac{1}{2}(3) = 1.5.$$

The exact area is

$$A = \int_2^4 \frac{1}{4}y\,dy = \frac{y^2}{8}\Big]_2^4 = 2 - \frac{1}{2} = 1.5.$$

(The Midpoint rule is exact for lines.)

19. Use the Midpoint Rule to complete the table in the textbook.

Solution:

$$\int_0^4 \sqrt{16 - x^2}\,dx$$

Number of Subintervals	2	4	6	8	10
Approximation	13.0375	12.7357	12.6591	12.6267	12.6096

21. Use the Midpoint Rule to complete the table in the textbook.

Solution:

$$\int_0^2 \sqrt{1 + x^3}\,dx$$

Number of Subintervals	2	4	6	8	10
Approximation	3.1523	3.2202	3.2320	3.2361	3.2380

23. *Trapezoidal Rule* Use the Trapezoidal Rule to approximate the given definite integral using $n = 8$ and compare the result with the exact value of the definite integral. Also approximate the integral using $n = 8$ and the Midpoint Rule. Which approximation technique appears to be better?

$$\int_0^2 x^3\,dx$$

Solution:

Exact:
$$\int_0^2 x^3\,dx = \frac{x^4}{4}\Big]_0^2 = 4$$

Trapezoidal:
$$\int_0^2 x^3\,dx \approx \frac{2-0}{2(8)}\left[(0)^3 + 2\left(\frac{1}{4}\right)^3 + 2\left(\frac{1}{2}\right)^3 + 2\left(\frac{3}{4}\right)^3 + 2(1)^3 \right.$$
$$+ 2\left(\frac{5}{4}\right)^3 +$$
$$\left. 2\left(\frac{3}{2}\right)^3 + 2\left(\frac{7}{4}\right)^3 + (2)^3\right]$$
$$= 4.0625$$

Midpoint: 3.9688

The Midpoint Rule is a better approximation in this example.

25. Use the Trapezoidal Rule to approximate the definite integral $\int_0^2 \frac{1}{x+1} dx$ with $n = 4$.

Solution:

$$\int_0^2 \frac{1}{x+1} dx \approx \frac{2-0}{2(4)} \left[1 + 2\left(\frac{2}{3}\right) + 2\left(\frac{1}{2}\right) + 2\left(\frac{2}{5}\right) + \frac{1}{3} \right] \approx 1.1167$$

(Exact answer is $\ln 3 \approx 1.0986$.)

27. Approximate the integral $\int_{-1}^1 \frac{1}{x^2+1} dx$ using the Trapezoidal Rule with $n = 4$.

Solution:

$$\int_{-1}^1 \frac{1}{x^2+1} dx \approx \frac{1-(-1)}{2(4)} \left[\frac{1}{(-1)^2} + 1 \right.$$
$$+ \frac{2}{(-1/2)^2+1} + \frac{2}{(0)^2+1}$$
$$\left. + \frac{2}{(1/2)^2+1} + \frac{1}{(1)^2+1} \right]$$
$$= 1.55$$

(Exact value is $\pi/2$.)

29. Use a computer or calculator to complete the following table of numerical approximations to the following integral.

$$\int_0^4 \sqrt{2+3x^2} \, dx$$

Solution:

n	Midpoint Rule	Trapezoidal Rule
4	15.3965	15.6055
8	15.4480	15.5010
12	15.4578	15.4814
16	15.4613	15.4745
20	15.4628	15.4713

31. Use the Trapezoidal Rule with $n = 10$ on a computer to approximate the area of the region bounded by the graphs of the given equations.

$$y = \sqrt{\frac{x^3}{4-x}}, \quad y = 0, \quad x = 3$$

Solution:

$$A = \int_0^3 \sqrt{\frac{x^3}{4-x}}\, dx \approx \frac{3-0}{2(10)}\Bigg[0$$

$$+ 2f\left(\frac{3}{10}\right) + 2f\left(\frac{3}{5}\right) + 2f\left(\frac{9}{10}\right)$$

$$+ 2f\left(\frac{6}{5}\right) + 2f\left(\frac{3}{2}\right) + 2f\left(\frac{9}{5}\right)$$

$$+ 2f\left(\frac{21}{10}\right) + 2f\left(\frac{12}{5}\right) + 2f\left(\frac{27}{10}\right) + f(3)\Bigg] \approx 4.81$$

33. *Velocity and Acceleration* The table lists the velocity v (in feet per second) of an accelerating car over a 20-second inverval. Use the Trapezoidal Rule to approximate the distance in feet that the car travels during the 20 seconds. (The distance is given by $s = \int_0^{20} v\, dt$).

Solution:

$$s = \int_0^{20} v\, dt \approx \frac{20-0}{2(4)}[v(0) + 2v(5) + 2v(10) + 2v(15) + v(20)]$$

$$\approx \frac{5}{2}[0 + 58.6 + 102.6 + 132 + 73.3] = \frac{5}{2}(366.5) = 916.25 \text{ feet}$$

Section 5.7   Volumes of Solids of Revolution

1. Find the volume of the solid formed by revolving the region bounded by the graph of $y = \sqrt{4 - x^2}$ about the x-axis.

Solution:

$$V = \pi \int_0^2 (\sqrt{4 - x^2})^2\, dx$$

$$= \pi \int_0^2 (4 - x^2)\, dx$$

$$= \pi \left(4x - \frac{x^3}{3}\right)\Bigg]_0^2 = \frac{16\pi}{3}$$

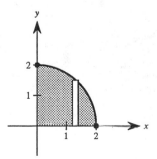

3. Find the volume of the solid formed by revolving the region bounded by the graph of $y = \sqrt{x}$ about the x-axis.

Solution:

$$V = \pi \int_1^4 (\sqrt{x})^2 \, dx$$

$$= \pi \int_1^4 x \, dx$$

$$= \pi \left(\frac{x^2}{2} \right) \Big]_1^4$$

$$= 8\pi - \frac{\pi}{2}$$

$$= \frac{15\pi}{2}$$

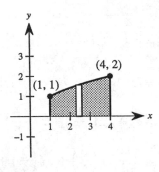

5. Find the volume of the solid formed by revolving the region bounded by the graphs of $y = 4 - x^2$, $y = 0$ about the x-axis.

Solution:

$$V = \pi \int_{-2}^2 (4 - x^2)^2 \, dx$$

$$= \pi \int_{-2}^2 (16 - 8x^2 + x^4) \, dx$$

$$= \pi \left[16x - \frac{8}{3}x^3 + \frac{x^5}{5} \right]_{-2}^2$$

$$= \frac{512\pi}{15}$$

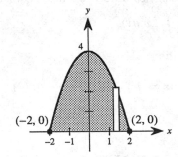

7. Find the volume of the solid formed by revolving the region bounded by the graphs of $y = 1 - \frac{1}{4}x^2$, $y = 0$ about the x-axis.

Solution:

$$V = \pi \int_{-2}^{2} \left(1 - \frac{x^2}{4}\right)^2 dx$$

$$= 2\pi \int_{0}^{2} \left(1 - \frac{x^2}{2} + \frac{x^4}{16}\right) dx$$

$$= 2\pi \left[x - \frac{1}{6}x^3 + \frac{1}{80}x^5\right]_{0}^{2}$$

$$= \frac{32\pi}{15}$$

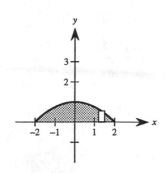

9. Find the volume of the solid formed by revolving the region bounded by the graphs of $y = -x + 1$, $y = 0$, $x = 0$ about the x-axis.

Solution:

$$V = \pi \int_{0}^{1} (-x + 1)^2 dx$$

$$= \pi \int_{0}^{1} (x^2 - 2x + 1) dx$$

$$= \pi \left(\frac{x^3}{3} - x^2 + x\right)\Big]_{0}^{1}$$

$$= \frac{\pi}{3}$$

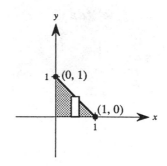

11. Find the volume of the solid formed by revolving the region bounded by the graphs of $y = \frac{1}{x} - \frac{1}{2}$, $y = -\frac{1}{2}x + 1$ about the x-axis.

Solution:

$$V = \pi \int_{1}^{2} \left[\left(-\frac{1}{2}x + 1\right)^2 - \left(\frac{1}{x} - \frac{1}{2}\right)^2\right] dx$$

$$= \pi \int_{1}^{2} \left[\left(\frac{1}{4}x^2 - x + 1\right) - \left(\frac{1}{x^2} + \frac{1}{4} - \frac{1}{x}\right)\right] dx$$

$$= \left[\frac{x^3}{12} - \frac{1}{2}x^2 + \frac{3}{4}x + \ln x + \frac{1}{x}\right]_{1}^{2}$$

$$= \pi \left[\ln 2 - \frac{2}{3}\right] \approx 0.0832$$

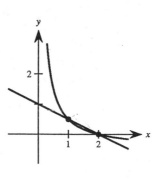

13. Find the volume of the solid formed by revolving the region bounded by the graphs of $y = 2x^2$, $y = 0$, and $x = 2$ about the x-axis.

Solution:

$$V = \pi \int_0^2 (2x^2)^2 \, dx$$

$$= \pi \int_0^2 4x^4 \, dx$$

$$= \pi \left(\frac{4x^5}{5} \right) \Bigg]_0^2$$

$$= \frac{128\pi}{5}$$

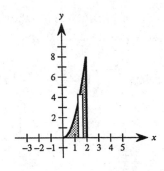

15. Find the volume of the solid formed by revolving the region bounded by the graphs of $y = e^x$, $y = 0$, $x = 0$, $x = 1$, about the x-axis.

Solution:

$$V = \pi \int_0^1 (e^x)^2 \, dx$$

$$= \pi \frac{1}{2} e^{2x} \Bigg]_0^1$$

$$= \frac{\pi}{2}(e^2 - 1)$$

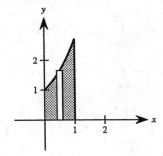

17. Find the volume of the solid formed by revolving the region bounded by the graphs of $y = x^2$, $y = 4$, and $x = 0$ about the y-axis.

Solution:

The points of intersection of the two graphs occur when $y = 0$ and $y = 4$.

$$V = \pi \int_0^4 (\sqrt{y})^2 \, dy$$

$$= \pi \int_0^4 y \, dy$$

$$= \pi \left(\frac{y^2}{2} \right) \Big]_0^4$$

$$= 8\pi$$

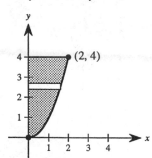

19. Find the volume of the solid formed by revolving the region bounded by the graphs of $x = 1 - \frac{1}{2}y$, $x = 0$, $y = 0$ about the y-axis.

Solution:

$$V = \pi \int_0^2 \left(1 - \frac{1}{2}y \right)^2 dy$$

$$= \pi \int_0^2 \left[1 - y + \frac{1}{4}y^2 \right] dy$$

$$= \pi \left[y - \frac{y^2}{2} + \frac{1}{12}y^3 \right]_0^2$$

$$= \pi \left[2 - 2 + \frac{1}{12} \cdot 8 \right] = \frac{2}{3}\pi$$

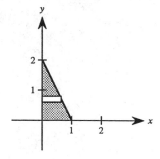

21. Find the volume of the solid formed by revolving the region bounded by the graphs of $y = x^{2/3}$, $y = 1$, and $x = 0$ about the y-axis.

Solution:

The points of intersection of the two graphs occur when $y = 0$ and $y = 1$.

$$V = \pi \int_0^1 (y^{3/2})^2 \, dy$$

$$= \pi \int_0^1 y^3 \, dy$$

$$= \pi \left(\frac{y^4}{4} \right) \Big]_0^1$$

$$= \frac{\pi}{4}$$

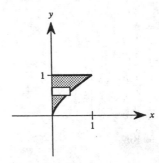

23. Find the volume of the solid formed by revolving the region bounded by the graphs of $y = \sqrt{4 - x}$, $y = 0$, and $x = 0$ about the y-axis.

Solution:

The points of intersection of the three graphs occur when $y = 0$ and $y = 2$.

$$V = \pi \int_0^2 (4 - y^2)^2 \, dy$$

$$= \pi \int_0^2 (16 - 8y^2 + y^4) \, dy$$

$$= \pi \left[16y - \frac{8y^3}{3} + \frac{y^5}{5} \right]_0^2$$

$$= \pi \left[32 - \frac{64}{3} + \frac{32}{5} \right]$$

$$= \frac{256\pi}{15}$$

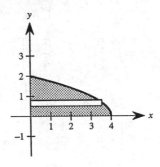

25. The line segment from $(0, 0)$ to $(6, 3)$ is revolved about the x-axis to form a cone. What is the volume of the cone?

Solution:

$$V = \pi \int_0^6 \left(\frac{1}{2}x\right)^2 dx$$

$$= \frac{\pi}{4} \int_0^6 x^2 \, dx$$

$$= \frac{\pi}{4} \left(\frac{x^3}{3}\right)\Big]_0^6$$

$$= 18\pi$$

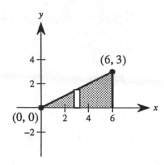

27. Use the Disc Method to verify that the volume of a sphere of radius r is $V = \frac{4}{3}\pi r^3$.

Solution:

A sphere of radius r can be formed by revolving the graph of $y = \sqrt{r^2 - x^2}$ about the x-axis.

$$V = \pi \int_{-r}^r (\sqrt{r^2 - x^2})^2 \, dx$$

$$= \pi \int_{-r}^r (r^2 - x^2) \, dx$$

$$= \pi \left[r^2 x - \frac{x^3}{3}\right]_{-r}^r$$

$$= \pi \left[\left(r^3 - \frac{r^3}{3}\right) - \left(-r^3 + \frac{r^3}{3}\right)\right]$$

$$= \frac{4\pi r^3}{3}$$

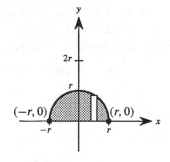

29. The upper half of the ellipse $9x^2 + 16y^2 = 144$ is revolved about the x-axis to form a prolate spheroid (shaped like a football). Find the volume of the spheroid.

Solution:

The upper half of the ellipse is given by

$$y = \sqrt{9 - \frac{9x^2}{16}}$$

$$V = \pi \int_{-4}^{4} \left(9 - \frac{9}{16}x^2\right) dx$$

$$= 18\pi \int_{0}^{4} \left(1 - \frac{x^2}{16}\right) dx$$

$$= 18\pi \left[x - \frac{x^3}{48}\right]_{0}^{4} = 18\pi \left[4 - \frac{4}{3}\right] = 48\pi$$

31. *Fish Population* A pond is to be stocked with a species of fish. The food supply in 500 cubic feet of pond water can adequately support one fish. The pond is nearly circular, is 20 feet deep at its center, and has a radius of 200 feet. The bottom of the pond can be modeled by

$$y = 20[(0.005x)^2 - 1].$$

(a) How much water is in the pond?

(b) Estimate the maximum number of fish the pond can support.

Solution:

$$y = 20[(0.005x)^2 - 1].$$

Solving for x, we obtain

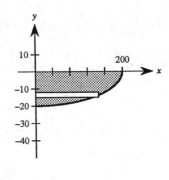

$$x = 200\sqrt{\frac{y}{20} + 1}$$

$$V = \pi \int_{-20}^{0} \left(200\sqrt{\tfrac{y}{20} + 1}\right)^2 dy$$

$$= 40,000\pi \int_{-20}^{0} \left(\frac{y}{20} + 1\right) dy$$

$$= 40,000\pi \left[\frac{y^2}{40} + y\right]_{-20}^{0} = 40,000\pi(10) \approx 1,256,637 \text{ cubic feet}$$

The maximum number of fish that can be supported is

$$\frac{1,256,637}{500} \approx 2513 \text{ fish.}$$

33. Use the Midpoint Rule with $n = 4$ to approximate the volume of the solid generated by revolving the region bounded by the graphs of the equations about the x-axis.

$y = \sqrt[3]{x+1}$, $y = 0$, $x = 0$, $x = 7$

Solution:

$$V = \pi \int_0^7 \left(\sqrt[3]{x+1}\right)^2 dx = \pi \int_0^7 (x+1)^{2/3} dx$$

$$\approx \pi \left(\frac{7}{4}\right)$$

$$\left[f\left(\frac{7}{8}\right) + f\left(\frac{21}{8}\right) + f\left(\frac{35}{8}\right) + f\left(\frac{49}{8}\right) \right]$$

$$= \frac{7\pi}{4} \left[\left(\frac{15}{8}\right)^{2/3} + \left(\frac{29}{8}\right)^{2/3} + \left(\frac{43}{8}\right)^{2/3} + \left(\frac{57}{8}\right)^{2/3} \right]$$

$$\approx 58.560 \text{ cubic units}$$

Chapter 5   Review Exercises

1. Find the indefinite integral of $\int 16\,dx$.

Solution:

$$\int 16\,dx = 16x + C$$

3. Find the indefinite integral of $\int (2x^2 + 5x)\,dx$.

Solution:

$$\int (2x^2 + 5x)\,dx = \frac{2}{3}x^3 + \frac{5}{2}x^2 + C$$

5. Find the indefinite integral of $\int \frac{2}{3\sqrt[3]{x}}\,dx$.

Solution:

$$\int \frac{2}{3\sqrt[3]{x}}\,dx = \int \frac{2}{3}x^{-1/3}\,dx = x^{2/3} + C$$

7. Find the indefinite integral of $\int \left(\sqrt[3]{x^4} + 3x\right)\,dx$.

Solution:

$$\int \left(\sqrt[3]{x^4} + 3x\right)\,dx = \int (x^{4/3} + 3x)\,dx = \frac{3}{7}x^{7/3} + \frac{3}{2}x^2 + C$$

9. Find the particular solution, $y = f(x)$, that satisfies the given conditions:
   $f'(x) = 3x + 1$, $f(2) = 6$.

   Solution:

   $$f(x) = \int (3x + 1)dx = \frac{3}{2}x^2 + x + C$$

   $$f(2) = 6 = \frac{3}{2}(2)^2 + 2C = 8 + C \Rightarrow C = -2$$

   Hence, $f(x) = \frac{3}{2}x^2 + x - 2$.

11. Find the particular solution $y = f(x)$ that satisfies the given conditions:
    $f''(x) = 2x^2$, $f'(3) = 10$, $f(3) = 6$.

    Solution:

    $$f'(x) = \int 2x^2 dx = \frac{2}{3}x^3 + C$$

    $$f'(3) = 10 = 18 + C_1 \Rightarrow C_1 = -8$$

    $$f'(x) = \frac{2}{3}x^3 - 8$$

    $$f(x) = \int \left(\frac{2}{3}x^3 - 8\right) dx = \frac{1}{6}x^4 - 8x + C_2$$

    $$f(3) = 6 = \frac{81}{6} - 24 + C_2 \Rightarrow C_2 = 30 - \frac{81}{6} = \frac{33}{2}$$

13. *Vertical Motion* An object is projected upward from the ground with an initial velocity of 80 feet per second.

    (a) How long does it take the object to rise to its maximum height?

    (b) What is the maximum height?

    (c) When is the velocity of the object half of its initial velocity?

    (d) What is the height of the object when its velocity is one-half the initial velocity?

    Solution:

    (a) $s(t) = -16t^2 + 80t$

    $v(t) = -32t + 80 = 0$

    $32t = 80$

    $t = 2.5$ seconds

    (b) $s(2.5) = 100$ feet

    (c) $v(t) = -32t + 80 = 40$

    $32t = 40$

    $t = 1.25$ seconds

    (d) $s(1.25) = 75$ feet

15. Find the indefinite integral of $\int (1+5x)^2 dx$.

Solution:

$$\int (1+5x)^2 dx = \int (1+10x+25x^2)dx = x + 5x^2 + \frac{25}{3}x^3 + C$$

Or $\int (1+5x)^2 dx = \frac{1}{5}(1+5x)^3/3 + C_1 = \frac{1}{15}(1+5x)^3 + C_1$

17. Find the indefinite integral of $\int \frac{1}{\sqrt{5x-1}}dx$.

Solution:

$$\int \frac{1}{\sqrt{5x-1}}dx = \frac{1}{5}\int (5x-1)^{-1/2}5dx = \frac{1}{5}(2)(5x-1)^{1/2} + C$$

$$= \frac{2}{5}\sqrt{5x-1} + C$$

19. Find the indefinite integral of $\int x(1-4x^2)dx$.

Solution:

$$\int x(1-4x^2)dx = \int (x-4x^3)dx = \frac{x^2}{2} - x^4 + C$$

21. Find the indefinite integral of $\int (x^4 - 2x)(2x^3 - 1)dx$.

Solution:

$$\int (x^4 - 2x)(2x^3 - 1)dx = \frac{1}{2}\int (x^4 - 2x)(4x^3 - 2)dx$$

$$= \frac{1}{2} \cdot \frac{1}{2}(x^4 - 2x)^2 + C = \frac{1}{4}(x^4 - 2x)^2 + C$$

23. *Production* The output P (in board feet) of a small sawmill changes according to the model

$$\frac{dP}{dt} = 2t(0.001t^2 + 0.5)^{1/4}, \qquad 0 \le t \le 40,$$

where t is measured in hours. Find the number of board feet produced in (a) 6 hours and (b) 12 hours.

Solution:

$$P = \int 2t(0.001t^2 + 0.5)^{1/4}dt = 800(0.001t^2 + 0.5)^{5/4} + C$$

$P(0) = 0 = 800(0.5)^{5/4} + C \Rightarrow C \approx -336.36$

$P = 800(0.001t^2 + 0.5)^{5/4} - 336.36$

(a) $P(6) \approx 30.5$ board feet

(b) $P(12) \approx 125.2$ board feet

25. Find the indefinite integral of $\int 3e^{-3x}dx$.

Solution:

$$\int 3e^{-3x}dx = -e^{-3x} + C$$

27. Find the indefinite integral of $\int (x-1)e^{x^2-2x}dx$.

Solution:

$$\int (x-1)e^{x^2-2x}dx = \frac{1}{2}e^{x^2-2x} + C$$

29. Find the indefinite integral of $\int \frac{x^2}{1-x^3}dx$.

Solution:

$$\int \frac{x^2}{1-x^3}dx = -\frac{1}{3}\int \frac{1}{1-x^3}(-3x^2)dx = -\frac{1}{3}\ln|1-x^3| + C$$

31. Find the indefinite integral of $\int \frac{(\sqrt{x}+1)^2}{\sqrt{x}}dx$.

Solution:

$$\int \frac{(\sqrt{x}+1)}{\sqrt{x}}dx = \int \frac{x+2\sqrt{x}+1}{\sqrt{x}}dx = \int (x^{1/2}+2+x^{-1/2})dx$$

$$= \frac{2}{3}x^{3/2} + 2x + 2x^{1/2} + C$$

33. Find the area of the region (shown in textbook) with $f(x) = 4 - 2x$.

Solution:

$$A = \int_0^2 (4-2x)dx$$

$$= \left[4x - x^2\right]_0^2 = 4$$

35. Find the area of the region (shown in textbook) with $f(y) = (y-2)^2$.

Solution:

$$A = \int_0^2 (y-2)^2 dy$$

$$= \left[\frac{y^3}{3} - 2y^2 + 4y - \frac{8}{3}\right]_0^2 = \frac{8}{3}$$

37. Find the area of the region (shown in textbook) with $f(x) = \dfrac{2}{x+1}$.

Solution:

$$A = \int_0^1 \frac{2}{x+1}\,dx = 2\ln(x+1)\Big]_0^1 = 2\ln 2$$

39. Evaluate $\displaystyle\int_0^4 (2+x)\,dx$.

Solution:

$$\int_0^4 (2+x)\,dx = \left[2x + \frac{x^2}{2}\right]_0^4 = 16$$

41. Evaluate $\displaystyle\int_{-1}^1 (4t^3 - 2t)\,dt$.

Solution:

$$\int_{-1}^1 (4t^3 - 2t)\,dt = \left[t^4 - t^2\right]_{-1}^1 = 0$$

43. Evaluate $\displaystyle\int_0^3 \frac{1}{\sqrt{1+x}}\,dx$.

Solution:

$$\int_0^3 \frac{1}{\sqrt{1+x}}\,dx = \int_0^3 (1+x)^{-1/2}\,dx = 2\sqrt{1+x}\,\Big]_0^3 = 2$$

45. Evaluate $\displaystyle\int_1^2 \left(\frac{1}{x^2} - \frac{1}{x^3}\right)dx$

Solution:

$$\int_1^2 \left(\frac{1}{x^2} - \frac{1}{x^3}\right)dx = \int_1^2 (x^{-2} - x^{-3})\,dx$$

$$= \left[\frac{x^{-1}}{-1} - \frac{x^{-2}}{-2}\right]_1^2$$

$$= \left[-\frac{1}{x} + \frac{1}{2x^2}\right]_1^2$$

$$= -\frac{3}{8} - \left(-\frac{1}{2}\right) = \frac{1}{8}$$

47. Evaluate $\displaystyle\int_1^3 \frac{(3 + \ln x)}{x}\,dx.$

Solution:

$$\int_1^3 \frac{3 + \ln x}{x}\,dx = \frac{1}{2}(3 + \ln x)^2 \Big]_1^3$$

$$= \frac{1}{2}[(3 + \ln 3)^2 - 3^2]$$

$$= \frac{1}{2}[6\ln 3 + (\ln 3)^2]$$

$$\approx 3.899$$

49. Evaluate $\displaystyle\int_{-1}^1 3xe^{x^2 - 1}\,dx.$

Solution:

$$\int_{-1}^1 3xe^{x^2 - 1}\,dx = \frac{3}{2}e^{x^2 - 1}\Big]_{-1}^1$$

$$= \frac{3}{2}(1 - 1) = 0$$

51. *Cost* The marginal cost for a typical additional client at a law firm can be modeled by

$$\frac{dC}{dx} = 675 + 0.5x,$$

where x is the number of clients. How does the cost C change when x increases from 50 to 51 clients? Illustrate your answer graphically.

Solution:

$$C = \int (675 + 0.5x)\,dx = 675x + \frac{1}{4}x^2 + C_1$$

$$C(51) - C(50) = \$700.25$$

53. Find the average value of the function $f(x) = \dfrac{4}{\sqrt{x-1}}$ on the closed interval [5, 10].
Then find the values of x in the interval where the function assumes its average value.

Solution:

$$\text{Average value} = \frac{1}{10-5}\int_5^{10}\frac{4}{\sqrt{x-1}}dx = \frac{4}{5}\int_5^{10}(x-1)^{-1/2}dx$$

$$= \frac{8}{5}(x-1)^{1/2}\Big]_5^{10} = \frac{8}{5}(3-2) = \frac{8}{5}$$

To find the values for which $f(x) = \dfrac{8}{5}$, solve for x in the equation.

$$\frac{4}{\sqrt{x-1}} = \frac{8}{5}$$

$$\frac{5}{2} = \sqrt{x-1}$$

$$x-1 = \frac{25}{4}$$

$$x = \frac{29}{4}$$

55. Find the average value of the function $f(x) = e^{5-x}$ on the closed interval [2, 5]. Then find the values of x in the interval where the function assumes its average value.

Solution:

$$\text{Average value} = \frac{1}{5-2}\int_2^5 e^{5-x}dx$$

$$= \frac{1}{3}\left[-e^{5-x}\right]_2^5 = \frac{1}{3}(-1+e^3) = 6.3618$$

To find the value of x for which $f(x) = \frac{1}{3}(-1+e^3)$, we solve $e^{5-x} = \frac{1}{3}(-1+e^3)$.
Using a graphing utility, we obtain $x \approx 3.150$.

57. *Checking Account* An interest-bearing checking account yields 4% interest compounded continuously. If you deposit $500 into such an account, and never write checks, what will the average value of the account be over a period of 2 years? Explain your reasoning.

Solution:

$$\text{Average value} = \frac{1}{b-a}\int_a^b f(t)dt$$

$$= \frac{1}{2-0}\int_0^2 500e^{0.04t}dt$$

$$= 250\left[\frac{e^{0.04t}}{0.04}\right]_0^2$$

$$= 6250[e^{0.08} - 1] \approx \$520.54$$

59. Explain how $\displaystyle\int_0^2 6x^5\,dx = 64$ can be used to evaluate $\displaystyle\int_{-2}^2 6x^5\,dx$.

Solution:

$$\int_{-2}^2 6x^5\,dx = 0 \text{ (odd function)}$$

61. Explain how $\displaystyle\int_1^2 \frac{4}{x^2}\,dx = 2$ can be used to evaluate $\displaystyle\int_{-2}^{-1} \frac{4}{x^2}\,dx$.

Solution:

$$\int_{-2}^{-1} \frac{4}{x^2}\,dx = \int_1^2 \frac{4}{x^2}\,dx = 2 \text{ (Symmetric about } y\text{-axis).}$$

63. Sketch the region bounded by the graphs $y = \dfrac{1}{x^2}$, $y = 4$, $x = 3$ and determine the area of the region.

Solution:

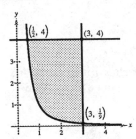

$$\text{Area} = \int_{1/2}^3 \left(4 - \frac{1}{x^2}\right) dx$$

$$= 4x + \frac{1}{x}\bigg]_{1/2}^3$$

$$= \left(12 + \frac{1}{3}\right) - (2+2) = \frac{25}{3}$$

65. Sketch the region bounded by the graphs of $y = 1 - \dfrac{1}{2}x$, $y = x - 2$, $y = 1$ and determine the area of the region.

Solution:

$$A = \int_0^1 [(y+2) - (2-2y)]\,dy$$

$$= \int_0^1 3y\,dy = \frac{3}{2}y^2\bigg]_0^1 = \frac{3}{2}$$

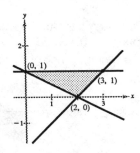

67. Sketch the region bounded by the graphs of $y = \sqrt{x}(x-1)$ and $y = 0$ and determine the area of the region.

Solution:

$$A = \int_0^1 [0 - \sqrt{x}(x-1)]\,dx$$

$$= \int_0^1 [-x^{3/2} + x^{1/2}]\,dx$$

$$= \left[-\frac{2}{5}x^{5/2} + \frac{2}{3}x^{3/2} \right]_0^1$$

$$= \frac{4}{15}$$

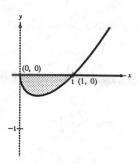

69. Sketch the region bounded by the graphs of $y = (x-3)^2$, $y = 8 - (x-3)^2$ and determine the area of the region.

Solution:

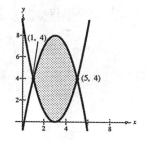

$$(x-3)^2 = 8 - (x-3)^2$$

$$2(x-3)^2 = 8$$

$$(x-3)^2 = 4$$

$$x - 3 = \pm 2$$

$$x = 1, 5$$

$$A = \int_1^5 [(8 - (x-3)^2) - (x-3)^2]\,dx = \int_1^5 [8 - 2(x-3)^2]\,dx$$

$$= 8x - \frac{2}{3}(x-3)^3 \Big]_1^5 = \left(40 - \frac{16}{3}\right) - \left(8 + \frac{16}{3}\right) = \frac{64}{3}$$

71. *Consumer and Producer Surplus* Find the consumer surplus and producer surplus for the demand function $p_1(x) = 1.25x + 162.5$ and supply function $p_2(x) = 500 - x$.

Solution:

Demand function = Supply function

$$500 - x = 1.25x + 162.5$$

$$2.25x = 337.5$$

$$x = 150 \Rightarrow \text{price} = 350$$

$$\text{Consumer surplus} = \int_0^{150} (\text{demand function} - \text{price}) dx$$

$$= \int_0^{150} [(500 - x) - 350] dx$$

$$= \left[150x - \frac{x^2}{2} \right]_0^{150} = 11{,}250$$

$$\text{Producer surplus} = \int_0^{150} (\text{price} - \text{supply function}) dx$$

$$- \int_0^{150} (350 - (1.25x + 162.5)) dx$$

$$= \left[187.5x - 1.25\frac{x^2}{2} \right]_0^{150} = 14, .062.5$$

73. *Ice Cream Consumption* The per capital consumption y (in pounds) of ice cream in the United States from 1981 through 1987, can be modeled by

$$y = 18.94 - \frac{5.175}{t} + \frac{3.632}{t^{3/2}}, \qquad 1 \le t \le 7,$$

where $t = 1$ represents December 31, 1981. The consumption from 1988 through 1990, can be modeled by

$$y = 0.019t^3 - 0.294t^2 + 26.465, \qquad 7 < t \le 10.$$

If the consumption had continued to follow the first model from 1988 through 1990, how much more or less ice cream would have been consumed?

Solution:

$$\int_8^{10} \left[\left(18.94 - \frac{5.175}{t} + \frac{3.632}{t^{3/2}} \right) - (0.019t^3 - 0.294t^2 + 26.465) \right] dt$$

$$= \left[-7.525t - 5.175 \ln t - 7.264t^{-1/2} - 0.00475t^4 - 0.098t^3 \right]_8^{10}$$

$$\approx 3.85 \text{ pounds}$$

75. Use the Midpoint Rule with $n = 4$ to approximate the definite integral $\int_0^2 (x^2 + 1)^2 dx$. Then use a programmable calculator or computer with $n = 20$. Compare the two approximations.

Solution:

$$\int_0^2 (x^2 + 1)^2 dx$$

$n = 4 : 13.3203$

$n = 20 : 13.7167$ (exact $13.7\overline{3}$)

77. Use the Midpoint Rule with $n = 4$ to approximate the definite integral $\int_0^1 \frac{1}{x^2 + 1} dx$. Then use a programmable calculator or computer with $n = 20$. Compare the two approximations.

Solution:

$$\int_0^1 \frac{1}{x^2 - 1} dx$$

$n = 4 : 0.7867$

$n = 20 : 0.7855$

79. Use the Disc Method to find the volume of the solid of revolution formed by revolving the region about the x-axis.

$$y = \frac{1}{\sqrt{x}}$$

Solution:

$$V = \pi \int_1^4 \left(\frac{1}{\sqrt{x}} \right)^2 dx = \pi \int_1^4 \frac{1}{x} dx = \pi \ln x \Big]_1^4 = \pi \ln 4 \approx 4.355$$

81. Use the Disc Method to find the volume of the solid of revolution formed by revolving the region about the x-axis.

$$y = e^{1-x}$$

Solution:

$$V = \pi \int_0^2 (e^{1-x})^2 dx = \pi \int_0^2 e^{2-2x} dx = -\frac{\pi}{2} \left[e^{2-2x} \right]_0^2$$

$$= -\frac{\pi}{2} [e^{-2} - e^2] = \frac{\pi}{2} (e^2 - e^{-2}) \approx 11.394$$

83. Use the Washer Method to find the volume of the solid of revolution formed by revolving the region about the x-axis.

$y = 2x + 1, y = 1$

Solution:

$$V = \pi \int_0^2 [(2x + 1)^2 - 1^2]dx = \pi \int_0^2 (4x^2 + 4x)dx$$

$$= \pi \left[\frac{4}{3}x^3 + 2x^2\right]_0^2 = \pi \left(\frac{32}{3} + 8\right) = \frac{56}{3}\pi$$

85. Use the Washer Method to find the volume of the solid of revolution formed by revolving the region about the x-axis.

$y = x^2, y = x^3$

Solution:

$$V = \pi \int_0^1 [(x^2)^2 - (x^3)^2]dx = \pi \left[\frac{x^5}{5} - \frac{x^7}{7}\right]_0^1 = \frac{2}{35}\pi$$

87. *Manufacturing* To create a part for an engine, a manufacturer drills a hole through the center of a metal sphere whose radius is 1 inch. The hole has a radius of 0.25 inch. What is the volume of the resulting ring?

Solution:

$$x^2 + y^2 = 1, y = \frac{1}{4}$$

$$x = \sqrt{1 - \left(\frac{1}{4}\right)^2} = \frac{\sqrt{15}}{4}$$

$$V = \pi \int_{-\sqrt{15/4}}^{\sqrt{15/4}} \left[(\sqrt{1 - x^2})^2 - \left(\frac{1}{4}\right)^2\right] dx$$

$$= 2\pi \int_0^{\sqrt{15/4}} \left(1 - x^2 - \frac{1}{16}\right) dx = \frac{5}{16}\pi\sqrt{15}$$

Practice Test for Chapter 5

1. Evaluate $\int (3x^2 - 8x + 5)\, dx$.

2. Evaluate $\int (x + 7)(x^2 - 4)\, dx$.

3. Evaluate $\int \dfrac{x^3 - 9x^2 + 1}{x^2}\, dx$.

4. Evaluate $\int x^3 \sqrt[4]{1 - x^4}\, dx$.

5. Evaluate $\int \dfrac{3}{\sqrt[3]{7x}}\, dx$.

6. Evaluate $\int \sqrt{6 - 11x}\, dx$.

7. Evaluate $\int (\sqrt[4]{x} + \sqrt[6]{x})\, dx$.

8. Evaluate $\int \left(\dfrac{1}{x^4} - \dfrac{1}{x^5}\right) dx$.

9. Evaluate $\int (1 - x^2)^3\, dx$.

10. Evaluate $\int \dfrac{5x}{(1 + 3x^2)^3}\, dx$.

11. Evaluate $\int e^{7x}\, dx$.

12. Evaluate $\int x e^{4x^2}\, dx$.

13. Evaluate $\int e^x (1 + 4e^x)^3\, dx$.

14. Evaluate $\int (e^x + 2)^2\, dx$.

15. Evaluate $\int \dfrac{e^{3x} - 4e^x + 1}{e^x}\, dx$.

16. Evaluate $\int \dfrac{1}{x + 6}\, dx$.

17. Evaluate $\int \dfrac{x^2}{8 - x^3}\, dx$.

18. Evaluate $\int \dfrac{e^x}{1 + 3e^x}\, dx$.

19. Evaluate $\int \dfrac{(\ln x)^6}{x}\, dx$.

20. Evaluate $\int \dfrac{x^2 + 5}{x - 1}\, dx$.

21. Evaluate $\int_0^3 (x^2 - 4x + 2)\, dx$.

22. Evaluate $\int_1^8 x\sqrt[3]{x}\, dx$.

23. Evaluate $\int_{\sqrt{5}}^{\sqrt{13}} \dfrac{x}{\sqrt{x^2 - 4}}\, dx$.

24. Sketch the region bounded by the graphs of $f(x) = x^2 - 6x$ and $g(x) = 0$ and find the area of the region.

25. Sketch the region bounded by the graphs of $f(x) = x^3 + 1$ and $g(x) = x + 1$ and find the area of the region.

26. Sketch the region bounded by the graphs of $f(y) = 1/y^2$, $x = 0$, $y = 1$, and $y = 3$ and find the area of the region.

27. Approximate the definite integral by the Midpoint Rule using $n = 4$.

$$\int_0^1 \sqrt{x^3 + 2}\,dx$$

28. Approximate the definite integral by the Midpoint Rule using $n = 4$.

$$\int_3^4 \frac{1}{x^2 - 5}\,dx$$

29. Find the volume of the solid generated by revolving the region bounded by the graphs of $f(x) = 1/\sqrt[3]{x}$, $x = 1$, $x = 8$, and $y = 0$ about the x-axis.

30. Find the volume of the solid generated by revolving the region bounded by the graphs of $y = \sqrt{25 - x}$, $y = 0$, $x = 0$ about the y-axis.

Graphing Calculator Required

31. Use a program similar to that on page 364 of the textbook to approximate $\int_0^4 \sqrt{1 + x^4}\,dx$ for $n = 50$ and $n = 100$.

32. Use a graphing calculator to sketch the region bounded by $f(x) = 3 - \sqrt{x}$ and $g(x) = 3 - \frac{1}{3}x$. Based on the graph alone (do no calculations) determine which value best approximates the bounded area.

   (a) 13   (b) 3   (c) 5   (c) 6

CHAPTER 6
Techniques of Integration

Section 6.1 Integration by Substitution

1. Evaluate $\displaystyle\int (x-2)^4\,dx$.

Solution:

$$\int (x-2)^4\,dx = \frac{(x-2)^5}{5} + C$$

3. Evaluate $\displaystyle\int \frac{2}{(t-9)^2}\,dt$.

Solution:

$$\int \frac{2}{(t-9)^2}\,dt = 2\int (t-9)^{-2}\,dt = (2)\frac{(t-9)^{-1}}{-1} + C = -\frac{2}{t-9} + C = \frac{2}{9-t} + C$$

5. Evaluate $\displaystyle\int \sqrt{1+x}\,dx$.

Solution:

$$\int \sqrt{1+x}\,dx = \int (1+x)^{1/2}\,dx = \frac{2}{3}(1+x)^{3/2} + C$$

7. Evaluate $\displaystyle\int \frac{12x+2}{3x^2+x}\,dx$.

Solution:

$$\int \frac{12x+2}{3x^2+x}\,dx = 2\int \frac{6x+1}{3x^2+x}\,dx = 2\ln|3x^2+x| + C = \ln(3x^2+x)^2 + C$$

9. Evaluate $\displaystyle\int \frac{1}{(5x+1)^3}\,dx$.

Solution:

$$\int \frac{1}{(5x+1)^3}\,dx = \frac{1}{5}\int (5x+1)^{-3}(5)\,dx = \left(\frac{1}{5}\right)\frac{(5x+1)^{-2}}{-2} + C = -\frac{1}{10(5x+1)^2} + C$$

11. Evaluate $\displaystyle\int \frac{1}{\sqrt{x+1}}dx$.

Solution:

$$\int \frac{1}{\sqrt{x+1}}dx = \int (x+1)^{-1/2}dx = 2(x+1)^{1/2} + C$$

13. Evaluate $\displaystyle\int \frac{e^{3x}}{1-e^{3x}}\,dx$.

Solution:

$$\int \frac{e^{3x}}{1-e^{3x}}\,dx = -\frac{1}{3}\int \frac{-3e^{3x}}{1-e^{3x}}\,dx = -\frac{1}{3}\ln|1-e^{3x}| + C$$

15. Evaluate $\displaystyle\int \frac{x^2}{x-1}\,dx$.

Solution:

$$\int \frac{x^2}{x-1}\,dx = \int \left[x+1+\frac{1}{x-1}\right]dx = \frac{x^2}{2} + x + \ln|x-1| + C$$

17. Evaluate $\displaystyle\int x\sqrt{x^2+4}\,dx$.

Solution:

$$\int x\sqrt{x^2+4}\,dx = \frac{1}{2}\int (x^2+4)^{1/2}2x\,dx = \frac{1}{3}(x^2+4)^{3/2} + C$$

19. Evaluate $\displaystyle\int e^{5x}\,dx$.

Solution:

$$\int e^{5x}\,dx = \frac{1}{5}\int e^{5x}(5)\,dx = \frac{1}{5}e^{5x} + C$$

21. Evaluate $\displaystyle\int \frac{x}{(x+1)^4}dx$.

Solution:

Let $u = x+1$, $du = dx$, $x = u-1$.

$$\int \frac{x}{(x+1)^4}dx \int \frac{u-1}{u^4}du = \int u^{-3}du - \int u^{-4}du$$

$$= \frac{u^2}{-2} - \frac{u^2}{-3} + C = \frac{-1}{2u^2} + \frac{1}{3u^3} + C$$

$$= \frac{-1}{2(x+1)^2} + \frac{1}{3(x+1)^3} + C$$

23. Evaluate $\displaystyle\int \frac{x}{(3x-1)^2}\,dx$.

Solution:

Let $u = 3x - 1$, then $x = (u+1)/3$ and $dx = (1/3)\,du$.

$$\int \frac{x}{(3x-1)^2}\,dx = \int \frac{(u+1)/3}{u^2}\left(\frac{1}{3}\right)du$$

$$= \frac{1}{9}\int \left(\frac{1}{u} + \frac{1}{u^2}\right)du$$

$$= \frac{1}{9}\left[\ln|u| - \frac{1}{u}\right] + C$$

$$= \frac{1}{9}\left[\ln|3x-1| - \frac{1}{3x-1}\right] + C$$

25. Evaluate $\displaystyle\int x(1-x)^4\,dx$.

Solution:

Let $u = 1 - x$, then $x = 1 - u$ and $dx = -du$.

$$\int x(1-x)^4\,dx = \int (1-u)u^4(-du)$$

$$= \int (u^5 - u^4)\,du$$

$$= \frac{u^6}{6} - \frac{u^5}{5} + C$$

$$= \frac{u^5}{30}(5u - 6) + C$$

$$= -\frac{(1-x)^5}{30}(1 + 5x) + C$$

27. Evaluate $\displaystyle\int \frac{x-1}{x^2 - 2x}\,dx$.

Solution:

$$\int \frac{x-1}{x^2-2x}\,dx = \frac{1}{2}\int \frac{2x-2}{x^2-2x}\,dx = \frac{1}{2}\ln|x^2 - 2x| + C$$

29. Evaluate $\displaystyle\int x\sqrt{x-3}\,dx$.

Solution:

Let $u = x - 3$, then $x = u + 3$ and $dx = du$.

$$\int x\sqrt{x-3}\,dx = \int (u+3)u^{1/2}\,du$$

$$= \int (u^{3/2} + 3u^{1/2})\,du$$

$$= \frac{2}{5}u^{5/2} + 2u^{3/2} + C$$

$$= \frac{2u^{3/2}}{5}(u+5) + C$$

$$= \frac{2}{5}(x-3)^{3/2}(x+2) + C$$

31. Evaluate $\displaystyle\int x^2\sqrt{1-x}\,dx$.

Solution:

Let $u = \sqrt{1-x}$, then $x = 1 - u^2$ and $dx = -2u\,du$.

$$\int x^2\sqrt{1-x}\,dx = \int (1-u^2)^2 u(-2u)\,du$$

$$= -2\int (u^6 - 2u^4 + u^2)\,du$$

$$= -2\left(\frac{u^7}{7} - \frac{2u^5}{5} + \frac{u^3}{3}\right) + C$$

$$= -\frac{2u^3}{105}(35 - 42u^2 + 15u^4) + C$$

$$= -\frac{2}{105}(1-x)^{3/2}(15x^2 + 12x + 8) + C$$

33. Evaluate $\int \dfrac{x^2 - 1}{\sqrt{2x - 1}}\, dx.$

Solution:

Let $u = \sqrt{2x - 1}$, then $x = (u^2 + 1)/2$ and $dx = u\,du$.

$$\int \frac{x^2 - 1}{\sqrt{2x - 1}}\, dx = \int \frac{[(u^2 + 1)/2]^2 - 1}{u}(u)\, du$$

$$= \frac{1}{4}\int (u^4 + 2u^2 - 3)\, du$$

$$= \frac{1}{4}\left(\frac{u^5}{5} + \frac{2u^3}{3} - 3u\right) + C$$

$$= \frac{u}{60}(3u^4 + 10u^2 - 45) + C$$

$$= \frac{\sqrt{2x - 1}}{60}[3(2x - 1)^2 + 10(2x - 1) - 45] + C$$

$$= \frac{\sqrt{2x - 1}}{60}[12x^2 + 8x - 52] + C$$

$$= \frac{\sqrt{2x - 1}}{15}(3x^2 + 2x - 13) + C$$

35. Evaluate $\int t\sqrt[3]{t + 1}\, dt.$

Solution:

Let $u = t + 1$, then $t = u - 1$ and $dt = du$.

$$\int t\sqrt[3]{t + 1}\, dt = \int (u - 1)\sqrt[3]{u}\, du = \int (u^{4/3} - u^{1/3})\, du = \frac{3}{7}u^{7/3} - \frac{3}{4}u^{4/3} + C$$

$$= \frac{3}{28}u^{4/3}(4u - 7) + C$$

$$= \frac{3}{28}(t + 1)^{4/3}[4(t + 1) - 7] + C$$

$$= \frac{3}{28}(t + 1)^{4/3}(4t - 3) + C$$

37. Evaluate $\int \dfrac{1}{\sqrt{t} - 1}\, dt.$

Solution:

Let $u = \sqrt{t} - 1, t = (u + 1)^2, dt = 2(u + 1)du$.

$$\int \frac{1}{\sqrt{t} - 1}\, dt \int \frac{2(u + 1)}{u}\, du = \int \left(2 + \frac{2}{u}\right) du$$

$$= 2u + 2\ln|u| + C$$

$$= 2(\sqrt{t} - 1) + 2\ln|\sqrt{t} - 1| + C$$

39. Evaluate $\int \dfrac{2\sqrt{t}+1}{t}\,dt$.

Solution:

$$\int \frac{2\sqrt{t}+1}{t}\,dt = \int \left(2t^{-1/2}+\frac{1}{t}\right) dt = 4t^{1/2}+\ln|t|+C = 4\sqrt{t}+\ln|t|+C$$

41. Evaluate $\int_0^4 \sqrt{2x+1}\,dx$.

Solution:

$$\int_0^4 \sqrt{2x+1}\,dx = \frac{1}{2}\int_0^4 (2x+1)^{1/2}(2)\,dx$$

$$= \frac{1}{2}\left(\frac{2}{3}\right)(2x+1)^{3/2}\Big]_0^4$$

$$= \frac{1}{3}(9)^{3/2}-\frac{1}{3}(1)^{3/2} = \frac{26}{3}$$

43. Evaluate $\int_0^1 3xe^{x^2}\,dx$.

Solution:

$$\int_0^1 3xe^{x^2}\,dx = \frac{3}{2}\int_0^1 2xe^{x^2}\,dx = \frac{3}{2}e^{x^2}\Big]_0^1 = \frac{3}{2}(e-1) \approx 2.577$$

45. Evaluate $\int_0^4 \dfrac{x}{(x+4)^2}\,dx$.

Solution:

Let $u = x+4$, $x = u-4$, $du = dx$. $u = 4$ when $x = 0$, $u = 8$ when $x = 4$.

$$\int_0^4 \frac{x}{(x+4)^2}\,dx \int_4^8 \frac{u-4}{u^2}\,du = \int_4^8 \left(\frac{1}{u}-4u^{-2}\right)$$

$$du = \left[\ln u + 4\frac{1}{u}\right]_4^8 = \left(\ln 8 + \frac{1}{2}\right) - (\ln 4 + 1)$$

$$= \ln 2 - \frac{1}{2} \approx 0.193$$

47. Evaluate $\displaystyle\int_0^{0.5} x(1-x)^3\,dx$.

Solution:

Let $u = 1 - x$, then $x = 1 - u$ and $dx = -du$. $u = 1$ when $x = 0$, and $u = 0.5$ when $x = 0.5$.

$$\int_0^{0.5} x(1-x)^3\,dx = \int_1^{0.5} (1-u)u^3(-du)$$

$$= \int_1^{0.5} (u^4 - u^3)\,du$$

$$= \left(\frac{u^5}{5} - \frac{u^4}{4}\right)\Bigg]_1^{0.5}$$

$$= \left(\frac{1}{160} - \frac{1}{64}\right) - \left(\frac{1}{5} - \frac{1}{4}\right)$$

$$= \frac{13}{320}$$

49. Evaluate $\displaystyle\int_3^7 x\sqrt{x-3}\,dx$.

Solution:

Let $u = \sqrt{x-3}$, then $x = u^2 + 3$ and $dx = 2u\,du$. $u = 0$ when $x = 3$, and $u = 2$ when $x = 7$.

$$\int_3^7 x\sqrt{x-3}\,dx = \int_0^2 (u^2 + 3)u(2u\,du)$$

$$= 2\int_0^2 (u^4 + 3u^2)\,du = 2\left(\frac{u^5}{5} + u^3\right)\Bigg]_0^2 = 2\left(\frac{32}{5} + 8\right) = \frac{144}{5}$$

51. Evaluate $\displaystyle\int_0^7 x\sqrt[3]{x+1}\,dx.$

Solution:

Let $u = \sqrt[3]{x+1}$, then $x = u^3 - 1$ and $dx = 3u^2\,du.$ $u = 1$ when $x = 0$, and $u = 2$ when $x = 7$.

$$\int_0^7 x\sqrt[3]{x+1}\,dx = 3\int_1^2 (u^3 - 1)u^3\,du$$

$$= 3\int_1^2 (u^6 - u^3)\,du$$

$$= 3\left(\frac{u^7}{7} - \frac{u^4}{4}\right)\Bigg]_1^2$$

$$= 3\left(\frac{128}{7} - 4\right) - 3\left(\frac{1}{7} - \frac{1}{4}\right)$$

$$= \frac{1209}{28}$$

53. Find the area of the region bounded by the graphs of the equation
$y = -x\sqrt{x+2},\ y = 0.$

Solution:

Let $u = x + 2,\ x = u - 2,\ du = 2x.$ $u = 0$ when $x = -2$, and $u = 2$, when $x = 0$.

$$\int_{-2}^0 -x\sqrt{x+2}\,dx = \int_0^2 -(u-2)\sqrt{u}\,du = \int_0^2 (-u^{3/2} + 2u^{1/2})\,du$$

$$= \left[-\frac{2}{5}u^{5/2} + \frac{4}{3}u^{3/2}\right]_0^2 = -\frac{2}{5}\cdot 2^{3/2} + \frac{4}{3}\cdot 2^{3/2}$$

$$= \sqrt{2}\left(\frac{8}{3} - \frac{8}{5}\right) = \frac{16\sqrt{2}}{15}$$

55. Find the area of the region bounded by the graph of $y^2 = x^2(1 - x^2)$.

Solution:

Use $y = x\sqrt{1 - x^2}$ and $y = 0$ and multiply by 4.

$$A = 4\int_0^1 x\sqrt{1 - x^2}\,dx$$

$$= \frac{4}{-2}\int_0^1 (1 - x^2)^{1/2}(-2x)\,dx$$

$$= -2\left(\frac{2}{3}\right)(1 - x^2)^{3/2}\bigg]_0^1$$

$$= -\frac{4}{3}[0 - 1] = \frac{4}{3} \text{ square units}$$

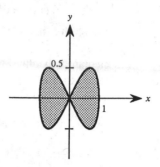

57. Find the volume of the solid generated by revolving the region bounded by the graph of $y = x\sqrt{1 - x^2}$ about the x-axis.

Solution:

$$V = 2\pi\int_0^1 [x\sqrt{1 - x^2}]^2\,dx$$

$$= 2\pi\int_0^1 x^2(1 - x^2)\,dx = 2\pi\left[\frac{x^3}{3} - \frac{x^5}{5}\right]_0^1 = 2\pi\left(\frac{1}{3} - \frac{1}{5}\right) = \frac{4\pi}{15} \text{ cubic unit}$$

59. Find the average amount by which the function $f(x)$ exceeds the function $g(x)$ on the interval $[0, 1]$.

$$f(x) = \frac{1}{x + 1}, \quad g(x) = \frac{x}{(x + 1)^2}$$

Solution:

$$\frac{1}{1 - 0}\int_0^1 [f(x) - g(x)]\,dx = \int_0^1 \left[\frac{1}{x + 1} - \frac{x}{(x + 1)^2}\right]dx$$

$$= \int_0^1 \frac{1}{(x + 1)^2}\,dx$$

$$= -\frac{1}{x + 1}\bigg]_0^1$$

$$= -\frac{1}{2} + 1 = \frac{1}{2}$$

61. *Probability* The probability of recall in a certain experiment is found to be

$$P(a \leq x \leq b) = \int_a^b \frac{15}{4} x\sqrt{1-x}\, dx$$

where x represents the percentage of recall.

(a) What is the probability that a randomly chosen individual will recall between 40% and 80% of the material?

(b) What is the median percentage recall? That is, for what value of b is it true that the probability from 0 to b is 0.5?

Solution:

Let $u = \sqrt{1-x}$, then $x = 1 - u^2$ and $dx = -2u\, du$.

$$\int \frac{15}{4} x\sqrt{1-x}\, dx = \frac{1}{2}(1-x)^{3/2}(-3x-2) + C$$

(a) $P(0.40 \leq x \leq 0.80) = \dfrac{1}{2}(1-x)^{3/2}(-3x-2)\Big]_{0.40}^{0.80} = 0.547$

(b) $P(0 \leq x \leq b) = \dfrac{1}{2}(1-x)^{3/2}(-3x-2)\Big]_0^b$

$$= \frac{1}{2}[(1-b)^{3/2}(-3b-2)+2] = 0.5$$

Solving this equation for b produces

$$(1-b)^{3/2}(-3b-2)+2 = 1$$

$$(1-b)^{3/2}(-3b-2) = -1$$

$$(1-b)^{3/2}(3b+2) = 1$$

$$(1-b)^3(3b+2)^2 = 1$$

$$b \approx 0.586.$$

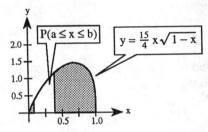

63. *Revenue* A company sells a seasonal product that has a daily revenue approximated by

$$R = 0.06t^2(365 - t)^{1/2} + 1250, \quad 0 \le t \le 365.$$

Find the average daily revenue over the period of one year.

Solution:

The average daily revenue is given by the following.

$$\frac{1}{365 - 0}\int_0^{365} [0.06t^2(365 - t)^{1/2} + 1250]\,dt = \frac{1}{365}\int_0^{365} [0.06t^2(365 - t)^{1/2}]$$

$$dt + \frac{1}{365}\int_0^{365} 1250\,dt$$

$$= \frac{1}{365}\int_{\sqrt{365}}^0 0.06(365 - u^2)^2 u(-2u)$$

$$du + 1250 \approx \$24,\,520.95$$

65. Use the Midpoint Rule with $n = 10$ on a computer to approximate the area of the region bounded by the graphs of the equations. (It is instructive to use the computer to sketch the graph of the region.)

$$y = \sqrt[3]{x}\,\sqrt{4 - x}, \quad y = 0$$

Solution:

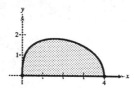

$$A = \int_0^4 \sqrt[3]{x}\,\sqrt{4 - x}\,dx$$

$$\approx \frac{4 - 0}{10}\left[f\!\left(\frac{1}{5}\right)\right.$$

$$+ f\!\left(\frac{3}{5}\right) + f(1) + f\!\left(\frac{7}{5}\right)$$

$$+ f\!\left(\frac{9}{5}\right) + f\!\left(\frac{11}{5}\right)$$

$$+ f\!\left(\frac{13}{5}\right) + f(3) +$$

$$\left. f\!\left(\frac{17}{5}\right) + f\!\left(\frac{19}{5}\right)\right]$$

$$\approx 5.885$$

Section 6.2   Integration by Parts and Present Value

1. Use integration by parts to evaluate $\int xe^{3x}\,dx$.

   Solution:

   Let $u = x$ and $dv = e^{3x}\,dx$, then $du = dx$ and $v = \frac{1}{3}e^{3x}$.

   $$\int xe^{3x}\,dx = \frac{1}{3}xe^{3x} - \int \frac{1}{3}e^{3x}\,dx = \frac{1}{3}xe^{3x} - \frac{1}{9}e^{3x} + C = \frac{1}{9}e^{3x}(3x-1) + C$$

3. Use integration by parts to evaluate $\int x^2 e^{-x}\,dx$.

   Solution:

   Let $u = x^2$ and $dv = e^{-x}\,dx$, then $du = 2x\,dx$ and $v = -e^{-x}$.

   $$\int x^2 e^{-x}\,dx = -x^2 e^{-x} + 2\int xe^{-x}\,dx$$

   Let $u = x$ and $dv = e^{-x}\,dx$, then $du = dx$ and $v = -e^{-x}$.

   $$\int x^2 e^{-x}\,dx = -x^2 e^{-x} + 2\left[-xe^{-x} + \int e^{-x}\,dx \right]$$

   $$= -x^2 e^{-x} - 2xe^{-x} - 2e^{-x} + C$$

   $$= -e^{-x}(x^2 + 2x + 2) + C$$

5. Use integration by parts to evaluate $\int \ln 2x\,dx$.

   Solution:

   Let $u = \ln 2x$ and $dv = dx$, then $du = (1/x)\,dx$ and $v = x$.

   $$\int \ln 2x\,dx = x\ln 2x - \int x\left(\frac{1}{x}\right)dx$$

   $$= x\ln 2x - \int dx$$

   $$= x\ln 2x - x + C$$

   $$= x(\ln 2x - 1) + C$$

7. Evaluate $\int e^{4x}\,dx$.

   Solution:

   $$\int e^{4x}\,dx = \frac{1}{4}\int e^{4x}(4)\,dx = \frac{1}{4}e^{4x} + C$$

9. Evaluate $\int xe^{4x}dx$.

Solution:

Let $u = x$ and $dv = e^{4x}dx$, then $du = dx$ and $v = \dfrac{1}{4}e^{4x}$.

$$\int xe^{4x}dx = \frac{1}{4}xe^{4x} - \frac{1}{4}\int e^{4x}dx = \frac{1}{4}xe^{4x} - \frac{1}{16}e^{4x} + C$$

$$= \frac{e^{4x}}{16}(4x - 1) + C$$

11. Evaluate $\int xe^{x^2}dx$.

Solution:

$$\int xe^{x^2}dx = \frac{1}{2}e^{x^2} + C$$

13. Evaluate $\int x^2e^xdx$.

Solution:

Let $u = x^2$ and $dv = e^xdx$, then $du = 2x\,dx$ and $v = e^x$.

$$\int x^2e^xdx = x^2e^x - \int 2xe^xdx$$

Let $u = 2x$ and $dv = e^xdx$, then $du = 2\,dx$ and $v = e^x$.

$$\int x^2e^xdx = x^2e^x - [2xe^x - \int e^x(2\,dx)] = (x^2 - 2x + 2)e^x + C$$

15. Evaluate $\int x^3e^x\,dx$.

Solution:

Let $u = x^3$ and $dv = e^x\,dx$, then $du = 3x^2\,dx$ and $v = e^x$.

$$\int x^3e^x\,dx = x^3e^x - 3\int x^2e^x\,dx$$

Let $u = x^2$ and $dv = e^x\,dx$, then $du = 2x\,dx$ and $v = e^x$.

$$\int x^3e^x\,dx = x^3e^x - 3\left(x^2e^x - 2\int xe^x\,dx\right) = x^3e^x - 3x^2e^x + 6\int xe^x\,dx$$

Let $u = x$ and $dv = e^x\,dx$, then $du = dx$ and $v = e^x$.

$$\int x^3e^x\,dx = x^3e^x - 3x^2e^x + 6\left(xe^x - \int e^x\,dx\right)$$

$$= x^3e^x - 3x^2e^x + 6xe^x - 6e^x + C = e^x(x^3 - 3x^2 + 6x - 6) + C$$

17. Evaluate $\int x^3 \ln x \, dx$.

Solution:

Let $u = \ln x$ and $dv = x^3 \, dx$, then $du = (1/x) \, dx$ and $v = x^4/4$.

$$\int x^3 \ln x \, dx = \frac{x^4}{4} \ln x - \frac{1}{4} \int x^3 \, dx = \frac{x^4}{4} \ln x - \frac{x^4}{16} + C = \frac{x^4}{16}(4 \ln x - 1) + C$$

19. Evaluate $\int t \ln(t + 1) \, dt$.

Solution:

Let $u = \ln(t + 1)$ and $dv = t \, dt$, then $du = [1/(t + 1)] \, dt$ and $v = t^2/2$.

$$\int t \ln(t + 1) \, dt = \frac{t^2}{2} \ln(t + 1) - \frac{1}{2} \int \frac{t^2}{t + 1} \, dt$$

$$= \frac{t^2}{2} \ln(t + 1) - \frac{1}{2} \int \left(t - 1 + \frac{1}{t + 1} \right) dt$$

$$= \frac{t^2}{2} \ln(t + 1) - \frac{1}{2} \left[\frac{t^2}{2} - t + \ln(t + 1) \right] + C$$

$$= \frac{1}{4}[2(t^2 - 1) \ln(t + 1) + t(2 - t)] + C$$

21. Evaluate $\int x(\ln x)^2 dx$.

Solution:

Let $u = (\ln x)^2$ and $dv = x \, dx$, then $du = \frac{2 \ln x}{x} dx$ and $v = \frac{x^2}{2}$.

$$\int x(\ln x)^2 dx = \frac{x^2}{2}(\ln x)^2 - \int x \ln x \, dx$$

Let $u = \ln x$ and $v = x \, dx$, then $du = \frac{1}{x} dx$ and $v = \frac{x^2}{2}$.

$$\int x(\ln x)^2 dx = \frac{x^2}{2}(\ln x)^2 - \left[\frac{x^2}{2} \ln x - \int \frac{x}{2} dx \right]$$

$$= \frac{x^2}{2}(\ln x)^2 - \frac{x^2}{2} \ln x + \frac{x^2}{4} + C$$

23. Evaluate $\int \frac{(\ln x)^2}{x} \, dx$.

Solution:

$$\int \frac{(\ln x)^2}{x} \, dx = \int (\ln x)^2 \left(\frac{1}{x} \right) dx = \frac{(\ln x)^3}{3} + C$$

25. Evaluate $\int x\sqrt{x-1}\,dx$.

Solution:

Let $u = x$ and $dv = \sqrt{x-1}\,dx$, then $du = dx$ and $v = \frac{2}{3}(x-1)^{3/2}$.

$$\int x\sqrt{x-1}\,dx = \frac{2}{3}x(x-1)^{3/2} - \frac{2}{3}\int (x-1)^{3/2}\,dx$$

$$= \frac{2}{3}x(x-1)^{3/2} - \frac{4}{15}(x-1)^{5/2} + C = \frac{2}{15}(x-1)^{3/2}(3x+2) + C$$

27. Evaluate $\int (x^2 - 1)e^x\,dx$.

Solution:

Let $u = x^2 - 1$ and $dv = e^x\,dx$, then $du = 2x\,dx$ and $v = e^x$.

$$\int (x^2 - 1)e^x\,dx = (x^2 - 1)e^x - 2\int xe^x\,dx$$

Let $u = x$ and $dv = e^x\,dx$, then $du = dx$ and $v = e^x$.

$$\int (x^2 - 1)e^x\,dx = (x^2 - 1)e^x - 2\left(xe^x - \int e^x\,dx \right)$$

$$= (x^2 - 1)e^x - 2xe^x + 2e^x + C$$

$$= e^x(x^2 - 2x + 1) + C$$

$$= (x-1)^2 e^x + C$$

29. Evaluate $\int \dfrac{xe^{2x}}{(2x+1)^2}\,dx$.

Solution:

Let $u = xe^{2x}$ and $dv = (2x+1)^{-2}\,dx$, then $du = e^{2x}(2x+1)\,dx$ and $v = -1/[2(2x+1)]$.

$$\int \frac{xe^{2x}}{(2x+1)^2}\,dx = -\frac{xe^{2x}}{2(2x+1)} + \frac{1}{2}\int e^{2x}\,dx$$

$$= -\frac{xe^{2x}}{2(2x+1)} + \frac{1}{4}e^{2x} + C$$

$$= \frac{e^{2x}}{4(2x+1)} + C$$

31. Evaluate $\displaystyle\int_0^1 x^2 e^x \, dx$.

Solution:

Let $u = x^2$ and $dv = e^x \, dx$, then $du = 2x \, dx$ and $v = e^x$.

$$\int_0^1 x^2 e^x \, dx = x^2 e^x \Big]_0^1 - 2\int_0^1 x e^x \, dx$$

Let $u = x$ and $dv = e^x \, dx$, then $du = dx$ and $v = e^x$.

$$\int_0^1 x^2 e^x \, dx = x^2 e^x \Big]_0^1 - 2\left(x e^x \Big]_0^1 - \int_0^1 e^x \, dx \right) = e - 2\left(e - e^x \Big]_0^1 \right)$$

$$= e - 2e + 2(e - 1)$$
$$= e - 2 \approx 0.718$$

33. Evaluate $\displaystyle\int_1^3 x^5 \ln x \, dx$.

Solution:

Let $u = \ln x$ and $dv = x^5 \, dx$, then $du = \dfrac{1}{x} \, dx$ and $v = \dfrac{x^6}{6}$.

$$\int_1^e x^5 \ln x \, dx = \frac{x^6}{6} \ln x \Big]_1^e - \int_1^e \frac{x^5}{6} \, dx$$

$$= \frac{e^6}{6} - \left[\frac{x^6}{36} \right]_1^e = \frac{e^6}{6} - \frac{e^6}{36} + \frac{1}{36} = \frac{5}{36} e^6 + \frac{1}{36}$$

$$\approx 56.060$$

35. Integrate the following (a) by parts, letting $dv = \sqrt{2x - 3}\,dx$, and (b) by substitution, letting $u = \sqrt{2x - 3}$.

$$\int 2x\sqrt{2x - 3}\,dx$$

Solution:

(a) Let $u = 2x$ and $dv = \sqrt{2x - 3}\,dx$, then $du = 2\,dx$ and $v = \frac{1}{3}(2x - 3)^{3/2}$.

$$\int 2x\sqrt{2x - 3}\,dx = \frac{2}{3}x(2x - 3)^{3/2} - \frac{2}{3}\int (2x - 3)^{3/2}\,dx$$

$$= \frac{2}{3}x(2x - 3)^{3/2} - \frac{2}{15}(2x - 3)^{5/2} + C$$

$$= \frac{2}{15}(2x - 3)^{3/2}(3x + 3) + C$$

$$= \frac{2}{5}(2x - 3)^{3/2}(x + 1) + C$$

(b) Let $u = \sqrt{2x - 3}$, then $x = (u^2 + 3)/2$ and $dx = u\,du$.

$$\int 2x\sqrt{2x - 3}\,dx = \int (u^2 + 3)u^2\,du$$

$$= \frac{u^5}{5} + u^3 + C$$

$$= \frac{u^3}{5}(u^2 + 5) + C$$

$$= \frac{2}{5}(2x - 3)^{3/2}(x + 1) + C$$

37. Integrate the following (a) by parts, letting $dv = 1/\sqrt{4+5x}\,dx$, and (b) by substitution, letting $u = \sqrt{4+5x}$.

$$\int \frac{x}{\sqrt{4+5x}}\,dx$$

Solution:

(a) Let $u = x$ and $dv = 1/\sqrt{4+5x}\,dx$, then $du = dx$ and $v = \frac{2}{5}\sqrt{4+5x}$.

$$\int \frac{x}{\sqrt{4+5x}}\,dx = \frac{2}{5}x\sqrt{4+5x} - \frac{2}{5}\int \sqrt{4+5x}\,dx$$

$$= \frac{2}{5}x\sqrt{4+5x} - \frac{4}{75}(4+5x)^{3/2} + C$$

$$= \frac{2}{75}\sqrt{4+5x}(5x-8) + C$$

(b) Let $u = \sqrt{4+5x}$, then $x = (u^2-4)/5$ and $dx = 2u/5\,du$.

$$\int \frac{x}{\sqrt{4+5x}}\,dx = \int \frac{(u^2-4)/5}{u}\left(\frac{2u}{5}\right)du$$

$$= \frac{2}{25}\int (u^2-4)\,du$$

$$= \frac{2}{25}\left(\frac{u^3}{3} - 4u\right) + C$$

$$= \frac{2}{75}\sqrt{4+5x}(5x-8) + C$$

39. Use integration by parts to verify the formula

$$\int x^n \ln x\,dx = \frac{x^{n+1}}{(n+1)^2}[-1 + (n+1)\ln x] + C, \quad n \neq -1.$$

Solution:

Let $u = \ln x$ and $dv = x^n\,dx$, then $du = 1/x\,dx$ and $v = x^{n+1}/(n+1)$.

$$\int x^n \ln x\,dx = \frac{x^{n+1}}{n+1}\ln x - \int \frac{1}{x}\cdot\frac{x^{n+1}}{n+1}\,dx = \frac{x^{n+1}}{n+1}\ln x - \frac{1}{n+1}\int x^n\,dx$$

$$= \frac{x^{n+1}}{n+1}\ln x - \frac{1}{n+1}\cdot\frac{x^{n+1}}{n+1} + C = \frac{x^{n+1}}{(n+1)^2}[-1 + (n+1)\ln x] + C$$

41. Evaluate $\int x^2 e^{5x}\, dx$. [Use Exercise 40.]

Solution:

Using $n = 2$ and $a = 5$, we have $\int x^2 e^{5x}\, dx = \dfrac{x^2 e^{5x}}{5} - \dfrac{2}{5}\int x e^{5x}\, dx$.

Now, using $n = 1$ and $a = 5$, we have the following.

$$\int x^2 e^{5x}\, dx = \frac{x^2 e^{5x}}{5} - \frac{2}{5}\left[\frac{x e^{5x}}{5} - \frac{1}{5}\int e^{5x}\, dx\right]$$

$$= \frac{x^2 e^{5x}}{5} - \frac{2x e^{5x}}{25} + \frac{2 e^{5x}}{125} + C$$

$$= \frac{e^{5x}}{125}(25x^2 - 10x + 2) + C$$

43. Evaluate $\int x^{-2} \ln x\, dx$.

Solution:

Using $n = -2$, Exercise 39 yields

$$\int x^{-2} \ln x\, dx = \frac{x^{-2+1}}{(-2+1)^2}[-1 + (-2+1)\ln x] + C$$

$$= \frac{1}{x}(-1 - \ln x) + C = -\frac{1}{x} - \frac{\ln x}{x} + C$$

45. Find the area of the region bounded by the graphs of $y = xe^{-x}$, $y = 0$, and $x = 4$.

Solution:

Letting $u = x$ and $dv = e^{-x}\, dx$, we have $du = dx$ and $v = -e^{-x}$, and the area is

$$A = \int_0^4 x e^{-x}\, dx$$

$$= -x e^{-x}\Big]_0^4 + \int_0^4 e^{-x}\, dx$$

$$= -4e^{-4} - \left[e^{-x}\right]_0^4$$

$$= -4e^{-4} - e^{-4} + 1$$

$$= 1 - 5e^{-4} \approx 0.908.$$

47. Given the region bounded by the graphs of $y = 2 \ln x$, $y = 0$, and $x = e$, find
(a) the area of the region.
(b) the volume of the solid generated by revolving the region about the x-axis.

Solution:

(a) Letting $u = 2 \ln x$ and $dv = dx$, we have $du = \dfrac{2}{x} dx$ and $v = x$.

$$\text{Area} = \int_1^e 2 \ln x \, dx = 2x \ln x \Big]_1^e - \int_1^e 2 dx$$

$$= 2e - \Big[2x \Big]_1^e = 2e - 2e + 2 = 2$$

(b) Letting $u = (2 \ln x)^2$ and $dv = dx$, we have $du = 8 \ln x \left(\dfrac{1}{x} \right) dx$ and $v = x$.

$$\text{Volume} = \pi \int_1^e (2 \ln x)^2 dx = \pi \left(\Big[x(2 \ln x)^2 \Big]_1^e - \int_1^e 8 \ln x \, dx \right)$$

$$= \pi \left(4e - \Big[8(x \ln x - x) \Big]_1^e \right)$$

$$= \pi (4e - [8]) = 4\pi (e - 2) \approx 9.026$$

49. Evaluate $\displaystyle\int_0^2 t^3 e^{-4t} dt$.

Solution:

$$\int_0^2 t^3 e^{-4t} dt = \frac{3}{128} - \frac{379}{128} e^{-8} \approx 0.022$$

51. Evaluate $\displaystyle\int_0^5 x^4 (25 - x^2)^{3/2} dx$.

Solution:

$$\int_0^5 x^4 (25 - x^2)^{3/2} dx = \frac{1{,}171{,}875}{256} \pi \approx 14{,}381{,}070$$

53. *Product Demand* The executive officers of a manufacturing company forecast that the demand for their product over the next 10 years will be approximated by the model $x = 500(20 + te^{-0.1t})$, $0 \leq t \leq 10$ where x is the number of units demanded and t is the time in years.

(a) Are the corporate officers forecasting an increase or decrease in demand over the next decade?

(b) If the model is correct, determine the total demand over the next 10 years.

(c) Find the average annual demand during the 10-year period.

Solution:

(a) $x = 500(20 + te^{-0.1t})$, $0 \leq t \leq 10$

$$\frac{dx}{dt} = 500(-0.1te^{-0.1t} + e^{-0.1t})$$

$$= 500e^{-0.1t}(-0.1t + 1)$$

On the interval $(0, 10)$, $dx/dt > 0$. Thus, x is increasing. The corporate officers are forecasting an increase in demand over the next decade.

(b) $\displaystyle\int_0^{10} 500(20 + te^{-0.1t})\, dt = 500\left[\int_0^{10} 20\, dt + \int_0^{10} te^{-0.1t}\, dt\right]$

$$= 500(200) + 500\int te^{-0.1t}\, dt$$

Let $u = t$ and $dv = e^{-0.1t}\, dt$, then $du = dt$ and $v = -10e^{-0.1t}$.

$$= 100,000 + 500\left[-10te^{-0.1t} + 10\int e^{-0.1t}\, dt\right]_0^{10}$$

$$= 100,000 + 500\left\{-100e^{-1} - \left[100e^{-0.1t}\right]_0^{10}\right\}$$

$$= 100,000 + 500[-100e^{-1} - 100e^{-1} + 100]$$

$$= 100,000 + 50,000(1 - 2e^{-1}) \approx 113,212 \text{ units}$$

(c) Average $= \dfrac{113,212}{10}$

$$\approx 11,321 \text{ per year}$$

55. *Learning Theory* A model for the ability M of a child to memorize, measured on a scale from 0 to 10, is given by $M = 1 + 1.6t \ln t$, $0 < t \le 4$, where t is the child's age in years. Find the average value of M (a) between the child's first and second birthdays, and (b) between the child's third and fourth birthdays.

Solution:

(a) Average $= \displaystyle\int_1^2 (1.6t \ln t + 1)\, dt = (0.8t^2 \ln t - 0.4t^2 + t) \Big]_1^2 = 3.2(\ln 2) - 0.2 \approx 2.0181$

(b) Average $= \displaystyle\int_3^4 (1.6t \ln t + 1)\, dt$

$$= (0.8t^2 \ln t - 0.4t^2 + t) \Big]_3^4$$

$$= 12.8(\ln 4) - 7.2(\ln 3) - 1.8 \approx 8.0346$$

57. Find the present value of the income $c = 5000$ over $t_1 = 4$ years at the given annual inflation rate $r = 5\%$.

Solution:

$$V = \int_0^{t_1} c(t)e^{-rt}\, dt = \int_0^4 5000 e^{-0.05t}\, dt$$

$$= \frac{5000}{-0.05} e^{-0.05t} \Big]_0^4 \approx \$18,126.92$$

59. Find the present value of the income $c = 150,000 + 2500t$ over $t_1 = 10$ years at the given annual inflation rate $r = 4\%$.

Solution:

$$V = \int_0^{t_1} c(t)e^{-rt} = \int_0^{10} (150,000 + 2500t)e^{-0.04t}\, dt$$

$$\approx \$1,332,474.72$$

61. Find the present value of income $c = 1000 + 50e^{t/2}$ over $t_1 = 4$ years at the given annual inflation rate of $r = 6\%$.

Solution:

$$V = \int_0^{t_1} c(t)e^{-rt}\, dt = \int_0^4 (1000 + 50e^{t/2})e^{-0.06t}\, dt \approx \$4103.07.$$

63. *Present Value* A company expects its income c during the next 4 years to be modeled by

$$c = 150,000 + 75,000t$$

(a) Find the actual income for the business over the 4 years.

(b) Assuming an annual inflation rate of 4%, what is the present value of this income?

Solution:

$$c = 150,000 + 75,000t$$

(a) $\displaystyle\int_0^4 (150,000 + 75,000t)\,dt = 150,000t + 37,500t^2 \Big]_0^4$

$$= \$1,200,000$$

(b) $\displaystyle V = \int_0^{t_1} c(t)e^{-rt}\,dt = \int_0^4 (150,000 + 75,000t)e^{-0.04t}\,dt$

$$\approx \$1,094,142.26$$

65. Use the Midpoint Rule with $n = 10$ to approximate

$$\int_1^4 \frac{4}{\sqrt{x} + \sqrt[3]{x}}\,dx.$$

Solution:

$$\int_1^4 \frac{4}{\sqrt{x} + \sqrt[3]{x}}\,dx = 4\int_1^4 \frac{1}{\sqrt{x} + \sqrt[3]{x}}\,dx$$

$$\approx 4\left(\frac{4-1}{10}\right)\left[f\left(\frac{23}{20}\right) + f\left(\frac{29}{20}\right) + f\left(\frac{35}{20}\right) + f\left(\frac{41}{20}\right)\right.$$

$$+ f\left(\frac{47}{20}\right) + f\left(\frac{53}{20}\right)$$

$$+ f\left(\frac{59}{20}\right) + f\left(\frac{65}{20}\right)$$

$$\left. + f\left(\frac{71}{20}\right) + f\left(\frac{77}{20}\right)\right] \approx 4.254$$

67. Find the future value of the income given by $f(t) = 3000$ over $t_1 = 10$ years at the annual rate of $r = 8\%$. If f represents an investment function over a period of t_1 years that is continuously invested at an annual interest rate of r (compounded continuously), then the **future value** of the investment is given by

$$\text{Future value} = e^{rt_1} \int_0^{t_1} f(t)e^{-rt}\, dt.$$

Solution:

$$\text{Future value} = e^{rt_1} \int_0^{t_1} f(t)e^{-rt}\, dt = e^{(0.08)10} \int_0^{10} 3000 e^{-0.08t}\, dt$$

$$= e^{0.8} \left[\frac{3000}{-0.08} e^{-0.08t} \right]_0^{10} \approx 45{,}957.78$$

69. *College Expenses* In 1993, the total cost to attend Notre Dame University for 1 year was estimated to be $19,937. If your grandparents had continuously invested in a college fund according to the model

$$f(t) = 250t$$

for 18 years, at an annual interest rate of 10%, would the fund have grown enough to allow you to cover 4 years of expenses at Notre Dame?

Solution:

$$\text{Future value} = e^{rt_1} \int_0^{t_1} f(t)e^{-rt}\, dt = e^{(0.1)18} \int_0^{18} (250t)e^{-0.1t}\, dt$$

$$\approx \$81{,}241.19$$

Four years at Notre Dame costs $(4)(19{,}937) = \$79{,}748$, so there would be enough money.

Section 6.3   Partial Fractions and Logistics Growth

1. Write $\dfrac{2(x+20)}{x^2-25}$ as a sum of partial fractions.

Solution:

$$\frac{2x+40}{(x-5)(x+5)} = \frac{A}{x-5} + \frac{B}{x+5}$$

Basic equation: $2x + 40 = A(x+5) + B(x-5)$

When $x = 5$: $50 = 10A$, $A = 5$.

When $x = -5$: $30 = -10B$, $B = -3$.

$$\frac{2(x+20)}{x^2-25} = \frac{5}{x-5} - \frac{3}{x+5}$$

3. Write $\dfrac{8x+3}{x^2-3x}$ as a sum of partial fractions.

Solution:

$$\frac{8x+3}{x(x-3)} = \frac{A}{x} + \frac{B}{x-3}$$

Basic equation: $8x + 3 = A(x-3) + Bx$

When $x = 0$: $3 = -3A$, $A = -1$.

When $x = 3$: $27 = 3B$, $B = 9$.

$$\frac{8x+3}{x^2-3x} = \frac{9}{x-3} - \frac{1}{x}$$

5. Write $\dfrac{4x-13}{x^2-3x-10}$ as a sum of partial fractions.

Solution:

$$\frac{4x-13}{(x-5)(x+2)} = \frac{A}{x-5} + \frac{B}{x+2}$$

Basic equation: $4x - 13 = A(x+2) + B(x-5)$

When $x = 5$: $7 = 7A$, $A = 1$.

When $x = -2$: $-21 = -7B$, $B = 3$.

$$\frac{4x-13}{x^2-3x-10} = \frac{1}{x-5} + \frac{3}{x+2}$$

7. Write $\dfrac{3x^2-2x-5}{x^3+x^2}$ as a sum of partial fractions.

Solution:

$$\frac{3x^2-2x-5}{x^2(x+1)} = \frac{A}{x} + \frac{B}{x^2} + \frac{C}{x+1}$$

Basic equation: $3x^2 - 2x - 5 = Ax(x+1) + B(x+1) + Cx^2$

When $x = 0$: $-5 = B$

When $x = 1$: $0 = C$

When $x = 1$: $-4 = 2A - 10 \Rightarrow A = 3$

$$\frac{3x^2-2x-5}{x^2(x+1)} = \frac{3}{x} - \frac{5}{x^2}$$

9. Write $\dfrac{x+1}{3(x-2)^2}$ as a sum of partial fractions.

Solution:

$$\frac{1}{3}\left[\frac{x+1}{(x-2)^2}\right] = \frac{1}{3}\left[\frac{A}{x-2} + \frac{B}{(x-2)^2}\right]$$

Basic equation: $x+1 = A(x-2) + B$

When $x = 2$: $3 = B$.

When $x = 3$: $4 = A + B \Rightarrow A = 1$.

$$\frac{x+1}{3(x-2)^2} = \frac{1}{3}\left[\frac{1}{x-2} + \frac{3}{(x-2)^2}\right] = \frac{1}{3(x-2)} + \frac{1}{(x-2)^2}$$

11. Write $\dfrac{8x^2+15x+9}{(x+1)^3}$ as a sum of partial fractions.

Solution:

$$\frac{8x^2+15x+9}{(x+1)^3} = \frac{A}{x+1} + \frac{B}{(x+1)^2} + \frac{C}{(x+1)^3}$$

Basic equation: $8x^2+15x+9 = A(x+1)^2+B(x+1)+C = Ax^2+(2A+B)x+(A+B+C)$

Therefore, $A = 8$, $2A + B = 15$, and $A + B + C = 9$. Solving these equations yields $A = 8$, $B = -1$, and $C = 2$.

$$\frac{8x^2+15x+9}{(x+1)^3} = \frac{8}{x+1} - \frac{1}{(x+1)^2} + \frac{2}{(x+1)^3}$$

13. Find $\displaystyle\int \frac{1}{x^2-1}\,dx$.

Solution:

$$\frac{1}{(x+1)(x-1)} = \frac{A}{x+1} + \frac{B}{x-1}$$

Basic equation: $1 = A(x-1) + B(x+1)$

When $x = -1$: $1 = -2A$, $A = -\frac{1}{2}$.

When $x = 1$: $1 = 2B$, $B = \frac{1}{2}$.

$$\int \frac{1}{x^2-1}\,dx = \frac{-1}{2}\int \frac{1}{x+1}\,dx + \frac{1}{2}\int \frac{1}{x-1}\,dx$$

$$= \frac{-1}{2}\ln|x+1| + \frac{1}{2}\ln|x-1| + C$$

$$= \frac{1}{2}\ln\left|\frac{x-1}{x+1}\right| + C$$

15. Find $\displaystyle\int \frac{-2}{x^2 - 16}\,dx.$

Solution:

$$\frac{-2}{(x+4)(x-4)} = \frac{A}{x+4} + \frac{B}{x-4}$$

Basic equation: $-2 = A(x-4) + B(x+4)$

When $x = -4$: $-2 = -8A$, $A = \frac{1}{4}$.

When $x = 4$: $-2 = 8B$, $B = -\frac{1}{4}$.

$$\int \frac{-2}{x^2 - 16}\,dx = \frac{1}{4}\int \frac{1}{x+4}\,dx - \frac{1}{4}\int \frac{1}{x-4}\,dx$$

$$= \frac{1}{4}\ln|x+4| - \frac{1}{4}\ln|x-4| + C$$

$$= \frac{1}{4}\ln\left|\frac{x+4}{x-4}\right| + C$$

17. Find $\displaystyle\int \frac{1}{3x^2 - x}\,dx.$

Solution:

$$\frac{1}{3x^2 - x} = \frac{1}{x(3x-1)} = \frac{A}{x} + \frac{B}{3x-1}$$

Basic equation: $1 = A(3x-1) + Bx$

When $x = 0: 1 = -A \Rightarrow A = -1$

When $x = \frac{1}{3}: 1 = B\left(\frac{1}{3}\right) \Rightarrow B = 3$

$$\int \frac{1}{3x^2 - x}\,dx = \int \frac{-1}{x}\,dx + \int \frac{3}{3x-1}\,dx = -\ln|x| + \ln|3x-1| + C$$

19. Find $\displaystyle\int \frac{1}{2x^2 + x}\,dx.$

Solution:

$$\frac{1}{x(2x+1)} = \frac{A}{x} + \frac{B}{2x+1}$$

Basic equation: $1 = A(2x+1) + Bx$

When $x = 0$: $A = 1$.

When $x = -\frac{1}{2}$: $B = -2$.

$$\int \frac{1}{2x^2 + x}\,dx = \int \frac{1}{x}\,dx - \int \frac{2}{2x+1}\,dx = \ln|x| - \ln|2x+1| + C = \ln\left|\frac{x}{2x+1}\right| + C$$

21. Find $\displaystyle\int \frac{3}{x^2+x-2}\,dx$.

Solution:

$$\frac{3}{(x-1)(x+2)} = \frac{A}{x-1} + \frac{B}{x+2}$$

Basic equation: $3 = A(x+2) + B(x-1)$

When $x = 1$: $3 = 3A$, $A = 1$.

When $x = -2$: $3 = -3B$, $B = -1$.

$$\int \frac{3}{x^2+x-2}\,dx = \int \frac{1}{x-1}\,dx - \int \frac{1}{x+2}\,dx$$

$$= \ln|x-1| - \ln|x+2| + C = \ln\left|\frac{x-1}{x+2}\right| + C$$

23. Find $\displaystyle\int \frac{5-x}{2x^2+x-1}\,dx$.

Solution:

$$\frac{5-x}{(2x-1)(x+1)} = \frac{A}{2x-1} + \frac{B}{x+1}$$

Basic equation: $5 - x = A(x+1) + B(2x-1)$

When $x = \frac{1}{2}$: $4.5 = 1.5A$, $A = 3$.

When $x = -1$: $6 = -3B$, $B = -2$.

$$\int \frac{5-x}{2x^2+x-1}\,dx = 3\int \frac{1}{2x-1}\,dx - 2\int \frac{1}{x+1}\,dx = \frac{3}{2}\ln|2x-1| - 2\ln|x+1| + C$$

25. Find $\displaystyle\int \frac{x^2+12x+12}{x^3-4x}\,dx$.

Solution:

$$\frac{x^2+12x+12}{x(x+2)(x-2)} = \frac{A}{x} + \frac{B}{x+2} + \frac{C}{x-2}$$

Basic equation: $x^2 + 12x + 12 = A(x+2)(x-2) + Bx(x-2) + Cx(x+2)$

When $x = 0$: $12 = -4A$, $A = -3$.

When $x = -2$: $-8 = 8B$, $B = -1$.

When $x = 2$: $40 = 8C$, $C = 5$.

$$\int \frac{x^2+12x+12}{x^3-4x}\,dx = 5\int \frac{1}{x-2}\,dx - \int \frac{1}{x+2}\,dx - 3\int \frac{1}{x}\,dx$$

$$= 5\ln|x-2| - \ln|x+2| - 3\ln|x| + C$$

27. Find $\displaystyle\int \frac{x+2}{x^2-4x}\,dx$.

Solution:

$$\frac{x+2}{x(x-4)} = \frac{A}{x-4} + \frac{B}{x}$$

Basic equation: $x+2 = Ax + B(x-4)$

When $x = 4$: $6 = 4A$, $A = \frac{3}{2}$.

When $x = 0$: $2 = -4B$, $B = -\frac{1}{2}$.

$$\int \frac{x+2}{x^2-4x}\,dx = \frac{1}{2}\left[3\int\frac{1}{x-4}\,dx - \int\frac{1}{x}\,dx\right] = \frac{1}{2}[3\ln|x-4| - \ln|x|] + C$$

29. Find $\displaystyle\int \frac{4-3x}{(x-1)^2}\,dx$.

Solution:

$$\frac{4-3x}{(x-1)^2} = \frac{A}{x-1} + \frac{B}{(x-1)^2}$$

Basic equation: $4 - 3x = A(x-1) + B$

When $x = 1$: $1 = B$

When $x = 0$: $4 = -A + 1 \Rightarrow A = -3$

$$\int \frac{4-3x}{(x-1)^2}\,dx = \int\frac{-3}{x-1}\,dx + \int\frac{1}{(x-1)^2}\,dx = -3\ln|x-1| - \frac{1}{x-1} + C$$

31. Find $\displaystyle\int \frac{4x^2-1}{2x(x^2+2x+1)}\,dx$.

Solution:

$$\frac{4x^2-1}{2x(x+1)^2} = \frac{A}{2x} + \frac{B}{x+1} + \frac{C}{(x+1)^2}$$

Basic equation: $4x^2 - 1 = A(x+1)^2 + B(2x)(x+1) + C(2x)$

$$= (A+2B)x^2 + (2A+2B+2C)x + A$$

Therefore, $A+2B = 4$, $2A+2B+2C = 0$, and $A = -1$.

Solving these equations we get $A = -1$, $B = \frac{5}{2}$, and $C = -\frac{3}{2}$.

$$\int \frac{4x^2-1}{2x(x^2+2x+1)}\,dx = \frac{-1}{2}\int\frac{1}{x}\,dx + \frac{5}{2}\int\frac{1}{x+1}\,dx - \frac{3}{2}\int\frac{1}{(x+1)^2}\,dx$$

$$= \frac{1}{2}\left[5\ln|x+1| - \ln|x| + \frac{3}{x+1}\right] + C$$

33. Evaluate $\displaystyle\int_4^5 \frac{1}{9-x^2}\,dx$.

Solution:

$$\frac{1}{9-x^2} = \frac{-1}{(x-3)(x+3)} = \frac{A}{x-3} + \frac{B}{x+3}$$

Basic equation: $-1 = A(x+3) + B)(x-3)$

When $x = 3$: $-1 = 6A \Rightarrow A = -\dfrac{1}{6}$

When $x = -3$: $-1 = -6B \Rightarrow B = \dfrac{1}{6}$

$$\int_4^5 \frac{1}{9-x^2}\,dx = \int_4^5 \frac{-\frac{1}{6}}{x-3}\,dx + \int_4^5 \frac{\frac{1}{6}}{x+3}\,dx$$

$$= \frac{1}{6}\Big[-\ln(x-3) + \ln(x+3)\Big]_4^5 = \frac{1}{6}[-\ln 2 + \ln 8 - \ln 7]$$

$$= \frac{1}{6}\ln\frac{4}{7} \approx -0.093$$

35. Evaluate $\displaystyle\int_1^5 \frac{x-1}{x^2(x+1)}\,dx$.

Solution:

$$\frac{x-1}{x^2(x+1)} = \frac{A}{x} + \frac{B}{x^2} + \frac{C}{x+1}$$

Basic equation: $x - 1 = Ax(x+1) + B(x+1) + Cx^2$

When $x = 0$: $B = -1$.

When $x = -1$: $C = -2$.

When $x = 1$: $0 = 2A + 2B + C$, $0 = 2A - 4$, $A = 2$.

$$\int_1^5 \frac{x-1}{x^2(x+1)}\,dx = 2\int_1^5 \frac{1}{x}\,dx - \int_1^5 \frac{1}{x^2}\,dx - 2\int_1^5 \frac{1}{x+1}\,dx$$

$$= \left[2\ln|x| + \frac{1}{x} - 2\ln|x+1|\right]_1^5 = \left[2\ln\left|\frac{x}{x+1}\right| + \frac{1}{x}\right]_1^5$$

$$= 2\ln\left(\frac{5}{3}\right) - \frac{4}{5} \approx 0.222$$

37. Evaluate $\displaystyle\int_0^1 \frac{x^3}{x^2-2}\,dx$.

Solution:

$$\frac{x^3}{x^2-2} = x + \frac{2x}{x^2-2}$$

$$\int_0^1 \left(x + \frac{2x}{x^2-2}\right)dx = \left[\frac{x^2}{2} + \ln|x^2-2|\right]_0^1 = \frac{1}{2} - \ln 2 \approx -0.193$$

39. Evaluate $\displaystyle\int_1^2 \frac{x^3 - 2x^2 + 1}{x^2 - 3x}\,dx$

Solution:

$$\frac{x^3 - 2x^2 + 1}{x^2 - 3x} = x + 1 + \frac{3x + 1}{x^2 - 3x}$$

$$\frac{3x + 1}{x^2 - 3x} = \frac{A}{x} + \frac{B}{x - 3}$$

Basic equation: $3x + 1 = A(x - 3) + Bx$

When $x = 0$ $1 = -3A \Rightarrow A = -\dfrac{1}{3}$

When $x = 3$ $10 = 3B \Rightarrow B = \dfrac{10}{3}$

$$\int_1^2 \frac{x^3 - 2x^2 + 1}{x^2 - 3x}\,dx = \int_1^2 \left(x + 1 - \frac{1}{3}\cdot\frac{1}{x} + \frac{10}{3}\cdot\frac{1}{x - 3} \right)dx$$

$$= \left[\frac{x^2}{2} + x - \frac{1}{3}\ln x + \frac{10}{3}\ln |x - 3| \right]_1^2$$

$$= \left(4 - \frac{1}{3}\ln 2 \right) - \left(\frac{3}{2} + \frac{10}{3}\ln 2 \right) = \frac{5}{2} - \frac{11}{3}\ln 2 \approx -0.042$$

41. Find by substitution $\displaystyle\int \frac{e^x}{(e^x - 1)(e^x + 4)}\,dx, u = e^x.$

Solution:

Let $u = e^x$, then $du = e^x\,dx$.

$$\int \frac{e^x}{(e^x - 1)(e^x + 4)}\,dx = \int \frac{1}{(u - 1)(u + 4)}\,du$$

$$= \frac{1}{5}\left[\int \frac{1}{u - 1}\,du - \int \frac{1}{u + 4}\,du \right]$$

$$= \frac{1}{5}\ln\left| \frac{u - 1}{u + 4} \right| + C = \frac{1}{5}\ln\left| \frac{e^x - 1}{e^x + 4} \right| + C$$

43. Find by substitution $\displaystyle \int \frac{1}{x\sqrt{4+x^2}}\,dx,\ u = \sqrt{4+x^2}$.

Solution:

Let $u = \sqrt{4+x^2}$, then $x^2 = u^2 - 4$ and $x\,dx = u\,du$.

$$\int \frac{1}{x\sqrt{4+x^2}}\,dx = \int \frac{x}{x^2\sqrt{4+x^2}}\,dx$$

$$= \int \frac{1}{(u^2-4)u}(u)\,du$$

$$= \int \frac{1}{u^2-4}\,du$$

$$= \frac{1}{4}\int \left(\frac{-1}{u+2} + \frac{1}{u-2}\right) du$$

$$= \frac{1}{4}(\ln|u-2| - \ln|u+2|) + C$$

$$= \frac{1}{4}\ln\left|\frac{u-2}{u+2}\right| + C$$

$$= \frac{1}{4}\ln\left|\frac{\sqrt{4+x^2}-2}{\sqrt{4+x^2}+2}\right| + C$$

45. Find by substitution $\displaystyle \int \frac{1}{\sqrt{3x}(\sqrt{3x}+2)^2}\,dx,\ u = \sqrt{3x}$.

Solution:

Let $u = \sqrt{3x}$, the $u^2 = 3x$ and $2u\,du = 3\,dx$.

$$\int \frac{1}{\sqrt{3x}(\sqrt{3x}2)^2}\,dx = \int \frac{\frac{2}{3}u}{u(u+2)^2}\,du = \frac{2}{3}\int (u+2)^{-2}\,du$$

$$= \frac{2}{3}\frac{-1}{u+2} + C = \frac{-2}{3\sqrt{3x}+2)} + C$$

47. Find the area of the shaded region.

$$y = \frac{14}{16 - x^2}$$

Solution:

To find the limits of integration, solve

$$2 = \frac{14}{16 - x^2}$$

$$32 - 2x^2 = 14$$

$$18 = 2x^2$$

$$x = \pm 3$$

$$A = \int_{-3}^{3} \left(2 - \frac{14}{16 - x^2} \right) dx = \int_{-3}^{3} \left(2 - \frac{7}{4} \cdot \frac{1}{x + 4} + \frac{7}{4} \cdot \frac{1}{x - 4} \right) dx$$

$$= \left[2x - \frac{7}{4} \ln |x + 4| + \frac{7}{4} \ln |x - 4| \right]_{-3}^{3}$$

$$= \left(6 - \frac{7}{4} \ln 7 \right) - \left(-6 + \frac{7}{4} \ln 7 \right) = 12 - \frac{7}{2} \ln 7 \approx 5.1893$$

49. Find the area of the shaded region.

$$y = \frac{x + 1}{x^2 - x}$$

Solution:

$$A = \int_{2}^{5} \frac{x + 1}{x^2 - x} dx = \int_{2}^{5} \left(-\frac{1}{x} + \frac{2}{x - 1} \right) dx$$

$$= \left[-\ln x + 2 \ln(x - 1) \right]_{2}^{5} = (-\ln 5 + 2 \ln 4) - (-\ln 2)$$

$$= 5 \ln 2 - \ln 5 \approx 1.8563$$

51. Write the ration expression $\dfrac{1}{a^2 - x^2}$ as a sum of partial fractions. Check your results algebraically. Then assign a value to the constant a to check the results graphically.

$$\int \frac{1}{a^2 - x^2} dx = \frac{1}{2a} \ln \left| \frac{a + x}{a - x} \right| + C.$$

Solution:

$$\frac{1}{a^2 - x^2} = \frac{1}{(a + x)(a - x)} = \frac{A}{a + x} + \frac{B}{a - x} = \frac{1}{2a} \left(\frac{1}{a + x} + \frac{1}{a - x} \right)$$

53. Write the rational expression $\dfrac{1}{x(a-x)}$ as a sum of partial fractions. Check your results algebraically. Then assign a value to the constant a to check the results graphically.

Solution:

$$\frac{1}{x(a-x)} = \frac{A}{x} + \frac{B}{a-x}$$

Basic equation: $1 = A(a-x) + Bx$

When $x = a : 1 = Ba \Rightarrow B = \dfrac{1}{a}$

When $x = 0 : 1 = Aa \Rightarrow A = \dfrac{1}{a}$

$$\frac{1}{x(a-x)} = \frac{1/a}{x} + \frac{1/a}{a-x}$$

55. Find the volume of the solid generated by revolving the region bounded by the graphs of
$y \quad = \quad 10/[x(x \quad + \quad 10)]$,
$y = 0, \quad x = 1$, and $x = 5$ about the x-axis.

Solution:

$$V = \pi \int_1^5 \left[\frac{10}{x(x+10)}\right]^2 dx = 100\pi \int_1^5 \frac{1}{x^2(x+10)^2}\, dx$$

Let $\dfrac{1}{x^2(x+10)^2} = \dfrac{A}{x} + \dfrac{B}{x^2} + \dfrac{C}{x+10} + \dfrac{D}{(x+10)^2}$.

Basic equation: $1 = Ax(x+10)^2 + B(x+10)^2 + Cx^2(x+10) + Dx^2$

When $x = 0 : \quad 1 = 100B \Rightarrow B = \frac{1}{100}$.

When $x = -10 : \quad 1 = 100D \Rightarrow D = \frac{1}{100}$.

When $x = 1 : \quad 1 = 121A + 121B + 11C + D$ $\Big\}$ $\quad A = -1/500$

When $x = -1 : 1 = -81A + 81B + 9C + D$ $\quad C = 1/500$

$$V = \pi \int_1^5 100 \left[\frac{-1/500}{x} + \frac{1/100}{x^2} + \frac{1/500}{x+10} + \frac{1/100}{(x+10)^2}\right] dx$$

$$= \pi \int_1^5 \left[-\frac{1}{5x} + \frac{1}{x^2} + \frac{1}{5(x+10)} + \frac{1}{(x+10)^2}\right] dx$$

$$= \pi \left[-\frac{1}{5}\ln|x| - \frac{1}{x} + \frac{1}{5}\ln|x+10| - \frac{1}{x+10}\right]_1^5$$

$$= \pi \left[\frac{1}{5}\ln\left|\frac{x+10}{x}\right| - \frac{2x+10}{x(x+10)}\right]_1^5$$

$$= \pi \left[\left(\frac{1}{5}\ln 3 - \frac{4}{15}\right) - \left(\frac{1}{5}\ln 11 - \frac{12}{11}\right)\right] \approx 1.773 \text{ cubic units}$$

57. Find the volume of the solid generated by revolving the region bounded by the graphs of
$y = \dfrac{2x}{x^3 - 4x}$, $x = 1$, $x = -1$, and $y = 0$ about the x-axis.

Solution:

$$V = \pi \int_{-1}^{1} \left(\frac{2x}{x^3 - 4x} \right)^2 dx$$

$$= \pi \int_{-1}^{1} \left(\frac{2}{(x-2)(x+2)} \right)^2 dx \quad \frac{4}{(x-2)(x+2)^2}$$

$$= \frac{A}{x-2} + \frac{B}{(x-2)^2} + \frac{C}{x+2} + \frac{D}{(x+2)^2} \; = \; \frac{4}{(x-2)^2(x+2)^2}$$

Basic equation: $4 = A(x-2)(x+2)^2 + B(x+2)^2 + C(x+2)(x-2)^2 + D(x-2)^2$

When $x = 2$: $4 = 16B \Rightarrow B = \dfrac{1}{4}$

When $x = -2$: $4 = 16D \Rightarrow D = \dfrac{1}{4}$

When $x = 0$: $4 = -8A + 4\left(\dfrac{1}{4}\right) + 8C + 4\left(\dfrac{1}{4}\right) \Rightarrow 1 = -4A + 4C$

When $x = 1$: $4 = -9A + 9\left(\dfrac{1}{4}\right) + 3C + \dfrac{1}{4} \Rightarrow 3 = -18A + 6C$

Solving for A and C, $A = -\dfrac{1}{8}$, $C = \dfrac{1}{8}$.

Hence,

$$V = \pi \int_{-1}^{1} \left(-\frac{1}{8} \cdot \frac{1}{x-2} + \frac{1}{4} \cdot \frac{1}{(x-2)^2} + \frac{1}{8} \cdot \frac{1}{x+2} + \frac{1}{4} \cdot \frac{1}{(x+2)^2} \right) dx$$

$$= \pi \left[-\frac{1}{8} \ln|x-2| - \frac{1}{4} \cdot \frac{1}{x-2} + \frac{1}{8} \ln|x+2| - \frac{1}{4} \cdot \frac{1}{x+2} \right]_{-1}^{1}$$

$$= \pi \left[\left(\frac{1}{4} + \frac{1}{8} \ln 3 - \frac{1}{12} \right) - \left(-\frac{1}{8} \ln 3 + \frac{1}{12} - \frac{1}{4} \right) \right]$$

$$= \pi \left[\frac{1}{3} + \frac{1}{4} \ln 3 \right] \approx 1.9100$$

59. *Population Growth* A conservation organization releases 100 animals of an endangered species into a game preserve. The organization believes that the preserve has a capacity of 1000 animals and that the growth of the herd will be logistic. That is, the size y of the herd will follow the equation

$$\int \frac{1}{y(1000 - y)} dy = \int k\, dt,$$

where t is measured in years. Find this logistic curve. (To solve for the constant of integration C and the proportionality constant k, assume that $y = 100$ when $t = 0$ and $y = 134$ when $t = 2$.) Sketch the graph of your solution.

Solution:

$$\frac{1}{y(1000 - y)} = \frac{A}{y} + \frac{B}{1000 - y}$$

Basic equation: $1 = A(1000 - y) + By$

When $y = 0$: $1 = 1000A$, $A = \dfrac{1}{1000}$.

When $y = 1000$: $1 = 1000B$, $B = \dfrac{1}{1000}$.

$$\int \frac{1}{y(1000 - y)}\, dy = \int k\, dt$$

$$\frac{1}{1000} \int \left(\frac{1}{y} + \frac{1}{1000 - y} \right) dy = \int k\, dt$$

$$\ln |y| - \ln |1000 - y| = 1000(kt + C_1)$$

$$\ln \left| \frac{y}{1000 - y} \right| = 1000(kt + C_1)$$

$$\frac{y}{1000 - y} = e^{1000(kt + C_1)} = e^{1000C_1} e^{1000kt}$$

$$\frac{y}{1000 - y} = Ce^{1000kt}$$

When $t = 0$, $y = 100$: $\dfrac{1}{9} = C$, $\dfrac{y}{1000 - y} = \dfrac{1}{9} e^{1000kt}$.

When $t = 2$, $y = 134$: $\dfrac{67}{433} = \dfrac{1}{9} e^{2000k}$, $\ln \dfrac{603}{433} = 2000k$, $k = \dfrac{1}{2000} \ln \dfrac{603}{433}$.

Thus, $\dfrac{y}{1000 - y} = \dfrac{1}{9} e^{(1/2) \ln(603/433)t}$. Solving for y yields

$$9y \approx e^{0.1656t}(1000 - y)$$

$$y(9 + e^{0.1656t}) = 1000 e^{0.1656t}$$

$$y = \frac{1000 e^{0.1656t}}{e^{0.1656t} + 9} = \frac{1000}{1 + 9e^{-0.1656t}}.$$

61. *Marketing* After test-marketing a new menu item, a fast-food restaurant predicts that sales of the new item will grow according to the model

$$\frac{dS}{dt} = \frac{2t}{(t+4)^2},$$

where t is the time in weeks and S is the sales in thousands of dollars. Find the sales of the menu item at 10 weeks.

Solution:

$$\frac{dS}{dt} = \frac{2t}{(t+4)^2}$$

$$\frac{2t}{(t+4)^2} = \frac{A}{t+4} + \frac{B}{(t+4)^2}$$

Basic equation: $2t = A(t+4) + B$

When $t = -4: -8 = B$

When $t = 0: 0 = 4A - 8 \Rightarrow A = 2$

$$S = \int \frac{2t}{(t+4)^2} dt = \int \left(\frac{2}{t+4} - \frac{8}{(t+4)^2} \right) dt = 2\ln(t+4) + \frac{8}{t+4} + C$$

When $t = 0$, $S = 0 \Rightarrow 0 = 2\ln 4 + 2 + C \Rightarrow C \approx -4.77259$

When $t = 10$, $S \approx 2\ln(14) + \frac{8}{14} - 4.77259 \approx 1.077$ thousand

63. *GMAT* The number of people between 1982 and 1992 who took the Graduate Management Admission Test (GMAT) each year can be modeled by

$$N = 242t^2 - 17{,}922t - 18{,}164$$

where t is the time in years, with $t = 0$ corresponding to the year beginning September 1, 1982, and N is the number of test-takers in thousands. Find the total number of people who took the test between September 1, 1983 and August 31, 1990.

Solution:

$$\int_1^8 N(t)\,dt = \int_1^8 \frac{242t^2 - 17{,}922t - 18{,}164}{4t^2 - 96t - 100}\,dt$$

$$= \int_1^8 \left(\frac{121}{2} - 6057\frac{1}{2t-5} \right) dt$$

$$= \left[\frac{121}{2}t - \frac{6057}{2} \ln|2t-5| \right]_1^8 \approx 1467.85 \text{ thousand}$$

Section 6.4   Integration Tables and Completing the Square

1. Find $\displaystyle\int \frac{x}{(2+3x)^2}\,dx$ using Formula 4.

Solution:

Formula 4: $u = x, \quad du = dx, \quad a = 2, \quad b = 3$

$$\int \frac{x}{(2+3x)^2}\,dx = \frac{1}{9}\left[\frac{2}{2+3x} + \ln|2+3x|\right] + C$$

3. Find $\displaystyle\int \frac{x}{\sqrt{2+3x}}\,dx$ using Formula 19.

Solution:

Formula 19: $u = x, \quad du = dx, \quad a = 2, \quad b = 3$

$$\int \frac{x}{\sqrt{2+3x}}\,dx = \frac{-2(4-3x)}{27}\sqrt{2+3x} + C = \frac{2(3x-4)}{27}\sqrt{2+3x} + C$$

5. Find $\displaystyle\int \frac{2x}{\sqrt{x^4-9}}\,dx$ using Formula 25.

Solution:

Formula 25: $u = x^2, \quad du = 2x\,dx, \quad a = 3$

$$\int \frac{2x}{\sqrt{x^4-9}}\,dx = \ln|x^2 + \sqrt{x^4-9}| + C$$

7. Find $\displaystyle\int x^3 e^{x^2}\,dx$ using Formula 35.

Solution:

Formula 35: $u = x^2, \quad du = 2x\,dx$

$$\int x^3 e^{x^2}\,dx = \frac{1}{2}\int x^2 e^{x^2} 2x\,dx = \frac{1}{2}(x^2 - 1)e^{x^2} + C$$

9. Find $\displaystyle\int x\ln(x^2+1)\,dx$ using Formula 39.

Solution:

Formula 39: $u = x^2 + 1, \quad du = 2x\,dx$

$$\int x\ln(x^2+1)\,dx = \frac{1}{2}\int \ln(x^2+1)(2x)\,dx = \frac{1}{2}(x^2+1)[-1+\ln(x^2+1)] + C$$

11. Find $\displaystyle\int \frac{1}{x(1+x)}\,dx$.

Solution:

Formula 10: $u = x, \quad du = dx, \quad a = b = 1$

$$\int \frac{1}{x(1+x)}\,dx = \ln\left|\frac{x}{1+x}\right| + C$$

13. Find $\displaystyle\int \frac{1}{x\sqrt{x^2+9}}\,dx$.

Solution:

Formula 26: $u = x, \quad du = dx, \quad a = 3$

$$\int \frac{1}{x\sqrt{x^2+9}}\,dx = -\frac{1}{3}\ln\left|\frac{1+\sqrt{x^2+1}}{x}\right| + C$$

15. Find $\displaystyle\int \frac{1}{x\sqrt{4-x^2}}\,dx$.

Solution:

Formula 32: $u = x, \quad du = dx, \quad a = 2$

$$\int \frac{1}{x\sqrt{4-x^2}}\,dx = -\frac{1}{2}\ln\left|\frac{2+\sqrt{4-x^2}}{x}\right| + C$$

17. Find $\displaystyle\int x\ln x\,dx$.

Solution:

Formula 40: $u = x, \quad du = dx$

$$\int x\ln x\,dx = \frac{x^2}{4}(-1+2\ln x) + C$$

19. Find $\displaystyle\int \frac{6x}{1+e^{3x^2}}\,dx$.

Solution:

Formula 37: $u = 3x^2 \quad du = 6x\,dx$

$$\int \frac{6x}{1+e^{3x^2}}\,dx = 3x^2 - \ln(1+e^{3x^2}) + C$$

21. Find $\int x\sqrt{x^4 - 9}\,dx$.

Solution:

Formula 21: $u = x^2$, $du = 2x\,dx$, $a = 3$

$$\int x\sqrt{x^4 - 9}\,dx = \frac{1}{2}\int \sqrt{(x^2)^2 - 3^2}\,(2x)\,dx$$

$$= \frac{1}{4}(x^2\sqrt{x^4 - 9} - 9\ln|x^2 + \sqrt{x^4 - 9}|) + C$$

23. Find $\int \frac{t^2}{(2 + 3t)^3}\,dt$.

Solution:

Formula 8: $u = t$, $du = dt$, $a = 2$, $b = 3$

$$\int \frac{t^2}{(2 + 3t)^3}\,dt = \frac{1}{27}\left[\frac{4}{2 + 3t} - \frac{4}{2(2 + 3t)^2} + \ln|2 + 3t|\right] + C$$

25. Find $\int \frac{s}{s^2\sqrt{3 + s}}\,ds$.

Solution:

Formula 15: $u = s$, $du = ds$, $a = 3$, $b = 1$

$$\int \frac{s}{s^2\sqrt{3 + s}}\,ds = \int \frac{1}{s\sqrt{3 + s}}\,ds = \frac{1}{\sqrt{3}}\ln\left|\frac{\sqrt{3 + s} - \sqrt{3}}{\sqrt{3 + s} + \sqrt{3}}\right| + C$$

27. Find $\int \frac{x^2}{(3 + 2x)^5}\,dx$.

Solution:

Formula 9: $u = x$, $du = dx$, $a = 3$, $b = 2$, $n = 5$

$$\int \frac{x^2}{(3 + 2x)^5}\,dx = \frac{1}{8}\left[\frac{-1}{(3 + 2x)^2} + \frac{6}{3(3 + 2x)^3} - \frac{9}{4(3 + 2x)^4}\right] + C$$

29. Find $\int \frac{1}{x^2\sqrt{1 - x^2}}\,dx$.

Solution:

Formula 23: $u = x$, $du = dx$, $a = 1$

$$\int \frac{1}{x^2\sqrt{1 - x^2}}\,dx = -\frac{\sqrt{1 - x^2}}{x} + C$$

31. Find $\displaystyle\int x^2 \ln x \, dx$.

Solution:

Formula 41: $u = x, \quad du = dx, \quad n = 2$

$$\int x^2 \ln x \, dx = \frac{x^3}{9}(-1 + 3 \ln x) + C$$

33. Find $\displaystyle\int \frac{x^2}{(3x-5)^2} \, dx$.

Solution:

Formula 7: $u = x, \quad du = dx, \quad a = -5, \quad b = 3$

$$\int \frac{x^2}{(3x-5)^2} \, dx = \frac{1}{27}\left[3x - \frac{25}{3x-5} + 10 \ln|3x-5|\right] + C$$

35. Find $\displaystyle\int x^2\sqrt{x^2+4} \, dx$.

Solution:

Formula 22: $u = x, \quad du = dx, \quad a = 2$

$$\int x^2\sqrt{x^2+4} \, dx = \frac{1}{8}[x(2x^2+4)\sqrt{x^2+4} - 16\ln|x + \sqrt{x^2+4}|] + C$$

$$= \frac{1}{4}[x(x^2+2)\sqrt{x^2+4} - 8\ln|x + \sqrt{x^2+4}|] + C$$

37. Find $\displaystyle\int \frac{2}{1+e^{4x}} \, dx$.

Solution:

Formula 37: $u = 4x, \quad du = 4\,dx$

$$2\int \frac{1}{1+e^{4x}} \, dx = \frac{1}{2}\int \frac{4}{1+e^{4x}} dx = \frac{1}{2}[4x - \ln(1+e^{4x})] + C$$

39. Find $\displaystyle\int \frac{\ln x}{x(4+3\ln x)} \, dx$.

Solution:

Formula 3: $u = \ln x, \quad du = \frac{1}{x}\,dx, \quad a = 4, \quad b = 3$

$$\int \frac{\ln x}{x(4+3\ln x)} \, dx = \int \frac{\ln x}{4+3\ln x}\left(\frac{1}{x}dx\right) = \frac{1}{9}[3\ln x - 4\ln|4 + 3\ln x|] + C$$

41. Evaluate $\displaystyle\int_0^5 \frac{x}{\sqrt{5+2x}}dx.$

Solution:

Formula 19: $u = x,\ du = dx,\ a = 5,\ b = 2$

$$\int_0^5 \frac{x}{\sqrt{5+2x}}dx = \frac{-2(10-2x)}{12}\sqrt{5+2x}\,\Big]_0^5$$

$$= 0 + \frac{5}{3}\sqrt{5} = \frac{5\sqrt{5}}{3}$$

43. Evaluate $\displaystyle\int_0^4 \frac{6}{1+e^{0.5x}}\,dx.$

Solution:

Formula 38: $u = x,\ du = dx,\ n = 0.5$

$$6\int_0^4 \frac{1}{1+e^{0.5x}}\,dx = 6\left[x - \frac{1}{0.5}\ln(1+e^{0.5x})\right]_0^4$$

$$= 6[(4 - 2\ln(1+e^2)) - (0 - 2\ln 2)] \approx 6.795$$

45. Evaluate $\displaystyle\int x^2 e^x\,dx$ by (a) using the tables, and (b) integration by parts.

Solution:

(a) Formula 36: $u = x,\ du = dx,\ n = 2$

$$\int x^2 e^x\,dx = x^2 e^x - 2\int x e^x\,dx$$

Formula 35: $u = x,\ du = dx$

$$\int x^2 e^x\,dx = x^2 e^x - 2(x-1)e^x + C = e^x(x^2 - 2x + 2) + C$$

(b) Let $u = x^2$ and $dv = e^x\,dx$, then $du = 2x\,dx$ and $v = e^x$.

$$\int x^2 e^x\,dx = x^2 e^x - 2\int x e^x\,dx$$

Let $u = x$ and $dv = e^x\,dx$, then $du = dx$ and $v = e^x$.

$$\int x^2 e^x\,dx = x^2 e^x - 2\left[x e^x - \int e^x\,dx\right] = x^2 e^x - 2x e^x + 2e^x + C = e^x(x^2 - 2x + 2) + C$$

47. Evaluate $\int \dfrac{1}{x^2(x+1)}\,dx$ by (a) using the tables, and (b) partial fractions.

Solution:

Formula 12: $u = x$, $du = dx$, $a = 1$, $b = 1$

(a) $\displaystyle\int \frac{1}{x^2(x+1)}\,dx = -\left[\frac{1}{x} + \ln\left|\frac{x}{1+x}\right|\right] + C$

(b) $\dfrac{1}{x^2(x+1)} = \dfrac{A}{x} + \dfrac{B}{x^2} + \dfrac{C}{x+1}$

Basic equation: $1 = Ax(x+1) + B(x+1) + Cx^2$

When $x = 0$: $1 = B$.

When $x = -1$: $1 = C$.

When $x = 1$: $1 = 2A + 2B + C = 2A + 3 \Rightarrow A = -1$.

$$\int \frac{1}{x^2(x+1)}\,dx = \int\left[-\frac{1}{x} + \frac{1}{x^2} + \frac{1}{x+1}\right]dx = -\ln|x| - \frac{1}{x} + \ln|x+1| + C$$

$$= -\left[\frac{1}{x} + \ln|x| - \ln|x+1|\right] + C = -\left[\frac{1}{x} + \ln\left|\frac{x}{x+1}\right|\right] + C$$

49. Complete the square to express each polynomial as the sum or difference of squares.

(a) $x^2 + 6x$

(b) $x^2 - 8x + 9$

(c) $x^4 + 2x^2 - 5$

(d) $3 - 2x - x^2$

Solution:

(a) $x^2 + 6x = x^2 + 6x + 9 - 9 = (x+3)^2 - 9$

(b) $x^2 - 8x + 9 = x^2 - 8x + 16 - 16 + 9 = (x-4)^2 - 7$

(c) $x^4 + 2x^2 - 5 = x^4 + 2x^2 + 1 - 1 - 5 = (x^2+1)^2 - 6$

(d) $3 - 2x - x^2 = -(x^2 + 2x - 3) = -(x^2 + 2x + 1 - 1 - 3)$

$$= -[(x+1)^2 - 4] = 4 - (x+1)^2$$

51. Complete the square and then use integration tables to find the indefinite integral.

$$\int \frac{1}{x^2 + 6x - 8}\,dx$$

Solution:

Formula 29: $u = x + 3$, $du = dx$, $a = \sqrt{17}$

$$\int \frac{1}{x^2 + 6x - 8}\,dx = \int \frac{1}{(x+3)^2 - 17}\,dx = \frac{1}{2\sqrt{17}} \ln\left|\frac{(x+3) - \sqrt{17}}{(x+3) + \sqrt{17}}\right| + C$$

53. Complete the square and then use integration tables to find the indefinite integral.

$$\int \frac{1}{(x-1)\sqrt{x^2-2x+2}}\,dx.$$

Solution:

Formula 26: $u = x - 1$, $du = dx$, $a = 1$

$$\int \frac{1}{(x-1)\sqrt{x^2-2x+2}}\,dx = \int \frac{1}{(x-1)\sqrt{(x-1)^2+1}}\,dx$$

$$= -\ln\left|\frac{1+\sqrt{x^2-2x+2}}{x-1}\right| + C$$

55. Complete the square and then use integration tables to find the indefinite integral.

$$\int \frac{1}{2x^2-4x-6}\,dx.$$

Solution:

Formula 29: $u = x - 1$, $du = dx$, $a = 2$

$$\int \frac{1}{2x^2-4x-6}\,dx = \frac{1}{2}\int \frac{1}{(x-1)^2-4}\,dx = \frac{1}{8}\ln\left|\frac{x-3}{x+1}\right| + C$$

57. Complete the square and then use integration tables to find the indefinite integral.

$$\int \frac{x}{\sqrt{x^4+2x^2+2}}\,dx.$$

Solution:

Formula 25: $u = x^2 + 1$, $du = 2x\,dx$, $a = 1$

$$\int \frac{x}{\sqrt{x^4+2x^2+2}}\,dx = \int \frac{x}{\sqrt{(x^2+1)^2+1}}\,dx$$

$$= \frac{1}{2}\int \frac{2x}{\sqrt{(x^2+1)^2+1}}\,dx$$

$$= \frac{1}{2}\ln|x^2+1+\sqrt{x^4+2x^2+2}| + C$$

59. Find the area of the region bounded by the graphs of $y = x/\sqrt{x+1}$, $y = 0$, and $x = 8$.

Solution:

Formula 19: $u = x$, $du = dx$, $a = b = 1$

$$A = \int_0^8 \frac{x}{\sqrt{x+1}}\,dx = -\frac{2(2-x)}{3}\sqrt{x+1}\,\bigg]_0^8 = \frac{40}{3} \text{ square units}$$

61. *Population Growth* Find the average value of $N = 50/(1 + e^{4.8-1.9t})$ over the interval [3, 4], where N is the size of a population and t is the time in days.

Solution:

Formula 38: $u = 4.8 - 1.9t$, $du = -1.9dt$, $n = 1$ (or Formula 37)

$$\text{Average} = \int_3^4 \frac{50}{1 + e^{4.8-1.9t}} dt$$

$$= -\frac{50}{1.9} \int_3^4 \frac{-1.9}{1 + e^{4.8-1.9t}} dt = -\frac{50}{1.9}\left[4.8 - 1.9t - \ln(1 + e^{4.8-1.9t})\right]_3^4 \approx 42.58 \approx 43$$

63. *Revenue* The marginal revenue (in dollars per year) for a new product is modeled by

$$\frac{dR}{dt} = 10,000\left[1 - \frac{1}{(1 + 0.1t^2)^{1/2}}\right],$$

where t is the time in years. Estimate the total revenue from sales of the product over its first 2 years on the market.

Solution:

$$R = \int_0^2 10,000\left[1 - \frac{1}{(1 + 0.1t^2)^{1/2}}\right] dt$$

$$= 10,000t \Big]_0^2 - 10,000 \int_0^2 \frac{1}{(1 + 0.1t^2)^{1/2}} dt$$

Formula 25: $u = \sqrt{0.1}t$, $du = \sqrt{0.1}dt$, $a = 1$

$$R = 20,000 - \frac{10,000}{\sqrt{0.1}} \ln|\sqrt{0.1}t + \sqrt{0.1t^2 + 1}| \Big]_0^2 \approx \$1138.43$$

Section 6.5   Numerical Integration

1. Use the Trapezoidal Rule and Simpson's Rule to approximate to four decimal places the value of the following definite integral. Compare these results with the exact value.

$$\int_0^2 x^2\, dx, \quad n = 4$$

Solution:

Exact:
$$\int_0^2 x^2\, dx = \frac{1}{3}x^3 \bigg]_0^2 = \frac{8}{3} \approx 2.6667$$

Trapezoidal Rule:
$$\int_0^2 x^2\, dx \approx \frac{1}{4}\left[0 + 2\left(\frac{1}{2}\right)^2 + 2(1)^2 + 2\left(\frac{3}{2}\right)^2 + (2)^2 \right]$$

$$= \frac{11}{4} = 2.7500$$

Simpson's Rule:
$$\int_0^2 x^2\, dx \approx \frac{1}{6}\left[0 + 4\left(\frac{1}{2}\right)^2 + 2(1)^2 + 4\left(\frac{3}{2}\right)^2 + (2)^2 \right]$$

$$= \frac{8}{3} \approx 2.6667$$

3. Use the Trapezoidal Rule and Simpson's Rule to approximate to four decimal places the value of the following definite integral. Compare these results with the exact value.

$$\int_0^2 (x^4 + 1)dx, \quad n = 4$$

Solution:

Exact:
$$\int (x^4 + 1)dx = \frac{x^5}{5} + x \Big]_0^2$$

$$= \frac{32}{5} + 2 = \frac{42}{5} = 8.4$$

Trapizoidal Rule:
$$\int_0^2 (x^4 + 1)dx \approx \frac{1}{4}$$

$$\left[1 + 2\left(\frac{1}{16} + 1 \right) + 2(1 + 1) + 2\left(\frac{81}{16} + 1 \right) + 17 \right]$$

$$= \frac{36.25}{4} = 9.0625$$

Simpson's Rule:
$$\int_0^2 (x^4 + 1)dx \approx \frac{1}{6}$$

$$\left[1 + 4\left(\frac{1}{16} + 1 \right) + 2(1 + 1) + 4\left(\frac{81}{16} + 1 \right) + 17 \right]$$

$$= \frac{50.5}{6} \approx 8.4167$$

5. Use the Trapezoidal Rule and Simpson's Rule to approximate to four decimal places the value of the following definite integral. Compare these results with the exact value.

$$\int_0^2 x^3 \, dx, \quad n = 8$$

Solution:

Exact:

$$\int_0^2 x^3 \, dx = \tfrac{1}{4}x^4 \Big]_0^2 = 4.0000$$

Trapezoidal Rule:

$$\int_0^2 x^3 \, dx \approx \tfrac{1}{8}\big[0 + 2\big(\tfrac{1}{4}\big)^3 + 2\big(\tfrac{2}{4}\big)^3$$

$$+ 2\big(\tfrac{3}{4}\big)^3 + 2(1)^3 + 2\big(\tfrac{5}{4}\big)^3 + 2\big(\tfrac{6}{4}\big)^3 +$$

$$2\big(\tfrac{7}{4}\big)^3 + 8\big] = 4.0625$$

Simpson's Rule:

$$\int_0^2 x^3 \, dx \approx \tfrac{1}{12}\big[0 + 4\big(\tfrac{1}{4}\big)^3$$

$$+ 2\big(\tfrac{2}{4}\big)^3 + 4\big(\tfrac{3}{4}\big)^3 + 2(1)^3 + 4\big(\tfrac{5}{4}\big)^3 + 2\big(\tfrac{6}{4}\big)^3$$

$$+ 4\big(\tfrac{7}{4}\big)^3 + 8\big] = 4.0000$$

7. Use the Trapezoidal Rule and Simpson's Rule to approximate to four decimal places the value of the following definite integral. Compare these results with the exact value.

$$\int_1^2 \frac{1}{x^2} \, dx, \quad n = 4$$

Solution:

Exact:

$$\int_1^2 \frac{1}{x^2} \, dx = \frac{-1}{x}\bigg]_1^2 = 0.5000$$

Trapezoidal Rule:

$$\int_1^2 \frac{1}{x^2} \, dx \approx \frac{1}{8}\left[1 + 2\left(\frac{4}{5}\right)^2 + 2\left(\frac{4}{6}\right)^2 + 2\left(\frac{4}{7}\right)^2 + \frac{1}{4}\right] \approx 0.5090$$

Simpson's Rule:

$$\int_1^2 \frac{1}{x^2} \, dx \approx \frac{1}{12}\left[1 + 4\left(\frac{4}{5}\right)^2 + 2\left(\frac{4}{6}\right)^2 + 4\left(\frac{4}{7}\right)^2 + \frac{1}{4}\right] \approx 0.5004$$

9. Use the Trapezoidal Rule and Simpson's Rule to approximate to four decimal places the value of the following definite integral. Compare these results with the exact value.

$$\int_0^1 \frac{1}{1+x}\,dx, \quad n=4$$

Solution:

Exact:
$$\int_0^1 \frac{1}{1+x}\,dx = \ln|1+x|\Big]_0^1 \approx 0.6931$$

Trapezoidal Rule:
$$\int_0^1 \frac{1}{1+x}\,dx \approx \frac{1}{8}\left[1+2\left(\frac{4}{5}\right)+2\left(\frac{2}{3}\right)+2\left(\frac{4}{7}\right)+\frac{1}{2}\right] \approx 0.6970$$

Simpson's Rule:
$$\int_0^1 \frac{1}{1+x}\,dx \approx \frac{1}{12}\left[1+4\left(\frac{4}{5}\right)+2\left(\frac{2}{3}\right)+4\left(\frac{4}{7}\right)+\frac{1}{2}\right] \approx 0.6933$$

11. Using (a) the Trapezoidal Rule and (b) Simpson's Rule, approximate the following definite integral to three significant digits.

$$\int_0^2 (1+x^3)\,dx, \quad n=4$$

Solution:

(a) Trapezoidal Rule:
$$\frac{1}{4}\left[1+2\left(1+\frac{1}{8}\right)+2(1+1)+2\left(1+\frac{27}{8}\right)+9\right]=\frac{25}{4}\approx 6.25$$

(b) Simpson's Rule:
$$\frac{1}{6}\,[\,1+4\left(1+\frac{1}{8}\right)+2$$

$$(1+1)+4\left(1+\frac{27}{8}\right)+9\,]$$

$$=\frac{36}{6}=6 \text{ (exact!)}$$

13. Using (a) the Trapezoidal Rule and (b) Simpson's Rule, approximate the following definite integral to three significant digits.

$$\int_0^1 \sqrt{x}\sqrt{1-x}\,dx, \quad n = 4$$

Solution:

$$\int_0^1 \sqrt{x}\sqrt{1-x}\,dx = \int_0^1 \sqrt{x(1-x)}\,dx$$

(a) Trapezoidal Rule: $\quad \frac{1}{8}\left[0 + 2\sqrt{\frac{1}{4}\left(1-\frac{1}{4}\right)} + 2\sqrt{\frac{1}{2}\left(1-\frac{1}{2}\right)} + 2\sqrt{\frac{3}{4}\left(1-\frac{3}{4}\right)} + 0\right] \approx 0.342$

(b) Simpson's Rule: $\quad \frac{1}{12}\left[0 + 4\sqrt{\frac{1}{4}\left(1-\frac{1}{4}\right)} + 2\sqrt{\frac{1}{2}\left(1-\frac{1}{2}\right)} + 4\sqrt{\frac{3}{4}\left(1-\frac{3}{4}\right)} + 0\right] \approx 0.372$

15. Using (a) the Trapezoidal Rule and (b) Simpson's Rule, approximate the following definite integral to three significant digits.

$$\int_0^1 \sqrt{1-x^2}\,dx, \quad n = 4$$

Solution:

(a) Trapezoidal Rule: $\quad \frac{1}{8}\left[1 + 2\sqrt{\frac{15}{16}} + 2\sqrt{\frac{3}{4}} + 2\sqrt{\frac{7}{16}} + 0\right] \approx 0.749$

(b) Simpson's Rule: $\quad \frac{1}{12}\left[1 + 4\sqrt{\frac{15}{16}} + 2\sqrt{\frac{3}{4}} + 4\sqrt{\frac{7}{16}} + 0\right] \approx 0.771$

17. Using (a) the Trapezoidal Rule and (b) Simpson's Rule, approximate the following definite integral to three significant digits.

$$\int_0^1 \sqrt{1 - x^2} \, dx, \quad n = 8$$

Solution:

(a) Trapezoidal Rule: $\frac{1}{16} [1 + 2\sqrt{\frac{63}{64}} + 2\sqrt{\frac{60}{64}}$

$$+2\sqrt{\frac{55}{64}} + 2\sqrt{\frac{48}{64}}$$

$$+2\sqrt{\frac{39}{64}} + 2\sqrt{\frac{28}{64}}$$

$$+2\sqrt{\frac{15}{64}} + 0 \,] \approx 0.772$$

(b) Simpson's Rule: $\frac{1}{24} [\, 1 + 4\sqrt{\frac{63}{64}} + 2\sqrt{\frac{60}{64}}$

$$+4\sqrt{\frac{55}{64}} + 2\sqrt{\frac{48}{64}}$$

$$+4\sqrt{\frac{39}{64}} + 2\sqrt{\frac{28}{64}}$$

$$+4\sqrt{\frac{15}{64}} + 0 \,] \approx 0.780$$

19. Using (a) the Trapezoidal Rule and (b) Simpson's Rule, approximate the following definite integral to three significant digits.

$$\int_0^3 \frac{1}{2 - 2x + x^2} dx$$

Solution:

(a) Trapezoidal Rule: $\frac{1}{4} [\, \frac{1}{2} + 2(0.8) + 2(1) + 2$

$$(0.8) + 2(0.5) + 2(0.30769) + 0.2 \,] \approx 1.88$$

(b) Simpson's Rule: $\frac{1}{6} [\, \frac{1}{2} + 4(0.8) + 2(1)$

$$+4(0.8) + 2(0.5) + 4(0.30769) + 0.2 \,] \approx 1.89$$

21. *Present Value* Use Simpson's Rule with $n = 8$ to approximate the present value of the income
$c(t) = 6000 + 200\sqrt{t}$ over $t_1 = 4$ years at the annual interest $r = 7\%$.

Solution:

$$V = \int_0^{t_1} c(t)e^{-rt}\, dt = \int_0^4 (6000 + 200\sqrt{t})e^{-0.07t}\, dt$$

$$\approx \frac{4 - 0}{24}\left[(6000 + 200\sqrt{0})e^0 + 4\left(6000 + 200\sqrt{\tfrac{1}{2}}\right)e^{-0.07(1/2)}\right.$$

$$+ 2(6000 + 200\sqrt{1})e^{-0.07}$$

$$+ 4\left(6000 + 200\sqrt{\tfrac{3}{2}}\right)e^{-0.07(3/2)}$$

$$+ 2(6000 + 200\sqrt{2})e^{-0.14}$$

$$+ 4\left(6000 + 200\sqrt{\tfrac{5}{2}}\right)e^{-0.07(5/2)}$$

$$+ 2(6000 + 200\sqrt{3})e^{-0.21}$$

$$+ 4\left(6000 + 200\sqrt{\tfrac{7}{2}}\right)e^{-0.07(7/2)}$$

$$\left. + (6000 + 200\sqrt{4})e^{-0.28}\right] \approx \$21,831.20$$

23. *Marginal Analysis* Use Simpson's Rule with $n = 4$ to approximate the change in revenue from the marginal revenue function dR/dx. Assume the number x of units sold increases from 14 to 16.

$$\frac{dR}{dx} = 5\sqrt{8000 - x^3}$$

Solution:

$$\Delta R = \int_{14}^{16} 5\sqrt{8000 - x^3}\, dx$$

$$\approx \frac{16 - 14}{12}\left[5\sqrt{8000 - 14^3} + 4(5)\sqrt{8000 - \left(\tfrac{29}{2}\right)^3} + 2(5)\sqrt{8000 - 15^3}\right.$$

$$+ 4(5)\sqrt{8000 - \left(\tfrac{31}{2}\right)^3}$$

$$\left. + 5\sqrt{8000 - 16^3}\right] \approx \$678.36$$

25. *Probability* Use Simpson's Rule with $n = 6$ to approximate the indicated normal probability given by $P(0 \le x \le 1)$. The standard normal probability density function is

$$f(x) = \frac{1}{\sqrt{2\pi}} e^{-x^2/2}.$$

Solution:

$$P(a \le x \le b) = \int_a^b \frac{1}{\sqrt{2\pi}} e^{-x^2/2} \, dx$$

$$P(0 \le x \le 1) = \frac{1}{\sqrt{2\pi}} \int_0^1 e^{-x^2/2} \, dx$$

$$\approx \frac{1}{\sqrt{2\pi}} \left(\frac{1}{18} \right) [e^0 + 4e^{-(1/6)^2/2} + 2e^{-(1/3)^2/2} + 4e^{-(1/2)^2/2}$$

$$+ 2e^{-(2/3)^2/2} + 4e^{-(5/6)^2/2} + e^{-1/2}]$$

$$= \frac{1}{18\sqrt{2\pi}} [1 + 4e^{-1/72} + 2e^{-1/18} + 4e^{-1/8} + 2e^{-2/9} + 4e^{-25/72} + e^{-1/2}]$$

$$\approx 0.3413 = 34.13\%$$

27. *Surveying* Use Simpson's Rule to estimate the number of square feet of land in the lot shown in the figure, where x and y are measured in feet. The land is bounded by a stream and two straight roads.

x	0	100	200	300	400	500	600	700	800	900	1000
y	125	125	120	112	90	90	95	88	75	35	0

Solution:

$$A \approx \frac{1000}{3(10)} [125 + 4(125) + 2(120) + 4(112) + 2(90) + 4(90) + 2(95) + 4(88)$$

$$+ 2(75) + 4(35) + 0]$$

$$= 89,500 \text{ square feet}$$

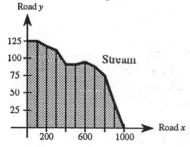

29. Find the maximum possible error in approximating the following definite integral using (a) the Trapezoidal Rule and (b) Simpson's Rule.

$$\int_0^2 x^4 \, dx, \quad n = 4$$

Solution:

$$f(x) = x^4$$
$$f'(x) = 4x^3$$
$$f''(x) = 12x^2$$
$$f'''(x) = 24x$$
$$f^{(4)}(x) = 24$$

(a) Trapezoidal Rule: Since $f''(x)$ is maximum in $[0, 2]$ when $x = 2$, we have

$$|\text{Error}| \le \frac{(2-0)^3}{48(4^2)}(48) = 0.2.$$

(b) Simpson's Rule: Since $f^{(4)}(x) = 24$, we have $|\text{Error}| \le \frac{(2-0)^5}{180(4^4)}(24) = 0.017.$

31. Find the maximum possible error in approximating the following definite integral using (a) the Trapezoidal Rule and (b) Simpson's Rule.

$$\int_0^1 e^{x^3} \, dx, \quad n = 4$$

Solution:

$$f(x) = e^{x^3}$$
$$f'(x) = 3x^2 e^{x^3}$$
$$f''(x) = 3(3x^4 + 2x)e^{x^3}$$
$$f'''(x) = 3(9x^6 + 18x^3 + 2)e^{x^3}$$
$$f^{(4)}(x) = 3(27x^8 + 108x^5 + 60x^2)e^{x^3}$$

(a) Trapezoidal Rule: Since $|f''(x)|$ is maximum in $[0, 1]$ when $x = 1$, we have

$$|\text{Error}| \le \frac{(1-0)^3}{12(4^2)}(15e) = \frac{5e}{64} \approx 0.212.$$

(b) Simpson's Rule: Since $|f^{(4)}(x)|$ is maximum in $[0, 1]$ when $x = 1$, we have

$$|\text{Error}| \le \frac{(1-0)^5}{180(4^4)}(585e) = \frac{13e}{1024} \approx 0.035.$$

33. Use the error formula to find n so that the error in the approximation of the definite integral is less than 0.0001 using (a) the Trapezoidal Rule and (b) Simpson's Rule.

$$\int_0^1 x^4 dx$$

Solution:

$$f(x) = x^4$$
$$f'(x) = 4x^3$$
$$f''(x) = 12x^2$$
$$f'''(x) = 24x$$
$$f^{(4)}(x) = 24$$

(a) Trapezoidal Rule: Since $|f''(x)|$ is maximum in [0, 1] when $x = 1$, and $|f''(1)|| = 12$, we have

$$|\text{ Error }| \le \frac{(1-0)^3}{12n^2}(12) \le 0.0001$$

$$\frac{1}{n^2} < 0.0001$$

$$n^2 > 10{,}000$$

$$n > 100$$

Let $n = 101$.

(b) Simpson's Rule: Since $|f^{(4)}(x)| = 24$ or [0, 1], we have

$$|\text{ Error }| \le \frac{1}{180n^4}24 < 0.0001$$

$$n^4 > 1333.33$$

$$n > 6.04$$

Let $n = 8$ (n must be even).

35. Use the error formula to find n so that the error in the approximation of the definite integral is less than 0.0001 using (a) the Trapezoidal Rule and (b) Simpson's Rule.

$$\int_1^3 e^{2x}\,dx$$

Solution:

$$f(x) = e^{2x}$$
$$f'(x) = 2e^{2x}$$
$$f''(x) = 4e^{2x}$$
$$f'''(x) = 8e^{2x}$$
$$f^{(4)}(x) = 16e^{2x}$$

(a) Trapezoidal Rule: Since $|f''(x)|$ is maximum in $[1, 3]$ when $x = 3$, and $|f''(3)| = 4e^6 \approx 1613.715$, we have

$$|\text{Error}| \le \frac{(3-1)^3}{12n^2}(1613.715) < 0.0001$$

$$n^2 > 10{,}758{,}100$$

$$n > 3279.95$$

Take $n = 3280$.

(b) Simpson's Rule: Since $|f^{(4)}(x)|$ is maximum in $[1, 3]$ when $x = 3$, and $|f^{(4)}(3)| = 16e^6 \approx 6454.861$, we have

$$|\text{Error}| \le \frac{(3-1)^5}{180n^4}(6454.861) < 0.0001$$

$$n^4 > 11{,}475{,}308.44$$

$$n > 58.2$$

Take $n = 60$ (n must be even).

37. Use the program for Simpson's Rule (on page 428 in the textbook) to approximate the integral.

$$\int_1^4 x\sqrt{x+4}\,dx$$

Solution:

$$\int_1^4 x\sqrt{x+4}\,dx \approx 19.5215 \qquad (n = 100)$$

39. Use the program for Simpson's Rule (on page 428 in the textbook) to approximate the integral.

$$\int_1^5 10xe^{-x}\,dx$$

Solution:

$$\int_2^5 10xe^{-x}\,dx \approx 3.6558 \qquad (n = 100)$$

41. Prove that Simpson's Rule is exact when used to approximate the integral of a cubic polynomial function, and demonstrate the result for

$$\int_0^1 x^3\,dx, \quad n = 2.$$

Solution:

$$P_3(x) = ax^3 + bx^2 + cx + d$$
$$P_3'(x) = 3ax^2 + 2bx + c$$
$$P_3''(x) = 6ax + 2b$$
$$P_3'''(x) = 6a$$
$$P_3{}^{(4)}(x) = 0$$

$$|\text{Error}| \le \frac{(b-a)^5}{180n^4}[\max|P_3{}^{(4)}(x)|] = \frac{(b-a)^5}{180n^4}(0) = 0$$

Therefore, Simpson's Rule is exact when used to approximate a cubic polynomial.

$$\int_0^1 x^3\,dx = \frac{1-0}{3(2)}\left[0^3 + 4\left(\frac{1}{2}\right)^3 + (1)^3\right] = \frac{1}{6}\left[0 + \frac{1}{2} + 1\right] = \frac{1}{4}$$

The exact value of this integral is

$$\int_0^1 x^3\,dx = \frac{x^4}{4}\Big]_0^1 = \frac{1}{4}$$

which is the same as the Simpson approximation.

43. *Arc Length* The suspension cable on a bridge that is 400 feet long is in the shape of a parabola whose equation is given by $y = x^2/800$ (see figure in text). Use Simpson's Rule with $n = 12$ and the definite integral

$$\int_a^b \sqrt{1 + [f'(x)]^2}\, dx$$

to approximate the length of the cable. Compare this result with the length obtained by using the table in Section 6.4 to perform the integration.

Solution:

$$y = \frac{x^2}{800}, \quad y' = \frac{x}{400}, \quad 1 + (y')^2 = 1 + \frac{x^2}{160,000}$$

$$S = \int_{-200}^{200} \sqrt{\frac{160,000 + x^2}{160,000}}\, dx$$

$$= \int_{-200}^{200} \frac{\sqrt{160,000 + x^2}}{400}\, dx = \frac{1}{200} \int_0^{200} \sqrt{160,000 + x^2}\, dx$$

$$\approx \frac{200 - 0}{36(200)} [400 + 4\sqrt{160,000 + \left(\frac{50}{3}\right)^2} + 2\sqrt{160,000 + \left(\frac{100}{3}\right)^2}$$

$$+ 4\sqrt{160,000 + (50)^2}$$

$$+ 2\sqrt{160,000 + \left(\frac{200}{3}\right)^2} + 4\sqrt{160,000 + \left(\frac{250}{3}\right)^2}$$

$$+ 2\sqrt{160,000 + (100)^2}$$

$$+ 4\sqrt{160,000 + \left(\frac{350}{3}\right)^2}$$

$$+ 2\sqrt{160,000 + \left(\frac{400}{3}\right)^2}$$

$$+ 4\sqrt{160,000 + (150)^2}$$

$$+ 2\sqrt{160,000 + \left(\frac{500}{3}\right)^2} + 4\sqrt{160,000 + \left(\frac{550}{3}\right)^2}$$

$$+ \sqrt{160,000 + (200)^2}\,] \approx 416.1 \text{ feet}$$

Using Formula 21: $u = x, \quad du = dx, \quad a = 40.$

$$\frac{1}{200} \int_0^{200} \sqrt{160,000 + x^2}\, dx = \frac{1}{400} \left[x\sqrt{160,000 + x^2} \right.$$

$$\left. + 160,000 \ln |x + \sqrt{160,000 + x^2}\,| \right]_0^{200}$$

$$= \frac{1}{400} [200\sqrt{200,000} + 160,000 \ln |200 +$$

$$\sqrt{200,000}\,| - 160,000 \ln \sqrt{160,000}]$$

$$\approx 416.1$$

45. *Medicine* A body assimilates a 12-hour cold tablet at a rate modeled by

$$\frac{dC}{ct} = 8 - \ln(t^2 - 2t + 4), \qquad 0 \le t \le 12,$$

where dC/dt is measured in grams per hour and t is the time (in hours). Find the total amount of the drug absorbed into the body during the 12 hours.

Solution:

$$C = \int_0^{12} (8 - \ln(t^2 - 2t + 4))dt \approx 58.876 \text{ grams.}$$

(Simpson's Rule with $n = 100$)

47. *Magazine Subscribers* The rate of change S of subscribers to a newly introduced magazine is modeled by

$$\frac{dS}{dt} = 1000t^2 e^{-t}, \qquad 0 \le t \le 6,$$

where t is the time in years. Find the total increase in the number of subscribers during the first 6 years.

Solution:

$$\int_0^6 1000t^2 e^{-t} dt \approx 1876 \text{ subscribers.}$$

(Simpson's Rule with $n = 100$)

Section 6.6   Improper Integrals

1. Evaluate $\int_0^\infty e^{-x}\, dx$.

Solution:

This integral converges since $\int_0^\infty e^{-x}\, dx = \lim_{b \to \infty} \left[-e^{-x} \right]_0^b = 0 + 1 = 1.$

3. Evaluate $\int_1^\infty \frac{1}{x^2}\, dx$.

Solution:

This integral converges since $\int_1^\infty \frac{1}{x^2}\, dx = \lim_{b \to \infty} \left[-\frac{1}{x} \right]_1^b = 0 + 1 = 1.$

5. Evaluate $\int_0^\infty e^{x/3}\,dx$.

Solution:

This integral diverges since $\int_0^\infty e^{x/3}\,dx = \lim_{b\to\infty}\left[3e^{x/3}\right]_0^b = \infty$.

7. Evaluate $\int_5^\infty \dfrac{x}{\sqrt{x^2-16}}\,dx$.

Solution:

This integral diverges since $\int_5^\infty \dfrac{x}{\sqrt{x^2-16}}\,dx = \lim_{b\to\infty}\left[\sqrt{x^2-16}\right]_5^b = \infty$.

9. Evaluate $\int_{-\infty}^0 e^{-x}\,dx$.

Solution:

This integral diverges since $\int_{-\infty}^0 e^{-x}\,dx = \lim_{a\to-\infty}\left[-e^{-x}\right]_a^0 = -1+\infty = \infty$.

11. Evaluate $\int_{-\infty}^\infty e^{|x|}\,dx$.

Solution:

This integral diverges since

$$\int_{-\infty}^\infty e^{|x|}\,dx = \int_{-\infty}^0 e^{-x}\,dx + \int_0^\infty e^x\,dx$$

$$= \lim_{a\to-\infty}\left[-e^{-x}\right]_a^0 + \lim_{b\to\infty}\left[e^x\right]_0^b = (-1+\infty) + (\infty-1) = \infty.$$

13. Evaluate $\int_{-\infty}^\infty 2xe^{-3x^2}\,dx$.

Solution:

This integral converges since

$$\int_{-\infty}^\infty 2xe^{-3x^2}\,dx = \int_{-\infty}^0 2xe^{-3x^2}\,dx + \int_0^\infty 2xe^{-3x^2}\,dx$$

$$= \lim_{a\to-\infty}\left[-\frac{1}{3}e^{-3x^2}\right]_a^0 + \lim_{b\to\infty}\left[-\frac{1}{3}e^{-3x^2}\right]_0^b$$

$$= \left(-\frac{1}{3}+0\right) + \left(0+\frac{1}{3}\right) = 0.$$

15. Evaluate $\displaystyle\int_0^4 \frac{1}{\sqrt{x}}\,dx$.

Solution:

This integral converges since $\displaystyle\int_0^4 \frac{1}{\sqrt{x}}\,dx = \lim_{b\to 0^+}\left[2\sqrt{x}\right]_b^4 = 4$.

17. Evaluate $\displaystyle\int_0^2 \frac{1}{(x-1)^{2/3}}\,dx$.

Solution:

This integral converges since

$$\int_0^2 \frac{1}{(x-1)^{2/3}}\,dx = \int_0^1 \frac{1}{(x-1)^{2/3}}\,dx + \int_1^2 \frac{1}{(x-1)^{2/3}}\,dx$$

$$= \lim_{b\to 1^-}\left[3(x-1)^{1/3}\right]_0^b + \lim_{a\to 1^+}\left[3(x-1)^{1/3}\right]_a^2 = 3+3 = 6.$$

19. Evaluate $\displaystyle\int_0^1 \frac{1}{1-x}\,dx$.

Solution:

This integral diverges since $\displaystyle\int_0^1 \frac{1}{1-x}\,dx = \lim_{b\to 1^-}\left[-\ln|1-x|\right]_0^b = \infty$.

21. Evaluate $\displaystyle\int_0^9 \frac{1}{\sqrt{9-x}}\,dx$.

Solution:

This integral converges since $\displaystyle\int_0^9 \frac{1}{\sqrt{9-x}}\,dx = \lim_{b\to 9^-}\left[-2\sqrt{9-x}\right]_0^b = 0-(-2\sqrt{9}) = 6$

23. Evaluate $\displaystyle\int_0^1 \frac{1}{x^2}\,dx$.

Solution:

This integral diverges since $\displaystyle\int_0^1 \frac{1}{x^2}\,dx = \lim_{b\to 0^+}\left[-\frac{1}{x}\right]_b^1 = \infty$.

25. Evaluate $\displaystyle\int_0^2 \frac{1}{\sqrt[3]{x-1}}\,dx$.

Solution:

This integral converges since

$$\int_0^2 \frac{1}{\sqrt[3]{x-1}}\,dx = \int_0^1 \frac{1}{\sqrt[3]{x-1}}\,dx + \int_1^2 \frac{1}{\sqrt[3]{x-1}}\,dx$$

$$= \lim_{b\to 1^-}\left[\frac{3}{2}(x-1)^{2/3}\right]_0^b + \lim_{a\to 1^+}\left[\frac{3}{2}(x-1)^{2/3}\right]_a^2 = -\frac{3}{2}+\frac{3}{2} = 0.$$

27. Evaluate $\int_3^4 \dfrac{1}{\sqrt{x^2 - 9}}\,dx$.

Solution:

This integral converges since

$$\int_3^4 \frac{1}{\sqrt{x^2 - 9}}\,dx = \lim_{a \to 3^+}\left[\ln(x + \sqrt{x^2 - 9})\right]_a^4$$

$$= \ln(4 + \sqrt{7}) - \ln 3 \approx 0.7954$$

29. Complete the table in the textbook for the specified values of a and n to demonstrate that $\lim\limits_{x \to \infty} x^n e^{-ax} = 0$, when $a = 1$ and $n = 1$.

Solution:

$a = 1, \ n = 1: \ \lim\limits_{x \to \infty} x e^{-x}$

x	1	10	25	50
xe^{-x}	0.3679	0.0005	0.0000	0.0000

31. Complete the table in the textbook for the specified values of a and n to demonstrate that $\lim\limits_{x \to \infty} x^n e^{-ax} = 0$ when $a = 1$, and $n = 1$.

Solution:

$a = \dfrac{1}{2}, \ n = 5: \ \lim\limits_{x \to \infty} x^5 e^{-1/2x}$

x	1	10	25	50
$x^2 e^{-(1/2)x}$	0.6065	0.6738	0.0023	0.0000

33. Evaluate the convergent improper integral using the fact that $\lim\limits_{x \to \infty} x^n e^{-ax} = 0$, $a > 0, \ n > 0$.

$$\int_0^\infty x^2 e^{-x}\,dx$$

Solution:

$$\int_0^\infty x^2 e^{-x}\,dx = \lim_{b \to \infty}\left[-x^2 e^{-x} - 2x e^{-x} - 2e^{-x}\right]_0^b = 2$$

35. Evaluate the convergent improper integral using the fact that $\lim\limits_{x \to \infty} x^n e^{-ax} = 0$, $a > 0$, $n > 0$.

$$\int_0^\infty xe^{-2x}\, dx$$

Solution:

$$\int_0^\infty xe^{-2x}\, dx = \lim_{b \to \infty}\left[-\frac{1}{2}xe^{-2x} - \frac{1}{4}e^{-2x}\right]_0^b = (0 - 0) - \left(0 - \frac{1}{4}\right) = \frac{1}{4}$$

37. *Present Value* You are asked to calculate the pay for a business that is forecast to yield a continuous flow of profit at the rate of $500,000 per year. If money will earn interest at the nominal rate of 9% per year compounded continuously, what is the present value of the business (a) for 20 years, and (b) forever (in perpetuity)?

Solution:

(a) Present value $= \displaystyle\int_0^{20} 500,000e^{-0.09t}\, dt = \frac{500,000}{-0.09}e^{-0.09t}\Big]_0^{20} \approx \$4,637,228.40$

(b) Present value $= \displaystyle\int_0^\infty 500,000e^{-0.09t}\, dt = \lim_{b \to \infty}\frac{500,000}{-0.09}e^{-0.09t}\Big]_0^b \approx \$5,555,555.56$

39. *Capitalized Cost* Find the capitalized cost C of an asset (a) for $n = 5$ years, (b) for $n = 10$ years, and (c) forever. The *capitalized cost* is given by

$$C = C_0 + \int_0^n c(t)e^{-rt}\, dt$$

where $C_0 = 650,000$ is the original investment, t is the time in years, $r = 10\%$ is the annual rate compounded continuously and $c(t) = \$25,000$ is the annual cost of maintenance.

Solution:

$$C = 650,000 + \int_0^n 25,000e^{-0.10t}\, dt = 650,000 - \left[250,000e^{-0.10t}\right]_0^n$$

(a) For $n = 5$, we have $C = 650,000 - [250,000(e^{-0.50} - 1)] \approx \$748,367.34$.

(b) For $n = 10$, we have $C = 650,000 - [250,000(e^{-1} - 1)] \approx \$808,030.14$.

(c) For $n = \infty$, we have

$$C = 650,000 - \lim_{n \to \infty}\left[250,000e^{-0.10t}\right]_0^n$$

$$= 650,000 - 250,000(0 - 1) = \$900,000$$

41. For $y = 1/x^2$, $y = 0$, $x \geq 1$, (a) find the area of the region bounded by the graphs, and (b) find the volume of the solid generated by revolving the region about the x-axis.

Solution:

(a) $A = \displaystyle\int_1^\infty \frac{1}{x^2}\,dx$

$= \displaystyle\lim_{b\to\infty}\left[-\frac{1}{x}\right]_1^b = 1$

(b) $V = \pi\displaystyle\int_1^\infty \left(\frac{1}{x^2}\right)^2 dx$

$= \pi\displaystyle\lim_{b\to\infty}\left[-\frac{1}{3x^3}\right]_1^b = \frac{\pi}{3}$

43. *Household Size* In 1991, the number of people per household in the United States was normally distributed with a mean of 3.07 and a standard deviation of 1.65. Find the probability that a person chosen at random lives

(a) alone.
(b) with 2 people.
(c) with 6 people.

Solution:

$$P(a \leq x \leq b) = \int_a^b \frac{1}{\sigma\sqrt{2\pi}}e^{-(x-u)^2/25^2}\,dx = \int_a^b h(x)\,dx$$

$u = 3.07$, $\sigma = 1.65$. Use numerical integration.

(a) alone: $P(0.5 \leq x \leq 1.5) = \displaystyle\int_{a.5}^{1.5} h(x)\,dx \approx 0.111$

(b) 2 people: $P(1.5 \leq x \leq 2.5) = \displaystyle\int_{1.5}^{2.5} h(x)\,dx \approx 0.194$

(c) 6 people: $P(5.5 \leq x \leq 6.5) = \displaystyle\int_{5.5}^{6.5} h(x)\,dx \approx 0.052$

Chapter 6   Review Exercises

1. Find the indefinite integral.

$$\int dt$$

Solution:

$$\int dt = t + C$$

3. Find the indefinite integral.

$$\int (x + 5)^3\,dx$$

Solution:

$$\int (x + 5)^3\,dx = \frac{(x + 5)^4}{4} + C$$

5. Find the indefinite integral.

$$\int e^{10x}\,dx$$

Solution:

$$\int e^{10x}\,dx = \frac{1}{10}e^{10x} + C$$

7. Find the indefinite integral.

$$\int \frac{1}{5x}\,dx$$

Solution:

$$\int \frac{1}{5x}\,dx = \frac{1}{5}\ln|x| + C$$

9. Find the indefinite integral.

$$\int x\sqrt{x^2 + 4}\,dx$$

Solution:

$$\int x\sqrt{x^2 + 4}\,dx = \frac{1}{2}(x^2 + 4)^{3/2}\left(\frac{2}{3}\right) + C = \frac{1}{3}(x^2 + 4)^{2/3} + C$$

11. Find the indefinite integral.

$$\int \frac{2e^x}{3 + e^x}\,dx$$

Solution:

$$\int \frac{2e^x}{3 + e^x}\,dx = 2\ln(3 + e^x) + C$$

13. Use substitution to find the indefinite integral.

$$\int x(x - 2)^3\,dx$$

Solution:

$$u = x - 2, \quad x = u + 2, \quad du = dx$$

$$\int x(x - 2)^3\,dx = \int (u + 2)u^3\,du = \int (u^4 + 2u^3)\,du$$

$$= \frac{u^5}{5} + \frac{u^4}{2} + C = \frac{(x - 2)^5}{5} + \frac{(x - 2)^4}{2} + C$$

15. Use substitution to find the indefinite integral.

$$\int x\sqrt{x+1}\,dx$$

Solution:

$$u = x+1, \quad x = u-1, \quad du = dx$$

$$\int x\sqrt{x+1}\,dx = \int (u-1)u^{1/2}du = \int (u^{3/2} - u^{1/2})du$$

$$= \frac{2}{5}u^{5/2}\frac{-2}{3}u^{3/2} + C = \frac{2}{5}(x+1)^{5/2} - \frac{2}{3}(x+1)^{3/2} + C$$

$$= \frac{2}{15}(x+1)^{3/2}[3(x+1) - 5] + C$$

$$= \frac{2}{15}(x+1)^{3/2}(3x-2) + C$$

17. Use substitution to find the indefinite integral.

$$\int 2x\sqrt{x-3}\,dx. \text{ Let } u = x-3, \text{ then } x = u+3 \text{ and } dx = du.$$

Solution:

$$\int 2x\sqrt{x-3}\,dx = 2\int (u+3)\sqrt{u}\,du = 2\int (u^{3/2} + 3u^{1/2})\,du$$

$$= 2\left(\frac{2}{5}u^{5/2} + 2u^{3/2}\right) + C$$

$$= \frac{4}{5}u^{3/2}(u+5) + C$$

$$= \frac{4}{5}(x-3)^{3/2}(x+2) + C$$

19. Use substitution to find the indefinite integral.

$$\int_{1/2}^{\infty} \frac{1}{\sqrt{2x-1}}\,dx.$$

Let $u = 1-x$, then $x = 1-u$ and $dx = -du$.

$$\int (x+1)\sqrt{1-x}\,dx = -\int (2-u)\sqrt{u}\,du = -\int (2u^{1/2} - u^{3/2})\,du$$

$$= -\left(\frac{4}{3}u^{3/2} - \frac{2}{5}u^{5/2}\right) + C = -\frac{2}{15}u^{3/2}(10 - 3u) + C$$

$$= -\frac{2}{15}(1-x)^{3/2}(3x+7) + C$$

21. Use substitution to evaluate the definite integral.

$$\int_2^3 x\sqrt{x-2}\,dx.$$

Solution:

$$u = x - 2, \ \ x = u + 2, \ \ du = dx$$

$$\int_2^3 x\sqrt{x-2}\,dx = \int_0^1 (u+2)u^{1/2}du = \int_0^1 (u^{3/2}+2u^{1/2})du$$

$$= \left[\frac{2}{5}u^{5/2}+\frac{4}{3}u^{3/2}\right]_0^1 = \frac{2}{5}+\frac{4}{3} = \frac{26}{15}$$

23. Use substitution to evaluate the definite integral.

$$\int_1^3 x^2(x-1)^3\,dx$$

Solution:

$$u = x - 1, x = u + 1, du = dx$$

$$\int_1^3 x^2(x-1)^3 dx = \int_0^2 (u+1)^2 u^3 du = \int_0^2 (u^5+2u^4+u^3)du$$

$$= \left[\frac{u^6}{6}+\frac{2u^5}{5}+\frac{u^4}{4}\right]_0^2 = \frac{32}{3}+\frac{64}{4}+4 = \frac{412}{15} \approx 27.467$$

25. *Probability* The probability of recall in an experiment is found to be

$$P(a \le x \le b) = \int_a^b \frac{105}{16} x^2 \sqrt{1-x}\,dx,$$

where x represents the percent of recall (see figure in textbook).

(a) Find the probability that a randomly chosen individual will recall 80% of the material.

(b) What is the median percent recall? That is, for what value of b is it true that $P(0 \le x \le b) = 0.5$?

Solution:

(a) $P(0 \le x \le 0.80) = \int_0^{0.8} \frac{105}{16} x^2 \sqrt{1-x}\,dx$

$u = 1 - x, \ x = 1 - u, \ du = -dx$

$$\int_1^{0.2} \frac{105}{16} (1-u)^2 u^{1/2}(-du) = -\frac{105}{16} \int_1^{0.2} (u^{1/2} - 2u^{3/2} + u^{5/2})du$$

$$= -\frac{105}{16} \left[\frac{2}{3} u^{3/2} - \frac{4}{5} u^{5/2} + \frac{2}{7} u^{7/2} \right]_1^{0.2}$$

$$\approx 0.696$$

(b) Solve the equation $\int_0^b \frac{105}{16} x^2 \sqrt{1-x}\,dx = 0.5$ for b.

From part (a),

$$\frac{-105}{16} \left[\frac{2}{3} u^{3/2} - \frac{4}{5} u^{5/2} + \frac{2}{7} u^{7/2} \right]_1^{1-b} = 0.5$$

$$\left[\frac{2}{3}(1-b)^{3/2} - \frac{4}{5}(1-b)^{5/2} + \frac{2}{7}(1-b)^{7/2} \right] - \left[\frac{2}{3} - \frac{4}{5} + df27 \right] = \frac{-8}{105}$$

$$\left[\frac{2}{3}(1-b)^{3/2} - \frac{4}{5}(1-b)^{5/2} + \frac{2}{7}(1-b)^{7/2} \right] = \frac{8}{105}$$

Using a graphing utility to solve for b, we obtain $b \approx 0.693$.

27. Use integration by parts to find the indefinite integral.

$$\int \frac{\ln x}{\sqrt{x}}\,dx$$

Solution:

Let $u = \ln x, \ dv = \frac{1}{\sqrt{x}}dx, \ du = \frac{1}{x}dx, \ v = 2\sqrt{x}$

$$\int \frac{\ln x}{\sqrt{x}}dx = 2\sqrt{x}\ln x - \int 2\sqrt{x}\frac{1}{x}dx$$

$$= 2\sqrt{x}\ln x - \int 2x^{-1/2}dx$$

$$= 2\sqrt{x}\ln x - 4\sqrt{x} + C$$

29. Use integration by parts to find the indefinite integral.

$$\int (x-1)e^x \, dx.$$

Solution:

Use integration by parts and let $u = x - 1$ and $dv = e^x \, dx$, then $du = dx$ and $v = e^x$.

$$\int (x-1)e^x \, dx = (x-1)e^x - \int e^x \, dx = (x-1)e^x - e^x + C = (x-2)e^x + C$$

31. Use integration by parts repeatedly to find the indefinite integral.

$$\int 2x^2 e^{2x} dx$$

Solution:

Let $u = 2x^2$, $dv = e^{2x}$, $du = 4x \, dx$, $v = \frac{1}{2}e^{2x}$.

$$\int 2x^2 e^{2x} dx = (2x^2)\left(\frac{1}{2}e^{2x}\right) - \int \frac{1}{2}e^{2x}(4x \, dx)$$

$$= x^2 e^{2x} - \int 2x e^{2x} dx$$

Use parts again for the integral on the right: $u = 2x$, $dv = e^{2x}$, $du = 2dx$, $v = \frac{1}{2}e^{2x}$.

$$\int 2x^2 e^{2x} dx = x^2 e^{2x} - \left[(2x)\left(\frac{1}{2}e^{2x}\right) - \int \frac{1}{2}e^{2x} 2 \, dx\right]$$

$$= x^2 e^{2x} - x e^{2x} + \int e^{2x} dx$$

$$= x^2 e^{2x} - x e^{2x} + \frac{1}{2}e^{2x} + C$$

33. Find the present value of the income $c(t) = 10{,}000$ (measured in dollars), over $t_1 = 5$ years at the annual inflation rate of $r = 4\%$.

Solution:

$$\text{Present value} = \int_0^{t_1} c(t)e^{-rt} \, dt$$

$$= \int_0^5 10{,}000 e^{-0.04t} dt$$

$$= -250{,}000 e^{-0.04t} \Big]_0^5 = \$45{,}317.31$$

35. Find the present value of the income $c(t) = 12,000t$ (measured in dollars), over $t_1 = 10$ years at the annual inflation rate of $r = 5\%$.

Solution:

$$\text{Present value} = \int_0^{t_1} c(t)e^{-rt}\,dt$$

$$= \int_0^{10} 12,000e^{-0.05t}\,dt$$

$$= (-240,000t - 4,800,000)e^{-0.05t}\Big]_0^{10} = \$432,979.25$$

37. Find $\displaystyle\int \frac{1}{x(x+5)}\,dx$ using partial fractions.

Solution:

Use partial fractions.

$$\frac{1}{x(x+5)} = \frac{A}{x} + \frac{B}{x+5}$$

Basic equation: $1 = A(x+5) + Bx$

When $x = 0$: $1 = 5A$, $A = \frac{1}{5}$.

When $x = -5$: $1 = -5B$, $B = -\frac{1}{5}$.

$$\int \frac{1}{x(x+5)}\,dx = \frac{1}{5}\int\left[\frac{1}{x} - \frac{1}{x+5}\right]dx = \frac{1}{5}[\ln|x| - \ln|x+5|] + C = \frac{1}{5}\ln\left|\frac{x}{x+5}\right| + C$$

39. Find $\displaystyle\int \frac{4x-13}{x^2-3x-10}\,dx$ using partial fractions.

Solution:

Partial fractions: $\dfrac{4x-13}{x^2-3x-10} - \dfrac{A}{(x-5)} + \dfrac{B}{(x+2)}$

Basic equation: $4x - 13 = A(x+2) + B(x-5)$

When $x = -2$: $-21 = -7B$, $B = 3$

When $x = 5$: $7 = 7A$, $A = 1$

$$\int \frac{4x-13}{x^2-3x-10}\,dx = \int\left(\frac{1}{x-5} + \frac{3}{x+2}\right)dx = \ln|x-5| + 3\ln|x+2| + C$$

41. Find $\displaystyle\int \frac{x^2}{x^2 + 2x - 15}\,dx$ using partial fractions.

Solution:

$$\frac{x^2}{x^2 + 2x - 15} = 1 - \frac{2x - 15}{(x + 5)(x - 3)}$$

Use partial fractions.

$$\frac{2x - 15}{(x + 5)(x - 3)} = \frac{A}{x + 5} + \frac{B}{x - 3}$$

Basic equation: $2x - 15 = A(x - 3) + B(x + 5)$

When $x = -5$: $-25 = -8A$, $A = \frac{25}{8}$.

When $x = 3$: $-9 = 8B$, $B = -\frac{9}{8}$.

$$\int \frac{x^2}{x^2 + 2x - 15}\,dx = \int \left[1 - \frac{25}{8}\left(\frac{1}{x + 5}\right) + \frac{9}{8}\left(\frac{1}{x - 3}\right) \right] dx$$

$$= x - \frac{25}{8}\ln|x + 5| + \frac{9}{8}\ln|x - 3| + C$$

43. *Sales Growth* When it is introduced to the market, a new product initially sells 1250 units per week. After 6 months, the number of sales increases to 6500. The sales can be modeled by logistics growth with a limit of 10,000 units per week.

(a) Find a logistics growth model for the number of units.

(b) Use the model to complete the table in the textbook.

(c) Use the graph in the textbook to approximate the year that sales will be 7500 units per week.

43. —CONTINUED—

Solution:

(a) $y = \dfrac{L}{1 + be^{-kt}} = \dfrac{10,000}{1 + be^{-kt}}$.

Since $y = 1250$ when $t = 0$, $\dfrac{10,000}{1+b} = 1250 \Rightarrow 1 + b = 8 \Rightarrow b = 7$.

When $t = 26$ (6 months), $y = 6500 = \dfrac{10,000}{1 + 7e^{-k(26)}}$

Solving for k, $\quad 1 + 7e^{-26k} = \dfrac{100}{65}$

$$ye^{-26k} = \dfrac{35}{65}$$

$$e^{26k} = \dfrac{5}{65} = \dfrac{1}{13}$$

$$k = \dfrac{-1}{26} \ln\left(\dfrac{1}{13}\right) \approx 0.098652$$

Thus, $y = \dfrac{10,000}{1 + 7e^{-0.098652t}}$

(b)

Time, t	0	3	6	12	24
Sales, y	1250	1611	2052	3182	6039

(c) The sales will be 7500 when $t \approx 31$ weeks.

45. Evaluate $\displaystyle\int \dfrac{\sqrt{x^2 + 9}}{x}\, dx$.

Solution:

Use Formula 23 from the tables and let $u = x$, $a = 5$, and $du = dx$.

$$\int \dfrac{\sqrt{x^2 + 25}}{x}\, dx = \sqrt{x^2 + 25} - 5\ln\left|\dfrac{5 + \sqrt{x^2 + 25}}{x}\right| + C$$

47. Evaluate $\int \frac{1}{(x^2 - 4)} dx$.

Solution:

Use Formula 29 and let $u = x$, $a = 2$.

$$\int \frac{1}{x^2 - 4} dx = \frac{1}{4} \ln \left| \frac{x - 2}{x + 2} \right| + C$$

49. Use Formula 19 from the tables and let $u = x$, $a = 1$, $b = 1$, and $du = dx$.

Solution:

$$\int_0^3 \frac{x}{\sqrt{1 + x}} dx = \left[-\frac{2(2 - x)}{3} \sqrt{1 + x} \right]_0^3 = \frac{8}{3}$$

51. Use a reduction formula found in the table of integrals in Section 6.4 to find the indefinite integral.

$$\int \frac{\sqrt{1 + x}}{x} dx$$

Solution:

Use Formula 17 and let $u = x$, $a = 1$, $b = 1$.

$$\int \frac{\sqrt{x + 1}}{x} dx = 2\sqrt{1 + x} + \int \frac{1}{x\sqrt{1 + x}} dx$$

$$= 2\sqrt{1 + x} + \ln \left| \frac{\sqrt{1 + x} - 1}{\sqrt{1 + x} + 1} \right| + C \text{ (Formula 15)}$$

53. Use a reduction formula found in the table of integrals in Section 6.4 to find the indefinite integral.

$$\int (x - 5)^3 e^{x - 5} dx$$

Solution:

Use Formula 36 and $u = x - 5$, $n = 3$, $du = dx$.

$$\int (x - 5)^3 e^{x - 5} dx = (x - 5)^3 e^{x - 5} - 3 \int (x - 5)^2 e^{x - 5} dx$$

$$= (x - 5)^3 e^{x - 5} - 3 \left[\int (x - 5)^2 e^{x - 5} - 2 \int (x - 5) e^{x - 5} dx \right]$$

$$= (x - 5)^3 e^{x - 5} - 3(x - 5)^2 e^{x - 5} + 6(x - 6) e^{x - 5} + C \text{ (Formula 35)}$$

55. Complete the square and then use the table of integrals given in Section 6.4 to find the indefinite integral.

$$\int \frac{1}{x^2 + 4x - 21} dx$$

Solution:

$$\frac{1}{x^2 + 4x - 21} = \frac{1}{x^2 + 4x + 4 - 25} = \frac{1}{(x+2)^2 - 25}$$

$$\int \frac{1}{(x+1)^2 - 25} dx = \frac{1}{10} \ln \left| \frac{(x+2) - 5}{(x+2) + 5} \right| + C \qquad \text{Formula 29}$$

$$= \frac{1}{10} \ln \left| \frac{x-3}{x+7} \right| + C$$

57. Complete the square and then use the table of integrals given in Section 6.4 to find the indefinite integral.

$$\int \sqrt{x^2 - 10x} dx$$

Solution:

$$x^2 - 10x = x^2 - 10x + 25 - 25 = (x-5)^2 - 25$$

$$\int \sqrt{x^2 - 10x} \, dx = \int \sqrt{(x-5)^2 - 5^2} \, dx$$

$$= \frac{1}{2} [(x-5)\sqrt{(x-5)^2 - 5^2} + 25 \ln |(x-5) + \sqrt{(x-5)^2 - 5^2}|] + C$$

(Formula 21)

59. Approximate $\int_1^3 \frac{1}{x^2} dx$, with $n = 4$ using the Trapezoidal Rule.

Solution:

$$\int_1^3 \frac{1}{x^2} dx \approx \frac{3-1}{2(4)} \left[1 + 2 \left(\frac{4}{9} \right) + 2 \left(\frac{1}{4} \right) + 2 \left(\frac{4}{25} \right) + \frac{1}{9} \right] = 0.705$$

61. Approximate $\int_1^2 \frac{1}{1 + \ln x} dx$ with $n = 4$ using the Trapezoidal Rule.

Solution:

$$\int_1^2 \frac{1}{1 + \ln x} dx \frac{1}{8} \left(1 + 2 \left[\frac{1}{1 + \ln(5/4)} \right] + 2 \left[\frac{1}{1 + \ln(3/2)} \right] + 2 \left[\frac{1}{1 + \ln(7/4)} \right] + \right.$$

$$\left. \frac{1}{1 + \ln 2} \right) \approx 0.741$$

63. Approximate $\int_{1}^{2} \frac{1}{x^3} dx$, with $n = 4$ using Simpson's Rule.

Solution:

$$\int_{1}^{2} \frac{1}{x^3} dx \approx \frac{2-1}{3(4)} \left[1 + 4\left(\frac{4}{5}\right)^3 + 2\left(\frac{2}{3}\right)^3 + 4\left(\frac{4}{7}\right)^3 + \frac{1}{8} \right] \approx 0.376$$

65. Approximate $\int_{0}^{1} \frac{x^{3/2}}{2 - x^2} dx$, with $n = 4$ using Simpson's Rule.

Solution:

$$\int_{0}^{1} \frac{x^{3/2}}{2 - x^2} dx \approx \frac{1}{12} \left[0 + \frac{8}{31} + \frac{2\sqrt{2}}{7} + \frac{24\sqrt{3}}{23} + 1 \right] \approx 0.289$$

67. Use the error formula to find bounds for the error in approximating the integral using the Trapezoidal Rule.

$$\int_{0}^{2} e^{2x} dx, \ n = 4$$

Solution:

$$f(x) = e^{2x}$$
$$f'(x) = 2e^{2x}$$
$$f''(x) = 4e^{2x}$$
$$|f''(x)| \leq 4e^{2(2)} \approx 219 \text{ on } [0, 2]$$
$$|E| \leq \frac{(2 - 0)^3}{12(4)^2}, (219) \leq 9.125$$

69. Use the error formula to find bounds for the error in approximating the integral using Simpson's Rule.

$$\int_{2}^{4} \frac{1}{x - 1} dx, \ n = 4$$

Solution:

$$f(x) = \frac{1}{x - 1} = (x - 1)^{-1}$$
$$f'(x) = -(x - 1)^{-2}$$
$$f''(x) = 2(x - 1)^{-3}$$
$$f'''(x) = -6(x - 1)^{-4}$$
$$f^{(4)}(x) = 24(x - 1)^{-5} = \frac{24}{(x - 1)^5}$$
$$|f^{(4)}(x)| \leq 24 \text{ on } [2, 4]$$
$$|E| \leq \frac{(4 - 2)^5}{180(4)^4} (24) \approx 0.017$$

71. Evaluate the improper integral.

$$\int_0^\infty 4xe^{-2x^2}\,dx$$

Solution:

$$\int_0^\infty 4xe^{-2x^2}\,dx = \lim_{b\to\infty} -\int_0^b e^{-2x^2}(-4x\,dx)$$

$$= \lim_{b\to\infty}\left[-e^{2x^2}\right]_0^b = 1$$

73. Evaluate the improper integral.

$$\int_{-\infty}^0 \frac{1}{3x^2}\,dx$$

Solution:

$$\int_{-\infty}^0 \frac{1}{3x^2}\,dx = \lim_{b\to-\infty}\int_b^{-1}\frac{1}{3}x^{-2}\,dx + \lim_{a\to 0^-}\int_{-1}^a \frac{1}{3}x^{-2}\,dx$$

$$= \lim_{b\to-\infty}\left[\frac{-1}{3x}\right]_b^{-1} + \lim_{x\to 0^-}\left[\frac{-1}{3x}\right]_{-1}^0 \quad \text{(diverges)}$$

75. Evaluate the improper integral.

$$\int_0^4 \frac{1}{\sqrt{4x}}\,dx$$

Solution:

$$\int_0^4 \frac{1}{\sqrt{4x}}\,dx = \lim_{a\to 0^+}\int_a^4 \frac{1}{2}x^{-1/2}\,dx = \lim_{a\to 0^+}\left[x^{1/2}\right]_a^4 = 2$$

77. Evaluate the improper integral.

$$\int_2^3 \frac{1}{\sqrt{x-2}}\,dx$$

Solution:

$$\int_2^3 \frac{1}{\sqrt{x-2}}\,dx = \lim_{b\to 2^+}\left[2(x-2)^{1/2}\right]_b^3 = 2$$

79. *Present Value* You are considering buying a franchise that yields a continuous income stream of $50,000 per year. Find the present value of the franchise (a) for 15 years and (b) forever. Assume that money earns 6% interest per year, compounded continuously.

Solution:

(a) Present Value $= \displaystyle\int_0^{15} 50{,}000e^{-0.06t}\,dt$

$\qquad\qquad\qquad = \left[\dfrac{50{,}000}{-0.06}e^{-0.06t}\right]_0^{15} \approx \$494{,}525.28$

(b) Present Value $= \displaystyle\int_0^{\infty} 50{,}000e^{-0.06t}\,dt$

$\qquad\qquad\qquad = \lim_{b\to\infty}\left[\dfrac{50{,}000}{-0.06}e^{-0.06t}\right]_0^{b} \approx \$833{,}333.33$

81. *Per Capita Income* In 1991, the per capita income per state was approximately normally distributed with a mean of $18,188.83 and a standard deviation of $2736.16 (see figure in textbook). Find the probability that a state has a per capita income of (a) $20,000 or greater, and (b) $30,000 or greater.

Solution:

$$P(a \le x \le b) = \int_a^b \frac{1}{2736.16\sqrt{2\pi}}e^{-(x-18,188.38)^2/2(2738.16)^2}\,dx$$

Using numerical integration or a graphing utility,

(a) $P(20{,}000 \le x) \approx 0.25$

(b) $P(30{,}000 \le x) \approx 0.79 \times 10^{-5}$ (essentially 0)

Practice Test for Chapter 6

1. Evaluate $\int x\sqrt{x+3}\,dx.$

2. Evaluate $\int \dfrac{x}{(x-2)^3}\,dx.$

3. Evaluate $\int \dfrac{1}{3x+\sqrt{x}}\,dx.$

4. Evaluate $\int \dfrac{\ln 7x}{x}\,dx.$

5. Evaluate $\int xe^{2x}\,dx.$

6. Evaluate $\int x^3 \ln x\,dx.$

7. Evaluate $\int x^2\sqrt{x-6}\,dx.$

8. Evaluate $\int x^2 e^{4x}\,dx.$

9. Evaluate $\int \dfrac{-5}{x^2+x-6}\,dx.$

10. Evaluate $\int \dfrac{x+12}{x^2+4x}\,dx.$

11. Evaluate $\int \dfrac{5x+3}{(x+2)^2}\,dx.$

12. Evaluate $\int \dfrac{3x^3+9x^2-x+3}{x(x+3)}\,dx.$

13. Evaluate $\int \dfrac{1}{x^2\sqrt{16-x^2}}\,dx.$ (Use tables.)   **14.** Evaluate $\int (\ln x)^3\,dx.$ (Use tables.)

15. Evaluate $\int \dfrac{1200}{1+e^{0.06x}}\,dx.$ (Use tables.)

16. Approximate the integral using (a) the Trapezoidal Rule and (b) Simpson's Rule.

$$\int_0^4 \sqrt{3+x^3}\,dx, \quad n=8$$

17. Approximate the integral using (a) the Trapezoidal Rule and (b) Simpson's Rule.

$$\int_0^2 e^{-x^2/2}\,dx, \quad n=4$$

18. Determine the divergence or convergence of the integral. Evaluate the integral if it converges.

$$\int_0^9 \dfrac{1}{\sqrt{x}}\,dx$$

19. Determine the divergence or convergence of the integral. Evaluate the integral if it converges.

$$\int_1^\infty \dfrac{1}{x-3}\,dx$$

20. Determine the divergence or convergence of the integral. Evaluate the integral if it converges.

$$\int_{-\infty}^0 e^{-3x}\,dx$$

Graphing Calculator Required

21. Use a program similar to that on page 428 of the textbook to approximate $\displaystyle\int_0^3 \frac{1}{\sqrt{x^3+1}}dx$ when $n = 50$ and $n = 100$.

22. Complete the following chart using Simpson's Rule to determine the convergence or divergence of $\displaystyle\int_0^1 \frac{1}{\sqrt{1-x^2}}dx$.

n	100	1000	10000
$\displaystyle\int_1^{0.9999999} \frac{1}{\sqrt{1-x^2}}dx$			

Note: The upper limit cannot equal 1 to avoid division by zero. Let $b = 0.9999999$.

CHAPTER 7
Functions of Several Variables

Section 7.1 The Three-Dimensional Coordinate System

1. Plot the points on the same three-dimensional coordinate system.

(a) $(2, 1, 3)$

(b) $(-1, 2, 1)$

Solution:

(a) See graph.

(b) See graph

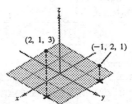

3. Plot the points on the same three-dimensional coordinate system.

(a) $(5, -2, 2)$

(b) $(5, -2, -2)$

Solution:

(a) See graph.

(b) See graph.

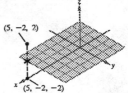

5. Find the distance between the points $(4, 1, 5)$ and $(8, 2, 6)$.

Solution:

$$d = \sqrt{(8-4)^2 + (2-1)^2 + (6-5)^2} = \sqrt{18} = 3\sqrt{2}$$

7. Find the distance between the points $(-1, -5, 7)$ and $(-3, 4, -4)$.

Solution:

$$d = \sqrt{(-3+1)^2 + (4+5)^2 + (-4-7)^2} = \sqrt{206}$$

9. Find the coordinates of the midpoint of the line segment joining the given points $(6, -9, 1)$, $(-2, -1, 5)$.

Solution:

$$\text{Midpoint} = \left(\frac{6+(-2)}{2}, \frac{-9+(-1)}{2}, \frac{1+5}{2} \right) = (2, -5, 3)$$

11. Find the coordinates of the midpoint of the line segment jointing the given points $(-5, -2, 5)$, $(6, 3, -7)$.

Solution:

$$\text{Midpoint} = \left(\frac{-5+6}{2}, \frac{-2+3}{2}, \frac{5+(-7)}{2} \right) = \left(\frac{1}{2}, \frac{1}{2}, -1 \right)$$

13. Find (x, y, z).

Solution:

$$(2, -1, 3) = \left(\frac{x+(-2)}{2}, \frac{y+1}{2}, \frac{z+1}{2} \right)$$

$$2 = \frac{x-2}{2} \qquad -1 = \frac{y+1}{2} \qquad 3 = \frac{z+1}{2}$$

$$4 = x - 2 \qquad -2 = y + 1 \qquad 6 = z + 1$$

$$x = 6 \qquad y = -3 \qquad z = 5(x, y, z) = (6, -3, 5)$$

15. Find (x, y, z).

Solution:

$$\left(\frac{3}{2}, 1, 2 \right) = \left(\frac{x+2}{2}, \frac{y+0}{2}, \frac{z+3}{2} \right)$$

$$\frac{3}{2} = \frac{x+2}{2} \qquad 1 = \frac{y}{2} \qquad 2 = \frac{2+3}{2}$$

$$x = 1 \qquad y = 2 \qquad z = 1(x, y, z) = (1, 2, 1)$$

17. Find the lengths of the sides of a triangle with vertices $(0, 0, 0)$, $(2, 2, 1)$, and $(2, -4, 4)$. Determine whether the triangle is a right triangle, an isosceles triangle, or neither of these.

Solution:

Let $A = (0, 0, 0)$, $B = (2, 2, 1)$, and $C = (2, -4, 4)$. Then we have the following.

$$d(AB) = \sqrt{(2-0)^2 + (2-0)^2 + (1-0)^2} = 3$$

$$d(AC) = \sqrt{(2-0)^2 + (-4-0)^2 + (4-0)^2} = 6$$

$$d(BC) = \sqrt{(2-2)^2 + (-4-2)^2 + (4-1)^2} = 3\sqrt{5}$$

The triangle is a right triangle since

$$d^2(AB) + d^2(AC) = (3)^2 + (6)^2 = 9 + 36 = 45 = d^2(BC).$$

19. Find the lengths of the sides of a triangle with vertices $(-2, 2, 4)$, $(-2, 2, 6)$, and $(-2, 4, 8)$. Determine whether the triangle is a right triangle, an isosceles triangle, or neither of these.

Solution:

Let $A = (-2, 2, 4)$, $B = (-2, 2, 6)$, $C = (-2, 4, 8)$. Then we have the following

$$d(AB) = \sqrt{(-2 - (-2))^2 + (2 - 2)^2 + (6 - 4)^2} = 2$$

$$d(AC) = \sqrt{(-2 - (-2))^2 + (4 - 2)^2 + (8 - 4)^2} = 2\sqrt{5}$$

$$d(BC) = \sqrt{(-2 - (-2))^2 + (4 - 2)^2 + (8 - 6)^2} = 2\sqrt{2}$$

The triangle is neither right nor isosceles.

21. Use the standard form of the equation of the sphere. (See graph in textbook.)

Solution:

$$x^2 + (y - 2)^2 + (z - 2)^2 = 4$$

23. Use the standard form of the equation of the sphere. (See graph in textbook.)

Solution:

The midpoint of the diameter is the center.

$$\text{Center} = \left(\frac{2+1}{2}, \frac{1+3}{2}, \frac{3-1}{2}\right) = \left(\frac{3}{2}, 2, 1\right)$$

The radius is the distance between the center and either endpoint.

$$\text{radius} = \sqrt{\left(2 - \frac{3}{2}\right)^2 + (1 - 2)^2 + (3 - 1)^2}$$

$$= \sqrt{\frac{1}{4} + 1 + 4}$$

$$= \frac{\sqrt{21}}{2} \left(x - \frac{3}{2}\right)^2 + (y - 2)^2 + (z - 1)^2 = \frac{21}{4}$$

25. Find the standard form of the equation of the sphere. Center: $(1, 1, 5)$; Radius: 3

Solution:

$$(x - 1)^2 + (y - 1)^2 + (z - 5)^2 = 9$$

27. Find the standard form of the equation of a sphere with endpoints of a diameter (2, 0, 0) and (0, 6, 0).

Solution:

The midpoint of the diameter is the center.

$$\text{Center} = \left(\frac{2+0}{2}, \frac{0+6}{2}, \frac{0+0}{2}\right) = (1, 3, 0)$$

The radius is the distance between the center and either endpoint.

$$\text{Radius} = \sqrt{(1-2)^2 + (3-0)^2 + (0-0)^2} = \sqrt{10}$$

$$(x-1)^2 + (y-3)^2 + (z-0)^2 = (\sqrt{10})^2$$

$$(x-1)^2 + (y-3)^2 + z^2 = 10$$

29. Find the center and radius of the sphere $x^2 + y^2 + z^2 - 2x + 6y + 8z + 1 = 0$.

Solution:

$$(x-1)^2 + (y+3)^2 + (z+4)^2 = 25$$

Center: $(1, -3, -4)$

Radius: 5

31. Find the center and radius of the sphere $x^2 + y^2 + z^2 - 8y = 0$.

Solution:

$$(x-0)^2 + (y-4)^2 + (z-0)^2 = 16$$

Center: (0, 4, 0)

Radius: 4

33. Find the center and radius of the sphere $2x^2 + 2y^2 + 2z^2 - 4x - 12y - 8z + 3 = 0$.

Solution:

$$(x-1)^2 + (y-3)^2 + (z-2)^2 = -\frac{3}{2} + 1 + 9 + 4 = \frac{25}{2}$$

Center: (1, 3, 2)

Radius: $\dfrac{5}{\sqrt{2}}$

35. Find the center and radius of the sphere $9x^2 + 9y^2 + 9z^2 - 6x + 18y + 1 = 0$.

Solution:

$$\left(x - \tfrac{1}{3}\right)^2 + (y+1)^2 + z^2 = 1$$

Center: $\left(\tfrac{1}{3}, -1, 0\right)$

Radius: 1

37. Sketch the xy-trace of the sphere $(x - 1)^2 + (y - 3)^2 + (z - 2)^2 = 25$.

Solution:

To find the xy-trace, we let $z = 0$.

$$(x - 1)^2 + (y - 3)^2 + (0 - 2)^2 = 25$$
$$(x - 1)^2 + (y - 3)^2 = 21$$

The xy-trace is a circle centered at $(1, 3)$ with radius of $\sqrt{21}$ in the xy-plane.

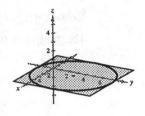

39. Sketch the yz-trace of the sphere $x^2 + y^2 + z^2 - 4x - 4y - 6z - 12 = 0$.

Solution:

$$(x - 2)^2 + (y - 2)^2 + (z - 3)^2 = 29$$

To find the yz-trace, we let $x = 0$.

$$(0 - 2)^2 + (y - 2)^2 + (z - 3)^2 = 29$$
$$4 + (y - 2)^2 + (z - 3)^2 = 29$$
$$(y - 2)^2 + (z - 3)^2 = 25$$

The yz-trace is a circle centered at $(2, 3)$ with a radius of 5 in the yz-plane.

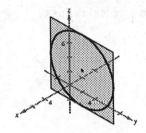

41. Sketch the trace of intersection of the sphere $x^2 + y^2 + z^2 = 25$ with each plane.

(a) $z = 3$ (b) $x = 4$

Solution:

(a) To find the trace with $z = 3$, replace z
with 3 in the equation of the sphere

$$x^2 + y^2 + 3^2 = 25$$
$$x^2 + y^2 = 16.$$

The trace is a circle centered at $(0, 0, 3)$
with a radius of 4.

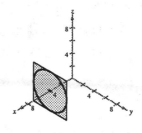

(b) To find the trace with $x = 4$, replace x
with 4 in the equation of the sphere

$$4^2 + y^2 + z^2 = 25$$
$$y^2 + z^2 = 9.$$

The trace is a circle centered at $(4, 0, 0)$
with a radius of 3.

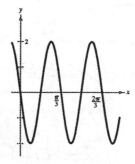

43. Sketch the trace of intersection of the sphere $x^2 + y^2 + z^2 - 4x - 6y + 9 = 0$ with each
plane.

(a) $x = 2$ (b) $y = 3$

Solution:

(a) Let $x = 2$.

$$4 + y^2 + z^2 - 8 - 6y + 9 = 0$$
$$(y - 3)^2 + z^2 = 2^2$$

(b) Let $y = 3$.

$$x^2 + 9 + z^2 - 4x - 18y + 9 = 0$$
$$(x - 2)^2 + z^2 = 2^2$$

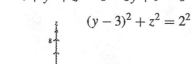

45. *Crystals* Crystals are classified according to their symmetry. Crystals shaped like cubes are classified as isometric. Suppose you have mapped the vertices of a crystal onto a three-dimensional coordinate system. Determine (x, y, z) if the crystal is isometric.

Solution:

Since the crystal is a cube, $A = (3, 3, 0)$. Thus, $(x, y, z) = (3, 3, 3)$

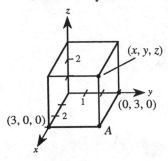

Section 7.2   Surfaces in Space

1. Find the intercepts and sketch the graph of $4x + 2y + 6z = 12$.

Solution:

To find the x-intercept, let $y = 0$ and $z = 0$.
$$4x = 12 \Rightarrow x = 3$$

To find the y-intercept, let $x = 0$ and $z = 0$.
$$2y = 12 \Rightarrow x = 6$$

To find the z-intercept, let $x = 0$ and $y = 0$.
$$6z = 12 \Rightarrow z = 2$$

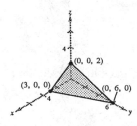

3. Find the intercepts and sketch the graph of $3x + 3y + 5z = 15$.

Solution:

To find the x-intercept, let $y = 0$ and $z = 0$.
$$3x = 15 \Rightarrow x = 5$$

To find the y-intercept, let $x = 0$ and $z = 0$.
$$3y = 15 \Rightarrow y = 5$$

To find the z-intercept, let $x = 0$ and $y = 0$.
$$5z = 15 \Rightarrow z = 3$$

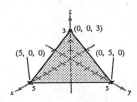

5. Find the intercepts and sketch the graph of $2x - y + 3z = 8$.

Solution:

To find the x-intercept, let $y = 0$ and $z = 0$.
$$2x = 8 \Rightarrow x = 4$$

To find the y-intercept, let $x = 0$ and $z = 0$.
$$-y = 8 \Rightarrow y = -8$$

To find the z-intercept, let $x = 0$ and $y = 0$.
$$3z = 8 \Rightarrow z = \tfrac{8}{3}$$

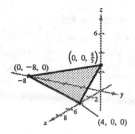

7. Find the intercepts and sketch the graph of $z = 3$.

Solution:

Since the coefficients of x and y are zero, the only intercept is the z-intercept of 3. The plane is parallel to the xy-plane.

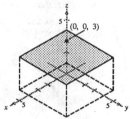

9. Find the intercepts and sketch the graph of $y + z = 5$.

Solution:

The y and z intercepts are both 5, and the plane is parallel to the x-axis.

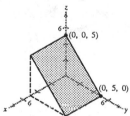

11. Find the intercepts and sketch the graph of $x + y - z = 0$.

Solution:

The only intercept is the origin.
The xy-trace is the line $x + y = 0$.
The xz-trace is the line $x - z = 0$.
The yz-trace is the line $y - z = 0$.

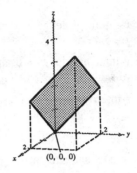

13. Find the intercepts and sketch the graph of $-x + 5y - 3z = 10$.

Solution:

To find the x-intercept, let $y = 0$ and $z = 0$.

$$-x = 10 \Rightarrow x = -10$$

To find the y-intercept, let $x = 0$ and $z = 0$.

$$5y = 10 \Rightarrow y = 2$$

To find the z-intercept, let $x = 0$ and $y = 0$.

$$-3z = 10 \Rightarrow z = -\frac{10}{3}$$

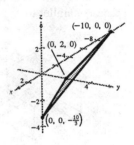

15. Find the intercepts and sketch the graph of $2y - 5z = 5$.

Solution:

The y-intercept is $\dfrac{5}{2}$, the z-intercept is -1, and the plane is parallel to the x-axis.

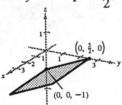

17. Determine whether the planes $5x - 3y + z = 4$ and $x + 4y + 7z = 1$ are parallel, perpendicular, or neither.

Solution:

For the first plane, $a_1 = 5$, $b_1 = -3$, and $c_1 = 1$, and for the second plane, $a_2 = 1$, $b_2 = 4$, and $c_2 = 7$. Therefore, we have

$$a_1 a_2 + b_1 b_2 + c_1 c_2 = (5)(1) + (-3)(4) + (1)(7) = 5 - 12 + 7 = 0$$

The planes are perpendicular.

19. Determine whether the planes $x - 5y - z = 1$ and $5x - 25y - 5z = -3$ are parallel, perpendicular, or neither.

Solution:

For the first plane, $a_1 = 1$, $b_1 = -5$, and $c_1 = -1$, and for the second plane, $a_2 = 5$, $b_2 = -25$, and $c_2 = -5$. Therefore, we have

$$a_2 = 5a_1, \quad b_2 = 5b_1, \quad c_2 = 5c_1.$$

The planes are parallel.

21. Determine whether the planes $x + 2y = 3$ and $4x + 8y = 5$ are parallel, perpendicular, or neither.

Solution:

For the first plane, $a_1 = 1$, $b_1 = 2$, and $c_1 = 0$, and for the second plane, $a_2 = 4$, $b_2 = 8$, and $c_2 = 0$. Therefore, we have

$$a_2 = 4a_1, \quad b_2 = 4b_1, \quad c_2 = 4c_1.$$

The planes are parallel.

23. Determine whether the planes $2x + y = 3$ and $3x - 5z = 0$ are parallel, perpendicular, or neither.

Solution:

For the first plane, $a_1 = 2$, $b_1 = 1$, and $c_1 = 0$, and for the second plane, $a_2 = 3$, $b_2 = 0$, and $c_2 = -5$. The planes are not parallel since

$$3a_1 = 2a_2 \quad \text{and} \quad 3b_1 \neq 2b_2$$

and the planes are not perpendicular since

$$a_1 a_2 + b_1 b_2 + c_1 c_2 = (2)(3) + (1)(0) + (0)(-5) = 6 \neq 0.$$

25. Find the distance between the point (0, 0, 0) and the plane $2x + 3y + z = 12$.

Solution:

$$D = \frac{|ax_0 + by_0 + cz_0 + d|}{\sqrt{a^2 + b^2 + c^2}}$$

$$= \frac{|2(0) + 3(0) + 1(0) - 12|}{\sqrt{(2)^2 + (3)^2 + (1)^2}}$$

$$= \frac{12}{\sqrt{4 + 9 + 1}} = \frac{12}{\sqrt{14}} = \frac{6\sqrt{14}}{7}$$

27. Find the distance between the point (1, 2, 3) and the plane $2x - y + z = 4$.

Solution:

$$D = \frac{|ax_0 + by_0 + cz_0 + d|}{\sqrt{a^2 + b^2 + c^2}} = \frac{|2(1) - 1(2) + 1(3) - 4|}{\sqrt{(2)^2 + (-1)^2 + (1)^2}} = \frac{1}{\sqrt{6}} = \frac{\sqrt{6}}{6}$$

29. Match $(x^2/9) + (y^2/16) + (z^2/9) = 1$ with the correct graph from the text.

Solution:

The graph is an ellipsoid that matches graph (c).

31. Match $4x^2 + 4y^2 - z^2 = 4$ with the correct graph.

Solution:

The graph of $x^2 + y^2 - \dfrac{z^2}{4} = 1$ is a hyperboloid of one sheet that matches graph (f).

33. Match $4x^2 - 4y + z^2 = 0$ with the correct graph from the text.

Solution:

The graph of $y = \dfrac{x^2}{1} + \dfrac{z^2}{4}$ is an elliptic paraboloid that matches graph (d).

35. Match $4x^2 - y^2 + 4z = 0$ with the correct graph from the text.

Solution:

The graph of $z = \dfrac{y^2}{4} - \dfrac{x^2}{1}$ is a hyperbolic paraboloid that matches graph (a).

37. Describe the trace of the surface $x^2 - y - z^2 = 0$ in xy-plane, $y = 1$, yz-plane.

Solution:

$$x^2 - y - z^2 = 0$$

Trace in xy-plane ($z = 0$):	$y = x^2$	Parabola
Trace in plane $y = 1$:	$x^2 - z^2 = 1$	Hyperbola
Trace in yz-plane ($x = 0$):	$y = -z^2$	Parabola.

39. Describe the trace of the surface $\dfrac{x^2}{4} + y^2 + z^2 = 1$ in xy-plane, xz-plane, yz-plane.

Solution:

$$\frac{x^2}{4} + y^2 + z^2 = 1$$

Trace in xy-plane ($z = 0$):	$\dfrac{x^2}{4} + y^2 = 1$	Ellipse
Trace in xz-plane ($y = 0$):	$\dfrac{x^2}{4} + z^2 = 1$	Ellipse
Trace in yz-plane ($x = 0$):	$y^2 + z^2 = 1$	Circle

41. Identify $x^2 + (y^2/4) + z^2 = 1$.

Solution:

The graph is an ellipsoid.

43. Identify $25x^2 + 25y^2 - z^2 = 5$.

Solution:

$$\frac{x^2}{1/5} + \frac{y^2}{1/5} - \frac{z^2}{5} = 1$$

The graph is a hyperboloid of one sheet.

45. Identify $x^2 - y + z^2 = 0$.

Solution:

The graph of $y = x^2 + z^2$ is an elliptic paraboloid.

47. Identify $x^2 - y^2 + z = 0$.

Solution:

The graph of $z = y^2 - x^2$ is a hyperbolic paraboloid.

49. Identify $4x^2 - y^2 + 4z^2 = -16$.

Solution:

The graph of $\dfrac{y^2}{16} - \dfrac{x^2}{4} - \dfrac{z^2}{4} = 1$ is a hyperboloid of two sheets.

51. Identify $z^2 = 9x^2 + y^2$.

Solution:

The graph of $-z^2 + 9x^2 + y^2 = 0$ is an elliptic cone.

53. Identify $3z = -y^2 + x^2$.

Solution:

The graph of $z = \dfrac{x^2}{3} - \dfrac{y^2}{3}$ is a hyperbolic paraboloid.

55. Identify $2x^2 + 2y^2 + 2z^2 - 3x + 4z = 10$.

Solution:

By completing the square, we find that the graph of $\left(x - \dfrac{3}{4}\right)^2 + y^2 + (z+1)^2 = \dfrac{105}{16}$ is a sphere.

57. Use a three-dimensional graphing utility to graph the function $z = y^2 - x^2 + 1$.

Solution:

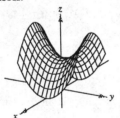

59. Use a three-dimensional graphing utility to graph the function $z = \dfrac{x^2}{2} + \dfrac{y^2}{4}$.

Solution:

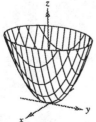

Section 7.3   Functions of Several Variables

1. When $f(x, y) = x/y$, find the following.

   (a) $f(3, 2)$ (b) $f(-1, 4)$ (c) $f(30, 5)$

   (d) $f(5, y)$ (e) $f(x, 2)$ (f) $f(5, t)$

   Solution:

   (a) $f(3, 2) = \dfrac{3}{2}$ (b) $f(-1, 4) = -\dfrac{1}{4}$ (c) $f(30, 5) = 6$

   (d) $f(5, y) = \dfrac{5}{y}$ (e) $f(x, 2) = \dfrac{x}{2}$ (f) $f(5, t) = \dfrac{5}{t}$

3. When $f(x, y) = xe^y$, find the following.

   (a) $f(5, 0)$ (b) $f(3, 2)$ (c) $f(2, -1)$

   (d) $f(5, y)$ (e) $f(x, 2)$ (f) $f(t, t)$

   Solution:

   (a) $f(5, 0) = 5$ (b) $f(3, 2) = 3e^2$ (c) $f(2, -1) = \dfrac{2}{e}$

   (d) $f(5, y) = 5e^y$ (e) $f(x, 2) = xe^2$ (f) $f(t, t) = te^t$

5. When $h(x, y, z) = xy/z$, find the following.

   (a) $h(2, 3, 9)$ (b) $h(1, 0, 1)$

   Solution:

   (a) $h(2, 3, 9) = \dfrac{2}{3}$ (b) $h(1, 0, 1) = 0$

7. When $V(r, h) = \pi r^2 h$, find the following.

   (a) $V(3, 10)$ (b) $V(5, 2)$

   Solution:

   (a) $V(3, 10) = \pi(3)^2(10) = 90\pi$ (b) $V(5, 2) = \pi(5)^2(2) = 50\pi$

9. Find (a) $A(100, 0.10, 10)$ and (b) $A(275, 0.0925, 40)$ when

$$A(P, r, t) = P\left[\left(1 + \frac{r}{12}\right)^{12t} - 1\right]\left(1 + \frac{12}{r}\right).$$

Solution:

(a) $A(100, 0.10, 10) = 100\left[\left(1 + \frac{0.10}{12}\right)^{120} - 1\right]\left(1 + \frac{12}{0.10}\right) \approx \$20, 655.20$

(b) $A(275, 0.0925, 40) = 275\left[\left(1 + \frac{0.0925}{12}\right)^{480} - 1\right]\left(1 + \frac{12}{0.0925}\right) \approx \$1, 397, 672.67$

11. Find (a) $f(1, 2)$ and (b) $f(1, 4)$ when

$$f(x, y) = \int_x^y (2t - 3)\, dt.$$

Solution:

(a) $f(1, 2) = \int_1^2 (2t - 3)\, dt = \left[(t^2 - 3t)\right]_1^2 = (-2) - (-2) = 0$

(b) $f(1, 4) = \int_1^4 (2t - 3)\, dt = \left[(t^2 - 3t)\right]_1^4 = 6$

13. When $f(x, y) = x^2 - 2y$, find the following.

(a) $f(x + \Delta x,\ y)$
(b) $\dfrac{f(x,\ y + \Delta y) - f(x,\ y)}{\Delta y}$

Solution:

(a) $f(x + \Delta x, y) = (x + \Delta x)^2 - 2y$

$\qquad = x^2 + 2x\Delta x + (\Delta x)^2 - 2y$

(b) $\dfrac{f(x, y + \Delta y) - f(x, y)}{\Delta y} = \dfrac{[x^2 - 2(y + \Delta y)] - (x^2 - 2y)}{\Delta y}$

$\qquad = \dfrac{x^2 - 2y - 2\Delta y - x^2 + 2y}{\Delta y} = -\dfrac{2\Delta y}{\Delta y} = -2,\ \Delta y \neq 0$

15. Describe the region R in the xy-coordinate plane that corresponds to the domain of $f(x, y) = \sqrt{16 - x^2 - y^2}$ and find the range of the function.

Solution:

The domain is the set of all points inside and on the circle $x^2 + y^2 = 16$ since $16 - x^2 - y^2 \geq 0$ and the range is $[0, 4]$.

17. Describe the region R in the xy-coordinate plane that corresponds to the domain of $f(x, y) = e^{x/y}$ and find the range of the function.

Solution:

The domain is the set of all points above or below the x-axis since $y \neq 0$. The range is $(0, \infty)$.

19. Describe the region R in the xy-coordinate plane that corresponds to the domain of $f(x, y) = \sqrt{9 - 9x^2 - y^2}$.

Solution:

The domain is the set of all points inside and on the ellipse $9x^2 + y^2 = 9$ since $9 - 9x^2 - y^2 \leq 0$.

21. Describe the region R in the xy-coordinate plane that corresponds to the domain of $f(x, \ y) = x/y$.

Solution:

Since $y \neq 0$, the domain is the set of all points above or below the x-axis.

23. Describe the region R in the xy-coordinate plane that corresponds to the domain of $f(x, y) = 1/xy$.

Solution:

The domain is the set of all points in the xy-plane except those on the x- and y-axes.

25. Describe the region R in the xy-coordinate plane that corresponds to the domain of $h(x, \ y) = x\sqrt{y}$.

Solution:

The domain is the set of all points in the xy-plane such that $y \geq 0$.

27. Describe the region R in the xy-coordinate plane that corresponds to the domain of $g(x, \ y) = \ln(4 - x - y)$.

Solution:

The domain is the half plane below the line $y = -x + 4$ since $4 - x - y > 0$.

29. Match the graph of the surface with one of the contour maps in the textbook.

$$f(x, y) = x^2 + \frac{y^2}{4}$$

Solution:

The contour map consists of ellipses $x^2 + \frac{y^2}{4} = C$. Matches (b).

31. Match the graph of the surface with one of the contour maps in the textbook.

$$f(x, y) = e^{1-x^2-y^2}$$

Solution:

The contour map consists of curves

$$e^{1-x^2-y^2} = C, \text{ or } 1 - x^2 - y^2 = \ln C$$

$$\Rightarrow x^2 + y^2 = 1 - \ln C, \text{ circles. Matches (a).}$$

33. Describe the level curves of the function $z = x + y$. Sketch the level curves for $c = -1, 0, 2, 4$.

Solution:

$$
\begin{array}{lll}
c = -1, & -1 = x + y & y = -x - 1 \\
c = 0, & 0 = x + y & y = -x \\
c = 2, & 2 = x + y & y = -x + 2 \\
c = 4, & 4 = x + y & y = -x + 4
\end{array}
$$

The level curves are parallel lines.

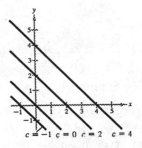

35. Describe the level curves of the function $z = \sqrt{16 - x^2 - y^2}$. Sketch the level curves for $c = 0, 1, 2, 3, 4$.

Solution:

$$
\begin{array}{lll}
c = 0, & 0 = \sqrt{16 - x^2 - y^2}, & x^2 + y^2 = 16 \\
c = 1, & 1 = \sqrt{16 - x^2 - y^2}, & x^2 + y^2 = 15 \\
c = 2, & 2 = \sqrt{16 - x^2 - y^2}, & x^2 + y^2 = 12 \\
c = 3, & 3 = \sqrt{16 - x^2 - y^2}, & x^2 + y^2 = 7 \\
c = 4, & 4 = \sqrt{16 - x^2 - y^2}, & x^2 + y^2 = 0
\end{array}
$$

The level curves are circles.

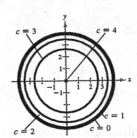

37. Describe the level curves of the function $f(x, y) = xy$. Sketch the level curves for $c = \pm 1, \pm 2, \ldots, \pm 6$.

Solution:

$c = 1,$ $xy = 1$

$c = -1,$ $xy = -1$

$c = 2,$ $xy = 2$

$c = -2,$ $xy = -2$

$c = \pm 3,$ $xy = \pm 3$

$c = \pm 4,$ $xy = \pm 4$

$c = \pm 5,$ $xy = \pm 5$

$c = \pm 6,$ $xy = \pm 6$

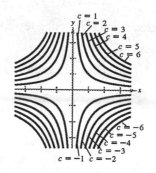

The level curves are hyperbolas.

39. Describe the level curves of the function $f(x, y) = \dfrac{x}{x^2 + y^2}$. Sketch the level curves for $c = \pm\frac{1}{2}, \pm 1, \pm\frac{3}{2}, \pm 2$.

Solution:

$c = \dfrac{1}{2},$ $\dfrac{1}{2} = \dfrac{x}{x^2 + y^2},$ $(x - 1)^2 + y^2 = 1$

$c = -\dfrac{1}{2},$ $-\dfrac{1}{2} = \dfrac{x}{x^2 + y^2},$ $(x + 1)^2 + y^2 = 1$

$c = 1,$ $1 = \dfrac{x}{x^2 + y^2},$ $\left(x - \dfrac{1}{2}\right)^2 + y^2 = \dfrac{1}{4}$

$c = -1,$ $-1 = \dfrac{x}{x^2 + y^2}$ $\left(x + \dfrac{1}{2}\right)^2 + y^2 = \dfrac{1}{4}$

$c = \dfrac{3}{2},$ $\dfrac{3}{2} = \dfrac{x}{x^2 + y^2},$ $\left(x - \dfrac{1}{3}\right)^2 + y^2 = \dfrac{1}{9}$

$c = -\dfrac{3}{2},$ $-\dfrac{3}{2} = \dfrac{x}{x^2 + y^2},$ $\left(x + \dfrac{1}{3}\right)^2 + y^2 = \dfrac{1}{9}$

$c = 2,$ $2 = \dfrac{x}{x^2 + y^2},$ $\left(x - \dfrac{1}{4}\right)^2 + y^2 = \dfrac{1}{16}$

$c = -2,$ $-2 = \dfrac{x}{x^2 + y^2},$ $\left(x + \dfrac{1}{4}\right)^2 + y^2 = \dfrac{1}{16}$

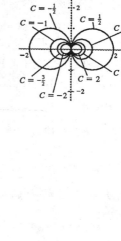

The level curves are circles.

41. *Cobb-Douglas Production Formula* A manufacturer estimates the Cobb-Douglas production function to be

$$f(x, y) = 100x^{0.75}y^{0.25}.$$

Estimate the production level when $x = 1500$ and $y = 1000$.

Solution:

$$f(1500, 1000) = 100(1500)^{0.75}(1000)^{0.25} \approx 135{,}540 \text{ units}$$

43. *Cost* A company manufactures two types of woodburning stoves: a free-standing model and a fireplace-insert model. The cost function for producing x free-standing stoves and y fireplace-insert stoves is

$$C(x, y) = 27\sqrt{xy} + 195x + 215y + 980.$$

Find the cost when $x = 80$ and $y = 20$.

Solution:

$$C(80, 20) = 27\sqrt{(80)(20)} + 195(80) + 215(20) + 980 \approx \$21{,}960.00$$

45. *Profit* A corporation manufactures a product at two locations. The costs of producing x_1 units at location 1 and x_2 units at location 2 are

$$C_1(x_1) - 0.02x_1^2 + 4x_1 + 500$$

and

$$C_2(x_2) = 0.05x_2^2 + 4x_2 + 275,$$

respectively. If the product sells for \$15 per unit, then the profit function for the product is

$$P(x_1, x_2) = 15(x_1 + x_2) - C_1(x_1) - C_2(x_2).$$

Find (a) $P(250, 150)$, and (b) $P(300, 200)$.

Solution:

$$P(x_1, \ x_2) = 15(x_1 + x_2) - (0.02x_1^2 + 4x_1 + 500) - (0.05x_2^2 + 4x^2 + 275)$$
$$= -0.02x_1^2 - 0.05x_2^2 + 11x_1 + 11x_2 - 775$$

(a) $P(250, \ 150) = \$1250.00$

(b) $P(300, \ 200) = \$925.00$

47. *Investment* In 1994, an investment of $1000 was made in a bond earning 10% compounded annually. Assume that the buyer pays tax at rate R and the annual rate of inflation is I. In the year 2004, the value V of the bond in constant 1994 dollars is

$$V(I, \ R) = 1000\left[\frac{1 + 0.10(1 - R)}{1 + I}\right]^{10}.$$

Use this function of two variables to complete the table.

Solution:

		I	
R	0	0.03	0.05
0	$2593.74	$1929.99	$1592.33
0.28	$2004.23	$1491.34	$1230.42
0.35	$1877.14	$1396.77	$1152.40

49. *Equity* The equity per share for Phillips Petroleum Company from 1986 through 1991 can be modeled by

$z = 1.085x + 0.779y - 10.778$,

where x is the total revenue (in billions of dollars) and y is the total assets (in billions of dollars).

(a) Find the equity per share when $x = 15$ and $y = 10$.

(b) Which of the two variables in this model has the greater influence on the equity per share of common stock? Explain your reasoning.

Solution:

(a) $z(15, 10) = 1.086(15) + 0.779(10) - 10.778 = 13.287$.

(b) The variable x has greater influence since its coefficient is larger.

Section 7.4   Partial Derivatives

1. For $f(x, \ y) = 2x - 3y + 5$, find the first partial derivatives with respect to x and with respect to y.

Solution:

$$f_x(x, \ y) = 2$$
$$f_y(x, \ y) = -3$$

3. For $f(x, y) = 5\sqrt{x} - 6y^2$, find the first partial derivatives with respect to x and with respect to y.

Solution:

$$f_x(x, y) = \frac{5}{2\sqrt{x}}$$

$$f_y(x, y) = -12y$$

5. For $f(x, y) = xy$, find the first partial derivatives with respect to x and with respect to y.

Solution:

$$f_x(x, y) = y$$

$$f_y(x, y) = x$$

7. For $z = x\sqrt{y}$, find the first partial derivatives with respect to x and with respect to y.

Solution:

$$\frac{\partial z}{\partial x} = \sqrt{y}$$

$$\frac{\partial z}{\partial y} = \frac{x}{2\sqrt{y}}$$

9. For $f(x, y) = \sqrt{x^2 + y^2}$, find the first partial derivatives with respect to x and with respect to y.

Solution:

$$f_x(x, y) = \frac{1}{2}(x^2 + y^2)^{-1/2}(2x) = \frac{x}{\sqrt{x^2 + y^2}}$$

$$f_y(x, y) = \frac{1}{2}(x^2 + y^2)^{-1/2}(2y) = \frac{y}{\sqrt{x^2 + y^2}}$$

11. For $z = x^2 e^{2y}$, find the first partial derivatives with respect to x and with respect to y.

Solution:

$$\frac{\partial z}{\partial x} = 2xe^{2y}$$

$$\frac{\partial z}{\partial y} = 2x^2 e^{2y}$$

13. For $h(x, y) = e^{-(x^2+y^2)}$, find the first partial derivatives with respect to x and with respect to y.

Solution:

$$h_x(x, y) = -2xe^{-(x^2+y^2)}$$

$$h_y(x, y) = -2ye^{-(x^2+y^2)}$$

15. For $z = \ln(x^2 + y^2)$, find the first partial derivatives with respect to x and with respect to y.

Solution:

$$\frac{\partial z}{\partial x} = \frac{2x}{x^2 + y^2}$$

$$\frac{\partial z}{\partial y} = \frac{2y}{x^2 + y^2}$$

17. For $z = \ln\dfrac{x - y}{(x + y)^2}$, find the first partial derivatives with respect to x and with respect to y.

Solution:

$$z = \ln\frac{x - y}{(x + y)^2} = \ln(x - y) - 2\ln(x + y)$$

$$\frac{\partial z}{\partial x} = \frac{1}{x - y} - \frac{2}{x + y} = \frac{3y - x}{x^2 - y^2}$$

$$\frac{\partial x}{\partial y} = \frac{-1}{x - y} - \frac{2}{x + y} = \frac{y - 3x}{x^2 - y^2}$$

19. Let $f(x, y) = 3x^2 ye^{x-y}$ and $g(x, y) = 3xy^2 e^{y-x}$. Find $f_x(x, y)$.

Solution:

$$f_x(x, y) = 6xye^{x-y} + 3x^2 ye^{x-y} = 3xye^{x-y}(2 + x)$$

21. Let $f(x, y) = 3x^2 ye^{x-y}$ and $g(x, y) = 3xy^2 e^{y-x}$. Find $g_x(x, y)$.

Solution:

$$g_x(x, y) = 3y^2 e^{y-x} - 3xy^2 e^{y-x} = 3y^2 e^{y-x}(1 - x)$$

23. Let $f_x(x, y) = 3x^2 ye^{x-y}$ and $g(x, y) = 3xy^2 e^{y-x}$. Find $f_x(1, 1)$.

Solution:

Using the solution from Exercise 19, $f_x(1, 1) = 9$.

25. When $f(x, \ y) = 3x^2 + xy - y^2$, evaluate f_x and f_y at point $(2, 1)$.

Solution:

$$f_x(x, \ y) = 6x + y, \qquad f_x(2, \ 1) = 13$$
$$f_y(x, \ y) = x - 2y, \qquad f_y(2, \ 1) = 0$$

27. When $f(x, y) = xy/(x - y)$, evaluate f_x and f_y at the point $(2, -2)$.

Solution:

$$f_x(x, y) = \frac{(x - y)y - xy}{(x - y)^2} = -\frac{y^2}{(x - y)^2} \qquad f_x(2, -2) = -\frac{4}{16} = -\frac{1}{4}$$

$$f_y(x, y) = \frac{(x - y)x - xy(-1)}{(x - y)^2} = \frac{x^2}{(x - y)^2} \qquad f_y(2, -2) = \frac{4}{16} = \frac{1}{4}$$

29. If $w = \sqrt{x^2 + y^2 + z^2}$, find the first partial derivatives with respect to x, y, and z, and evaluate these partial derivatives at the point $(2, -1, 2)$.

Solution:

$$w_x = \frac{x}{\sqrt{x^2 + y^2 + z^2}}, \quad \text{at } (2, -1, 2), \quad w_x = \frac{2}{3}$$

$$w_y = \frac{y}{\sqrt{x^2 + y^2 + z^2}}, \quad \text{at } (2, -1, 2), \quad w_y = -\frac{1}{3}$$

$$w_z = \frac{z}{\sqrt{x^2 + y^2 + z^2}}, \quad \text{at } (2, -1, 2), \quad w_z = \frac{2}{3}$$

31. If $w = \ln\sqrt{x^2 + y^2 + z^2}$, find the first partial derivatives with respect to x, y, and z and evaluate these partial derivatives at point $(3, 0, 4)$.

Solution:

$$w = \ln\sqrt{x^2 + y^2 + z^2} = \frac{1}{2}\ln(x^2 + y^2 + z^2)$$

$$w_x = \frac{x}{x^2 + y^2 + z^2}, \qquad w_x(3, 0, 4) = \frac{3}{25}$$

$$w_y = \frac{y}{x^2 + y^2 + z^2}, \qquad w_y(3, 0, 4) = 0$$

$$w_z(x, y, z) = \frac{z}{x^2 + y^2 + z^2}, \qquad w_z(3, 0, 4) = \frac{4}{25}$$

33. Evaluate $w = 2xz^2 + 3xyz - 6y^2z$ at the point $(1, -1, 2)$.

Solution:

$$w_x = 2z^2 + 3yz \qquad\qquad w_x(1, -1, 2) = 8 - 6 = 2$$

$$w_y = 3xz - 12yz \qquad\qquad w_y(1, -1, 2) = 6 + 24 = 30$$

$$w_z = 4xz + 3xy - 6y^2 \qquad w_z(1, -1, 2) = 8 - 3 - 6 = -1$$

35. Evaluate $w = \dfrac{x + 2z}{(x + y + z)^2}$ at the point $(2, 1, 2)$.

Solution:

$$w_x = \frac{y - x - 3z}{(x + y + z)^3} \qquad w_x(2, 1, 2) = \frac{7}{125}$$

$$w_y = -2\frac{x + 2z}{(x + y + 2)^3} \qquad w_x(2, 1, 2) = -\frac{12}{125}$$

$$w_z = 2\frac{y - 2}{(x + y + z)^3} \qquad w_z(2, 1, 2) = -\frac{2}{125}$$

37. For $f(x, y) = x^2 + 4xy + y^2 - 4x + 16y + 3$, find the solution(s) to the system of equations $f_x(x, y) = 0$ and $f_y(x, y) = 0$.

Solution:

$$\left. \begin{array}{l} f_x(x, y) = 2x + 4y - 4 = 0 \\ f_y(x, y) = 4x + 2y + 16 = 0 \end{array} \right\} \quad \begin{array}{r} -4x - 8y = -8 \\ 4x + 2y = -16 \\ \hline \end{array}$$

$$\begin{array}{r} -6y = -24 \\ y = 4 \\ x = -6 \end{array}$$

Solution: $(-6, 4)$

39. Find the solution(s) to the system of equations $f_x(x, y) = 0$ and $f_y(x, y) = 0$ for the following.

$$f(x, y) = \frac{1}{x} + \frac{1}{y} + xy$$

Solution:

$$\left. \begin{array}{l} f_x(x, y) = -\dfrac{1}{x^2} + y = 0 \Rightarrow x^2 y = 1 \\ f_y(x, y) = -\dfrac{1}{y^2} + x = 0 \Rightarrow y^2 x = 1 \end{array} \right\} \quad x = y = 1$$

Solution: $(1, 1)$

41. For $z = 2x - 3y + 5$, find the slope of the surface at the point $(2, 1, 6)$ in (a) the x-direction and (b) the y-direction.

Solution:

(a) $\dfrac{\partial z}{\partial x} = 2;$ at $(2, 1, 6)$, $\dfrac{\partial z}{\partial x} = 2$ \qquad (b) $\dfrac{\partial z}{\partial y} = -3;$ at $(2, 1, 6)$, $\dfrac{\partial z}{\partial y} = -3$

43. For $z = x^2 = 9y^2$, find the slope of the surface at the point $(3, 1, 0)$ in (a) the x-direction and (b) the y-direction.

Solution:

(a) $\dfrac{\partial z}{\partial x} = 2x$; at $(3, 1, 0)$, $\dfrac{\partial z}{\partial x} = 6$

(b) $\dfrac{\partial z}{\partial y} = -18y$; at $(3, 1, 0)$, $\dfrac{\partial z}{\partial y} = -18$

45. For $z = \sqrt{25 - x^2 - y^2}$, find the slope of the surface at the point $(3, 0, 4)$ in (a) the x-direction and (b) the y-direction.

Solution:

(a) $\dfrac{\partial z}{\partial x} = -\dfrac{x}{\sqrt{25 - x^2 - y^2}}$;   at $(3, 0, 4)$, $\dfrac{\partial z}{\partial x} = -\dfrac{3}{4}$

(b) $\dfrac{\partial z}{\partial y} = -\dfrac{y}{\sqrt{25 - x^2 - y^2}}$;   at $(3, 0, 4)$, $\dfrac{\partial z}{\partial y} = 0$

47. For $z = 4 - x^2 - y^2$, find the slope of the surface at the point $(1, 1, 2)$ in (a) the x-direction and (b) the y-direction.

Solution:

(a) $\dfrac{\partial z}{\partial x} = -2x$; at $(1, 1, 2)$, $\dfrac{\partial z}{\partial x} = -2$

(b) $\dfrac{\partial z}{\partial y} = -2y$; at $(1, 1, 2)$, $\dfrac{\partial z}{\partial y} = -2$

49. Show that $\partial^2 z/\partial x \partial y = \partial^2 z/\partial y \partial x$ for $z = x^2 - 2xy + 3y^2$.

Solution:

$\dfrac{\partial z}{\partial x} = 2x - 2y$ $\dfrac{\partial^2 z}{\partial y \partial x} = -2$

$\dfrac{\partial z}{\partial y} = -2x + 6y$ $\dfrac{\partial^2 z}{\partial x \partial y} = -2$

51. Show that $\partial^2 z/\partial x \partial y = \partial^2 z/\partial y \partial x$ for $z = \dfrac{e^{2xy}}{4x}$.

Solution:

$\dfrac{\partial z}{\partial x} = \dfrac{e^{2xy}(2xy - 1)}{4x^2}$ $\dfrac{\partial^2 z}{\partial y \partial x} = ye^{2xy}$

$\dfrac{\partial z}{\partial y} = \dfrac{1}{2}e^{2xy}$ $\dfrac{\partial^2 z}{\partial x \partial y} = ye^{2xy}$

53. Find the second partial derivatives for $\dfrac{\partial^2 z}{\partial x^2}, \dfrac{\partial^2 z}{\partial y^2}, \dfrac{\partial^2 z}{\partial y \partial z}$ and $\dfrac{\partial^2 z}{\partial x \partial y}$ for $z = x^3 - 4y^2$.

Solution:

The first partial derivatives are

$$\frac{\partial z}{\partial x} = 3x^2 \quad \text{and} \quad \frac{\partial z}{\partial y} = -8y$$

and the second partial derivatives are

$$\frac{\partial^2 z}{\partial x^2} = 6x, \qquad \frac{\partial^2 z}{\partial y \partial x} = 0 = \frac{\partial^2 z}{\partial x \partial y}, \quad \text{and} \quad \frac{\partial^2 z}{\partial y^2} = -8.$$

55. Find the second partial derivatives for $\dfrac{\partial^2 z}{\partial x^2}, \dfrac{\partial^2 z}{\partial y^2}, \dfrac{\partial^2 z}{\partial y \partial z}$ and $\dfrac{\partial^2 z}{\partial x \partial y}$ for $z = 4x^3 + 3xy^2 - 4y^3$.

Solution:

The first partial derivatives are

$$\frac{\partial z}{\partial x} = 12x^2 + 3y^2 \quad \text{and} \quad \frac{\partial z}{\partial y} = 6xy - 12y^2$$

and the second partial derivatives are

$$\frac{\partial^2 z}{\partial x^2} = 24x, \qquad \frac{\partial^2 z}{\partial y \partial x} = 6y = \frac{\partial^2 z}{\partial x \partial y}, \quad \text{and} \quad \frac{\partial^2 z}{\partial y^2} = 6x - 24y.$$

57. Find the second partial derivatives for $\dfrac{\partial^2 z}{\partial x^2}, \dfrac{\partial^2 z}{\partial y^2}, \dfrac{\partial^2 z}{\partial y \partial z}$ and $\dfrac{\partial^2 z}{\partial x \partial y}$ for $z = 9 + 4x - 6y - x^2 - y^2$.

Solution:

The first partial derivatives are

$$\frac{\partial z}{\partial x} = 4 - 2x \quad \text{and} \quad \frac{\partial z}{\partial y} = -6 - 2y$$

and the second partial derivatives are

$$\frac{\partial^2 z}{\partial x^2} = -2, \qquad \frac{\partial^2 z}{\partial y \partial x} = 0 = \frac{\partial^2 z}{\partial x \partial y}, \quad \text{and} \quad \frac{\partial^2 z}{\partial y^2} = -2.$$

59. Find the second partial derivatives for $\dfrac{\partial^2 z}{\partial x^2}, \dfrac{\partial^2 z}{\partial y^2}, \dfrac{\partial^2 z}{\partial y \partial z}$ and $\dfrac{\partial^2 z}{\partial x \partial y}$ for $z = \dfrac{xy}{x-y}$.

Solution:

From Exercise 27, the first partial derivatives are

$$\frac{\partial z}{\partial x} = \frac{-y^2}{(x-y)^2} \quad \text{and} \quad \frac{\partial z}{\partial y} = \frac{x^2}{(x-y)^2}$$

and the second partial derivatives are

$$\frac{\partial^2 z}{\partial x^2} = \frac{2y^2}{(x-y)^3}, \qquad \frac{\partial^2 z}{\partial y \partial x} = \frac{-2xy}{(x-y)^3} = \frac{\partial^2 z}{\partial x \partial y}, \quad \text{and} \quad \frac{\partial^2 z}{\partial y^2} = \frac{2x^2}{(x-y)^3}.$$

61. Find the second partial derivatives for $\dfrac{\partial^2 z}{\partial x^2}, \dfrac{\partial^2 z}{\partial y^2}, \dfrac{\partial^2 z}{\partial y \partial z}$ and $\dfrac{\partial^2 z}{\partial x \partial y}$ for $z = \sqrt{x^2 + y^2}$.

Solution:

The first partial derivatives are

$$\frac{\partial z}{\partial x} = \frac{x}{\sqrt{x^2 + y^2}} \quad \text{and} \quad \frac{\partial z}{\partial y} = \frac{y}{\sqrt{x^2 + y^2}}$$

and the second partial derivatives are

$$\frac{\partial^2 z}{\partial x^2} = \frac{\sqrt{x^2 + y^2} - x(x/\sqrt{x^2 + y^2})}{x^2 + y^2} = \frac{y^2}{(x^2 + y^2)^{3/2}},$$

$$\frac{\partial^2 z}{\partial y \partial x} = -\frac{1}{2}x(x^2 + y^2)^{-3/2}(2y) = -\frac{xy}{(x^2 + y^2)^{3/2}} = \frac{\partial^2 z}{\partial x \partial y}, \quad \text{and}$$

$$\frac{\partial^2 z}{\partial y^2} = \frac{\sqrt{x^2 + y^2} - y(y/\sqrt{x^2 + y^2})}{x^2 + y^2} = \frac{x^2}{(x^2 + y^2)^{3/2}}.$$

63. Find the second partial derivatives for $\dfrac{\partial^2 z}{\partial x^2}, \dfrac{\partial^2 z}{\partial y^2}, \dfrac{\partial^2 z}{\partial y \partial z}$ and $\dfrac{\partial^2 z}{\partial x \partial y}$ for $z = xe^{-y^2}$.

Solution:

The first partial derivatives are

$$\frac{\partial z}{\partial x} = e^{-y^2} \quad \text{and} \quad \frac{\partial z}{\partial y} = -2xye^{-y^2}$$

and the second partial derivatives are

$$\frac{\partial^2 z}{\partial x^2} = 0,$$

$$\frac{\partial^2 z}{\partial y \partial x} = -2ye^{-y^2} = \frac{\partial^2 z}{\partial x \partial y}, \quad \text{and}$$

$$\frac{\partial^2 z}{\partial y^2} = -2xe^{-y^2} + 4xy^2e^{-y^2} = 2xe^{-y^2}(2y^2 - 1).$$

65. Find the first partial derivatives of $w = 3x^2y - 5xyz + 10yz^2$ with respect to x, y, and z.

Solution:

$$w_x = 6xy - 5yz$$
$$w_y = 3x^2 - 5xz + 10z^2$$
$$w_z = -5xy + 20yz$$

67. Find the first partial derivatives of $w = \dfrac{xy}{x+y+z}$ with respect to x, y, and z.

Solution:

$$w_x = \frac{y(y+z)}{(x+y+z)^2}$$
$$w_y = \frac{x(x+z)}{(x+y+z)^2}$$
$$w_z = \frac{-xy}{(x+y+z)^2}$$

69. *Marginal Cost* A company manufactures two models of bicycles: a mountain bike and a racing bike. The cost function for producing x mountain bikes and y racing bikes is

$$C = 10\sqrt{xy} + 149x + 189y + 675.$$

Find the marginal costs ($\partial C/\partial x$ and $\partial C/\partial y$) when $x = 120$ and $y = 160$.

Solution:

$$\frac{\partial C}{\partial x} = \frac{5y}{\sqrt{xy}} + 149; \text{ at } (120, 160), \frac{\partial C}{\partial x} \approx 154.77$$

$$\frac{\partial C}{\partial y} = \frac{5x}{\sqrt{xy}} + 189: \text{ at } (120, 160), \frac{\partial C}{\partial y} \approx 193.33$$

71. *Marginal Productivity* Let $x = 1000$ and $y = 500$ in the Cobb-Douglas production function

$$f(x, \ y) = 100x^{0.6}y^{0.4}.$$

(a) Find the marginal productivity of labor, $\partial f/\partial x$.

(b) Find the marginal productivity of capital, $\partial f/\partial y$.

Solution:

(a) $\dfrac{\partial f}{\partial x} = 60x^{-0.4}y^{0.4} = 60\left(\dfrac{y}{x}\right)^{0.4}, \quad$ at $(1000, \ 500), \quad \dfrac{\partial f}{\partial x} \approx 45.47.$

(b) $\dfrac{\partial f}{\partial y} = 40x^{0.6}y^{-0.6} = 40\left(\dfrac{x}{y}\right)^{0.6}, \quad$ at $(1000, \ 500), \quad \dfrac{\partial f}{\partial y} \approx 60.63.$

73. *Complementary and Substitute Products* Let x_1 and x_2 be the demands for Products 1 and 2, respectively, and p_1 and p_2 the prices of Products 1 and 2, respectively. Determine if the following demand functions describe complementary or substitute product relationships.

(a) $x_1 = 150 - 2p_1 - \left(\dfrac{5}{2}\right)p_2, \quad x_2 = 350 - \left(\dfrac{3}{2}\right)p_1 - 3p_2$

(b) $x_1 = 150 - 2p_1 + 1.8p_2, \quad x_2 = 350 + 0.75p_1 - 1.9p_2$

(c) $x_1 = \dfrac{1000}{\sqrt{p_1 p_2}}, \quad x_2 = \dfrac{750}{p_2\sqrt{p_1}}$

Solution:

(a) Complementary since $\dfrac{\partial x_1}{\partial p_2} = -\dfrac{5}{2} < 0$ and $\dfrac{\partial x_2}{\partial p_1} = -\dfrac{3}{2} < 0.$

(b) Substitute since $\dfrac{\partial x_1}{\partial p_2} = 1.8 > 0$ and $\dfrac{\partial x_2}{\partial p_1} = 0.75 > 0.$

(c) Complementary since $\dfrac{\partial x_1}{\partial p_2} = \dfrac{-500}{p_1{}^2 p_2\sqrt{p_1 p_2}} < 0$ and $\dfrac{\partial x_2}{\partial p_1} = \dfrac{-375}{p_1 p_2\sqrt{p_1}} < 0.$

75. *University Admissions* Let N be the number of applicants to a university, p the charge for food and housing at the university, and t the tuition. Suppose that N is a function of p and t such that $\partial N/\partial p < 0$ and $\partial N/\partial t < 0$. How would you interpret the fact that both partials are negative?

Solution:

Since both first partials are negative, an increase in the charge for food and housing or tuition will cause a decrease in the number of applicants.

77. *Marginal Utility* The utility function $U = f(x, y)$ is a measure of the utility (or satisfaction) derived by a person from the consumption of two goods x and y. Suppose the utility function is

$$U = -5x^2 + xy - 3y^2.$$

(a) Determine the marginal utility of good x.

(b) Determine the marginal utility of good y.

(c) When $x = 2$ and $y = 3$, should a person consume one more unit of good x or one more unit of good y? Explain your reasoning.

(d) Use a three-dimensional graphing utility to graph the function. Interpret the marginal utilities of goods x and y graphically.

Solution:

(a) $U_x = -10x + y$

(b) $U_y = x - 6y$

(c) When $x = 2$ and $y = 3$, $U_x = -17$ and $U_y = -16$. The person should consume one more unit of good y, since the rate of decrease of satisfaction is less for y.

(d)

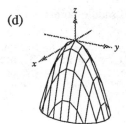

Graph of $U = -5x^2 + xy - 3y^2$

Section 7.5   Extrema of Functions of Two Variables

1. Find any critical points and relative extrema of the function
$$f(x, y) = x^2 - y^2 + 4x - 8y - 11.$$

Solution:

The first partial derivatives of f, $f_x(x, y) = 2x + 4$ and $f_y(x, y) = -2y - 8$, are zero at the point $(-2, -4)$. Moreover, since

$$f_{xx}(x, y) = 2, \quad f_{yy}(x, y) = -2, \text{ and } f_{xy}(x, y) = 0,$$

it follows that

$$f_{xx}(2, 4)f_{yy}(2, 4) - [f_{xy}(2, 4)]^2 = -4 < 0.$$

Thus, $(-2, -4, 1)$ is a saddle point. There are no relative extrema.

3. Find any critical points and relative extrema of the function $f(x, y) = \sqrt{x^2 + y^2 + 1}$.

   Solution:

   The first partial derivatives of f,

   $$f_x(x, y) = \frac{x}{\sqrt{x^2 + y^2 + 1}} \quad \text{and} \quad f_y(x, y) = \frac{y}{\sqrt{x^2 + y^2 + 1}},$$

   are zero at the point $(0, 0)$. Moreover, since

   $$f_{xx}(x, y) = \frac{y^2 + 1}{(x^2 + y^2 + 1)^{3/2}}, \quad f_{yy}(x, y) = \frac{x^2 + 1}{(x^2 + y^2 + 1)^{3/2}}, \text{ and}$$

   $$f_{xy}(x, y) = \frac{-xy}{(x^2 + y^2 + 1)^{3/2}},$$

   it follows that

   $$f_{xx}(0, 0) = 1 > 0 \text{ and } f_{xx}(0, 0)f_{yy}(0, 0) - [f_{xy}(0, 0)]^2 = 1 > 0.$$

   Thus, $(0, 0, 1)$ is a relative minimum.

5. Examine $f(x, y) = (x - 1)^2 + (y - 3)^2$ for relative extrema and saddle points.

   Solution:

   The first partial derivatives of f, $f_x(x, y) = 2(x - 1)$ and $f_y(x, y) = 2(y - 3)$, are zero at the point $(1, 3)$. Moreover, since

   $$f_{xx}(x, y) = 2, \quad f_{yy}(x, y) = 2, \quad \text{and} \quad f_{xy}(x, y) = 0,$$

   it follows that

   $$f_{xx}(1, 3) > 0 \text{ and } f_{xx}(1, 3)f_{yy}(1, 3) - [f_{xy}(1, 3)]^2 = 4 > 0.$$

   Thus, $(1, 3, 0)$ is a relative minimum.

7. Examine $f(x, y) = 2x^2 + 2xy + y^2 + 2x - 3$ for relative extrema and saddle points.

   Solution:

   The first partial derivatives of f, $f_x(x, y) = 4x + 2y + 2$ and $f_y(x, y) = 2x + 2y$, are zero at the point $(-1, 1)$. Moreover, since

   $$f_{xx}(x, y) = 4, \quad f_{yy}(x, y) = 2, \quad \text{and} \quad f_{xy}(x, y) = 2,$$

   it follows that

   $$f_{xx}(-1, 1) > 0 \text{ and } f_{xx}(-1, 1)f_{yy}(-1, 1) - [f_{xy}(-1, 0)]^2 = 4 > 0.$$

   Thus, $(-1, 1, -4)$ is a relative minimum.

9. Examine $f(x, \ y) = -5x^2 + 4xy - y^2 + 16x + 10$ for relative extrema and saddle points.

Solution:

The first partial derivatives of f, $f_x(x, \ y) = -10x + 4y + 16$ and $f_y(x, \ y) = 4x - 2y$, are zero at the point $(8, 16)$. Moreover, since

$$f_{xx}(x, \ y) = -10, \quad f_{yy}(x, \ y) = -2, \quad \text{and} \quad f_{xy}(x, \ y) = 4,$$

it follows that

$$f_{xx}(8, \ 16) < 0 \text{ and } f_{xx}(8, \ 16)f_{yy}(8, \ 16) - [f_{xy}(8, \ 16)]^2 = 4 > 0.$$

Thus, $(8, 16, 74)$ is a relative maximum.

11. Examine $f(x, y) = 3x^2 + 2y^2 - 12x - 4y + 7$ for relative extrema and saddle points.

Solution:

The first partial derivatives of f, $fx(x, y) = 6x - 12$ and $f_y(x, y) = 4y - 4$, are zero at the point $(2, 1)$. Moreover, since

$$f_{xx}(x, y) = 6, f_{yy}(x, y) = 4 \text{ and } f_{xy}(x, y) = 0$$

it follows that

$$f_{xx}(2, 1) > 0 \text{ and } f_{xx}(2, 1)f_{yy}(2, 1) - [f_{xy}(2, 1)]^2 = 24 > 0. \text{ Thus } (2, 1, -7) \text{ is a}$$
relative minimum.

13. Examine $f(x, \ y) = x^2 - y^2 + 4x - 4y - 8$ for relative extrema and saddle points.

Solution:

The first partial derivatives of f, $f_x(x, \ y) = 2x + 4$ and
$f_y(x, \ y) = -2y - 4 = -2(y + 2)$, are zero at the point $(-2, \ -2)$. Moreover, since

$$f_{xx}(x, \ y) = 2, \quad f_{yy}(x, \ y) = -2, \text{ and } f_{xy}(x, \ y) = 0,$$

it follows that

$$f_{xx}(1, \ -2)f_{yy}(1, \ -2) - [f_{xy}(1, \ -2)]^2 = -4 < 0.$$

Thus, $(-2 \ -2, \ -8)$ is a saddle point.

15. Example $f(x, y) = xy$ for relative extrema and saddle points.

    Solution:

    The first partial derivatives of f, $f_x(x, y) = y$ and $f_y(x, y) = x$, are zero at the point $(0, 0)$. Moreover, since

    $$f_{xx}(x, y) = 0, \quad f_{yy}(x, y) = 0, \text{ and } f_{xy}(x, y) = 1,$$

    it follows that

    $$f_{xx}(0, 0)f_{yy}(0, 0) - [f_{xy}(0, 0)]^2 = -1 < 0.$$

    Thus, $(0, 0, 0)$ is a saddle point.

17. Examine $f(x, y) = (x^2 + 4y^2)e^{1-x^2-y^2}$ for relative extrema and saddle points.

    Solution:

    The first partial derivatives of f,

    $$f_x(x, y) = 2xe^{1-x^2-y^2}(1 - x^2 - 4y^2) \text{ and } f_y(x, y) = 2ye^{1-x^2-y^2}(4 - x^2 - 4y^2)$$

    are zero at $(0, 0)$, $(0, \pm 1)$, and $(\pm 1, 0)$. Moreover, since

    $$f_{xx}(x, y) = 2e^{1-x^2-y^2}(1 - 5x^2 + 2x^4 - 4y^2 + 8x^2y^2),$$

    $$f_{yy}(x, y) = 2e^{1-x^2-y^2}(4 - x^2 - 20y^2 + 8y^4 + 2x^2y^2), \text{ and}$$

    $$f_{xy}(x, y) = -4xye^{1-x^2-y^2}(5 - x^2 - 4y^2),$$

    we can determine that $(0, 0, 0)$ is a relative minimum, $(0, \pm 1, 4)$ are relative maxima, and $(\pm 1, 0, 1)$ are saddle points.

19. Examine $f(x, y) = e^{xy}$ for relative extrema and saddle points.

    Solution:

    The first partial derivatives of f, $f_x(x, y) = ye^{xy}$ and $f_y(x, y) = xe^{xy}$, are zero at the point $(0, 0)$. Moreover, since

    $$f_{xx}(x, y) = y^2e^{xy}, \quad f_{yy}(x, y) = x^2e^{xy}, \text{ and } f_{xy}(x, y) = e^{xy}(1 + xy),$$

    it follows that $f_{xx}(0, 0) = 0$ and

    $$f_{xx}(0, 0)f_{yy}(0, 0) - [f_{xy}(0, 0)]^2 = -1 < 0.$$

    Thus, $(0, 0, 1)$ is a saddle point.

21. Determine whether there is a relative maximum, a relative minimum, a saddle point, or insufficient information to determine the nature of the function $f(x, y)$ at the critical point (x_0, y_0).

$f_{xx}(x_0, y_0) = 16$

$f_{yy}(x_0, y_0) = 4$

$f_{xy}(x_0, y_0) = 8$

Solution:

Since $d = f_{xx}(x_0, y_0) f_{yy}(x_0, y_0) - [f_{xy}(x_0, y_0)]^2 = (16)(4) - (8)^2 = 0$, there is insufficient information.

23. Determine whether there is a relative maximum, a relative minimum, a saddle point, or insufficient information to determine the nature of the function $f(x, y)$ at the critical point (x_0, y_0).

$f_{xx}(x_0, y_0) = -7$

$f_{yy}(x_0, y_0) = 4$

$f_{xy}(x_0, y_0) = 9$

Solution:

Since $d = f_{xx}(x_0, y_0) f_y(x_0, y_0) - [f_{xy}(x_0, y_0)]^2 = (-7)(4) - (9)^2 < 0$, $f(x_0, y_0)$ is a saddle point.

25. Find the critical points and test the relative extrema of the function $f(x, y) = (xy)^2$. List the critical points for which the Second-Partials Test fails.

Solution:

The first partial derivatives of f, $f_x(x, y) = 2xy^2$ and $f_y(x, y) = 2x^2 y$, are zero at the points $(a, 0)$ and $(0, b)$ where a and b are any real numbers. Since

$$f_{xx}(x, y) = 2y^2, \quad f_{yy}(x, y) = 2x^2, \text{ and } f_{xy}(x, y) = 4xy,$$

it follows that

$$f_{xx}(a, 0) f_{yy}(a, 0) - [f_{xy}(a, 0)]^2 = 0 \quad \text{and} \quad f_{xx}(0, b) f_{yy}(0, b) - [f_{xy}(0, b)]^2 = 0$$

and the Second Derivative Test fails. We note that $f(x, y) = (xy)^2$ is nonnegative for all $(a, 0, 0)$ and $(0, b, 0)$ where a and b are real numbers. Therefore, $(a, 0, 0)$ and $(0, b, 0)$ are relative minima.

27. Find the critical points and test the relative extrema of the function $f(x, y) = x^3 + y^3$. List the critical points for which the Second- Partials Test fails.

Solution:

The first partial derivatives of f, $f_x(x, y) = 3x^2$ and $f_y(x, y) = 3y^2$, are zero at $(0, 0)$. Moreover, since

$$f_{xx}(x, y) = 6x, \quad f_{yy}(x, y) = 6y, \quad f_{xy}(x, y) = 0, \text{ and}$$

$$f_{xx}(0, 0)f_{yy}(0, 0) - [f_{xy}(0, 0)]^2 = 0,$$

the Second-Partials Test fails. By testing "nearby" points, we conclude that $(0, 0, 0)$ is a saddle point.

29. Find the critical points and test the relative extrema of the function $f(x, y) = x^{2/3} + y^{2/3}$. List the critical points for which the Second–Partials Test fails.

Solution:

The first partial derivatives of f,

$$f_x(x, y) = \frac{2}{3\sqrt[3]{x}} \text{ and } f_y(x, y) = \frac{2}{3\sqrt[3]{y}},$$

are undefined at the point $(0, 0)$. Since

$$f_{xx}(x, y) = -\frac{2}{9x^{4/3}}, \quad f_{yy}(x, y) = -\frac{2}{9y^{4/3}}, \quad f_{xy}(x, y) = 0$$

and $f_{xx}(0, 0)$ is undefined, the Second-Derivative Test fails. Since $f(x, y) \geq 0$ for all points in the xy-coordinate plane, $(0, 0, 0)$ is a relative minimum.

31. Find the critical points of the function and from the form of the function determine whether each critical point is a relative maximum or a relative minimum.

$$f(x, y, z) = (x - 1)^2 + (y + 3)^2 + z^2$$

Solution:

Critical point: $(x, y, z) = (1, -3, 0)$, a relative minimum.

33. Determine whether the statement is true or false. If it is false, explain why or give an example that shows it is false.

If $d > 0$ and $f_x(a, b) < 0$, then $f(a, b)$ is a relative minimum.

Solution:

False. (a, b) must be a critical point.

35. Determine whether the statement is true or false. If it is false, explain why or give an example that shows it is false.

If $f(x, y)$ has a relative maximum at (x_0, y_0, z_0), then $f_x(x_0, y_0) = f_y(x_0, y_0) = 0$.

Solution:

False. The function need not have partial derivatives.

37. When the sum is 30 and the product is maximum, find three positive numbers x, y, and z that satisfy these conditions.

Solution:

Let x, y, and z be the numbers. The sum is given by

$$x + y + z = 30 \text{ and } z = 30 - x - y$$

and the product is given by $P = xyz = 30xy - x^2y - xy^2$. The first partial derivatives of P are

$$P_x = 30y - 2xy - y^2 = y(30 - 2x - y)$$
$$P_y = 30x - x^2 - 2xy = x(30 - x - 2y).$$

Setting these equal to zero produces the system

$$2x + \ y = \ 30$$
$$x + 2y = 30.$$

Solving the system, we have $x = 10$, $y = 10$, and $z = 10$.

39. When the sum is 30 and the sum of the squares is minimum, find three positive numbers x, y, and z that satisfy these conditions.

Solution:

The sum is given by

$$x + y + z = 30$$
$$z = 30 - x - y$$

and the sum of the squares is given by $S = x^2 + y^2 + z^2 = x^2 + y^2 + (30 - x - y)^2$. The first partial derivatives of S are

$$S_x = 2x - 2(30 - x - y) = 4x + 2y - 60 \text{ and } S_y = 2y - 2(30 - x - y) = 2x + 4y - 60.$$

Setting these equal to zero produces the system

$$2x + \ y = \ 30$$
$$x + 2y = 30.$$

Solving this system yields $x = 10$ and $y = 10$. Thus, the sum of squares is a minimum when $x = y = z = 10$.

41. *Revenue* A company manufactures two products. The total revenue from x_1 units of Product 1 and x_2 units of Product 2 is $R = -5x_1{}^2 - 8x_2{}^2 - 2x_1x_2 + 42x_1 + 102x_2$. Find x_1 and x_2 so as to maximize the revenue.

Solution:

The first partial derivatives of R are

$$R_{x_1} = -10x_1 - 2x_2 + 42 \text{ and } R_{x_2} = -16x_2 - 2x_1 + 102.$$

Setting these equal to zero produces the system

$$5x_1 + x_2 = 21$$

$$x_1 + 8x_2 = 51$$

which yields $x_1 = 3$ and $x_2 = 6$. By the Second-Partials Test, it follows that the revenue is maximized when $x_1 = 3$ and $x_2 = 6$.

43. *Revenue* Find p_1 and p_2 so as to maximize the total revenue $R = x_1p_1 + x_2p_2$ for a retail outlet that sells two competitive products with the demand functions $x_1 = 1000 - 2p_1 + p_2$ and $x_2 = 1500 + 2p_1 - 1.5p_2$.

Solution:

The revenue function is given by

$$R = x_1p_1 + x_2p_2 = 1000p_1 + 1500p_2 + 3p_1p_2 - 2p_1{}^2 - 1.5p_2{}^2$$

and the first partials of R are $R_{p_1} = 1000 + 3p_2 - 4p_1$ and $R_{p_2} = 1500 + 3p_1 - 3p_2$. Setting these equal to zero produces the system

$$4p_1 - 3p_2 = 1000$$

$$-3p_1 + 3p_2 = 1500.$$

Solving this system yields $p_1 = 2500$ and $p_2 = 3000$, and by the Second-Partials Test, we conclude that the revenue is maximized when $p_1 = 2500$ and $p_2 = 3000$.

45. *Profit* A corporation manufactures a product at two locations. The costs of producing x_1 units at location 1 and x_2 units at location 2 are $C_1 = 0.04x_1^2 + 5x_1 + 375$ and $C_2 = 0.07x_2^2 + 3.1x_2 + 295$ respectively. If the product sells for \$15 per unit, find the quantity that must be produced at each location to maximize the profit

$$P = 15(x_1 + x_2) - C_1 - C_2.$$

Solution:

The profit function is given by

$$P = 15(x_1 + x_2) - C_1 - C_2$$
$$= 15(x_1 + x_2) - (0.04x_1^2 + 5x_1 + 375) - (0.07x_2^2 + 3.1x_2 + 295)$$
$$= -0.04x_1^2 + 10x_1 - 0.07x_2^2 + 11.9x_2 - 670.$$

The first partials of P are

$$P_{x_1}(x_1, x_2) = -0.08x_1 + 10 \text{ and } P_{x_2}(x_1, x_2) = -0.14x_2 + 11.9.$$

The first partials are zero at $(125, 85)$. By the Second-Partials Test, this is a relative maximum. The profit is maximum when $x_1 = 125$ and $x_2 = 85$.

47. *Profit* A corporation manufactures a certain product at two locations. The cost functions for producing x_1 units at location 1 and x_2 units at location 2 are given by $C_1 = 0.05x_1^2 + 15x_1 + 5400$ and $C_2 = 0.03x_2^2 + 15x_2 + 6100$, respectively. The demand function for the product is given by $p = 225 - 0.4(x_1 + x_2)$ and therefore, the total revenue function is $R = [225 - 0.4(x_1 + x_2)](x_1 + x_2)$. Find the production levels at the two locations that will maximize the profit $P = R - C_1 - C_2$.

Solution:

The profit is given by

$$P = R - C_1 - C_2$$
$$= [225 - 0.4(x_1 + x_2)](x_1 + x_2) - (0.05x_1^2 + 15x_1 + 5400)$$
$$- (0.03x_2^2 + 15x_2 + 6100)$$
$$= -0.45x_1^2 - 0.43x_2^2 - 0.8x_1x_2 + 210x_1 + 210x_2 - 11500$$

and the first partial derivatives of P are $P_{x_1} = -0.9x_1 - 0.8x_2 + 210$ and $P_{x_2} = -0.86x_2 - 0.8x_1 + 210$. By setting these equal to zero, we obtain the system

$$0.9x_1 + 0.8x_2 = 210$$
$$0.8x_1 + 0.86x_2 = 210.$$

Solving this system yields $x_1 \approx 94$ and $x_2 \approx 157$, and by the Second-Partials Test, we conclude that the profit is maximum when $x_1 \approx 94$ and $x_2 \approx 157$.

49. *Volume* Find the dimensions of a rectangular package of largest volume that may be sent by parcel post assuming that the sum of the length and the girth (perimeter of a cross section) cannot exceed 108 inches.

Solution:

Let x = length, y = width, and z = height. The sum of length and girth is given by

$$x + (2y + 2z) = 108$$
$$x = 108 - 2y - 2z$$

and the volume of the package is given by $V = xyz = 108yz - 2zy^2 - 2yz^2$. The first partial derivatives of V are

$$V_y = 108z - 4yz - 2z^2 = (108 - 4y - 2z) \text{ and}$$
$$V_z = 108y - 2y^2 - 4yz = y(108 - 2y - 4z).$$

Setting these equal to zero produces the system

$$4y + 2z = 108$$
$$2y + 4z = 108.$$

which yields the solution $x = 36$ inches, $y = 18$ inches, and $z = 18$ inches.

51. *Hardy-Weinberg Law* Common blood types are determined by genetically by three alleles A, B, and O. (An allele is any of a group of possible mutational forms of a gene.) A person whose blood type is AA< BB, or OO is homozygous. A person whose blood type is AB, AO or BO is heterozygous. The Hardy-Weinberg Law states that the proportion P of heterozygous individuals in any given population is

$$P(p, q, r) = 2pq + 2pr + 2qr,$$

where p represents the percent of allele A in the population, q represents the percent of allele B in the population, and r represents the percent of allele O in the population. Use the fact that $p + q + r = 1$ (the sum of the three must equal 100%) to show that the maximum proportion of heterozygous individuals in any population is $\frac{2}{3}$.

Solution:

$$P(p, q, r) = 2pq + 2pr + 2qr. \text{ Since } p + q + r = 1, r = 1 - p - q \text{ and}$$
$$P = 2pq + 2p(1 - p - q) + 2q(1 - p - q)$$
$$= -2p^2 + 2p - 2q^2 + 2q - 2pq$$
$$P_p = -4p + 2 - 2q \text{ and } P_q = -4q + 2 - 2p$$

Solving $P_p = P_q = 0$, we obtain $p = q = \frac{1}{3}$, and hence $r = \frac{1}{3}$. Finally, the maximum proportion is

$$P = 2\left(\frac{1}{3}\right)\left(\frac{1}{3}\right) + 2\left(\frac{1}{3}\right)\left(\frac{1}{3}\right) + 2\left(\frac{1}{3}\right)\left(\frac{1}{3}\right)$$
$$= \frac{6}{9} = \frac{2}{3}$$

Section 7.6   Lagrange Multipliers

1. Assuming that x and y are positive, use Lagrange multipliers to maximize $f(x, \ y) = xy$ subject to the constraint $x + y = 10$.

Solution:

$$F(x, \ y, \ \lambda) = xy - \lambda(x + y - 10)$$

$$F_x = y - \lambda = 0, \qquad\qquad y = \lambda$$

$$F_y = x - \lambda = 0, \qquad\qquad x = \lambda$$

$$F_\lambda = -(x + y - 10) = 0, \qquad 2\lambda = 10$$

Thus, $\lambda = 5$, $x = 5$, and $y = 5$, and $f(x, \ y)$ is maximum at $(5, 5)$. The maximum is $f(5, \ 5) = 25$.

3. Assuming that x and y are positive, use Lagrange multipliers to minimize $f(x, \ y) = x^2 + y^2$ subject to the constraint $x + y - 4 = 0$.

Solution:

$$F(x, \ y, \ \lambda) = x^2 + y^2 - \lambda(x + y - 4)$$

$$F_x = 2x - \lambda = 0, \qquad\qquad x = \tfrac{1}{2}\lambda$$

$$F_y = 2y - \lambda = 0, \qquad\qquad y = \tfrac{1}{2}\lambda$$

$$F_\lambda = -(x + y - 4) = 0, \qquad \lambda = 4$$

Thus, $\lambda = 4$, $x = 2$, $y = 2$, and $f(x, \ y)$ is minimum at $(2, 2)$. The minimum is $f(2, \ 2) = 8$.

5. Assuming that x and y are positive, use Lagrange multipliers to maximize $f(x, \ y) = x^2 - y^2$ subject to the constraint $y - x^2 = 0$.

Solution:

$$F(x, \ y, \ \lambda) = x^2 - y^2 - \lambda(y - x^2)$$

$$F_x = 2x + 2x\lambda = 0, \qquad 2x(1 + \lambda) = 0$$

$$F_y = -2y - \lambda = 0, \qquad\qquad y = -\tfrac{1}{2}\lambda$$

$$F_\lambda = -(y - x^2) = 0, \qquad\qquad x = \sqrt{y}$$

Thus, $\lambda = -1$, $x = \sqrt{2}/2$, $y = 1/2$. $f(x, \ y)$ is maximum at $(\sqrt{2}/2, \ 1/2)$. The maximum is $f(\sqrt{2}/2, \ 1/2) = 1/4$.

7. Assuming that x and y are positive, use Lagrange multipliers to maximize $f(x, y) = 3x + xy + 3y$ subject to the constraint $x + y = 25$.

Solution:

$$F(x, y, \lambda) = 3x + xy + 3y - \lambda(x + y - 25)$$

$$F_x = 3 + y - \lambda = 0, \qquad\qquad y = \lambda - 3$$

$$F_y = 3 + x - \lambda = 0, \qquad\qquad x = \lambda - 3$$

$$F_\lambda = -(x + y - 25) = 0, \qquad 2\lambda - 6 = 25$$

Thus, $\lambda = \dfrac{31}{2}$, $x = \dfrac{25}{2}$, $y = \dfrac{25}{2}$, and $f(x, y)$ is maximum at $\left(\dfrac{25}{2}, \dfrac{25}{2}\right)$. The maximum is $f\left(\dfrac{25}{2}, \dfrac{25}{2}\right) = 231.25$.

9. Assuming that x and y are positive, use Lagrange multipliers to maximize $f(x, y) = \sqrt{6 - x^2 - y^2}$ subject to the constraint $x + y - 2 = 0$.

Solution:

Note: $f(x, y)$ has a maximum value when $g(x, y) = 6 - x^2 - y^2$ is maximum.

$$F(x, y, \lambda) = 6 - x^2 - y^2 - \lambda(x + y - 2)$$

$$\left.\begin{array}{ll} F_x = -2x - \lambda = 0, & -2x = \lambda \\ F_y = -2y - \lambda = 0, & -2y = \lambda \end{array}\right\} x = y$$

$$F_\lambda = -(x + y - 2) = 0, \qquad 2x = 2$$

Thus, $x = y = 1$ and $f(x, y)$ is maximum at $(1, 1)$. The maximum is $f(1, 1) = 2$.

11. Assuming that x and y are positive, use Lagrange multipliers to maximize $f(x, y) = e^{xy}$ subject to the constraint $x^2 + y^2 - 8 = 0$.

Solution:

$$F(x, y, \lambda) = e^{xy} - \lambda(x^2 + y^2 - 8)$$

$$\left.\begin{array}{ll} F_x = ye^{xy} - 2x\lambda = 0, & e^{xy} = 2x\lambda/y \\ F_y = xe^{xy} - 2y\lambda = 0, & e^{xy} = 2y\lambda/x \end{array}\right\} x = y$$

$$F_\lambda = -(x^2 + y^2 - 8) = 0, \qquad 2x^2 = 8$$

Thus, $x = y = 2$ and $f(x, y)$ is maximum at $(2, 2)$. The maximum is $f(2, 2) = e^4$.

13. Use Lagrange multipliers to find the indicated extrema. Assume that x, y, and z are positive.

Minimize $f(x, y, z) = 2x^2 + 3y^2 + 2z^2$

Constraint: $x + y + z - 24 = 0$

Solution:

$$F(x, y, z, \lambda) = 2x^2 + 3y^2 + 2z^2 - \lambda(x + y + z - 24)$$

$$F_x = 4x - \lambda = 0, \qquad \lambda = 4x$$

$$F_y = 6y - \lambda = 0, \qquad \lambda = 6y$$

$$F_z = 4z - \lambda = 0, \qquad \lambda = 4z$$

$$F_\lambda = -(x + y + z - 24) = 0$$

$$\frac{\lambda}{4} + \frac{\lambda}{6} + \frac{\lambda}{4} = 24$$

$$8\lambda = 24 \cdot 12$$

$$\lambda = 36$$

Thus, $x = 9$, $y = 6$, $z = 9$ and $f(x, y, z)$ is minimum at $(9, 6, 9)$. The minimum is $f(9, 6, 9) = 432$.

15. Use Lagrange multipliers to find the indicated extrema. Assume that x, y, and z are positive.

Minimize $f(x, y, z) = x^2 + y^2 + z^2$ subject to the constraint $x + y + z = 1$. (Assume x, y, and z are positive.)

Solution:

$$F(x, y, z, \lambda) = x^2 + y^2 + z^2 - \lambda(x + y + z - 1)$$

$$\left.\begin{array}{l} F_x = 2x - \lambda = 0 \\[4pt] F_y = 2y - \lambda = 0 \\[4pt] F_z = 2z - \lambda = 0 \end{array}\right\} \qquad x = y = z$$

$$F_\lambda = -(x + y + z - 1) = 0, \qquad 3x = 1$$

Thus, $x = y = z = \frac{1}{3}$ and $f(x, y, z)$ is minimum at $f\left(\frac{1}{3}, \frac{1}{3}, \frac{1}{3}\right) = \frac{1}{3}$.

17. Use Lagrange multipliers to find the indicated extrema. Assume that x, y, and z are positive.

Maximize $f(x, y, z) = x + y + z$ subject to the constraint $x^2 + y^2 + z^2 = 1$. (Assume x, y and z are positive.)

Solution:

$$F(x, y, z, \lambda) = x + y + z - \lambda(x^2 + y^2 + z^2 - 1)$$

$$\left.\begin{aligned} F_x &= 1 - 2x\lambda = 0 \\ F_y &= 1 - 2y\lambda = 0 \\ F_z &= 1 - 2z\lambda = 0 \end{aligned}\right\} x = y = z$$

$$F_\lambda = -(x^2 + y^2 + z^2 - 1) = 0$$

$$3x^2 = 1 \Rightarrow x = \frac{1}{\sqrt{3}} = y = z$$

19. Use the Lagrange multipliers with the objective function
$f(x, y, z, w) = 2x^2 + y^2 + z^2 + 2w^2$ to maximize $f(x, y, z, w)$ subject to the constraint $2x + 2y + z + w = 2$. (Assume x, y, z, and w are nonnegative.)

Solution:

$$F(x, y, z, w, \lambda) = 2x^2 + y^2 + z^2 + 2x^2 - \lambda(2x + 2y + z + w - z)$$

$$F_x = 4x - 2\lambda = 0 \qquad x = \tfrac{1}{2}\lambda$$

$$F_y = 2y - 2\lambda = 0 \qquad y = \lambda = 2x$$

$$F_z = 2z - \lambda = 0 \qquad z = \tfrac{1}{2}\lambda = x$$

$$F_w = 4w - \lambda = 0 \qquad w = \tfrac{1}{4}\lambda = \tfrac{1}{2}x$$

$$F_\lambda = -(2x + 2y + z + w) = 0$$

$$2x + 2(2x) + x + \frac{1}{2}x = 2 \Rightarrow x = \frac{4}{15}$$

The maximum is $f\left(\dfrac{4}{15}, \dfrac{8}{15}, \dfrac{4}{15}, \dfrac{2}{15}\right) = \dfrac{8}{15}$.

21. Assuming that x, y, and z are positive, use Lagrange multipliers to maximize $f(x, y, z) = xyz$ subject to the constraints $x + y + z = 32$ and $x - y + z = 0$.

Solution:

$$F(x, y, z, \lambda, \eta) = xyz - \lambda(x + y + z - 24) - \eta(x - y + z - 12)$$

$$\left.\begin{array}{l} F_x = yz - \lambda - \eta = 0 \\ F_y = xz - \lambda + \eta = 0 \\ F_z = xy - \lambda - \eta = 0 \end{array}\right\} \qquad x = z$$

$$F_\lambda = -(x + y + z - 24) = 0, \quad x + (2x - 12) + x = 24$$

$$F_\eta = -(x - y + z - 12) = 0, \quad y = 2x - 12$$

Thus, $x = 9$, $y = 6$, and $z = 9$. The maximum is $f(9, 6, 9) = 486$.

23. Assuming that x, y, and z are positive, use Lagrange multipliers to maximize $f(x, y, z) = xyz$ subject to the constraints $x^2 + z^2 = 5$ and $x - 2y = 0$.

Solution:

$$F(x, y, z, \lambda, \eta) = xyz - \lambda(x^2 + z^2 - 5) - \eta(x - 2y)$$

$$\begin{array}{ll} F_x = yz - 2x\lambda - \eta = 0 & \\ F_y = xz + 2\eta = 0, & \eta = -xz/2 \\ F_z = xy - 2z\lambda = 0, & \lambda = xy/2z \\ F_\lambda = -(x^2 + z^2 - 5) = 0, & z = \sqrt{5 - x^2} \\ F_\eta = -(x - 2y) = 0, & y = x/2 \end{array}$$

From F_x, we can write $\dfrac{x\sqrt{5 - x^2}}{2} - \dfrac{x^3}{2\sqrt{5 - x^2}} + \dfrac{x\sqrt{5 - x^2}}{2} = 0$

$$x\sqrt{5 - x^2} = \dfrac{x^3}{2\sqrt{5 - x^2}}$$

$$2x(5 - x^2) = x^3$$

$$3x^3 - 10x = 0$$

$$x(3x^2 - 10) = 0.$$

Since x, y, and z are positive, we have $x = \sqrt{10/3}$, $y = (1/2)\sqrt{10/3}$, and $z = \sqrt{5/3}$.

$$f\left(\sqrt{\dfrac{10}{3}}, \dfrac{1}{2}\sqrt{\dfrac{10}{3}}, \sqrt{\dfrac{5}{3}}\right) = \dfrac{5\sqrt{15}}{9}$$

25. Find three positive numbers x, y, and z such that the sum is 120 and the product is maximum.

Solution:

Maximize $f(x, y, z) = xyz$ subject to the constraint $x + y + z = 120$.

$F(x, y, z, \lambda) = xyz - \lambda(x + y + z - 120)$

$$\left. \begin{array}{l} F_x = yz - \lambda = 0 \\ F_y = xz - \lambda = 0 \\ F_z = xy - \lambda = 0 \end{array} \right\} \ yz = xz = xy \Rightarrow x = y = z$$

$F_\lambda = -(x + y + z - 120) = 0, \qquad 3x = 120$

Thus, $x = y = z = 40$.

27. Find three positive numbers x, y, and z such that the sum is S and the product is maximum.

Solution:

Maximize $f(x, y, z) = xyz$ subject to the constraint $x + y + z = S$.

$F(x, y, z, \lambda) = xyz - \lambda(x + y + z - S)$

$$\left. \begin{array}{l} F_x = yz - \lambda = 0 \\ F_y = xz - \lambda = 0 \\ F_z = xy - \lambda = 0 \end{array} \right\} \ yz = xz = xy \Rightarrow x = y = z$$

$F_\lambda = -(x + y + z - S) = 0, \qquad 3x = S$

Thus, $x = y = z = S/3$.

29. Find the minimum distance from the line $x + 2y = 5$ to the point $(0, 0)$. Start by minimizing $d^2 = x^2 + y^2$.

Solution:

$F(x, y, \lambda) = x^2 + y^2 - \lambda(x + 2y - 5)$

$F_x = 2x - \lambda = 0 \qquad\qquad x = \dfrac{\lambda}{2}$

$F_y = 2y - 2\lambda = 0 \qquad\qquad y = \lambda = 2x$

$F_\lambda = -(x + 2y - 5) = \qquad 0$

$x + 2(2x) = 5 \Rightarrow x = 1, y = 2$

The minimum distance is $\sqrt{x^2 + y^2} = \sqrt{1 + 4} = \sqrt{5}$.

31. Find the minimum distance from the plane $x + y + z = 1$ to the point $(2, 1, 1)$. Start by minimizing
$d^2 = (x - 2)^2 + (y - 1)^2 + (z - 1)^2$.

Solution:

$F(x, \ y, \ z, \ \lambda) = (x - 2)^2 + (y - 1)^2 + (z - 1)^2 - \lambda(x + y + z - 1)$

$\left.\begin{array}{l} F_x = 2(x - 2) - \lambda = 0 \\[2mm] F_y = 2(y - 1) - \lambda = 0 \\[2mm] F_z = 2(z - 1) - \lambda = 0 \end{array}\right\}$ $\begin{array}{l} x - 2 = y - 1 = z - 1 \\[2mm] x - 1 = y = z \end{array}$

$F_\lambda = -(x + y + z - 1) = 0$

Thus, $x = 1, \quad y = z = x - 1 = 0$, and $d = \sqrt{(1 - 2)^2 + (0 - 1)^2 + (0 - 1)^2} = \sqrt{3}$.

33. *Volume* Find the dimensions of the rectangular package of largest volume. Assume that the sum of the length and the girth cannot exceed 108 inches. (Maximize $V = xyz$ subject to the constraint $x + 2y + 2z = 108$.)

Solution:

$F(x, \ y, \ z, \ \lambda) = xyz - \lambda(x + 2y + 2z - 108)$

$\left.\begin{array}{l} F_x = yz - \lambda = 0 \\[2mm] F_y = xz - 2\lambda = 0 \end{array}\right\}$ $x = 2y$

$F_z = xy - 2\lambda = 0,$ $y = z$

$F_\lambda = -(x + 2y + 2z - 108) = 0,$ $6y = 108$

Thus, $x = 36, \quad y = 18$, and $z = 18$. The volume is maximum when the dimensions are $36 \times 18 \times 18$ inches.

35. *Cost* A cargo container (in the shape of a rectangular solid) must have a volume of 480 cubic feet. Use Lagrange multipliers to find the dimensions of the container of this size which has a minimum cost, if the bottom will cost $5 per square foot to construct and the sides and top will cost $3 per square foot to construct.

Solution:

Minimize $C(x, \ y, \ z) = 5xy + 3(xy + 2xz + 2yz) = 8xy + 6xz + 6yz$ subject to the constraint $xyz = 480$.

$F(x, \ y, \ z, \ \lambda) = 8xy + 6xz + 6yz - \lambda(xyz - 480)$

$$\left.\begin{array}{l} F_x = 8y + 6z - \lambda yz = 0 \\[4pt] F_y = 8x + 6y - \lambda xy = 0 \\[4pt] F_z = 6x + 6y - \lambda xy = 0 \end{array}\right\} \quad \begin{array}{l} x = y \\[8pt] 4y = 3z \end{array}$$

$F_\lambda = -(xyz - 480) = 0, \ y(y)(\tfrac{4}{3}y) = 480, \ y = 2\sqrt[3]{45}$

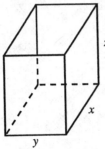

Thus, the dimensions are $2\sqrt[3]{45}$ feet $\times 2\sqrt[3]{45}$ feet $\times \tfrac{8}{3}\sqrt[3]{45}$ feet.

37. *Cost* A manufacturer has an order for 2000 units that can be produced at two locations. Let x_1 and x_2 be the numbers of units produced at the two plants. The cost function is modeled by

$$C = 0.25x_1^2 + 10x + 0.15x_2^2 + 12xz.$$

Solution:

$$F(x_1, x_2, \lambda) = 0.25x_1^2 + 25x_1 + 0.05\lambda_2^2 + 12x_2 - \lambda(x_1 + x_2 - 2000)$$

$$F_{x1} = 0.5x_1 + 10 - \lambda = 0, \qquad x_1 = \ 2\lambda - 20$$

$$F_{x2} = 0.3x_2 + 12 - \lambda = 0, \qquad x_2 = \frac{10}{3}\lambda - 40$$

$$F_\lambda = -(x_1 + x_2 - 2000)$$

$$(2\lambda - 20) + \left(\frac{10}{3}\lambda - 40\right) = 2000$$

$$\frac{16}{3}\lambda = 2060$$

$$\lambda = 386.25$$

Hence, $x_1 = 725.5$ and $x_2 = 1287.5$. To minimize cost, let $x_1 = 753$ units and $x_2 = 1287$ units.

39. *Least-Cost Rule*   The production function for a company is $f(x, \ y) = 100x^{0.25}y^{0.75}$ where x is the number of units of labor and y is the number of units of capital. Suppose that labor costs \$48 per unit, capital costs \$36 per unit, and management sets a production goal of 20,000 units.

(a) Find the number of units of labor and capital needed to meet the production goal while minimizing the cost.

(b) Show that the conditions of part (a) are met when

$$\frac{\text{Marginal productivity of labor}}{\text{Marginal productivity of capital}} = \frac{\text{unit price of labor}}{\text{unit price of capital}}.$$

This proportion is called the **Least-Cost Rule** (or Equimarginal Rule).

Solution:

(a) $F(x, \ y, \ \lambda) = 48x + 36y - \lambda(x^{0.25}y^{0.75} - 200)$

$\qquad F_x = 48 - 0.25\lambda x^{-0.75}y^{0.75} = 0$

$\qquad F_y = 36 - 0.75\lambda x^{0.25}y^{-0.25} = 0$

$\qquad F_\lambda = -(x^{0.25}y^{0.75} - 200) = 0$

This produces

$$\left(\frac{y}{x}\right)^{0.75} = \frac{48}{0.25\lambda} \quad \text{and} \quad \left(\frac{y}{x}\right)^{0.25} = \frac{0.75\lambda}{36}.$$

Thus, $\dfrac{y}{x} = \left(\dfrac{48}{0.25\lambda}\right)\left(\dfrac{0.75\lambda}{36}\right) = 4$

$\qquad x = \dfrac{200}{4^{0.75}} = \dfrac{200}{2\sqrt{2}} = 50\sqrt{2} \approx 71$

$\qquad y = 4x = 200\sqrt{2} \approx 283.$

(b) $\qquad \dfrac{f_x(x, \ y)}{f_y(x, \ y)} = \dfrac{48}{36}$

$\qquad \dfrac{25x^{-0.75}y^{0.75}}{75x^{0.25}y^{-0.25}} = \dfrac{48}{36}$

$\qquad\qquad \dfrac{y}{x} = 4$

Thus, $y = 4x$ and the conditions of part (a) are met.

41. *Production* The production function for a company is $f(x, y) = 100x^{0.25}y^{0.75}$ where x is the number of units of labor and y is the number of units of capital. Suppose that labor costs $48 per unit and capital costs $36 per unit. The total cost of labor and capital is limited to $100,000.

(a) Find the maximum production level for this manufacturer.

(b) Find the marginal productivity of money.

(c) Use the marginal productivity of money to find the maximum number of units that can be produced if $125,000 is available for labor and capital.

Solution:

(a) From Exercise 39, we have $y = 4x$.

$$F(x, y, \lambda) = 100x^{0.25}y^{0.75} - \lambda(48x + 36y - 100,000)$$

$$F_\lambda = -(48x + 36y - 100,000) = 0$$

Thus, $x = \dfrac{3125}{6}$, $y = \dfrac{6250}{3}$, and $f\left(\dfrac{3125}{6}, \dfrac{6250}{3}\right) \approx 147,313.91 \approx 147,314$.

(b) $F_x = 25x^{-0.75}y^{0.75} - 48\lambda = 0$

$$\lambda = \frac{25x^{-0.75}y^{0.75}}{48} = \frac{25}{48}\left(\frac{3125}{6}\right)^{-0.75}\left(\frac{6250}{3}\right)^{0.75} \approx 1.4731$$

(c) $147,314 + 25,000\lambda \approx 147,314 + 25,000(1.4731) \approx 184,141.5 \approx 184,142$ units

43. *Bacteria Culture* A microbiologist must prepare a culture medium in which to grow a certain type of bacteria. The percent of sale contained in this medium is $S = 12xyz$, where x, y, and z are the nutrient solutions to be mixed in the medium. For the bacteria to grow, the medium must be 13% salt. The nutrient solutions cost $1, $2, and $3 per liter. How much of each nutrient solution should be used to minimize the cost of the culture medium?

Solution:

Minimize cost $= x + 2y + 3z$

Constraint: $12xyz = 0.13$

$$F(x, y, z, \lambda) = x + 2y + 3z - \lambda(12xyz - 0.13)$$

$$\begin{aligned}
F_x &= 1 - 12\lambda yz = 0, & 12\lambda yz &= 1 \\
F_y &= 2 - 12\lambda xz = 0, & 12\lambda xz &= 2 \\
F_z &= 3 - 12\lambda xy = 0, & 12\lambda xy &= 3
\end{aligned}\right\} \quad \begin{aligned} x &= 2y \\ x &= 3z \end{aligned}$$

$$F_\lambda = -(12xyz - 0.13) = 0$$

$$12x\left(\frac{x}{2}\right)\left(\frac{x}{3}\right) = 0.13 \qquad x = \sqrt[3]{0.065} \approx 0.402$$

$$2x^3 = 0.13 \qquad y = \frac{1}{2}\sqrt[3]{0.065} \approx 0.201$$

$$z = \frac{1}{3}\sqrt[3]{0.065} \approx 0.134$$

45. Investment Strategy An investor is considering three different stocks in which to invest $300,000. The average annual dividends for the stocks are

Dow Chemicals (D)   3.9%

CIGNA Corp. (C)   4.5%

Pennzoil Company (P)   4.0%.

The amount invested in Pennzoil must follow the equation

$$3000D - 3000C + P^2 = 0.$$

How much should be invested in each stock to yield a maximum of dividends?

Solution:

Maximize $F(D, C.P) = 0.039D + 0.045C + 0.040P$

Constraints: $D + C + P = 300,000$

$$3000D - 3000C + P^2 = 0$$

$$0.039 = \lambda + 3000\mu$$

$$0.045 = \lambda - 3000\mu$$

$$0.040 = \lambda + 2P\mu$$

From equations 1 and 2, $\lambda = 0.042$ and $0.039 = 0.042 + 3000\mu \Rightarrow \mu = \dfrac{-0.003}{3000}$

From equation 3,

$$0.040 = 0.042 + 2P\left(\frac{-0.003}{3000}\right)$$

$$0.002 = 2P\left(\frac{0.003}{3000}\right)$$

$$P = \$3000$$

Finally, $C = \$150,000$ and $D = \$147,000$

Section 7.7   Least Squares Regression Analysis

1. (a) Use the method of least squares to find the least squares regression line, and (b) calculate the sum of the squared errors.

   Solution:

   (a) $\sum x_i = 0$

   $\sum y_i = 4$

   $\sum x_i y_i = 6$

   $\sum x_i^2 = 8$

   $a = \dfrac{3(6) - 0(4)}{3(8) - 0^2} = \dfrac{3}{4}$

   $b = \dfrac{1}{3}\left[4 - \dfrac{3}{4}(0)\right] = \dfrac{4}{3}$

   The regression line is $y = \frac{3}{4}x + \frac{4}{3}$.

   (b) $\left(-\dfrac{3}{2} + \dfrac{4}{3} - 0\right)^2$

   $+ \left(\dfrac{4}{3} - 1\right)^2$

   $+ \left(\dfrac{3}{2} + \dfrac{4}{3} - 3\right)^2 = \dfrac{1}{6}$

3. (a) Use the method of least squares to find the least squares regression line, and (b) calculate the sum of the squared errors.

   Solution:

   (a) $\sum x_i = 4$

   $\sum y_i = 8$

   $\sum x_i y_i = 4$

   $\sum x_i^2 = 6$

   $a = \dfrac{4(4) - 4(8)}{4(6) - 4^2} = -2$

   $b = \dfrac{1}{4}[8 + 2(4)] = 4$

   The regression line is $y = -2x + 4$.

   (b) $(4-4)^2 + (2-3)^2 + (2-1)^2 + (0-0)^2 = 2$

5. Find the least squares regression line for $(-2, 0)$, $(-1, 1)$, $(0, 1)$, $(1, 2)$, and $(2, 3)$.

Solution:

$$\sum x_i = 0$$
$$\sum y_i = 7$$
$$\sum x_i y_i = 7$$
$$\sum x_i^2 = 10$$

Since $a = \frac{7}{10}$ and $b = \frac{7}{5}$, the regression line is $y = \frac{7}{10}x + \frac{7}{5}$.

7. Find the least squares regression line for $(-2, 2)$, $(2, 6)$, and $(3, 7)$.

Solution:

$$\sum x_i = 3$$
$$\sum y_i = 15$$
$$\sum x_i y_i = 29$$
$$\sum x_i^2 = 17$$

Since $a = 1$ and $b = 4$, the regression line is $y = x + 4$.

9. Find the least squares regression line for $(-3, 4)$, $(-1, 2)$, $(1, 1)$, and $(3, 0)$.

Solution:

$$\sum x_i = 0$$
$$\sum y_i = 7$$
$$\sum x_i y_i = -13$$
$$\sum x_i^2 = 20$$

Since $a = -\frac{13}{20}$ and $b = \frac{7}{4}$, the regression line is $y = -\frac{13}{20}x + \frac{7}{4}$.

11. Find the least squares regression line for $(0, 0)$, $(1, 1)$, $(3, 4)$, $(4, 2)$, and $(5, 5)$.

Solution:

$$\sum x_i = 13$$
$$\sum y_i = 12$$
$$\sum x_i y_i = 46$$
$$\sum x_i^2 = 51$$

Since $a = \frac{37}{43}$ and $b = \frac{7}{43}$, the regression line is $y = \frac{37}{43}x + \frac{7}{43}$.

13. Find the least squares regression line for $(0, 6)$, $(4, 3)$, $(5, 0)$, $(8, -4)$, and $(10, -5)$.

Solution:

$$\sum x_i = 27$$

$$\sum y_i = 0$$

$$\sum x_i y_i = -70$$

$$\sum x_i^2 = 205$$

Since $a = -\frac{175}{148}$ and $b = \frac{945}{148}$, the regression line is $y = -\frac{175}{148}x + \frac{945}{148}$.

15. Use partial derivatives to find the values of a and b such that the linear model $f(x) = ax + b$ has a minimum sum of the squared errors for the points $(-2, -1)$, $(0, 0)$, $(2, 3)$.

Solution:

The sum of the squared errors is as follows.

$$S = (-2a + b + 1)^2 + (0a + b)^2 + (2a + b - 3)^2$$

$$\frac{\partial S}{\partial a} = 2(-2a + b + 1)(-2) + 2(2a + b - 3)(2) = 16a - 16$$

$$\frac{\partial S}{\partial b} = 2(-2a + b + 1) + 2b + 2(2a + b - 3) = 6b - 4$$

Setting these partial derivatives equal to zero produces $a = 1$ and $b = \frac{2}{3}$.
Thus, $y = x + \frac{2}{3}$.

17. Use partial derivatives to find the values of a and b such that the linear model $f(x) = ax + b$ has a minimum sum of the squared errors for the points $(-2, 4)$, $(-1, 1)$, $(0, -1)$, $(1, -3)$.

Solution:

The sum of the squared errors is as follows.

$$S = (-2a + b - 4)^2 + (-a + b - 1)^2 + (b + 1)^2 + (a + b + 3)^2$$

$$\frac{\partial S}{\partial a} = -4(-2a + b - 4) - 2(-a + b - 1) + 2(a + b + 3) = 12a - 4b + 24$$

$$\frac{\partial S}{\partial b} = 2(-2a + b - 4) + 2(-a + b - 1) + 2(b + 1) + 2(a + b + 3) = -4a + 8b - 2$$

Setting these partial derivatives equal to zero produces

$$12a - 4b = -24$$

$$-4a + 8b = 2$$

Thus, $a = -2.3$ and $b = -0.9$, and $y = -2.3x - 0.9$.

19. Find the least squares regression quadratic for the points $(-2, 0)$, $(-1, 0)$, $(0, 1)$, $(1, 2)$, and $(2, 5)$. Then plot these points and sketch the graph of the least squares quadratic.

Solution:

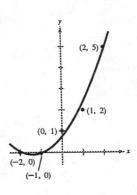

$$\sum x_i = 0$$

$$\sum y_i = 8$$

$$\sum x_i^2 = 10$$

$$\sum x_i^3 = 0$$

$$\sum x_i^4 = 34$$

$$\sum x_i y_i = 12$$

$$\sum x_i^2 y_i = 22$$

This produces the system
$$34a \quad\quad +10c = 22$$
$$10b \quad\quad = 12$$
$$10a \quad\quad +5c = 8$$

which yields $a = \frac{3}{7}$, $b = \frac{6}{5}$, and $c = \frac{26}{35}$, and we have $y = \frac{3}{7}x^2 + \frac{6}{5}x + \frac{26}{35}$.

21. Find the least squares regression quadratic for the points $(1, 0)$, $(2, 1)$, $(3, 7)$ and $(4, 13)$. Then plot these points and sketch the graph of the least squares quadratic.

Solution:

$$\sum x_i = 10$$

$$\sum y_i = 21$$

$$\sum x_i^2 = 30$$

$$\sum x_i^3 = 100$$

$$\sum x_i^4 = 354$$

$$\sum x_i y_i = 75$$

$$\sum x_i^2 y_i = 275$$

This produces the system

$$354a + 100b + 30c = 275$$
$$100a + 30b + 10c = 75$$
$$30a + 10c + 4c = 21$$

which yields $a = 1.25$, $b = -1.75$, and $c = 0.25$, and we have $y = 1.25x^2 - 1.75x + 0.25$.

23. Find a model (linear and quadratic) for the data $(-4, 1)$, $(-3, 2)$, $(-2, 2)$, $(-1, 4)$, $(0, 6)$, $(1, 8)$, $(2, 9)$. State which model best fits the data.

Solution:

Linear: $y = 1.4286x + 6$

Quadratic: $y = 0.1190x^2 + 1.6667x + 5.6429$

25. Find a model (linear and quadratic) for the data $(0, 769)$, $(1, 677)$, $(2, 601)$, $(3, 543)$, $(4, 489)$, $(5, 411)$. State which model best fits the data.

Solution:

Linear: $y = -68.9143x + 753.9524$

Quadratic: $y = 2.8214x^2 - 83.0214x + 763.3571$

27. *Demand* A store manager wants to know the demand for a certain product as a function of price. The daily sales for three prices, x, of the product are \$1.00, \$1.25, and \$1.50 for demands, y, of 450, 375, and 330.

(a) Find the least squares regression line for these data.

(b) Estimate the demand when the price is \$1.40.

(c) What price will create a demand of 500 products?

Solution:

$(1, 450)$, $(1.25, 375)$, $(1.5, 330)$

(a) $\sum x_i = 3.75$

  $\sum y_i = 1155$

  $\sum x_i y_i = 1413.75$

  $\sum x_i^2 = 4.8125$

  Thus, $a = -240$, $b = 685$, and $y = -240x + 685$.

(b) When $x = 1.4$, $y = 349$.

(c) $y = 500$ when $x \approx 0.77$

29. *Crop Yield* A farmer used four test plots to determine the relationship between wheat yield in bushels per acre and the amount of fertilizer in hundreds of pounds per acre. The results are given in the table in the textbook.

(a) Find the least squares regression line for the data.

(b) Estimate the yield for a fertilizer application of 160 pounds per acre.

Solution:

(a) Using a graphing utility, the least squares regression line is $y = 13.8x + 22.1$.

(b) If $x = 1.6$, $y \approx 44.18$ bushels per acre.

31. *Infant Mortality* To study the number of infant deaths per 1000 live births in the United States, a medical researcher obtains the data shown in the textbook.

(a) Find the least squares regression line for the data and use it to estimate the number of infant deaths in 1998. Let $t = 0$ represent 1970.

(b) Find the least squares regression quadratic for the data and use it to estimate the number of infant deaths in 1998.

Solution:

(a) Using a graphing utility, the least squares regression line is $y = 0.5267t + 19.4677$ ($t = 0$ is 1970).

In 1998, $t = 28$ and $y \approx 4.7$ deaths.

(b) The least squares regression quadratic is

$$y = -0.000545t^2 - 0.5255t + 19.5881.$$

In 1988, $t = 28$ and $y \approx 4.4$ deaths.

33. *Engine Desing* After developing a new turbocharger for an automobile engine, the following experimental data was obtained for speed in miles per hour at 2-second intervals. (See table in textbook.)

(a) Find a least squares regression quadratic for the data.

(b) Use the model to estimate the speed after 5 seconds.

Solution:

(a) (0, 0), (2, 15), (4, 30), (6, 50), (8, 65), (10, 70)

$$\sum x_i = 30$$
$$\sum y_i = 230$$
$$\sum x_i^2 = 220$$
$$\sum x_i^3 = 1800$$
$$\sum x_i^4 = 15{,}664$$
$$\sum x_i y_i = 1670$$
$$\sum x_i^2 y_i = 13{,}500$$

$$15{,}664a + 1800b + 220c = 13{,}500$$
$$1800a + 220b + 30c = 1670$$
$$220a + 30b + 6c = 230$$

Thus, $a = -\frac{25}{112}$, $b = \frac{541}{56}$, and $c = -\frac{25}{14}$ and we have $y = -\frac{25}{112}x^2 + \frac{541}{56}x - \frac{25}{14}$.

(b) When $x = 5$, $y \approx 40.9$ mph.

35. Find any model that best fits the data points (1, 13), (2, 16.5), (4, 24), (5, 28), (8, 39), (11, 50.25), (17, 72), (20, 85).

Solution:

Linear: $y = 3.7569x + 9.0347$

Quadratic: $y = 0.006316x^2 + 3.6252x + 9.4282$

37. Find any model that best fits the data points (1, 1.5), (2.5, 8.5), (5, 13.5), (8, 16.7), (9, 18), (20, 22).

Solution:

Linear: $y = 0.9374x + 6.2582$

Quadratic: $y = -0.08715x^2 + 2.8159x + 0.3975$

39. Plot the points (1, 4), (2, 6), (3, 8), (4, 11), (5, 13), (6, 15) and determine whether the data has positive, negative, or no correlation.

Solution:

Positive correlation

$r = 0.9981$

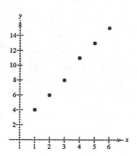

41. Plot the points (1, 3), (2, 6), (3, 2), (4, 3), (5, 9), (6, 1) and determine whether the data has positive, negative, or no correlation.

Solution:

No correlation

$r = 0$

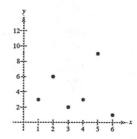

43. Determine whether the statement is true or false.

Data that is modeled by $y = 3.29x - 4.17$ has a negative correlation.

Solution:

No, the slope is positive.

45. Determine whether the statement is true or false.

If the correlation coefficient $r \approx -0.98781$, the model is a good fit.

Solution:

Yes, $|r| \approx 1$.

Section 7.8 Double Integrals and Area in the Plane

1. Evaluate $\displaystyle\int_0^x (2x - y)\, dy$.

Solution:

$$\int_0^x (2x - y)\, dy = \left(2xy - \frac{y^2}{2}\right)\Big]_0^x = \frac{3x^2}{2}$$

3. Evaluate $\displaystyle\int_1^{2y} \frac{y}{x}\, dx$.

Solution:

$$\int_1^{2y} \frac{y}{x}\, dx = y\ln|x|\,\Big]_1^{2y} = y\ln|2y|$$

5. Evaluate $\displaystyle\int_0^{\sqrt{9-x^2}} x^2 y\, dy$.

Solution:

$$\int_0^{\sqrt{9-x^2}} x^2 y\, dy = \frac{x^2 y^2}{2}\Big]_0^{\sqrt{9-x^2}} = \frac{x^2(9 - x^2)}{2} = \frac{9x^2 - x^4}{2}$$

7. Evaluate $\displaystyle\int_{e^y}^{y} \frac{y\ln x}{x}\, dx$.

Solution:

$$\int_{e^y}^{y} \frac{y\ln x}{x}\, dx = \frac{y(\ln x)^2}{2}\Big]_{e^y}^{y} = \frac{y}{2}[(\ln y)^2 - y^2]$$

9. Evaluate $\displaystyle\int_0^{x^3} ye^{-y/x}\,dy$.

Solution:

Using integration by parts, we have the following.

$$\int_0^{x^3} ye^{-y/x}\,dy = -xye^{-y/x}\Big]_0^{x^3} + x\int_0^{x^3} e^{-y/x}\,dy$$

$$= -x^4 e^{-x^2} - \left[x^2 e^{-y/x}\right]_0^{x^3} = -x^4 e^{-x^2} - x^2 e^{-x^2} + x^2$$

$$= x^2(1 - e^{-x^2} - x^2 e^{-x^2})$$

11. Evaluate $\displaystyle\int_0^2\int_0^1 (x-y)\,dy\,dx$

Solution:

$$\int_0^2\int_0^1 (x-y)\,dy\,dx = \int_0^2 \left[xy - \frac{y^2}{2}\right]_0^1 dx$$

$$= \int_0^2 \left(x - \frac{1}{2}\right) dx$$

$$= \left[\frac{x^2}{2} - \frac{1}{2}x\right]_0^2 = 2 - 1 = 1$$

13. Evaluate $\displaystyle\int_0^4\int_0^3 xy\,dy\,dx$.

Solution:

$$\int_0^4\int_0^3 xy\,dy\,dx = \int_0^4 \left[\frac{xy^2}{2}\right]_0^3 dx = \frac{9}{2}\int_0^4 x\,dx = \frac{9}{2}\left[\frac{x^2}{2}\right]_0^4 = 36$$

15. Evaluate $\displaystyle\int_0^1\int_0^{\sqrt{1-y^2}} (x+y)\,dx\,dy$.

Solution:

$$\int_0^1\int_0^{\sqrt{1-y^2}} (x+y)\,dx\,dy = \int_0^1 \left[\frac{x^2}{2} + xy\right]_0^{\sqrt{1-y^2}} dy$$

$$= \int_0^1 \left[\frac{1}{2}(1-y^2) + y\sqrt{1-y^2}\right] dy$$

$$= \left[\frac{1}{2}\left(y - \frac{y^3}{3}\right) - \frac{1}{2}\left(\frac{2}{3}\right)(1-y^2)^{3/2}\right]_0^1$$

$$= \frac{1}{2}\left[y - \frac{y^3}{3} - \frac{2}{3}(1-y^2)^{3/2}\right]_0^1 = \frac{2}{3}$$

17. Evaluate $\displaystyle\int_1^2 \int_0^4 (x^2 - 2y^2 + 1)\, dx\, dy$.

Solution:

$$\int_1^2 \int_0^4 (x^2 - 2y^2 + 1)\, dx\, dy = \int_1^2 \left[\frac{x^3}{3} - 2xy^2 + x\right]_0^4 dy$$

$$= \int_1^2 \left(\frac{64}{3} - 8y^2 + 4\right) dy$$

$$= \left[\frac{76}{3}y - \frac{8y^3}{3}\right]_1^2$$

$$= \left[\frac{4}{3}(19y - 2y^3)\right]_1^2 = \frac{20}{3}$$

19. Evaluate $\displaystyle\int_0^2 \int^{\sqrt{1-y^2}}_{0} - 5xy\, dx\, dy$.

Solution:

$$\int_0^2 \int^{\sqrt{1-y^2}} - 5xy\, dx\, dy = -5\int_0^2 \left[\frac{x^2}{2}y\right]_0^{\sqrt{1-y^2}} dy$$

$$= -5\int_0^2 \frac{(1-y^2)y}{2} dy = -\frac{5}{2}\left[\frac{y^2}{2} - \frac{y^4}{4}\right]_0^2$$

$$= -\frac{5}{2}[2 - 4] = 5$$

21. Evaluate $\displaystyle\int_0^2 \int_0^{4-x^2} x^3\, dy\, dx$.

Solution:

$$\int_0^2 \int_0^{4-x^2} x^3\, dy\, dx = \int_0^2 x^3 y\Big]_0^{4-x^2} dx = \int_0^2 (4x^3 - x^5)\, dx = \left[\left(x^4 - \frac{x^6}{6}\right)\right]_0^2 = \frac{16}{3}$$

23. Evaluate $\displaystyle\int_0^\infty \int_0^\infty e^{-(x+y)/2}\, dy\, dx$.

Solution:

Since (for fixed x) $\displaystyle\lim_{b\to\infty}\left[-2e^{-(x+y)/2}\right]_0^b = 2e^{-x/2}$, we have the following.

$$\int_0^\infty \int_0^\infty e^{-(x+y)/2}\, dy\, dx = \int_0^\infty 2e^{-x/2}\, dx = \lim_{b\to\infty}\left[-4e^{-x/2}\right]_0^b = 4$$

25. Sketch the region R whose area is given by the following double integral. Then switch the order of integration and show that both orders yield the same area.

$$\int_0^1 \int_0^2 dy\,dx.$$

Solution:

$$\int_0^1 \int_0^2 dy\,dx = \int_0^1 2\,dx = 2$$

$$\int_0^2 \int_0^1 dx\,dy = \int_0^2 dy = 2$$

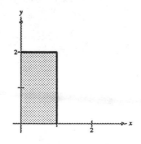

27. Sketch the region R whose area is given by the following double integral. Then switch the order of integration and show that both orders yield the same area.

$$\int_0^1 \int_{2y}^2 dx\,dy.$$

Solution:

$$\int_0^1 \int_{2y}^2 dx\,dy = \int_0^1 (2 - 2y)\,dy = (2y - y^2)\Big]_0^1 = 1$$

$$\int_0^2 \int_0^{x/2} dy\,dx = \int_0^2 \frac{x}{2}\,dx = \frac{x^2}{4}\Big]_0^2 = 1$$

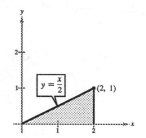

29. Sketch the region R whose area is given by the following double integral. Then switch the order of integration and show that both orders yield the same area.

$$\int_0^2 \int_{x/2}^1 dy\,dx.$$

Solution:

$$\int_0^2 \int_{x/2}^1 dy\,dx = \int_0^2 \left(1 - \frac{x}{2}\right) dx = \left(x - \frac{x^2}{4}\right)\Big]_0^2 = 1$$

$$\int_0^1 \int_0^{2y} dx\,dy = \int_0^1 2y\,dy = y^2\Big]_0^1 = 1$$

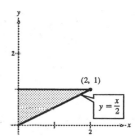

31. Sketch the region R whose area is given by the following double integral. Then switch the order of integration and show that both orders yield the same area.

$$\int_0^1 \int_{y^2}^{\sqrt[3]{y}} dx\, dy.$$

Solution:

$$\int_0^1 \int_{y^2}^{\sqrt[3]{y}} dx\, dy = \int_0^1 (\sqrt[3]{y} - y^2)\, dy$$

$$= \left[\left(\frac{3}{4} y^{4/3} - \frac{y^3}{3} \right) \right]_0^1 = \frac{5}{12}$$

$$\int_0^1 \int_{x^3}^{\sqrt{x}} dy\, dx = \int_0^1 (\sqrt{x} - x^3)\, dx$$

$$= \left[\left(\frac{2}{3} x^{3/2} - \frac{x^4}{4} \right) \right]_0^1 = \frac{5}{12}$$

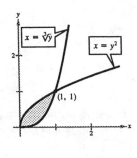

$x = \sqrt[3]{y}$

$x = y^2$

$(1, 1)$

33. Evaluate the double integral.

$$\int_0^3 \int_y^3 e^{x^2} dx\, dy$$

Solution:

$$\int_0^3 \int_y^3 e^{x^2} dx\, dy = \int_0^3 \int_0^x e^{x^2} dy\, dx$$

$$= \int_0^3 \left[y e^{x^2} \right]_0^x dx$$

$$= \int_0^3 x e^{x^2} dx$$

$$= \frac{1}{2} e^{x^2} \bigg]_0^3$$

$$= \frac{1}{2} [e^9 - 1] \approx 4051.042$$

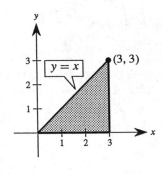

$y = x$

$(3, 3)$

35. Use a double integral to find the area of the specified region.

Solution:

$$A = \int_0^8 \int_0^3 dy\, dx$$

$$= \int_0^8 3\, dx$$

$$= 3x \Big]_0^8 = 24$$

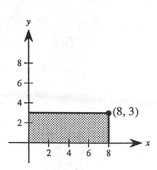

37. Use a double integral to find the area of the specified region.

Solution:

$$A = \int_0^2 \int_0^{4-x^2} dy\, dx$$

$$= \int_0^2 (4 - x^2)\, dx$$

$$= \left[4x - \frac{x^3}{3} \right]_0^2 = \frac{16}{3}$$

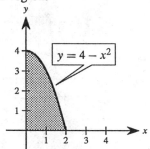

39. Use a double integral to find the area of the specified region.

Solution:

$$A = \int_0^4 \int_{(2-\sqrt{x})^2}^{} dy\, dx$$

$$= \int_0^4 (4 - 4\sqrt{x} + x)\, dx$$

$$= \left[4x - \frac{8}{3}x^{3/2} + \frac{x^2}{2} \right]_0^4$$

$$= \frac{8}{3}$$

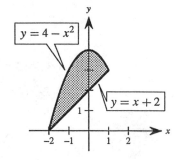

41. Use a double integral to find the area of the region bounded by the graphs of $y = 25 - x^2$ and $y = 0$.

Solution:

$$A = \int_{-5}^{5} \int_{0}^{25-x^2} dy \, dx$$

$$= \int_{-5}^{5} (25 - x^2) \, dx$$

$$= \left[25x - \frac{x^3}{3} \right]_{-5}^{5}$$

$$= \left(125 - \frac{125}{3} \right) - \left(-125 + \frac{125}{3} \right) = \frac{500}{3}$$

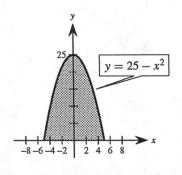

43. Use a double integral to find the area of the region bounded by the graphs of $5x - 2y = 0$, $y = -x + 3$, $y = 0$.

Solution:

The point of intersection of the two graphs is found by equating $y = \frac{5}{2}x$ and $y = 3 - x$, which yields $x = \frac{6}{7}$ and $y = \frac{15}{7}$.

$$A = \int_{0}^{15/7} \int_{2y/5}^{3-y} dx \, dy = \int_{0}^{15/7} \left(3 - y - \frac{2y}{5} \right) dy$$

$$= \int_{0}^{15/7} \left(3 - \frac{7y}{5} \right) dy \left[3y - \frac{7y^2}{10} \right]_{0}^{15/7}$$

$$= 3 \left(\frac{15}{7} \right) - \frac{7}{10} \left(\frac{15}{7} \right)^2 = \frac{45}{14}$$

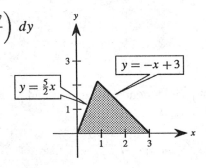

Note: Area of triangle is $\frac{1}{2}(3) \left(\frac{15}{7} \right) = \frac{45}{14}$

45. Use a double integral to find the area of the region bounded by the graphs of $y = x$, $y = 2x$, and $x = 2$.

Solution:

$$A = \int_0^2 \int_x^{2x} dy\,dx$$

$$= \int_0^2 (2x - x)\,dx$$

$$= \int_0^2 x\,dx$$

$$= \frac{x^2}{2}\Big]_0^2 = 2$$

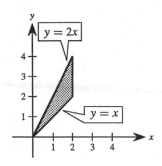

47. Evaluate the double integral $\int_0^1 \int_0^2 e^{-x^2 - y^2} dx\ dy$.

Solution:

$$\int_0^1 \int_0^2 e^{-x^2 - y^2} dx\ dy \approx 0.65876$$

49. Evaluate the double integral $\int_1^2 \int_0^x e^{xy} dy\ dx$.

Solution:

$$\int_1^2 \int_0^x e^{xy} dy\ dz \approx 8.1747.$$

51. Evaluate the double integral $\int_0^1 \int_x^1 \sqrt{1 - x^2} dy\ dx$.

Solution:

$$\int_0^1 \int_x^1 \sqrt{1 - x^2} dy\ dx = \frac{\pi}{4} - \frac{1}{3} \approx 0.4521$$

53. Determine whether the statement is true or false.

Changing the color of integration will sometimes change the value of a double integral.

Solution:

False.

Section 7.9   Applications of Double Integrals

1. Evaluate $\displaystyle\int_0^2 \int_0^1 (3x + 4y)\,dy\,dx$.

    Solution:

$$\int_0^2 \int_0^1 (3x + 4y)\,dy\,dx = \int_0^2 (3xy + 2y^2)\Big]_0^1 dx$$

$$= \int_0^2 (3x + 2)\,dx$$

$$= \left[\left(\tfrac{2}{3}x^2 + 2x\right)\right]_0^2 = 10$$

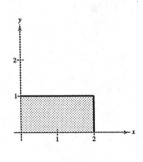

3. Evaluate $\displaystyle\int_0^1 \int_y^{\sqrt{y}} x^2 y^2 \,dx\,dy$.

    Solution:

$$\int_0^1 \int_y^{\sqrt{y}} x^2 y^2 \,dx\,dy = \int_0^1 \frac{x^3 y^2}{3}\bigg]_y^{\sqrt{y}} dy$$

$$= \frac{1}{3}\int_0^1 (y^{7/2} - y^5)\,dy$$

$$= \frac{1}{3}\left[\frac{2}{9}y^{9/2} - \frac{1}{6}y^6\right]_0^1 = \frac{1}{54}$$

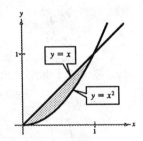

5. Evaluate $\displaystyle\int_0^1 \int_0^{\sqrt{1-x^2}} y\,dy\,dx$.

    Solution:

$$\int_0^1 \int_0^{\sqrt{1-x^2}} y\,dy\,dx = \int_0^1 \frac{y^2}{2}\bigg]_0^{\sqrt{1-x^2}} dx$$

$$= \frac{1}{2}\int_0^1 (1 - x^2)\,dx$$

$$= \frac{1}{2}\left(x - \frac{x^3}{3}\right)\bigg]_0^1 = \frac{1}{3}$$

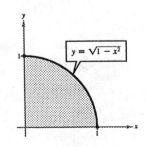

7. Set up a double integral for both orders of integration and use the more convenient order to integrate $f(x, y) = xy$ over rectangular region with vertices at $(0, 0)$, $(0, 5)$, $(3, 5)$, and $(3, 0)$.

Solution:

$$\int_0^3 \int_0^5 xy \, dy \, dx = \int_0^5 \int_0^3 xy \, dx \, dy$$

$$\int_0^3 \int_0^5 xy \, dy \, dx = \int_0^3 \frac{xy^2}{2} \Big]_0^5 dx = \int_0^3 \frac{25}{2} x \, dx = \frac{25}{4} x^2 \Big]_0^3 = \frac{225}{4}$$

9. Set up a double integral for both orders of integration and use the more convenient order to integrate $f(x, y) = y/(1 + x^2)$ over the region bounded by the graphs of $y = 0$, $y = \sqrt{x}$, and $x = 4$.

Solution:

$$\int_0^4 \int_0^{\sqrt{x}} \frac{y}{1 + x^2} \, dy \, dx = \int_0^2 \int_{y^2}^4 \frac{y}{1 + x^2} \, dx \, dy$$

$$\int_0^4 \int_0^{\sqrt{x}} \frac{y}{1 + x^2} \, dy \, dx = \int_0^4 \left[\frac{y^2}{2(1 + x^2)} \right]_0^{\sqrt{x}} dx$$

$$= \int_0^4 \frac{x}{2(1 + x^2)} \, dx = \frac{1}{4} \ln(1 + x^2) \Big]_0^4$$

$$= \frac{1}{4} \ln 17 \approx 0.708$$

11. Evaluate the following double integral. Note that it is necessary to switch the order of integration.

$$\int_0^1 \int_{y/2}^{1/2} e^{-x^2} \, dx \, dy$$

Solution:

$$\int_0^1 \int_{y/2}^{1/2} e^{-x^2} \, dx \, dy = \int_0^{1/2} \int_0^{2x} e^{-x^2} \, dy \, dx$$

$$= \int_0^{1/2} 2x e^{-x^2} \, dx = -e^{-x^2} \Big]_0^{1/2}$$

$$= 1 - e^{-1/4} \approx 0.2212$$

13. Use a double integral to find the volume of the specified solid.

Solution:

$$V = \int_0^2 \int_0^4 \frac{y}{2}\, dx\, dy$$

$$= \int_0^2 \frac{xy}{2}\bigg]_0^4 dy$$

$$= \int_0^2 2y\, dy$$

$$= y^2\bigg]_0^2 = 4$$

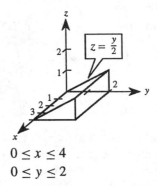

$$z = \frac{y}{2}$$

$$0 \le x \le 4$$
$$0 \le y \le 2$$

15. Use a double integral to find the volume of the specified solid.

Solution:

$$V = \int_0^3 \int_x^3 (8 - x - y)\, dy\, dx$$

$$= \int_0^3 \left(8y - xy - \frac{y^2}{2}\right) \Big]_x^3 dx$$

$$= \int_0^3 \left[\left(24 - 3x - \frac{9}{2}\right) - \left(8x - x^2 - \frac{x^2}{2}\right)\right] dx$$

$$= \int_0^3 \left(\frac{39}{2} - 11x + \frac{3}{2}x^2\right) dx$$

$$= \left[\frac{39}{2}x - \frac{11x^2}{2} + \frac{x^3}{2}\right]_0^3 = 22.5$$

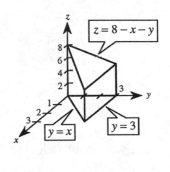

$$z = 8 - x - y$$

$$y = x \qquad y = 3$$

17. Use a double integral to find the volume of the specified solid.

Solution:

$$V = \int_0^6 \int_0^{4-(2x/3)} \left(3 - \frac{x}{2} - \frac{3y}{4}\right) dy\, dx$$

$$= \int_0^6 \left[3y - \frac{xy}{2} - \frac{3y^2}{8}\right]_0^{4-(2x/3)} dx$$

$$= \int_0^6 \left(6 - 2x + \frac{x^2}{6}\right) dx$$

$$= \left[6x - x^2 + \frac{x^3}{18}\right]_0^6 = 12$$

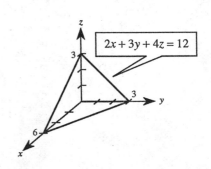

$$2x + 3y + 4z = 12$$

19. Use a double integral to find the volume of the specified solid.

    Solution:

$$V = \int_0^1 \int_0^y (1 - xy)\,dx\,dy$$

$$= \int_0^1 \left[x - \frac{x^2 y}{2} \right]_0^y dy$$

$$= \int_0^1 \left(y - \frac{y^3}{2} \right) dy$$

$$= \left[\frac{y^2}{2} - \frac{y^4}{8} \right]_0^1 = \frac{3}{8}$$

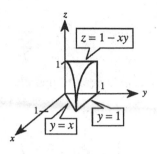

21. Use a double integral to find the volume of the specified solid.

    Solution:

$$V = 4\int_0^1 \int_0^1 (4 - x^2 - y^2)\,dy\,dx$$

$$= 4\int_0^1 \left[4y - x^2 y - \frac{y^3}{3} \right]_0^1 dx$$

$$= 4\int_0^1 \left[4 - x^2 - \frac{1}{3} \right] dx$$

$$= 4\int_0^1 \left(\frac{11}{3} - x^2 \right) dx$$

$$= 4\left[\frac{11x}{3} - \frac{x^3}{3} \right]_0^1 = 4\left(\frac{11}{3} - \frac{1}{3} \right) = 4\left(\frac{10}{3} \right) = \frac{40}{3}$$

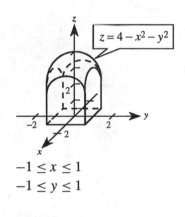

$$-1 \le x \le 1$$
$$-1 \le y \le 1$$

23. Use a double integral to find the volume of the specified solid.

    Solution:

$$V = \int_0^1 \int_0^x \sqrt{1 - x^2}\,dy\,dx$$

$$= \int_0^1 x\sqrt{1 - x^2}\,dx$$

$$= -\frac{1}{3}(1 - x^2)^{3/2} \Big]_0^1 = \frac{1}{3}$$

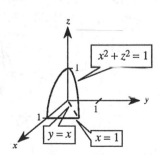

25. Use a double integral to find the volume of the solid bounded by the graphs of
$z = xy$, $z = 0$, $y = 0$, $y = 4$, $x = 0$, and $x = 1$.

Solution:

$$V = \int_0^4 \int_0^1 xy \, dx \, dy = \int_0^4 \left[\frac{x^2 y}{2}\right]_0^1 dy = \frac{1}{2}\int_0^4 y \, dy = \frac{y^2}{4}\bigg]_0^4 = 4$$

27. Use a double integral to find the volume of the solid bounded by the graphs of
$z = x^2$, $z = 0$, $x = 0$, $x = 2$, $y = 0$, and $y = 4$.

Solution:

$$V = \int_0^2 \int_0^4 x^2 \, dy \, dx = \int_0^2 \left[x^2 y\right]_0^4 dx = \int_0^2 4x^2 \, dx = \frac{4x^3}{3}\bigg]_0^2 = \frac{32}{3}$$

29. Find the average value of $f(x, y) = x$ over the rectangular region with vertices $(0, 0)$, $(4, 0)$, $(4, 2)$, and $(0, 2)$.

Solution:

$$\text{Average} = \frac{1}{8}\int_0^4 \int_0^2 x \, dy \, dx = \frac{1}{8}\int_0^4 2x \, dx = \frac{x^2}{8}\bigg]_0^4 = 2$$

31. Find the average value of $f(x, y) = x^2 + y^2$ over the rectangular region with vertices $(0, 0)$, $(2, 0)$, $(2, 2)$, and $(0, 2)$.

Solution:

$$\text{Average} = \frac{1}{4}\int_0^2 \int_0^2 (x^2 + y^2) \, dx \, dy$$

$$= \frac{1}{4}\int_0^2 \left[\frac{x^3}{3} + xy^2\right]_0^2 dy = \frac{1}{4}\int_0^2 \left(\frac{8}{3} + 2y^2\right) dy = \left[\frac{1}{4}\left(\frac{8}{3}y + \frac{2}{3}y^3\right)\right]_0^2 = \frac{8}{3}$$

33. *Average Revenue* A company sells two products whose demand functions are
$x_1 = 500 - 3p_1$ and $x_2 = 750 - 2.4p_2$. Therefore, the total revenue is given by $R = x_1 p_1 + x_2 p_2$. Estimate the average revenue if the price p_1 varies between \$50 and \$75 and the price p_2 varies between \$100 and \$150.

Solution:

$$\text{Average} = \frac{1}{1250}\int_{100}^{150} \int_{50}^{75} [(500 - 3p_1)p_1 + (750 - 2.4p_2)p_2] \, dp_1 \, dp_2$$

$$= \frac{1}{1250}\int_{100}^{150} \int_{50}^{75} [-3p_1^2 + 500p_1 - 2.4p_2^2 + 750p_2] \, dp_1 \, dp_2$$

$$= \frac{1}{1250}\int_{100}^{150} \left[-p_1^3 + 250p_1^2 - 2.4p_1 p_2^2 + 750p_1 p_2\right]_{50}^{75} dp_2$$

$$= \frac{1}{1250}\int_{100}^{150} [484{,}375 - 60p_2^2 + 18{,}750p_2] \, dp_2$$

$$= \frac{1}{1250}\left[484{,}375p_2 - 20p_2^3 + 9375p_2^2\right]_{100}^{150} = \$75{,}125$$

Chapter 7   Review Exercises

1. Plot the points $(2, -1, 4)$, $(-1, 3, -3)$.

   Solution:

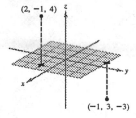

3. Find the distance between $(0, 0, 0)$ and $(2, 5, 9)$.

   Solution:

$$d = \sqrt{(2 - 0)^2 + (5 - 0)^2 + (9 - 0)^2} = \sqrt{4 + 25 + 81} = \sqrt{110}$$

5. Find the midpoint of the line segment joining $(2, 6, 4)$ and $(-4, 2, 8)$

   Solution:

$$\text{Midpoint} = \left(\frac{2 - 4}{2}, \frac{6 + 2}{2}, \frac{4 + 8}{2}\right) = (-1, 4, 6)$$

7. Find the standard form of the equation of the sphere.

   Center: $(0, 1, 0)$; Radius: 5

   Solution:

$$(x - 0)^2 + (y - 1)^2 + (z - 0)^2 = 5^2$$
$$x^2 + (y - 1)^2 + z^2 = 25$$

9. Find the standard form of the equation of the sphere.

   Diameter endpoints: $(3, 4, 0)$, $(5, 8, 2)$

   Solution:

$$\text{Center} = \left(\frac{3 + 5}{2}, \frac{4 + 8}{2}, \frac{0 + 2}{2}\right) = (4, 6, 1)$$

Radius $= \sqrt{(4 - 3)^2 + (6 - 4)^2 + (1 - 0)^2} = \sqrt{6}$

Circle: $(x - 4)^2 + (y - 6)^2 + (z - 1)^2 = 6$

11. Find the center and radius of the sphere.

$$x^2 + y^2 + z^2 + 4x - 2y - 8z + 5 = 0$$

Solution:

$$x^2 + 4x + 4 + y^2 - 2y + 1 + z^2 - 8z + 16 = -5 + 4 + 1 + 16$$
$$(x + 2)^2 + (y - 1)^2 + (z - 4)^2 = 16 = 4^2$$

Center: $(-2, 1, 4)$ Radius: 4

13. Sketch the xy-trace of the sphere.

$$(x + 2)^2 + (y - 1)^2 + (z - 3)^2 = 25$$

Solution:

Let $z = 0$: $(x + 2)^2 + (y - 1)^2 + (0 - 3)^2 = 25$
$$(x + 2)^2 + (y - 1)^2 = 16 = 4^2$$

Circle of radius 4

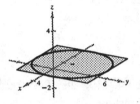

15. Find the intercepts and sketch the graph of the plane $x + 2y + 3z = 6$.

Solution:

x-intercept: $(6, 0, 0)$
y-intercept: $(0, 3, 0)$
z-intercept: $(0, 0, 2)$

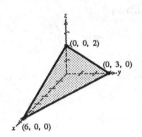

17. Find the intercepts and sketch the graph of the plane.

$$6x + 3y - 6z = 12$$

Solution:

x-intercept: $(2, 0, 0)$
y-intercept: $(0, 4, 0)$
z-intercept: $(0, 0, -2)$

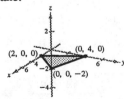

19. When $x^2 + y^2 + z^2 - 2x + 4y - 6z + 5 = 0$, identify the surface.

Solution:

The graph is a sphere whose standard equation is $(x - 1)^2 + (y + 2)^2 + (z - 3)^2 = 9$.

21. When $x^2 + \dfrac{y^2}{16} + \dfrac{z^2}{9} = 1$, identify the surface.

Solution:

The graph is an ellipsoid.

23. Identify the surface. $z = \dfrac{x^2}{9} + y^2$

Solution:

The graph is an elliptic paraboloid.

25. When $z = \sqrt{x^2 + y^2}$, identify the surface.

Solution:

The graph is the top half of a circular cone whose standard equation is $x^2 + y^2 - z^2 = 0$.

27. Find the function values.

$f(x, y) = xy^2$

(a) $f(2, 3)$ (b) $f(0, 1)$

(c) $f(-5, 7)$ (d) $f(-2, -4)$

Solution:

$f(x, y) = xy^2$

(a) $f(2, 3) = 2(3)^2 = 18$ (b) $f(0, 1) = 0(1)^2 = 0$

(c) $f(-5, 7) = -5(7)^2 = -245$ (d) $f(-2, -4) = -2(-4)^2 = -32$

29. Describe the region R in the xy-plane that corresponds to the domain of

$f(x, y) = \sqrt{1 - x^2 - y^2}$. Then find the range of the function.

Solution:

The domain is the set of all points inside or on the circle $x^2 + y^2 = 1$ and the range is $[0, 1]$.

31. Describe the level curves of the function. Sketch the level curves for the given c-values.

$z = 10 - 2x - 5y, \; c = 0, 2, 4, 5, 10$

Solution:

The level curves are lines of slope $-\dfrac{2}{5}$.

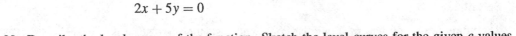

$$c = 0: 10 - 2x - 5y = 0$$
$$2x + 5y = 10$$
$$c = 2: 10 - 2x - 5y = 2$$
$$2x + 5y = 8$$
$$c = 4: 10 - 2x - 5y = 4$$
$$2x + 5y = 6$$
$$c = 5: 10 - 2x - 5y = 5$$
$$2x + 5y = 5$$
$$c = 10: 10 - 2x - 5y = 10$$
$$2x + 5y = 0$$

33. Describe the level curves of the function. Sketch the level curves for the given c-values.

$z = (xy)^2, c = 1, 4, 9, 12, 16$

Solution:

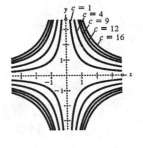

$$z = (xy)^2 \qquad\qquad y^2 = \frac{1}{x^2}, y = \pm\frac{1}{x}$$
$$c = 1: (xy)^2 = 1, \qquad\quad y = \pm\frac{3}{x}$$
$$c = 4: (xy)^2 = 4,$$
$$c = 9: (xy)^2 = 9, \qquad\quad y = \pm\frac{2\sqrt{3}}{x}$$
$$c = 12: (xy)^2 = 12,$$
$$c = 16: (xy)^2 = 16, \qquad y = \pm\frac{4}{x}$$

The level curves are hyperbolas.

35. *Average Precipitation* The contour map shown below represents the average yearly precipitation for Iowa.

(a) Discuss the use of color to represent the level curves.

(b) Which part of Iowa receives the most precipitation?

(c) Which part of Iowa receives the least precipitation?

Solution:

(a) The level curves represent lines of equal rainfall, and separate the 4 colors.

(b) The small eastern portion containing Davenport.

(c) The northwestern portion containing Sioux City.

37. *Equation of Exchange* Economists use an equation of exchange to express the relation among money, prices, and business transactions. This equation can be written as

$$P = \frac{x}{MV}T,$$

where M is the money supply, V is the velocity of circulation, T is the total number of transactions, and P is the price level. Find P when $M = \$2500$, $V = 6$, and $T = 6000$.

Solution:

$$P = \frac{MV}{T} = \frac{(2500)6}{6000} = \$2.50$$

39. Find the first partial derivatives.

$$f(x, y) = x^2y + 3xy + 2x - 5y$$

Solution:

$$f(x, y) = x^2y + 3xy + 2x - 5y$$
$$f_x = 2xy + 3y + 2$$
$$f_y = x^2 + 3x - 5$$

41. Find the first partial derivatives.

$$z = 6x^2\sqrt{y} + 3\sqrt{xy} - 7xy$$

Solution:

$$z = 6x^2\sqrt{y} + 3\sqrt{xy} - 7xy$$
$$z_x = 12x\sqrt{y} + \frac{3}{2}\sqrt{\frac{y}{x}} - 7y$$
$$z_y = 3\frac{x^2}{\sqrt{y}} + \frac{3}{2}\sqrt{\frac{x}{y}} - 7x$$

43. Find the first partial derivatives.

$$f(x, y) = \ln(2x + 3y)$$

Solution:

$$f(x, y) = \ln(2x + 3y)$$
$$fx = \frac{2}{2x + 3y}$$
$$fy = \frac{3}{2x + 3y}$$

45. Find the first partial derivatives.

$$f(x, y) = x^2e^y - y^2e^x$$

Solution:

$$f_x = 2xe^y - y^2e^x$$
$$f_y = x^2e^y - 2ye^x$$

47. Find the first partial derivatives.

$w = xyz^2$

Solution:

$$\frac{\partial w}{\partial x} = yz^2$$

$$\frac{\partial w}{\partial y} = xz^2$$

$$\frac{\partial w}{\partial z} = 2xyz$$

49. Find the slope of $z = 3x - 4y + 9$, at the point (3, 2, 10) in (a) the x-direction and (b) the y-direction.

Solution:

(a) $z_x = 3$ (b) $z_y = -4$

51. Find the slope of $z = 8 - x^2 - y^2$, at the point (1, 2, 3) in (a) the x-direction and (b) the y-direction.

Solution:

(a) $z_x = -2x$ At (1, 2, 3), $z_x = -2$

(b) $z_y = -2y$ At (1, 2, 3), $z_y = -4$

53. Find all second partial derivatives.

$f(x, y) = x^3 - 4xy^2 + y^3$

Solution:

$$f_x = 3x^2 - 4y^2, \qquad f_y = -8xy + 3y^2$$
$$f_{xx} = 6x, \qquad f_{yy} = -8x + 6y, \qquad f_{xy} = f_{yx} = -8y$$

55. Find all second partial derivatives.

$f(x, y) = \sqrt{64 - x^2 - y^2}$

Solution:

$$f_x = \frac{-x}{\sqrt{64 - x^2 - y^2}} \qquad f_y = \frac{-y}{\sqrt{64 - x^2 - y^2}}$$

$$f_{xx} = \frac{y^2 - 64}{(64 - x^2 - y^2)^{3/2}} \qquad f_{yy} = \frac{x^2 - 64}{(64 - x^2 - y^2)^{3/2}}$$

$$f_{xy} = \frac{-xy}{(64 - x^2 - y^2)^{3/2}} = f_{yx}$$

57. *Marginal Cost*   A company manufactures two models of skis: cross-country skis and downhill skis. The cost function for producing x cross-country skis and y downhill skis is

$$C = 15(xy)^{1/3} + 99x + 139y + 2293$$

Find the marginal cost when $x = 250$ and $y = 175$.

Solution:

$$C_x = 5x^{-2/3}y^{1/3} + 99 \qquad C_x(250, 175) \approx 99.70$$
$$C_y = 5x^{1/3}y^{-2/3} + 139 \qquad C_y(250, 175) \approx 140.04$$

59. Find any critical points and relative extrema of the function $f(x, y) = x^2 + 2xy + y^2$

Solution:

The first partial derivatives of f, $f_x(x, y) = 2x + 2y$ and $f_y(x, y) = 2x + 2y$, are zero when $y = -x$. The points $(x, -x, 0)$ are relative minima.

Note: The Second-Partials Test fails since $d = 0$.

61. Find any critical points and relative extrema of the function $f(x, y) = x^2 + 6xy + 3y^2 + 6x + 8$.

Solution:

The first partial derivative of f, $f_x = 2x + 6y + 6$ and $f_y = 6x + 6y$, are zero at $\left(\dfrac{3}{2}, -\dfrac{3}{2}\right)$.

The second partials are

$$f_{xx} = 2, \; f_{xy} = 6, \text{ and } f_{yy} = 6$$

Since $f_{xx} > 0$ and $d = f_{xx}f_{yy} - (f_{xy})^2 < 0$, $f\left(\frac{3}{2}, -\frac{3}{2}\right)$ is a saddle point. No relative extrema.

63. Find any critical points and relative extrema of the function $f(x, y) = x^3 + y^2 - xy$.

Solution:

The first partial derivatives of f, $f_x = 3x^2 - y$ and $f_y = 2y - x$, are zero at $\left(\dfrac{1}{6}, \dfrac{1}{12}\right)$ and $(0, 0)$. The second partials are

$$f_{xx} = 6x \qquad f_{yy} = 2 \qquad f_{xy} = 1.$$

At $(0, 0)$, $d < 0 \Rightarrow$ saddle point.

At $\left(\dfrac{1}{6}, \dfrac{1}{12}\right)$, $f_{xx} > 0$ and $d > 0 \Rightarrow$ relative minimum.

65. Find any critical points and relative extrema of the function
$f(x, y) = x^3 + y^3 - 3x - 3y + 2$.

Solution:

The first partial derivatives of f, $f_x = 3x^2 - 3$ and $f_y = 3y^2 - 3$, are zero at $(\pm 1, \pm 1)$, $(\pm 1, \mp 1)$.

The second partials are

$$f_{xx} = 6x \qquad f_{yy} = 6y, \, and \qquad f_{xy} = 0.$$

$(1, 1)$: fxx > 0, d $> 0 relative minimum$

$(1, -1)$: fxx > 0, $\qquad$ d $< 0 saddle point$

$(-1, 1)$: fxx < 0, $\qquad$ d $< 0 saddle point$

$(-1, -1)$: fxx < 0, d $> 0 relative maximum$

67. *Revenue* A company manufactures and sells two products. The demand functions for the products are

$p_1 = 100 - x_1$ and $p_2 = 200 - 0.5x_2$.

(a) Find the total revenue functions for x_1 and x_2.

(b) Find x_1 and x_2 so that the revenue is maximized.

(c) What is the maximum revenue?

Solution:

(a) $R = x_1 p_1 + z_2 p_2 = x, (100 - x_1) + x_2(200 - 0.5x_2)$

$$= -x_1^2 - \frac{1}{2}x_2^2 + 100x_1 + 200x_2$$

(b) $R_{x_1} = -2x_1 + 100 = 0 \Rightarrow x_1 = 50$

$R_{x_2} = -x_2 + 200 = 0 \Rightarrow x_2 = 200$

By the Second-Partials Test, $(50, 200)$ is a maximum.

(c) $R(50, 200) = \$22,500.00$

69. Using Lagrange multipliers, locate any extrema of $f(x_1 y) = x^2 y$ subject to the constraint $x + 2y = 2$.

Solution:

$$F(x, y, \lambda) = x^2 y - \lambda(x + 2y - 2)$$

$$\left. \begin{array}{l} F_x(x, y, \lambda) = 2xy - \lambda = 0 \\ F_y(x, y, \lambda) = x^2 - 2\lambda = 0 \end{array} \right\} \qquad 4xy = x^2$$

$$F_\lambda(x, y, \lambda) = -(x + 2y - 2) = 0, \qquad y = \frac{2 - x}{2}$$

Thus, $x = 0$ or $x = \frac{4}{3}$ and the corresponding y-values are $y = 1$ or $y = \frac{1}{3}$. This implies that the extrema occur at $(0, 1, 0)$ (relative minimum) and $\left(\frac{4}{3}, \frac{1}{3}, \frac{16}{27}\right)$ (relative minimum).

71. Using Lagrange multipliers, locate any extrema of $f(x, y, z) = xyx$, subject to the constraint $x + 2y + z - 4 = 0$.

Solution:

$$F(x, y, z, \lambda) = xyz - \lambda(x + 2y + z - 4)$$

$$\left. \begin{array}{l} F_x = yz - \lambda = 0 \\ F_y = xz - 2\lambda = 0 \\ F_z = xy - \lambda = 0 \end{array} \right\} \qquad \begin{array}{l} xz = 2yz = 2xy \Rightarrow x = 2y \\ \\ z = 2y \end{array}$$

$$F_\lambda = -(x + 2y + z - 4) = 0$$

$$2y + 2y + 2y - 4 = 0 \Rightarrow y = \frac{2}{3}, x = \frac{4}{3}, z = \frac{4}{3}. \text{ At } \left(\frac{4}{3}, \frac{2}{3}, \frac{4}{3}\right),$$

the relative maximum value is $\frac{32}{27}$.

73. Using Lagrange multipliers, locate any extrema of $f(x, y, z) = x^2 + y^2 + z^2$, subject to the constraints $x + z = 6$, and $y + z = 8$.

Solution:

$$F(x, y, z, \lambda, \mu) = x^2 + y^2 + z^2 - \lambda(x + z - 6) - \mu(y + z - 8)$$

$$F_x = 2x - \lambda = 0 \qquad\qquad\qquad x = \frac{\lambda}{2}$$

$$F_y = 2y - \mu = 0 \qquad\qquad\qquad y = \frac{\mu}{2}$$

$$F_z = 2z - \lambda - \mu = 0$$

$$f_\lambda = -(x + z - 6) = 0 \qquad\qquad z = (\lambda + \mu)/2 = x + y$$

$$f_\mu = -(y + z - 8) = 0 \qquad \left. \begin{array}{l} x + z = 6 \Rightarrow 2x + y = 6 \\ y + z = 8 \Rightarrow x + 2y = 8 \end{array} \right\}$$

$$x = \frac{4}{3}, y = \frac{10}{3}, z = \frac{14}{3}$$

$f\left(\frac{4}{3}, \frac{10}{3}, \frac{14}{3}\right) = 34\frac{2}{3}$ is a relative minimum.

75. *Maximum Production Level* The production function for a manufacturer is $f(x, y) = 4x + xy + 2y$. Assume that the total amount available for labor x and capital y is \$2000 and that units of labor and capital cost \$20 and \$4, respectively. Find the maximum production level for this manufacturer.

Solution:

Maximize $f(x, y) = 4x + xy + 2y$, subject to the constraint $20x + 4y = 2000$.

$$F(x, y, \lambda) = 4x + xy + 2y - \lambda(20x + 4y - 2000)$$

$$\left. \begin{array}{l} F_x(x, y, \lambda) = 4 + y - 20\lambda = 0 \\ F_y(x, y, \lambda) = x + 2 - 4\lambda = 0 \end{array} \right\} \qquad \begin{array}{l} 4 + y = 5(x + 2) \\ y = 5x + 6 \end{array}$$

$$F_\lambda(x, y, \lambda) = -(20x + 4y - 2000) = 0, \qquad y = 500 - 5x$$

Thus, $x = 49.4$ and $y = 5(49.4) + 6 = 253$ which implies that the maximum production level is $f(49.4, \ 253) \approx 13,202$.

77. (a) Use the method of least squares to find the least squares regression line and (b) calculate the sum of the squared errors.

$(-2, -3), (-1, -1), (1, 2), (3, 2)$

Solution:

(a) $\sum x_i = 1$

$\sum y_i = 0$

$\sum x_i^2 = 15$

$\sum x_i y_i = 15$

$a = \dfrac{4(15) - (1)(0)}{4(15) - (1)^2} = \dfrac{60}{59}$

$b = \dfrac{1}{4}\left(0 - \dfrac{60}{59}(1)\right) = -\dfrac{15}{59}$

$y = \dfrac{60}{59}x - \dfrac{15}{59}.$

(b) $\left(\dfrac{60}{59}(-2) - \dfrac{15}{59} + 3\right)^2 + \left(\dfrac{60}{59}(-1) - \dfrac{15}{59} + 1\right)^2 + \left(\dfrac{60}{59}(1) - \dfrac{15}{59} - 2\right)^2$

$+ \left(\dfrac{60}{59}(3) - \dfrac{15}{59} - 2\right)^2 \approx 2.746$

79. *Biotechnology* The biotechnology industry, which includes genetic engineering, has produced over 27 new wonder drugs. The biotechnology industry product sales (in billions of dollars) from 1990 to 1993 are listed in the table in the textbook.

(a) Use a graphing utility with a built-in least squares regression program to find a linear model for the data.

(b) Use the model to estimate the product sales of the biotechnology industry in the year 2000.

Solution:

(a) Sales $= S = 1.42t + 2.82$ ($t = 0$ is 1990)

(b) $S(10) \approx 17.02$ billion dollars

81. Find the least squares regression quadratic for the points $(-1, 9)$, $(0, 7)$, $(1, 5)$, $(2, 6)$, and $(4, 23)$. Plot the points and sketch the least squares quadratic on the same coordinate axes.

Solution:

$$\sum x_i = 6$$

$$\sum y_i = 50$$

$$\sum x_i^2 = 22$$

$$\sum x_i y_i = 100$$

$$\sum x_i^3 = 72$$

$$\sum x_i^2 y_i = 406$$

$$\sum x_i^4 = 274$$

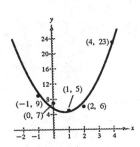

The system

$$274a + 74b + 22c = 406$$

$$74a + 22b + 6c = 100$$

$$22a + 6b + 5c = 50$$

has approximate solutions $a = 1.71$, $b = -2.57$, and $c = 5.56$. Therefore, the least squares quadratic is $y = 1.71x^2 - 2.57x + 5.56$.

83. Evaluate $\displaystyle\int_0^1 \int_0^{1+x} (3x + 2y)\, dy\, dx$.

Solution:

$$\int_0^1 \int_0^{1+x} (3x + 2y)\, dy\, dx = \int_0^1 \left[(3xy + y^2) \right]_0^{1+x} dx = \int_0^1 [3x(1+x) + (1+x)^2]\, dx$$

$$= \int_0^1 (4x^2 + 5x + 1)\, dx = \left[\frac{4x^3}{3} + \frac{5x^2}{2} + x \right]_0^1$$

$$= \frac{4}{3} + \frac{5}{2} + 1 = \frac{29}{6}$$

85. Evaluate $\displaystyle\int_1^2 \int_1^{2y} \frac{x}{y^2}\, dx\, dy$.

Solution:

$$\int_1^2 \int_1^{2y} \frac{x}{y^2}\, dx\, dy = \int_1^2 \left[\frac{x^2}{2y^2} \right]_1^{2y} dy$$

$$= \int_1^2 \left[\frac{4y^2}{2y^2} - \frac{1}{2y^2} \right] dy = \int_1^2 \left(2 - \frac{1}{2}y^{-2} \right) dy$$

$$= \left[2y + \frac{1}{2y} \right]_1^2 = \left(4 + \frac{1}{4} \right) - \left(2 + \frac{1}{2} \right) = \frac{7}{4}$$

87. Use a double integral to find the area of the region shown in the textbook. Compute the area of R by letting $f(x, y) = 1$ and integrating.

$$\iint_R f(x, y) \, dA$$

Solution:

$$A = \int_{-2}^{2} \int_{5}^{9-x^2} dy \, dx = \int_{5}^{9} \int_{-\sqrt{9-y}}^{\sqrt{9-y}} dx \, dy$$

$$\int_{-2}^{2} \int_{5}^{9-x^2} dy \, dx = \int_{-2}^{2} [(9 - x^2) - 5] \, dx$$

$$= \int_{-2}^{2} (4 - x^2) \, dx = \left[\left(4x - \frac{x^3}{3} \right) \right]_{-2}^{2} = \left(8 - \frac{8}{3} \right) - \left(-8 + \frac{8}{3} \right)$$

$$= \frac{32}{3}$$

89. Use a double integral to find the area of the region shown in the textbook.

Solution:

$$A = \int_{-3}^{6} \int_{1/3(x+3)}^{\sqrt{x+3}} - dy \, dx = \int_{-3}^{6} \left(\sqrt{x+3} - \frac{1}{3}(x+3) \right) dx$$

$$= \left[\frac{2}{3}(x+3)^{3/2} - \frac{x^2}{6} - x \right]_{-3}^{6} = (18 - 6 - 6) - \left(0 - \frac{3}{2} + 3 \right) = \frac{9}{2}$$

91. Use an appropriate double integral to find the volume of a solid bounded by the graphs of $z = (xy)^2$, $z = 0$, $y = 0$, $y = 4$, $x = 0$, and $x = 4$.

Solution:

$$V = \int_{0}^{4} \int_{0}^{4} (xy)^2 \, dy \, dx = \int_{0}^{4} \int_{0}^{4} x^2 y^2 \, dy \, dx = \int_{0}^{4} \frac{x^2 y^3}{3} \Big]_{0}^{4} dx$$

$$= \int_{0}^{4} \frac{64x^2}{3} \, dx = \frac{64x^3}{9} \Big]_{0}^{4} = \frac{4096}{9}$$

93. *Average Elevation* In a triangular coastal area, the elevation in miles above sea level at the point (x, y) is $f(x, y) = 0.25 - 0.025x - 0.01y$, where x and y are measured in miles (see figure in textbook). Find the average elevation of the triangular area.

Solution:

$$\text{Average} = \frac{\int_{0}^{10} \int_{0}^{25-2.5x} (0.25 - 0.025x - 0.01y) dy dx}{\text{area}}$$

$$= \frac{10^5/12}{125} = 0.083\overline{3} \text{ miles}$$

Practice Test for Chapter 7

1. Find the distance between the points $(3, -7, 2)$ and $(5, 11, -6)$ and find the midpoint of the line segment joining the two points.

2. Find the standard form of the equation of the sphere whose center is $(1, -3, 0)$ and radius is $\sqrt{5}$.

3. Find the center and radius of the sphere whose equation is
$$x^2 + y^2 + z^2 - 4x + 2y + 8z = 0.$$

4. Sketch the graph of the plane.
   (a) $3x + 8y + 6z = 24$ (b) $y = 2$

5. Identify the surface.
   (a) $\dfrac{x^2}{16} + \dfrac{y^2}{4} - \dfrac{z^2}{9} = 1$ (b) $z = \dfrac{x^2}{25} + y^2$

6. Find the domain of the function.
   (a) $f(x, y) = \ln(3 - x - y)$ (b) $f(x, y) = \dfrac{1}{x^2 + y^2}$

7. Find the first partial derivatives of $f(x, y) = 3x^2 + 9xy^2 + 4y^3 - 3x - 6y + 1$.

8. Find the first partial derivatives of $f(x, y) = \ln(x^2 + y^2 + 5)$.

9. Find the first partial derivatives of $f(x, y, z) = x^2 y^3 \sqrt{z}$.

10. Find the second partial derivatives of $z = \dfrac{x}{x^2 + y^2}$.

11. Find the relative extrema of $f(x, y) = 3x^2 + 4y^2 - 6x + 16y - 4$.

12. Find the relative extrema of $f(x, y) = 4xy - x^4 - y^4$.

13. Use Lagrange multipliers to find the minimum of $f(x, y) = xy$ subject to the constraint $4x - y = 16$.

14. Use Lagrange multipliers to find the minimum of $f(x, y) = x^2 - 16x + y^2 - 8y + 12$ subject to the constraint $x + y = 4$.

15. Find the least squares regression line for the points $(-3, 7)$, $(1, 5)$, $(8, -2)$, and $(4, 4)$.

16. Find the least squares regression quadratic for the points $(-5, 8)$, $(-1, 2)$, $(1, 3)$, and $(5, 5)$.

17. Evaluate $\displaystyle\int_0^3 \int_0^{\sqrt{x}} xy^3 \, dy \, dx$.

18. Evaluate $\displaystyle\int_{-1}^2 \int_0^{3y} (x^2 - 4xy) \, dx \, dy$.

19. Set up a double integral to find the area of the indicated region.

(a)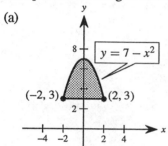

(b)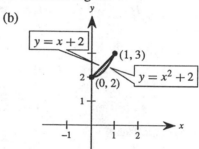

20. Find the volume of the solid bounded by the first octant and the plane $x + y + z = 4$.

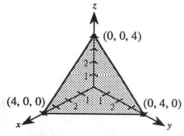

Graphing Calculator Required

21. Use a program similar to the one given on page 514 of the textbook to find the least square regression line and the correlation coefficient for the given data points. $(0, 20.4)$, $(1, 21.3)$, $(2, 22.9)$, $(3, 23.4)$, $(4, 24)$, $(5, 24.2)$, $(6, 24.9)$, $(7, 25.3)$, $(8, 26.2)$, $(9, 27.5)$, $(10, 29)$, $(11, 30.3)$, and $(12, 31.1)$.

22. Use a graphing calculator or a computer algebra system to approximate $\displaystyle\int_2^3 \int_0^{x+2} e^{x^2 y} \, dy \, dx$.

CHAPTER P
Probability and Calculus

Section P.1 Discrete Probability

1. List the elements in the following set.

   A coin is tossed three times.

   (a) The sample space S
   (b) The event A that at least two heads occur
   (c) The event B that no more than one head occurs
   Solution:

   (a) $S = \{HHH, \ HHT, \ HTH, \ THH, \ HTT, \ THT, \ TTH, \ TTT\}$
   (b) $A = \{HHH, \ HHT, \ HTH, \ THH\}$
   (c) $B = \{HTT, \ THT, \ TTH, \ TTT\}$

3. List the elements in the following set.

   An integer is selected from the set of all integers between 1 and 50 that are divisible by 3.

   (a) The sample space S
   (b) The event A that the integer is divisible by 12
   (c) The event B that the integer is a perfect square
   Solution:

   (a) $S = \{3, 6, 9, 12, 15, 18, 21, 24, 27, 30, 33, 36, 39, 42, 45, 48\}$
   (b) $A = \{12, \ 24, \ 36, \ 48\}$
   (c) $B = \{9, 36\}$

5. *Election Poll* Three people have been nominated for president of a college class. From a small poll it is estimated that Jane has a probability of 0.29 of winning and the probability of Larry winning is 0.47. What is the probability of the third candidate winning the election?

   Solution:

   $$1 - 0.29 - 0.47 = 0.24$$

7. *Quality Control* In one component of a spacecraft there is a main system and a backup system. The probability of at least one of the systems performing satisfactorily throughout the duration of the flight is 0.9855. What is the probability they both fail?

Solution:

$$1 - 0.9855 = 0.0145$$

9. *Tossing Coins* Two coins are tossed. A random variable assigns the number 0, 1, or 2 to each possible outcome, depending on the number of heads that turn up. Find the frequencies of 0, 1, and 2.

Solution:

Random Variable	0	1	2
Frequency	1	2	1

11. *True-False Exam* Three students answer a true-false question on an examination. A random variable assigns the number 0, 1, 2, or 3 to each outcome, depending on the number of answers of *true* among the three students. Find the frequencies of 0, 1, 2, and 3.

Solution:

Random Variable	0	1	2	3
Frequency	1	3	3	1

13. Sketch the probability histogram for the given distribution and find the required probabilities.

x	0	1	2	3	4
$P(x)$	$\frac{1}{20}$	$\frac{3}{20}$	$\frac{6}{20}$	$\frac{6}{20}$	$\frac{4}{20}$

(a) $P(1 \leq x \leq 3)$

(b) $P(x \geq 2)$

Solution:

(a) $P(1 \leq x \leq 3) = P(1) + P(2) + P(3)$

$$= \tfrac{3}{20} + \tfrac{6}{20} + \tfrac{6}{20}$$

$$= \tfrac{15}{20}$$

$$= \tfrac{3}{4}$$

(b) $P(x \geq 2) = P(2) + P(3) + P(4)$

$$= \tfrac{6}{20} + \tfrac{6}{20} + \tfrac{4}{20}$$

$$= \tfrac{16}{20}$$

$$= \tfrac{4}{5}$$

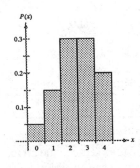

15. See the table in the textbook, sketch a graph of the probability distribution and find the required probabilities.

(a) $P(x \leq 3)$

(b) $P(x \geq 3)$

Solution:

(a) $P(x \leq 3) = 0.041 + 0.189 + 0.247 + 0.326$

$$= 0.803$$

(b) $P(x > 3) = 0.159 + 0.038$

$$= 0.197$$

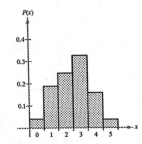

17. *Boy or Girl?* A couple has four children. Assume that it is equally likely that each child will be a girl or a boy.

(a) What is the sample space?

(b) Complete a table to form the probability distribution if the random variable x is the number of girls in the family.

(c) Use the table of part (b) to graph the probability distribution.

(d) Use the table of part (b) to find the probability of having at least one boy.

Solution:

(a) $S = \{gggg,\ gggb,\ ggbg,\ gbgg,\ bggg,\ ggbb,\ gbbg,$

       $gbgb,\ bgbg,\ bbgg,\ bggb,\ gbbb,\ bgbb,\ bbgb,$

       $bbbg,\ bbbb\}$

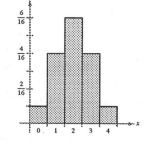

(b)

Random Variable, x	0	1	2	3	4
Probability of x, $P(x)$	$\frac{1}{16}$	$\frac{4}{16}$	$\frac{6}{16}$	$\frac{4}{16}$	$\frac{1}{16}$

(c) See accompanying graph.

(d) Probability of at least one boy $= 1 -$ probability of all girls.

$$P = 1 - \tfrac{1}{16} = \tfrac{15}{16}$$

19. Find $E(x)$, $V(x)$, and σ for the given probability distribution. (Use the table in the textbook.)

Solution:

$$E(x) = 1\left(\frac{1}{16}\right) + 2\left(\frac{3}{16}\right) + 3\left(\frac{8}{16}\right) + 4\left(\frac{3}{16}\right) + 5\left(\frac{1}{16}\right) = \frac{48}{16} = 3$$

$$V(x) = (1-3)^2\left(\frac{1}{16}\right) + (2-3)^2\left(\frac{3}{16}\right) + (3-3)^2\left(\frac{8}{16}\right) + (4-3)^2\left(\frac{3}{16}\right)$$

$$+ (5-3)^2\left(\frac{1}{16}\right)$$

$$= 14\left(\frac{1}{16}\right) = \frac{7}{8} = 0.875$$

$$\sigma = \sqrt{V(x)} = 0.9354$$

21. Find $E(x)$, $V(x)$, and σ for the given probability distribution.

x	-3	-1	0	3	5
$P(x)$	$\frac{1}{5}$	$\frac{1}{5}$	$\frac{1}{5}$	$\frac{1}{5}$	$\frac{1}{5}$

Solution:

$$E(x) = -3\left(\tfrac{1}{5}\right) + (-1)\left(\tfrac{1}{5}\right) + 0\left(\tfrac{1}{5}\right) + 3\left(\tfrac{1}{5}\right) + 5\left(\tfrac{1}{5}\right) = \tfrac{4}{5}$$

$$V(x) = \left(-3 - \tfrac{4}{5}\right)^2\left(\tfrac{1}{5}\right) + \left(-1 - \tfrac{4}{5}\right)^2\left(\tfrac{1}{5}\right) + \left(0 - \tfrac{4}{5}\right)^2\left(\tfrac{1}{5}\right) + \left(3 - \tfrac{4}{5}\right)^2\left(\tfrac{1}{5}\right) + \left(5 - \tfrac{4}{5}\right)^2\left(\tfrac{1}{5}\right)$$

$$= 8.16$$

$$\sigma = \sqrt{V(x)} \approx 2.857$$

23. Find the mean and variance of the discrete random variable x when x is (a) the number of points when the four-sided die is tossed once, and (b) the sum of the points when the four-sided die is tossed twice.

Solution:

(a) $E(x) = 1\left(\tfrac{1}{4}\right) + 2\left(\tfrac{1}{4}\right) + 3\left(\tfrac{1}{4}\right) + 4\left(\tfrac{1}{4}\right) = \tfrac{10}{4} = 2.5$

$$V(x) = (1 - 2.5)^2\left(\tfrac{1}{4}\right) + (2 - 2.5)^2\left(\tfrac{1}{4}\right) + (3 - 2.5)^2\left(\tfrac{1}{4}\right) +](4 - 2.5)^2\left(\tfrac{1}{4}\right)$$

(b) $E(x) = 2\left(\tfrac{1}{16}\right) + 3\left(\tfrac{2}{16}\right) + 4\left(\tfrac{3}{16}\right) + 5\left(\tfrac{4}{16}\right) + 6\left(\tfrac{3}{16}\right) + 7\left(\tfrac{2}{16}\right) + 8\left(\tfrac{1}{16}\right) = \tfrac{80}{16} = 5$

$$V(x) = (2 - 5)^2\left(\tfrac{1}{16}\right) + (3 - 5)^2\left(\tfrac{2}{16}\right) + (4 - 5)^2\left(\tfrac{3}{16}\right) + (5 - 5)^2\left(\tfrac{4}{16}\right) + (6 - 7)^2\left(\tfrac{5}{36}\right)$$

$$+ (7 - 7)^2\left(\tfrac{6}{36}\right)$$

$$+ (8 - 5)^2\left(\tfrac{1}{16}\right)$$

$$= \tfrac{5}{2} = 2.5$$

25. *Revenue* A publishing company introduces a new weekly magazine that sells for $1.50 on the newsstand. The marketing group of the company estimates that sales x in thousands will be approximated by the following probability function.

x	10	15	20	30	40
$P(x)$	0.25	0.30	0.25	0.15	0.05

(a) Find $E(x)$ and σ.   (b) Find the expected revenue.

Solution:

(a) $E(x) = 10(0.25) + 15(0.30) + 20(0.25) + 30(0.15) + 40(0.05) = 18.50$

$$V(x) = (10 - 18.50)^2(0.25) + (15 - 18.50)^2(0.30) + (20 - 18.50)^2(0.25)$$

$$+ (30 - 18.50)^2(0.15) + (40 - 18.50)^2(0.05) = 65.25$$

$$\sigma = \sqrt{V(x)} \approx 8.078$$

(b) Expected revenue: $R = \$1.50(18.50)(1000) = \$27,750$

27. *Insurance* An insurance company needs to determine the annual premium required to break even on fire protection policies with a face value of $90,000. If x is the claim size on these policies and the analysis is restricted to the losses $30,000, $60,000, and $90,000, then the probability distribution of x is given by the following table.

x	0	30,000	60,000	90,000
$P(x)$	0.995	0.0036	0.0011	0.0003

What premium should customers be charged for the company to break even?

Solution:

$$E(x) = 0(0.995) + 30{,}000(0.0036) + 60{,}000(0.0011) + 90{,}000(0.0003) = 201$$

Each customer should be charged $201.

29. *Games of Chance* In roulette, the wheel has the 38 numbers 00, 0, 1, 2, ..., 34, 35, and 36, marked on equally spaced slots. If a player bets $1 on a number and wins, then he keeps the dollar and receives an additional 35 dollars. Otherwise, he loses his dollar. Find the expected net gain to the player for one play.

Solution:

$$E(x) = 35\left(\frac{1}{38}\right) + (-1)\left(\frac{37}{38}\right) = -\frac{2}{38} \approx -\$0.05$$

OR

$$E(x) = 36\left(\frac{1}{38}\right) + 0\left(\frac{37}{38}\right) = \frac{36}{38}$$

$$\frac{36}{38} - 1 = -\$0.05$$

31. *Market Analysis* After considerable market study, a sporting goods company has decided on two possible cities in which to open a new store. Management estimates that city 1 will yield $20 million in revenues if successful and will lose $4 million if not, whereas city 2 will yield $50 million in revenues if successful and lost $9 million if not. City 1 has a 0.3 probability of being successful and City 2 has a 0.2 probability of being successful. In which city should the sporting goods company open the new store with respect to the expected return from each store?

Solution:

City 1: Expected value $= 0.3(20) + 0.7(-4) = 3.2$ million

City 2: Expected value $= 0.2(50) + 0.8(-9) = 2.8$ million

The company should open the store in City 1.

33. Use a graphing utility to find the mean and standard deviation of the data in the textbook, which gives the ages of 50 residents of a long-term-care nursing facility.

Solution:

Mean $= 77.3$

Standard deviation $= 8.198$

Section P.2   Continuous Random Variables

1. Verify that $f(x) = \frac{1}{8}$ is a probability density function over the interval $[0, 8]$.

Solution:

$$\int_0^8 \frac{1}{8}\, dx = \frac{1}{8}x \Big]_0^8 = 1 \text{ and}$$

$$f(x) = \frac{1}{8} \geq 0 \text{ on } [0, 8].$$

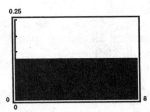

3. Verify that $f(x) = \dfrac{4 - x}{8}$ is a probability density function over the interval $[0, 4]$.

Solution:

$$\int_0^4 \frac{4 - x}{8}\, dx = \frac{1}{8}\left(4x - \frac{x^2}{2}\right)\Big]_0^4 = 1 \text{ and}$$

$$f(x) = \frac{4 - x}{8} \geq 0 \text{ on } [0, 4].$$

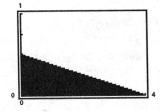

5. Verify that $f(x) = 6x(1-x)$ is a probability density function over the interval $[0, 1]$.

Solution:

$$\int_0^1 6x(1-x)\,dx = \int_0^1 (6x - 6x^2)\,dx$$

$$= \left[3x^2 - 2x^3\right]_0^1 = 1 \text{ and}$$

$$f(x) = 6x(1-x) \geq 0 \text{ on } [0,\ 1].$$

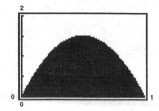

7. Verify that $f(x) = \frac{1}{5}e^{-x/5}$ is a probability density function over the interval $[0,\ \infty)$.

Solution:

$$\int_0^\infty \frac{1}{5}e^{-x/5}\,dx = \left[\lim_{b\to\infty} -e^{-x/5}\right]_0^b = 0 + 1 = 1 \text{ and}$$

$$f(x) = \frac{1}{5}e^{-x/5} \geq 0 \text{ on } [0,\ \infty).$$

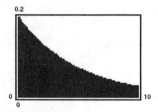

9. Verify that $f(x) = \frac{3}{8}x\sqrt{4-x^2}$ is a probability density function over the interval $[0, 2]$.

Solution:

$$\int_0^2 \frac{3}{8}x\sqrt{4-x^2}\,dx = -\frac{1}{2}\left(\frac{3}{8}\right)\left(\frac{2}{3}\right)(4-x^2)^{3/2}\bigg]_0^2 = 1$$

and

$$f(x) = \frac{3}{8}x\sqrt{4-x^2} \geq 0 \text{ on } [0, 2].$$

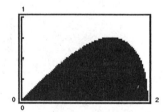

11. Verify that $f(x) = \frac{4}{27}x^2(3 - x)$ is a probability density function over the interval $[0, 3]$.

Solution:

$$\int_0^3 \frac{4}{27}x^2(3 - x)\,dx = \frac{4}{27}\int_0^3 (3x^2 - x^3)\,dx$$

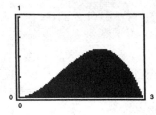

$$= \frac{4}{27}\left[x^3 - \frac{x^4}{4}\right]_0^3$$

$$= \frac{4}{27}\left(27 - \frac{81}{4}\right) = 1$$

and

$$f(x) = \frac{4}{27}x^2(3 - x) \geq 0 \text{ on } [0,\ 3].$$

13. Verify that $f(x) = \frac{1}{3}e^{-x/3}$ is a probability density function over the interval $[0,\ \infty)$.

Solution:

$$\int_0^\infty \frac{1}{3}e^{-x/3}\,dx = \lim_{b\to\infty}\left[-e^{-x/3}\right]_0^b = 0 - (-1) = 1$$

and

$$f(x) = \frac{1}{3}e^{-x/3} \geq 0 \text{ on } [0,\ \infty).$$

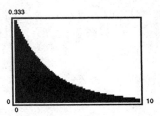

15. Find the constant k so that $f(x) = kx$ is a probability density function over the interval $[1, 4]$.

Solution:

$$\int_1^4 kx\,dx = \left[\frac{kx^2}{2}\right]_1^4 = \frac{15}{2}k = 1 \Rightarrow k = \frac{15}{2}$$

17. Find the constant k so that $f(x) = k(4 - x^2)$ is a probability density function over the interval $[-2,\ 2]$.

Solution:

$$\int_{-2}^2 k(4 - x^2)\,dx = k\left(4x - \frac{x^3}{3}\right)\Bigg]_{-2}^2 = \frac{32k}{3} = 1$$

$$k = \frac{3}{32}$$

19. Find the constant k so that $f(x) = ke^{-x/2}$ is a probability density function over the interval $[0, \infty)$.

Solution:

$$\int_0^\infty ke^{-x/2}\,dx = \lim_{b\to\infty}\left[-2ke^{-x/2}\right]_0^b = 2k = 1 \Rightarrow k = \frac{1}{2}$$

21. Sketch the graph of $f(x) = \frac{1}{10}$ over the interval $[0, 10]$ and find the indicated probabilities.

(a) $P(0 < x < 6)$ (b) $P(4 < x < 6)$

(c) $P(8 < x < 10)$ (d) $P(x \geq 2)$

Solution:

$$\int_a^b \frac{1}{10}\,dx = \frac{x}{10}\Big]_a^b = \frac{b-a}{10}$$

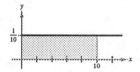

(a) $P(0 < x < 6) = \dfrac{6-0}{10} = \dfrac{3}{5}$

(b) $P(4 < x < 6) = \dfrac{6-4}{10} = \dfrac{1}{5}$

(c) $P(8 < x < 10) = \dfrac{10-8}{10} = \dfrac{1}{5}$

(d) $P(x \geq 2) = P(2 < x < 10) = \dfrac{10-2}{10} = \dfrac{4}{5}$

23. Sketch the graph of $f(x) = \frac{3}{16}\sqrt{x}$ over the interval $[0, 4]$ and find the indicated probabilities.

(a) $P(0 < x < 2)$ (b) $P(2 < x < 4)$

(c) $P(1 < x < 3)$ (d) $P(x \leq 3)$

Solution:

$$\int_a^b \frac{3}{16}\sqrt{x}\,dx = \left(\frac{3}{16}\right)\frac{2}{3}x^{3/2}\Big]_a^b = \frac{1}{8}[b\sqrt{b} - a\sqrt{a}]$$

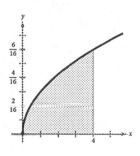

(a) $P(0 < x < 2) = \dfrac{\sqrt{2}}{4} \approx 0.354$

(b) $P(2 < x < 4) = 1 - \dfrac{\sqrt{2}}{4} \approx 0.646$

(c) $P(1 < x < 3) = \dfrac{1}{8}(3\sqrt{3} - 1) \approx 0.525$

(d) $P(x \leq 3) = \dfrac{3\sqrt{3}}{8} \approx 0.650$

25. Sketch the graph of the probability density function over the indicated interval and find the indicated probabilities.

$$f(t) = \frac{1}{3}e^{-t/3}, \ [0, \infty)$$

(a) $P(t < 2)$ (b) $P(t \geq 2)$
(c) $P(1 < t < 4)$ (d) $P(t = 3)$

Solution:

$$\int_a^b \frac{1}{3}e^{-t/3}dt = e^{-t/3} \Big]_a^b = e^{-a/3} - e^{-b/3}$$

(a) $P(t < 2) = e^{-0/3} - e^{-2/3} \approx 0.4866$

(b) $P(t \geq 2) = e^{-2/3} - 0 \approx 0.5134$

(c) $P(1 < t < 4) = e^{-1/3} - e^{-4/3} \approx 0.4529$

(d) $P(t = 3) = 0$

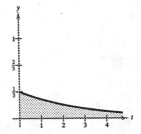

27. *Transportation* Buses arrive and depart from a college every 20 minutes. The probability density function for the waiting time t (in minutes) for a person arriving at random at the bus stop is

$$f(t) = \frac{1}{30}, \ [0, 30].$$

Find the probability that the person will wait (a) no more than 5 minutes and (b) at least 12 minutes.

Solution:

$$P(a < t < b) = \int_a^b \frac{1}{30}dt = \frac{b-a}{30}$$

(a) $P(0 \leq t \leq 5) = \frac{5-0}{30} = \frac{1}{6}$

(b) $P(18 < t < 30) = \frac{30-18}{30} = \frac{2}{5}$

29. *Waiting Time* The waiting time (in minutes) for service at the checkout at a certain grocery store is exponentially distributed with $\lambda = 3$. Using the exponential density function

$$f(t) = \frac{1}{\lambda}e^{-t/\lambda}, \quad [0, \infty)$$

find the probability of waiting (a) less than 2 minutes, (b) more than 2 minutes but less than 4 minutes, and (c) at least 2 minutes.

Solution:

$$\int_a^b \frac{1}{3}e^{-t/3}\,dt = -e^{-t/3}\Big]_a^b = e^{-a/3} - e^{-b/3}$$

(a) $P(0 < t < 2) = e^{-0/3} - e^{-2/3} = 1 - e^{-2/3} \approx 0.487$

(b) $P(2 < t < 4) = e^{-2/3} - e^{-4/3} \approx 0.250$

(c) $P(t > 2) = 1 - P(0 < t < 2) = e^{-2/3} \approx 0.513$

31. *Waiting Time* The length of time (in hours) required to unload trucks at a depot is distributed with $\lambda = \frac{3}{4}$. Using the exponential density function

$$f(t) = \frac{1}{\lambda}e^{-t/\lambda}, \quad [0, \infty)$$

what proportion of the trucks can be unloaded in less than one hour?

Solution:

$$P(0 < t < 1) = \int_0^1 \frac{4}{3}e^{-4t/3}\,dt = -e^{-4t/3}\Big]_0^1 = 1 - e^{-4/3} \approx 0.736$$

33. *Demand* The weekly demand x (in tons) for a certain product is a continuous random variable with the density function

$$f(x) = \frac{1}{36}xe^{-x/6}, \quad [0, \infty).$$

Find the following.

(a) $P(x < 6)$ \qquad\qquad\qquad\qquad (b) $P(6 < x < 12)$

(c) $P(x > 12) = 1 - P(x \le 12)$

Solution:

$$\int_a^b \frac{1}{36}xe^{-x/6}\,dx = -\frac{1}{6}e^{-x/6}(x + 6)\Big]_a^b$$

(a) $P(x < 6) = -\frac{1}{6}e^{-x/6}(x + 6)\Big]_0^6 = -\frac{1}{6}[12e^{-1} - 6] \approx 0.264$

(b) $P(6 < x < 12) = -\frac{1}{6}x^{-x/6}(x + 6)\Big]_6^{12} = 2e^{-1} - 3e^{-2} \approx 0.330$

(c) $P(x > 12) = 1 - P(x \le 12) = 1 - (1 - 3e^{-2}) \approx 0.406$

35. *Learning Theory* The probability density function for the percentage of recall in a certain learning experiment is found to be

$$f(x) = \frac{15}{4}x\sqrt{1-x}, \quad [0, \ 1].$$

What is the probability that a randomly chosen individual in the experiment will recall between (a) 0% and 25% of the material, and (b) 50% and 75% of the material?

Solution:

$$\int_a^b \frac{15}{4}x\sqrt{1-x}\,dx = -\frac{1}{2}(1-x)^{3/2}(3x+2)\bigg]_a^b$$

(a) $P(0 < x < 0.25) = -\frac{1}{2}(1-x)^{3/2}(3x+2)\bigg]_0^{0.25} = -\frac{1}{2}[(0.75)^{3/2}(2.75) - 2] \approx 0.1069$

(b) $P(0.50 < x < 0.75) = -\frac{1}{2}(1-x)^{3/2}(3x+2)\bigg]_{0.50}^{0.75}$

$$= -\frac{1}{2}[(0.25)^{3/2}(4.25) - (0.50)^{3/2}(3.50)] \approx 0.3531$$

37. Use a computer or graphing utility and Simpson's Rule with $n = 12$ to approximate the integral in the Introductory Example. This integral yields the probability of obtaining 49, 50, or 51 heads when a fair coin is tossed 100 times.

Solution:

$$P(49 \le x \le 51) \approx \int_{48.5}^{51.5} \frac{1}{5\sqrt{2\pi}} e^{-(x-50)^2/50}\,dx$$

$$= \frac{1}{5\sqrt{2\pi}} \int_{48.5}^{51.5} e^{-(x-50)^2/50}\,dx$$

$$\approx \frac{51.5 - 48.5}{3(12)}\left(\frac{1}{5\sqrt{2\pi}}\right)[f(48.50)$$

$$+ 4f(48.75) + 2f(49) + 4f(49.25)$$

$$+ 2f(49.50) + 4f(49.75) + 2f(50) + 4f(50.25)$$

$$+ 2f(50.50) + 4f(50.75) + 2f(51) + 4f(51.25) + f(51.50)]$$

$$\approx 0.236 \ (\text{where } f(x) = e^{-(x-50)^2/50}).$$

Section P.3   Expected Value and Variance

1. Use the probability density function $f(x) = \frac{1}{8}$ over the interval $[0, 8]$ to find (a) the mean, (b) the variance, and (c) the standard deviation of the random variable. Sketch and locate the mean on the graph of the density function.

Solution:

(a) $\mu = \int_a^b x f(x)\,dx = \int_0^8 x\left(\frac{1}{8}\right) dx = \frac{x^2}{16}\Big]_0^8 = 4$

(b) $\sigma^2 = \int_a^b x^2 f(x)\,dx - \mu^2$

$= \int_0^8 x^2\left(\frac{1}{8}\right) dx - (4)^2$

$= \frac{x^3}{24}\Big]_0^8 - 16$

$= \frac{64}{3} - 16 = \frac{16}{3}$

(c) $\sigma = \dfrac{4}{\sqrt{3}}$

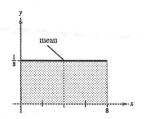

3. Use the probability density function $f(t) = \dfrac{t}{18}$, over the interval $[0, 6]$ to find (a) the mean, (b) the variance, and (c) the standard deviation of the random variable. Sketch and locate the mean on the graph of the density function.

Solution:

(a) $\mu = \int_a^b t f(t)\,dt = \int_0^6 t\left(\frac{t}{18}\right) dt = \frac{t^3}{54}\Big]_0^6 = 4$

(b) $\mu^2 = \int_a^b t^2 f(t) - \mu^2$

$= \int_0^6 t^2\left(\frac{t}{18}\right) dt - 4^2$

$= \frac{t^4}{72}\Big]_0^6 - 4^2 = 18 - 16 = 2$

(c) $\sigma = \sqrt{2}$

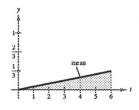

5. Use the probability density function $f(x) = 6x(1-x)$ over the interval $[0, 1]$ to find (a) the mean, (b) the variance, and (c) the standard deviation of the random variable. Sketch and locate the mean on the graph of the density function.

Solution:

(a) $\mu = \int_a^b xf(x)\,dx = \int_0^1 x[6x(1-x)]\,dx = \int_0^1 (6x^2 - 6x^3)\,dx = \left[2x^3 - \frac{3}{2}x^4\right]_0^1 = \frac{1}{2}$

(b) $\sigma^2 = \int_a^b x^2 f(x)\,dx - \mu^2$

$= \int_0^1 x^2[6x(1-x)]\,dx - \left(\frac{1}{2}\right)^2 = \int_0^1 (6x^3 - 6x^4)\,dx - \frac{1}{4}$

$= \left[\frac{3}{2}x^4 - \frac{6}{5}x^5\right]_0^1 - \frac{1}{4}$

$= \frac{3}{2} - \frac{6}{5} - \frac{1}{4} = \frac{1}{20}$

(c) $\sigma = \frac{1}{2\sqrt{5}}$

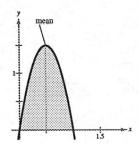

7. Use the probability density function $f(x) = \frac{5}{2}x^{3/2}$ over the interval $[0, 1]$ to find (a) the mean, (b) the variance, and (c) the standard deviation of the random variable. Sketch and locate the mean on the graph of the density function.

Solution:

(a) $\mu = \displaystyle\int_a^b xf(x)\,dx$

$= \displaystyle\int_0^1 x\left(\frac{5}{2}x^{3/2}\right)dx$

$= \dfrac{5}{2}\displaystyle\int_0^1 x^{5/2}\,dx$

$= \left(\dfrac{5}{2}\right)\dfrac{2}{7}x^{7/2}\Big]_0^1$

$= \dfrac{5}{7} \approx 0.714$

(b) $\sigma^2 = \displaystyle\int_a^b x^2 f(x)\,dx - \mu^2$

$= \displaystyle\int_0^1 x^2\left(\frac{5}{2}x^{3/2}\right)dx - \left(\frac{5}{7}\right)^2 = \frac{5}{2}\int_0^1 x^{7/2}\,dx - \frac{25}{49}$

$= \left(\dfrac{5}{2}\right)\dfrac{2}{9}x^{9/2}\Big]_0^1 - \dfrac{25}{49} = \dfrac{5}{9} - \dfrac{25}{49} = \dfrac{20}{441}$

(c) $\sigma = \dfrac{2\sqrt{5}}{21}$

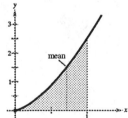

9. Use the probability density function

$$f(x) = \frac{4}{3(x+1)^2}$$

over the interval [0, 3] to find (a) the mean, (b) the variance, and (c) the standard deviation of the random variable. Sketch and locate the mean on the graph of the density function.

Solution:

(a) $\displaystyle \mu = \int_a^b x f(x)\,dx = \int_0^3 \frac{4x}{3(x+1)^2}\,dx = \frac{4}{3}\left[\frac{1}{x+1} + \ln|x+1|\right]_0^3$ (Formula 4)

$\displaystyle = \frac{4}{3}\left[\left(\frac{1}{4} + \ln 4\right) - (1+0)\right] = \frac{4}{3}(\ln 4) - 1 \approx 0.848$

(b) $\displaystyle \sigma^2 = \int_a^b x^2 f(x)\,dx - \mu^2 = \int_0^3 \frac{4x^2}{3(x+1)^2}\,dx - \left[\frac{4}{3}(\ln 4) - 1\right]^2$

$\displaystyle = \frac{4}{3}\left[x - \frac{1}{x+1} - 2\ln|x+1|\right]_0^3 - \left[\frac{4}{3}(\ln 4) - 1\right]^2$ (Formula 7)

$\displaystyle = \frac{4}{3}\left[\left(3 - \frac{1}{4} - 2\ln 4\right) - (0 - 1 - 0)\right] - \left[\frac{4}{3}(\ln 4) - 1\right]^2$

$\displaystyle = \left[5 - \frac{8}{3}\ln 4\right] - \left[\frac{4}{3}(\ln 4) - 1\right]^2 = 4 - \left(\frac{4}{3}\ln 4\right)^2 \approx 0.583$

(c) $\sigma \approx 0.764$

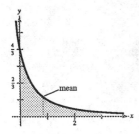

11. Find the median of the exponential probability density function.

$$f(t) = \frac{1}{9}e^{-t/9}, [0, \infty)$$

Solution:

$$\text{Median} = \int_0^m \frac{1}{9}e^{-t/9}dt = -e^{t/9}\Big]_0^m = 1 - e^{m/9} = \frac{1}{2}$$

$$e^{-m/9} = \frac{1}{2} \Rightarrow -\frac{m}{9} = \ln\frac{1}{2}$$

$$m = -9\ln\frac{1}{2} \approx 6.238$$

13. Use the results from the table of special probability density functions to identify the density function and find its expected value (mean), variance, and standard deviation for $f(x) = \frac{1}{10}$ over $[0, 10]$.

Solution:

$$f(x) = \frac{1}{10}, \quad [0, 10] \text{ is a uniform density function.}$$

Expected value (mean): $\dfrac{a+b}{2} = \dfrac{0+10}{2} = 5$

Variance: $\dfrac{(b-a)^2}{12} = \dfrac{(10-0)^2}{12} = \dfrac{100}{12} = \dfrac{25}{3}$

Standard deviation: $\dfrac{b-a}{\sqrt{12}} = \dfrac{10-0}{\sqrt{12}} \approx 2.887$

15. Use the results from the table of special probability density functions to identify the density function and find its expected value (mean), variance, and standard deviation for $f(x) = \frac{1}{8}e^{-x/8}, \quad [0, \infty)$.

Solution:

$$f(x) = \frac{1}{8}e^{-x/8}, \quad [0, \infty) \text{ is an exponential density function with } a = \frac{1}{8}.$$

Expected value (mean): $\dfrac{1}{a} = 8$

Variance: $\dfrac{1}{a^2} = 64$

Standard deviation: $\dfrac{1}{a} = 8$

17. Use the results from the table of special probability density functions to identify the density function and find its expected value (mean), variance, and standard deviation for

$$f(x) = \frac{1}{11\sqrt{2\pi}} e^{-(x-100)^2/242}, \quad (-\infty, \infty).$$

Solution:

$f(x) = \frac{1}{11\sqrt{2\pi}} e^{-(x-100)^2/242}, \quad (-\infty, \infty)$ is a normal density function with $\mu = 100$ and $\sigma = 11$.

Expected value (mean): $\mu = 100$

Variance: $\sigma^2 = 121$

Standard deviation: $\sigma = 11$

19. Use a symbolic differentiation utility to find the mean, standard deviation of $f(x) = \frac{1}{\sqrt{2\pi}} e^{-x^2/2}$, and indicated probability $P(0 \le x \le 0.85)$.

Solution:

Mean $= 0$

Standard deviation $= 1$

$P(0 \le x \le 0.85) \approx 0.3023$

21. Use a symbolic differentiation utility to find the mean, standard deviation of $f(x) = \frac{1}{6} e^{-x/6}$, and indicated probability $P(x \ge 2.23)$.

Solution:

Mean $= \dfrac{1}{6}$

Standard deviation $= \dfrac{1}{6}$

$P(x \ge 2.23) \approx 0.6896$

23. Use a symbolic differentiation utility to find the mean, standard deviation of $f(x) = \frac{1}{2\sqrt{2\pi}} e^{-(x-8)^2/8}$, and indicated probability $P(3 \le x \le 13)$.

Solution:

Mean $= 8$

Standard deviation $= 2$

$P(3 \le x \le 13) \approx 0.9876$

25. Let x be a random variable that is normally distributed with a mean of 60 and a standard deviation of 12. Find the required probabilities using a symbolic integration utility.

(a) $P(x > 64)$

(b) $P(x > 70)$

(c) $P(x < 70)$

(d) $P(33 < x < 65)$

Solution:

$\mu = 60, \sigma = 12$

(a) $P(x > 64) \approx 0.3694$

(b) $P(x > 70) \approx 0.2023$

(c) $P(x < 70) \approx 0.7977$

(d) $P(33 < x < 65) \approx 0.6493$

27. *Arrival Time* The arrival time t of a bus at a bus stop is uniformly distributed between the times of 10:00 A.M. and 10:10 A.M.

(a) Find the mean and standard deviation of the random variable t.

(b) What is the probability that you will miss the bus if you arrive at the bus stop at 10:03 A.M.?

Solution:

$$f(t) = \frac{1}{10}, \quad [0, \ 10] \text{ where } t = 0 \text{ corresponds to 10:00 A.M.}$$

(a) Mean: $\dfrac{10}{2} = 5$. The mean is 10:05 A.M. (b) $1 - \displaystyle\int_3^{10} \frac{1}{10} \, dx = 1 - \frac{7}{10} = \frac{3}{10} = 0.30$

Standard deviation: $\dfrac{10}{\sqrt{12}} \approx 2.887$ minutes

29. *Useful Life* The time t until failure of an appliance is exponentially distributed with a mean of 2 years.

(a) Find the probability density function for the random variable t.

(b) Find the probability that the appliance will fail in less than 1 year.

Solution:

(a) $f(t) = \dfrac{1}{2} e^{-t/2}$, since mean $= 2$

(b) $P(0 < t < 1) = \displaystyle\int_0^1 \frac{1}{2} e^{-t/2} dt = -e^{-t/2} \Big]_0^1 = 1 - e^{-1/2} \approx 0.3935$

31. *Waiting Time* The waiting time t for service at a customer service desk in a department store is exponentially distributed, with a mean of 5 minutes.

(a) Find the probability density function for the random variable t.

(b) Find $P(\mu - \sigma < t < \mu + \sigma)$.

Solution:

(a) Since $\mu = 5$, we have $f(t) = \dfrac{1}{5}e^{-t/5}$.

(b) $P(\mu - \sigma < t < \mu + \sigma) = P(0 < t < 10)$

$$\int_0^{10} \frac{1}{5}e^{-t/5}\, dt = -e^{-t/5}\Big]_0^{10} = 1 - e^{-2} \approx 0.865 = 86.5\%$$

33. *Standardized Test Scores* The scores on a national exam are normally distributed with a mean of 150 and a standard deviation of 16. You scored 174 on the exam.

(a) How far, in standard deviations, did your score exceed the national mean?

(b) What fraction of those who have taken the exam had scores lower than yours?

Solution:

(a) $\dfrac{174 - 150}{16} = \dfrac{3}{2} = 1.5$

Your score exceeded the national mean by 1.5 standard deviations.

(b) $P(x < 174) = 0.9332$

Thus, $0.9332 = 93.32\%$ of those who took the exam had scores lower than yours.

35. *Demand* The daily demand x for a certain product (in hundreds of pounds) is a random variable with the probability density function

$$f(x) = \frac{1}{36}x(6-x), \quad [0, \ 6].$$

(a) Determine the expected value and the standard deviation of demand.

(b) Determine the median of the random variable.

(c) Find $P(\mu - \sigma < x < \mu + \sigma)$.

Solution:

(a) $\mu = \displaystyle\int_0^6 \frac{1}{36}x^2(6-x)\,dx = \frac{1}{36}\int_0^6 (6x^2 - x^3)\,dx = \frac{1}{36}\left[2x^3 - \frac{x^4}{4}\right]_0^6 = 3$

$\sigma^2 = \displaystyle\int_0^6 \frac{1}{36}x^3(6-x)\,dx - (3)^2 = \frac{1}{36}\int_0^6 (6x^3 - x^4)\,dx - 9$

$= \dfrac{1}{36}\left[\dfrac{3x^4}{2} - \dfrac{x^5}{5}\right]_0^6 - 9 = \dfrac{54}{5} - 9 = \dfrac{9}{5}$

$\sigma = \sqrt{\dfrac{9}{5}} = \dfrac{3\sqrt{5}}{5} \approx 1.342$

(b) $\displaystyle\int_0^m \frac{1}{36}x(6-x)\,dx = \frac{1}{36}\int_0^m (6x - x^2)\,dx = \frac{1}{36}\left[3x^2 - \frac{x^3}{3}\right]_0^m$

$= \dfrac{1}{36}\left[3m^2 - \dfrac{m^3}{3}\right] = \dfrac{1}{2}$

$3m^2 - \dfrac{m^3}{3} = 18 \Rightarrow 0 = (m-3)(m^2 - 6m - 18)$

$m = 3 \text{ or } m = \dfrac{6 \pm \sqrt{108}}{2} = \dfrac{6 \pm 6\sqrt{3}}{2} = 3 \pm 3\sqrt{3}$

In the interval $[0, \ 6]$, $m = 3$.

(c) $P(\mu - \sigma < x < \mu + \sigma) = P\left(3 - \dfrac{3\sqrt{5}}{5} < x < 3 + \dfrac{3\sqrt{5}}{5}\right)$

$\approx P(1.6584 < x < 4.3416) = \displaystyle\int_{1.6584}^{4.3416} \frac{1}{36}x(6-x)\,dx$

$= \dfrac{1}{36}\left[3x^2 - \dfrac{x^3}{3}\right]_{1.6584}^{4.3416}$

$\approx 0.626 = 62.6\%$

37. *Learning Theory* The percentage recall x in a learning experiment is a random variable with the probability density function

$$f(x) = \frac{15}{4}x\sqrt{1-x}, \quad [0, \ 1].$$

Determine the mean and variance of the random variable x.

Solution:

$$\mu = \int_0^1 \frac{15}{4}x^2\sqrt{1-x}\,dx$$

$$= \frac{15}{4}\left(\frac{2}{-7}\right)\left[x^2(1-x)^{3/2} - 2\left(\frac{2}{-5}\right)\left[x(1-x)^{3/2} + \frac{2}{3}(1-x)^{3/2}\right]\right]_0^1$$

$$= -\frac{15}{14}\left[0 - \frac{4}{5}\left(\frac{2}{3}\right)\right] = \frac{4}{7}$$

$$\sigma^2 = \int_0^1 \frac{15}{4}x^3\sqrt{1-x}\,dx - \left(\frac{4}{7}\right)^2 = \frac{15}{4}\left(\frac{2}{-9}\right)$$

$$\left[\left[x^3(1-x)^{3/2}\right]_0^1 - 3\int_0^1 x^2\sqrt{1-x}\,dx\right] - \frac{16}{49}$$

$$= -\frac{5}{6}\left[0 - 3\left(\frac{4}{7}\right)\left(\frac{4}{15}\right)\right] - \frac{16}{49} = \frac{8}{21} - \frac{16}{49} = \frac{8}{147}$$

39. *Demand* The daily demand x for a certain product (in thoudands of units) is a random variable with the probability density function

$$f(x) = \frac{1}{25}xe^{-x/5}, \ [0, \infty).$$

(a) Determine the expected daily demand.

(b) Find $P(x \le 4)$.

Solution:

Using a graphing utility,

(a) $\mu = \int_0^\infty xf(x)dx = \int_0^\infty \frac{1}{25}x^2e^{-x/5}dx = 10$

(b) $P(x \le 4) \approx 0.1912$

41. Find the mean $f(x) = \frac{1}{11}$ and median $[0, 11]$.

Solution:

Mean $= \frac{11}{2} =$ Median

43. Find the mean $f(x) = 4(1 - 2x)$ and median $\left[0, \dfrac{1}{2}\right]$.

Solution:

$$\text{Mean} = \int_0^{1/2} x4(1 - 2x)\,dx = \frac{1}{6}$$

Median: $\displaystyle\int_0^m 4(1 - 2x)\,dx = \frac{1}{2}$

$$4x - 4x^2 \Big]_0^m = \frac{1}{2}$$

$$4m - 4m^2 = \frac{1}{2} \Rightarrow m \approx 0.1465$$

($m \approx 0.8536$ is not in the interval $[0, \frac{1}{2}]$.)

45. Find the mean $f(x) = \dfrac{1}{5}e^{-x/5}$ and median $[0, \infty]$.

Solution:

Mean $= 5$

Median $= 5\ln 2 \approx 3.4657$

47. *Cost of Electricity* The daily cost of electricity x in a city is a random variable with the probability density function

$$f(x) = 0.28e^{-0.28x}, \; 0 \le x < \infty.$$

Find the median daily cost of electricity.

Solution:

$$\int_0^m f(x)\,dx = \int_0^m 0.28e^{-0.28x}\,dx = 0.5$$

$$-e^{-0.28m} + 1 = 0.5$$

$$e^{-0.28m} = 0.5$$

$$m = \frac{1}{-0.28}\ln 0.5 \approx 2.4755$$

49. *Demand* The daily demand x for water (in millions of gallons) in a town is a random variable with the probability density function

$$f(x) = \frac{1}{9}xe^{-x/3}, \; [0, \infty).$$

(a) Determine the expected value and the standard deviation of the demand.

(b) Find the probability that the demand is greater than 4 million gallons on a given day.

Solution:

(a) $\mu = \displaystyle\int_0^\infty \frac{1}{9}x^2 e^{-x/3}\, dx$ (Use integration by parts)

$$= \lim_{b \to \infty} -3\left[\frac{x^2}{9}e^{-x/3} - 2\left(-\frac{x}{3} - 1\right)e^{-x/3}\right]_0^b = 6$$

$$\sigma^2 = \int_0^\infty \frac{1}{9}x^3 e^{-x/3}\, dx - (6)^2 \quad \text{(Use integration by parts)}$$

$$= \lim_{b \to \infty}\left[-\frac{x^3}{3}e^{-x/3}\right]_0^b + 9\int_0^\infty \frac{1}{9}x^2 e^{-x/3}\, dx - 36 = 0 + 9(6) - 36 = 18$$

    (Use part (a))

$$\sigma = \sqrt{18} = 3\sqrt{2} \approx 4.243$$

(b) $P(x > 4) = 1 - P(x < 4) = 1 - \displaystyle\int_0^4 \frac{1}{9}xe^{-x/3}\, dx = 1 - \left[-\frac{1}{3}e^{-x/3}(x + 3)\right]_0^4 \approx 0.615$

51. *Machine Precision* An automatic filling machine fills cans so that the weights are normally distributed with a mean of μ and a standard deviation of σ. The value of μ can be controlled by settings on the machine, but σ depends on the precision and design of the machine. For a particular substance, $\sigma = 0.15$ ounce. If 12-ounce cans are being filled, determine the setting for μ so that no more than 5% of the cans weigh less than the stated weight.

Solution:

$$P(x < 12) = 0.05$$

$$P\left(z < \frac{12 - \mu}{0.15}\right) = 0.05$$

$$0.5000 - P\left(\frac{12 - \mu}{0.15} < z < 0\right) = 0.05$$

$$P\left(\frac{12 - \mu}{0.15} < z < 0\right) = 0.4500$$

$$\frac{12 - \mu}{0.15} \approx -1.645$$

$$\mu \approx 12.25$$

53. *Wages* The employees of a large corporation are paid an average wage of $12.30 per hour with a standard deviation of $1.50. Assume that these wages are normally distributed. Use a computer or calculator and Simpson's Rule (with $n = 10$) to approximate the percent of employees that earn hourly wages of $9.00 to $12.00.

Solution:

$$\mu = 12.30, \quad \sigma = 1.50$$

$$f(x) = \frac{1}{1.50\sqrt{2\pi}} e^{-(x-12.30)^2/4.5}$$

$$P(9 < x < 12) = \frac{1}{1.50\sqrt{2\pi}} \int_9^{12} e^{-(x-12.30)^2/4.5}\, dx \approx 0.4068 = 40.68\%$$

55. *Intelligence Quotient* The IQs of students in a school are normally distributed with a mean of 110 and a standard deviation of 10. Use a symbolic integration utility to find the probability that a student selected at random will have an IQ within one standard defiation of the mean.

Solution:

$$f(x) = \frac{1}{10\sqrt{2\pi}} e^{-(x-110)^2/200} \quad \text{since } \mu = 110 \text{ and } \sigma = 10.$$

$$P(100 < x < 120) = \int_{100}^{120} \frac{1}{10\sqrt{2\pi}} e^{-(x-110)^2/200}\, dx$$

$$= \frac{1}{10\sqrt{2\pi}} \int_{100}^{120} e^{-(x-110)^2/200}\, dx \approx 0.6828 = 68.28\%$$

Chapter P   Review Exercises

1. Describe the sample space of the experiment.

   A month of the year is chosen for a vacation.

   Solution:

   The sample space consists of the twelve months of the year.

   $S = \{$January, February, March, April, May, June, July, August, September, October, November, December$\}$

3. Describe the sample space of the experiment.

   A student must answer three questions from a selection of four essay questions.

   Solution:

   If the questions are numbered 1, 2, 3, and 4,

   $S = \{123, 124, 134, 234.\}$

5. Describe the sample space of the experiment.

Three numbers are drawn in a lottery. Each number is a digit from 0 to 9. Find the sample space giving the number of 7's drawn.

Solution:

$S = \{0, 1, 2, 3\}$

7. Complete the table in the textbook to form the frequency distribution of the random variable x. Then construct a bar graph to represent the result.

A computer randomly selects a three-digit bar code. Each digit can be 0 or 1, and x is the number of 1's in the bar code.

Solution:

x	0	1	2	3
$n(x)$	1	3	3	1

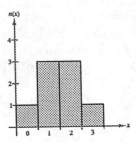

9. Sketch a graph of the given probability distribution (shown in the textbook) and find the required probabilities.

(a) $P(2 \leq x \leq 4)$ (b) $P(x \geq 3)$

Solution:

(a) $P(2 \leq x \leq 4) = P(2) + P(3) + P(4)$

$$= \frac{7}{18} + \frac{5}{18} + \frac{3}{18} = \frac{15}{18} = \frac{5}{6}$$

(b) $P(x \geq 3) = P(3) + P(4) + P(5)$

$$= \frac{5}{18} + \frac{3}{18} + \frac{2}{18} = \frac{10}{18} = \frac{5}{9}$$

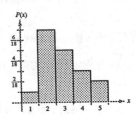

11. *Tossing Dice* Consider an experiment in which two six-sided dice are tossed. Find the indicated probability.

(a) The probability that the total is 8.

(b) The probability that the total is greater than 4.

(c) The probability that doubles are thrown.

(d) The probability of getting double sixes.

Solution:

x	2	3	4	5	6	7	8	9	10	11	12
$n(x)$	1	2	3	4	5	6	5	4	3	2	1

$n(S) = 36$

(a) $P(x = 8) = \dfrac{5}{36}$

(b) $P(x > 4) = 1 - P(x \le 4) = 1 - \dfrac{6}{36} = \dfrac{5}{6}$

(c) $P \text{ (doubles)} = \dfrac{6}{36} = \dfrac{1}{6}$

(d) $P \text{ (double sixes)} = \dfrac{1}{36}$

13. *Quiz Scores* An instructor gave a 25-point quiz to 52 students. Use the frequency distribution of quiz scores shown in the textbook to find the mean quiz score.

Solution:

Mean = 19.5

15. *Revenue* A publishing company introduces a new weekly newspaper that sells for 75 cents. The marketing group of the company estimates that sales x in thousands will be approximated by the following probability function.

x	10	15	20	30	40
$P(x)$	0.10	0.20	0.50	0.15	0.05

(a) Find $E(x)$.   (b) Find the expected revenue.

Solution:

(a) $E(x) = 10(0.10) + 15(0.20) + 20(0.50) + 30(0.15) + 40(0.05) = 20.5$

(b) $R = 20.5(1000)(0.75) = \$15,375$

17. *Sales Volume* A company sells five different models of personal computers. During one month the sales for the five models were as shown in textbook. Find the variance and standard deviation of the prices.

Solution:

$$E(x) = \frac{[24(1200) + 12(1500) + 35(2000) + 5(2200) + 4(3000)]}{18}$$

$$= \frac{139,800}{18} = 1747.50$$

$$V(x) = [(1200 - 1747.50)^2(24) + (1500 - 1747.50)^2(12)$$

$$+ (2000 - 1747.50)^2(35) + (2200 - 1747.50)^2(5)$$

$$+ \frac{(3000 - 1747.50)^2(4)]}{80}$$

$$= 218,243.7500$$

$$\sigma = \sqrt{V(x)} \approx 467.1657$$

19. *Car Ownership* A random survey of households recorded the number of cars per household. The results of the survey are shown in the table in the textbook.

Find the variance and standard deviation of x.

Solution:

$$E(x) = 0(0.10) + 1(0.28) + 2(0.39) + 3(0.17) + 4(0.04) + 5(0.02)$$

$$= 1.83$$

$$V(x) = (0 - 1.83)^2(0.10) + (1 - 1.83)^2(0.28) + (2 - 1.83)^2(0.39)$$

$$+ (3 - 1.83)^2(0.17) + (4 - 1.83)^2(0.04) + (5 - 1.83)^2(0.02)$$

$$\approx 1.1611$$

$$\sigma = \sqrt{V(x)} \approx 1.0775$$

21. Use a graphing utility to graph the function $f(x) = \frac{1}{8}(4 - x)$, $[0, 4]$. Then verify that f is a probability density function.

Solution:

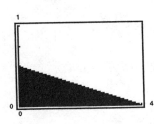

$$\int_0^4 \frac{1}{8}(4 - x)dx = \left[\frac{1}{2}x - \frac{x^2}{16}\right]_0^4$$

$$= (2 - 1) = 1$$

23. Use a graphing utility to graph the function $f(x) = \dfrac{1}{4\sqrt{x}}$, $[1, 9]$. Then verify that f is a probability density function $[1, 9]$.

Solution:

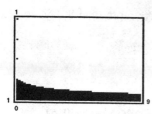

$$\int_1^9 \frac{1}{4\sqrt{x}} dx = \frac{1}{4}\left[2\sqrt{x}\right]_1^9 = 1$$

25. Find $P(0 < x < 2)$ for the probability density function $f(x) = \dfrac{2}{(x+1)^2}$, $[0, 1]$.

Solution:

$$P(0 < x < 2) = \int_0^2 \frac{1}{50}(10 - x)dx = \frac{1}{50}\left[10x - \frac{x^2}{x}\right]_0^2 = \frac{9}{25}$$

27. Find $P(0 < x < \frac{1}{2})$ for the probability density function.

$$f(x) = 2/(x+1)^2, \quad [0, \ 1]$$

Solution:

$$P\left(0 < x < \frac{1}{2}\right) = \int_0^{1/2} \frac{2}{(x+1)^2} dx = -\frac{2}{x+1}\Bigg]_0^{1/2} = -\frac{4}{3} + 2 = \frac{2}{3}$$

29. *Transportation* Buses arrive and depart from a college every 20 minutes. The probability density function for the waiting time t (in minutes) for a person arriving at the bus stop is

$$f(t) = \frac{1}{20}, \ [0, 20].$$

Find the probability that the person will wait (a) no more than 10 minutes, and (b) at least 15 minutes.

Solution:

(a) $P(t \le 10) = \displaystyle\int_0^{10} \frac{1}{20}dt = \frac{1}{20}t\Bigg]_0^{10} = \frac{1}{2}$

(b) $P(t \ge 15) = \displaystyle\int_{15}^{20} \frac{1}{20}dt = \frac{1}{20}t\Bigg]_{15}^{20} = 1 - \frac{3}{4} = \frac{1}{4}$

31. *Recovery Time* The time t (in days) until recovery after a certain medical procedure is a random variable with the probability density function

$$f(t) = \frac{1}{4\sqrt{t-4}}, \ [5, 13].$$

Find the probability that a patient selected at random will take more than 8 days to recover.

Solution:

$$P(t > 8) = \int_8^{13} \frac{1}{4\sqrt{t-4}}dt = \frac{1}{2}\sqrt{t-4}\Big]_8^{13} = \frac{1}{2}$$

33. Find the means of the continuous probability density function $f(x) = \frac{1}{5}$, $[0, 5]$.

Solution:

$$\text{Mean} = \frac{5-0}{2} = 2.5$$

35. Find the mean of the continuous probability density function $f(x) = \frac{1}{6}e^{-x/6}$, $[0, \infty)$.

Solution:

$$\text{Mean} = 6$$

37. Find the variance and standard deviation of the continuous probability density function $f(x) = \frac{2}{9}x(3-x)$, $[0, 3]$.

Solution:

$$\text{Mean} = \int_0^3 x\frac{2}{9}x(3-x)dx = \frac{2}{9}\left[x^3 - \frac{x^4}{4}\right]_0^3 = \frac{3}{2}$$

$$\text{Variance} = \int_0^3 \left(x - \frac{3}{2}\right)^2 \frac{2}{9}x(3-x)dx = \frac{9}{20}$$

$$\text{Standard deviation} = \sqrt{V(x)} = \frac{3}{2\sqrt{5}}$$

39. Find the variance and standard deviation of the continuous probability density function $f(x) = \frac{1}{2}e^{-x/2}$, $[0, \infty)$

Solution:

$$\text{Mean} = \int_0^\infty x\left[\frac{1}{2}e^{-x/2}\right]dx = 2$$

$$\text{Variance} = 4$$

$$\text{Standard deviation} = 2$$

41. Find the median of the continuous probability density function $f(x) = 6x(1 - x)$, $[0, 1]$.

Solution:

$$\int_0^m 6x(1 - x)dx = 3x^2 - 2x^3 \Big]_0^m = 3m^2 - 2m^3 = \frac{1}{2} \Rightarrow m = \frac{1}{2}$$

43. Find the median of the continuous probability density function.

$f(x) = 0.25e^{-x/4}$, $[0, \infty)$

Solution:

$$\int_0^m 0.25e^{-x/4}dx = 1 - e^{-m/4} = \frac{1}{2} \Rightarrow \approx 2.7726$$

45. *Waiting Time* The waiting time t (in minutes) for service at the checkout at a grocery store is exponentially distributed with the probability density function

$f(t) = \frac{1}{3}e^{-t/3}$, $[0, \infty)$.

Find the probability of waiting (a) less than 2 minutes, and (b) more than 2 minutes but less than 4 minutes.

Solution:

$$f(t) = \frac{1}{3}e^{-1/3}dt, 0 \leq t < \infty$$

(a) $P(t < 2) = \int_0^2 f(t)dt \approx 0.4866$

(b) $P(2 < t < 4) = \int_2^4 f(t)dt \approx 0.2498$

47. *Botany* In a botany experiment, plants are grown in a nutrient solution. The heights of the plants are found to be normally distributed with a mean of 42 centimeters and a standard deviation of 3 centimeters. Find the probability that a plant in the experiment is at least 50 centimeters tall.

Solution:

$$f(x) = \frac{1}{\sigma\sqrt{2\pi}}e^{-(x-\mu)^2/2\sigma^2} P(x \geq 50) = \int_{50}^{\infty} + (x)dx \approx 0.00383.$$

49. *Meteorology* The monthly rainfall x in a certain state is normally distributed with a mean of 3.75 inches and a standard deviation of 0.5 inch. Use Simpson's Rule (with $n = 12$) to approximate the probability that in a randomly selected month the rainfall is between 3.5 and 4 inches.

Solution:

$\mu = 3.75$, $\omega = 0.5$. By Simpson's Rule with $n = 12$, $P(3.5 < x < 4) \approx 0.3829$

Practice Test for Chapter P

1. A coin is tossed four times. What is the probability that at least two heads occur?

2. A card is chosen at random from a standard 52-card deck of playing cards. What is the probability that the card will be red and not a face card?

3. Find $E(x)$, $V(x)$, and σ for the given probability distribution.

x	-2	-1	0	3	4
$P(x)$	$\frac{2}{10}$	$\frac{1}{10}$	$\frac{4}{10}$	$\frac{2}{10}$	$\frac{1}{10}$

4. Find the constant k so that $f(x) = ke^{-x/4}$ is a probability density function over the interval $[0, \infty)$.

5. Find (a) $P(0 < x < 5)$ and (b) $P(x > 1)$ for the probability density function
   $f(x) = x/32$, $[0, 8]$.

6. Find (a) the mean, (b) the standard deviation, and (c) the median for the probability density function

$$f(x) = \frac{3}{256}x(8 - x), \quad [0, 8].$$

7. Find (a) the mean, (b) the standard deviation, and (c) the median for the probability density function

$$f(x) = \frac{6}{x^2}, \quad [2, 3].$$

8. Find the expected value, median, and standard deviation of the exponential density function
   $f(x) = 7e^{-7x}$, $[0, \infty)$.

Technology Required

9. Find $P(1.67 < x < 3.24)$ using the standard normal probability density function.

10. The monthly revenue x (in thousands of dollars) of a given shop is normally distributed with $\mu = 20$ and $\sigma = 4$. Approximate $P(19 < x < 24)$.

CHAPTER D
Differential Equations

Section D.1   Solutions of Differential Equations

1. Verify that $y = x^3 + 5$ is a solution of the differential equation $y' = 3x^2$.

   Solution:

   $$y' = 3x^2$$

3. Verify that $y = e^{-2x}$ is a solution of the differential equation $y' + 2y = 0$.

   Solution:

   $$y' = -2e^{-2x} \text{ and } y' + 2y = -2e^{-2x} + 2(e^{-2x}) = 0$$

5. Verify that $y = 2x^3$ is a solution of the differential equation $y' - \dfrac{3}{x}y = 0$.

   Solution:

   $$y' = 6x^2 \text{ and } y' - \frac{3}{x}y = 6x^2 - \frac{3}{x}(2x^3) = 0$$

7. Verify that $y = x^2$ is a solution of the differential equation $x^2 y'' - 2y = 0$.

   Solution:

   $$y'' = 2 \text{ and } x^2 y'' - 2y = x^2(2) - 2(x^2) = 0.$$

9. Verify that $y = 2e^{2x}$ is a solution of the differential equation $y'' - y' - 2y = 0$.

   Solution:

   $$y' = ye^{2x}$$
   $$y'' = 8e^{2x} \text{ and } y'' - y' - 2y = 8e^{2x} - 4e^{2x} - 2(2x^{2x}) = 0$$

11. Verify that $y = (1/x) + C$ is a solution of the differential equation $dy/dx = -1/x^2$.

    Solution:

    By differentiation, we have

    $$\frac{dy}{dx} = -\frac{1}{x^2}.$$

13. Verify that $y = Ce^{4x}$ is a solution of the differential equation $dy/dx = 4y$.

Solution:

By differentiating, we have

$$\frac{dy}{dx} = 4Ce^{4x} = 4y.$$

15. Verify that $y = Ce^{-t/3} + 7$ is a solution of the differential equation $3\dfrac{dy}{dt} + y - 7 = 0$.

Solution:

Since $\dfrac{dy}{dt} = -\left(\dfrac{1}{3}\right)Ce^{-t/3}$, we have $3\dfrac{dy}{dt} + y - 7 = 3\left(-\dfrac{1}{3}Ce^{-t/3}\right) + (Ce^{-t/3} + 7) - 7 = 0$.

17. Verify that $y = Cx^2 - 3x$ is a solution of the differential equation $xy' - 3x - 2y = 0$.

Solution:

Since $y' = 2Cx - 3$, we have

$$xy' - 3x - 2y = x(2Cx - 3) - 3x - 2(Cx^2 - 3x) = 0.$$

19. Verify that $y = x^2 + 2x + (C/x)$ is a solution of the differential equation $xy' + y = x(3x + 4)$.

Solution:

Since $y' = 2x + 2 - (C/x^2)$, we have

$$xy' + y = \left(2x^2 + 2x - \frac{C}{x}\right) + \left(x^2 + 2x + \frac{C}{x}\right) = 3x^2 + 4x = x(3x + 4).$$

21. Verify that $y = C_1 e^{x/2} + C_2 e^{-2x}$ is a solution of the differential equation $2y'' + 3y' - 2y = 0$.

Solution:

Since $y' = \frac{1}{2}C_1 e^{x/2} - 2C_2 e^{-2x}$, we have $y'' = \frac{1}{4}C_1 e^{x/2} + 4C_2 e^{-2x}$, and it follows that

$$2y'' + 3y' - 2y = \frac{1}{2}C_1 e^{x/2} + 8C_2 e^{-2x} + \frac{3}{2}C_1 e^{x/2} - 6C_2 e^{-2x} - 2C_1 e^{x/2} - 2C_2 e^{-2x} = 0.$$

23. Verify the $y = (bx^4)/(4 - a) + Cx^a$ is a solution of the differential equation $y' - (ay/x) = bx^3$.

Solution:

Since $y' = 4bx^3/(4 - a) + aCx^{a-1}$, we have

$$y' - \frac{ay}{x} = \left[\frac{4bx^3}{4 - a} + aCx^{a-1}\right] - \frac{a}{x}\left[\frac{bx^4}{4 - a} + Cx^a\right]$$

$$= \frac{4bx^3}{4 - a} + aCx^{a-1} - \frac{abx^3}{4 - a} - aCx^{a-1} = \frac{bx^3(4 - a)}{4 - a} = bx^3.$$

25. Verify that $y = 2/(1 + Ce^{x^2})$ is a solution of the differential equation $y' + 2xy = xy^2$.

Solution:

Since

$$y' = -2(1 + Ce^{x^2})^{-2} 2xCe^{x^2} = -\frac{4xCe^{x^2}}{(1 + Ce^{x^2})^2}$$

we have

$$y' + 2xy = -\frac{4xCe^{x^2}}{(1 + Ce^{x^2})^2} + \frac{4x}{1 + Ce^{x^2}}$$

$$= \frac{-4xCe^{x^2} + 4x + 4xCe^{x^2}}{(1 + Ce^{x^2})^2} = x\left(\frac{2}{1 + Ce^{x^2}}\right)^2 = xy^2$$

27. Verify that $y = x\ln x + Cx + 4$ is a solution of the differential equation $x(y' - 1) - (y - 4) = 0$.

Solution:

Since $y' = \ln x + 1 + C$, we have $x(y' - 1) - (y - 4) = x(\ln x + 1 + C - 1) - (x\ln x + Cx + 4 - 4) = 0$.

29. Verify that $x^2 + y^2 = Cy$ is a solution of the differential equation $y' = 2xy/(x^2 - y^2)$.

Solution:

By implicit differentiation, we have $2x + 2yy' = Cy'$, which implies that $2x = y'(C - 2y)$ and

$$y' = \frac{2x}{C - 2y} = \frac{2xy}{Cy - 2y^2} = \frac{2xy}{(x^2 + y^2) - 2y^2} = \frac{2xy}{x^2 - y^2}.$$

31. Verify that $x^2 + xy = C$ is a solution of the differential equation $x^2 y'' - 2(x + y) = 0$.

Solution:

$$2x + y + xy' = 0 \Rightarrow y' = \frac{-2x - y}{x} = -2 - \frac{y}{x}$$

$$y'' = -\frac{y'}{x} + \frac{y}{x^2} = \frac{2}{x} + \frac{2y}{x^2}$$

$$x^2 y'' - 2(x + y) = x^2\left(\frac{2}{x} + \frac{2y}{x^2}\right) - 2(x + y) = 0$$

33. Determine whether $y = e^{-2x}$ is a solution of the differential equation $y^{(4)} - 16y = 0$.

Solution:

$$y' = -2e^{-2x}$$
$$y'' = 4e^{-2x}$$
$$y''' = -8e^{-2x}$$
$$y^{(4)} = 16e^{-2x}$$

Therefore, we have $y^{(4)} - 16y = 16e^{-2x} - 16(e^{-2x}) = 0$.

35. Determine whether $y = 4/x$ is a solution of the differential equation $y^{(4)} - 16y = 0$.

Solution:

$$y = 4x^{-1}$$
$$y' = -4x^{-2}$$
$$y'' = 8x^{-3}$$
$$y''' = -24x^{-4}$$
$$y^{(4)} = 96x^{-5}$$

Therefore, we have $y^{(4)} - 16y = 96x^{-5} - 16(4x^{-1}) \neq 0$ and y is not a solution of the given differential equation.

37. Determine whether $y = \frac{2}{9}xe^{-2x}$ is a solution to the differential equation $y''' - 3y' + 2y = 0$.

Solution:

$$y = \frac{2}{9}xe^{-2x}$$
$$y' = -\frac{4}{9}xe^{-2x} + \frac{2}{9}e^{-2x}$$
$$y'' = \frac{8}{9}xe^{-2x} - \frac{8}{9}e^{-2x}$$
$$y''' = -\frac{16}{9}xe^{-2x} + \frac{24}{9}e^{-2x}$$

Therefore,

$$y''' - 3y' + 2y = \left(-\frac{16}{9}xe^{-2x} + \frac{24}{9}e^{-2x}\right) - 3\left(-\frac{4}{9}xe^{-2x} + \frac{2}{9}e^{-2x}\right) + 2\left(\frac{2}{9}xe^{-2x}\right) = 2e^{-2x}.$$

This is *not* a solution to $y''' - 3y' + 2y = 0$.

39. Determine whether $y = xe^x$ is a solution to the differential equation $y''' - 3y' + 2y = 0$.

Solution:

$$y = xe^x$$
$$y' = xe^x + e^x$$
$$y'' = xe^x + 2e^x$$
$$y''' = xe^x + 3e^x$$

Therefore, $y''' - 3y' + 2y = (xe^x + 3e^x) - 3(xe^x + e^x) + 2(xe^x) = 0$. This *is* a solution to $y''' - 3y' + 2y = 0$.

41. Verify that $y = Ce^{-2x}$ satisfies the differential equation $y' + 2y = 0$. Then find the particular solution satisfying the initial condition of $y = 3$ when $x = 0$.

Solution:

Since $y' = -2Ce^{-2x} = -2y$, it follows that $y' + 2y = 0$. To find the particular solution, we use the fact that $y = 3$ when $x = 0$. That is, $3 = Ce^0 = C$. Thus, $C = 3$ and the particular solution is $y = 3e^{-2x}$.

43. Verify that $y = C_1 + C_2 \ln x (x > 0)$ satisfies the differential equation $xy'' + y' = 0$. Then find the particular solution satisfying the initial conditions of $y = 5$ and $y' = 1/2$ when $x = 1$.

Solution:

Since $y' = C_2(1/x)$ and $y'' = -C_2(1/x^2)$, it follows that $xy'' + y' = 0$. To find the particular solution, we use the fact that $y = 5$ and $y' = 1/2$ when $x = 1$. That is,

$$\frac{1}{2} = C_2\frac{1}{1} \qquad \Rightarrow \qquad C_2 = \frac{1}{2}$$
$$5 = C_1 + \frac{1}{2}(0) \qquad \Rightarrow \qquad C_1 = 5$$

Thus, the particular solution is $y = 5 + \frac{1}{2}\ln|x| = 5 + \ln\sqrt{|x|}$.

45. Verify that $y = C_1e^{4x} + C_2e^{-3x}$ satisfies the differential equation $y'' - y' - 12y = 0$. Then find the particular solution satisfying the initial conditions of $y = 5$ and $y' = 6$ when $x = 0$.

Solution:

Since $y' = 4C_1e^{4x} - 3C_2e^{-3x}$ and $y'' = 16C_1e^{4x} + 9C_2e^{-3x}$, it follows that $y'' - y' - 12y = 0$. To find the particular solution, we use the fact that $y = 5$ and $y' = 6$ when $x = 0$. That is,

$$C_1 + C_2 = 5$$
$$4C_1 - 3C_2 = 6$$

which implies that $C_1 = 3$ and $C_2 = 2$. The particular solution is

$$y = 3e^{4x} + 2e^{-3x}$$

47. Verify that $y = e^{2x/3}(C_1 + C_2 x)$ satisfies the differential equation $9y'' - 12y' + 4y = 0$. Then find the particular solution satisfying the initial conditions of $y = 4$ when $x = 0$ and $y = 0$ when $x = 3$.

Solution:

Since

$$y' = e^{2x/3}\left(\tfrac{2}{3}C_1 + \tfrac{2}{3}C_2 x + C_2\right)$$
$$y'' = e^{2x/3}\left(\tfrac{4}{9}C_1 + \tfrac{4}{9}C_2 x + \tfrac{4}{3}C_2\right)$$

it follows that $9y'' - 12y' + 4y = 0$. To find the particular solution, we use the fact that $y = 4$ when $x = 0$, and $y = 0$ when $x = 3$. That is,

$$4 = e^0[C_1 + C_2(0)] \quad \Rightarrow \quad C_1 = 4$$
$$0 = e^2[4 + C_2(3)] \quad \Rightarrow \quad C_2 = -\tfrac{4}{3}$$

Therefore, the particular solution is $y = e^{2x/3}\left(4 - \tfrac{4}{3}x\right) = \tfrac{4}{3}e^{2x/3}(3 - x)$.

49. The general solution of $y = Cx^2$ is $xy' - 2y = 0$. Sketch the particular solutions corresponding to 1, 2, 4.

Solution:

When $C = 1$, the graph is a parabola $y = x^2$.

When $C = 2$, the graph is a parabola $y = 2x^2$.

When $C = 4$, the graph is a parabola $y = 4x^2$.

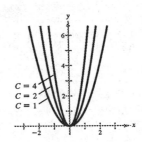

51. The general solution of $(x + 2)y' - 2y = 0$ is $y = C(x + 2)^2$. Sketch the particular solutions corresponding to $C = 0$, $C = \pm 1$, and $C = \pm 2$.

Solution:

When $C = 0$, the graph is a straight line.

When $C = 1$, the graph is a parabola opening upward with a vertex at $(-2, 0)$.

When $C = -1$, the graph is a parabola opening downward with a vertex at $(-2, 0)$.

When $C = 2$, the graph is a parabola opening upward with a vertex at $(-2, 0)$.

When $C = -2$, the graph is a parabola opening downward with a vertex at $(-2, 0)$.

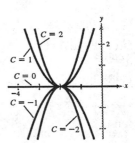

53. Use integration to find the general solution of the differential equation $dy/dx = 3x^2$.

Solution:

$$y = \int 3x^2 \, dx = x^3 + C$$

55. Use integration to find the general solution of $\dfrac{dy}{dx} = \dfrac{x+3}{x}$.

Solution:

$$y = \int \frac{x+3}{x} dx = \int \left(1 + \frac{3}{x}\right) dx = x + 3 \ln|x| + C$$

57. Use integration to find the general solution of the differential equation $\dfrac{dy}{dx} = x\sqrt{x-3}$.

Solution:

Letting $u = x - 3$, we have the following.

$$y = \int x\sqrt{x-3}\, dx$$

$$= \int (u+3)u^{1/2}\, du$$

$$= \int (u^{3/2} + 3u^{1/2})\, du = \tfrac{2}{5}u^{5/2} + 2u^{3/2} + C = \tfrac{2}{5}u^{3/2}(u+5) + C$$

$$= \tfrac{2}{5}(x-3)^{3/2}(x+2) + C$$

59. The general solution of $2xy' - 3y = 0$ is $y^2 = Cx^3$. Find the particular solution that passes through the point $(4, 4)$.

Solution:

Since $y = 4$ when $x = 4$, we have $4^2 = C4^3$ which implies that $C = \tfrac{1}{4}$ and the particular solution is $y^2 = x^3/4$.

61. The general solution of $y' - y = 0$ is $y = Ce^x$. Find the particular solution that passes through the point
$(0, 3)$.

Solution:

Since $y = 3$ when $x = 0$, we have $3 = Ce^0$ which implies that $C = 3$ and the particular solution is $y = 3e^x$.

63. *Population Growth* The limiting capacity of the habitat for a particular wildlife herd is 750. The growth rate dN/dt of the herd is proportional to the unutilized opportunity for growth, as described by the differential equation $dN/dt = k(750 - N)$. The general solution to this differential equation is $N = 750 - Ce^{-kt}$. When $t = 0$, the population of the herd is 100. After 2 years, the herd has grown to 160 animals.

(a) Find the population function N in terms of the time t in years.

(b) Sketch the graph of this population function using a graphing utility.

(c) What is the population of the herd after 4 years?

Solution:

(a) Since $N = 100$ when $t = 0$, it follows that $C = 650$. Therefore, the population function is $N = 750 - 650e^{-kt}$. Moreover, since $N = 160$ when $t = 2$, it follows that

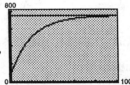

$$160 = 750 - 650e^{-2k}$$

$$e^{-2k} = \frac{59}{65}$$

$$k = -\tfrac{1}{2} \ln \tfrac{59}{65} \approx -0.0484$$

Thus, the population function is $N = 750 - 650e^{-0.0484t}$.

(b) See accompanying graph.

(c) When $t = 4$, $N \approx 214$.

65. *Marketing* You are working in the marketing department of a computer software company. Your marketing team determines that a maximum of 30,000 units of a new product can be sold in a year. You hypothesize that the rate of growth of the sales x is proportional to the difference between the maximum sales and the current sales. That is,

$$\frac{dx}{dt} = k(30{,}000 - x).$$

The general solution of this differential equation is $x = 30{,}000 - Ce^{-kt}$, where t is the time in years. During the first year, 2000 units are sold. Complete the table in the textbook showing the number of units sold in subsequent years.

Solution:

$x = 30{,}000 - Ce^{-kt}$. Since the product is new, $x = 0$ when $t = 0 \Rightarrow C = 30{,}000$.
When $t = 1, x = 2000 \Rightarrow$

$$2000 = 30{,}000 - 30{,}000e^{-k}$$

$$\frac{1}{15} = 1 - e^{-k}$$

$$e^{-k} = \frac{14}{15}$$

$$k = -\ln\left(\frac{14}{15}\right) \approx 0.06899$$

$$x = 30{,}000 - 30{,}000e^{-0.06899t}$$

Year, t	2	4	6	8	10
Units, x	3867	7235	10,169	12,725	14,951

67. A differential equation can have more than one solution.

Solution:

True

69. Show that $y = a + Ce^{k(1-b)t}$ is a solution of the differential equation

$$y = a + b(y - a) + \frac{1}{k}\frac{dy}{dt}$$

where k is a constant.

Solution:

$$y = a + Ce^{k(1-b)t}$$

$$\frac{dy}{dt} = Ck(1 - b)e^{k(1-b)t}$$

$$a + b(y - a) + \frac{1}{k}\frac{dy}{dt} = a + b[(a + Ce^{k(1-b)t}) - a] + \frac{1}{k}[Ck(1 - b)e^{k(1-b)t}]$$

$$= a + bCe^{k(1-b)t} + C(1 - b)e^{k(1-b)t}$$

$$= a + Ce^{k(1-b)t}[b + (1 - b)] = a + Ce^{k(1-b)t} = y$$

71. *Snow Removal* Assume that the rate of change in the number of miles s of road cleared per hour by a snow plow is inversely proportional to the depth h of the snow. This rate of change is described by the differential equation

$$\frac{ds}{dh} = \frac{k}{h}.$$

Show that

$$s = 25 - \frac{13}{\ln 3} \ln \frac{h}{2}$$

is a solution of this differential equation. Since

$$\frac{ds}{dh} = -\frac{13}{\ln 3} \left(\frac{1/2}{h/2} \right) = -\frac{13}{\ln 3} \frac{1}{h}$$

and $-13/\ln 3$ is a constant, we can conclude that the equation is a solution to

$$\frac{ds}{dh} = \frac{k}{h} \quad \text{where } k = -\frac{13}{\ln 3}.$$

Section D.2   Separation of Variables

1. Decide whether the variables $\dfrac{dy}{dx} = \dfrac{x}{y+3}$ can be separated.

Solution:

Yes, $\dfrac{dy}{dx} = \dfrac{x}{y+3}$

$(y+3)dy = xdx$

3. Decide whether the variables $\dfrac{dy}{dx} = \dfrac{1}{x} + 1$ can be separated.

Solution:

Yes, $\dfrac{dy}{dx} = \dfrac{1}{x} + 1$

$dy = \left(\dfrac{1}{x} + 1 \right) dx$

5. Decide whether the variables $\dfrac{dy}{dx} = x - y$ can be separated.

Solution:

No, the variables cannot be separated.

7. Find the general solution of $\dfrac{dy}{dx} = 2x$.

   Solution:
   $$\frac{dy}{dx} = 2x$$
   $$\int dy = \int 2x\,dx$$
   $$y = x^2 + C$$

9. Find the general solution of $\dfrac{dy}{dx} = \dfrac{1}{x}$.

   Solution:
   $$\frac{dy}{dx} = \frac{1}{x}$$
   $$\int dy = \int \frac{1}{x}\,dx$$
   $$y = \ln|x| + C$$

11. Find the general solution of $3y^2\dfrac{dy}{dx} = 1$.

    Solution:
    $$3y^2\frac{dy}{dx} = 1$$
    $$\int 3y^2\,dy = \int dx$$
    $$y^3 = x + C$$
    $$y = \sqrt[3]{x + C}$$

13. Find the general solution of $y' - xy = 0$.

    Solution:
    $$\frac{dy}{dx} = xy$$
    $$\int \frac{1}{y}\,dy = \int x\,dx$$
    $$\ln|y| = \frac{1}{2}x^2 + C_1$$
    $$y = e^{(x^2/2)+C_1} = e^{C_1}e^{x^2/2} = Ce^{x^2/2}$$

15. Find the general solution of $\dfrac{dy}{dt} = \dfrac{e^t}{4y}$.

Solution:

$$\frac{dy}{dt} = \frac{e^t}{4y}$$

$$\int 4y\,dy = \int e^t\,dt$$

$$2y^2 = e^t + C_1$$

$$y^2 = \frac{1}{2}e^t + C$$

17. Find the general solution of $e^y \dfrac{dy}{dt} = 3t^2 + 1$.

Solution:

$$e^y \frac{dy}{dt} = 3t^2 + 1$$

$$\int e^y\,dy = \int (3t^2 + 1)\,dt$$

$$e^y = t^3 + t + C$$

$$y = \ln|t^3 + t + C|$$

19. Find the general solution of $(2+x)y' = 2y$.

Solution:

$$(2+x)\frac{dy}{dx} = 2y$$

$$\int \frac{1}{2y}\,dy = \int \frac{1}{2+x}\,dx$$

$$\frac{1}{2}\ln|y| = \ln|C_1(2+x)|$$

$$\sqrt{y} = C_1(2+x)$$

$$y = C(2+x)^2$$

21. Find the general solution of $\dfrac{dy}{dx} = \sqrt{1-y}$.

Solution:

$$\frac{dy}{dx} = \sqrt{1-y}$$

$$\int (1-y)^{-1/2}dy = \int dx$$

$$-2(1-y)^{1/2} = x + C_1$$

$$\sqrt{1-y} = \frac{-x}{2} + C$$

$$1-y = \left(C - \frac{x}{2}\right)^2$$

$$y = 1 - \left(C - \frac{x}{2}\right)^2$$

23. Find the general solution of $y' = (2x-1)(y+3)$.

Solution:

$$y' = \frac{dy}{dx} = (2x-1)(y+3)$$

$$\int \frac{1}{y+3}dy = \int (2x-1)dx$$

$$\ln|y+3| = x^2 - x + C_1$$

$$y + 3 = e^{x^2 - x + C_1}$$

$$y = -3 + Ce^{x^2 - x}$$

25. Find the general solution of $y' = \dfrac{x}{y} - \dfrac{x}{1+y}$.

Solution:

$$y' = \frac{dy}{dx} = \frac{x}{y} - \frac{x}{1+y} = x\left(\frac{1}{y+y^2}\right)$$

$$\int (y + y^2)dy = \int x\,dx$$

$$\frac{y^2}{2} + \frac{y^3}{3} = \frac{x^2}{2} + C_1$$

$$3y^2 + 2y^3 = 3x^2 + C$$

27. Find the particular solution of $yy' - e^x = 0$ that satisfies the initial condition $y = 4$ when $x = 0$.

Solution:

$$y\frac{dy}{dx} = e^x$$

$$\int y\,dy = \int e^x\,dx$$

$$\frac{y^2}{2} = e^x + C$$

When $x = 0$, $y = 4$. Therefore, $C = 7$ and the particular solution is $y^2 = 2e^x + 14$.

29. Find the particular solution of $x(y+4) + y' = 0$ that satisfies the initial condition $y = -5$ when $x = 0$.

Solution:

$$\frac{dy}{dx} = -x(y + 4)$$

$$\int \frac{1}{y+4}dy = \int -x\,dx$$

$$\ln|y + 4| = -\frac{x^2}{2} + C_1$$

$$|y + 4| = e^{-x^2/2 + C_1}$$

$$y = -4 + Ce^{-x^2/2}$$

When $x = 0$, $y = -5 \Rightarrow C = -1$ and $y = -4 - e^{-x^2/2}$.

31. Find the particular solution of $\dfrac{dy}{dx} = x^2(1 + y)$ that satisfies the initial condition $y = 3$ when $x = 0$.

Solution:

$$\frac{dy}{dx} = x^2(1 + y)$$

$$\frac{dy}{1+y} = x^2\,dx$$

$$\ln(1 + y) = x^2 + C_1$$

$$y + 1 = e^{x^2 + C_1} = Ce^{x^2}$$

$$y = Ce^{x^2} - 1$$

$$y = 4e^{x^2} - 1$$

33. Find an equation for the graph that passes through the point $(-1, 1)$ and has the specified slope $y' = \dfrac{6x}{5y}$.

Solution:

$$\frac{dy}{dx} = \frac{6x}{5y}$$

$$\int 5y\,dy = \int 6x\,dx$$

$$\frac{5}{2}y^2 = 3x^2 + C_1 \Rightarrow 5y^2 = 6x^2 + C$$

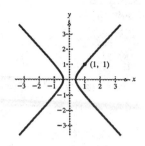

When $x = -1$, $y = 1 \Rightarrow 5 = 6 + C \Rightarrow C = -1$ $5y^2 = 6x^2 - 1$ or $6x^2 - 5y^2 = 1$ (hyperbola).

35. *Velocity* Solve $12.5(dv/dt) = 43.2 - 1.25v$ to find velocity v as a function of time if $v = 0$ when $t = 0$. The differential equation was derived to describe the motion of two people on a toboggan after considering the force of gravity, friction, and air resistance.

Solution:

$$\frac{dv}{dt} = 3.456 - 0.1v$$

$$\int \frac{dv}{3.456 - 0.1v} = \int dt$$

$$-10 \ln |3.456 - 0.1v| = t + C_1$$

$$(3.456 - 0.1v)^{-10} = C_2 e^t$$

$$3.456 - 0.1v = Ce^{-0.1t}$$

$$v = -10Ce^{-0.1t} + 34.56$$

When $t = 0$, $v = 0$. Therefore, $C = 3.456$ and the solution is $v = 34.56(1 - e^{-0.1t})$.

37. Use Newton's Law of Cooling, which states that the rate of change in the temperature T of an object is proportional to the difference between the temperature T of the object and the temperature of the surrounding environment T_0. This is described by the differential equation

$\dfrac{dT}{dt} = k(T - t_0)$. From the above, we have $T = Ce^{kt} + T_0$. We have $T_0 = 90$, and when $t = 0$, $T = 1500$. Thus, $1500 = Ce^0 + 90$ which implies that $C = 1410$. When $t = 1$, $T = 1120$ which implies that

$$1120 = 1410e^k + 90$$

$$k = \ln \frac{1030}{1410} = \ln \frac{103}{141}.$$

Therefore, $T = 1410e^{[\ln(103/141)]t} + 90$. When $t = 5$, we have $T \approx 383.298°$.

39. Use Newton's Law of Cooling, which states that the rate of change in the temperature T of an object is proportional to the difference between the temperature T of the object and the temperature of the surrounding environment T_0. This is described by the differential equation

$\dfrac{dT}{dt} = k(T - t_0)$. From the above, we have $T = Ce^{kt} + T_0$. Since $T_0 = 0$ and $T = 70$ when $t = 0$, we have $T = 70e^{kt}$. When $t = 1$, $T = 48$ and we have $48 = 70e^k$ which implies that $k = \ln\frac{48}{70} = \ln\frac{24}{35}$. Therefore, $T = 70e^{[\ln(24/35)]t}$.

(a) When $t = 6$, we have $T \approx 7.277°$.

(b) When $T = 10$, we have

$$10 = 70e^{[\ln(24/35)]t}$$

$$\ln\left(\frac{1}{7}\right) = \ln\left(\frac{24}{35}\right) t$$

$$t = \frac{\ln(1/7)}{\ln(24/35)} \approx 5.158 \text{ hours.}$$

41. *Learning Theory* The management at a certain factory has found that a worker can produce at most 30 units in a day. The number of units N per day produced by a new employee will increase at a rate proportional to the difference between 30 and N. This is described by the differential equation

$$\frac{dN}{dt} = k(30 - N),$$

where t is the time in days. Find the solution of this differential equation.

Solution:

$$\int \frac{dN}{30 - N} = \int k \, dt$$

$$-\ln|30 - N| = kt + C_1$$

$$30 - N = e^{-(kt + C_1)}$$

$$30 - N = C_2 e^{-kt}$$

$$N = 30 + Ce^{-kt}$$

43. *Pareto's Law* According to the economist Vilfredo Pareto (1848–1923), the rate of decrease of the number of people y in a stable economy have an income of at least x dollars is directly proportional to the number of such people and inversely proportional to their income x. This is modeled by the differential equation

$$\frac{dy}{dx} = -k\frac{y}{x}.$$

Solve this differential equation.

Solution:

$$\frac{dy}{dx} = -k\frac{y}{x}$$

$$\int \frac{dy}{y} = \int \frac{-k}{x}dx$$

$$\ln|y| = -k\ln|x| + C_1 = \ln|x|^{-k} + \ln C = \ln(C|x|^{-k})$$

$$y = cx^{-k}$$

Section D.3   First-Order Linear Differential Equations

1. Write the linear differential equation in standard form.

$$x^3 - 2x^2y' + 3y = 0$$

Solution:

$$x^3 - 2x^2y' + 3y = 0$$

$$-2x^2y' + 3y = -x^3$$

$$y' + \frac{-3}{2x^2}y = \frac{x}{2}$$

3. Write the linear differential equation in standard form.

$$xy' + y = xe^x$$

Solution:

$$xy' + y = xe^x$$

$$y' + \frac{1}{x}y = e^x$$

5. Write the linear differential equation in standard form.

$$y + 1 = (x - 1)y'$$

Solution:

$$y + 1 = (x - 1)y'$$

$$(1 - x)y' + y = -1$$

$$y' + \frac{1}{1 - x}y = \frac{1}{x - 1}$$

7. Solve the differential equation $\dfrac{dy}{dx} + 3y = 6$.

Solution:

For this linear differential equation, we have $P(x) = 3x$ and $Q(x) = 6x$. Therefore, the integrating factor is $u(x) = e^{\int 3x\,dx} = e^{3x}$ and the general solution is

$$y = \frac{1}{u(x)} \int Q(x)u(x)\,dx = e^{-3x} \int 6e^{3x}\,dx = e^{-3x}(2e^{3x} + C) = 2 + Ce^{-3x}.$$

9. Solve the differential equation $\dfrac{dy}{dx} + y = e^{-x}$.

Solution:

For this linear differential equation, we have $P(x) = 1$ and $Q(x) = e^{-x}$. Therefore, the integrating factor is $u(x) = e^{\int dx} = e^x$ and the general solution is

$$y = \frac{1}{u(x)} \int Q(x)u(x)\,dx = e^{-x} \int e^{-x}e^x dx = e^{-x}(x + C) \ .$$

11. Solve the differential equation $\dfrac{dy}{dx} + (y/x) = 3x + 4$.

Solution:

For this linear differential equation, we have $P(x) = 1/x$ and $Q(x) = 3x + 4$. Therefore, the integrating factor is

$$u(x) = e^{\int 1/x\,dx} = e^{\ln x} = x$$

and the general solution is

$$y = \frac{1}{u(x)} \int Q(x)u(x)\,dx = \frac{1}{x} \int (3x + 4)x\,dx = \frac{1}{x}(x^3 + 2x^2 + C) = x^2 + 2x + \frac{C}{x}.$$

13. Solve the differential equation $y' + 5xy = x$.

Solution:

For this linear differential equation, we have $P(x) = 5x$ and $Q(x) = x$. Therefore, the integrating factor is

$$u(x) = e^{\int 5x\,dx} = e^{\frac{5}{2}x^2}$$

and the general solution is

$$y = \frac{1}{u(x)} \int Q(x)u(x)\,dx = \frac{1}{e^{\frac{5}{2}x^2}} \int xe^{\frac{5}{2}x^2}\,dx$$

$$= \frac{1}{e^{\frac{5}{2}x^2}} \left(\frac{1}{5}e^{\frac{5}{2}x^2} + C \right) = \frac{1}{5} + Ce^{-\frac{5}{2}x^2}$$

15. Solve the differential equation $(x - 1)y' + y = x^2 - 1$.

Solution:

For this linear differential equation

$$y' + y\left(\frac{1}{x-1}\right) = x + 1$$

we have $P(x) = 1/(x - 1)$ and $Q(x) = x + 1$. Therefore, the integrating factor is $u(x) = e^{\int 1/(x-1)\,dx} = e^{\ln(x-1)} = x - 1$ and the general solution is

$$y = \frac{1}{u(x)} \int Q(x)u(x)\,dx = \frac{1}{x-1} \int (x+1)(x-1)\,dx = \frac{1}{x-1}\left(\frac{x^3}{3} - x + C_1\right)$$

$$= \frac{x^3 - 3x + C}{3(x-1)}.$$

17. Solve the differential equation $xy' + y = x^2 + 1$.

Solution:

For this linear differential equation, $y' + \frac{1}{x}y = x + \frac{1}{x}$, we have $P(x) = \frac{1}{x}$ and $Q(x) = x + \frac{1}{x}$. Therefore, the integrating factor is

$$u(x) = e^{\int \frac{1}{x}dx} = e^{\ln x} = x$$

and the general solution is

$$y = \frac{1}{u(x)} \int Q(x)u(x)dx = \frac{1}{x} \int \left(x + \frac{1}{x}\right) x\,dx$$

$$= \frac{1}{x}\left[\frac{x^3}{3} + x + C\right] = \frac{x^2}{3} + 1 + \frac{C}{x}$$

19. Solve $y' + y = 4$ in two ways.

Solution:

Separation of Variables:
$$\frac{dy}{dx} = 4 - y$$
$$\int \frac{dy}{4 - y} = \int dx$$
$$-\ln|4 - y| = x + C_1$$
$$4 - y = e^{-(x+C_1)}$$
$$4 - y = C_2 e^{-x}$$
$$y = 4 - C_2 e^x = 4 + Ce^{-x}$$

First-Order Linear:
$$P(x) = 1, \quad Q(x) = 4$$
$$u(x) = e^{\int 1\, dx} = e^x$$
$$y = \frac{1}{e^x} \int 4e^x\, dx = \frac{1}{e^x}[4e^x + C] = 4 + Ce^{-x}$$

21. Solve $y' - 2xy = 2x$ in two ways.

Solution:

Separation of Variables:
$$\frac{dy}{dx} = 2x(1 + y)$$
$$\int \frac{dy}{1 + y} = \int 2x\, dx$$
$$\ln|1 + y| = x^2 + C_1$$
$$1 + y = e^{x^2 + C_1}$$
$$y = Ce^{x^2} - 1$$

First-Order Linear:
$$P(x) = -2x, \quad Q(x) = 2x$$
$$u(x) = e^{\int -2x\, dx} = e^{-x^2}$$
$$y = \frac{1}{e^{-x^2}} \int 2xe^{-x^2}\, dx = e^{x^2}[-e^{-x^2} + C] = Ce^{x^2} - 1$$

23. Find the particular solution $y' + y = 6e^x$ that satisfies the initial condition of $y(0) = 3$.

Solution:

Since $P(x) = 1$ and $Q(x) = 6e^x$, the integrating factor is

$$u(x) = e^{\int dx} = e^x$$

and the general solution is

$$y = \frac{1}{e^x} \int 6e^x(e^x)dx = \frac{1}{e^x}[3e^{2x} + C] = 3e^x + Ce^{-x}.$$

Since $y = 3$ when $x = 0$, it follows that $C = 0$, and the particular solution is $y = 3e^x$.

25. Find the particular solution of $xy' + y = 0$ that satisfies the initial condition of $y(2) = 2$.

Solution:

Since $P(x) = 1/x$ and $Q(x) = 0$, the integrating factor is $u(x) = e^{\int 1/x \, dx} = e^{\ln x} = x$ and the general solution is

$$y = \frac{1}{x} \int 0 \, dx = \frac{C}{x}.$$

Since $y = 2$ when $x = 2$, it follows that $C = 4$, and the particular solution is $y = 4/x$ or $xy = 4$.

27. Find the particular solution of $y' + y = x$ that satisfies the initial condition of $y(0) = 4$.

Solution:

Since $P(x) = 1$ and $Q(x) = x$, the integrating factor is $u(x) = e^{\int dx} = e^x$ and the general solution is

$$y = e^{-x} \int xe^x \, dx = e^{-x}(xe^x - e^x + C) = x - 1 + Ce^{-x}.$$

Since $y = 4$ when $x = 0$, it follows that $C = 5$, and the particular solution is $y = x - 1 + 5e^{-x}$.

29. Find the particular solution of $xy' - 2y = -x^2$ that satisfies the initial condition of $y(1) = 5$.

Solution:

Since $P(x) = -2/x$ and $Q(x) = -x$, the integrating factor is

$$u(x) = e^{\int -2/x\, dx} = e^{-2\ln x} = \frac{1}{x^2}$$

and the general solution is

$$y = x^2 \int (-x)\left(\frac{1}{x^2}\right) dx = x^2(-\ln|x| + C).$$

Since $y = 5$ when $x = 1$, it follows that $C = 5$, and the particular solution is $y = x^2(5 - \ln|x|)$.

31. *Sales* The rate of change (in thousands of units) in sales S is estimated to be

$$\frac{dS}{dt} = 0.2(100 - S) + 0.2t,$$

where t is the time in years. Solve the differential equation and complete a table to estimate the sales of a new product for the first 10 years. (Assume that $S = 0$ when $t = 0$.)

Solution:

Since $P(t) = 0.2$ and $Q(t) = 20 + 0.2t$, the integrating factor is $u(t) = e^{\int 0.2\, dt} = e^{t/5}$ and the general solution is

$$S = e^{-t/5} \int e^{t/5}\left(20 + \frac{t}{5}\right) dt.$$

Using integration by parts, the integral is

$$S = e^{-t/5}(100e^{t/5} + te^{t/5} - 5e^{t/5} + C) = 100 + t - 5 + Ce^{-t/5} = 95 + t + Ce^{-t/5}.$$

Since $S = 0$ when $t = 0$, it follows that $C = -95$, and the particular solution is $S = t + 95(1 - e^{-t/5})$. During the first 10 years, the sales are as follows.

t	0	1	2	3	4	5
S	0	18.22	33.32	45.86	56.31	65.05

t	6	7	8	9	10
S	72.39	78.57	83.82	88.30	92.14

33. *Elasticity of Demand* Find the demand function $p = f(x)$, given $\eta = 1 - \dfrac{400}{3x}$, $p = 340$ when $x = 20$, and $\eta = (p/x)(dp/dx)$.

Solution:

$$\frac{dp}{dx}\left(1 - \frac{400}{3x}\right) = \frac{p}{x}$$

$$\frac{dp}{dx}\left(x - \frac{400}{3}\right) = p$$

$$\int \frac{dp}{p} = \int \frac{dx}{x - (400/3)}$$

$$\ln|p| = \ln\left|x - \frac{400}{3}\right| + \ln|C|$$

$$p = C\left(x - \frac{400}{3}\right)$$

$$340 = C\left(20 - \frac{400}{3}\right) \Rightarrow C = -3$$

$$p = -3\left(x - \frac{400}{3}\right) = 400 - 3x$$

35. *Price* Write the price of a product as a function of time using the given demand and supply functions and the initial condition. Follow the steps shown in the Introductory Example.

$$\begin{aligned}
D(t) &= 480 + 5p(t) - 2p'(t) && \text{Demand function} \\
S(t) &= 300 + 8p(t) + p'(t) && \text{Supply function} \\
p(0) &= \$75.00 && \text{Initial condition}
\end{aligned}$$

Solution:

$$D(t) = S(t)$$

$$480 + 5p(t) - 2p'(t) = 300 + 8p(t) + p'(t)$$

$$180 = 3p'(t) + 3p(t)$$

$$60 = p'(t) + p(t)$$

$$P(t) = 1, \quad Q(t) = 60$$

$$u(t) = e^{\int 1\, dt} = e^t$$

$$p(t) = \frac{1}{e^t}\int 60e^t \, dt = \frac{1}{e^t}[60e^t + C] = 60 + Ce^{-t}$$

$$p(0) = 60 + C = 75 \Rightarrow C = 15$$

$$p(t) = 60 + 15e^{-t} = 15(4 + e^{-t})$$

37. *Investment Growth* A brokerage firm opens a new real estate investment plan for which the earnings are equivalent to continuous compounding at the rate of r. The firm estimates that deposits from investors will create a net cash flow of Pt dollars, where t is the time in years. The rate of increase in the amount A in the real estate investment is

$$\frac{dA}{dt} = rA + Pt.$$

(a) Solve the differential equation and find the amount A as a function of t. Assume that $A = 0$ when $t = 0$.

(b) Find the total investment A after 10 years given that $P = \$500,000$ and $r = 9\%$.

Solution:

(a) Since $P(t) = -r$ and $Q(t) = Pt$, the integrating factor is $u(t) = e^{\int -r\,dt} = e^{-rt}$ and the general solution is

$$A = e^{rt} \int Pte^{-rt}\,dt = Pe^{rt}\left(-\frac{t}{r}e^{-rt} - \frac{1}{r^2}e^{-rt} + C_1\right) = \frac{P}{r^2}(-rt - 1 + Ce^{rt}).$$

Since $A = 0$ when $t = 0$, it follows that $C = 1$, and the particular solution is

$$A = \frac{P}{r^2}(e^{rt} - rt - 1).$$

(b) When $t = 10$, $P = 500{,}000$ and $r = 0.09$, $A \approx \$34{,}543{,}402$.

Section D.4   Applications of Differential Equations

1. Solve the differential equation $dy/dx = ky$ and find the particular solution that passes through the points $(0, 1)$ and $(3, 2)$.

Solution:

The general solution is $y = Ce^{kx}$. Since $y = 1$ when $x = 0$, it follows that $C = 1$. Thus, $y = e^{kx}$. Since $y = 2$ when $x = 3$, it follows that $2 = e^{3k}$ which implies that

$$k = \frac{\ln 2}{3} \approx 0.2310.$$

Thus, the particular solution is $y \approx e^{0.2310x}$.

3. Solve the differential equation $dy/dx = ky$ and find the particular solution that passes through the points
(0, 4) and (4, 1).

Solution:

The general solution is $y = Ce^{kx}$. Since $y = 4$ when $x = 0$, it follows that $C = 4$. Thus, $y = 4e^{kx}$. Since $y = 1$ when $x = 4$, it follows that $\frac{1}{4} = e^{4k}$ which implies that

$$k = \frac{1}{4} \ln \frac{1}{4} \approx -0.3466.$$

Thus, the particular solution is $y \approx 4e^{-0.3466x}$.

5. Solve the differential equation $dy/dx = ky$ and find the particular solution that passes through the points
(2, 2) and (3, 4).

Solution:

The general solution is $y = Ce^{kx}$. Since $y = 2$ when $x = 2$ and $y = 4$ when $x = 3$, it follows that $2 = Ce^{2k}$ and $4 = Ce^{3k}$. By equating C-values from these two equations, we have the following.

$$2e^{-2k} = 4e^{-3k}$$

$$\frac{1}{2} = e^{-k} \quad \Rightarrow \quad k = \ln 2 \approx 0.6931$$

This implies that

$$C = 2e^{-2\ln 2} = 2e^{\ln(1/4)} = 2\left(\frac{1}{4}\right) = \frac{1}{2}.$$

Thus, the particular solution is

$$y = \frac{1}{2}e^{x\ln 2} \approx \frac{1}{2}e^{0.6931x}.$$

7. *Growth of an Investment* The rate of growth of an investment is proportional to the amount A of the investment at any time t. An investment of \$2000 increases to a value of \$2983.65 in 5 years. Find its value after 10 years.

Solution:

The general solution is $y - Ae^{kt}$ with $A = 2000$. Since $y = 2983.65$ when $t = 5$, we have

$$2983.65 = 2000e^{5k}$$

$$k = \frac{\ln(1.491825)}{5} \approx 0.08.$$

Thus, the particular solution is $y = 2000e^{0.08t}$. When $t = 10$,
$y = 2000e^{0.08(10)} \approx \$4451.08.$

9. *Sales Increase* The rate of increase in sales S (in thousands of units) of a new product is proportional to the difference between L and S (in thousands of units) at any time t. If L is the estimated maximum level of sales and $S = 0$ when $t = 0$, write and solve the differential equation for this sales model.

Solution:

$$\frac{dS}{dt} = k(L - S)$$

$$\int \frac{dS}{L - S} = \int k\,dt$$

$$-\ln|L - S| = kt + C_1$$

$$L - S = e^{-kt - C_1}$$

$$S = L + Ce^{-kt}$$

Since $S = 0$ when $t = 0$, we have $0 = L + C \Rightarrow C = -L$. Thus, $S = L(1 - e^{-kt})$.

11. Solve the differential equation $dy/dx = ky(20 - y)$ and find the particular solution that passes through the points $(0, 1)$ and $(5, 10)$.

Solution:

The general solution is $y = Ce^{20kx}(20 - y)$. Since $y = 1$ when $x = 0$, it follows that $C = \frac{1}{19}$. Thus,

$$y = \frac{1}{19}e^{20kx}(20 - y).$$

Since $y = 10$ when $x = 5$, it follows that

$$19 = e^{100k}$$

$$20k = \frac{\ln 19}{5} \approx 0.5889.$$

Thus, the particular solution is

$$y = \frac{1}{19}e^{0.5889x}(20 - y)$$

$$y(19 + e^{0.5889x}) = 20e^{0.5889x}$$

$$y = \frac{20e^{0.5889x}}{19 + e^{0.5889x}} = \frac{20}{1 + 19e^{-0.5889x}}.$$

13. Solve the differential equation $dy/dx = ky(5000 - y)$ and find the particular solution that passes through the points (0, 250) and (25, 2000).

Solution:

The general solution is $y = Ce^{5000kx}(5000 - y)$. Since $y = 250$ when $x = 0$, it follows that $C = \frac{1}{19}$. Thus,

$$y = \frac{1}{19}e^{5000kx}(5000 - y).$$

Since $y = 2000$ when $x = 25$, it follows that

$$\frac{38}{3} = e^{125000k}$$

$$5000k = \frac{\ln(38/3)}{25} \approx 0.10156.$$

Thus, the particular solution is

$$y = \frac{1}{19}e^{0.10156x}(5000 - y)$$

$$y(19 + e^{0.10156x}) = 5000e^{0.10156x}$$

$$y = \frac{5000e^{0.10156x}}{19 + e^{0.10156x}} = \frac{5000}{1 + 19e^{-0.10156x}}.$$

15. *Logistics Growth* At any time t, the rate of growth of the population N of deer in a state part is proportional to the product of N and $L - N$ where $L = 500$ is the maximum number of deer the park can maintain. Write N as a function of t if $N = 100$ when $t = 0$ and $N = 200$ when $t = 4$.

Solution:

$$\frac{dN}{dt} = kN(500 - N)$$

$$\int \frac{dN}{N(500 - N)} = \int k \, dt$$

$$\frac{1}{500} \int \left[\frac{1}{N} + \frac{1}{500 - N} \right] dN = \int k \, dt$$

$$\ln |N| - \ln |500 - N| = 500(kt + C_1)$$

$$\frac{N}{500 - N} = e^{500kt + C_2} = Ce^{500kt}$$

$$N = \frac{500Ce^{500kt}}{1 + Ce^{500kt}}$$

When $t = 0$, $N = 100$. Thus, $100 = \dfrac{500C}{1 + C} \Rightarrow C = 0.25$. Thus, $N = \dfrac{125e^{500kt}}{1 + 0.25e^{500kt}}$.

When $t = 4$, $N = 200$. Thus, $200 = \dfrac{125e^{2000k}}{1 + 0.25e^{2000k}} \Rightarrow k = \dfrac{\ln(8/3)}{2000} \approx 0.00049$.

Therefore,

$$N = \frac{125e^{0.2452t}}{1 + 0.25e^{0.2452t}} = \frac{500}{1 + 4e^{-0.2452t}}.$$

17. *Learning Theory* Assume that the rate of change in the proportion P of correct responses after n trials is proportional to P and $L - P$, where L is the limiting proportion of correct responses. Write and solve the differential equation for this learning theory model.

Solution:

The differential equation is given by the following.

$$\frac{dP}{dn} = kP(L - P)$$

$$\int \frac{1}{P(L - P)} \, dP = \int k \, dn$$

$$\frac{1}{L}[\ln |P| - \ln |L - P|] = kn + C_1$$

$$\frac{P}{L - P} = Ce^{Lkn}$$

$$P = \frac{CLe^{Lkn}}{1 + Ce^{Lkn}} = \frac{CL}{e^{-Lkn} + C}$$

19. *Chemical Reaction* Use the chemical reaction model in Example 2 to find the amount y as a function of t, and use a graphing utility to graph the function.

$y = 45$ grams when $t = 0$; $y = 4$ grams when $t = 2$.

Solution:

The general solution is $y = \dfrac{-1}{kt + C}$. Since $y = 45$ when

$t = 0$, it follows that $45 = \dfrac{-1}{C}$ and $C = \dfrac{-1}{45}$. Therefore

$$y = -\dfrac{1}{kt - \left(\frac{1}{45}\right)} = \dfrac{45}{1 - 45kt}$$

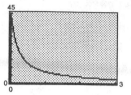

Since $y = 4$ when $t = 2$, we have $4 = \dfrac{45}{1 - 45k(2)} \Rightarrow k = -\dfrac{45}{360}$.

Thus,

$$y = \dfrac{45}{1 + \frac{41}{8}t} = \dfrac{360}{8 + 41t}.$$

21. Use the Gompertz growth model $y = 500e^{-Ce^{-kt}}$ to find the amount y as a function of time and sketch the graph of y. Use the initial conditions $y = 100$ when $t = 0$ and $y = 150$ when $t = 2$.

Solution:

Since $y = 100$ when $t = 0$, it follows that $100 = 500e^{-C}$, which implies that $C = \ln 5$. Therefore, we have $y = 500e^{(-\ln 5)e^{-kt}}$. Since $y = 150$ when $t = 2$, it follows that

$$150 = 500e^{(-\ln 5)e^{-2k}}$$

$$e^{-2k} = \dfrac{\ln 0.3}{\ln 0.2}$$

$$k = -\dfrac{1}{2}\ln\dfrac{\ln 0.3}{\ln 0.2} \approx 0.1452.$$

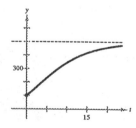

Therefore, y is given by $y = 500e^{-1.6904e^{-0.1451t}}$.

23. *Gompertz Growth Model* A population of eight beavers has been introduced to a new wetlands area. Biologists estimate that the maximum population the wetlands can sustain is 60 beavers. After 3 years, the population is 15 beavers. If the population follows a Gompertz growth model, how many beavers will be in the wetlands in 10 years?

Solution:

From Example 3, the general solution is

$$y = 60e^{-Ce^{-kt}}.$$

Since $y = 8$ when $t = 0$,

$$8 = 60e^{-C} \Rightarrow C = \ln\frac{15}{2} \approx 2.0149.$$

Since $y = 15$ when $t = 3$,

$$15 = 60e^{-2.0149e^{-3k}}$$

$$\frac{1}{4} + e^{-2.0149e^{-3k}}$$

$$\ln\frac{1}{4} = -2.0419e^{-3k}$$

$$k = -\frac{1}{3}\ln\left(\frac{\ln\frac{1}{4}}{-2.0149}\right) \approx 0.1246.$$

Thus,

$$y = 60e^{-2.0149e^{-0.1246t}}.$$

When $t = 10$, $y \approx 34$ beavers.

25. *Hybrid Selection* You are studying a population of mayflies to determine how quickly characteristic A will pass from one generation to the next. At the start of the study, half the population has characteristic A. After four generations, 75% of the population has characteristic A. Find the percent of the population that will have characteristic A after 10 generations. (Assume $a = 2$ and $b = 1$.) Use the hybrid selection model in Example 4 to find the percent of the population that has the indicated characteristic.

Solution:

Following Example 4, the differential equation is

$$\frac{dy}{dt} = ky(1 - y)(2 - y)$$

and its general solution is

$$\frac{y(2 - y)}{(1 - y)^2} = Ce^{2kt}$$

$$y = \frac{1}{2} \text{ when } t = 0 \Rightarrow \frac{\frac{1}{2}\left(\frac{3}{2}\right)}{\left(\frac{1}{2}\right)^2} = C \Rightarrow C = 3$$

$$y = 0.75 = \frac{3}{4} \text{ when } t = 4 \Rightarrow \frac{\frac{3}{4}\left(\frac{5}{4}\right)}{\left(\frac{1}{4}\right)^2} = 15 = 3e^{2k(4)}$$

$$\Rightarrow k = \frac{1}{8} \ln 5 \approx 0.2012.$$

Hence, the particular solution is

$$\frac{y(2 - y)}{(1 - y)^2} = 3e^{0.4024t}.$$

Using a symbolic algebra utility or graphing utility, you find that when $t = 10$,

$$\frac{y(2 - y)}{(1 - y)^2} = 3e^{0.4024(10)}$$

and $y \approx 0.92$.

27. *Mixture* A 100-gallon tank is full of a solution containing 25 pounds of a concentrate. Starting at time $t = 0$, distilled water is admitted to the tank at the rate of 5 gallons per minute, and the well-stirred solution is withdrawn at the same rate.

(a) Find the amount Q of the concentrate in the solution as a function of t, $[Q' + (Q/20) = 0]$.

(b) Find the time when the amount of concentrate in the tank reaches 15 pounds.

Solution:

(a) $$\frac{dQ}{dt} = -\frac{Q}{20}$$

$$\int \frac{dQ}{Q} = \int -\frac{1}{20}\, dt$$

$$\ln |Q| = -\frac{1}{20}t + C_1$$

$$Q = e^{-(1/20)t + C_1} = Ce^{-(1/20)t}$$

Since $Q = 25$ when $t = 0$, we have $25 = C$, thus, the particular solution is $Q = 25e^{-(1/20)t}$.

(b) When $Q = 15$, we have $15 = 25e^{-(1/20)t}$.

$$\frac{3}{5} = e^{-(1/20)t}$$

$$\ln\left(\frac{3}{5}\right) = -\frac{1}{20}t$$

$$-20\ln\left(\frac{3}{5}\right) = t$$

$$t \approx 10.217 \text{ minutes}$$

29. *Snow Removal* Assume that the rate of change in the number of miles s of road cleared of snow per hour by a snowplow is inversely proportional to the height h of snow. That is $ds/dh = k/h$. Find s as a function of h if $s = 25$ miles when $h = 2$ inches and $s = 12$ miles when $h = 6$ inches ($2 \le h \le 15$).

Solution:

$$\frac{ds}{dh} = \frac{k}{h}$$

$$\int ds = \int \frac{k}{h}\, dh$$

$$s = k \ln h + C_1 = k \ln Ch$$

Since $s = 25$ when $h = 2$ and $s = 12$ when $h = 6$, it follows that $25 = k \ln 2C$ and $12 = k \ln 6C$, which implies

$$C = \frac{1}{2} e^{-(25/13) \ln 3} \approx 0.0605 \quad \text{and} \quad k = \frac{25}{\ln 2C} = \frac{-13}{\ln 3} \approx -11.8331.$$

Therefore, s is given by the following.

$$s = -\frac{13}{\ln 3} \ln \left[\frac{h}{2} e^{-(25/13)\ln 3} \right]$$

$$= -\frac{13}{\ln 3}\left[\ln \frac{h}{2} - \frac{25}{13} \ln 3 \right] = -\frac{1}{\ln 3}\left[13 \ln \frac{h}{2} - 25 \ln 3 \right]$$

$$= 25 - \frac{13 \ln(h/2)}{\ln 3},$$

$$2 \le h \le 15$$

31. *Growth Rate* Let x and y be the sizes of two internal organs of a particular mammal at time t. Empirical data indicate that the relative growth rates of these two organs are equal, and hence, we have

$$\frac{1}{x}\frac{dx}{dt} = \frac{1}{y}\frac{dy}{dt}.$$

Solve this differential equation, writing y as a function of x.

Solution:

$$\int \left(\frac{1}{y}\frac{dy}{dt} \right) dt = \int \left(\frac{1}{x}\frac{dx}{dt} \right) dt$$

$$\int \frac{1}{y}\, dy - \int \frac{1}{x}\, dx$$

$$\ln |y| = \ln |x| + C_1 = \ln |Cx|$$

$$y = Cx$$

33. *Investment Growth* A large corporation starts at time $t = 0$ to invest part of its receipts at a rate of P dollars per year in a fund for future corporate expansion. Assume that the fund earns r percent per year compounded continuously. Thus, the rate of growth of the amount A in the fund is given by $dA/dt = rA + P$, where $A = 0$ when $t = 0$. Solve this differential equation for A as a function of t.

Solution:

$$\int \frac{1}{rA + P} \, dA = \int dt$$

$$\frac{1}{r} \ln |rA + P| = t + C_1$$

$$rA + P = Ce^{rt}$$

$$A = \frac{1}{r}(Ce^{rt} - P)$$

Since $A = 0$ when $t = 0$, it follows that $C = P$. Therefore, we have

$$A = \frac{P}{r}(e^{rt} - 1).$$

35. *Investment Growth* Use the result of Exercise 33 to find P if the corporation needs $120,000,000 in 8 years and the fund earns $16\frac{1}{4}\%$ compounded continuously.

Solution:

Since $A = 120,000,000$ when $t = 8$ and $r = 0.1625$, we have

$$P = \frac{(0.1625)(120,000,000)}{e^{(0.1625)(8)} - 1} \approx \$7,305,295.15.$$

37. *Mixture* A medical researcher wants to determine the concentration C (in moles per liter) of a tracer drug injected into a moving fluid. We can start solving this problem by considering a single-compartment dilution model. If the tracer is injected instantaneously at time $t = 0$, then the concentration of the fluid in the compartment begins diluting according to the differential equation $dC/dt = -(R/V)C$, $\quad C = C_0$ when $t = 0$.

(a) Solve this differential equation to find the concentration as a function of time.

(b) Find the limit of C as $t \to \infty$.

Solution:

(a) $\displaystyle \int \frac{dC}{C} = \int -\frac{R}{V} \, dt$

$$\ln |C| = -\frac{R}{V}t + K_1$$

$$C = Ke^{-Rt/V}$$

Since $C = C_0$ when $t = 0$, it follows that $K = C_0$ and the function is $C = C_0 e^{-Rt/V}$.

(b) Finally, as $t \to \infty$, we have $\displaystyle \lim_{t \to \infty} C = \lim_{t \to \infty} C_0 e^{-Rt/V} = 0.$

39. *Mixture* In Exercise 37, we assumed that there was a single initial injection of the trace drug into the compartment. Now let us consider the case in which the tracer is continuously injected (beginning at $t = 0$) at the rate of Q moles per minute. By considering Q to be negligible compared with R, we have the differential equation $dC/dt = (Q/V) - (R/V)C$, $C = 0$ when $t = 0$.

(a) Solve this differential equation to find the concentration as a function of time.

(b) Find the limit of C as $t \to \infty$.

Solution:

(a) $\displaystyle \int \frac{1}{Q - RC}\, dC = \int \frac{1}{V}\, dt$

$\displaystyle -\frac{1}{R} \ln|Q - RC| = \frac{t}{V} + K_1$

$\displaystyle Q - RC = e^{-R[(t/V)+K_1]}$

$\displaystyle C = \frac{1}{R}(Q - e^{-R[(t/V)+K_1]}) = \frac{1}{R}(Q - Ke^{-Rt/V})$

Since $C = 0$ when $t = 0$, it follows that $K = Q$ and we have $C = \dfrac{Q}{R}(1 - e^{-Rt/V})$.

(b) As $t \to \infty$, the limit of C is Q/R.

Chapter D   Review Exercises

1. Verify that $y = 3x^{2/3}$ is a solution of the differential equation $\dfrac{3}{2}xy' - y = 0$.

Solution:

Since $y' = 2x^{-1/3}$, we have

$$\frac{3}{2}xy' - y = \frac{3}{2}x(2x^{-1/3}) - y = 3x^{2/3} - 3x^{2/3} = 0.$$

3. Verify that $y = -(1/3) + Ce^{-3/x}$ is a solution of the differential equation $y' - (3y/x^2) = 1/x^2$.

Solution:

Since $y' = (3/x^2)Ce^{-3/x}$, we have

$$y' - \frac{3y}{x^2} = \frac{3}{x^2}Ce^{-3/x} - \frac{3[-(1/3) + Ce^{-3/x}]}{x^2} = \frac{3}{x^2}Ce^{-3/x} + \frac{1}{x^2} - \frac{3}{x^2}Ce^{-3/x} = \frac{1}{x^2}.$$

5. Verify that $y = C(x - 4)^2$ is a solution of the differential equation $\dfrac{dy}{dx} - \dfrac{2y}{x} = \dfrac{4\,dy}{x\,dx}$.

Solution:

Since $\dfrac{dy}{dx} = 2C(x - 4)$, we have

$$\dfrac{dy}{dx} - \dfrac{2y}{x} = 2C(x - 4) - 2\left(\dfrac{C(x - 4)^2}{x}\right) = 2C(x - 4)\left[1 - \dfrac{x - 4}{x}\right]$$

$$= 2C(x - 4)\left(\dfrac{4}{x}\right) = \dfrac{4\,dy}{x\,dx}.$$

7. Verify that $y = e^{x^3}(x + C)$ is a solution of the differential equation $\dfrac{dy}{dx} - 3x^2 y = e^{x^3}$.

Solution:

Since $\dfrac{dy}{dx} = e^{x^3} + 3x^2(x + C)e^{x^3} = e^{x^3} + 3x^2 y$,

we have $\dfrac{dy}{dx} - 3x^2 y = e^{x^3} + 3x^2 y - 3x^2 y = e^{x^3}$.

9. Verify that the general solution $y = Ce^{-x/5}$ satisfies the given differential equation $5y' + y = 0$. Then find the particular solution that satisfies the initial condition $y = 5$ when $x = 0$.

Solution:

Since $y' = -\dfrac{1}{5}Ce^{-x/5}$, $5y' + y = 5\left(-\dfrac{1}{5}Ce^{-x/5}\right) + Ce^{-x/5} = 0$. To find the particular solution, use $y = 5$ when $x = 0$:

$$5 = Ce^\circ = C$$

Thus, $y = 5e^{-x/5}$.

11. Verify that the general solution $y = \dfrac{1}{2}e^x + Ce^{-x}$ satisfies the given differential equation $y' + y = e^x$. Then find the particular solution that satisfies the initial condition $y = \dfrac{3}{2}$ when $x = 0$

Solution:

Since $y' = \dfrac{1}{2}e^x - Ce^{-x}$, it follows that $y' + y = e^x$. To find the particular solution, use the fact that $y = \dfrac{3}{2}$ when $x = 0$. That is, $\dfrac{3}{2} = \dfrac{1}{2} + C$ which implies $C = 1$. Thus, the particular solution is $y = \dfrac{1}{2}e^x + e^{-x}$.

13. Verify that $y = x^2 + 2x + (C/x)$ satisfies the differential equation $y' + (y/x) = 3x + 4$. Then find the particular solution satisfying the initial condition of $y = 3$ when $x = 1$.

Solution:

Since $y' = 2x + 2 - (C/x^2)$, it follows that $y' + (y/x) = 3x + 4$. To find the particular solution, we use the fact that $y = 3$ when $x = 1$. That is, $3 = 1^2 + 2(1) + (C/1)$ which implies $C = 0$. Thus, the particular solution is $y = x^2 + 2x$.

15. Verify that $y = \dfrac{x^3 - 3x + C}{3(x-1)}$ satisfies the differential equation $(x - 1)y' + y = x^2 - 1$.
Then find the particular solution satisfying the initial condition of $y = 4$ when $x = 2$.

Solution:

Since $y' = \dfrac{3(x-1)(3x^2 - 3) - (x^3 - 3x + C)(3)}{9(x-1)^2} = \dfrac{2x^3 - 3x^2 + 3 - C}{3(x-1)^2}$ it follows that

$$(x - 1)y' + y = \dfrac{2x^3 - 3x^2 + 3 - C}{3(x-1)} + \dfrac{x^3 - 3x + C}{3(x-1)} = \dfrac{3(x^2 - 1)(x-1)}{3(x-1)} = x^2 - 1.$$

To find the particular solution, we use the fact that $y = 4$ when $x = 2$. That is,
$4 = (2 + C)/3$ which implies that $C = 10$. Thus, the particular solution is

$$y = \dfrac{x^3 - 3x + 10}{3(x-1)}.$$

17. *Population Growth* A population of fruit flies is modeled by

$$\dfrac{dy}{dt} = ky.$$

(a) Show that the solution to the differential equation is $y = Ce^{kt}$.

(b) There were 180 fruit flies after 2 days and 300 after 4 days. How many were there after 10 days?

Solution:

(a) $y' = Cke^{kt} = ky$

(b) Let 2 days corrspond to $t = 0$. Then $180 = C$. When $t = 2$ (4 days), $y = 300$:

$$300 = 180e^{2k} \Rightarrow k = \dfrac{1}{2} \ln\left(\dfrac{5}{3}\right).$$

After 10 days, $t = 8$ and

$$y = 180e^{\frac{1}{2} \ln(5/3)(8)} \approx 1389 \text{ flies}.$$

19. Find the general solution of the differential equation $yy' - 3x^2 = 0$.

Solution:

$$y\left(\dfrac{dy}{dx}\right) - 3x^2 = 0$$

$$\int y \, dy = \int 3x^2 \, dx$$

$$\dfrac{y^2}{2} = x^3 + C_1$$

$$y^2 = 2x^3 + C$$

21. Find the general solution of the differential equation $y' = x^2y^2 - 9x^2$.

Solution:

$$\frac{dy}{dx} = x^2(y^2 - 9)$$

$$\int \frac{1}{y^2 - 9} \, dy = \int x^2 \, dx$$

$$\int \left(\frac{1}{y-3} - \frac{1}{y+3} \right) dy = \int 6x^2 \, dx$$

$$\ln|y - 3| - \ln|y + 3| = 2x^3 + C_1$$

$$\frac{y-3}{y+3} = Ce^{2x^3}$$

Solving for y produces $y = \dfrac{3(1 + Ce^{2x^3})}{1 - Ce^{2x^3}}$.

23. Find the general solution of the differential equation $xyy' - (1 + 2y^2 + y^4) = 0$.

Solution:

$$xy\frac{dy}{dx} = 1 + 2y^2 + y^4$$

$$\int \frac{y}{1 + 2y + y^4} \, dy = \int \frac{1}{x} \, dx$$

$$\int \frac{y}{(y^2 + 1)^2} \, dy = \int \frac{1}{x} \, dx$$

$$-\frac{1}{2(y^2 + 1)} = \ln|x| + C$$

$$-1 = 2(y^2 + 1)(\ln|x| + C)$$

$$0 = 2(y^2 + 1)(\ln|x| + C) + 1$$

25. *Chemical Reaction* In a chemical reaction a certain compound changes into another compound at a rate proportional to the unchanged amount according to the model $\frac{dy}{dt} = ky$. (a) Solve the differential equation. (b) If initially there were 20 grams of the original compound and 16 grams after 1 hour, when will 75% of the compound be changed?

Solution:

(a) Let $y =$ amount of compound. Then dy/dt is the rate the compound changes. Since $dy/dt = ky$, we have the following.

$$\int \frac{1}{y} \, dy = \int k \, dt$$

$$\ln |y| = kt + C_1$$

$$y = Ce^{kt}$$

(b) Since $y = 20$ when $t = 0$, it follows that $C = 20$. Thus, we have $y = 20e^{kt}$. Since $y = 16$ when $t = 1$, it follows that $k = \ln \frac{4}{5}$. Thus, the solution is $y = 20e^{[\ln(4/5)]t}$. After 75% has been changed, we have $y = 5$ which implies that $5 = 20e^{[\ln(4/5)]t}$ and solving for t produces

$$t = \frac{\ln(1/4)}{\ln(4/5)} \approx 6.213 \text{ hours.}$$

27. Solve the first-order linear differential equation $\frac{dy}{dx} + 6y = 9$.

Solution:

The integrating factor is $\mu(x) = e^{\int P(x)dx} = e^{6x}$. The solution is

$$y = \frac{1}{u(x)} \int Q(x)u(x)dx = \frac{1}{e^{6x}} \int 9e^{6x}dx \ .$$

$$= \frac{1}{e^{6x}} \left(\frac{3}{2}e^{6x} + C \right)$$

$$= \frac{3}{2} + Ce^{-6x}$$

29. Solve the first-order linear differential equation $\frac{dy}{dx} - xy = 6x$.

Solution:

The integrating factor is $u(x) = e^{\int -xdx} = e^{-x^2/2}$. The solution is

$$y = \frac{1}{e^{-x^2/2}} \int e^{-x^2/2}(6x)dx = e^{x^2/2}(-6e^{-x^2/2} + C)$$

$$= -6 + Ce^{x^2/2}$$

31. Solve the differential equation $\dfrac{dy}{dx} - (3y/x^2) = 1/x^2$.

Solution:

For this linear differential equation, we have $P(x) = -3/x^2$ and $Q(x) = 1/x^2$. Therefore, the integrating factor is

$$u(x) = e^{\int -3/x^2 \, dx} = e^{3/x}$$

and the solution is

$$y = e^{-3/x} \int \frac{1}{x^2} e^{3/x} \, dx = e^{-3/x}\left(-\frac{1}{3}e^{3/x} + C\right) = -\frac{1}{3} + Ce^{-3/x}.$$

33. Solve the differential equation $2xy' - y = x^3 - x$.

Solution:

This linear differential equation

$$y' - \frac{y}{2x} = \frac{x^2}{2} - \frac{1}{2}$$

has $P(x) = -1/(2x)$ and $Q(x) = (x^2/2) - (1/2)$. Therefore, the integrating factor is

$$u(x) = e^{\int -1/(2x) \, dx} = \frac{1}{\sqrt{x}}$$

and the solution is

$$y = \sqrt{x} \int \frac{1}{2}(x^2 - 1)\frac{1}{\sqrt{x}} \, dx$$

$$= \sqrt{x} \int \frac{1}{2}(x^{3/2} - x^{-1/2}) \, dx = \frac{1}{2}\sqrt{x}\left(\frac{2}{5}x^{5/2} - 2x^{1/2} + C_1\right) = \frac{1}{5}x^3 - x + C\sqrt{x}.$$

35. *Investment* Let $A(t)$ be the amount in a fund earning interest at the annual rate of r percent compounded continuously. If a continuous cash flow of P dollars per year is withdrawn from the fund, then the rate of decrease of A is given by the differential equation $dA/dt = rA - P$ where $A = A_0$ when $t = 0$.

(a) Solve this differential equation for A as a function of t.

(b) Use the result of part (a) to find A when $A_0 = \$2,000,000$, $r = 7\%$, $P = \$250,000$ and $t = 5$ years.

(c) Find A_0 if a retired person wants a continuous cash flow of \$40,000 per year for 20 years. Assume that the person's investment will earn 8%, compounded continuously.

Solution:

(a) For this linear differential equation, w have $P(t) = -r$ and $Q(t) = -P$. Therefore, the integrating factor is

$$u(x) = e^{\int -r\,dt} = e^{-rt}$$

and the solution is

$$A = e^{rt}\int - Pe^{-rt}\,dt = e^{rt}\left(\frac{P}{r}e^{-rt} + C\right) = \frac{P}{r} + Ce^{rt}.$$

Since $A = A_0$ when $t = 0$, we have $C = A_0 - (P/r)$ which implies that

$$A = \frac{P}{r} + \left(A_0 - \frac{P}{r}\right)e^{rt}.$$

(b) When $A_0 = \$2,000,000$, $r = 7\%$, $P = \$250,000$ and $t = 5$ years, we have

$$A = \frac{250,000}{0.07} + \left(2,000,000 - \frac{250,000}{0.07}\right)e^{(0.07)(5)} \approx \$1,341,465.28.$$

(c) Since $A = 0$ when $t = 20$, we have $0 = \dfrac{40,000}{0.08} + \left(A_0 - \dfrac{40,000}{0.08}\right)e^{0.08(20)}.$

Solving for A_0 with a graphing utility, we obtain

$$A_0 \approx \$399,051.74.$$

37. *Barometric Pressure* The barometric pressure y (in inches of mercury) at an altitude of x miles above sea level decreases at a rate proportional to the current pressure according to the model

$$\frac{dy}{dx} = -0.2y,$$

where $y = 29.92$ inches when $x = 0$. Find the barometric pressure at the top of Mt. St. Helens (8364 feet) and at the top of Mt. McKinley (20,320 feet).

Solution:

$$\frac{dy}{dx} = -0.2y \Rightarrow \int \frac{dy}{y} = \int -0.2dx$$

$$\ln|y| = -0.2x + C_1$$

$$y = Ce^{-0.2x}$$

Since $y = 29.92$ when $x = 0$, $C = 29.92$.

Mt. St. Helen (8364 feet = 1.584 miles): $y = 21.769$ inches.

Mt. McKinley (20,320 feet = 3.848 miles): $y = 13.859$ inches.

39. *Population Growth* The rate of growth in the number N of chickens on a poultry farm varies at a rate directly proportional to N and $(L - N)$, where L is the limiting size of the flock.

(a) Write a differential equation to model the situation.

(b) Suppose a farm had 500 chickens when $t = 0$ and 1000 chickens when $t = 4$. If $L = 5000$, how large will the flock be when $t = 8$?

Solution:

(a) $\dfrac{dN}{dt} = kN(L - N)$

(b) The general solution to this logistics equation is obtained as follows:

$$\int \frac{dN}{N(L - N)} = \int k \, dt$$

$$\int \left(\frac{\frac{1}{L}}{N} + \frac{\frac{1}{L}}{L - N} \right) dN = \int k \, dt$$

$$\frac{1}{L} \ln \left(\frac{N}{L - N} \right) = kt + C_1$$

$$Ce^{Lkt} = \frac{N}{L - N}$$

$$LCe^{Lkt} - NCe^{Lkt} = N$$

$$N = \frac{LCe^{Lkt}}{1 + Ce^{Lkt}} = \frac{L}{1 + \frac{1}{C}e^{-Lkt}}$$

$$L = 5000 \text{ and } 500 = \frac{5000}{1 + \frac{1}{C}} \Rightarrow 1 + \frac{1}{C} = 10 \ .$$

$$\Rightarrow C = \frac{1}{9}$$

Hence $N = \dfrac{5000}{1 + 9e^{-5000kt}}$.

Since $N = 1000$ when $t = 4$, we obtain $k = 4.05465 \times 10^{-5}$ and

$$N = \frac{5000}{1 + 9e^{-0.2027t}}.$$

When $t = 8$, $N \approx 1800$ chickens.

Practice Test for Chapter D

1. Verify that $y = x^3 - 4x + \dfrac{C}{x}$ is a solution of $xy' + y = 4x(x^2 - 2)$.

2. Verify that $y = Ce^{-5x}$ is a solution of $y''' + 125y = 0$.

3. Find the general solution of $y^3 y' = x + 2$.

4. Find the general solution of $y' = \dfrac{y+4}{x-1}$.

5. Find the general solution of $y' \ln y = xe^x$.

6. Find the general solution of $y' + 4y = e^{-2x}$.

7. Find the general solution of $x^3 y' + 2y = e^{1/x^2}$.

8. Find the general solution of $xy' - 4y = 6x^2 - 1$.

9. Assume that the rate of change of y (with respect to time t) is proportional to $(30 - y)$. Find the particular solution that passes through the points $(0, 4)$ and $(6, 11)$.

10. Use the Gompertz growth model
$$\frac{dy}{dt} = ky \ln \frac{1000}{y}$$
to find the growth function given $y = 50$ when $t = 0$ and $y = 200$ when $t = 4$.

Graphing Calculator Required

11. Find the general solution of $\dfrac{1}{y}\dfrac{dy}{dx} = 3x^2$ and use a graphing utility to sketch several solutions.

12. Using a TI-85 or similar calculator in the differential equation mode, graph several solutions to $Q'(t) = -\dfrac{t}{Q}$ by using different initial conditions.

CHAPTER S
Series and Taylor Polynomials

Section S.1   Sequences

1. Write the first five terms of $\{2^n\}$.

   Solution:

   2, 4, 8, 16, 32

3. Write the first five terms of $\left\{\left(-\dfrac{1}{2}\right)^n\right\}$.

   Solution:

   $-\dfrac{1}{2},\ \dfrac{1}{4},\ -\dfrac{1}{8},\ \dfrac{1}{16},\ -\dfrac{1}{32}$

5. Write the first five terms of $\left\{\dfrac{3^n}{n!}\right\}$.

   Solution:

   $3,\ \dfrac{9}{2},\ \dfrac{27}{6},\ \dfrac{81}{24},\ \dfrac{243}{120}$

7. Write the first five terms of $\left\{\dfrac{(-1)^n}{n^2}\right\}$.

   Solution:

   $-1,\ \dfrac{1}{4},\ -\dfrac{1}{9},\ \dfrac{1}{16},\ -\dfrac{1}{25}$

9. Determine the convergence or divergence of $a_n = 5/n$. If the sequence converges, find its limit.

   Solution:

   This sequence converges since $\displaystyle\lim_{n\to\infty}\dfrac{5}{n} = 0$.

11. Determine the convergence or divergence of the following. If the sequence converges, find its limit.

$$a_n = \frac{n+1}{n}$$

Solution:

This sequence converges since $\lim_{n \to \infty} \frac{n+1}{n} = 1$.

13. Determine the convergence or divergence of the following. If the sequence converges, find its limit.

$$a_n = \frac{n^2 + 3n - 4}{2n^2 + n - 3}$$

Solution:

This sequence converges since $\lim_{n \to \infty} = \frac{n^2 + 3n - 4}{2n^2 + n - 3} = \frac{1}{2}$.

15. Determine the convergence or divergence of the following. If the sequence converges, find its limit.

$$a_n = \frac{n^2 - 25}{n + 25}$$

Solution:

This sequence diverges since $\lim_{n \to \infty} \frac{n^2 - 25}{n + 25} = \frac{\lim_{n \to \infty}}{n} - 5) = \infty$.

17. Determine the convergence or divergence of the following. If the sequence converges, find its limit.

$$a_n = \frac{1 + (-1)^n}{n}$$

Solution:

This sequence converges since $\lim_{n \to \infty} \frac{1 + (-1)^n}{n} = 0$.

19. Determine the convergence or divergence of the following. If the sequence converges, find its limit.

$$a_n = 3 - \frac{1}{2^n}$$

Solution:

This sequence converges since $\lim_{n \to \infty} \left(3 - \frac{1}{2^n} \right) = 3$.

21. Determine the convergence or divergence of the following. If the sequence converges, find its limit.

$$a_n = \frac{3^n}{4^n}$$

Solution:

This sequence converges since $\lim\limits_{n\to\infty} \dfrac{3^n}{4^n} = \lim\limits_{n\to\infty} \left(\dfrac{3}{4}\right)^n = 0$.

23. Determine the convergence or divergence of the following. If the sequence converges, find its limit.

$$a_n = \frac{(n+1)!}{n!}$$

Solution:

This sequence diverges since $\lim\limits_{n\to\infty} \dfrac{(n+1)!}{n!} = \lim\limits_{n\to\infty} \dfrac{(n+1)n!}{n!} = \lim\limits_{n\to\infty} (n+1) = \infty$.

25. Determine the convergence or divergence of the following. If the sequence converges, find its limit.

$$a_n = (-1)^n \frac{n}{n+1}$$

Solution:

This sequence diverges since $\lim\limits_{n\to\infty} (-1)^n \dfrac{n}{n+1}$ does not exist.

27. Use the graph of the sequence in the textbook to decide whether the sequence converges. Then verify your result analytically.

Solution:

The sequence $a_n = (-1)^n + 2$ oscillates between 1 and 3. Hence, $\lim\limits_{n\to\infty} a_n$ does not exist.

29. Write an expression for the nth term of the sequence $1, 4, 7, 10, \ldots$.

Solution:

$$a_n = 3n - 2$$

31. Write an expression for the nth term of the sequence $-1, 4, 9, 14, \ldots$.

Solution:

$$a_n = 5n - 6$$

33. Write an expression for the n term of the sequence $\frac{2}{3}, \frac{3}{4}, \frac{4}{5}, \frac{5}{6}, \ldots$.

Solution:

$$a_n = \frac{n+1}{n+2}$$

35. Write an expression for the nth term of the sequence $2, -1, \frac{1}{2}, -\frac{1}{4}, \frac{1}{8}, \ldots$.

Solution:

$$a_n = \frac{(-1)^{n-1}}{2^{n-2}}$$

37. Write an expression for the nth term of the sequence $2, 1+\frac{1}{2}, 1+\frac{1}{3}, 1+\frac{1}{4}, \ldots$.

Solution:

$$a_n = 1 + \frac{1}{n} = \frac{n+1}{n}$$

39. Write an expression for the nth term of the sequence $-2, 2, -2, 2, \ldots$.

Solution:

$$a_n = 2(-1)^n$$

41. Write an expression for the nth term of the sequence $1, \frac{1}{2}, \frac{1}{6}, \frac{1}{24}, \frac{1}{120}, \ldots$.

Solution:

$$a_n = \frac{1}{n!}$$

43. Write the next two terms of the arithmetic sequence $2, 5, 8, 11, \ldots$.

Solution:

Since $a_n = 3n - 1$, the next two terms are $a_5 = 14$ and $a_6 = 17$.

45. Write the next two terms of the arithmetic sequence $1, \frac{5}{3}, \frac{7}{3}, 3, \ldots$.

Solution:

Since $a_n = \frac{1}{3} + \frac{2n}{3}$, we have $a_s = \frac{11}{3}$ and $a_6 = \frac{13}{3}$.

47. Write the next two terms of the geometric sequence $3, -\frac{3}{2}, \frac{3}{4}, -\frac{3}{8}, \ldots$.

Solution:

Since $a_n = 3\left(-\frac{1}{2}\right)^{n-1}$, the next two terms are $a_5 = \frac{3}{16}$ and $a_6 = -\frac{3}{32}$.

49. Write the next two terms of the geometric sequence $2, 6, 18, 54, \ldots$.

Solution:

Since $a_n = 2(3^{n-1})$, the next two terms are 162 and 486.

51. Determine whether the sequence $20, 10, 5, \frac{5}{2}, \ldots$ is arithmetic or geometric.

Solution:

Since $a_n = 20 \left(\frac{1}{2}\right)^{n-1}$, the sequence is geometric.

53. Determine whether the sequence $\frac{8}{3}, \frac{10}{3}, 4, \frac{14}{3}, \ldots$ is arithmetic or geometric.

Solution:

Since $a_n = \frac{2}{3}n + 2$, the sequence is arithmetic.

55. Give an example of a sequence satisfying the given condition:

A sequence that converges to $\frac{3}{4}$. (There is more than one correct answer.)

Solution:

One example is $a_n = \dfrac{3n+1}{4n}$.

57. *Compound Interest* Consider the sequence $\{A_n\}$, whose nth term is given by $A_n = P[1 + (r/12)]^n$, where P is the principal, A_n is the amount at compound interest after n months, and r is the annual percentage rate. Find the first ten terms of the sequence for $P = \$9000$ and $r = 0.06$.

Solution:

$$A_n = P[1 + (5/12)]^n = 9000\left[1 + \frac{0.06}{12}\right]^n = 9000[1.005]^n.$$ The first 10 terms are

9045.00, 9090.23, 9135.68, 9181.35, 9227.26, 9273.40, 9319.76,

9366.36, 9413.20, 9460.26

59. *Individual Retirement Account* A deposit of \$2000 is made each year in an account that earns 11% interest compounded annually. The balance after n years is given by $A_n = 2000(11)[(1.1)^n - 1]$.

(a) Compute the first six terms of the sequence.

(b) Find the balance after 20 years by finding the twentieth term of the sequence.

(c) Find the balance after 40 years by finding the fortieth term of the sequence.

Solution:

(a) $A_n = 2000(11)[(1.1)^n - 1]$

$A_1 = \$2200$

$A_2 = \$4620$

$A_3 = \$7282$

$A_4 = \$10,210.20$

$A_5 = \$13,431.22$

$A_6 \approx \$16,974.34$

(b) $A_{20} \approx \$126,005.00$

(c) $A_{40} \approx \$973,703.62$

61. *Hospital Costs* The average cost per day for a semiprivate hospital room from 1980 to 1990 is approximated by the model

$$a_n = 127.42 + 17.37n, \qquad n = 0, 1, 2, \ldots, 10,$$

where a_n is the average cost in dollars and n is the year with $n = 0$ corrsponding to 1980. Find the terms of this finite sequence and construct a bar graph that represents the sequence. Use the model to predict the cost in 1995.

Solution:

1980: $a_0 = 127.42$

1981: $a_1 = 144.79$

1982: $a_2 = 162.16$

1983: $a_3 = 179.53$

1984: $a_4 = 196.90$

1985: $a_5 = 214.27$

1986: $a_6 = 231.27$

1987: $a_7 = 249.01$

1988: $a_8 = 266.38$

1989: $a_9 = 283.75$

1990: $a_{10} = 301.12$

In 1995, $a_{15} = \$387.97$

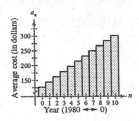

63. *Investment* A deposit of $100 is made each month in an account that earns 6% interest compounded monthly. The balance in the account after n months is given by

$A_n = 100(201)[(1.005)^n - 1]$.

(a) Compute the first six terms of this sequence.

(b) Find the balance after 5 years by computing the 60th term of the sequence.

(c) Find the balance after 20 years by computing the 240th term of the sequence.

Solution:

$A_n = 100(201)[(1.005)^n - 1]$

(a) $A_1 = \$100.50$

$A_2 = \$201.50$

$A_3 \approx \$303.01$

$A_4 \approx \$405.03$

$A_5 \approx \$507.55$

$A_6 \approx \$610.59$

(b) $A_{60} \approx \$7011./89$

(c) $A_{240} \approx \$46,435.11$

65. The sum of the squares of the first n positive integers is given by

$$S_n = \frac{n(n+1)(2n+1)}{6}, \qquad n = 1, 2, 3, \ldots$$

(a) Compute the first five terms of the sequence and verify that each term gives the correct sum.

(b) Find the sum of the squares of the first 20 positive integers.

Solution:

(a) $S_1 = 1 = 1^2$

$S_2 = 5 = 1^2 + 2^2$

$S_3 = 14 = 1^2 + 2^2 + 3^2$

$S_4 = 30 = 1^2 + 2^2 + 3^2 + 4^2$

$S_5 = 55 = 1^2 + 2^2 + 3^2 + 4^2 + 5^2$

(b) $S_{20} = 2870$

67. *Governmental Expenditures* A government program that currently costs taxpayers \$1.3 billion per year is to be cut back by 15% per year.

(a) Write an expression for the amount budgeted for this program after n years.

(b) Compute the budget amounts for the first four years.

(c) Determine the convergence or divergence of the sequence of reduced budgets. If the sequence converges, find its limit.

Solution:

(a) $A_1 = 1.3 - 0.15(1.3) = 1.3(0.85)$

$A_2 = A_1 - 0.15A_1 = 0.85A_1 = 1.3(0.85)^2$

$A_3 = 1.3(0.85)^3$

$\vdots$

$A_n = 1.3(0.85)^n$

(b) $A_1 = \$1.105$ billion

$A_2 = \$0.939$ billion

$A_3 = \$0.798$ billion

$A_4 = \$0.679$ billion

(c) The sequence converges to 0 : $\lim\limits_{n \to \infty} 1.3(0.85)^n = 0.$

69. Consider the sequence whose nth term a_n is given by

$$a_n = \left(1 + \frac{1}{n}\right)^n.$$

Demonstrate that the terms of this sequence approach e by finding a_1, a_{10}, a_{100}, a_{1000}, and $a_{10,000}$.

Solution:

$$a_n = \left(1 + \frac{1}{n}\right)^n$$

$a_1 = 2$

$a_{10} \approx 2.593742460$

$a_{100} \approx 2.704813829$

$a_{1000} \approx 2.716923932$

$a_{10000} \approx 2.718145927$

Note: $e \approx 2.718281828$

71. *Job Offer* A person accepts a position with a company at a salary of \$32,800 for the first year. The person is guaranteed a raise of 5% per year for the first four years. Determine the person's salary during the fourth year of employment.

Solution:

Year 1: \$32,800

Year 2: $(1.05)(32,800) = \$34,440$

Year 3: $(1.05)(34,400) = \$36,162$

Year 4: $(1.05)(36,162) = \$37,970.10$

Section S.2   Series and Convergence

1. Find the first five terms of $\displaystyle\sum_{n=1}^{\infty} \frac{1}{n^2} = 1 + \frac{1}{4} + \frac{1}{9} + \frac{1}{16} + \frac{1}{25} + \cdots .$

Solution:

$$S_1 = 1$$

$$S_2 = \frac{5}{4} = 1.25$$

$$S_3 = \frac{49}{36} \approx 1.361$$

$$S_4 = \frac{205}{144} \approx 1.424$$

$$S_5 = \frac{5269}{3600} \approx 1.464$$

3. Find the first five terms of $\displaystyle\sum_{n=1}^{\infty} \frac{3}{2^{n-1}} = 3 + \frac{3}{2} + \frac{3}{4} + \frac{3}{8} + \frac{3}{16} + \cdots .$

Solution:

$$S_1 = 3$$

$$S_2 = \frac{9}{2} = 4.5$$

$$S_3 = \frac{21}{4} = 5.25$$

$$S_4 = \frac{45}{8} = 5.625$$

$$S_5 = \frac{93}{16} = 5.8125$$

5. Verify that the following infinite series diverges.

$$\sum_{n=1}^{\infty} \frac{n}{n+1} = \frac{1}{2} + \frac{2}{3} + \frac{3}{4} + \frac{4}{5} + \cdots$$

Solution:

This series diverges by the nth-Term Test since $\lim\limits_{n\to\infty} \dfrac{n}{n+1} = 1 \neq 0$.

7. Verify that the following infinite series diverges.

$$\sum_{n=1}^{\infty} \frac{n^2}{n^2+1} = \frac{1}{2} + \frac{4}{5} + \frac{9}{10} + \frac{16}{17} + \cdots$$

Solution:

This series diverges by the nth-Term Test since $\lim\limits_{n\to\infty} \dfrac{n^2}{n^2+1} = 1 \neq 0$.

9. Verify that the following infinite series diverges.

$$\sum_{n=0}^{\infty} 3\left(\frac{3}{2}\right)^n = 3 + \frac{9}{2} + \frac{27}{4} + \frac{81}{8} + \cdots$$

Solution:

This series diverges by the Test for Convergence of a Geometric Series since $|r| = |\frac{3}{2}| > 1$.

11. Verify that the following infinite series diverges.

$$\sum_{n=0}^{\infty} 1000(1.055)^n = 1000 + 1055 + 1113.025 + \cdots$$

Solution:

This series diverges by the Test for Convergence of a Geometric Series since $|r| = |1.055| > 1$.

13. Verify that the following geometric series converges.

$$\sum_{n=0}^{\infty} 2\left(\frac{3}{4}\right)^n = 2 + \frac{3}{2} + \frac{9}{8} + \frac{27}{32} + \frac{81}{128} + \cdots$$

Solution:

This series converges by the Test for Convergence of a Geometric Series since $|r| = |\frac{3}{4}| < 1$.

15. Verify that the following geometric series converges.

$$\sum_{n=0}^{\infty} (0.9)^n = 1 + 0.9 + 0.81 + 0.729 + \cdots$$

Solution:

This series converges by the Test for Convergence of a Geometric Series since $|r| = |0.9| < 1$.

17. Find the sum of $\displaystyle\sum_{n=0}^{\infty} \left(\frac{1}{2}\right)^n = 1 + \frac{1}{2} + \frac{1}{4} + \frac{1}{8} + \cdots$.

Solution:

Since $a = 1$ and $r = \dfrac{1}{2}$, we have $S = \dfrac{1}{1-(1/2)} = 2$.

19. Find the sum of $\displaystyle\sum_{n=0}^{\infty} \left(-\frac{1}{2}\right)^n = 1 - \frac{1}{2} + \frac{1}{4} - \frac{1}{8} + \cdots$.

Solution:

Since $a = 1$ and $r = -\dfrac{1}{2}$, we have $S = \dfrac{1}{1+(1/2)} = \dfrac{2}{3}$.

21. Find the sum of $\displaystyle\sum_{n=0}^{\infty} 2\left(\frac{1}{\sqrt{2}}\right)^n = 2 + \sqrt{2} + 1 + \frac{1}{\sqrt{2}} + \cdots$.

Solution:

Since $a = 2$ and $r = \dfrac{1}{\sqrt{2}}$, we have

$$S = \frac{2}{1-(1/\sqrt{2})} = \frac{2\sqrt{2}}{\sqrt{2}-1}\left(\frac{\sqrt{2}+1}{\sqrt{2}+1}\right) = 4 + 2\sqrt{2} \approx 6.828.$$

23. Find the sum of $1 + 0.1 + 0.01 + 0.001 + \cdots$.

Solution:

Since $a = 1$ and $r = 0.1$, we have $S = \dfrac{1}{1-0.1} = \dfrac{1}{0.9} = \dfrac{10}{9}$.

25. Find the sum of $2 - \frac{2}{3} + \frac{2}{9} - \frac{2}{27} + \cdots$.

Solution:

Since $a = 2$ and $r = -\dfrac{1}{3}$, we have $S = \dfrac{2}{1+(1/3)} = \dfrac{3}{2}$.

27. Find the sum of $\displaystyle\sum_{n=0}^{\infty} \left(\frac{1}{2^n} - \frac{1}{3^n}\right)$.

Solution:

$$\sum_{n=0}^{\infty} \left(\frac{1}{2^n} - \frac{1}{3^n}\right) = \sum_{n=0}^{\infty} \left(\frac{1}{2}\right)^n - \sum_{n=0}^{\infty} \left(\frac{1}{3}\right)^n = \frac{1}{1 - (1/2)} - \frac{1}{1 - (1/3)} = 2 - \frac{3}{2} = \frac{1}{2}$$

29. Find the sum of $\displaystyle\sum_{n=0}^{\infty} \left(\frac{1}{3^n} + \frac{1}{4^n}\right)$.

Solution:

$$\sum_{n=0}^{\infty} \left(\frac{1}{3^n} + \frac{1}{4^n}\right) = \sum_{n=0}^{\infty} \left(\frac{1}{3}\right)^n + \sum_{n=0}^{\infty} \left(\frac{1}{4}\right)^n = \frac{1}{1 - (1/3)} + \frac{1}{1 - (1/4)} = \frac{3}{2} + \frac{4}{3} = \frac{17}{6}$$

31. Determine the convergence or divergence of $\displaystyle\sum_{n=1}^{\infty} \frac{n + 10}{10n + 1}$.

Solution:

This series diverges by the nth-Term Test since $\displaystyle\lim_{n\to\infty} \frac{n + 10}{10n + 1} = \frac{1}{10} \neq 0$.

33. Determine the convergence or divergence of $\displaystyle\sum_{n=1}^{\infty} \frac{n! + 1}{n!}$.

Solution:

This series diverges by the nth-Term Test since $\displaystyle\lim_{n\to\infty} \frac{n! + 1}{n!} = 1 \neq 0$.

35. Determine the convergence or divergence of $\displaystyle\sum_{n=1}^{\infty} \frac{3n - 1}{2n + 1}$.

Solution:

This series diverges by the nth-Term Test since $\displaystyle\lim_{n\to\infty} \frac{3n - 1}{2n + 1} = \frac{3}{2} \neq 0$.

37. Determine the convergence or divergence of $\displaystyle\sum_{n=0}^{\infty} (1.075)^n$.

Solution:

This series diverges by the Test for Convergence of a Geometric Series since $r = 1.075 > 1$.

39. Determine the convergence or divergence of $\displaystyle\sum_{n=0}^{\infty} \frac{3}{4^n}$.

Solution:

This series converges by the Test for Convergence of a Geometric Series since $r = \dfrac{1}{4} < 1$.

41. Find the sum of the geometric series given by the following.

$$0.66\overline{6} = 0.6 + 0.06 + 0.006 + 0.0006 + \cdots$$

Solution:

$$0.66\overline{6} = \sum_{n=0}^{\infty} 0.6(0.1)^n = \frac{0.6}{1 - 0.1} = \frac{0.6}{0.9} = \frac{2}{3}$$

43. Find the sum of the geometric series given by the following.

$$0.81\overline{81} = 0.81 + 0.0081 + 0.000081 + \cdots$$

Solution:

$$0.81\overline{81} = \sum_{n=o}^{\infty} 0.81(0.01)^n$$

$$= \frac{0.81}{1 - 0.01} = \frac{0.81}{0.99} = \frac{9}{11}$$

45. *Sales* A company produces a new product for which it estimates the annual sales to be 8000 units. Suppose that in any given year, 10% of the units (regardless of age) will become inoperative. (a) How many units will be in use after n years? (b) Find the market stabilization level of the product.

Solution:

(a) $\displaystyle\sum_{i=0}^{n-1} 8000(0.9)^i = \frac{8000[1 - (0.9)^{(n-1)+1}]}{1 - 0.9}$ (b) $\displaystyle\sum_{i=0}^{\infty} 8000(0.9)^i = \frac{8000}{1 - 0.9} = 80{,}000$

$$= 80{,}000(1 - 0.9^n)$$

47. *Bouncing Ball* A ball is dropped from a height of 16 feet. Each time it drops h feet, it rebounds $0.64h$ feet. Find the total distance traveled by the ball.

Solution:

$$D_1 = 16$$

$$D_2 = 0.64(16) + 0.64(16) = 32(0.64)$$

$$D_3 = 32(0.64)^2$$

$$\vdots$$

$$D = -16 + \sum_{n=0}^{\infty} 32(0.64)^n = -16 + \frac{32}{1 - 0.64}$$

$$= -16 + \frac{32}{0.36} = \frac{2624}{36} \approx 72.89 \text{ feet}$$

49. *Annuity* A deposit of $100 is made at the beginning of each month for 5 years into an account that pays 10% interest compounded monthly. What is the balance A in the account at the end of the 5 years?

$$A = 100\left(1 + \frac{0.10}{12}\right) + \cdots + 100\left(1 + \frac{0.10}{12}\right)^{60}$$

Solution:

$$A = \sum_{n=1}^{60} 100\left(1 + \frac{0.10}{12}\right)^n$$

$$= -100 + \sum_{n=0}^{60} 100\left(1 + \frac{0.10}{12}\right)^n$$

$$= -100 + \frac{100\left[1 - \left(1 + \frac{0.10}{12}\right)^{61}\right]}{1 - \left(1 + \frac{0.10}{12}\right)}$$

$$\approx \$7808.24$$

51. *Multiplier Effect* The annual spending by tourists in a resort city is 100 million dollars. Approximately 75% of that revenue is again spent in the resort city, and of that amount approximately 75% is again spent in the resort city. If this pattern continues, write the geometric series that gives the total amount of spending generated by the 100 million dollars and find the sum of the series.

Solution:

$$A = \sum_{n=0}^{\infty} 100(0.75)^n = \frac{100}{1 - 0.75} = \$400 \text{ million}$$

53. *Wages* Suppose that an employer offered to pay you 1 cent the first day, and then double your wages each day thereafter. Find your total wages for working 20 days.

Solution:

$$A = \sum_{n=0}^{19} 0.01(2)^n = \frac{0.01(1 - 2^{20})}{1 - 2} = \$10,485.75$$

55. *Probability* Use a symbolic algebra utility to estimate the number of tosses required until the first head occurs in the experiment in Exercise 54 in the textbook.

Solution:

$$\sum_{n=1}^{\infty} n \left(\tfrac{1}{2}\right)^n = \tfrac{1}{2} + 2\left(\tfrac{1}{4}\right) + 3\left(\tfrac{1}{8}\right) + 4\left(\tfrac{1}{16}\right) + 5\left(\tfrac{1}{32}\right) + 6\left(\tfrac{1}{64}\right) + \cdots$$

$$= \tfrac{1}{2} + \tfrac{1}{2} + \tfrac{3}{8} + \tfrac{1}{4} + \tfrac{5}{32} + \tfrac{3}{32} + \cdots \approx 2$$

57. Use a symbolic algebra utility to evaluate the summation $\sum_{n=1}^{\infty} n^2 \left(\dfrac{1}{2}\right)^n$

Solution:

$$\sum_{n=1}^{\infty} n^2 \left(\frac{1}{2}\right)^n = 6$$

59. Use a symbolic algebra utility to evaluate the summation $\sum_{n=1}^{\infty} \dfrac{n!}{(n!)^2}$

Solution:

$$\sum_{n=1}^{\infty} \frac{n!}{(n!)^2} = \sum_{n=1}^{\infty} \frac{1}{n!} = e - 1 \approx 1.7183$$

61. Use a symbolic algebra utility to evaluate the summation $\sum_{n=1}^{\infty} e^2 \left(\dfrac{1}{e}\right)^n$

Solution:

$$\sum_{n=1}^{\infty} e^2 \left(\frac{1}{e}\right)^n = \frac{e^2}{3 - 1} \approx 4.3003$$

Section S.3   p-Series and the Ratio Test

1. Determine whether the series $\sum_{n=1}^{\infty} \dfrac{1}{n^2}$ is a *p*-series.

Solution:

The series $\sum_{n=1}^{\infty} \dfrac{1}{n^2}$ is a *p*-series with $p = 2$.

3. Determine whether the series $\displaystyle\sum_{n=1}^{\infty} \frac{1}{3^n}$ is a p-series.

Solution:

The series

$$\sum_{n=1}^{\infty} \frac{1}{3^n} = \sum_{n=0}^{\infty} \frac{1}{3}\left(\frac{1}{3}\right)^n$$

is *not* a p-series. This series is geometric with $r = \frac{1}{3}$.

5. Determine whether the series $\displaystyle\sum_{n=1}^{\infty} \frac{1}{n^n}$ is a p-series.

Solution:

The series

$$\sum_{n=1}^{\infty} \frac{1}{n^n} = 1 + \frac{1}{2^2} + \frac{1}{3^3} + \frac{1}{4^4} + \cdots$$

is *not* a p-series. The exponent changes with each term.

7. Determine the convergence or divergence of the p-series $\displaystyle\sum_{n=1}^{\infty} \frac{1}{n^3}$.

Solution:

This series converges since $p = 3 > 1$.

9. Determine the convergence or divergence of the p-series $\displaystyle\sum_{n=1}^{\infty} \frac{1}{\sqrt[3]{n}}$.

Solution:

This series diverges since $p = \frac{1}{3} < 1$.

11. Determine the convergence or divergence of the p-series $\displaystyle\sum_{n=1}^{\infty} \frac{1}{n^{1.03}}$.

Solution:

This series converges since $p = 1.03 > 1$.

13. Determine the convergence or divergence of the following p-series.

$$1 + \frac{1}{\sqrt{2}} + \frac{1}{\sqrt{3}} + \frac{1}{\sqrt{4}} + \cdots$$

Solution:

$$1 + \frac{1}{\sqrt{2}} + \frac{1}{\sqrt{3}} + \frac{1}{\sqrt{4}} + \cdots = \sum_{n=1}^{\infty} \frac{1}{\sqrt{n}} = \sum_{n=1}^{\infty} \frac{1}{n^{1/2}}$$

Therefore, this series diverges since $p = \frac{1}{2} < 1$.

15. Determine the convergence or divergence of the following p-series.

$$1 + \frac{1}{2\sqrt{2}} + \frac{1}{3\sqrt{3}} + \frac{1}{4\sqrt{4}} + \cdots$$

Solution:

$$1 + \frac{1}{2\sqrt{2}} + \frac{1}{3\sqrt{3}} + \frac{1}{4\sqrt{4}} + \cdots = \sum_{n=1}^{\infty} \frac{1}{n^{3/2}}$$

Therefore, the series converges since $p = \frac{3}{2} > 1$.

17. Use the Ratio Test to determine the convergence or divergence of $\displaystyle\sum_{n=0}^{\infty} \frac{3^n}{n!}$.

Solution:

Since $a_n = 3^n/n!$, we have

$$\lim_{n \to \infty} \left| \frac{a_{n+1}}{a_n} \right| = \lim_{n \to \infty} \left| \frac{3^{n+1}}{(n+1)!} \cdot \frac{n!}{3^n} \right| = \lim_{n \to \infty} \frac{3}{n+1} = 0$$

and the series converges.

19. Use the Ratio Test to determine the convergence or divergence of $\displaystyle\sum_{n=0}^{\infty} \frac{n!}{3^n}$.

Solution:

Since $a_n = n!/3^n$, we have

$$\lim_{n \to \infty} \left| \frac{a_{n+1}}{a_n} \right| = \lim_{n \to \infty} \left| \frac{(n+1)!}{3^{n+1}} \cdot \frac{3^n}{n!} \right| = \lim_{n \to \infty} \frac{n+1}{3} = \infty$$

and the series diverges.

21. Use the Ratio Test to determine the convergence or divergence of $\displaystyle\sum_{n=1}^{\infty} \frac{n}{4^n}$.

Solution:

Since $a_n = n/4^n$, we have

$$\lim_{n\to\infty} \left| \frac{a_{n+1}}{a^n} \right| = \lim_{n\to\infty} \left| \frac{n+1}{4^{n+1}} \cdot \frac{4^n}{n} \right| = \lim_{n\to\infty} \frac{n+1}{4n} = \frac{1}{4}$$

and the series converges.

23. Use the Ratio Test to determine the convergence or divergence of $\displaystyle\sum_{n=1}^{\infty} \frac{2^n}{n^5}$.

Solution:

Since $a_n = 2^n/n^5$, we have

$$\lim_{n\to\infty} \left| \frac{a_{n+1}}{a_n} \right| = \lim_{n\to\infty} \left| \frac{2^{n+1}}{(n+1)^5} \cdot \frac{n^5}{2^n} \right| = \lim_{n\to\infty} \frac{2n^5}{(n+1)^5} = 2$$

and the series diverges.

25. Use the Ratio Test to determine the convergence or divergence of $\displaystyle\sum_{n=0}^{\infty} \frac{(-1)^n 2^n}{n!}$.

Solution:

Since $a_n = [(-1)^n 2^n]/n!$, we have

$$\lim_{n\to\infty} \left| \frac{a_{n+1}}{a_n} \right| = \lim_{n\to\infty} \left| \frac{(-1)^{n+1} 2^{n+1}}{(n+1)!} \cdot \frac{n!}{(-1)^n 2^n} \right| = \lim_{n\to\infty} \left| \frac{-2}{n+1} \right| = 0$$

and the series converges.

27. Use the Ratio Test to determine the convergence or divergence of $\displaystyle\sum_{n=0}^{\infty} \frac{4^n}{3^n + 1}$.

Solution:

Since $a_n = \dfrac{4^n}{3^n + 1}$, we have

$$\lim_{n\to\infty} \left| \frac{a_{n+1}}{a_n} \right| = \lim_{n\to\infty} \left| \frac{4^{n+1}}{3^{n+1} + 1} \cdot \frac{3^n + 1}{4^n} \right| = \frac{4}{3} > 1$$

and the series diverges.

29. Use the Ratio Text to determine the convergence or divergence of $\displaystyle\sum_{n=0}^{\infty} \frac{n5^n}{n!}$.

Solution:

Since $a_n = \dfrac{n5^n}{n!}$, we have

$$\lim_{n\to\infty}\left|\frac{a_{n+1}}{a_n}\right| = \lim_{n\to\infty}\left|\frac{(n+1)5^{n+1}}{(n+1)!}\cdot\frac{n!}{n5^n}\right| = \lim_{n\to\infty}\left|\frac{5}{n}\right| = 0 < 1$$

and the series converges.

31. Approximate the sum of $\displaystyle\sum_{n=1}^{\infty} \frac{1}{n^3}$ using four terms. Estimate the maximum error of your approximation.

Solution:

$$\sum_{n=1}^{\infty}\frac{1}{n^3} \approx \frac{1}{1} + \frac{1}{2^3} + \frac{1}{3^3} + \frac{1}{4^3} = \frac{2035}{1728} \approx 1.1777$$

The error is less than $\dfrac{1}{(p-1)N^{p-1}} = \dfrac{1}{(3-1)4^{3-1}} = \dfrac{1}{32}.$

33. Using ten terms, approximate the sum of the following convergent series. Include an estimate of the maximum error for your approximation.

$$\sum_{n=1}^{\infty} \frac{1}{n^{3/2}}$$

Solution:

$$\sum_{n=1}^{\infty}\frac{1}{n^{3/2}} \approx 1 + \frac{1}{2\sqrt{2}} + \frac{1}{3\sqrt{3}} + \cdots + \frac{1}{10\sqrt{10}} \approx 1.995.$$

The error is less than

$$\frac{1}{(p-1)N^{p-1}} = \frac{1}{(\frac{3}{2}-1)10^{(\frac{3}{2}-1)}}$$

$$= \frac{2}{\sqrt{10}}$$

$$\approx 0.6325$$

35. Verify that the Ratio Test is inconclusive for the p-series.

$$\sum_{n=1}^{\infty} \frac{1}{n^{3/2}}$$

Solution:

$$\lim_{n\to\infty} \left| \frac{a_{n+1}}{A_n} \right| = \lim_{n\to\infty} \frac{\frac{1}{(n+1)^{3/2}}}{\frac{1}{n^{3/2}}} = \lim_{n\to\infty} \left(\frac{n}{n+1} \right)^{3/2} = 1,$$

and the ratio test is inconclusive. (The series is a convergent p-series).

37. Test for convergence or divergence using any appropriate test from this chapter.

$$\sum_{n=1}^{\infty} \frac{2n}{n+1}$$

Solution:

This series diverges by the nth-Term Test since $\displaystyle\lim_{n\to\infty} \frac{2n}{n+1} = 2 \neq 0$.

39. Test for convergence or divergence using any appropriate test from this chapter.

$$\sum_{n=1}^{\infty} \frac{1}{n\sqrt[3]{n}} = \sum_{n=1}^{\infty} \frac{1}{n^{4/3}}$$

Solution:

This series converges by the p-series test since $p = \frac{4}{3} > 1$.

41. Test for convergence or divergence using any appropriate test from this chapter.

$$\sum_{n=0}^{\infty} \frac{(-1)^n 2^n}{3^n} = \sum_{n=0}^{\infty} \left(-\frac{2}{3} \right)^n$$

Solution:

This series converges by the Geometric Series Test since $|r| = \left| -\frac{2}{3} \right| = \frac{2}{3} < 1$.

43. Test for convergence or divergence using any appropriate test from this chapter.

$$\sum_{n=1}^{\infty} \left(\frac{1}{n^2} - \frac{1}{n^3} \right) = \sum_{n=1}^{\infty} \frac{1}{n^2} - \sum_{n=1}^{\infty} \frac{1}{n^3}$$

Solution:

Since both series are convergent p-series, their difference is convergent.

45. Test for convergence or divergence using any appropriate test from this chapter.

$$\sum_{n=0}^{\infty} \left(\frac{5}{4}\right)^n$$

Solution:

This series diverges by the Geometric Series Test since $r = \frac{5}{4} > 1$.

47. Test for convergence or divergence using any appropriate test from this chapter.

$$\sum_{n=1}^{\infty} \frac{n!}{3^{n-1}}$$

Solution:

This series diverges by the Ratio Test since $a_n = n!/(3^{n-1})$, and

$$\lim_{n\to\infty} \left|\frac{a_{n+1}}{a_n}\right| = \lim_{n\to\infty} \left|\frac{(n+1)!}{3^n} \cdot \frac{3^{n-1}}{n!}\right| = \lim_{n\to\infty} \frac{n+1}{3} = \infty.$$

49. Use a computer to confirm the sum of the convergent series.

$$\sum_{n=1}^{\infty} \frac{1}{n^2} = \frac{\pi^2}{6}$$

Solution:

$$\sum_{n=1}^{100} \frac{1}{n^2} = \frac{1}{1} + \frac{1}{2^2} + \frac{1}{3^2} + \frac{1}{4^2} + \cdots + \frac{1}{100^2} \approx 1.635, \quad \frac{\pi^2}{6} \approx 1.644934$$

51. *Research Express* The table lists the research and development expenses at universities for environmental sciences (in millions of dollars) for the years 1989 to 1992. (See table in textbook.)

(a) Use an infinite series to model the data.

(b) Can you determine whether the series is converging or diverging by using the Ratio Test? Explain.

Solution:

(a) Observe that the amounts differ by approximately 0.06 million each year. Hence, one model for the *cumulative* expenses is

$$E(n) = \sum_{k=1}^{n} [1.00 + 0.06(k - 1)]$$

where $n = 1$ corresponds to 1989.

(b) Although this series diverges, you cannot tell so by the Ratio Test:

$$\lim_{k\to\infty} \frac{1.00 + 0.06(k)}{1.00 + 0.06(k - 1)} = 1.$$

Section S.4 Power Series and Taylor's Theorem

1. Write the first five terms of the power series.

$$\sum_{n=0}^{\infty} \left(\frac{x}{4}\right)^n$$

Solution:

$$\sum_{n=0}^{\infty} \left(\frac{x}{4}\right)^n = 1 + \frac{x}{4} + \left(\frac{x}{4}\right)^2 + \left(\frac{x}{4}\right)^3 + \left(\frac{x}{4}\right)^4 + \cdots$$

3. Write the first five terms of the power series.

$$\sum_{n=0}^{\infty} \frac{(-1)^{n+1}(x+1)^n}{n!}$$

Solution:

$$\sum_{n=0}^{\infty} \frac{(-1)^{n+1}(x+1)^n}{n!} = -1 + (x+1) - \frac{(x+1)^2}{2} + \frac{(x+1)^3}{6} - \frac{(x+1)^4}{24} + \cdots$$

5. Find the radius of convergence for $\displaystyle\sum_{n=0}^{\infty} \left(\frac{x}{2}\right)^n = \sum_{n=0}^{\infty} \left(\frac{1}{2}\right)^n x^n$.

Solution:

$$R = \lim_{n\to\infty} \left| \frac{a_n}{a_{n+1}} \right| = \lim_{n\to\infty} \left| \frac{1}{2^n}\left(\frac{2^{n+1}}{1}\right) \right| = 2$$

7. Find the radius of convergence for $\displaystyle\sum_{n=1}^{\infty} \frac{(-1)^n x^n}{3n}$.

Solution:

$$R = \lim_{n\to\infty} \left| \frac{a_n}{a_{n+1}} \right| = \lim_{n\to\infty} \left| \frac{(-1)^n}{3n}\left(\frac{3(n+1)}{(-1)^{n+1}}\right) \right| = \lim_{n\to\infty} \frac{n+1}{n} = 1$$

9. Find the radius of convergence for $\displaystyle\sum_{n=0}^{\infty} \frac{(-1)^n x^n}{n!}$.

Solution:

$$R = \lim_{n\to\infty} \left| \frac{a_n}{a_{n+1}} \right| = \lim_{n\to\infty} \left| \frac{1}{n!}\left(\frac{(n+1)!}{1}\right) \right| = \lim_{n\to\infty} (n+1) = \infty$$

11. Find the radius of convergence for $\displaystyle\sum_{n=0}^{\infty} n!\left(\frac{x}{2}\right)^n$.

Solution:

$$R = \lim_{n\to\infty} \left| \frac{a_n}{a_{n+1}} \right| = \lim_{n\to\infty} \left| \frac{n!}{2^n} \cdot \frac{2^{n+1}}{(n+1)!} \right| = \lim_{n\to\infty} \frac{2}{n+1} = 0$$

13. Find the radius of convergence for $\displaystyle\sum_{n=1}^{\infty} \frac{(-1)^{n+1}x^n}{4^n}$.

Solution:

$$R = \lim_{n\to\infty} \left|\frac{a_n}{a_{n+1}}\right| = \lim_{n\to\infty} \left|\frac{(-1)^{n+1}}{4^n}\left(\frac{4^{n+1}}{(-1)^{n+2}}\right)\right| = 4$$

15. Find the radius of convergence for $\displaystyle\sum_{n=1}^{\infty} \frac{(-1)^{n+1}(x-5)^n}{n5^n}$.

Solution:

$$R = \lim_{n\to\infty} \left|\frac{a_n}{a_{n+1}}\right| = \lim_{n\to\infty} \left|\frac{(-1)^{n+1}}{n5^n}\left(\frac{(n+1)5^{n+1}}{(-1)^{n+2}}\right)\right| = 5$$

17. Find the radius of convergence for $\displaystyle\sum_{n=0}^{\infty} \frac{(-1)^{n+1}(x-1)^{n+1}}{n+1}$.

Solution:

$$R = \lim_{n\to\infty} \left|\frac{a_n}{a_{n+1}}\right| = \lim_{n\to\infty} \left|\frac{(-1)^{n+1}}{n+1}\left(\frac{n+2}{(-1)^{n+2}}\right)\right| = 1$$

19. Find the radius of convergence for $\displaystyle\sum_{n=1}^{\infty} \frac{(x-c)^{n-1}}{c^{n-1}}, 0 < c$.

Solution:

$$R = \lim_{n\to\infty} \left|\frac{a_n}{a_{n+1}}\right| = \lim_{n\to\infty} \left|\frac{1}{c^{n-1}}\left(\frac{c^n}{1}\right)\right| = c$$

21. Find the radius of convergence for $\displaystyle\sum_{n=1}^{\infty} \frac{n}{n+1}(-2x)^{n-1}$.

Solution:

$$R = \lim_{n\to\infty} \left|\frac{a_n}{a_{n+1}}\right| = \lim_{n\to\infty} \left|\frac{(-2)^{n-1}n}{(n+1)!}\left(\frac{(n+2)!}{(-2)^n(n+1)}\right)\right| = \infty$$

23. Find the radius of convergence for $\displaystyle\sum_{n-0}^{\infty} \frac{x^{2n+1}}{(2n+1)!}$.

Solution:

$$R = \lim_{n\to\infty} \left|\frac{a_n}{a_{n+1}}\right| = \lim_{n\to\infty} \left|\frac{1}{(2n+1)!}\left(\frac{(2n+3)!}{1}\right)\right| = \lim_{n\to\infty} |(2n+3)(2n+2)| = \infty$$

25. Apply Taylor's Theorem to find the power series (centered at 0) for $f(x) = e^x$ and find the radius of convergence.

Solution:

$$
\begin{aligned}
f(x) &= e^x & f(0) &= 1 \\
f'(x) &= e^x & f'(0) &= 1 \\
f''(x) &= e^x & f''(0) &= 1 \\
&\;\vdots & &\;\vdots \\
f^{(n)}(x) &= e^x & f^{(n)}(0) &= 1
\end{aligned}
$$

The power series for f is

$$
e^x = f(0) + f'(0)x + \frac{f''(0)x^2}{2!} + \cdots = 1 + x + \frac{x^2}{2!} + \frac{x^3}{3!} + \cdots = \sum_{n=0}^{\infty} \frac{x^n}{n!}
$$

and the radius of convergence is

$$
R = \lim_{n \to \infty} \left| \frac{1}{n!} \cdot \frac{(n+1)!}{1} \right| = \lim_{n \to \infty} (n+1) = \infty.
$$

27. Apply Taylor's Theorem to find the power series (centered at 0) for $f(x) = e^{2x}$ and find the radius of convergence.

Solution:

$$
\begin{aligned}
f(x) &= e^{2x} & f(0) &= 1 \\
f'(x) &= 2e^{2x} & f'(0) &= 2 \\
f''(x) &= 4e^{2x} & f''(0) &= 4 \\
f'''(x) &= 8e^{2x} & f'''(0) &= 8 \\
& & &\;\vdots \\
& & f^{(n)}(0) &= 2^n
\end{aligned}
$$

The power series for f is

$$
e^{2x} = f(0) + f'(0)(x) + \frac{f''(0)(x)^2}{2!} + \cdots = 1 + 2x + \frac{4x^2}{2!} + \frac{8x^3}{3!} + \cdots = \sum_{n=0}^{\infty} \frac{(2x)^n}{n!}
$$

and the radius of convergence is

$$
R = \lim_{n \to \infty} \left| \frac{2^n}{n!} \cdot \frac{(n+1)!}{2^{n+1}} \right| = \lim_{n \to \infty} \left(\frac{n+1}{2} \right) = \infty.
$$

29. Apply Taylor's Theorem to find the power series (centered at 0) for $f(x) = 1/(x+1)$ and find the radius of convergence.

Solution:

$$f(x) = \frac{1}{x+1} \qquad\qquad f(0) = 1$$

$$f'(x) = \frac{-1}{(x+1)^2} \qquad\qquad f'(0) = -1$$

$$f''(x) = \frac{2}{(x+1)^3} \qquad\qquad f''(0) = 2$$

$$f'''(x) = \frac{-6}{(x+1)^4} \qquad\qquad f'''(0) = -6$$

$$\vdots$$

$$f^{(n)}(0) = (-1)^n n!$$

The power series for f is

$$\frac{1}{x+1} = f(0) + f'(0)x + \frac{f''(0)x^2}{2!} + \cdots$$

$$= 1 - x + \frac{2x^2}{2!} - \frac{6x^3}{3!} + \cdots + \frac{(-1)^n n! x^n}{n!} + \cdots = 1 - x + x^2 - x^3 + \cdots$$

$$= \sum_{n=0}^{\infty} (-1)^n x^n$$

and the radius of convergence is $R = \lim_{n \to \infty} \left| \frac{(-1)^n}{(-1)^{n+1}} \right| = \lim_{n \to \infty} |-1| = 1$.

31. Apply Taylor's Theorem to find the power series (centered at 2) for $f(x) = \sqrt{x}$ and find the radius of convergence.

Solution:

$$f(x) = \sqrt{x} \qquad\qquad f(2) = \sqrt{2}$$

$$f'(x) = \frac{1}{2\sqrt{x}} \qquad\qquad f'(2) = \frac{1}{2\sqrt{2}} = \frac{1}{4}\sqrt{2}$$

$$f''(x) = -\frac{1}{4x\sqrt{x}} \qquad\qquad f''(2) = -\frac{1}{8\sqrt{2}} = -\frac{1}{16}\sqrt{2}$$

$$f'''(x) = \frac{3}{8x^2\sqrt{x}} \qquad\qquad f'''(2) = \frac{3}{32\sqrt{2}} = \frac{3}{64}\sqrt{2}$$

$$f^4(x) = -\frac{15}{16x^3\sqrt{x}} \qquad\qquad f^4(2) = \frac{-15}{128\sqrt{2}} = \frac{-15}{256}\sqrt{2}$$

The general pattern (for $n \geq 2$) is

$$f^{(n)}(2) = \frac{(-1)^{n+1} 1 \cdot 3 \cdot 5 \cdots (2n-3)}{2^{2n}}\sqrt{2}$$

The power series for $f(x) = \sqrt{x}$ is

$$\sqrt{x} = f(2) + f'(2)(x-2) + f''(2)(x-2)^2/2! + \cdots$$

$$= \sqrt{2} + \frac{1}{4}\sqrt{2}(x-2) + \sum_{n=2}^{\infty} \frac{(-1)^{n+1} 1 \cdot 3 \cdots (2n-3)}{2^{2n} n!}\sqrt{2}(x-2)^n$$

The radius of convergence is

$$R = \lim_{n \to \infty}\left|\frac{a_n}{a_{n+1}}\right| = \lim_{n \to \infty}\left[\frac{1 \cdot 3 \cdots (2n-3)\sqrt{2}}{2^{2n} n!} \cdot \frac{2^{(2n+1)}(n+1)!}{1 \cdot 3 \cdots (2n-3)(2n-1)\sqrt{2}}\right]$$

$$= \lim_{n \to \infty}\left[\frac{2^2(n+1)}{2n-1}\right] = 2$$

33. Apply Taylor's Theorem to find the binomial series (centered at 0) for $f(x) = \dfrac{1}{(1+x)^3}$ and find the radius of convergence.

Solution:

$$
\begin{aligned}
f(x) &= (1+x)^{-3} & f(0) &= 1 \\
f'(x) &= -3(1+x)^{-4} & f'(0) &= -3 \\
f''(x) &= 12(1+x)^{-5} & f''(0) &= 12 \\
f'''(x) &= -60(1+x)^{-6} & f'''(0) &= -60
\end{aligned}
$$

In general, $f^{(n)}(0) = (-1)^n \dfrac{(n+2)!}{2}$. The power series is

$$\frac{1}{(1+x)^3} = f(0) + f'(0)x + \frac{f''(0)x^2}{2!} + \cdots$$

$$= 1 - 3x + 6x^2 - 10x^3 + \cdots = \sum_{n=0}^{\infty} (-1)^n \frac{(n+2)(n+1)}{2} x^n.$$

$$R = \lim_{n\to\infty} \left| \frac{a_n}{a_{n+1}} \right| = \lim_{n\to\infty} \frac{(n+2)(n+1)}{(n+3)(n+2)} = 1.$$

35. Apply Taylor's Theorem to find the binomial series (centered at 0) for $f(x) = 1/(\sqrt{1+x})$ and find the radius of convergence.

Solution:

$$
\begin{aligned}
f(x) &= (1+x)^{-1/2} & f(0) &= 1 \\
f'(x) &= -\frac{1}{2}(1+x)^{-3/2} & f'(0) &= -\frac{1}{2} \\
f''(x) &= \frac{3}{4}(1+x)^{-5/2} & f''(0) &= \frac{3}{4} \\
f'''(x) &= -\frac{15}{8}(1+x)^{-7/2} & f'''(0) &= -\frac{15}{8}
\end{aligned}
$$

Thus, the general pattern is given by $f^{(n)}(0) = (-1)^n \left(\dfrac{1 \cdot 3 \cdot 5 \cdots (2n-1)}{2^n} \right)$. The power series for f is

$$\frac{1}{\sqrt{1+x}} = f(0) + f'(0)x + \frac{f''(0)x^2}{2!} + \frac{f'''(0)x^3}{3!} + \cdots$$

$$= 1 - \frac{1}{2}x + \frac{1 \cdot 3x^2}{2^2 2!} - \frac{1 \cdot 3 \cdot 5x^3}{2^3 3!} + \cdots$$

$$= 1 + \sum_{n=1}^{\infty} \frac{(-1)^n 1 \cdot 3 \cdot 5 \cdots (2n-1)}{2^n n!} x^n$$

and the radius of convergence is

$$R = \lim_{n\to\infty} \left| \frac{1 \cdot 3 \cdot 5 \cdots (2n-1)}{2^n n!} \left(\frac{2^{n+1}(n+1)!}{1 \cdot 3 \cdot 5 \cdots (2n+1)} \right) \right| = \lim_{n\to\infty} \frac{2(n+1)}{2n+1} = 1.$$

37. Find the radius of convergence of (a) $f(x)$, (b) $f'(x)$, (c) $f''(x)$, and (d) $\int f(x)\,dx$ when

$$f(x) = \sum_{n=0}^{\infty} \left(\frac{x}{2}\right)^n.$$

Solution:

(a) $f(x) = \sum_{n=0}^{\infty} \left(\frac{x}{2}\right)^n = \sum_{n=0}^{\infty} \frac{x^n}{2^n}$

$$R = \lim_{n\to\infty} \left| \frac{1}{2^n} \cdot \frac{2^{n+1}}{1} \right| = \lim_{n\to\infty} 2 = 2$$

(b) $f'(x) = \sum_{n=1}^{\infty} \frac{nx^{n-1}}{2^n}$

$$R = \lim_{n\to\infty} \left| \frac{n}{2^n} \cdot \frac{2^{n+1}}{n+1} \right| = \lim_{n\to\infty} \frac{2n}{n+1} = 2$$

(c) $f''(x) = \sum_{n=2}^{\infty} \frac{n(n-1)x^{n-2}}{2^n}$

$$R = \lim_{n\to\infty} \left| \frac{n(n-1)}{2^n} \cdot \frac{2^{n+1}}{(n+1)n} \right| = \lim_{n\to\infty} \frac{2(n-1)}{n+1} = 2$$

(d) $\int f(x)\,dx = C + \sum_{n=0}^{\infty} \frac{x^{n+1}}{2^n(n+1)}$

$$R = \lim_{n\to\infty} \left| \frac{1}{2^n(n+1)} \cdot \frac{2^{n+1}(n+2)}{1} \right| = \lim_{n\to\infty} \frac{2(n+2)}{n+1} = 2$$

39. Find the radius of convergence of (a) $f(x)$, (b) $f'(x)$, (c) $f''(x)$, and (d) $\int f(x)\,dx$ when

$$f(x) = \sum_{n=0}^{\infty} \frac{(x+1)^{n+1}}{n+1}.$$

Solution:

(a) $f(x) = \sum_{n=0}^{\infty} \frac{(x-1)^{n+1}}{n+1}$

$$R = \lim_{n \to \infty} \left| \frac{1}{n+1} \cdot \frac{n+2}{1} \right| = \lim_{n \to \infty} \frac{n+2}{n+1} = 1$$

(b) $f'(x) = \sum_{n=0}^{\infty} \frac{(n+1)(x+1)^n}{n+1} = \sum_{n=0}^{\infty} (x+1)^n$

$$R = \lim_{n \to \infty} 1 = 1$$

(c) $f''(x) = \sum_{n=1}^{\infty} n(x+1)^{n-1}$

$$R = \lim_{n \to \infty} \left| \frac{n}{n+1} \right| = 1$$

(d) $\int f(x)\,dx = C + \sum_{n=0}^{\infty} \frac{(x+1)^{n+2}}{(n+1)(n+2)}$

$$R = \lim_{n \to \infty} \left| \frac{1}{(n+1)(n+2)} \cdot \frac{(n+2)(n+3)}{1} \right| = \lim_{n \to \infty} \frac{n+3}{n+1} = 1$$

41. Use the power series for e^x to find the power series for $f(x) = e^{x^3}$.

Solution:

Since the power series for e^x is

$$e^x = \sum_{n=0}^{\infty} \frac{x^n}{n!}$$

it follows that the power series for e^{x^3} is

$$e^{x^3} = \sum_{n=0}^{\infty} \frac{(x^3)^n}{n!} = \sum_{n=0}^{\infty} \frac{x^{3n}}{n!}.$$

43. Differentiate the series found in Exercise 41 to find the power series for $f(x) = 3x^2 e^{x^3}$.

Solution:

$$3x^2 e^x = \frac{d}{dx}[e^{x^3}] = \sum_{n=1}^{\infty} \frac{3nx^{3n-1}}{n!} = 3\sum_{n=1}^{\infty} \frac{x^{3n-1}}{(n-1)!} = 2\sum_{n=0}^{\infty} \frac{x^{3n+2}}{n!}$$

45. Use the power series for $1/(1+x)$ to find the power series for $f(x) = 1/(1+x^4)$.

Solution:

Since the power series for $1/(1+x)$ is

$$f(x) = \frac{1}{1+x} = \sum_{n=0}^{\infty} (-1)^n x^n$$

it follows that the power series for $1/(1+x^4)$ is

$$f(x^4) = \frac{1}{1+x^4} = \sum_{n=0}^{\infty} (-1)^n x^{4n}.$$

47. Integrate the following series for $\dfrac{1}{+x}$ to find the power series for $f(x) = \ln(1+x^2)$.

$$\sum_{n=0}^{\infty} (-1)^n x^n$$

Solution:

$$\frac{1}{1+x^2} = \sum_{n=0}^{\infty} (-1)^n x^{2n}$$

$$\frac{2x}{1+x^2} = \sum_{n=0}^{\infty} (-1)^n (2x)x^{2n} = 2\sum_{n=0}^{\infty} (-1)^n x^{2n+1}$$

$$\ln(1+x^2) = \int \frac{2x}{1+x^2}\, dx = 2\sum_{n=0}^{\infty} \frac{(-1)^n x^{2n+2}}{2n+2} = \sum_{n=0}^{\infty} \frac{(-1)^n x^{2n+2}}{n+1}$$

49. Integrate the series for $1/x$ to find the power series for $f(x) = \ln x$.

Solution:

$$\frac{1}{x} = \sum_{n=0}^{\infty} (-1)^n (x-1)^n$$

$$\ln x = \int \frac{1}{x}\, dx = \sum_{n=0}^{\infty} \frac{(-1)^n (x-1)^{n+1}}{n+1}$$

51. Differentiate the series for $-1/x$ to find the power series for $f(x) = \dfrac{1}{x^2}$.

Solution:

$$-\frac{1}{x} = \sum_{n=0}^{\infty} (-1)^{n+1}(x-1)^n. \text{ Differentiating,}$$

$$\frac{1}{x^2} = \sum_{n=1}^{\infty} (-1)^{n+1} n(x-1)^{n-1}.$$

53. Use the Taylor series for the exponential function and the process in the Introductory Example to approximate $e^{1/2}$ to four decimal places.

Solution:

$$e^x = 1 + x + \frac{x^2}{2!} + \frac{x^3}{3!} + \frac{x^4}{4!} + \frac{x^5}{5!} + \cdots$$

$$e^{1/2} = 1 + \frac{1}{2} + \frac{1}{2!(2^2)} + \frac{1}{3!(2^3)} + \frac{1}{4!(2^4)} + \frac{1}{5!(2^5)} + \cdots$$

Since $1/[6!(2^6)] \approx 0.00002$, the first six terms are sufficient to approximate $e^{1/2}$ to four decimal places.

$$e^{1/2} \approx 1 + \frac{1}{2} + \frac{1}{8} + \frac{1}{48} + \frac{1}{384} + \frac{1}{3840} \approx 1.6487$$

55. Use a computer or calculator and 50 terms of the following series to approximate $f(0.5)$. The actual sum is $\ln 0.5$.

$$f(x) = \sum_{n=1}^{\infty} \frac{(-1)^{n+1}(x-1)^n}{n}, \quad 0 < x \le 2$$

Solution:

$$f(0.5) = \sum_{n=1}^{\infty} \frac{(-1)^{n+1}(0.5-1)^n}{n} = \sum_{n=1}^{\infty} \frac{(-1)^{n+1}(-1)^n(1/2)^n}{n} = \sum_{n=1}^{\infty} \frac{(-1)^{2n+1}}{2^n n}$$

$$= -\sum_{n=1}^{\infty} \frac{1}{2^n n} \approx -0.6931$$

Section S.5   Taylor Polynomials

1. Find the Taylor polynomial (centered at 0) of degree (a) 1, (b) 2, (c) 3, and (d) 4 for $f(x) = e^x$.

Solution:

$$e^x = \sum_{n=0}^{\infty} \frac{1}{n!} x^n$$

(a) $S_1(x) = 1 + x$

(b) $S_2(x) = 1 + x + \dfrac{x^2}{2}$

(c) $S_3(x) = 1 + x + \dfrac{x^2}{2} + \dfrac{x^3}{6}$

(d) $S_4(x) = 1 + x + \dfrac{x^2}{2} + \dfrac{x^3}{6} + \dfrac{x^4}{24}$

3. Find the Taylor polynomial (centered at 0) of degree (a) 1, (b) 2, (c) 3, and (d) 4 for
$f(x) = \sqrt{x+1}$.

Solution:

$$\frac{1}{\sqrt{x+1}} = 1 + \frac{x}{2^1 \cdot 1!} - \frac{x^2}{2^2 \cdot 2!} + \frac{3x^3}{2^3 \cdot 3!} - \frac{3 \cdot 5x^4}{2^4 \cdot 4!}$$

(a) $S_1(x) = 1 + \dfrac{x}{2}$ (b) $S_2(x) = 1 + \dfrac{x}{2} - \dfrac{x^2}{8}$

(c) $S_3(x) = 1 + \dfrac{x}{2} - \dfrac{x^2}{8} + \dfrac{3x^3}{48}$ (d) $S_4(x) = 1 + \dfrac{x}{2} - \dfrac{x^2}{8} + \dfrac{3x^3}{48} - \dfrac{15x^4}{384}$

5. Find the Taylor polynomial (centered at 0) of degree (a) 1, (b) 2, (c) 3, and (d) 4 for
$f(x) = \dfrac{x}{x+1}$.

Solution:

$$f(x) = \frac{x}{x+1} = 1 - \frac{1}{x+1}$$

(a) $S_1(x) = x$

(b) $S_2(x) = x - x^2$

(c) $S_3(x) = x - x^2 + x^3$

(d) $S_4(x) = x - x^2 + x^2 - x^4$

7. Complete the table using the Taylor polynomial as an approximation to $f(x) = e^{x/2}$.

Solution:

$$S_1(x) = 1 + \frac{x}{2}$$

$$S_2(x) = 1 + \frac{x}{2} + \frac{x^2}{8}$$

$$S_3(x) = 1 + \frac{x}{2} + \frac{x^2}{8} + \frac{x^3}{48}$$

$$S_4(x) = 1 + \frac{x}{2} + \frac{x^2}{8} + \frac{x^3}{48} + \frac{x^4}{384}$$

x	0	0.25	0.50	0.75	1.0
$f(x)$	1.0000	1.1331	1.2840	1.4550	1.6487
$S_1(x)$	1.0000	1.1250	1.2500	1.3750	1.5000
$S_2(x)$	1.0000	1.1328	1.2813	1.4453	1.6250
$S_3(x)$	1.0000	1.1331	1.2839	1.4541	1.6458
$S_4(x)$	1.0000	1.1331	1.2840	1.4549	1.6484

9. Find the Taylor polynomial (centered at 0) of degree (a) 2, (b) 4, (c) 6, and (d) 8 for $f(x) = 1/(1 + x^2)$.

   Solution:

   $$\frac{1}{1 + x^2} = \sum_{n=0}^{\infty} (-1)^n x^{2n}$$

   (a) $S_2(x) = 1 - x^2$ (b) $S_4(x) = 1 - x^2 + x^4$

   (c) $S_6(x) = 1 - x^2 + x^4 - x^6$ (d) $S_8(x) = 1 - x^2 + x^4 - x^6 + x^8$

11. Use a symbolic differentiation utility to find the 4th-degree Taylor polynomial (centered at 0).

    $$f(x) = \frac{1}{x^2 + 1}$$

    Solution:

    $$S_4(x) = 1 - x^2 + x^4$$

13. Match the Taylor polynomial approximation of the function $f(x) = e^{-x^2/2}$ with its graph (shown in the textbook).

    $$y = -\frac{1}{2}x^2 + 1$$

    Solution:

    $y = -\frac{1}{2}x^2 + 1$ is a parabola through $(0, 1)$; matches (d).

15. Match the Taylor polynomial approximation of the function $f(x) = e^{-x\ 2/2}$ with its graph (shown in the textbook).

    $$y = e^{=-1/2}[(x + 1) + 1]$$

    Solution:

    $y = e^{-1/2}[(x + 1) + 1]$ is a line, matches (a).

17. Use a sixth-degree Taylor polynomial centered at $c = 0$ for the function $f(x) = e^{-x}$ to approximate $f(\frac{1}{2})$.

    Solution:

    $$S_6(x) = 1 - x + \frac{x^2}{2} - \frac{x^3}{6} + \frac{x^4}{24} - \frac{x^5}{120} + \frac{x^6}{720}$$

    $$f\left(\frac{1}{2}\right) \approx 1 - \frac{1}{2} + \frac{1}{8} - \frac{1}{48} + \frac{1}{384} - \frac{1}{3840} + \frac{1}{46,080} \approx 0.607$$

19. Use a sixth-degree Taylor polynomial centered at $c = 2$ for the function $f(x) = \ln x$ to approximate $f\left(\frac{3}{2}\right)$.

Solution:

$$f(x) = \ln x, c = 2$$

$$S_6(x) = \ln 2 + \frac{1}{2}(x-2) - \frac{1}{8}(x-2)^2 + \frac{1}{24}(x-2)^3 - \frac{1}{64}(x-2)^4 + \frac{1}{160}(x-2)^5$$

$$- \frac{1}{384}(x-2)^6 f\left(\frac{3}{2}\right)$$

$$\approx \ln 2 + \frac{1}{2}\left(-\frac{1}{2}\right) - \frac{1}{8}\left(\frac{1}{4}\right) + \frac{1}{24}\left(-\frac{1}{8}\right) - \frac{1}{64}\left(\frac{1}{16}\right) - \frac{1}{160}\left(\frac{1}{32}\right)$$

$$- \frac{1}{384}\left(\frac{1}{64}\right)$$

$$= 0.4055$$

21. Use a sixth-degree Taylor polynomial centered at $c = 0$ for the function $f(x) = e^{-x^2}$ to approximate

$$\int_0^1 e^{-x^2}\, dx.$$

Solution:

$$S_6(x) = 1 - x^2 + \frac{x^4}{2} - \frac{x^6}{6}$$

$$\int_0^1 e^{-x^2}\, dx \approx \int_0^1 \left(1 - x^2 + \frac{x^4}{2} - \frac{x^6}{6}\right) dx = \left[x - \frac{x^3}{3} + \frac{x^5}{10} - \frac{x^7}{42}\right]_0^1 \approx 0.74286$$

23. Use a sixth-degree Taylor polynomial centered at $c = 0$ for the function $f(x) = 1/\sqrt{1+x^2}$ to approximate

$$\int_0^{1/2} \frac{1}{\sqrt{1+x^2}}\, dx.$$

Solution:

$$S_6(x) = 1 - \frac{1}{2}x^2 + \frac{3}{8}x^4 - \frac{5}{16}x^6$$

$$\int_0^{1/2} \frac{1}{\sqrt{1+x^2}}\, dx \approx \int_0^{1/2} \left(1 - \frac{1}{2}x^2 + \frac{3}{8}x^4 - \frac{5}{16}x^6\right) dx$$

$$= \left[x - \frac{x^3}{6} + \frac{3x^5}{40} - \frac{5x^7}{112}\right]_0^{1/2} = \frac{1}{2} - \frac{1}{48} + \frac{3}{1280} - \frac{5}{14,336} \approx 0.481$$

25. Determine the degree c the Taylor polynomial centered at c to approximate $f(x) = e^x$ in the interval $[0, 2]$ to an accuracy of ± 0.001.

Solution:

Since the $(n + 1)$ derivative of $f(x) = e^x$ is e^x, the maximum value of $|f^{n+1}(x)|$ on the interval $[0, 2]$ is $e^2 < 8$. Therefore, the nth remainder is bounded by

$$|R_n| \le \left| \frac{8}{(n + 1)!}(x - 1)^{n+1} \right|, \qquad 0 \le x \le 2$$

$$|R_n| \le \frac{8}{(n + 1)!}(1)$$

with $n = 7$, $\dfrac{8}{(7 + 1)!} = 1.98 \times 10^{-4} < 0.001$.

Thus, $n = 7$ will approximate e^x with an error less than 0.001.

27. Determine the maximum error guaranteed by Taylor's Remainder Theorem when

$$1 - x + \frac{x^2}{2!} - \frac{x^3}{3!} + \frac{x^4}{4!} - \frac{x^5}{5!}$$

is used to approximate $f(x) = e^{-x}$ in the interval $[0, 1]$.

Solution:

$$|R_5| \le \frac{f^{(6)}(z)}{6!}x^6 = \frac{e^{-z}}{6!}x^6$$

Since $e^{-z} \le 1$ in the interval $[0, 1]$, it follows that

$$R_5 \le \frac{1}{6!} \approx 0.00139.$$

29. *Profit* Let n be a random variable representing the number of units of a certain commodity sold per day in a given store. The probability distribution of n is given in the following table.

n	0	1	2	3	$4, \cdots$
$P(n)$	$\dfrac{1}{2}$	$\left(\dfrac{1}{2}\right)^2$	$\left(\dfrac{1}{2}\right)^3$	$\left(\dfrac{1}{2}\right)^4$	$\left(\dfrac{1}{2}\right)^5, \cdots$

Use Example 5 as a model for each of the following.

(a) Show that $\displaystyle\sum_{n=0}^{\infty} P(n) = 1$.

(b) Find the expected value of the random variable n.

(c) If there is a \$10 profit on each unit sold, what is the expected daily profit on this commodity?

Solution:

(a) $\displaystyle\sum_{n=0}^{\infty} P(n) = \sum_{n=0}^{\infty} \left(\frac{1}{2}\right)^{n+1} = \sum_{n=0}^{\infty} \frac{1}{2}\left(\frac{1}{2}\right)^{n} = \frac{1/2}{1-(1/2)} = 1$

(b) Expected value $= \displaystyle\sum_{n=0}^{\infty} n\,P(n) = \sum_{n=0}^{\infty} n\left(\frac{1}{2}\right)^{n+1} = 1$ (See Example 5.)

(c) The expected daily profit is $\$10(1) = \$10$.

Section S.6   Newton's Method

1. Complete one iteration of Newton's Method for the function $f(x) = x^2 - 5$ using $x_1 = 2.2$.

Solution:

$$x_2 = x_1 - \frac{f(x_1)}{f'(x_1)} = 2.2 - \frac{(2.2)^2 - 5}{2(2.2)} \approx 2.2364$$

3. Approximate the indicated zero(s) of $f(x) = x^3 + x - 1$. Use Newton's Method, continuing until two successive approximations differ by less than 0.001. (See graph in textbook.)

Solution:

$$f'(x) = 3x^2 + 1$$

n	x_n	$f(x_n)$	$f'(x_n)$	$\dfrac{f(x_n)}{f'(x_n)}$	$x_n - \dfrac{f(x_n)}{f'(x_n)}$
1	0.5000	−0.3750	1.7500	−0.2143	0.7143
2	0.7143	0.0787	2.5306	0.0311	0.6832
3	0.6832	0.0021	2.4002	0.0009	0.6823

Approximation: $x \approx 0.682$

5. Approximate the indicated zero(s) of the function $y = 5\sqrt{x - 1} - 2x$. Use Newton's Method, continuing until two successive approximations differ by less than 0.001. (See graphs in textbook.)

Solution:

$$f'(x) = \frac{5}{2\sqrt{x - 1}} - 2$$

n	x_n	$f(x_n)$	$f'(x_n)$	$\dfrac{f(x_n)}{f'(x_n)}$	$x_n - \dfrac{f(x_n)}{f'(x_n)}$
1	1.2	−0.1639	3.5902	−0.0457	1.2457
2	1.2457	−0.0131	3.0440	−0.0043	1.2500
3	1.2500	−0.000094	3.0003	−0.00003	1.25

Approximation: $x \approx 1.25$ (exact!)

7. Approximate the indicated zero(s) of $f(x) = \ln x + x$. Use Newton's Method, continuing until two successive approximations differ by less than 0.001. (See graph in textbook.)

Solution:

$$f'(x) = \frac{1}{x} + 1$$

n	x_n	$f(x_n)$	$f'(x_n)$	$\dfrac{f(x_n)}{f'(x_n)}$	$x_n - \dfrac{f(x_n)}{f'(x_n)}$
1	0.6000	0.0892	2.1667	0.4120	0.5588
2	0.5588	−0.0231	2.7895	−0.0083	0.5671
3	0.5671	−0.0002	3.7634	−0.0001	0.5672

Approximation: $x \approx 0.567$

9. Approximate the indicated zero(s) of $f(x) = e^{-x^2} - x^2$. Use Newton's Method, continuing until two successive approximations differ by less than 0.001. (See graph in textbook.)

Solution:

$$f'(x) = -2xe^{-x^2} - 2x = -2x(e^{-x^2} + 1)$$

n	x_n	$f(x_n)$	$f'(x_n)$	$\dfrac{f(x_n)}{f'(x_n)}$	$x_n - \dfrac{f(x_n)}{f'(x_n)}$
1	0.8000	−0.1127	−2.4437	0.0461	0.7539
2	0.7539	−0.0019	−2.3619	0.0008	0.7531

Approximations: $x \approx \pm 0.753$

11. Approximate the indicated zero(s) of $f(x) = x^3 - 27x - 27$. Use Newton's Method, continuing until two successive approximations differ by less than 0.001. (See graph in textbook.)

Solution:

$$f'(x) = 3x^2 - 27$$

n	x_n	$f(x_n)$	$f'(x_n)$	$\dfrac{f(x_n)}{f'(x_n)}$	$x_n - \dfrac{f(x_n)}{f'(x_n)}$
1	−5.0000	−17.0000	48.0000	−0.3542	−4.6458
2	−4.6458	−1.8371	37.7513	−0.0487	−4.5972
3	−4.5972	−0.0329	36.4019	−0.0009	−4.5963

n	x_n	$f(x_n)$	$f'(x_n)$	$\dfrac{f(x_n)}{f'(x_n)}$	$x_n - \dfrac{f(x_n)}{f'(x_n)}$
1	−1.0000	−1.0000	−24.0000	0.0417	−1.0417
2	−1.0417	−0.0053	−23.7448	0.0002	−1.0419

n	x_n	$f(x_n)$	$f'(x_n)$	$\dfrac{f(x_n)}{f'(x_n)}$	$x_n - \dfrac{f(x_n)}{f'(x_n)}$
1	6.0000	27.0000	81.0000	0.3333	5.6667
2	5.6667	1.9630	69.3333	0.0283	5.6384
3	5.6384	0.0136	68.3731	0.0002	5.6382

Approximations: $x \approx -4.596, \ -1.042, \ 5.638$

13. Approximate, to three decimal places, the x-value of the point of intersection of the graphs shown in the textbook.

$$f(x) = 4 - x,$$
$$g(x) = \ln x$$

Solution:

Let $h(x) = f(x) - g(x) = 4 - x - \ln x$. Then $h'(x) = -1 - \dfrac{1}{x}$. Starting with $x_1 = 3$, you obtain

$$x_1 = 3$$
$$x_2 = 2.926$$
$$x_3 = 2.92627$$
$$x \approx 2.926$$

Series and Taylor Polynomials

15. Approximate, to three decimal places, the x-value of the point of intersection of the graphs shown in the textbook.

$f(x) = 3 - x,$

$g(x) = 1/(x^2 + 1)$

Solution:

Let $3 - x = 1/(x^2 + 1)$ and define

$$h(x) = \frac{1}{x^2 + 1} + x - 3 \quad \text{then} \quad h'(x) = -\frac{2x}{(x^2 + 1)^2} + 1.$$

n	x_n	$h(x_n)$	$h'(x_n)$	$\dfrac{h(x_n)}{h'(x_n)}$	$x_n - \dfrac{h(x_n)}{h'(x_n)}$
1	3.0000	0.1000	0.9400	0.1064	2.8936
2	2.8936	0.0003	0.9341	0.0003	2.8933

Approximation: $x \approx 2.893$

17. Apply Newton's Method to $y = 2x^3 - 6x^2 + 6x - 1$, using the initial estimate $x_1 = 1$ and explain why the method fails.

Solution:

Newton's Method fails because $f'(x_1) = 0$.

19. Apply Newton's Method to $y = -x^3 + 3x^2 - x + 1$, using the initial estimate $x_1 = 1$ and explain why the method fails.

Solution:

Newton's Method fails because

$$\lim_{x \to \infty} x_n = \begin{cases} 1 = x_1 = x_3 = \dots \\ 0 = x_2 = x_4 = \dots \end{cases}$$

Therefore, the limit does not exist.

21. Use Newton's Method to obtain a general rule for approximating $\sqrt{a}$. [*Hint:* Consider $f(x) = x^2 - a$.]

Solution:

Let $f(x) = x^2 - a$, then $f'(x) = 2x$.

$$x_{n+1} = x_n - \frac{x_n^2 - a}{2x_n} = \frac{x_n^2 + a}{2x_n}$$

23. Use the result of Exercise 21 to approximate $\sqrt{7}$ to three decimal places.

Solution:

$$x_{i+1} = \frac{x_i^2 + 7}{2x_i}$$

i	1	2	3	4	5
x_i	2.0000	2.7500	2.6477	2.6458	2.6458

Approximation: $\sqrt{7} \approx 2.646$

25. Use the result of Exercise 22 to approximate $\sqrt[4]{6}$ to three decimal places.

Solution:

Let $f(x) = x^4 - 6$, then $f'(x) = 4x^3$.

$$x_{i+1} = x_i - \frac{x_i^4 - 6}{4x_i^3} = \frac{3x_i^4 + 6}{4x_i^3}$$

i	1	2	3	4	5
x_i	2.0000	1.6875	1.5778	1.5652	1.5651

Approximation: $\sqrt[4]{6} \approx 1.565$

27. Use Newton's Method to show that the equation $x_{n+1} = x_n(2 - ax_n)$ can be used to approximate $1/a$ if x_1 is an initial guess of the reciprocal of a. Note that this method of approximating reciprocals uses only the operations of multiplication and subtractions. [*Hint:* Consider $f(x) = (1/x) - a$.]

Solution:

Let $f(x) = (1/x) - a$, then $f'(x) = -1/x^2$.

$$x_{n+1} = x_n - \frac{(1/x_n) - a}{-1/(x_n^2)} = x_n + (x_n - ax_n^2) = x_n(2 - ax_n)$$

29. *Optimal Time*   A man is in a boat 2 miles from the nearest point on the coast, as shown in the figure. He is to go to a point Q, which is 3 miles down the coast and 1 mile inland. If he can row at 3 mi/hr and walk at 4 mi/hr, toward what point on the coast should he row in order to reach point Q in the least time?

Solution:

The time is given by

$$T = \frac{\sqrt{x^2 + 4}}{3} + \frac{\sqrt{x^2 - 6x + 10}}{4}.$$

To minimize the time, we set dT/dx equal to zero and solve for x. This produces the equation

$$7x^4 - 42x^3 + 43x^2 + 216x - 324 = 0.$$

Let $f(x) = 7x^4 - 42x^3 + 43x^2 + 216x - 324$. Since $f(1) = -100$ and $f(2) = 56$, the solution is in the interval $(1, 2)$.

n	x_n	$f(x_n)$	$f'(x_n)$	$\dfrac{f(x_n)}{f'(x_n)}$	$x_n - \dfrac{f(x_n)}{f'(x_n)}$
1	1.7000	19.5887	135.6240	0.1444	1.5556
2	1.5556	−1.0414	150.2782	−0.0069	1.5625
3	1.5629	−0.0092	149.5693	−0.0001	1.5626

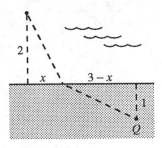

Approximation: $x \approx 1.563$ miles

31. *Chemical Concentration* The concentration C of a certain chemical in the bloodstream t hours after injection into muscle tissue is given by

$$C = \frac{3t^2 + t}{50 + t^3}.$$

When is the concentration the greatest?

Solution:

To maximize C, we set dC/dt equal to zero and solve for t. This produces

$$C' = -\frac{3t^4 - 2t^3 + 300t + 50}{(50 + t^3)^2} = 0.$$

Let $f(t) = 3t^4 + 2t^3 - 300t - 50$. Since $f(4) = -354$ and $f(5) = 575$, the solution is in the interval $(4, 5)$.

n	t_n	$f(t_n)$	$f'(t_n)$	$\dfrac{f(t_n)}{f'(t_n)}$	$t_n - \dfrac{f(t_n)}{f'(t_n)}$
1	4.5000	12.4375	915.0000	0.0136	4.4864
2	4.4864	0.0658	904.3822	0.0001	4.4863

Approximation: $t \approx 4.486$ hours

33. *Forestry* The value of a tract of timber is given by $V(t) = 100,000e^{0.8\sqrt{t}}$ where t is the time in years with $t = 0$ corresponding to 1990. If money earns interest at a rate $r = 10\%$ compounded continuously, then the present value of the timber at any time t is given by $A(t) = V(t)e^{-0.10t}$. Assume the cost of maintenance of the timber to be a constant cash flow at the rate of \$1000 per year. Then the total present value of this cost for t years is given by

$$C(t) = \int_0^t 1000e^{-0.10u}\, du$$

and the net present value of the tract of timber is given by $P(t) = A(t) - C(t)$. Find the year when the timber should be harvested to maximize the present value function P.

Solution:

$$P(t) = A(t) - C(t) = 100,000e^{0.8\sqrt{t}}e^{-0.10t} - \int_0^t 1000e^{-0.10u}\, du$$

$$= 100,000e^{0.8\sqrt{t}-0.10t} - 1000\int_0^t e^{-0.10u}\, du$$

$$P'(t) = 100,000\left(\frac{0.4}{\sqrt{t}} - 0.10\right)e^{0.8\sqrt{t}-0.10t} - 1000e^{-0.10t}$$

$$= 1000e^{-0.10t}\left[100\left(\frac{0.4}{\sqrt{t}} - 0.10\right)e^{0.8\sqrt{t}} - 1\right] = 0$$

Let $f(t) = \left(\dfrac{40}{\sqrt{t}} - 10\right)e^{0.8\sqrt{t}} - 1$, then

$$f'(t) = \left(\frac{40}{\sqrt{t}} - 10\right)\left(\frac{0.4}{\sqrt{t}}e^{0.8\sqrt{t}}\right) + e^{0.8\sqrt{t}}\left(-\frac{20}{t\sqrt{t}}\right) = e^{0.8\sqrt{t}}\left(\frac{16}{t} - \frac{4}{\sqrt{t}} - \frac{20}{t\sqrt{t}}\right)$$

$$t_{n+1} = t_n - \frac{f(t_n)}{f'(t_n)}$$

n	1	2	3	4
t_n	16	15.8696	15.8686	15.8686

The timber should be harvested in 15.8686 years.

35. Use a graphing utility to approximate all the real zeros of the function
$f(x) = \frac{1}{4}x^3 - 3x^2 + \frac{3}{4}x - 2$ by Newton's Method. Graph the function in order to make the initial estimate of a zero.

Solution:

From the graph we see that the function has one zero and it is in the interval (11, 12). Let $x_1 = 12$.

$$f(x) = \frac{1}{4}x^3 - 3x^2 + \frac{3}{4}x - 2$$

$$f'(x) = \frac{3}{4}x^2 - 6x + \frac{3}{4}$$

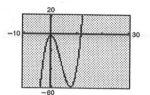

$$x_{n+1} = x_n - \frac{f(x_n)}{f'(x_n)}$$

$$= x_n - \frac{(1/4)x_n^3 - 3x_n^2 + (3/4)x_n - 2}{(3/4)x_n^2 - 6x_n + (3/4)}$$

$$= x_n - \frac{x_n^3 - 12x_n^2 + 3x_n - 8}{3x_n^2 - 24x_n + 3}$$

$$= \frac{2x_n^3 - 12x_n^2 + 8}{2x_n^2 - 24x_n + 3}$$

n	1	2	3	4
x_n	12.0000	11.8095	11.8033	11.8033

Zero: $x \approx 11.8033$

37. Use a graphing utility to approximate all the real zeros of $f(x) = -x^4 + 5x^2 - 5$ by Newton's Method. Graph the function to make the initial estimate of a zero.

Solution:

$$f(x) = -x^4 + 5x^2 - 5. \qquad x \approx \pm 1.9021, \pm 1.1756$$

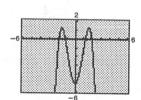

39. Use a graphing utility to approximate all the real zeros of $f(x) = x^2 - \ln x - \dfrac{3}{2}$ by Newton's Method. Graph the function to make the initial estimate of a zero.

Solution:

$$f(x) = x^2 - \ln x - \frac{3}{2}. \qquad x \approx 1.3385, \, 0.2359$$

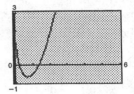

Chapter S   Review Exercises

1. Write out the first five terms of the specified sequence. (Begin with $n = 1$.)

$$a_n = \left(-\frac{1}{3}\right)^n$$

Solution:

$$a_n = \left(-\frac{1}{3}\right)^n: -\frac{1}{3}, \frac{1}{9}, \frac{-1}{27}, \frac{1}{81}, \frac{-1}{243}$$

3. Write out the first five terms of the specified sequence. (Begin with $n = 1$.)

$$a_n = \frac{4^n}{n!}: \ 4, \ 8, \ 10 \tfrac{2}{3}, \ 10 \tfrac{2}{3}, \ \frac{128}{15}$$

5. Determine the convergence or divergence of the sequence with the general term

$$a_n = \frac{2n + 3}{n^2}$$

Solution:

The sequence converges since $\displaystyle \lim_{n \to \infty} \frac{2n + 3}{n^2} = 0$.

7. Determine the convergence or divergence of the sequence with the general term

$$a_n = \frac{n^3}{n^2 + 1}.$$

Solution:

The sequence diverges since $\displaystyle \lim_{n \to \infty} \frac{n^3}{n^2 + 1} = \infty$.

9. Determine the convergence or divergence of the sequence with the general term

$$a_n = 5 + \frac{1}{3^n}.$$

Solution:

The sequence converges since $\lim\limits_{n \to \infty} \left(5 + \frac{1}{3^n} \right) = 5 + 0 = 5.$

11. Determine the convergence or divergence of the sequence with the general term

$$a_n = \frac{1}{n^{4/3}}$$

Solution:

The sequence converges, since $\lim\limits_{n \to \infty} \frac{1}{n^{4/3}} = 0.$

13. Find the general term of $\frac{1}{3}, \frac{2}{6}, \frac{3}{9}, \frac{4}{12} \cdots$.

Solution:

$$a_n = \frac{n}{3n} \text{ or } a_n = \frac{1}{3}$$

15. Find the general term of the sequence $\frac{1}{3}, -\frac{2}{9}, \frac{4}{27}, -\frac{8}{81}, \ldots$.

Solution:

$$a_n = (-1)^{n-1} \left(\frac{2^{n-1}}{3^n} \right), \quad n = 1, 2, 3, \ldots$$

OR

$$a_n = (-1)^n \left(\frac{2^n}{3^{n+1}} \right), \quad n = 0, 1, 2, \ldots$$

17. *Sales Increases* A mail-order company sells \$15,000 worth of products during its first year. The company's goal is to increase sales by \$10,000 each year for 9 years. (See graph in textbook.)

(a) Write an expression for the amount of sales during the nth year.

(b) Compute the total sales for the first 5 years that the mail-order company is in business.

Solution:

(a) $a_1 = 15,000$

$a_2 = 15,000 + 10,000$

$\vdots$

$a_n = 15,000 + 10,000(n - 1)$

(b) $a_1 + a_2 + a_3 + a_4 + a_5 = \sum\limits_{n=1}^{15} [15,000 + 10,000(n-1)] = (15,000)5 + 100,000 = \$175,000$

19. Find the first five terms of the sequence of partial sums for the following series.

$$\sum_{n=0}^{\infty} \left(\frac{3}{2}\right)^n$$

Solution:

$$S_0 = 1$$

$$S_1 = 1 + \frac{3}{2} = \frac{5}{2} = 2.5$$

$$S_2 = 1 + \frac{3}{2} + \frac{9}{4} = \frac{19}{4} = 4.75$$

$$S_3 = 1 + \frac{3}{2} + \frac{9}{4} + \frac{27}{8} = \frac{65}{8} = 8.125$$

$$S_4 = 1 + \frac{3}{2} + \frac{9}{4} + \frac{27}{8} + \frac{81}{16} = \frac{211}{16} = 13.1875$$

21. Find the first five terms of the sequence of partial sums for the following series.

$$\sum_{n=1}^{\infty} \frac{(-1)^{n+1}}{(2n)!}$$

Solution:

$$S_1 = \frac{1}{2!} = \frac{1}{2} = 0.5$$

$$S_2 = \frac{1}{2!} - \frac{1}{4!} = \frac{11}{24} \approx 0.4583$$

$$S_3 = \frac{1}{2!} - \frac{1}{4!} + \frac{1}{6!} = \frac{331}{720} \approx 0.4597$$

$$S_4 = \frac{1}{2!} - \frac{1}{4!} + \frac{1}{6!} - \frac{1}{8!} = \frac{18,535}{40,320} \approx 0.4597$$

$$S_5 = \frac{1}{2!} - \frac{1}{4!} + \frac{1}{6!} - \frac{1}{8!} + \frac{1}{10!} = \frac{1,668,151}{3,628,800} \approx 0.4597$$

23. Determine the convergence or divergence of the series $\displaystyle\sum_{n=1}^{\infty} \frac{n^2 + 1}{n(n + 1)}$.

Solution:

This series diverges by the nth-Term Test since $\displaystyle\lim_{n \to \infty} \frac{n^2 + 1}{n(n + 1)} = 1 \neq 0$.

25. Determine the convergence or divergence of the series $\displaystyle\sum_{n=0}^{\infty} 2(0.25)^{n+1}$.

Solution:

This geometric series converges since $r = (0.25) < 1$.

27. Use the nth-Term Test to verify that the series diverges.

$$\sum_{n=1}^{\infty} \frac{2n}{n+5}$$

Solution:

$$\lim_{n \to \infty} \frac{2n}{n+5} = 2 \neq 0, \text{ and the series diverges.}$$

29. Use the nth-Term Test to verify that the series diverges.

$$\sum_{n=0}^{\infty} \left(\frac{5}{4}\right)^n$$

Solution:

$$\lim_{n \to \infty} \left(\frac{5}{4}\right)^n = \infty \neq 0, \text{ and the series diverges.}$$

31. Find the nth partial sum of the series.

$$\sum_{n=0}^{\infty} \left(\frac{1}{5}\right)^n$$

Solution:

$$S_n = \sum_{k=0}^{n} \left(\frac{1}{5}\right)^k = \frac{1 - \left(\frac{1}{5}\right)^{n+1}}{1 - \frac{1}{5}} = \frac{5}{4}\left(1 - \left(\frac{1}{5}\right)^{n+1}\right)$$

33. Find the nth partial sum of the series.

$$\sum_{n=0}^{\infty} \left(\frac{1}{2^n} + \frac{1}{4^n}\right)$$

Solution:

$$S_n = \sum_{k=0}^{n} \frac{1}{2^n} + \sum_{k=0}^{n} \frac{1}{4^n} = \frac{1 - \left(\frac{1}{2}\right)^{n+1}}{1 - \frac{1}{2}} + \frac{1 - \left(\frac{1}{4}\right)^n}{1 - \frac{1}{4}}$$

$$= 2\left(1 - \left(\frac{1}{2}\right)^{n+4}\right) + \frac{4}{3}\left(1 - \left(\frac{1}{4}\right)^{n+1}\right)$$

35. Decide whether $\sum_{n=0}^{\infty} = \frac{1}{4}(4)^n$ converges or diverges. If it converges, find its sum.

Solution:

$$\sum_{n=0}^{\infty} \frac{1}{4}(4^n) \text{ diverges since } \lim_{n \to \infty} a_n \neq 0.$$

37. Decide whether $\displaystyle\sum_{n=0}^{\infty} [(0.5)^n + (0.2)^n]$ converges or diverges. If it converges, find its sum.

Solution:

$$\sum_{n=0}^{\infty}[(0.5)^n + (0.2)^n] = \frac{1}{1 - 0.5} + \frac{1}{1 - 0.2} = 2 + \frac{5}{4} = \frac{13}{4}.$$

39. *Bouncing Ball* A ball is dropped from a height of 8 feet. Each time it drops h feet, it rebounds $0.7h$ feet.

(a) Write a model for the distance traveled by the ball.

(b) Find the total distance traveled by the ball.

Solution:

(a) $D_1 = 8$

$D_2 = 0.7(8) + 0.7(8) = 16(0.7)$

$D_3 = 16(0.7)^2$

$D = -8 + 16 + 16(0.7) + 16(0.7)^2 + \cdots$

(b) $D = -8 + \displaystyle\sum_{n=0}^{\infty} 16(0.7)^n = -8 + \frac{16}{1 - 0.7} = -8 + \frac{160}{3} = \frac{136}{3}$ feet.

41. Determine the convergence or divergence of the p-series.

$$\sum_{n=1}^{\infty} \frac{1}{n^4}$$

Solution:

$\displaystyle\sum_{n=1}^{\infty}\frac{1}{n^4}$ converges by the p-series test since $p = 4 > 1$.

43. Determine the convergence or divergence of the p-series.

$$\sum_{n=1}^{\infty} \frac{1}{n\sqrt[4]{n}}$$

Solution:

$\displaystyle\sum_{n=1}^{\infty} \frac{1}{n\sqrt[4]{n}} = \sum_{n=1}^{\infty} \frac{1}{n^{5/4}}$ converges by the p-series test since $p = \frac{5}{4} > 1$.

45. Approximate the sum of $\displaystyle\sum_{n=1}^{\infty} \frac{1}{n^6}$ using four terms. Include an estimate of the maximum error for your approximation.

Solution:

$$\sum_{n=1}^{\infty} \frac{1}{n^6} \approx 1 + \frac{1}{2^6} + \frac{1}{3^6} + \frac{1}{4^6} \approx 1.0172$$

$$\text{error} < \frac{1}{(5)4^5} \approx 1.9531 \times 10^{-4}$$

47. Approximate the sum of $\displaystyle\sum_{n=1}^{\infty} \frac{1}{n^{5/4}}$ using six terms. Include an estimate of the maximum error for your approximation.

Solution:

$$\sum_{n=1}^{\infty} \frac{1}{n^{5/4}} \approx 1 + \frac{1}{2^{5/4}} + \cdots + \frac{1}{7^{5/4}} \approx 2.17857$$

$$\text{error} < \frac{1}{\frac{1}{4}(7)^{1/4}} < 2.4592$$

49. Determine the convergence or divergence of the series $\displaystyle\sum_{n=1}^{\infty} \frac{n4^n}{n!}$ by using the Ratio Test.

Solution:

This series converges by the Ratio Test since

$$\lim_{n\to\infty} \left| \frac{(n+1)4^{n+1}}{(n+1)!} \cdot \frac{n!}{n4^n} \right| = \lim_{n\to\infty} \frac{4}{n} = 0 < 1.$$

51. Determine the convergence or divergence of the series $\displaystyle\sum_{n=1}^{\infty} \frac{(-1)^n 3^n}{n}$ by using the Ratio Test.

Solution:

This series diverges by the Ratio Test since

$$\lim_{n\to\infty} \left| \frac{(-1)^{n+1} 3^{n+1}}{n+1} \cdot \frac{n}{(-1)^n 3^n} \right| = \lim_{n\to\infty} \left| 3\frac{n}{n+1} \right| = 3 > 1$$

53. Determine the convergence or divergence of the series $\displaystyle\sum_{n=1}^{\infty} \frac{n2^n}{n!}$ by using the Ratio Test.

Solution:

This series converges by the Ratio Test since

$$\lim_{n\to\infty} \left| \frac{(n+1)2^{n+1}}{(n+1)!} \cdot \frac{n!}{n2^n} \right| = \lim_{n\to\infty} \frac{2}{n} = 0 < 1.$$

55. Find the radius of convergence of the power series $\displaystyle\sum_{n=0}^{\infty} \frac{(-1)^n (x-2)^n}{(n+1)^2}$.

Solution:

$$R = \lim_{n\to\infty} \left| \frac{(-1)^n}{(n+1)^2} \cdot \frac{(n+2)^2}{(-1)^{n+1}} \right| = \lim_{n\to\infty} \left| -\frac{n^2+4n+4}{n^2+2n+1} \right| = 1$$

57. Find the radius of convergence of the power series $\displaystyle\sum_{n=0}^{\infty} n!(x-2)^n$.

Solution:

$$R = \lim_{n\to\infty} \left| \frac{n!}{(n+1)!} \right| = \lim_{n\to\infty} \frac{1}{n+1} = 0$$

59. Apply Taylor's Theorem to find the power series for $f(x) = e^{-0.5x}$, centered at $c = 0$.

Solution:

$$f(x) = e^{-0.5x} \qquad\qquad f(0) = 1$$

$$f'(x) = -\frac{1}{2}e^{-1/2x} \qquad f'(0) = -\frac{1}{2}$$

$$f''(x) = \frac{1}{4}e^{-1/2} \qquad\quad f'(0) = \frac{1}{4}$$

$$\vdots \qquad\qquad\qquad \vdots$$

$$f^{(n)}(0) = \left(-\frac{1}{2}\right)^n$$

$$e^{-0.5x} = 1 - \frac{1}{2}x + \frac{1}{4} \cdot \frac{x^2}{2} - \frac{1}{8} \cdot \frac{x^3}{3!} + \cdots = \sum_{n=0}^{\infty} \left(-\frac{1}{2}\right)^n \frac{x^n}{n!}$$

61. Apply Taylor's Theorem to find the power series for $f(x) = 1/x$ centered at $c = -1$.

Solution:

$$f(x) = \frac{1}{x} \qquad\qquad f(-1) = -1$$

$$f'(x) = -\frac{1}{x^2} \qquad\qquad f'(-1) = -1$$

$$f''(x) = \frac{2}{x^3} \qquad\qquad f''(-1) = -2$$

$$f'''(x) = -\frac{6}{x^4} \qquad\qquad f'''(-1) = -6$$

$$\vdots$$

$$f^{(n)}(-1) = -(n!)$$

The power series for f is

$$\frac{1}{x} = f(-1) + f'(-1)(x+1) + \frac{f''(-1)(x+1)^2}{2!} + \cdots$$

$$= -1 - (x+1) - \frac{2(x+1)^2}{2!} - \frac{6(x+1)^3}{3!} - \cdots$$

$$= -[1 + (x+1) + (x+1)^2 + (x+1)^3 + \cdots] = -\sum_{n=0}^{\infty}(x+1)^n.$$

63. Find the series representation of $f(x) = \ln(x+2)$. Assume the series is centered at 0.

Solution:

$$\ln(x+2) = \ln\left(2(\tfrac{x}{2}+1)\right) = \ln 2 + \ln\left(\frac{x}{2}+1\right)$$

$$= \ln(2) + \frac{1}{2}x - \frac{1}{8}x^2 + \frac{1}{24}x^3 - \frac{1}{64}x^4 + \cdots = \ln 2 + \sum_{n=1}^{\infty}(-1)^{n+1}\frac{(x/2)^2}{n}$$

65. Find the series representation of $f(x) = (1+x^2)^2$. Assume the series is centered at 0.

Solution:

$$(1+x^2)^2 = 1 + 2x^2 + \frac{2(1)x^4}{2!} + \cdots = 1 + 2x^2 + x^4 + \cdots$$

67. Use a sixth-degree Taylor polynomial to approximate the function in
$$f(x) = \frac{1}{(x+3)^2}, [-1, 1].$$

Solution:

$$\frac{1}{(x+3)^2} \approx \frac{1}{9} - \frac{2}{27}x + \frac{1}{27}x^2 - \frac{4}{243}x^3 + \frac{5}{729}x^4 - \frac{2}{729}x^5 + \frac{7}{6561}x^6$$

69. Use a sixth-degree Taylor polynomial to approximate the function in $f(x) = \ln(x + 2)$, $[0, 2]$.

Solution:

$$\ln(x + 2) \approx \ln 3 + \frac{1}{3}(x - 1) - \frac{1}{18}(x - 1)^2 + \frac{1}{81}(x - 1)^3$$

$$- \frac{1}{324}(x - 1)^4 + \frac{1}{1215}(x - 1)^5 - \frac{1}{4374}(x - 1)^6$$

71. Use a sixth-degree Taylor polynomial centered at c for the function f to obtain the desired approximation.

$$f(x) = e^{x^2}, c = 1, \text{ approximate } f(1.25)$$

Solution:

$$f(1.25) \approx 4.770479903$$

73. Use a sixth-degree Taylor polynomial centered at c for the function f to obtain the desired approximation.

$$f(x) = \ln(1 + x), c = 1, \text{ approximate } f(1.5)$$

Solution:

$$f(1.5) \approx 0.9162835738$$

75. Determine the maximum error guaranteed by Taylor's Remainder Theorem when the given 5th-degree polynomial is used to approximate f in the indicated interval.

$$f(x) = \frac{2}{x}, \left[1, \frac{3}{2}\right]$$

$$P_5(x) = 2[1 - (x - 1) + (x - 1)^2 - (x - 1)^3 + (x - 1)^4 - (x - 1)^5]$$

Solution:

$$\text{error} = R_n = \frac{f^{(n+1)}(z)}{(n + 1)!}(x - c)^{n+1}$$

$$f(x) = \frac{2}{x} \Rightarrow f^{(6)}(x) = \frac{1440}{x^7} \leq 1440 \text{ on } \left[1, \frac{3}{2}\right]$$

$$R_n \leq \frac{1440}{6!}(x - 1)^6 < 2\left(\frac{1}{2}\right)^6 = \frac{1}{32}$$

77. Use a Taylor polynomial of sixth-degree to approximate $\int_0^{0.3} \sqrt{1 + x^3}\, dx$ centered at $c = 0$.

Solution:

$$\sqrt{1 + x^3} = 1 + \frac{x^3}{2} - \frac{x^6}{8} + \cdots$$

$$\int_0^{0.3} \sqrt{1 + x^3}\, dx \approx \left[x + \frac{x^4}{8} - \frac{x^7}{56}\right]_0^{0.3} = 0.3 + \frac{(0.3)^4}{8} - \frac{(0.3)^7}{56} \approx 0.301$$

79. Use a Taylor polynomial of sixth-degree to approximate $\sum\limits_{0}^{0.75} \ln(x^2+1)dx$.

Solution:

$$\ln(x^2+1) = x^2 - \frac{1}{2}x^4 + \frac{1}{3}x^6 - \cdots$$

$$\sum_{0}^{0.75} \ln(x^2+1)dx \approx \sum_{0}^{0.75} \left(x^2 - \frac{1}{2}x^4 + \frac{1}{3}x^6 \right) dx$$

$$= \left[\frac{x^3}{3} - \frac{x^5}{10} + \frac{x^7}{21} \right]_{0}^{0.75} \approx 0.12325$$

81. Find the expected value of the random variable n, and determine the expected production costs if each unit costs $23.00 to make.

$$P(n) = \left(\frac{1}{3}\right)^{n+1}$$

Solution:

$$\text{Expected Value} = \sum_{n=0}^{\infty} n P(n) = \sum_{n=0}^{\infty} n \left(\frac{1}{3}\right)^{n+1}$$

$$= 0\left(\frac{1}{3}\right) + 1\left(\frac{1}{3}\right)^2 + 2\left(\frac{1}{3}\right)^3 + \cdots$$

Since $(1-x)^{-2} = 1 + 2x + 3x^2 + 4x^3 + \cdots$ (Bionomial series)

$$\left(1 - \frac{1}{3}\right)^{-2} = 1 + 2\left(\frac{1}{3}\right) + 3\left(\frac{1}{3}\right)^2 + \cdots = \frac{9}{4} \text{ and}$$

$$\text{Expected Value} = 1\left(\frac{1}{3}\right)^2 + 2\left(\frac{1}{3}\right)^3 + 3\left(\frac{1}{3}\right)^4 + \cdots$$

$$= \left(\frac{1}{3}\right)^2 \left[1 + 2\left(\frac{1}{3}\right) + 3\left(\frac{1}{3}\right)^2 + \cdots \right]$$

$$= \left(\frac{1}{3}\right)^2 \left(\frac{9}{4}\right) = \frac{1}{4} = 0.25 \text{ units}$$

Expected Production Cost $= (23.00)(0.25) = \$5.75$.

83. Use Newton's Method to approximate to three decimal places the zero(s) of $f(x) = 2x^3 + 3x - 1$.

Solution:

$$f(x) = 2x^3 + 3x - 1$$

$$f'(x) = 6x^2 + 3$$

$$x_{n+1} = x_n - \frac{f(x_n)}{f'(x_n)} = x_n - \frac{2x_n^3 + 3x_n - 1}{6x_n^2 + 3}$$

$x_1 = 0$ (initial guess)

$$x_2 = \frac{1}{3}$$

$x_3 = 0.31\overline{31}$

$x_4 = 0.3129$

$x \approx 0.313$

85. Use Newton's Method to approximate to three decimal places the zero(s) of $f(x) = \ln 3x + x$.

Solution:

$$f(x) = \ln 3x + x$$

$$f'(x) = \frac{1}{x} + 1$$

$$x_{n+1} = x_n - \frac{f(x_n)}{f'(x_n)}$$

$x_1 = 0.5$ (initial guess)

$x_2 = 0.1982$

$x_3 = 0.2514$

$x_4 = 0.2576$

$x \approx 0.258$

87. Apply Newton's Method to approximate to three decimal places the x-value of the point of intersection of the graphs of $f(x) = x^5$, $g(x) = x + 3$.

Solution:

Let $h(x) = f(x) - g(x) = x^5 - (x + 3)$

$$h'(x) = 5x^4 - 1$$

$x_1 = 1.5$ (initial guess)

$x_2 = 1.37275$

$x_3 = 1.34279$

$x_4 = 1.3413$

$x \approx 1.341$

89. Apply Newton's Method to approximate to three decimal places the x-value of the point of intersection of the graphs of $f(x) = x^3$, $g(x) = e^{-x}$.

Solution:

$$\text{Let } h(x) = f(x) - g(x) = x^3 - e^{-x}$$

$$h'(x) = 3x^2 + e^{-x}$$

$$x_1 = 1 \text{ (initial guess)}$$

$$x_2 = 0.8123$$

$$x_3 = 0.7743$$

$$x_4 = 0.7729$$

$$x \approx 0.773$$

Practice Test for Chapter S

1. Find the general term of the sequence $\frac{1}{2}$, $\frac{2}{5}$, $\frac{3}{10}$, $\frac{4}{17}$, $\frac{5}{26}$, $\ldots$.

2. Find the general term of the sequence 5, -7, 9, -11, 13, $\ldots$.

3. Determine the convergence or divergence of the sequence whose general term is

$$a_n = \frac{n^2}{3n^2 + 4}.$$

4. Determine the convergence or divergence of the sequence whose general term is

$$a_n = \frac{4n}{\sqrt{n^2 + 1}}.$$

5. Find the sum of the series $\displaystyle\sum_{n=0}^{\infty} \left(\frac{1}{5^n} - \frac{1}{7^n} \right).$

6. Determine the convergence or divergence of the series $\displaystyle\sum_{n=1}^{\infty} \frac{3^n}{n!}.$

7. Determine the convergence or divergence of the series $\displaystyle\sum_{n=1}^{\infty} \frac{1}{n\sqrt[3]{n}}.$

8. Determine the convergence or divergence of the series $\displaystyle\sum_{n=1}^{\infty} \frac{n}{2n + 3}.$

9. Determine the convergence or divergence of the series $\displaystyle\sum_{n=0}^{\infty} \frac{(-1)^n 6^n}{5^n}.$

10. Determine the convergence or divergence of the series $\displaystyle\sum_{n=1}^{\infty} \frac{\sqrt[3]{n}}{\sqrt{n}}.$

11. Determine the convergence or divergence of the series $\displaystyle\sum_{n=1}^{\infty} \frac{5^n n!}{(n + 1)!}.$

12. Determine the convergence or divergence of the series $\displaystyle\sum_{n=0}^{\infty} 4(0.27)^n.$

13. Determine the convergence or divergence of the series $\displaystyle\sum_{n=1}^{\infty} \left(1 + \frac{1}{3^n} \right).$

14. Find the radius of convergence of the power series $\displaystyle\sum_{n=0}^{\infty} \frac{(-1)^n (x - 3)^n}{(n + 4)^2}.$

15. Find the radius of convergence of the power series $\displaystyle\sum_{n=0}^{\infty} \frac{x^n}{(n+1)!}$.

16. Apply Taylor's Theorem to find the power series (centered at 0) for $f(x) = e^{-4x}$.

17. Apply Taylor's Theorem to find the power series (centered at 1) for $f(x) = \dfrac{1}{\sqrt[3]{x}}$.

18. Use the ninth-degree Taylor polynomial for e^{x^3} to approximate the value of

$$\int_0^{0.213} e^{x^3}\, dx.$$

19. Use Newton's Method to approximate the zero of the function $f(x) = x^3 + x - 3$. (Make your approximation good to three decimal places.)

20. Use Newton's Method to approximate $\sqrt[4]{10}$ to three decimal places.

Graphing Calculator Required

21. Use SUM SEQ to evaluate the following sums.

(a) $\displaystyle\sum_{n=0}^{10} \frac{4}{2^n}$

(b) $\displaystyle\sum_{n=1}^{8} 3n!$

22. Graph the function $y = e^{2x}$ as well as the Taylor Polynomials of degree 2, 4, and 6 on the same set of axes.

23. Use a program similar to the one on page S-54 in the textbook to approximate the real roots of $3x^4 - 2x^3 + 5x^2 + 6x - 10 = 0$.

CHAPTER T
Trigonometric Functions

Section T.1   Radian Measure of Angles

1. Determine two coterminal angles (one positive and one negative) for (a) 45° and
(b) −41°. Give the answers in degrees.

Solution:

(a) Positive: $45° + 360° = 405°$

   Negative: $45° - 360° = -315°$

(b) Positive: $-41° + 360° = 319°$

   Negative: $-41° - 360° = -401$

3. Determine two coterminal angles (one positive and one negative) for (a) 300° and
(b) 740°. Give the answers in degrees.

Solution:

(a) Positive: $300° + 360° = 660°$

   Negative: $300° - 360° = -60°$

(b) Positive: $740° - 2(360°) = 20°$

   Negative: $740° - 3(360°) = -340°$

5. Determine two coterminal angles (one positive and one negative) for (a) $\pi/9$ and
(b) $2\pi/3$. Give the answers in radians.

Solution:

(a) Positive: $(\pi/9) + 2\pi = 19\pi/9$

   Negative: $(\pi/9) - 2\pi = -17\pi/9$

(b) Positive: $(2\pi/3) + 2\pi = 8\pi/3$

   Negative: $(2\pi/3) - 2\pi = -4\pi/3$

7. Determine two coterminal angles (one positive and one negative) for (a) $-9\pi/4$ and
(b) $-2\pi/15$. Give the answers in radians.

Solution:

(a) Positive: $(-9\pi/4) + 2(2\pi) = 7\pi/4$

   Negative: $(-9\pi/4) + 2\pi = -\pi/4$

(b) Positive: $(-2\pi/15) + 2\pi = 28\pi/15$

   Negative: $(-2\pi/15) - 2\pi = -32\pi/15$

9. Express 30° in radian measure as a multiple of π.

Solution:

$$30°\left(\frac{\pi \text{ radians}}{180°}\right) = \frac{\pi}{6} \text{ radians}$$

11. Express $315°$ in radian measure as a multiple of π.

Solution:

$$315°\left(\frac{\pi \text{ radians}}{180°}\right) = \frac{7\pi}{4} \text{ radians}$$

13. Express $-30°$ in radian measure as a multiple of π.

Solution:

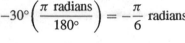

$$-30°\left(\frac{\pi \text{ radians}}{180°}\right) = -\frac{\pi}{6} \text{ radians}$$

15. Express $-270°$ in radian measure as a multiple of π.

Solution:

$$-270°\left(\frac{\pi \text{ radians}}{180°}\right) = -\frac{3\pi}{2} \text{ radians}$$

17. Express $3\pi/2$ in degree measure.

Solution:

$$\frac{3\pi}{2}\left(\frac{180°}{\pi}\right) = 270°$$

19. Express $-7\pi/12$ in degree measure.

Solution:

$$-\frac{7\pi}{12}\left(\frac{180°}{\pi}\right) = -105°$$

21. Express the angle in degree measure.

$$\frac{11\pi}{2}$$

Solution:

$$\frac{11\pi}{2}\left(\frac{180°}{\pi}\right) = 990°$$

23. Express the angle in degree measure.

$$-\frac{11\pi}{30}$$

Solution:

$$-\frac{11\pi}{30}\left(\frac{180°}{\pi}\right) = -66°$$

25. Solve the triangle for θ and c.

Solution:

The angle θ is $\theta = 90° - 30° = 60°$. Since the vertical side is $c/2$, we can use the Pythagorean Theorem to find the length of the hypotenuse as follows.

$$c^2 = (5\sqrt{3})^2 + \left(\frac{c}{2}\right)^2$$

$$\frac{3c^2}{4} = 75$$

$$c^2 = 100$$

$$c = 10$$

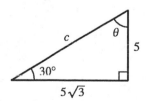

27. Solve the triangle for θ and a.

Solution:

The angle θ is $\theta = 90° - 60° = 30°$. By the Pythagorean Theorem, the value of a is

$$a = \sqrt{8^2 - 4^2}$$
$$= \sqrt{64 - 16}$$
$$= \sqrt{48}$$
$$= 4\sqrt{3}$$

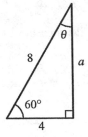

29. Solve the triangle for θ.

Solution:

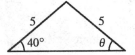

Since the triangle is isosceles, we have $\theta = 40°$.

31. Solve the triangle for θ.

Solution:

Since the large triangle is similar to the two smaller triangles, $\theta = 60°$. The hypotenuse of the large triangle is $\sqrt{2^2 + (2\sqrt{3})^2} = \sqrt{16} = 4$, and by similar triangles we have

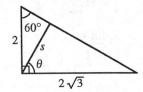

$$\frac{s}{2} = \frac{2\sqrt{3}}{4} \Rightarrow s = \sqrt{3}.$$

33. Find the area of the equilateral triangle with sides of length 6 inches.

Solution:

$$h^2 + 3^2 = 6^2$$
$$h^2 = 27$$
$$h = 3\sqrt{3}$$
$$A = \frac{1}{2}bh = \frac{1}{2}(6)(3\sqrt{3}) = 9\sqrt{3} \text{ square inches}$$

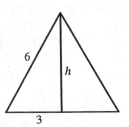

35. Find the area of the equilateral triangle with sides of length 5 feet.

Solution:

$$h^2 + \left(\frac{5}{2}\right)^2 = 5^2$$

$$h^2 = \frac{25}{2}$$

$$h = \frac{5\sqrt{2}}{2}$$

$$A = \frac{1}{2}bh$$

$$= \frac{1}{2}(5)\left(\frac{5\sqrt{2}}{2}\right) = \frac{25\sqrt{2}}{4} \text{ square feet}$$

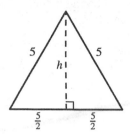

37. Determine whether the statement, "An angle whose measure is 75° is obtuse" is true or false. Explain.

Solution:

False. An obtuse angle is between 90° and 180°.

39. Determine whether the statement, "A right triangle can have one angle whose measure is 89°" is true or false. Explain.

Solution:

True. The angles would be 90°, 89°, and 1°.

41. *Height* A person 6 feet tall standing 12 feet from a streetlight casts a shadow 8 feet long. What is the height of the streetlight?

Solution:

Using similar triangles, we have $h/24 = 6/8$ which implies that $h = 18$ feet.

43. Let r represent the radius of a circle, θ the central angle (measured in radians), and s the length of the arc subtended by the angle. Use the relationship $\theta = s/r$ to complete the following table.

Solution:

r	8 ft	15 in.	85 cm	24 in.	$12{,}963/\pi$ mi
s	12 ft	24 in.	200.28 cm	96 in.	8642 mi
θ	1.5	1.6	$3\pi/4$	4	$2\pi/3$

45. *Distance* A man bends his elbow through 75°. The distance from his elbow to the tip of his index finger is $18\frac{3}{4}$ inches. (a) Find the radian measure of this angle. (b) Find the distance the tip of the index finger moves.

Solution:

(a) The radian measure is $75° \left(\dfrac{\pi \text{ radians}}{180°} \right) = \dfrac{5\pi}{12}$ radians.

(b) The distance moved is $S = \dfrac{5\pi}{12}(18.75) = 7.8125\pi$ in ≈ 24.54 in.

47. *Latitude* Assuming that the earth is a sphere of radius 4000 miles, what is the difference in latitude of two cities, one of which is 325 miles due north of the other? [Latitude lines on the earth run parallel to the equator and measure the angle from the equator to a point north or south of the equator.]

Solution:

Using the equation $\theta = s/r$, we have the following.

$$\theta = \frac{325}{4000} = \frac{13}{160} = \frac{13}{160} \left(\frac{180°}{\pi} \right) = \left(\frac{117}{8\pi} \right)^{\circ} \approx 4.655°$$

Section T.2   The Trigonometric Functions

1. Determine all six trigonometric functions for θ.

Solution:

Since $x = 3$ and $y = 4$, it follows that $r = \sqrt{3^2 + 4^2} = 5$. Therefore, we have the following.

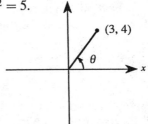

$$\sin \theta = \tfrac{4}{5} \qquad \csc \theta = \tfrac{5}{4}$$

$$\cos \theta = \tfrac{3}{5} \qquad \sec \theta = \tfrac{5}{3}$$

$$\tan \theta = \tfrac{4}{3} \qquad \cot \theta = \tfrac{3}{4}$$

3. Determine all six trigonometric functions for θ.

Solution:

Since $x = -12$ and $y = -5$, it follows that $r = \sqrt{(-12)^2 + (-5)^2} = 13$. Therefore, we have the following.

$$\sin \theta = -\frac{5}{13} \qquad \csc \theta = -\frac{13}{5}$$

$$\cos \theta = -\frac{12}{13} \qquad \sec \theta = -\frac{13}{12}$$

$$\tan \theta = \frac{5}{12} \qquad \cot \theta = \frac{12}{5}$$

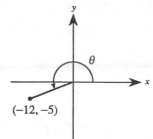

5. Determine all six trigonometric functions for θ.

Solution:

Since $x = -\sqrt{3}$ and $y = 1$, it follows that $r = \sqrt{3 + 1^2} = 2$. Therefore, we have the following.

$$\sin \theta = \frac{1}{2} \qquad \csc \theta = 2$$

$$\cos \theta = -\frac{\sqrt{3}}{2} \qquad \sec \theta = -\frac{2\sqrt{3}}{3}$$

$$\tan \theta = -\frac{\sqrt{3}}{3} \qquad \cot \theta = -\sqrt{3}$$

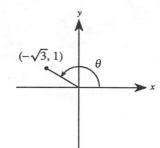

7. Find $\csc\theta$ given $\sin\theta = \frac{1}{2}$.

Solution:

$$\csc\theta = \frac{1}{\sin\theta} = \frac{1}{1/2} = 2$$

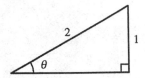

9. Find $\cot\theta$ given $\cos\theta = \frac{4}{5}$.

Solution:

Since $x = 4$ and $r = 5$, the length of the opposite side is $y = \sqrt{5^2 - 4^2} = 3$. Therefore, we have

$$\cot\theta = \frac{x}{y} = \frac{4}{3}.$$

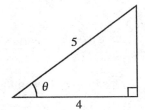

11. Find $\sec\theta$ given $\cot\theta = \frac{15}{8}$.

Solution:

Since $x = 15$ and $y = 8$, the length of the hypotenuse is $r = \sqrt{15^2 + 8^2} = 17$. Therefore, we have the following.

$$\sec\theta = \frac{r}{x} = \frac{17}{15}$$

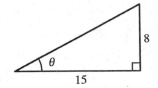

13. Sketch a right triangle corresponding to $\sin \theta = \dfrac{1}{3}$ and find the other five trigonometric functions of θ.

Solution:

The length of the third side of the triangle is

$$x^2 = 3^2 - 1^2 = 8$$

$$x = 2\sqrt{2}$$

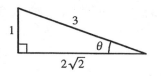

Therefore,

$$\sin \theta = \frac{1}{3} \qquad \csc \theta = 3$$

$$\cos \theta = \frac{2\sqrt{2}}{3} \qquad \sec \theta = \frac{3}{2\sqrt{2}}$$

$$\tan \theta = \frac{1}{2\sqrt{2}} \qquad \cot \theta = 2\sqrt{2}.$$

15. Sketch a right triangle corresponding to $\sec \theta = 2$ and find the other five trigonometric functions of θ.

Solution:

Since $x = 1$ and $r = 2$, the length of the opposite side is $y = \sqrt{2^2 - 1^2} = \sqrt{3}$.
Therefore,

$$\sin \theta = \frac{\sqrt{3}}{2} \qquad \csc \theta = \frac{2\sqrt{3}}{3}$$

$$\cos \theta = \frac{1}{2} \qquad \sec \theta = 2$$

$$\tan \theta = \sqrt{3} \qquad \cot \theta = \frac{\sqrt{3}}{3}.$$

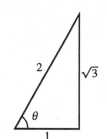

17. Sketch a right triangle corresponding to $\tan\theta = 3$ and find the other five trigonometric functions of θ.

Solution:

Since $x = 1$ and $y = 3$, the length of the hypotenuse is $r = \sqrt{1^2 + 3^2} = \sqrt{10}$. Therefore,

$$\sin\theta = \frac{3\sqrt{10}}{10} \qquad \csc\theta = \frac{\sqrt{10}}{3}$$

$$\cos\theta = \frac{\sqrt{10}}{10} \qquad \sec\theta = \sqrt{10}$$

$$\tan\theta = 3 \qquad \cot\theta = \frac{1}{3}.$$

19. Given that $\sin\theta > 0$ and $\cos\theta < 0$, determine the quadrant in which θ lies.

Solution:

Since the sinc is negative and the cosine is positive, θ must lie in Quadrant IV.

21. Given that $\sin\theta > 0$ and $\sec\theta > 0$, determine the quadrant in which θ lies.

Solution:

Since the sine is positive and the secant is positive, θ must lie in Quadrant I.

23. Given that $\csc\theta > 0$ and $\tan\theta < 0$, determine the quadrant in which θ lies.

Solution:

Since the cosecant is positive and the tangent is negative, θ must lie in Quadrant II.

25. Evaluate the sine, cosine, and tangent of (a) $60°$ and (b) $-2\pi/3$. Do not use a calculator.

Solution:

(a) $\sin 60° = \dfrac{\sqrt{3}}{2}$

$\cos 60° = \dfrac{1}{2}$

$\tan 60° = \sqrt{3}$

(b) $\sin\left(\dfrac{-2\pi}{3}\right) = \dfrac{-\sqrt{3}}{2}$

$\cos\left(\dfrac{-2\pi}{3}\right) = -\dfrac{1}{2}$

$\tan\left(\dfrac{-2\pi}{3}\right) = \sqrt{3}$

27. Evaluate the sine, cosine, and tangent of (a) $-\pi/6$ and (b) 150°. Do not use a calculator.

Solution:

(a) $\sin\left(-\dfrac{\pi}{6}\right) = -\dfrac{1}{2}$

$\cos\left(-\dfrac{\pi}{6}\right) = \dfrac{\sqrt{3}}{2}$

$\tan\left(-\dfrac{\pi}{6}\right) = -\dfrac{\sqrt{3}}{3}$

(b) $\sin 150° = \dfrac{1}{2}$

$\cos 150° = -\dfrac{\sqrt{3}}{2}$

$\tan 150° = -\dfrac{\sqrt{3}}{3}$

29. Evaluate the sine, cosine, and tangent of (a) 225° and (b) −225°. Do not use a calculator.

Solution:

(a) $\sin 225° = -\dfrac{\sqrt{2}}{2}$

$\cos 225° = -\dfrac{\sqrt{2}}{2}$

$\tan 225° = 1$

(b) $\sin(-225°) = \dfrac{\sqrt{2}}{2}$

$\cos(-225°) = -\dfrac{\sqrt{2}}{2}$

$\tan(-225°) = -1$

31. Evaluate the sine, cosine, and tangent of (a) 750° and (b) 510°. Do not use a calculator.

Solution:

(a) $\sin 750° = \dfrac{1}{2}$

$\cos 750° = \dfrac{\sqrt{3}}{2}$

$\tan 750° = \dfrac{\sqrt{3}}{3}$

(b) $\sin 510° = \dfrac{1}{2}$

$\cos 510° = -\dfrac{\sqrt{3}}{2}$

$\tan 510° = -\dfrac{\sqrt{3}}{3}$

33. Use a calculator to evaluate the trigonometric function to four decimal places.

(a) $\sin 12°$

(b) $\csc 12°$

Solution:

(a) $\sin 12° \approx 0.2079$

(b) $\csc 12° \approx 4.8097$

35. Use a calculator to evaluate the trigonometric function to four decimal places.

(a) $\tan\left(\dfrac{\pi}{9}\right)$

(b) $\tan\left(\dfrac{10\pi}{9}\right)$

Solution:

(a) $\tan\left(\dfrac{\pi}{9}\right) \approx 0.3640$

(b) $\tan\left(\dfrac{10\pi}{9}\right) \approx 0.3640$

37. Use a calculator to evaluate the trigonometric function to four decimal places.

(a) $\cos(-110°)$

(b) $\cos 250°$

Solution:

(a) $\cos(-110°) \approx -0.3420$

(b) $\cos 250° \approx -0.3420$

39. Use a calculator to evaluate the trigonometric function to four decimal places.

(a) $\csc 2.62$

(b) $\csc 150°$

Solution:

(a) $\csc 2.62 = \dfrac{1}{\sin 2.62} \approx 2.0070$

(b) $\csc 150° = \dfrac{1}{\sin 150°} = 2.0000$

41. Find two values of θ, $(0 \le \theta \le 2\pi)$, for (a) $\sin\theta = \frac{1}{2}$ and (b) $\sin\theta = -\frac{1}{2}$.

Solution:

(a) $\theta = \dfrac{\pi}{6}$ or $\theta = \dfrac{5\pi}{6}$

(b) $\theta = \dfrac{7\pi}{6}$ or $\theta = \dfrac{11\pi}{6}$

43. Find two values of θ, $(0 \le \theta \le 2\pi)$, for (a) $\csc\theta = 2\sqrt{3}/3$ and (b) $\cot\theta = -1$.

Solution:

(a) $\theta = \dfrac{\pi}{3}$ or $\theta = \dfrac{2\pi}{3}$

(b) $\theta = \dfrac{3\pi}{4}$ or $\theta = \dfrac{7\pi}{4}$

45. Find two values of θ, $(0 \le \theta \le 2\pi)$, for (a) $\tan\theta = 1$ and (b) $\cot\theta = -\sqrt{3}$.

Solution:

(a) $\theta = \dfrac{3\pi}{4}$ or $\theta = \dfrac{7\pi}{4}$

(b) $\theta = \dfrac{5\pi}{6}$ or $\theta = \dfrac{11\pi}{6}$

47. Solve for θ, $(0 \le \theta \le 2\pi)$, in the equation $2 \sin^2 \theta = 1$.

Solution:

Solving for $\sin \theta$ produces the following.

$$\sin \theta = \pm \frac{\sqrt{2}}{2}$$

$$\theta = \frac{\pi}{4}, \frac{3\pi}{4}, \frac{5\pi}{4}, \frac{7\pi}{4}$$

49. Solve for θ, $(0 \le \theta \le 2\pi)$, in the equation $\tan^2 \theta - \tan \theta = 0$.

Solution:

$$\tan \theta (\tan \theta - 1) = 0$$

$\tan \theta = 0$ $\qquad$ or $\quad$ $\tan \theta = 1$

$\theta = 0, \; \pi, \; 2\pi$ $\qquad\qquad$ $\theta = \frac{\pi}{4}, \frac{5\pi}{4}$

51. Solve for θ, $(0 \le \theta \le 2\pi)$, in the equation $\sin 2\theta - \cos \theta = 0$.

Solution:

$$\sin 2\theta - \cos \theta = 0$$

$$2 \sin \theta \cos \theta - \cos \theta = 0$$

$$\cos \theta (2 \sin \theta - 1) = 0$$

$\cos \theta = 0$ $\qquad$ or $\qquad$ $2 \sin \theta = 1$

$\theta = \frac{\pi}{2}, \frac{3\pi}{2}$ $\qquad\qquad$ $\theta = \frac{\pi}{6}, \frac{5\pi}{6}$

53. Solve for θ, $(0 \le \theta \le 2\pi)$, in the equation $\sin \theta = \cos \theta$.

Solution:

Dividing both sides by $\cos \theta$ produces the following.

$$\tan \theta = 1$$

$$\theta = \frac{\pi}{4}, \; \frac{5\pi}{4}$$

55. Solve for θ, $(0 \leq \theta \leq 2\pi)$, in the equation $\cos^2 \theta + \sin \theta = 1$.

Solution:

Using the identity $\cos^2 \theta = 1 - \sin^2 \theta$ produces the following.

$$1 - \sin^2 \theta + \sin \theta = 1$$

$$\sin^2 \theta - \sin \theta = 0$$

$$\sin \theta (\sin \theta - 1) = 0$$

$$\sin \theta = 0 \qquad\qquad \text{or} \quad \sin \theta = 1$$

$$\theta = 0, \ \pi, \ 2\pi \qquad\qquad \theta = \frac{\pi}{2}$$

57. Solve for y.

Solution:

Since

$$\tan 30° = \frac{1}{\sqrt{3}} = \frac{y}{100}$$

it follows that

$$y = \frac{100}{\sqrt{3}} = \frac{100\sqrt{3}}{3}.$$

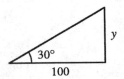

59. Solve for x.

Solution:

Since

$$\cot 60° = \frac{1}{\sqrt{3}} = \frac{x}{25}$$

it follows that

$$x = \frac{25}{\sqrt{3}} = \frac{25\sqrt{3}}{3}.$$

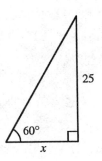

61. Solve for r.

Solution:

Since

$$\sin 40° = \frac{10}{r} \approx 0.6428$$

it follows that

$$r = \frac{10}{0.6428} \approx 15.5572.$$

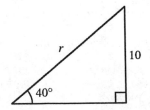

63. *Length* A 20-foot ladder leaning against the side of a house makes a 75° angle with the ground. How far up the side of the house does the ladder reach?

Solution:

Let h be the height of the ladder. Then

$$\sin 75° = \frac{h}{20} \approx 0.9659$$

and

$$h = 20(0.9659) \approx 19.3185 \text{ feet.}$$

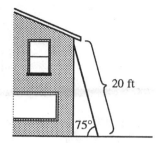

20 ft

75°

65. *Distance* From a 150-foot observation tower on the coast, a Coast Guard officer sights a boat in difficulty. The angle of depression of the boat is 3°. How far is the boat from the shoreline?

Solution:

Let x be the distance from the shore. Then

$$\cot 3° = \frac{x}{150} \approx 19.0811$$

and

$$x = 150(19.0811) \approx 2862.2 \text{ feet.}$$

3°

67. *Average Temperature* The average daily temperature (in degrees Fahrenheit) for a certain city is given by

$$T(t) = 45 - 23 \cos\left[\frac{2\pi}{365}(t - 32)\right],$$

where t is the time in days with $t = 1$ corresponding to January 1. Find the average temperature on (a) January 1 and (b) July 4 ($t = 185$).

Solution:

(a) For January 1, we have $t = 1$ and the average temperature is

$$T(1) = 45 - 23 \cos\left[\frac{2\pi}{365}(-31)\right] \approx 45 - 23 \cos(-0.5336) \approx 45 - 19.8 = 25.2°$$
Fahrenheit.

(b) For July 4, we have $t = 185$ and the average temperature is

$$T(185) = 45 - 23 \cos\left[\frac{2\pi}{365}(153)\right] \approx 45 - 23 \cos(2.6338) \approx 45 + 20.1 = 65.1°$$
Fahrenheit.

69. Use a graphing utility to complete a table for the function

$$f(x) = \frac{2}{5}x + 2\sin\frac{\pi x}{5}.$$

Solution:

x	0	2	4	6	8	10
$f(x)$	0	2.7021	2.7756	1.2244	1.2979	4

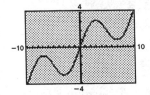

Section T.3   Graphs of Trigonometric Functions

1. Find the period and amplitude of $y = 2\sin 2x$.

Solution:

Period: $\dfrac{2\pi}{2} = \pi$

Amplitude: 2

3. Find the period and amplitude of $y = (3/2)\cos(x/2)$.

Solution:

Period: $\dfrac{2\pi}{1/2} = 4\pi$

Amplitude: $\dfrac{3}{2}$

5. Find the period and amplitude of $y = \frac{1}{2}\cos \pi x$.

Solution:

Period: $\dfrac{2\pi}{\pi} = 2$

Amplitude: $\dfrac{1}{2}$

7. Find the period and amplitude of $y = -2 \sin x$.

Solution:

Period: $\dfrac{2\pi}{1} = 2\pi$

Amplitude: 2

9. Find the period and amplitude of $y = -2 \sin 10x$.

Solution:

Period: $\dfrac{2\pi}{10} = \dfrac{\pi}{5}$

Amplitude: 2

11. Find the period and amplitude of $y = (1/2) \cos(2x/3)$.

Solution:

Period: $\dfrac{2\pi}{2/3} = 3\pi$

Amplitude: $\dfrac{1}{2}$

13. Find the period and amplitude of $y = 3 \sin 4\pi x$.

Solution:

Period: $\dfrac{2\pi}{4\pi} = \dfrac{1}{2}$

Amplitude: 3

15. Find the period of $y = 5 \tan 2x$.

Solution:

Period: $\dfrac{\pi}{2}$

17. Find the period of $y = 3 \sec 5x$.

Solution:

Period: $\dfrac{2\pi}{5}$

19. Find the period of $y = \cot(\pi x/6)$.

Solution:

Period: $\dfrac{\pi}{\pi/6} = 6$

21. Match $y = \sec 2x$ with the correct graph from the text.

Solution:

The graph of this function has a period of π and matches graph (c).

23. Match $y = \cot\left(\dfrac{\pi x}{2}\right)$ with the correct graph from the text.

Solution:

The graph of this function has a period of 2 and matches graph (f).

25. Match $y = 2\csc(x/2)$ with the correct graph from the text.

Solution:

The graph of this function has a period of 4π and matches graph (b).

27. Sketch the graph of $y = \sin(x/2)$.

Solution:

Period: 4π
Amplitude: 1
x-intercepts: $(0,\ 0),\ (2\pi,\ 0),\ (4\pi,\ 0)$
Maximum: $(\pi,\ 1)$
Minimum: $(3\pi,\ -1)$

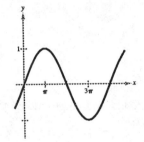

29. Sketch the graph of $y = 2\cos\dfrac{2x}{3}$.

Solution:

Period: 3π

Amplitude: 2

x-intercepts: $\left(\dfrac{3\pi}{4},\ 0\right),\ \left(\dfrac{9\pi}{4}, 0\right),\ \left(\dfrac{15\pi}{4},\ 0\right)$

Maxima: $(0, 2),\ (3\pi, 2)$

Minima: $\left(\dfrac{3\pi}{2},\ -2\right)$

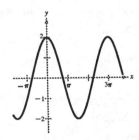

31. Sketch the graph of $y = -2 \sin 6x$.

Solution:

Period: $\dfrac{\pi}{3}$

Amplitude: 2

x-intercepts: $(0, 0)$, $\left(\dfrac{\pi}{6}, 0\right)$, $\left(\dfrac{\pi}{3}, 0\right)$, $\left(\dfrac{\pi}{2}, 0\right)$, $\left(\dfrac{2\pi}{3}, 0\right)$

Maxima: $\left(\dfrac{\pi}{4}, 2\right)$, $\left(\dfrac{7\pi}{4}, 2\right)$

Minimum: $\left(\dfrac{\pi}{12}, -2\right)$, $\left(\dfrac{5\pi}{12}, -2\right)$

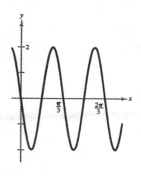

33. Sketch the graph of $y = \cos 2\pi x$.

Solution:

Period: 1

Amplitude: 1

x-intercepts: $\left(-\dfrac{3}{4}, 0\right)$, $\left(-\dfrac{1}{4}, 0\right)$, $\left(\dfrac{1}{4}, 0\right)$, $\left(\dfrac{3}{4}, 0\right)$

Maxima: $(-1, 1)$, $(0, 1)$, $(1, 1)$

Minima: $\left(-\dfrac{1}{2}, -1\right)$, $\left(\dfrac{1}{2}, 1\right)$

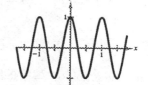

35. Sketch the graph of $y = -\sin(2\pi x/3)$.

Solution:

Period: 3

Amplitude: 1

x-intercepts: $(0, 0)$, $\left(\dfrac{3}{2}, 0\right)$, $(3, 0)$

Maximum: $\left(\dfrac{9}{4}, 1\right)$

Minimum: $\left(\dfrac{3}{4}, -1\right)$

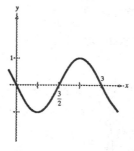

37. Sketch the graph of $y = 2\tan x$.

Solution:

Period: π

x-intercepts: $(0, 0)$, $(\pi, \ 0)$

Asymptotes: $x = -\dfrac{\pi}{2}$, $x = \dfrac{\pi}{2}$, $x = \dfrac{3\pi}{2}$

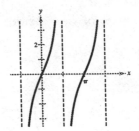

39. Sketch the graph of $y = \cot 2x$.

Solution:

Period: $\dfrac{\pi}{2}$

x-intercepts: $\left(-\dfrac{3\pi}{4}, 0\right)$, $\left(-\dfrac{\pi}{4}, 0\right)$, $\left(\dfrac{\pi}{4}, 0\right)$, $\left(\dfrac{3\pi}{4}, 0\right)$

Asymptotes: $x = -\dfrac{\pi}{2}$, $x = 0$, $x = \dfrac{\pi}{2}$

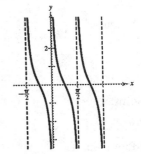

41. Sketch the graph of $y = \csc\left(\dfrac{2x}{3}\right)$.

Solution:

Period: 3π

Asymptotes: $x = 0$, $x = \dfrac{2\pi}{2}, 3\pi$

Relative minimum: $(\dfrac{3\pi}{4}, \ 1)$

Relative maximum: $(\dfrac{9\pi}{4}, \ -1)$

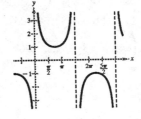

43. Sketch the graph of $y = 2\sec 2x$.

Solution:

Period: π

Asymptotes: $x = -\dfrac{\pi}{4}$, $x = \dfrac{\pi}{4}$, $x = \dfrac{3\pi}{4}$,

$x = \dfrac{5\pi}{4}$, $x = \dfrac{7\pi}{4}$

Relative minima: $(0, \ 2)$, $(\pi, \ 2)$

Relative maxima: $\left(\dfrac{\pi}{2}, \ -2\right)$, $\left(\dfrac{3\pi}{2}, \ -2\right)$

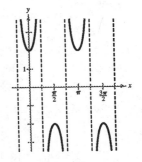

45. Sketch the graph of $y = \csc 2\pi x$.

Solution:

Period: 1

Asymptotes: $x = -\frac{3}{2}$, $x = -1$, $x = -\frac{1}{2}$, $x = 0$,

$x = \frac{1}{2}$, $x = 1$, $x = \frac{3}{2}$

Relative minima: $\left(-\frac{7}{4}, 1\right)$, $\left(-\frac{3}{4}, 1\right)$, $\left(\frac{1}{4}, 1\right)$, $\left(\frac{5}{4}, 1\right)$

Relative maxima: $\left(-\frac{5}{4}, -1\right)$, $\left(-\frac{1}{4}, -1\right)$, $\left(\frac{3}{4}, -1\right)$, $\left(\frac{7}{4}, -1\right)$

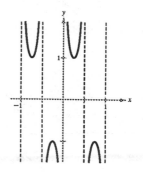

47. Complete a table (using a calculator set in radian mode) to estimate

$$\lim_{x \to 0} \frac{1 - \cos x}{x}.$$

Solution:

x	-0.1	-0.01	-0.001	0.001	0.01	0.1
$f(x)$	-0.05	-0.005	-0.0005	0.0005	0.005	0.05

From this table, we estimate that $\lim\limits_{x \to 0} \dfrac{1 - \cos x}{x} = 0$.

49. Complete a table (using a calculator set in radian mode) to estimate

$$\lim_{x \to 0} \frac{\sin x}{5x}.$$

Solution:

x	-0.1	-0.01	-0.001	0.001	0.01	0.1
$f(x)$	0.2	0.20	0.200	0.200	0.20	0.2

From this table, we estimate that $\lim\limits_{x \to 0} \dfrac{\sin x}{5x} = \dfrac{1}{5}$.

51. Determine whether the statement "The amplitude of $f(x) = -3\cos 2x$ is -3", is true or false. Explain your reasoning.

Solution:

False, the amplitude is 3 (must be positive).

53. Determine whether the statement "$\lim\limits_{x \to 0} \dfrac{\sin 5x}{3x} = \dfrac{5}{3}$", is true or false. Explain your reasoning.

Solution:

True, $\lim\limits_{x \to 0} \dfrac{\sin 5x}{3x} = \dfrac{5}{3}\left(\lim\limits_{x \to 0} \dfrac{\sin 5x}{5x}\right) = \dfrac{5}{3}(1) = \dfrac{5}{3}$.

55. *Respiratory Cycle* For a person at rest, the velocity v (in liters per second) of air flow into and out of the lungs during a respiratory cycle is

$$v(t) = 0.9 \sin \frac{\pi t}{3}$$

where t is the time in seconds. Inhalation occurs when $v > 0$ and exhalation occurs when $v < 0$.

(a) Find the time for one full respiratory cycle.

(b) Find the number of cycles per minute.

(c) Sketch the graph of the velocity function.

Solution:

(a) Period $= \dfrac{2\pi}{\pi/3} = 6$ seconds

(b) Cycles per minute $= \dfrac{60}{6} = 10$

(c) See accompanying graph.

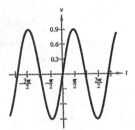

57. *Piano Tuning* When tuning a piano, a technician strikes a tuning fork for the A above middle C and sets up wave motion that can be approximated by $y = 0.001 \sin 880\pi t$ where t is the time in seconds.

(a) What is the period p of this function?

(b) What is the frequency f of this note ($f = 1/p$)?

(c) Sketch the graph of this function.

Solution:

(a) Period: $\dfrac{2\pi}{880\pi} = \dfrac{1}{440}$

(b) Frequency = 1/period = 440 (c) See accompanying graph.

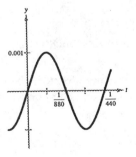

59. *Predator-Prey Cycle* The population P of a predator at time t (in months) is modeled by

$$P = 8000 + 2500 \sin \frac{2\pi t}{24},$$

and the population p of its prey is modeled by

$$p = 12{,}000 + 4000 \cos \frac{2\pi t}{24}.$$

Graph both models on the same set of axes and explain the oscillations in the size of each population.

Solution:

$$\text{(Graphs of) } P = 8000 + 2500 \sin \frac{2\pi t}{24}$$

$$p = 12{,}000 + 4000 \cos \frac{2\pi t}{24}$$

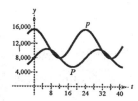

61. *Sales* Sketch the graph of the sales function

$$S(t) = 22.3 - 3.4 \cos \frac{\pi t}{6}$$

over one year where S is sales in thousands of units and t is the time in months with $t = 1$ corresponding to January.

Solution:

The graph has a period of 12, an amplitude of 3.4, and oscillates about the line $y = 22.3$, as shown in the graph.

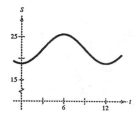

63. *Biorhythms* For the person born in July 20, 1964, use the biorhythm cycles given in Example 6 to calculate this person's three energy level on December 25, 1994.

Solution:

December 25, 2000 is the 13,673rd day of this person's life.

Days in 1964:	165
9 leap years:	+ 9(366)
27 non-leap years:	+ 27(365)
Days in 2000:	+ 360
	13,674
	−1
	13,673 (Do not count both first and last day.)

Therefore,

$$P(13,673) = \sin\frac{2\pi(13,673)}{23} \approx 0.1362$$

$$E(13,673) = \sin\frac{2\pi(13,673)}{28} \approx -0.9010$$

$$I(13,673) = \sin\frac{2\pi(13,673)}{33} \approx -0.8660.$$

65. Use a graphing utility or graphics calculator to sketch the graph of the given functions on the same coordinate axes where x is in the interval $[0, 2]$.

(a) $y = \dfrac{4}{\pi}\sin\pi x$

(b) $y = \dfrac{4}{\pi}\left(\sin\pi x + \dfrac{1}{3}\sin 3\pi x\right)$

Solution:

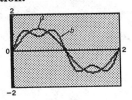

67. Use a graphing utility to sketch the graph of the function f and find $\lim\limits_{x \to 0} f(x)$ (if it exists).

$$f(x) = \frac{\sin x}{x}, \quad x \neq 0$$

Solution:

$$\lim_{x \to 0} \frac{\sin x}{x} = 1$$

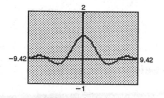

69. *Sales* Sales, S, in thousands of units, of a seasonal product is given by

$$S = 58.3 + 32.5 \cos \frac{\pi t}{6}$$

where t is the time in months (with $t = 1$ corresponding January and $t = 12$ corresponding to December). (a) Use a graphing utility to sketch the graph of S and (b) determine the months when sales exceed 75,000 units.

Solution:

(a)
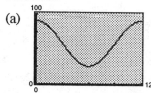

(b) Sales exceed 75,000 units during the months of January, February, November, and December.

Section T.4   Derivatives of Trigonometeic Functions

1. Find the derivative of $y = x^2 - \cos x$.

Solution:

$$y' = 2x + \sin x$$

3. Find the derivative of $y = \dfrac{1}{2} - 3\sin x$.

Solution:

$$y' = -3\cos x$$

5. Find the derivative of $f(x) = 4\sqrt{x} + 3\cos x$.

Solution:

$$f'(x) - \frac{2}{\sqrt{x}} - 3\sin x$$

7. Find the derivative of $f(t) = t^2 \cos t$.

Solution:

$$f'(t) = -t^2 \sin t + 2t \cos t$$

9. Find the derivative of $g(t) = (\cos t)/t$.

Solution:

$$g'(t) = \frac{t(-\sin t) - (\cos t)(1)}{t^2} = -\frac{t \sin t + \cos t}{t^2}$$

11. Find the derivative of $y = \tan x + x^2$.

Solution:

$$y' = \sec^2 x + 2x$$

13. Find the derivative of $y = 5x \sec x$.

Solution:

$$y' = 5x(\sec x \tan x) + 5 \sec x$$
$$= 5 \sec x(x \tan x + 1)$$

15. Find the derivative of $y = \sin 4x$.

Solution:

$$y' = 4 \cos 4x$$

17. Find the derivative of $y = \csc x^2$.

Solution:

$$y' = -\csc x^2 \cot x^2 (2x)$$
$$= -2x \csc x^2 \cot x^2$$

19. Find the derivative of $y = \frac{1}{2} \csc 2x$.

Solution:

$$y' = \tfrac{1}{2}(2)(-\csc 2x \cot 2x) = -\csc 2x \cot 2x$$

21. Find the derivative of $y = x \sin(1/x)$.

Solution:

$$y' = x\left(\frac{1}{x^2}\right)\left(-\cos\frac{1}{x}\right) + \left(\sin\frac{1}{x}\right)(1) = \sin\frac{1}{x} - \frac{1}{x}\cos\frac{1}{x}$$

23. Find the derivative of $y = 3\tan 4x$.

Solution:

$$y' = 12\sec^2 4x$$

25. Find the derivative of $y = \cos^2 x$.

Solution:

$$y = (\cos x)^2$$
$$y' = 2(\cos x)(-\sin x) = -2\cos x \sin x = -\sin 2x$$

27. Find the derivative of $y = \cos^2 x - \sin^2 x$.

Solution:

$$y' = -2\cos x \sin x - 2\cos x \sin x = -4\cos x \sin x = -2\sin 2x$$

29. Find the derivative of $y = (\cos x)/(\sin x)$.

Solution:

$$y = \cot x$$
$$y' = -\csc^2 x$$

31. Find the derivative of $y = \ln|\sin x|$.

Solution:

$$y' = \frac{\cos x}{\sin x} = \cot x$$

33. Find the derivative of $y = \ln|\csc x^2 - \cot x^2|$ and simplify your answer by using the trigonometric identies listed in Section T-2 in the textbook.

Solution:

$$y' = \frac{1}{\csc x^2 - \cot x^2}(-2x\csc x^2 \cot x^2 + 2x\csc^2 x^2)$$
$$= \frac{2x\csc x^2(\csc x^2 - \cot x^2)}{\csc x^2 - \cot x^2}$$
$$= 2x\csc x^2$$

35. Find the derivative of $y = \tan x - x$.

Solution:

$$y' = \sec^2 x - 1 = \tan^2 x$$

37. Find the derivative of $y = \sqrt{\sin x}$.

Solution:

$$y' = \frac{1}{2}(\sin x)^{-1/2} \cos x = \frac{\cos x}{2\sqrt{\sin x}}$$

39. Find the derivative of $y = \frac{1}{2}(x \tan x - \sec x)$.

Solution:

$$y' = \frac{1}{2}(x \sec^2 x + \tan x - \sec x \tan x)$$

41. Use implicit differentiation to find $\dfrac{dy}{dx}$ in the equation $\sin x + \cos 2y = 1$.

Evaluate $\dfrac{dy}{dx}$ at $(\pi/2, \pi/4)$.

Solution:

$$\sin x + \cos 2y = 1$$

$$\cos x - 2 \sin 2y \frac{dy}{dx} = 0$$

$$\frac{dy}{dx} = \frac{\cos x}{2 \sin 2y}$$

At $\left(\dfrac{\pi}{2}, \dfrac{\pi}{4}\right)$, we have $\dfrac{dy}{dx} = 0$.

43. Verify that $y = 2 \sin x + 3 \cos x$ is a solution of the differential equation $y'' + y = 0$.

Solution:

Since $y' = 2 \cos x - 3 \sin x$ and $y'' = -2 \sin x + 3 \cos x$, it follows that $y'' + y = 0$.

45. Verify that $y = \cos 2x + \sin 2x$ is a solution of the differential equation $y'' + 4y = 0$.

Solution:

Since $y' = -2 \sin 2x + 2 \cos 2x$ and $y'' = -4 \cos 2x - 4 \sin 2x$, it follows that $y'' + 4y = 0$.

47. Find the slope of the tangent line to $y = \sin \dfrac{5x}{4}$ at the point $(0, 0)$. Compare this to the number of complete cycles in the interval $[0, 2\pi]$.

Solution:

Since $y' = \dfrac{5}{4} \cos \left(\dfrac{5x}{4}\right)$, the slope of the tangent line at $(0, 0)$ is $\dfrac{5}{4}$. There is 1 complete cycle of the graph in the interval $[0, 2\pi]$.

49. Find the slope of the tangent line to $y = \sin 2x$ at the point $(0, 0)$. Compare this to the number of complete cycles in the interval $[0, 2\pi]$.

Solution:

Since $y' = 2\cos 2x$, the slope of the tangent line at $(0, 0)$ is 2. There are 2 complete cycles of the graph in the interval $[0, 2\pi]$.

51. Find the slope of the tangent line to $y = \sin x$ at the point $(0, 0)$. Compare this to the number of complete cycles in the interval $[0, 2\pi]$.

Solution:

Since $y' = \cos x$, the slope of the tangent line at $(0, 0)$ is 1. There is 1 complete cycle of the graph in the interval $[0, 2\pi]$.

53. Find an equation of the tangent line to the graph of $f(x) = \tan x$ at the point $(-\pi/4, -1)$.

Solution:

Since $y' = \sec^2 x$, the slope of the tangent line at $(-\pi/4, -1)$ is $m = \sec^2(-\pi/4) = 2$. Therefore, the equation of the tangent line is

$$y + 1 = 2\left(x - \frac{\pi}{4}\right)$$

$$y = 2x + \left(\frac{\pi}{2} - 1\right).$$

55. Sketch the graph of $f(x) = 2\sin x + \sin 2x$ on the interval $[0, 2\pi]$.

Solution:

The first derivative is zero when

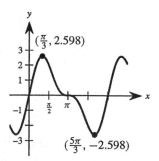
$(\frac{\pi}{3}, 2.598)$

$(\frac{5\pi}{3}, -2.598)$

$$2\cos x + 2\cos 2x = 0$$

$$2[\cos x + 2\cos^2 x - 1] = 0$$

$$2\cos^2 x + \cos x - 1 = 0$$

$$(2\cos x - 1)(\cos x + 1) = 0$$

$$\cos x = \frac{1}{2} \text{ or } \cos x = -1.$$

Critical numbers: $x = \dfrac{\pi}{3}, \dfrac{5\pi}{3}, \pi$

Relative maximum: $\left(\dfrac{\pi}{3}, \dfrac{3\sqrt{3}}{2}\right)$

Relative minimum: $\left(\dfrac{5\pi}{3}, -\dfrac{3\sqrt{3}}{2}\right)$

Points of inflection: $(0, 0)$, $(1.8235, 1.4524)$, $(\pi, 0)$, $(4.4597, -1.4524)$, $(2\pi, 0)$

57. Sketch the graph of $f(x) = x - 2\sin x$ on the interval $[0, 2\pi]$.

Solution:

The first derivative is zero when $1 - 2\cos x = 0$

$$\cos x = \frac{1}{2}.$$

Critical numbers: $x = \dfrac{\pi}{3}, \dfrac{5\pi}{3}, \dfrac{7\pi}{3}, \dfrac{11\pi}{3}$

Relative minima: $\left(\dfrac{\pi}{3}, \dfrac{\pi}{3} - \sqrt{3}\right)$

Relative maxima: $\left(\dfrac{5\pi}{3}, \dfrac{5\pi}{3} + \sqrt{3}\right)$

Points of inflection: $(0, 0), (\pi, \pi)$

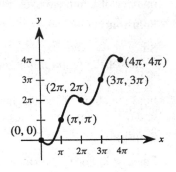

59. Sketch the graph of $y = e^{-x}\cos x$ on the interval $[0, 2\pi]$.

Solution:

The first derivative is zero when

$$f'(x) = e^{-x}(-\sin x) - e^{-x}\cos x = 0$$

$$e^{-x}(\sin x + \cos x) = 0$$

$$\tan x = -1$$

Critical numbers: $x = \dfrac{3\pi}{4}, \dfrac{7\pi}{4}$

Relative maximum: $\left(\dfrac{7\pi}{4}, 0.0029\right)$

Relative minimum: $\left(\dfrac{3\pi}{4}, -0.0670\right)$

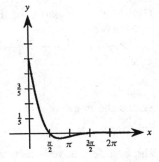

61. *Sales* Sales of electricity in the United States have had both an increasing annual sales pattern and a seasonal monthly sales pattern. For the years 1983–1985, the sales pattern can be approximated by the model $S = 180.6 + 0.55t + 13.60 \cos \dfrac{\pi t}{3}$, where S is the sales (per month) in billions of kilowatt hours and t is the time in months, with $t = 1$ corresponding to January 1983. (a) Find the relative extrema of this function for the years 1983 and 1984, and (b) use this model to predict the sales in August 1985. (Use $t = 31.5$.)

Solution:

(a) Since $S' = 0.55 - (13.60\pi/3) \sin(\pi t/3)$, it follows that $S' = 0$ when $t = 0.0369 + 3n$. Therefore, the relative extrema are as follows.

Maxima	Minima
(0.0369, 194.21)	(3.0369, 168.68)
(6.0369, 197.51)	(9.0369, 171.98)
(12.0369, 200.81)	(15.0369, 175.28)
(18.0369, 204.11)	(21.0369, 178.58)

(b) When $t = 31.5$, the sales are $S = 180.6 + 0.55(31.5) + 13.60 \cos \dfrac{\pi(31.5)}{3} \approx 197.925$ billion kilowatt hours.

63. *Average Temperature* The normal average daily temperature in degrees Fahrenheit for a certain city is given by

$$T(t) = 55 - 2 \cos \frac{2\pi(t - 32)}{365},$$

where t is the time in days with $t = 1$ corresponding to January 1. Find the expected date of (a) the warmest day, and (b) the coldest day.

Solution:

The derivative of T is

$$T'(t) = 21 \left(\frac{2\pi}{365} \right) \sin \frac{2\pi(t - 32)}{365}$$

which is zero when

$$\sin \frac{2\pi(t - 32)}{365} = 0$$

which implies that $t = 32$ or $t = \frac{365}{2} + 32 = 214.5$.

(a) The warmest day occurs when $t = 214.5$ on August 2 and August 3.

(b) The coldest day occurs when $t = 32$ on February 1.

65. Apply Taylor's Theorem to verify the power series centered at $c = 0$ for $\sin x$, and find the radius of convergence.

$$\sin x = x - \frac{x^3}{3!} + \frac{x^5}{5!} - \frac{x^7}{7!} + \cdots + \frac{(-1)^n x^{2n+1}}{(2n+1)!} + \cdots$$

Solution:

$$\begin{aligned}
f(x) &= \sin x & f(0) &= 0 \\
f'(x) &= \cos x & f'(0) &= 1 \\
f''(x) &= -\sin x & f''(0) &= 0 \\
f'''(x) &= -\cos x & f'''(0) &= -1
\end{aligned}$$

Therefore, the Taylor series is $f(x) = f(0) + f'(0)x + \dfrac{f''(0)x^2}{2!} + \cdots$

$$= x - \frac{x^3}{3!} + \frac{x^5}{5!} - \frac{x^7}{7!} + \cdots + \frac{(-1)^n x^{2n+1}}{(2n+1)!} + \cdots$$

$$= \sum_{n=0}^{\infty} (-1)^n \cdot \frac{x^{2n+1}}{(2n+1)!}$$

The radius of convergence is given by $R = \lim\limits_{n \to \infty} \left| \dfrac{1}{(2n+1)!} \cdot \dfrac{(2n+3)!}{1} \right| = \infty$.

67. Use the power series for $\sin x$ to find the power series of $f(x) = \sin x^2$.

Solution:

$$\sin x^2 = \sum_{n=0}^{\infty} (-1)^n \cdot \frac{(x^2)^{2n+1}}{(2n+1)!} = \sum_{n=0}^{\infty} (-1)^n \cdot \frac{x^{4n+2}}{(2n+1)!}$$

69. Use the power series for $\cos x$ to find the power series of $h(x) = \cos 2x$.

Solution:

$$\cos 2x = \sum_{n=0}^{\infty} (-1)^n \cdot \frac{(2x)^{2n}}{(2n)!}$$

71. Differentiate the appropriate power series to verify the derivative formula

$$\frac{d}{dx}[\sin x] = \cos x.$$

Solution:

Since $\sin x = x - \dfrac{x^3}{3!} + \dfrac{x^5}{5!} - \dfrac{x^7}{7!} + \cdots$ it follows that $\dfrac{d}{dx}[\sin x] = 1 - \dfrac{x^2}{2!} + \dfrac{x^4}{4!} - \dfrac{x^6}{6!} + \cdots$ which is the power series for $\cos x$.

73. Use a graphing utility (a) to sketch the graph of f and f' on the same coordinate axes over the specified interval, (b) to find the critical numbers of f, and (c) to find the interval(s) on which f' is positive and the interval(s) on which it is negative. Note the behavior of f in relation to the sign of f'.

$$f(t) = t^2 \sin t, \quad (0, 2\pi)$$

Solution:

(a) $f(t) = t^2 \sin t$

$\quad f'(t) = t^2 \cos t + 2t \sin t$

$\quad\quad = t(t \cos t + 2 \sin t)$

(b) $f'(t) = 0$ when $t = 0$, $t \approx 2.289$, and $t \approx 5.087$.

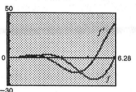

(c)

Intervals	(0, 2.289)	(2.289, 5.087)	(5.087, 2π)
Sign of f'	+	−	+
Conclusion	f is increasing	f is decreasing	f is increasing

75. Use a graphing utility (a) to sketch the graph of f and f' on the same coordinate axes over the specified interval, (b) to find the critical numbers of f, and (c) to find the interval(s) on which f' is positive and the interval(s) on which it is negative. Note the behavior of f in relation to the sign of f'.

$$f(x) = \sin x - \tfrac{1}{3} \sin 3x + \tfrac{1}{5} \sin 5x, \quad (0, \pi)$$

Solution:

(a) $f(x) = \sin x - \tfrac{1}{3} \sin 3x + \tfrac{1}{5} \sin 5x$

$\quad f'(x) = \cos x - \cos 3x + \cos 5x$

(b) $f'(x) = 0$ when $x \approx 0.524$, $x \approx 1.571$, and $x \approx 2.618$.

(c)

Intervals	(0, 0.524)	(0.524, 1.571)	(1.571, 2.618	(2.618, π)
Sign of f'	+	+	−	−
Conclusion	f is increasing	f is increasing	f is decreasing	f is decreasing

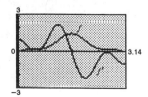

77. Use a graphing utility (a) to sketch the graph of f and f' on the same coordinate axes over the specified interval, (b) to find the critical numbers of f, and (c) to find the interval(s) on which f' is positive and the interval(s) on which it is negative. Note the behavior of f in relation to the sign of f'.

$$f(x) = \sqrt{2x}\,\sin x, \quad [0, 2\pi]$$

Solution:

(a) $f(x) = \sqrt{2x}\,\sin x$

$$f'(x) = \sqrt{2x}\,\cos x + \frac{\sin x}{\sqrt{2x}}$$

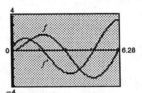

(b) $f'(x) = 0$ when $x \approx 1.837$ and $x \approx 4.816$.

(c)

Intervals	$(0, 1.837)$	$(1.837, 4.816)$	$(4.816, 2\pi)$
Sign of f'	$+$	$-$	$+$
Conclusion	f is increasing	f is decreasing	f is increasing

79. Use Newton's Method to approximate all the real zeros of $f(x) = x \sin x - \cos 2x$ for x in the interval $[0, 10]$. Sketch the graph of f in order to make the initial estimate of a zero.

Solution:

$$f(x) = x \sin x - \cos 2x$$

$$f'(x) = x \cos x + \sin x + 2 \sin 2x$$

$$x_{n+1} = x_n - \frac{x_n \sin x_n - \cos 2x_n}{x_n \cos x_n + \sin x_n + 2 \sin 2x_n}$$

From the graph we see that there are four zeros.

n	x_n
1	0.5
2	0.6156
3	0.6081
4	0.6080

n	x_n
1	2.8
2	2.8455
3	2.8457
4	2.8457

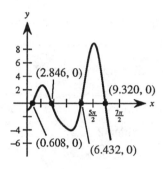

n	x_n
1	6.5
2	6.4337
3	6.4323
4	6.4323

n	x_n
1	9.5
2	9.3159
3	9.3196
4	9.3196

The zeros of f in the interval $[0, 10]$ are approximately 0.608, 2.846, 6.432, and 9.320.

81. Use a graphing utility to find the relative extrema of $f(x) = \dfrac{x}{\sin x}$. Let $0 < x < 2\pi$.

Solution:

Relative maximum: $(4.49, -4.60)$

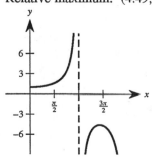

83. Use a graphing utility to find the relative extrema of $f(x) = \ln x \cos x$. Let $0 < x < 2\pi$.

Solution:

Relative maximum: $(1.27, 0.07)$

Relative minimum: $(3.38, -1.18)$

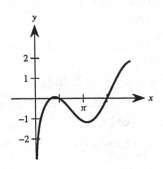

85. Use a graphing utility to find the relative extrema of $f(x) = \sin(0.1x^2)$. Let $0 < x < 2\pi$.

Solution:

Relative maximum: $(3.96, 1)$

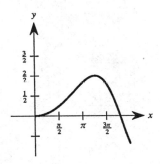

Section T.5 Integrals of Trigonometric Functions

1. Evaluate $\int (2\sin x + 3\cos x)\, dx$.

Solution:

$$\int (2\sin x + 3\cos x)\, dx = -2\cos x + 3\sin x + C$$

3. Evaluate $\int (1 - \csc t \cot t)\, dt$.

Solution:

$$\int (1 - \csc t \cot t)\, dt = t + \csc t + C$$

5. Evaluate $\int (\csc^2 \theta - \cos \theta)d\theta$.

Solution:

$$\int (\csc^2 \theta - \cos \theta)d\theta = -\cot \theta - \sin \theta + C$$

7. Evaluate $\int \sin 2x \, dx$.

Solution:

$$\int \sin 2x \, dx = \frac{1}{2}\int 2 \sin 2x \, dx = -\frac{1}{2} \cos 2x + C$$

9. Evaluate $\int x \cos x^2 \, dx$.

Solution:

$$\int x \cos x^2 \, dx = \frac{1}{2}\int 2x \cos x^2 \, dx = \frac{1}{2} \sin x^2 + C$$

11. Evaluate $\int \sec^2 \frac{x}{2} \, dx$.

Solution:

$$\int \sec^2 \frac{x}{2} \, dx = 2\int \frac{1}{2} \sec^2 \frac{x}{2} \, dx = 2 \tan \frac{x}{2} + C$$

13. Evaluate $\int \tan 3x \, dx$.

Solution:

$$\int \tan 3x \, dx = \frac{1}{3}\int 3 \tan 3x \, dx = -\frac{1}{3} \ln |\cos 3x| + C$$

15. Evaluate $\int \tan^4 x \sec^2 x \, dx$.

Solution:

$$\int \tan^3 x \sec^2 x \, dx = \frac{\tan^4 x}{4} + C$$

17. Evaluate $\int \cot \pi x \, dx$.

Solution:

$$\int \cot \pi x \, dx = \frac{1}{\pi}\int \pi \cot \pi x \, dx = \frac{1}{\pi} \ln |\sin \pi x| + C$$

19. Evaluate $\int \csc 2x \, dx$.

Solution:

$$\int \csc 2x \, dx = \frac{1}{2} \int 2 \csc 2x \, dx = \frac{1}{2} \ln|\csc 2x - \cot 2x| + C$$

21. Evaluate $\int \frac{\sec^2 2x}{\tan 2x} dx$.

Solution:

$$\int \frac{\sec^2 2x}{\tan 2x} dx = \frac{1}{2} \int \frac{1}{\tan 2x} (2 \sec^2 2x \, dx) = \frac{1}{2} \ln|\tan 2x| + C$$

23. Evaluate $\int \frac{\sec x \tan x}{\sec x - 1} dx$.

Solution:

$$\int \frac{\sec x \tan x}{\sec x - 1} dx = \ln|\sec x - 1| + C$$

25. Evaluate $\int \frac{\sin x}{1 + \cos x} dx$.

Solution:

$$\int \frac{\sin x}{1 + \cos x} dx = -\ln|1 + \cos x| + C$$

27. Evaluate $\int \frac{\csc^2 x}{\cot^3 x} dx$.

Solution:

$$\int \frac{\csc^2 x}{\cot^3 x} dx = -\int \cot^{-3} x(-\csc^2 x) \, dx = -\frac{\cot^{-2} x}{-2} + C = \frac{1}{2} \tan^2 x + C$$

29. Evaluate $\int e^x \sin e^x \, dx$.

Solution:

$$\int e^x \sin e^x \, dx = -\cos e^x + C$$

31. Evaluate $\int e^{-x} \tan e^{-x} \, dx$.

Solution:

$$\int e^{-x} \tan e^{-x} \, dx = -\int (-e^{-x}) \tan e^{-x} \, dx = \ln|\cos e^{-x}| + C$$

33. Evaluate $\displaystyle\int (\sin 2x + \cos 2x)^2\, dx$.

Solution:

$$\int (\sin 2x + \cos 2x)^2\, dx = \int (\sin^2 2x + 2\sin 2x \cos 2x + \cos^2 2x)\, dx$$

$$= \int (1 + \sin 4x)\, dx = x - \frac{1}{4}\cos 4x + C$$

35. Evaluate $\displaystyle\int x \cos x\, dx$.

Solution:

Using integration by parts, we let $u = x$ and $dv = \cos x\, dx$. Then $du = dx$ and $v = \sin x$.

$$\int x \cos x\, dx = x \sin x - \int \sin x\, dx = x \sin x + \cos x + C$$

37. Evaluate $\displaystyle\int x \sec^2 x\, dx$.

Solution:

Using integration by parts, we let $u = x$ and $dv = \sec^2 x\, dx$. Then $du = dx$ and $v = \tan x$.

$$\int x \sec^2 x\, dx = x \tan x - \int \tan x\, dx = x \tan x + \ln|\cos x| + C$$

39. Evaluate $\displaystyle\int_0^{\pi/4} \cos \frac{4x}{3}\, dx$.

Solution:

$$\int_0^{\pi/4} \cos \frac{4x}{3}\, dx = \frac{3}{4} \sin \frac{4x}{3} \Big]_0^{\pi/4} = \frac{3}{4}\left(\sin \frac{\pi}{3}\right) = \frac{3\sqrt{3}}{8} \approx 0.6495$$

41. Evaluate $\displaystyle\int_{\pi/2}^{2\pi/3} \sec^2 \frac{x}{2}\, dx$.

Solution:

$$\int_{\pi/2}^{2\pi/3} \sec^2 \frac{x}{2}\, dx = 2 \tan \frac{x}{2} \Big]_{\pi/2}^{2\pi/3} = 2(\sqrt{3} - 1) \approx 1.4641$$

43. Evaluate $\displaystyle\int_{\pi/12}^{\pi/4} \csc 2x \cot 2x\, dx$.

Solution:

$$\int_{\pi/12}^{\pi/4} \csc 2x \cot 2x\, dx = -\frac{1}{2} \csc 2x \Big]_{\pi/12}^{\pi/4} = -\frac{1}{2}\left[\csc \frac{\pi}{2} - \csc \frac{\pi}{6}\right] = -\frac{1}{2}[1 - 2] = \frac{1}{2}$$

45. Evaluate $\int_0^1 \tan(1-x)dx$.

Solution:

$$\int_0^1 \tan(1-x)\,dx = \ln|\cos(1-x)|\Big]_0^1 = \ln(\cos 0) - \ln(\cos 1) \approx 0.6156$$

47. Determine the area of the region. (See textbook for graph.)

$$y = \cos\frac{x}{4}$$

Solution:

$$\int_0^{2\pi} \cos\frac{x}{4}\,dx = 4\sin\frac{x}{4}\Big]_0^{2\pi} = 4$$

49. Determine the area of the region. (See textbook for graph.)

$$y = x + \sin x$$

Solution:

$$\text{Area} = \int_0^\pi (x+\sin x)\,dx = \left[\frac{x^2}{2} - \cos x\right]_0^\pi = \frac{\pi^2}{2} + 2 \approx 6.9348 \text{ square units}$$

51. Find the area of the region bounded by the graphs of $y = \sin x + \cos 2x$ and $y = 0$, $0 \le x \le \pi$.

Solution:

$$\text{Area} = \int_0^\pi (\sin x + \cos 2x)\,dx = \left[-\cos x + \frac{1}{2}\sin 2x\right]_0^\pi = 2 \text{ square units}$$

53. Find the volume of the solid generated by revolving the region bounded by the graphs of $y = \sec x$, $y = 0$, $x = 0$, and $x = \pi/4$ about the x-axis.

Solution:

$$V = \pi\int_0^{\pi/4} \sec^2 x\,dx = \pi\tan x\Big]_0^{\pi/4} = \pi \text{ cubic units}$$

55. Find the general solution of the first-order linear differential equation $y' + 2y = \sin x$.

Solution:

Since $P(x) = 2$ and $Q(x) = \sin x$, the integrating factor is $u(x) = e^{\int 2\,dx} = e^{2x}$ and the solution is

$$y = e^{-2x}\int e^{2x}\sin x\,dx.$$

Using integration by parts, we find the solution to be

$$y = e^{-2x}\left[\left(\frac{1}{5}\right)e^{2x}(2\sin x - \cos x) + C\right] = \frac{1}{5}(2\sin x - \cos x) + Ce^{-2x}.$$

57. Use the Taylor polynomial of degree 6 to approximate the integral of $\dfrac{\sin x}{x}$ over $\left[0, \dfrac{\pi}{2}\right]$.

Solution:

$$\frac{\sin x}{x} \approx 1 - \frac{x^2}{6} + \frac{x^4}{120} - \frac{x^6}{5040}$$

$$\int_0^{\pi/2} \frac{\sin x}{x}\, dx \approx \left[x - \frac{x^3}{18} + \frac{x^5}{600} - \frac{x^7}{35,280}\right]_0^{\pi/2} \approx 1.3707$$

59. Approximate the following integral, letting $n = 4$ and using (a) the Trapezoidal Rule and (b) Simpson's Rule.

$$\int_0^{\pi/2} f(x)\, dx, \qquad f(x) = \begin{cases} (\sin x)/x, & x > 0 \\ 1, & x = 0 \end{cases}$$

Solution:

(a) $\dfrac{\pi/2}{8}\left[f(0) + 2f\left(\dfrac{\pi}{8}\right) + 2f\left(\dfrac{\pi}{4}\right) + 2f\left(\dfrac{3\pi}{8}\right) + f\left(\dfrac{\pi}{2}\right)\right] \approx 1.3655$

(b) $\dfrac{\pi/2}{12}\left[f(0) + 4f\left(\dfrac{\pi}{8}\right) + 2f\left(\dfrac{\pi}{4}\right) + 4f\left(\dfrac{3\pi}{8}\right) + f\left(\dfrac{\pi}{2}\right)\right] \approx 1.3708$

61. *Average Value* The minimum stockpile level of gasoline in the United States can be approximated by the model

$$Q(t) = 217 + 13 \cos \frac{\pi(t-3)}{6}$$

where Q is measured in millions of barrels of gasoline and t is the time in months, with $t = 1$ corresponding to January. Find the average minimum level given by this model during (a) the first quarter $(0 \le t \le 3)$,
(b) the second quarter $(3 \le t \le 6)$, and (c) the entire year $(0 \le t \le 12)$.

Solution:

(a) $\dfrac{1}{3}\displaystyle\int_0^3 \left[217 + 13 \cos \frac{\pi(t-3)}{6}\right] dt = \dfrac{1}{3}\left[217t + \frac{78}{\pi} \sin \frac{\pi(t-3)}{6}\right]_0^3$

$$= \frac{1}{3}\left(651 + \frac{78}{\pi}\right) \approx 225.28 \text{ million barrels}$$

(b) $\dfrac{1}{3}\displaystyle\int_3^6 \left[217 + 13 \cos \frac{\pi(t-3)}{6}\right] dt = \dfrac{1}{3}\left[217t + \frac{78}{\pi} \sin \frac{\pi(t-3)}{6}\right]_3^6$

$$= \frac{1}{3}\left(1302 + \frac{78}{\pi} - 651\right) \approx 225.28 \text{ million barrels}$$

(c) $\dfrac{1}{12}\displaystyle\int_0^{12} \left[217 + 13 \cos \frac{\pi(t-3)}{6}\right] dt = \dfrac{1}{12}\left[217t + \frac{78}{\pi} \sin \frac{\pi(t-3)}{6}\right]_0^{12}$

$$= \frac{1}{12}\left(2604 - \frac{78}{\pi} + \frac{78}{\pi}\right) \approx 217 \text{ million barrels}$$

63. *Air-Conditioning Cost* Suppose that the temperature (in degrees Fahrenheit) is given by

$$T = 72 + 12\sin\frac{\pi(t-8)}{12},$$

where t is the time in hours, with $t = 0$ representing midnight. Furthermore, suppose that it costs $0.10 to cool a particular house 1° for one hour.

(a) Find the cost C of cooling this house if the thermostat is set at 72° and the cost is given by

$$C = 0.1\int_8^{20}\left[72 + 12\sin\frac{\pi(t-8)}{12} - 72\right]dt.$$

(b) Find the savings in resetting the thermostat to 78° by evaluating the integral

$$C = 0.1\int_{10}^{18}\left[72 + 12\sin\frac{\pi(t-8)}{12} - 78\right]dt.$$

Solution:

(a) $C = 0.1\displaystyle\int_8^{20} 12\sin\frac{\pi(t-8)}{12}\,dt = -\frac{14.4}{\pi}\cos\frac{\pi(t-8)}{12}\bigg]_8^{20} = -\frac{14.4}{\pi}(-1-1) \approx \$9.17$

(b) $C = 0.1\displaystyle\int_{10}^{18}\left[12\sin\frac{\pi(t-8)}{12} - 6\right]dt = \left[-\frac{14.4}{\pi}\cos\frac{\pi(t-8)}{12} - 0.6t\right]_{10}^{18} \approx \$3.14$

Savings $\approx 9.17 - 3.14 = \$6.03$

65. *Respiratory Cycle* After exercising for a few minutes, a person has a respiratory cycle for which the velocity of air flow is approximated by

$$v = 1.75\sin\frac{\pi t}{2}.$$

How much does the lung capacity of a person increase as a result of exercising? In other words, how much more air is inhaled during a cycle after exercising than is inhaled during a cycle at rest? (See Exercise 64.) (Note that the cycle is shorter and you must integrate over the inverval [0, 2].)

Solution:

$$V = \int_0^2 1.75\sin\frac{\pi t}{2}\,dt = -\frac{3.5}{\pi}\cos\frac{\pi t}{2}\bigg]_0^2 \approx 2.2282 \text{ liters}$$

Capacity increases by $2.2282 - 1.7189 = 0.5093$ liter.

67. Use a graphing utility and Simpson's Rule with $n = 8$ to approximate the following definite integral.

$$\int_0^{\pi/2}\sqrt{x}\sin x\,dx$$

Solution:

$$\int_0^{\pi/2}\sqrt{x}\sin x\,dx \approx 0.9777$$

69. Use a graphing utility and Simpson's Rule with $n = 20$ to approximate the following definite integral.

$$\int_0^\pi \sqrt{1 + \cos^2 x}\, dx$$

Solution:

$$\int_0^\pi \sqrt{1 + \cos^2 x}\, dx \approx 3.8202$$

Section T.6   L'Hôpital's Rule

1. Decide whether $\displaystyle\lim_{x \to 0} \frac{2x + \sqrt{x}}{x}$ produces an indeterminate form.

Solution:

Yes, $\dfrac{0}{0}$

3. Decide whether $\displaystyle\lim_{x \to -\infty} \frac{4}{x^2 + e^x}$ produces an indeterminate form.

Solution:

No, $\dfrac{4}{\infty} \to 0$

5. Decide whether $\displaystyle\lim_{x \to \infty} \frac{2xe^{2x}}{3e^x}$ produces an indeterminate form.

Solution:

Yes, $\dfrac{\infty}{\infty}$

7. Complete the table in the textbook to estimate $\displaystyle\lim_{x} \to 0 \frac{e^{-x} - 1}{3x}$ numerically.

Solution:

x	-0.1	-0.01	-0.001	0	0.001	0.01	0.1
$f(x)$	-0.35	-0.335	-0.3335		-0.3332	-0.332	-0.32

$$\lim_{x \to 0} \frac{e^{-x} - 1}{3x} = \frac{-1}{3}$$

9. Complete the table in the textbook to estimate $\lim\limits_{x \to 0} \dfrac{\sin x}{5x}$ numerically.

Solution:

x	-0.1	-0.01	-0.001	0	0.001	0.01	0.1
$f(x)$	0.1997	0.2	0.2		0.2	0.2	0.1997

$$\lim_{x \to 0} \frac{\sin x}{5x} = \frac{1}{5}$$

11. Use a graphing utility to find $\lim\limits_{x \to \infty} \dfrac{\ln x}{x^2}$.

Solution:

$$\lim_{x \to \infty} \frac{\ln x}{x^2} = \infty$$

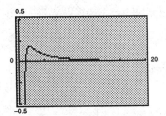

13. Use a graphing utility to find $\lim\limits_{x \to 2} \dfrac{x^2 - x - 2}{x^2 - 5x + 6}$.

Solution:

$$\lim_{x \to 2} \frac{x^2 - x - 2}{x^2 - 5x + 6} = -3$$

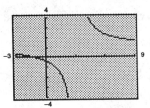

15. Use L'Hôpital's Rule to find $\lim\limits_{x \to 0} \dfrac{e^{-x} - 1}{x}$.

Solution:

$$\lim_{x \to 0} \frac{e^{-x} - 1}{x} = \lim_{x \to 0} \frac{-e^{-x}}{1} = -1 \text{ (See Exercise 7)}$$

17. Use L'Hôpital's Rule to find $\lim\limits_{x \to 0} \dfrac{\sin x}{5x}$.

Solution:

$$\lim_{x \to 0} \frac{\sin x}{5x} = \lim_{x \to 0} \frac{\cos x}{5} = \frac{1}{5} \text{ (See Exercise 9)}$$

19. Use L'Hôpital's Rule to find $\lim\limits_{x\to\infty} \dfrac{\ln x}{x^2}$.

Solution:

$$\lim_{x\to\infty} \frac{\ln x}{x^2} = \lim_{x\to\infty} \frac{\frac{1}{x}}{2x} = 0.$$

21. Use L'Hôpital's Rule to find $\lim\limits_{x\to 2} \dfrac{x^2 - x - 2}{x^2 - 5x + 6}$.

Solution:

$$\lim_{x\to 2} \frac{x^2 - x - 2}{x^2 - 5x + 6} = \lim_{x\to 2} \frac{2x - 1}{2x - 5} = \frac{3}{-1} = -3. \text{ (See Exercise 13)}$$

23. Use L'Hôpital's Rule to find $\lim\limits_{x\to 0} \dfrac{2x + 1 - e^x}{x}$.

Solution:

$$\lim_{x\to 0} \frac{2x + 1 - e^x}{x} = \lim_{x\to 0} \frac{2 - e^x}{1} = 1$$

25. Use L'Hôpital's Rule to find $\lim\limits_{x\to\infty} \dfrac{\ln x}{e^x}$.

Solution:

$$\lim_{x\to\infty} \frac{\ln x}{e^x} = \lim_{x\to\infty} \frac{\frac{1}{x}}{e^x} = 0$$

27. Use L'Hôpital's Rule to find $\lim\limits_{x\to\infty} \dfrac{4x^2 + 2x - 1}{3x^2 - 7}$.

Solution:

$$\lim_{x\to\infty} \frac{4x^2 + 2x - 1}{3x^2 - 7} = \lim_{x\to\infty} \frac{8xz - 2}{6x} = \lim_{x\to\infty} \frac{8}{6} = \frac{4}{3}$$

29. Use L'Hôpital's Rule to find $\lim\limits_{x\to\infty} \dfrac{1 - x}{e^x}$.

Solution:

$$\lim_{x\to\infty} \frac{1 - x}{e^x} = \lim_{x\to\infty} \frac{-1}{e^x} = 0$$

31. Use L'Hôpital's Rule to find $\lim\limits_{x\to 1} \dfrac{\ln x}{x^2 - 1}$.

Solution:

$$\lim_{x\to 1} \frac{\ln x}{x^2 - 1} = \lim_{x\to 1} \frac{\frac{1}{x}}{2x} - \frac{1}{2}$$

33. Use L'Hôpital's Rule to find $\lim\limits_{x \to 0} \dfrac{\sin 2x}{\sin 5x}$.

Solution:

$$\lim_{x \to 0} \frac{\sin 2x}{\sin 5x} = \lim_{x \to 0} \frac{2 \cos 2x}{5 \cos 5x} = \frac{2}{5}$$

35. Use L'Hôpital's Rule to find $\lim\limits_{x \to 0} \dfrac{\sin x}{e^x - 1}$.

Solution:

$$\lim_{x \to 0} \frac{\sin x}{e^x - 1} = \lim_{x \to 0} \frac{\cos x}{e^x} = 1$$

37. Use L'Hôpital's Rule to find $\lim\limits_{x \to \infty} \dfrac{x}{\sqrt{x + 1}}$.

Solution:

$$\lim_{x \to \infty} \frac{x}{\sqrt{x + 1}} = \lim_{x \to \infty} \frac{\frac{x}{x}}{\sqrt{\frac{1}{x} + \frac{1}{x^2}}} = \lim_{x \to \infty} \frac{1}{\sqrt{\frac{1}{x} + \frac{1}{x}}} = \infty$$

39. Use L'Hôpital's Rule to find $\lim\limits_{x \to \infty} \dfrac{e^{3x}}{x^3}$.

Solution:

$$\lim_{x \to \infty} \frac{e^{3x}}{x^3} = \lim_{x \to \infty} \frac{3e^{3x}}{3x^2} = \lim_{x \to \infty} \frac{3e^{3x}}{2x} = \lim_{x \to \infty} \frac{9e^{3x}}{2} = \infty$$

41. Find $\lim\limits_{x \to \infty} \dfrac{x^2 + 2x + 1}{x^2 + 3}$.

Solution:

$$\lim_{x \to \infty} \frac{x^2 + 2x + 1}{x^2 + 3} = \lim_{x \to \infty} \frac{2x + 2}{2x} = \lim_{x \to \infty} \frac{2}{2} = 1$$

43. Find $\lim\limits_{x \to -1} \dfrac{x^3 + 3x^2 - 6x - 8}{2x^3 - 3x^2 - 5x + 6}$.

Solution:

$$\lim_{x \to -1} \frac{x^3 + 3x^2 - 6x - 8}{2x^3 - 3x^2 - 5x + 6} = \frac{0}{6} = 0$$

45. Find $\lim\limits_{x \to 3} \dfrac{\ln(x - 2)}{x - 2}$.

Solution:

$$\lim_{x \to 3} \frac{\ln(x - 2)}{x - 2} = \frac{\ln(1)}{1} = 0$$

47. Find $\lim\limits_{x\to 1} \dfrac{2\ln x}{e^x}$.

Solution:

$$\lim_{x\to 1} \frac{2\ln x}{e^x} = \frac{2(0)}{e} = 0$$

49. Use L'Hôpital's Rule to compare the rate of growth of the numerator and the denominator.

$$\lim_{x\to\infty} \frac{x^2}{e^{4x}}$$

Solution:

$$\lim_{x\to\infty} \frac{x^2}{e^{4x}} = \lim_{x\to\infty} \frac{2x}{4e^{4x}} = \lim_{x\to\infty} \frac{2}{16e^{4x}} = 0$$

51. Use L'Hôpital's Rule to compare the rate of growth of the numerator and the denominator.

$$\lim_{x\to\infty} \frac{(\ln x)^4}{x}.$$

Solution:

$$\lim_{x\to\infty} \frac{(\ln x)^4}{x} = \lim_{x\to\infty} \frac{4(\ln x)^3(\frac{1}{x})}{1} = \lim_{x\to\infty} \frac{12(\ln x)^2(\frac{1}{x})}{1}$$

$$= \lim_{x\to\infty} \frac{24(\ln x)\frac{1}{x}}{1} = \lim_{x\to\infty} \frac{24(\frac{1}{x})}{1} = 0$$

53. Use L'Hôpital's Rule to compare the rate of growth of the numerator and the denominator.

$$\lim_{x\to\infty} \frac{(\ln x)^n}{x^m}.$$

Solution:

$$\lim_{x\to\infty} \frac{(\ln x)^n}{x^m} = 0. \text{ (The log term eventually disappears.)}$$

55. Complete the table in the textbook to show that x eventually "overpowers" $(\ln x)^5$.

Solution:

x	10	10^2	10^3	10^4	10^5	10^6
$\dfrac{(\ln x)^5}{x}$	6.47	20.71	15.73	6.63	2.02	0.503

$$\lim_{x\to\infty} \frac{(\ln x)^5}{x} = 0$$

57. Describe the error in $\lim\limits_{x \to 0} \dfrac{e^{3x} - 1}{e^x} = \lim\limits_{x \to 0} \dfrac{3e^{3x}}{e^x} = \lim\limits_{x \to 0} 3e^{2x} = 3.$

Solution:

The limit of the denominator is not 0.

59. Describe the error in $\lim\limits_{x \to 1} \dfrac{e^x - 1}{\ln x} = \lim\limits_{x \to 1} \dfrac{e^x}{(1/x)} = \lim\limits_{x \to 1} x e^x = e.$

Solution:

The limit of the numerator is not 0.

61. (a) Graph the function $\lim\limits_{x \to 2} \dfrac{x - 2}{\ln(3x - 5)}$ and (b) find the limit (if it exists).

Solution:

(a) 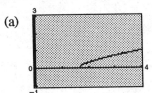   (b) $\lim\limits_{x \to 2} \dfrac{x - 2}{\ln(3x - 5)} = \dfrac{1}{3}$

63. (a) Graph the function $\lim\limits_{x \to -2} \dfrac{\sqrt{x^2 - 4} - 5}{x + 2}$ and (b) find the limit (if it exists).

Solution:

(a) 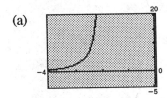   (b) $\lim\limits_{x \to -2} \dfrac{\sqrt{x^2 - 4} - 5}{x + 2}$

does not exist.

65. Determine whether the statement is true or false.

$$\lim_{x \to 0} \frac{x^2 + 3x - 1}{x + 1} = \lim_{x \to 0} \frac{2x + 3}{1} = 3$$

Solution:

False, $\lim\limits_{x \to 0} \dfrac{x^2 + 3x - 1}{x + 1} = \dfrac{-1}{1} = -1.$

67. Determine whether the statement is true or false.

If $\lim\limits_{x \to \infty} \dfrac{f(x)}{g(x)} = 0$, then $g(x)$ has a more rapid growth rate than $f(x)$.

Solution:

True

69. Determine whether the statement is true or false.

Show that L'Hôpital's Rule fails for the limit $\lim\limits_{x \to \infty} \dfrac{x}{\sqrt{x^2 + 1}}$.

What is the limit?

Solution:

$$\lim_{x \to \infty} \frac{x}{\sqrt{x^2 + 1}} = \lim_{x \to \infty} \frac{\sqrt{x^2 + 1}}{x} = \lim_{x \to \infty} \frac{x}{\sqrt{x^2 + 1}}$$

and repeated applications of L'Hôpital's Rule continue in this pattern.

$$\lim_{x \to \infty} \frac{x}{\sqrt{x^2 + 1}} = \lim_{x \to \infty} \frac{\frac{x}{x}}{\sqrt{\frac{x^2}{x^2} + \frac{1}{x^2}}} = \lim_{x \to \infty} \frac{1}{\sqrt{x + \frac{1}{x^2}}} = 1$$

71. *Sales Growth* The growth in sales for the years 1986 through 1992 for two major toy companies is modeled by

$f(t) = 1289.75 + 17.22t^2 + 1.67e^t$ *Hasbro*
$g(t) = 2419.55 + 774.58t,$ *Toys R Us*

where $t = 0$ corrsponds to 1986.

(a) Which company has the faster rate of growth of sales?

(b) Use a graphing utility to graph the models f and g for $0 \le x \le 10$. If the rate of growth of the sales of each company continues according to the model, when will the sales of the faster growing company exceed the sales of the slower growing company?

Solution:

(a) Hasbro has the faster rate of growth of sales because of the e^t term.

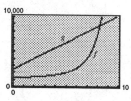

The Hasbro Company will exceed Toys R Us in 1994 ($t = 8.2$).

Chapter T   Review Exercises

1. Sketch the angle $\theta = 11\pi/4$ in standard position and give a positive and negative coterminal angle.

Solution:

Positive coterminal angle:
$$\frac{11\pi}{4} - 2\pi = \frac{3\pi}{4}$$

Negative coterminal angle:
$$\frac{11\pi}{4} - 2(2\pi) = -\frac{5\pi}{4}$$

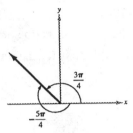

3. Sketch the angle $110°$ in standard position and give a positive and negative coterminal angle.

Solution:

Positive coterminal angle:
$$110° + 360° = 470°$$

Negative coterminal angle:
$$110° - 360° = -250°$$

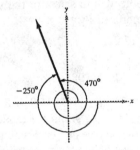

5. Convert the angle $\theta = 210°$ from degree to radian measure.

$210°$

Solution:
$$210° \left(\frac{\pi \text{ radians}}{180°} \right) = \frac{7\pi}{6} \text{ radians}$$

7. Convert the angle $\theta = -480°$ from degree to radian measure.

Solution:
$$-480° \left(\frac{\pi \text{ radians}}{180°} \right) = -\frac{8\pi}{3} \text{ radians} \approx -8.38$$

9. Convert the angle $\theta = \dfrac{7\pi}{3}$ from radian to degree measure.

$\dfrac{7\pi}{3}$

Solution:

$$\frac{7\pi}{3}\left(\frac{180°}{\pi}\right) = 420°$$

11. Convert the angle $\theta = -\dfrac{3\pi}{5}$ from radian to degree measure.

$-\dfrac{3\pi}{5}$

Solution:

$$-\frac{3\pi}{5}\left(\frac{180°}{\pi}\right) = -108°$$

13. Solve the triangle for the indicated side and/or angle. (See textbook.)

Solution:

$$b = \sqrt{8^2 - 4^2} = \sqrt{48} = 4\sqrt{3}; \ \theta = 90° - 30° = 60°$$

15. Solve the triangle for the indicated side and/or angle. (See textbook.)

Solution:

$C = 5, \theta = 60°$ (equilateral triangle)

$$a = \sqrt{5^2 - \left(\frac{5}{2}\right)^2} = \frac{5}{2}\sqrt{3}$$

17. *Height* A ladder of length 16 feet leans against the side of a house. The bottom of the ladder is 4.4 feet from the house (see figure in textbook). Find the height h of the top of the ladder.

Solution:

$$h = \sqrt{16^2 - 4.4^2} = \sqrt{236.64} \approx 15.38 \text{ feet}$$

19. Find the reference angle for $\dfrac{18\pi}{3}$.

Solution:

The reference angle is 0.

21. Find the reference angle for $252°$.

Solution:

The reference angle is $252° - 180° = 72°$.

23. Evaluate the trigonometric function $\cos 45°$ without using a calculator.

Solution:

$$\cos 45° = \frac{\sqrt{2}}{2}$$

25. Evaluate the trigonometric function $\tan \frac{\pi}{3}$ without using a calculator.

Solution:

$$\tan \frac{\pi}{3} = \sqrt{3}$$

27. Evaluate the trigonometric function $\sin \frac{5\pi}{3}$ without using a calculator.

Solution:

$$\sin \left(\frac{5\pi}{3} \right) = -\frac{\sqrt{3}}{2}$$

29. Evaluate the trigonometric function $\sec(-180°)$ without using a calculator.

Solution:

$$\sec(-180°) = 1$$

31. Evaluate $\tan 33°$.

Solution:

$$\tan 33° \approx 0.6494$$

33. Evaluate $\sin \left(-\frac{\pi}{9} \right)$.

Solution:

$$\sin \left(-\frac{\pi}{9} \right) \approx -0.3420$$

35. Solve for x, y, or r as indicated in graph in textbook.

Solution:

$$\cos 70° = \frac{50}{r} \Rightarrow = \frac{50}{\cos 70°} \approx 146.19$$

37. Solve for x, y, or r as indicated in graph in textbook.

Solution:

$$\tan 20° = \frac{25}{x} \Rightarrow x = \frac{25}{\tan 20°} \approx 68.69$$

39. Solve the trigonometric equation $2\cos x + 1 = 0$.

Solution:

$$2\cos x + 1 = 0$$

$$\cos x = -\frac{1}{2}$$

$$x = \frac{2\pi}{3} + 2k\pi, \ \frac{4\pi}{3} + 2k\pi$$

41. Solve the trigonometric equation $2\sin^2 x + 3\sin x + 1 = 0$.

Solution:

$$2\sin^2 x + 3\sin x + 1 = 0$$

$$(2\sin x + 1)(\sin x + 1) = 0$$

$$\sin x = -\frac{1}{2} \text{ or } \sin x = -1$$

$$x = \frac{7\pi}{6} + 2k\pi, \ \frac{11\pi}{6} + 2k\pi, \text{ or } x = \frac{3\pi}{2} + 2k\pi$$

43. Solve the trigonometric equation $\sec^2 x - \sec x - 2 = 0$.

Solution:

$$\sec^2 x - \sec x - 2 = 0$$

$$(\sec x - 2)(\sec x + 1) = 0$$

$$\sec x = 2 \text{ or } \sec x = -1$$

$$\cos x = \frac{1}{2} \text{ or } \cos x = -1$$

$$x = \frac{\pi}{3} + 2k\pi \text{ or } \frac{5\pi}{3} + 2k\pi \text{ or } x = \pi + 2k\pi$$

45. *Height* The length of a shadow of a tree is 125 feet when the angle of elevation of the sun is 33° (see figure). Approximate the height h of the tree. (See figure in textbook.)

Solution:

$$h \approx 125\tan 33° \approx 81.18 \text{ feet}$$

47. Graph the trigonometric function $y = 2\cos 6x$.

   Solution:

   $y = 2\cos 6x$

   Period: $\dfrac{2\pi}{6} = \dfrac{\pi}{3}$

   Amplitude: 2

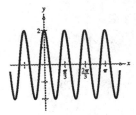

49. Graph the trigonometric function $y = \dfrac{1}{3}\tan x$.

   Solution:

   $y = \dfrac{1}{3}\tan x$

   Period: π

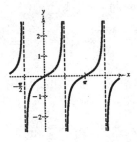

51. Sketch the graph of $y = 3\sin\dfrac{2x}{5}$.

   Solution:

   Period: $\dfrac{2\pi}{2/5} = 5\pi$

   Amplitude: 3

   x-intercepts: $(0,\ 0)$, $\left(\dfrac{5\pi}{2},\ 0\right)$, $(5\pi,\ 0)$

   Maximum: $\left(\dfrac{5\pi}{4},\ 3\right)$

   Minimum: $\left(\dfrac{15\pi}{4},\ -3\right)$

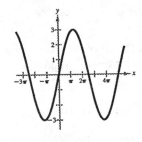

53. Sketch the trigonometric function $y = \sec 2\pi x$.

Solution:

Period: 1

Asymptotes: $x = -\frac{1}{4}$, $x = \frac{1}{4}$, $x = \frac{3}{4}$,

$x = \frac{5}{4}$

Maximum: $(\frac{1}{2}, -1)$, $(\frac{3}{2}, -1)$

Minimum: $(0, 1)$, $(1, 1)$

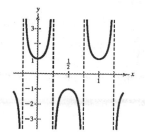

55. *Sales* The daily sales S (in thousands of units) of a seasonal product is modeled by

$$S = 74 + \frac{3}{365}t + 40\sin\frac{2\pi t}{365},$$

where t is the time in days, with $t = 1$ corresponding to January 1. Graph this model over a 1-year period.

Solution:

$$S = 74 + \frac{3}{365}t + 40\sin\frac{2\pi t}{365}$$

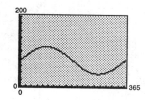

57. Find the derivative of $y = \sin 5\pi x$.

Solution:

$$y = \sin 5\pi x$$
$$y' = 5\pi \cos 5\pi x$$

59. Find the derivative of $y = -x \tan x$.

Solution:

$$y' = -x \sec^2 x - \tan x$$

61. Find the derivative of $y = \dfrac{\cos x}{x^2}$.

Solution:

$$y' = \frac{x^2(-\sin x) - \cos x(2x)}{(x^2)^2}$$
$$= \frac{-x \sin x - 2\cos x}{x^3}$$

63. Find the derivative of $y = 3\sin^2 4x + x$.

Solution:

$$y' = 6\sin 4x(4\cos 4x) + 1$$
$$= 24\sin 4x \cos 4x + 1 = 12\sin 8x + 1$$

65. Find the derivative of $y = 2\csc^3 x$.

Solution:

$$y' = 6\csc^2 x(-\csc x \cot x)$$
$$= -6\csc^3 x \cot x$$

67. Find the derivative of $y = e^x \cot x$.

Solution:

$$y' = e^x(-\csc^2 x) + e^x \cot x$$
$$= e^x(\cot x - \csc^2 x)$$

69. Find the relative extrema of the function $f(x) = \dfrac{x}{2} + \cos x$ on the interval $(0, 2\pi)$.

Solution:

Relative maximum: $(0.523, 1.128)$

Relative minimum: $(2.616, 0.443)$

71. Find the relative extrema of the function $f(x) = \sin^2 x + \sin x$.

Solution:

$$f(x) = \sin x(\sin x + 1)$$

Relative maxima: $\left(\dfrac{\pi}{2}, 2\right), \left(\dfrac{3\pi}{2}, 0\right)$

Relative minima: $\left(\dfrac{7\pi}{6}, -\dfrac{1}{4}\right), \left(\dfrac{11\pi}{6}, -\dfrac{1}{4}\right)$

73. *Sales* Refer to the model given in Exercise 55.

  (a) Find the maximum daily sales of the product. On what day of the year does the maximum daily sales occur?

  (b) Find the minimum daily sales of the product. On what day of the year does the minimum daily sales occur?

Solution:

  (a) Maximum daily sales of 114.75 thousand units occurs on the 92nd day of the year.

  (b) Minimum daily sales of 36.25 thousand units occurs on the 273rd day of the year.

75. Evaluate $\int (3\sin x - 2\cos x)\,dx$

Solution:

$$\int (3\sin x - 2\cos x)\,dx = -3\cos x - 2\sin x + C$$

77. Evaluate $\int \sin^3 x \cos x\,dx$

Solution:

$$\int \sin^3 x \cos x\,dx = \frac{\sin^4 x}{4} + C$$

79. Evaluate $\int_0^\pi (1 + \sin x)\,dx$

Solution:

$$\int_0^\pi (1 + \sin x)\,dx = \left[x - \cos x \right]_0^\pi = (\pi - (-1)) - (-1) = \pi + 2$$

81. Evaluate $\int_{-\pi/3}^{\pi/3} 4\sec x \tan x\,dx$

Solution:

$$\int_{-\pi/3}^{\pi/6} 4\sec x \tan x\,dx = 4\sec x \Big]_{-\pi/3}^{\pi/3} = 0$$

83. Find the area of the region.

$y = \sin 2x$

Solution:

$$\int_0^{\pi/2} \sin 2x\,dx = -\frac{1}{2}\cos 2x \Big]_0^{\pi/2} = -\frac{1}{2}(-1 - 1) = 1$$

85. Find the area of the region.

$y = 2\sin x + \cos 3x$

Solution:

$$\int_0^{\pi/2} (2\sin x + \cos 3x)\,dx = \left[-2\cos x + \frac{1}{3}\sin 3x \right]_0^{\pi/2}$$

$$= \left(-\frac{1}{3} \right) - (-2) = \frac{5}{3}$$

87. *Energy Consumption* Domestic energy consumption in the United States is seasonal. Assume that consumption is approximated by the model

$$Q = 6.9 + \cos \frac{\pi(2t - 1)}{12},$$

when Q is the total consumption (in quadrillion BTUs) and t is the time in months, with $0 < t \le 1$ corresponding to January (see figure). Find the average consumption rate of domestic energy during a year.

Solution:

$$\text{Average} = \frac{1}{12 - 0} \int_0^{12} \left[6.9 + \cos \frac{\pi(2t - 1)}{12} \right] dt$$

$$= \frac{1}{12} \left[6.9t + \frac{6}{\pi} \sin \frac{\pi(2t - 1)}{12} \right]_0^{12} = 6.9 \text{ quads}$$

89. Find $\lim\limits_{x \to 1} \dfrac{3x - 1}{5x + 5}$.

Solution:

$$\lim_{x \to 1} \frac{3x - 1}{5x + 5} = \frac{2}{10} = \frac{1}{5}$$

91. Find $\lim\limits_{x \to 1} \dfrac{x^3 - x^2 + 4x - 4}{x^3 - 6x^2 + 5x}$.

Solution:

$$\lim_{x \to 1} \frac{x^3 - x^2 + 4x - 4}{x^3 - 6x^2 + 5x} = \lim_{x \to 1} \frac{3x^2 - 2x + 4}{3x^2 - 12x + 5} = \frac{5}{-4} = -\frac{5}{4}$$

93. Find $\lim\limits_{x \to 0} \dfrac{\sin \pi x}{\sin 2\pi x}$.

Solution:

$$\lim_{x \to 0} \frac{\sin \pi x}{\sin 2\pi x} = \lim_{x \to 0} \frac{\pi \cos \pi x}{2\pi \cos 2\pi x} = \frac{\pi}{2\pi} = \frac{1}{2}$$

95. Find $\lim\limits_{x \to 0} \dfrac{\sin^2 x}{e^x}$.

Solution:

$$\lim_{x \to 0} \frac{\sin^2 x}{e^x} = \frac{0}{1} = 0$$

97. Given $\lim\limits_{x \to \infty} \dfrac{f(x)}{g(x)} = 0$, what can you say about the growth of f and g?.

Solution:

$g(x)$ grows faster than $f(x)$.

Practice Test for Chapter T

1. (a) Express $\dfrac{12\pi}{23}$ in degree measure.   (b) Express $105°$ in radian measure.

2. Determine two coterminal angles (one positive and one negative) for the given angle.

    (a) $-220°$; give your answers in degrees.   (b) $\dfrac{7\pi}{9}$; give your answers in radians.

3. Find the six trigonometric functions of the angle θ if it is in standard position and the terminal side passes through the point $(12, -5)$.

4. Solve for θ, $(0 \le \theta < 2\pi)$: $\sin^2 \theta + \cos \theta = 1$.

5. Sketch the graph of the given function.

    (a) $y = 3 \sin \dfrac{x}{4}$ (b) $y = \tan 2\pi x$

6. Find the derivative of $y = 3x - 3 \cos x$.

7. Find the derivative of $f(x) = x^2 \tan x$.

8. Find the derivative of $g(x) = \sin^3 x$.

9. Find the derivative of $y = \dfrac{\sec x}{x^2}$.

10. Find the derivative of $y = \sin 5x \cos 5x$.

11. Find the derivative of $y = \sqrt{\csc x}$.

12. Find the derivative of $y = \ln|\sec x + \tan x|$.

13. Find the derivative of $f(x) = \cot e^{2x}$.

14. Find dy/dx: $\sin(x^2 + y) = 3x$.

15. Find dy/dx: $\tan x - \cot 3y = 4$.

16. Evaluate $\int \cos 4x \, dx$.

17. Evaluate $\int \csc^2 \dfrac{x}{8} \, dx$.

18. Evaluate $\int x \tan x^2 \, dx$.

19. Evaluate $\int \sin^5 x \cos x \, dx$.

20. Evaluate $\int \dfrac{\cos^2 x}{\sin x} \, dx$.

21. Evaluate $\int e^{\tan x} \sec^2 x \, dx$.

22. Evaluate $\int \dfrac{\sin x}{1 + \cos x} \, dx$.

23. Evaluate $\int (\sec x - \tan x)^2 \, dx$.

24. Evaluate $\int x \cos x \, dx$.

25. Evaluate $\displaystyle\int_0^{\pi/4} (2x - \cos x) \, dx$.

26. Use L'Hôpital's Rule to find the limit: $\displaystyle\lim_{x \to \infty} \dfrac{e^{2x}}{x^2}$.

27. Use L'Hôpital's Rule to find the limit: $\displaystyle\lim_{x \to 0} \dfrac{\sin 7x}{3x}$.

28. Use L'Hôpital's Rule to find the limit: $\displaystyle\lim_{x \to \infty} \dfrac{5x^3 + 7x^2 - 8}{9x^3 + 2x + 4}$.

Graphing Calculator Required

29. Use a graphing utility to graph $f(x) = \sin x + \cos 2x$. What are the minimum and maximum values that $f(x)$ takes on?

30. Use a graphing utility to find $\displaystyle\lim_{x \to \infty} \dfrac{x}{\sqrt{x^2 + 4}}$. Try using L'Hôpital's Rule on this limit – what happens?

Appendix A Exercises

1. Left Riemann Sum: 0.518
   Right Riemann Sum: 0.768

3. Left Riemann Sum: 0.746
   Right Riemann Sum: 0.646

5. Left Riemann Sum: 0.859
   Right Riemann Sum: 0.659

7. Midpoint Rule: 0.673

9.

n	5	10	50	100
Left Sum S_L	1.6	1.8	1.96	1.98
Right Sum S_R	2.4	2.2	2.04	2.02

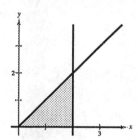

11. $\displaystyle\int_0^5 3\,dx$

13. $\displaystyle\int_{-4}^4 (4 - |x|)\,dx = \int_{-4}^0 (4 + x)\,dx + \int_0^4 (4 - x)\,dx$

15. $\displaystyle\int_{-2}^2 (4 - x^2)\,dx$

17. $A = 12$

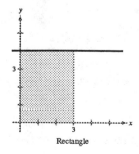

Rectangle

19. $A = 8$

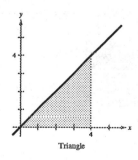

Triangle

21. $A = 14$

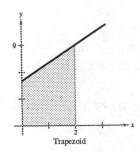

Trapezoid

23. $A = 1$

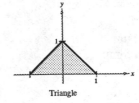

Triangle

25. $A = \dfrac{9\pi}{2}$

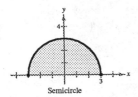

Semicircle

Appendix C Exercises

1.

3.

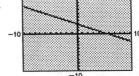

5.

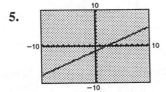

7.

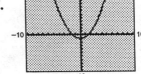

9.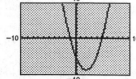

11.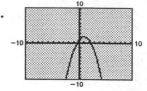

13.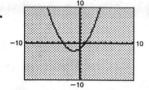

15.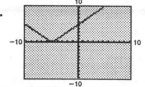

17.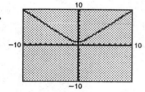

19.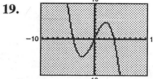

21. (d)   **23.** (a)   **25.** (i)   **27.** (j)   **29.** (e)

31.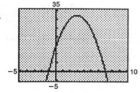

33.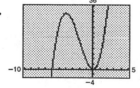

35. Xmin = −10
Xmax = 10
Xscl = 1
Ymin = −12
Ymax = 30
Yscl = 6
Xres = 1

37. Xmin = −10
Xmax = 10
Xscl = 1
Ymin = −10
Ymax = 10
Yscl = 1
Xres = 1

39. No intercepts

41. Three x-intercepts

43. Square

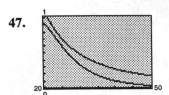

45. Circle

47.

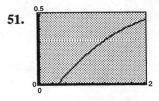

49. 0.59

51.

53. (b)

Practice Test Solutions for Chapter 0

1. Rational   (Sec. 0.1)

2. (Sec. 0.1)
  (a) Satisfies
  (b) Does not satisfy
  (c) Satisfies
  (d) Satisfies

3. $x \geq 3$ (Sec. 0.1)

4. $-1 < x < 7$ (Sec. 0.1)

5. $\sqrt{19} > \frac{13}{3}$ (Sec. 0.1)

6. (Sec. 0.2)
  (a) $d = 10$
  (b) Midpoint: 2

7. $-\frac{11}{3} \leq x \leq 3$ (Sec. 0.2)

8. $x < -5$ or $x > \frac{33}{5}$ (Sec. 0.2)

9. $-\frac{25}{2} < x < \frac{55}{2}$ (Sec. 0.2)

10. $|x - 1| \leq 4$ (Sec. 0.2)

11. $3x^5$ (Sec. 0.3)

12. 1   (Sec. 0.3)

13. $2xy\sqrt[3]{4x}$ (Sec. 0.3)

14. $\frac{1}{4}(x + 1)^{-1/3}(x + 7)$ (Sec. 0.3)

15. $x < 5$ (Sec. 0.3)

16. $(3x + 2)(x - 7)$ (Sec. 0.4)

17. $(5x + 9)(5x - 9)$ (Sec. 0.4)

18. $(x + 2)(x^2 - 2x + 4)$ (Sec. 0.4)

19. $-3 \pm \sqrt{11}$ (Sec. 0.4)

20. $-1, 2, 3$ (Sec. 0.4)

21. $\dfrac{-3}{(x - 1)(x + 3)}$ (Sec. 0.5)

22. $\dfrac{x + 13}{2\sqrt{x + 5}}$ (Sec. 0.5)

23. $\dfrac{1}{\sqrt{x}(x + 2)^{3/2}}$ (Sec. 0.5)

24. $\dfrac{3y\sqrt{y^2 + 9}}{y^2 + 9}$ (Sec. 0.5)

25. $-\dfrac{1}{2(\sqrt{x} - \sqrt{x + 7})}$ (Sec. 0.5)

26. $-1, 2, 4$ (Sec. 0.4)

Practice Test Solutions for Chapter 1

1. $d = \sqrt{82}$ (Sec. 1.1)

2. Midpoint: (1, 3)   (Sec. 1.1)

3. Collinear   (Sec. 1.1)

4. $x = \pm3\sqrt{5}$ (Sec. 1.1)

5. x-intercepts: $(\pm2, 0)$ (Sec. 1.2)
y-intercept: (0, 4)

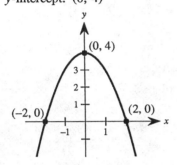

6. x-intercept: (2, 0)   (Sec. 1.2)
No y-intercept

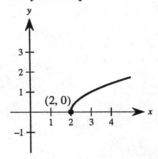

7. x-intercept: (3, 0)   (Sec. 1.2)
y-intercept: (0, 3)

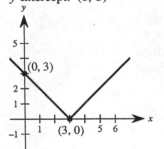

8. $(x - 4)^2 + (y + 1)^2 = 9$ (Sec. 1.2)
Center: (4, −1)
Radius: 3

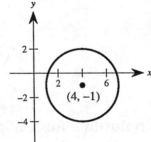

9. (0, −5) and (4, −3)   (Sec. 1.2)

10. $6x - y - 38 = 0$ (Sec. 1.3)

11. $2x - 3y + 1 = 0$ (Sec. 1.3)

12. $x - 6 = 0$ (Sec. 1.3)

13. $5x + 2y - 6 = 0$ (Sec. 1.3)

14. (a) 4   (Sec. 1.4)
(b) 31
(c) $x^2 - 10 + 20$
(d) $x^2 + 2x(\Delta x) + (\Delta x)^2 - 5$

15. Domain: $(-\infty, 3]$ (Sec. 1.4)
Range: $[0, \infty)$

16. (a) $2x^2 + 1$ (Sec. 1.4)
(b) $4(x+1)(x+2)$

17. $f^{-1}(x) = \sqrt[3]{x-6}$ (Sec. 1.4)

18. 22   (Sec. 1.5)

19. 12   (Sec. 1.5)

20. Does not exist   (Sec. 1.5)

21. $\dfrac{\sqrt{5}}{10}$ (Sec. 1.5)

22. 5   (Sec. 1.5)

23. Discontinuities: $x = \pm 8$ (Sec. 1.6)
$x = 8$ is removable.

24. $x = 3$ is a nonremovable discontinuity.
(Sec. 1.6)

25. (Sec. 1.6)

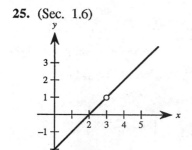

26. $y = \pm\sqrt{-x^2 - 6x - 5}$ (Sec. 1.2)
Domain: $[-5, -1]$

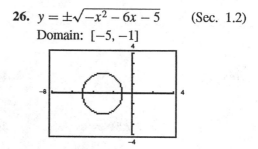

27. The graph does **not** show that the function does not exist at $x = 3$ on many
graphing utilities.

$\lim\limits_{x \to 3} f(x) = 6$ (Sec. 1.5)

Practice Test Solutions for Chapter 2

1. $\lim\limits_{\Delta x \to 0} \dfrac{f(x + \Delta x) - f(x)}{\Delta x} = \lim\limits_{\Delta x \to 0} (4x + 2\Delta x + 3)$

$= 4x + 3$

(Sec. 2.1)

2. $\lim\limits_{\Delta x \to 0} \dfrac{f(x + \Delta x) - f(x)}{\Delta x} = \lim\limits_{\Delta x \to 0} \dfrac{-1}{(x + \Delta x + 4)(x + 4)}$

$= -\dfrac{1}{(x - 4)^2}$

(Sec. 2.1)

3. $x - 4y + 2 = 0$ (Sec. 2.1)

4. $15x^2 - 12x + 15$ (Sec. 2.2)

5. $\dfrac{4x - 2}{x^3}$ (Sec. 2.2)

6. $\dfrac{2}{3\sqrt[3]{x}} + \dfrac{3}{5\sqrt[5]{x^2}}$ (Sec. 2.2)

7. (Sec. 2.3)
Average rate of change: 4
Instantaneous rates of change:
    $f'(0) = 0, \quad f'(2) = 12$

8. (Sec. 2.3)
Marginal cost: $4.31 - 0.0002x$

9. $5x^4 + 28x^3 - 39x^2 - 56x + 36$
(Sec. 2.4)

10. $-\dfrac{x^2 + 14x + 8}{(x^2 - 8)^2}$ (Sec. 2.4)

11. $\dfrac{3x^4 + 14x^3 - 45x^2}{(x + 5)^2}$ (Sec. 2.4)

12. $-\dfrac{3x^2 + 4x + 1}{2\sqrt{x}(x^2 + 4x - 1)^2}$ (Sec. 2.4)

13. $72(6x - 5)^{11}$ (Sec. 2.5)

14. $-\dfrac{12}{\sqrt{4 - 3x}}$ (Sec. 2.5)

15. $\dfrac{18x}{(x^2 + 1)^4}$ (Sec. 2.5)

16. $\dfrac{\sqrt{10x}}{x(x + 2)^{3/2}}$ (Sec. 2.5)

17. $24x - 54$ (Sec. 2.6)

18. $-\dfrac{15}{16(3 - x)^{7/2}}$ (Sec. 2.6)

19. $-\dfrac{x^4}{y^4}$ (Sec. 2.7)

20. $-\dfrac{2(xy^3 + 1)}{3(x^2y^2 - 1)}$ (Sec. 2.7)

21. $\dfrac{8\sqrt{xy + 4} + y}{10\sqrt{xy + 4} - x} = \dfrac{41y - 32x}{50y - 41x}$
(Sec. 2.7)

22. $-\dfrac{8x^2}{y^2(x^3 - 4)^2}$ (Sec. 2.7)

23. $\frac{5}{12}$ (Sec. 2.8)

24. $\dfrac{dA}{dt} = 2\pi r \dfrac{dr}{dt}$ (Sec. 2.8)

    $\dfrac{dr}{dt} = \dfrac{5}{4\pi}$

25. (Sec. 2.8)

$$V = \frac{4}{3}\pi h^3$$

$$\frac{dV}{dt} = 4\pi h^2 \frac{dh}{dt}$$

$$\frac{dh}{dt} = \frac{1}{8\pi}$$

26. (Sec. 2.4)

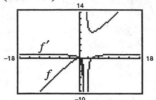

Horizontal Tangents at $x = 0$ and $x = 4$.
$f'(0) = f'(4) = 0$

27. (Sec. 2.7)

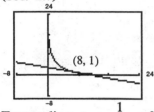

Tangent line: $y = -\frac{1}{4}x + 3$

Practice Test Solutions for Chapter 3

1. Increasing: $(-\infty,\ 0),\ (4,\ \infty)$
Decreasing: $(0, 4)$
(Sec. 3.1)

2. Increasing: $\left(-\infty,\ \frac{2}{3}\right)$ (Sec. 3.1)
Decreasing: $\left(\frac{2}{3},\ 1\right)$

3. Relative minimum: $(2,\ -45)$
(Sec. 3.2)

4. Relative minimum: $(-3,\ 0)$
(Sec. 3.2)

5. Maximum: $(5, 0)$ (Sec. 3.2)
Minimum: $(2,\ -9)$

6. No inflection points   (Sec. 3.6)

7. Points of inflection: (Sec. 3.6)
$$\left(-\frac{1}{\sqrt{3}},\ \frac{1}{4}\right),\ \left(\frac{1}{\sqrt{3}},\ \frac{1}{4}\right)$$

8. $S = x + \dfrac{600}{x}$ (Sec. 3.4)
First number: $10\sqrt{6}$
Second number: $\dfrac{10\sqrt{6}}{3}$

9. $A = 3xy = 3x\left(\dfrac{3000 - 6x}{4}\right)$

$3x = 750$ feet, $y = 375$ feet

(Sec. 3.4)

10. $x \approx 13{,}333$ units   (Sec. 3.5)

11. $p = \$14{,}088$ (Sec. 3.5)

12. -1 (Sec. 3.5)

13. $-\infty$ (Sec. 3.6)

14. -2 (Sec. 3.6)

15. (Sec. 3.7)

Intercept: $(0, 0)$

Vertical asymptotes: $x = \pm 3$

Horizontal asymptote: $y = 1$

Relative maximum: $(0, 0)$

No inflection points

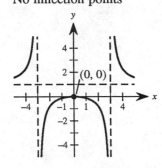

16. (Sec. 3.7)

Intercepts: $(-2, 0)$, $\left(0, \tfrac{2}{5}\right)$

Horizontal asymptote: $y = 0$

Relative maximum: $\left(1, \tfrac{1}{2}\right)$

Relative minimum: $\left(-5, -\tfrac{1}{10}\right)$

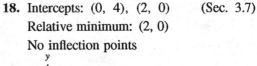

17. Intercept: $(0, -1)$ (Sec. 3.7)

No relative extrema

Inflection point: $(-1, -2)$

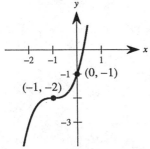

18. Intercepts: $(0, 4)$, $(2, 0)$ (Sec. 3.7)

Relative minimum: $(2, 0)$

No inflection points

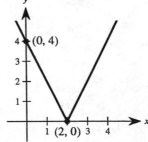

19. (Sec. 3.7)

Intercepts: $(2, 0)$, $(0, \sqrt[3]{4})$

Relative minimum: $(2, 0)$

No inflection points

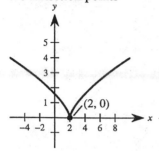

20. $\sqrt[3]{65} \approx 4.0208$ (Sec.3.8)

21.

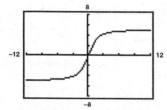

(Sec. 3.7)

Horizontal asymptotes at $y = \pm 5$.

No relative extrema.

22.

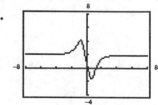

Yes, the graph crosses the horizontal asymptote $y = 2$.

(Sec. 3.7)

Practice Test Solutions for Chapter 4

1. (a) 81   (Sec. 4.1)

(b) $\frac{1}{32}$

(c) 1

2. (a) $x = 2$ (Sec. 4.1)

(b) $x = 32$

(c) $x = 5$

3. (a)

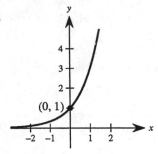

(b)

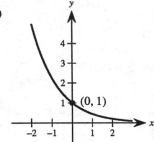

(Sec. 4.1)

4. (Sec. 4.1)

(a) $A \approx \$3540.28$

(b) $A \approx \$3618.46$

(c) $A \approx \$3626.06$

5. $6xe^{3x^2}$ (Sec. 4.2)

6. $\dfrac{e^{\sqrt[3]{x}}}{3\sqrt[3]{x^2}}$ (Sec. 4.2)

7. $\dfrac{e^x - e^{-x}}{2\sqrt{e^x + e^{-x}}}$ (Sec. 4.2)

8. $x^2 e^{2x}(2x + 3)$ (Sec. 4.2)

9. $\dfrac{xe^x - e^x - 3}{4x^2}$ (Sec. 4.2)

10. $e^{1.6094\ldots} = 5$ (Sec. 4.3)

11. (a)

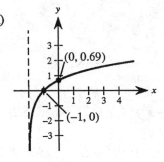

(b)

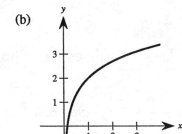

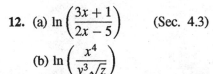
(Sec. 4.3)

12. (a) $\ln\left(\dfrac{3x + 1}{2x - 5}\right)$ (Sec. 4.3)

(b) $\ln\left(\dfrac{x^4}{y^3 \sqrt{z}}\right)$

13. (a) $x = e^{17}$ (Sec. 4.3)

(b) $x = \dfrac{\ln 2}{3\ln 5}$

14. $\dfrac{6}{6x-7}$ (Sec. 4.4)

15. $\dfrac{4x+15}{x(2x+5)}$ (Sec. 4.4)

16. $\dfrac{1}{x(x+3)}$ (Sec. 4.4)

17. $x^3(1+4\ln x)$ (Sec. 4.4)

18. $\dfrac{1}{2x\sqrt{\ln x+1}}$ (Sec. 4.4)

19. (a) $y=7e^{-0.7611t}$ (Sec. 4.5)
(b) $y=0.1501e^{0.4970t}$

20. $t\approx 5.776$ years   (Sec. 4.5)

21.

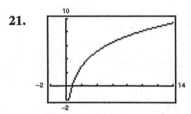

(Sec. 4.5)
The graphs are the same.

22.

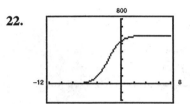

(Sec. 4.1)
$$\lim_{t\to\infty} f(t)=600$$
$$\lim_{x\to-\infty} f(t)=0$$

Practice Test Solutions for Chapter 5

1. x^3-4x^2+5x+C (Sec. 5.1)

2. (Sec. 5.1)
$$\frac{x^4}{4}+\frac{7x^3}{3}-2x^2-28x+C$$

3. $\dfrac{x^2}{2}-9x-\dfrac{1}{x}+C$ (Sec. 5.1)

4. $-\frac{1}{5}(1-x^4)^{5/4}+C$ (Sec. 5.2)

5. $\frac{9}{14}(7x)^{2/3}+C$ (Sec. 5.2)

6. $-\frac{2}{33}(6-11x)^{3/2}+C$ (Sec. 5.2)

7. $\frac{4}{5}x^{5/4}+\frac{6}{7}x^{7/6}+C$ (Sec. 5.1)

8. $-\dfrac{1}{3x^3}+\dfrac{1}{4x^4}+C$ (Sec. 5.1)

9. $x-x^3+\frac{3}{5}x^5-\frac{1}{7}x^7+C$ (Sec. 5.1)

10. $-\dfrac{5}{12(1+3x^2)^2}+C$ (Sec. 5.2)

11. $\left(\frac{1}{7}\right)e^{7x}+C$ (Sec. 5.3)

12. $\left(\frac{1}{8}\right)e^{4x^2}+C$ (Sec. 5.3)

13. $\left(\frac{1}{16}\right)(1 + 4e^x)^4 + C$ (Sec. 5.3)

14. $\left(\frac{1}{2}\right)e^{2x} + 4e^x + 4x + C$ (Sec. 5.3)

15. $\left(\frac{1}{2}\right)e^{2x} - 4x - e^{-x} + C$ (Sec. 5.3)

16. $\ln|x + 6| + C$ (Sec. 5.3)

17. $-\left(\frac{1}{3}\right)\ln|8 - x^3| + C$ (Sec. 5.3)

18. $\frac{1}{3}\ln(1 + 3e^x) + C$ (Sec. 5.3)

19. $\dfrac{(\ln x)^7}{7} + C$ (Sec. 5.3)

20. $\dfrac{x^2}{2} + x + 6\ln|x - 1| + C$ (Sec. 5.3)

(Use long division first)

21. -3 (Sec. 5.4)

22. $\frac{381}{7}$ (Sec. 5.4)

23. 2   (Sec. 5.4)

24. $A = 36$ (Sec. 5.5)

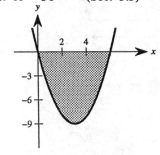

25. $A = \frac{1}{2}$ (Sec. 5.5)

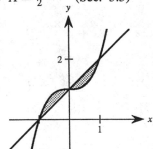

26. $A = \frac{2}{3}$ (Sec. 5.5)

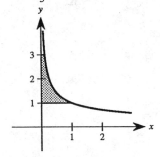

27. 1.4949   (Sec. 5.6)

28. 0.1472   (Sec. 5.6)

29. 3π (Sec. 5.7)

30. $\dfrac{5000\pi}{3}$ (Sec. 5.7)

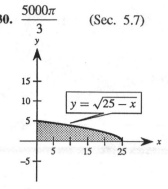

31. $n = 50$: 22.442278   (Sec. 5.6)

   $n = 100$: 22.443875

32. (c) Actual area is 4.5   (Sec. 5.5)

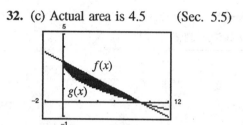

Practice Test Solutions for Chapter 6

1. $\frac{2}{5}(x+3)^{3/2}(x-2) + C$ (Sec. 6.1)

2. $-\dfrac{x-1}{(x-2)^2} + C$ (Sec., 6.1)

3. $\frac{2}{3}\ln|3\sqrt{x}+1| + C$ (Sec. 6.1)

4. $\dfrac{(\ln 7x)^2}{2} + C$ (Sec. 6.1)

5. $\frac{1}{4}e^{2x}(2x-1) + C$ (Sec. 6.2)

6. $\dfrac{x^4}{16}[4(\ln x) - 1] + C$ (Sec. 6.2)

7. $\frac{2}{35}(x-6)^{3/2}(5x^2 + 24x + 96) + C$ (Sec. 6.2)

8. $\frac{1}{32}e^{4x}(8x^2 - 4x + 1) + C$ (Sec. 6.2)

9. $\ln\left|\dfrac{x+3}{x-2}\right| + C$ (Sec. 6.3)

10. $\ln\left|\dfrac{x^3}{(x+4)^2}\right| + C$ (Sec. 6.3)

11. $5\ln|x+2| + \dfrac{7}{x+2} + C$ (Sec. 6.3)

12. $\frac{3}{2}x^2 + \ln\dfrac{|x|}{(x+2)^2} + C$ (Sec. 6.3)

Chapter 7

13. $-\dfrac{\sqrt{16-x^2}}{16x}+C$ (Sec. 6.4)

14. $x[(\ln x)^3 - 3(\ln x)^2 + 6(\ln x) - 6] + C$
(Sec. 6.4)

15. $1200x - 20,000\ln(1 + e^{0.06x}) + C$
(Sec. 6.4)

16. (a) 15.567   (Sec. 6.5)
     (b) 15.505

17. (a) 1.191   (Sec. 6.5)
     (b) 1.196

18. Convergent; 6   (Sec. 6.6)

19. Divergent   (Sec. 6.6)

20. Divergent   (Sec. 6.6)

21. $n = 50 : 1.652674$ (Sec. 6.5)
     $n = 100 : 1.652674$

22. $n = 100 : 8.935335$ (Sec. 6.5 and 6.6)
     $n = 1000 : 2.288003$
     $n = 10,000 : 1.636421$
     Converges $\left(\text{Actual answer is } \dfrac{\pi}{2}\right)$

Practice Test Solutions for Chapter 7

1. (a) $d = 14\sqrt{2}$ (Sec. 7.1)
     (b) Midpoint: $(4,\ 2,\ -2)$

2. $(x-1)^2 + (y+3)^2 + z^2 = 5$ (Sec. 7.1)

3. Center: $(2,\ -1,\ -4)$ (Sec. 7.1)
     Radius: $\sqrt{21}$

4. (Sec. 7.2)
     (a) x-intercept: $(8, 0, 0)$
     y-intercept: $(0, 3, 0)$ z-intercept: $(0, 0, 4)$

(b) $y = 2$
Parallel to xz-plane

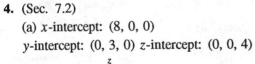

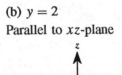

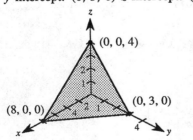

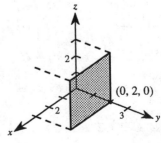

5. (Sec. 7.2)

(a) Hyperboloid of one sheet

(b) Elliptic paraboloid

6. (a) Domain: $x + y < 3$ (Sec. 7.3)

(b) Domain: all points in the
xy-plane except the origin

7. $f_x(x, y) = 6x + 9y^2 - 3$ (Sec. 7.4)

$f_y(x, y) = 18xy + 12y^2 - 6$

8. $f_x(x, y) = \dfrac{2x}{x^2 + y^2 + 5}$ (Sec. 7.4)

$f_y(x, y) = \dfrac{2y}{x^2 + y^2 + 5}$

9. $\dfrac{\partial w}{\partial x} = 2xy^3 \sqrt{z}$ (Sec. 7.4)

$\dfrac{\partial w}{\partial y} = 3x^2 y^2 \sqrt{z}$

$\dfrac{\partial w}{\partial z} = \dfrac{x^2 y^3}{2\sqrt{z}}$

10. $\dfrac{\partial^2 z}{\partial x^2} = 2x\left(\dfrac{x^2 - 3y^2}{(x^2 + y^2)^3}\right)$ (Sec. 7.4)

$\dfrac{\partial^2 z}{\partial y \partial x} = 2y\left(\dfrac{3x^2 - y^2}{(x^2 + y^2)^3}\right)$

$\dfrac{\partial^2 z}{\partial x \partial y} = 2y\left(\dfrac{3x^2 - y^2}{(x^2 + y^2)^3}\right)$

$\dfrac{\partial^2 z}{\partial y^2} = 2x\left(\dfrac{3y^2 - x^2}{(x^2 + y^2)^3}\right)$

11. (Sec. 7.5)

Relative minimum: $(1, -2, -23)$

12. Saddle point: $(0, 0, 0)$ (Sec. 7.5)

Relative maxima: $(1, 1, 2), (-1, -1, 2)$

13. $f(2, -8) = -16$ (Sec. 7.6)

14. $f(4, 0) = -36$ (Sec. 7.6)

15. $y = \frac{1}{65}(-51x + 355)$ (Sec. 7.7)

16. $y = \frac{1}{6}x^2 - \frac{7}{26}x + \frac{7}{3}$ (Sec. 7.7)

17. $\frac{81}{16}$ (Sec. 7.8)

18. $-\frac{135}{4}$ (Sec. 7.8)

19. (a) $A = \displaystyle\int_{-2}^{2}\int_{3}^{7-x^2} dy\, dx = \int_{3}^{7}\int_{-\sqrt{7-y}}^{\sqrt{7-y}} dx\, dy$ (Sec. 7.8)

(b) $A = \displaystyle\int_{0}^{1}\int_{x^2+2}^{x+2} dy\, dx = \int_{2}^{3}\int_{y-2}^{\sqrt{y-2}} dx\, dy$

20. $V - \displaystyle\int_{0}^{4}\int_{0}^{4-x}(4 - x - y)dy\, dx = \dfrac{32}{3}$ (Sec. 7.9)

21. $y \approx 0.832t + 20.432$ (Sec. 7.7)

$r \approx 0.983$

22. 1.028531×10^{17} (Sec. 7.8)

Practice Test Solutions for Chapter P

1. $\frac{11}{16}$ (Sec. P.1)

2. $\frac{5}{13}$ (Sec. P.1)

3. $E(x) = \frac{1}{2}$ (Sec. P.1)
$V(x) = 4.05$
$\sigma \approx 2.012$

4. $k = \frac{1}{4}$ (Sec. P.2)

5. (a) $\frac{25}{64}$ (Sec. P.2)
(b) $\frac{63}{64}$

6. (a) 4   (Sec. P.3)
(b) $\frac{4\sqrt{5}}{5}$
(c) 4

7. (a) $6\ln\left(\frac{3}{2}\right) \approx 2.433$ (Sec. P.3)
(b) $\sqrt{6 - 36\left(\ln\frac{3}{2}\right)^2} \approx 0.286$
(c) $\frac{12}{5}$

8. $\mu = \frac{1}{7}$ (Sec. P.3)
Median: $\frac{\ln 2}{7}$
$\sigma = \frac{1}{7}$

9. 0.0469   (Sec. P.3)

10. $P(19 < x < 24) = 0.4401$ (Sec. P.3)

Practice Test Solutions for Chapter D

1. $y' = 3x^2 - 4 - \dfrac{C}{x^2}$ (Sec. D.1)

$xy' + y = x\left(3x^2 - 4 - \dfrac{C}{x^2}\right) + \left(x^3 - 4x + \dfrac{C}{x}\right)$

$= 3x^3 - 4x - \dfrac{C}{x} + x^3 - 4x + \dfrac{C}{x}$

$= 4x^3 - 8x = 4x(x^2 - 2)$

2. $y' = -5Ce^{-5x}$ (Sec. D.1)

$y'' = 25Ce^{-5x}$

$y''' = -125Ce^{-5x}$

$y''' + 125y = -125Ce^{-5x} + 125Ce^{-5x} = 0$

3. $y^4 = 2x^2 + 8x + C$ (Sec. D.2)

4. $y = C(x - 1) - 4$ (Sec. D.2)

5. $y(\ln y - 1) = e^x(x - 1) + C$ (Sec. D.2) **6.** $y = \left(\frac{1}{2}\right)e^{-2x} + Ce^{-4x}$ (Sec. D.3)

7. $y = -\dfrac{e^{1/x^2}}{2x^2} + Ce^{1/x^2}$ (Sec. D.3) **8.** $y = -3x^2 + \frac{1}{4} + Cx^4$ (Sec. D.3)

9. $y = 30 - 26e^{-0.0523t}$ (Sec. D.4) **10.** $y = 1000e^{-2.9957e^{-0.1553t}}$ (Sec. D.4)

11. $y = Ce^{x^3}$ (Sec. D.2) **12.** $t^2 + Q^2 = C$ (Sec. D.2)

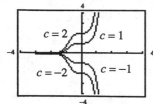 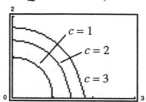

Practice Test Solutions for Chapter S

1. $a_n = \dfrac{n}{n^2 + 1}$ (Sec. S.1) **2.** $a_n = (-1)^{n-1}(2n + 3)$ (Sec. S.1)

3. Converges to $\frac{1}{3}$ (Sec. S.1) **4.** Converges to 4 (Sec. S.1)

5. $\frac{1}{12}$ (Sec. S.2) **6.** Converges by the Ratio Test
(Sec. S.3)

7. Converges since it is a p-series with $p = \frac{4}{3} > 1$.
(Sec. S.3) **8.** Diverges by the nth-Term Test
(Sec. S.2)

9. Diverges since it is a geometric series with $|r| = \left|-\frac{6}{5}\right| = \frac{6}{5} > 1$.
(Sec. S.2) **10.** Diverges since it is a p-series with $p = \frac{1}{6} < 1$.
(Sec. S.3)

11. Diverges by the Ratio Test
(Sec. S.3) **12.** Converges since it is a geometric series with $|r| = |0.27| = 0.27 < 1$.
(Sec. S.2)

13. Diverges by the nth-Term Test

(Sec. S.2)

14. $R = 1$ (Sec. S.4)

15. $R = \lim\limits_{n \to \infty} (n + 2) = \infty$ (Sec. S.4)

16. $e^{-4x} = \sum\limits_{n=0}^{\infty} \dfrac{(-4x)^n}{n!}$ (Sec. S.5)

17. $\dfrac{1}{\sqrt[3]{x}} = 1 + \sum\limits_{n=1}^{\infty} \dfrac{(-1)^n 1 \cdot 4 \cdot 7 \cdots (3n - 2)(x - 1)^n}{3^n n!}$ (Sec. S.5)

18. 0.214 (Sec. S.5)

19. $x \approx 1.213$ (Sec. S.6)

20. $\sqrt[4]{10} \approx 1.778$ (Sec. S.6)

21. (Sec. S.2)   (a) 7.9961 (b) $138,699$

22.

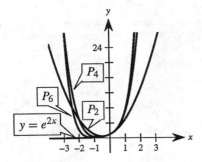

(Sec. S.5)

23. -1.2090 and 0.9021 (Sec. S.6)

Practice Test Solutions for Chapter T

1. (a) $93.913°$ (Sec. T.1)

  (b) $\dfrac{7\pi}{12}$

2. (a) $140°, -580°$ (Sec. T.1)

  (b) $\dfrac{25\pi}{9}, -\dfrac{11\pi}{9}$

3. $\sin\theta = \dfrac{y}{r} = -\dfrac{5}{13}$ $\csc\theta = \dfrac{r}{y} = -\dfrac{13}{5}$

  $\cos\theta = \dfrac{x}{r} = \dfrac{12}{13}$ $\sec\theta = \dfrac{r}{x} = \dfrac{13}{12}$

  $\tan\theta = \dfrac{y}{x} = -\dfrac{5}{12}$ $\cot\theta = \dfrac{x}{y} = -\dfrac{12}{5}$

  (Sec. T.2)

4. $\theta = 0, \dfrac{\pi}{2}, \dfrac{3\pi}{2}$ (Sec. T.2)

5. (a) Period: 8π (Sec. T.3)

Amplitude: 3

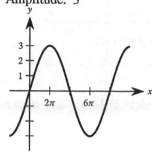

(b) Period: $\frac{1}{2}$

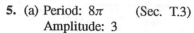

6. $3(1 + \sin x)$ (Sec. T.4)

7. $x(x \sec^2 x + 2 \tan x)$ (Sec. T.4)

8. $3 \sin^2 x \cos x$ (Sec. T.4)

9. $\dfrac{\sec x(x \tan x - 2)}{x^3}$ (Sec. T.4)

10. $5 \cos 10x$ (Sec. T.4)

11. $-\frac{1}{2}\sqrt{\csc x}\, \cot x$ (Sec. T.4)

12. $\sec x$ (Sec. T.4)

13. $-2e^{2x} \csc^2 e^{2x}$ (Sec. T.4)

14. $3 \sec(x^2 + y) - 2x$ (Sec. T.4)

15. $-\frac{1}{3} \sin^2 3y \sec^2 x$ (Sec. T.4)

16. $\frac{1}{4} \sin 4x + C$ (Sec. T.5)

17. $-8 \cot \dfrac{x}{8} + C$ (Sec. T.5)

18. $-\frac{1}{2} \ln |\cos x^2| + C$ (Sec. T.5)

19. $\dfrac{\sin^6 x}{6} + C$ (Sec. T.5)

20. $\ln |\csc x - \cot x| + \cos x + C$ (Sec. T.5)

21. $e^{\tan x} + C$ (Sec. T.5)

22. $-\ln |1 + \cos x| + C$ (Sec. T.5)

23. $2 \tan x - 2 \sec x - x + C$ (Sec. T.5)

24. $x \sin x + \cos x + C$ (Sec. T.5)

25. $\dfrac{\pi^2 - 8\sqrt{2}}{16}$ (Sec. T.5)

26. ∞ (Sec. T.6)

27. $\dfrac{7}{3}$ (Sec. T.6)

28. $\dfrac{5}{9}$ (Sec. T.6)

29.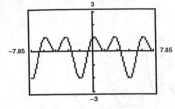

Minimum: -2

Maximum: 1.125

(Sec. T.3)

30.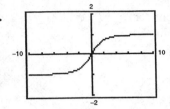

The limit is 1. L'Hôpital's Rule fails.

(Sec. T.6)

```
    </xsl:choose>
  </xsl:variable>
  <xsl:number format="{$format}" />
  ...
</xsl:for-each>
```

9. What different values can the level attribute on <xsl:number> take and how does its value change the numbering of a node?